Business Essentials

Third Edition

Ronald J. Ebert
University of Missouri-Columbia

Ricky W. Griffin
Texas A&M University

Prentice Hall, Upper Saddle River, New Jersey 07458

Editor-in-Chief: Natalie Anderson
Senior Editor: Linda Schreiber
Editorial Assistant: Susan Galle
Senior Development Editor: Ron Librach
Director of Development: Steve Deitmer
Marketing Manager: Debbie Clare
Associate Managing Editor: Judy Leale
Permissions Coordinator: Monica Stipanov
Manufacturing Supervisor: Arnold Vila
Manufacturing Manager: Vincent Scelta
Design Manager: Patricia Smythe
Interior Design: Lorraine Castellano
Photo Research Supervisor: Melinda Lee Reo
Image Permission Supervisor: Kay Dellosa
Image Permission Coordinator: Zina Arabia
Photo Researcher: Melinda Alexander
Cover Design: Pat Smythe
Cover Illustration: Sam Krieger
Composition: Carlisle Communications, Ltd.

Library of Congress Cataloging-in-Publication Data
Ebert, Ronald J.
Business essentials/Ronald J. Ebert, Ricky W. Griffin.—3rd ed.
p. cm.
Includes bibliographical references and index.
ISBN 0-13 084255-9 (pbk)
1. Industrial management—United States. 2. Business enterprises—
–United States. I. Griffin, Ricky W. II. Title.
HD70.U5E2 1999
658—dc21

99-13224
CIP

Prentice-Hall International (UK) Limited, London
Prentice-Hall of Australia Pty. Limited, Sydney
Prentice-Hall Canada, Inc., Toronto
Prentice-Hall Hispanoamericana, S.A., Mexico
Prentice-Hall of India Private Limited, New Delhi
Prentice-Hall of Japan, Inc., Tokyo
Prentice-Hall (Singapore) Pte. Ltd.
Editora Prentice-Hall do Brasil, Ltda., Rio de Janeiro

Printed in the United States of America

10 9 8 7 6 5 4 3 2 1

To some outstanding teachers—
Gene Groff, William Morris, and Stan Stockton
Jack Ivancevich and Skip Szilagyi
Thanks for your enduring influence on our lives.

R.J.E.

R.W.G.

OVERVIEW

CONTENTS

PREFACE

Each year, *Fortune* magazine publishes two prestigious lists: "The Best Companies to Work For" and "America's Most Admired Companies." Entering into this third edition of *Business Essentials*, we realize that you, our readership audience, deserve similar recognition on two counts. First, for us you are "The Best Students and Instructors to Work For." Second, for your role in widening the understanding of business, we include you and your institutions on our list of "Most Admired Contributors to Society." The enthusiastic reception for *Business Essentials* among instructors and students has stimulated this third edition of the book. For this revision, as with earlier editions, we have conceived *Business Essentials* as a new product with a unique purpose. The book reflects more than just changes that are occurring in the practice of business. It also reflects the changing needs of students and teachers of business.

MEETING CUSTOMER NEEDS

Business Essentials is an alternative for those who want a no-nonsense approach to the introduction-to-business course. It presents the "no-frills" essentials of business for those instructors who want focused coverage in a low-priced book.

In creating this third edition of *Business Essentials*, we drew upon our experiences in developing the previous editions and upon even earlier experiences in developing five successful editions of *Business*. The new edition of *Business Essentials* has been thoroughly updated, and we are most proud of *Business Essentials* because its development enabled us to practice what we preach by addressing the significant but previously unmet needs of an important market segment. Prentice Hall, the authors, and a panel of advisors who teach business listened closely to our customers, both students and instructors, in creating a successful new product. Not surprisingly, the twofold mandate of *Business Essentials*—brevity and high quality—involved sometimes challenging, often difficult decisions about content and orientation. Very early in the project, we learned to appreciate the difficulties of being selective; deciding upon which subject matter to emphasize and which materials to exclude was painful (you can't have a shorter book of high quality without cutting). Ultimately, our decisions for this third edition, as for the previous ones, were guided by suggestions from teachers and students, as well as by our own experiences in the practice of business.

■ MEETING OBJECTIVES

This third edition of *Business Essentials* was guided by the same fundamental objectives that we established for the book at the outset:

- We wanted it to be an affordable, lower-price alternative for students in the introductory course.
- We wanted it to be reduced in length while retaining high quality in its coverage of the essential facets of business.
- We wanted it to be accurate, with all statements of fact based on scientific research and/or managerial practice.
- We wanted it to be current, with illustrative examples and cases drawn from business stories that are still unfolding.
- We wanted it to be readable so that students could appreciate the experience of encountering and thinking about life in the world of business.

We believe that we have met all of these objectives. The price of *Business Essentials* is lower than that of most major, high-quality books designed for the introductory course. The book offers significant coverage of business essentials, including both traditional topics and newer ideas. All of our examples are drawn from today's business world, and we added and updated information and examples right up to the moment we went to press.

■ A NEW ORGANIZATION

One way that a textbook—or any successful product, for that matter—succeeds in the long term is by close reevaluation on a regular basis. We have done this with *Business Essentials;* the third edition has been reorganized according to both reviewer feedback and our own observations of the market. *Business Essentials* now consists of 16 chapters organized into 6 parts, plus 2 appendixes. This streamlined organization should make the material more manageable for both semester- and quarter-length courses.

Part One introduces the basics of the business system in the United States and now includes coverage of two of the most contemporary influences in business today: global business and ethics/social responsibility.

Part One: Introducing the Contemporary Business Environment
- Chapter 1: Understanding the U.S. Business System
- Chapter 2: Conducting Business in the United States
- Chapter 3: Understanding the Global Context of Business
- Chapter 4: Conducting Business Ethically and Responsibly

Part Two addresses the management side of business from a mostly macro perspective. In this part, we devote the first two chapters to the subjects of managing and organizing the business enterprise. In the next chapter, we look closely at an increasingly important aspect of the U.S. business scene—entrepreneurship and the small business.

Part Two: Understanding the Business of Managing
- Chapter 5: Managing the Business Enterprise
- Chapter 6: Organizing the Business Enterprise
- Chapter 7: Understanding Entrepreneurship and the Small Business

Part Three looks at a key element in any successful business—human resources. The two chapters in this part introduce students to the key elements of managing people. Topics addressed include: motivation, leadership, group dynamics, and labor and management relations issues.

Part Three: Understanding People in Organizations
- Chapter 8: Motivating, Satisfying, and Leading Employees
- Chapter 9: Managing Human Resources and Labor Relations

Part Four covers a topic that is often fun for students—marketing. Typically students can relate personally to the topics covered. In our experience, for example, all students can identify with an advertisement of some type, usually a television commercial (so do we, for that matter!). The chapters in this part discuss such topics as consumer behavior, pricing, and promoting and distributing products.

Part Four: Understanding Principles of Marketing
- Chapter 10: Understanding Marketing Processes and Consumer Behavior
- Chapter 11: Developing and Pricing Products
- Chapter 12: Promoting and Distributing Products

Part Five looks at the way businesses manage operations for the production of both goods and services and examines the ways they manage information. This part also examines the goals and methods of managing for quality and explains basic accounting as an element in a firm's information system.

Part Five: Managing Operations and Information
- Chapter 13: Managing Production and Improving Quality
- Chapter 14: Understanding Accounting and Information Systems

Part Six introduces the financial elements of business. Because these can be tricky topics for beginning business students, we stress the fundamentals in these chapters with an even and consistent style. Our goal is to address the key topics in a context that lets the student see their applications. Topics that we cover in this part are money and banking, securities, and other investments.

Part Six: Understanding Financial Issues
- Chapter 15: Understanding Money and Banking
- Chapter 16: Understanding Securities and Investments

In the appendices, we cover two important topics: financial and risk management and the legal aspects of business. Most reviewers of the second edition of *Business Essentials* told us that although these topics did not require complete chapter-length coverage, they should be made available to both students and teachers. We know that you might differ with this assessment; if so, let us know and we will reconsider for the fourth edition.

Appendix 1: Understanding Financial and Risk Management
Appendix 2: Understanding the Legal Context of Business

Finally, we have moved the topic of business careers and the job search onto the Prentice Hall Web site for quick access by students who are interested in looking into this important aspect of business life.

■ CONTEMPORARY THEMES

To be fully prepared for business in the third millennium, students must be aware of the business-world trends that will affect them as they start their careers. For this reason, we have concentrated on bringing several important themes to their attention.

- **The Growth of International Business.** Many businesspeople and observers of the business world see globalization of the economy as the great challenge in the coming century. To keep students aware of this challenge, we have based many of the examples, vignettes, and assignments in this book on the experiences of global companies. Chapter 3, "Understanding the Global Context of Business," provides full coverage of this important topic.
- **The Signficance of Small Business.** Because we recognize that many students will not go to work for large corporations, we have provided balanced coverage of both small and large companies throughout the text. Chapter 7, "Understanding Entrepreneurship and the Small Business," is comprehensive. In addition, examples throughout the book deal with small businesses, and many chapters contain sections that apply

specific practices and issues to the special concerns of small businesses. In addition, the *Business PlanPro* software (see below) is available for integrating chapter information into the development of a business plan for a small business.

- **The Growth of the Service Sector.** The service sector will continue to grow significantly around the globe. We stress the importance of this sector by giving it equal billing with manufacturing in Chapter 13, "Managing Production and Improving Quality." Throughout, the book also provides prominent coverage of service businesses in the examples, vignettes, visuals, and end-of-chapter exercises.
- **The Need to Manage Information and Communications Technology.** In our information-based society, the people and organizations that learn how to obtain and use information will be the ones that succeed. The explosive growth in information systems stems from the emergence of communications technologies such as multimedia communications systems. We cover this important topic in detail in Chapter 14, "Understanding Accounting and Information Systems," where the discussion has been completely reworked for accuracy and currency.
- **The Role of Ethics and Social Responsibility.** Because business ethics and social responsibility have been generating much discussion in recent years, we devote a full chapter to these topics (Chapter 4, "Conducting Business Ethically and Responsibily"). We also treat issues of business ethics and social responsibility in our examples, cases, and other features.
- **The Quality Imperative.** Quality improvement continues to be of special interest as we pass beyond the year 2000. We initiated coverage of this subject in Chapter 11, "Managing Production and Improving Quality," in response to the requests and suggestions of instructors. We also present quality considerations where they relate to other materials throughout the book.

User-Friendly Features and a Realistic Picture of Business

A textbook must be packaged effectively and engagingly if it is to accomplish its objectives. We have thus designed a number of features to make this book as user-friendly, and with as many hands-on applications, as possible.

- The third edition of *Business Essentials* introduces a brand-new feature called the **Web Vignette**, which puts the dynamic technology of the World Wide Web at the head of each part of the book. These comprehensive case studies present detailed discussions of real companies or industries, and to help students pursue questions and conduct further research, key Web addresses are included. As always, we also integrate discussion questions. *Web Vignettes* cover such topics as Beanie Babies, Southwest Airlines, NASCAR, and the Y2K problem. See the table of contents for a complete listing of topics and page numbers.
- Every chapter begins with a compelling **two-part case** that introduces a current real-world business situation by engaging student interest in the content and issues that follow in the chapter. Next comes a list of **learning objectives** for the chapter—a simple blueprint to alert students to the key subjects of study in the chapter. At the close of each chapter, we wrap up the two-part case. Here we incorporate questions for discussion so that students can analyze the case, either on their own or in class as a group.
- New to the third edition of *Business Essentials* is a feature entitled **CRAFTING YOUR BUSINESS PLAN.** We are pleased to introduce our partnership with Palo Alto Software and the addition of ***Business PlanPro*** into the third edition of *Business Essentials.* Developing a business plan is increasingly popular as an application experience in the introduction-to-business course, and *Business PlanPro* offers the ideal environment for doing so. Featuring 20 sample plans from real start-up companies, *Business PlanPro* 3.0 (BPP) is a powerful vehicle that offers the first-time planner a structured step-by-step approach to the process of building a comprehensive business plan. At the same time, it is quite suitable for commercial-

grade planning applications; the student who works with BPP gains a practical and saleable business skill for his or her business career.

Crafting Your Business Plan is a chapter-ending exercise that applies chapter material to the task of developing a business plan. The exercise lists the purpose of each planning assignment, guides the planner to the appropriate section of BPP, such as goal setting, projecting sales, start-up activities, competitive assessments, marketing and financial planning, information on where to go for start-up help, and many other areas. Students are encouraged first to examine sample plans and then to personalize their own plans in the BPP environment—writing them, storing and accessing them; gathering and entering data into BPP spreadsheets; using BPP graphics for class presentations and written reports; adding new sections as they progress through the textbook; and crafting final plans into coherent refined documents. The instructor, too, enjoys a great deal of flexibility in the level of student involvement with BPP. Students, for example, may be asked merely to examine business plans for some of BPP's 20 sample firms, or they may be encouraged to immerse themselves in a semester-long planning activity culminating in formal reports or other presentations. We have found that the BPP environment is a real eye-opener for students: The planning process brings together all of the course material from the textbook and vividly exposes the ways in which various topics relate to one another to fashion an integrated picture of any business.

- **BUILDING YOUR BUSINESS SKILLS** exercises give students an opportunity to apply both their knowledge and their critical-thinking skills to extended problems drawn from a wide range of realistic business experiences. Each exercise begins with a list of specific goals. A business situation is then described, and a step-by-step method for proceeding is outlined. Follow-up questions help students focus on the topic at hand.

  All of the *Building Your Business Skills* exercises are brand-new to this edition and have been specifically designed to satisfy the pedagogical criteria laid out in the **Secretary of Labor's Commission on Achieving Necessary Skills (SCANS).** SCANS was developed to identify the competencies that will be needed by students preparing to assume their roles in the workplace, and the exercises in this feature have been designed to foster in-depth involvement and problem solving in a format suitable for both out-of-class preparation and in-class discussion. To help students apply classroom and textbook lessons to the real world of business, *Building Your Business Skills* exercises emphasize the following areas in which students are encouraged to practice their skills: resources, interpersonal skills, information, systems, and technology.

- The prominence of the Internet as an information medium stimulated the continuation of our EXPLORING THE NET feature at the end of each chapter. The highly favorable user response from the second edition encouraged us to create some new examples while retaining and upgrading some of the more popular ones. Students are directed toward Internet information sources and hands-on network activities that enhance and reinforce understanding of important topics in each chapter. As in *Building Your Business Skills*, the *Exploring the Net* exercises are specifically designed to foster in-depth involvement and problem solving. The format is hands-on, and activities are designed to accommodate both out-of-class preparation and in-class discussion.

  Note that although we waited until the last possible minute to finalize the installments in this feature, we understand that users will undoubtedly encounter problems in accessing the same home pages and subdirectories that we used in creating these exercises. The reason will almost always be the same: a content provider has exercised his or her option to make changes. But of course, change and flexibility are integral features of the Internet. To work around these changes, we urge everyone to be flexible and creative. There are numerous sources for most types of information, and both we and our colleagues have found that when faced with glitches, determined students not only find they what they want but gain valuable experience in working with search engines. We are convinced that inventive students will not only locate alternative solutions to most exercise problems but will gain in enthusiasm in the process.

- Also new to the third edition are our **video cases.** First comes ***Showtime!***, a set of video cases featuring Showtime Networks Inc. In keeping with our tradition of integrating business information straight from the front lines, we worked with the managers and executives of one of the leading cable-TV networks in the country. During our visits with Showtime, we gathered information that applies directly to all of the core areas of the introduction-to-business course. We wanted to be sure to create an environment in which students can see the application of business concepts.

  Each part also includes a comprehensive video case from the acclaimed PBS series ***Small Business 2000.*** We have selected installments from this series because we wanted to give students a realistic balance between large, often global operations and small, more entrepreneurial settings. Here students can see how different small business owners apply the core concepts of business in order to survive and prosper in a highly competitive environment.

  Note that the video cases in this edition of *Business Essentials*, like the *Building Your Business Skills* and *Exploring the Net* exercises, have been designed for pedagogical effectiveness. The videos themselves are now the part-ending "cases," and the material placed in the text itself is designed to direct or focus student activities:

  - *Learning Objectives* tell students what information to look for and what concepts to focus on as they watch the video
  - *Background Information* provides context and supplements facts where needed
  - A description of *The Video* previews the content of the segment
  - *Discussion Questions* help students organize their thoughts on the material shown
  - *Follow-Up Assignments* furnish an opportunity for further study about the video topic
  - Where applicable, a section designed *For Further Exploration* encourages supplemental activities, many of which are geared to further research on the Internet.
- Within each chapter are **figures, tables,** and **photographs** to illustrate a point or convey a message. The selective inclusion of these visuals increases the reader's involvement in the text. All photos are inspired by the text material; captions expand upon text content.
- Each chapter includes a **thematic box** on "Trends and Challenges" designed to provide additional perspectives on the material. Various topics include reports on high-interest events, analyses of newly emerging problems, and examinations of controversial issues in today's business environment.
- To emphasize fundamental concepts, each **key term** is printed in boldface in the text and defined in the margin of the page where it is introduced. A comprehensive glossary at the end of the book provides readily accessible definitions as well as a reference to the text page where the word first occurs.
- Selected **cartoons** and **quotation callouts** are used occasionally to stimulate interest and enhance understanding of certain key points.
- Several useful features are found toward the end of each chapter. A concise ***Summary of Learning Objectives*** is followed by pedagogical features that both review what's been learned and ask students to apply what they've learned. ***Study Questions and Exercises*** are divided into three categories: **Review** (which tests recall of material), **Analysis** (which tests understanding), and **Application Exercises** (which ask students to apply concepts to basic problems).

SUPPLEMENTS

Because we recognize both the excitement and the challenge of teaching, we have endeavored to provide you with a text that will make your work more enjoyable. Toward this end, we have assembled what we believe is the best total instructional system available for a business text. Each component of the teaching and learning package has been carefully crafted to ensure that this first course in business is a rewarding experience for both instructors and students.

- *Instructor's Manual*
- *Study Guide*
- Test Item File
- *Prentice Hall Custom Test*
- Powerpoint Transparencies
- Color Transparencies
- Stock Market and Investment Practice Set
- *Beginning Your Career Search*
- Prentice Hall/*New York Times* "Themes of the Times" for Business
- *Threshold Competitor: A Management Simulation*
- PHLIP/CW Companion Website
- *Surfing for Success in Business: An Internet Guide*
- *Hot Topics in Introduction to Business*
- *The Business Student Writer's Manual*
- Prentice Hall Self-Assessment Library CD-ROM

We would like to highlight the following elements in the package for the third edition of *Business Essentials:*

- ***Prentice Hall Custom Test*** (Windows version) is based on the number-one best-selling test-generating software program developed by Engineering Software Associates. This state-of-the-art test-creation program is not only suitable for established courses but is customizable according to individual needs. It is user-friendly, and this powerful program permits instructors to originate error-free tailor-made tests quickly and easily. Exams can be administered either on-line or traditionally, and *Custom Test* also tracks students' results and analyzes the success of specific tests.
- ***Threshold Competitor: A Management Simulation*** (Second Edition) is the only Windows-based introduction-to-business simulation currently available. Using Threshold, students work in groups to manage small manufacturing companies competing in the same marketplace. They decide on company missions, goals, policies, and strategies in areas ranging from marketing to finance and manufacturing. They practice skills in planning, organizing, directing, and controlling and get responses to both questions and decisions. *Threshold Competitor* is now available in three versions: The Solo Version, in which individual students compete against computer-managed companies; the Team Version, in which students work in groups to make decisions; and the Team and Solo Combined Version.
- ***PHLIP/CW Companion Website*** is a Web-based learning environment that contains numerous links to discipline-specific Websites. In addition to the wealth of resources and information posted on the companion Website designed for both teachers and students, the PHLIP/CW site features a faculty-support section that provides instructors with access to textual and media material in the Prentice Hall Business Publishing archive. The purpose of PHLIP/CW is to furnish up-to-date classroom support through state-of-the-art technology and resources. Instructors and students can access PHLIP at

  http://www.prenhall.com/ebert

- ***Beginning Your Career Search*** is a concise discussion of the essentials of career planning. Chapters cover résumé preparation, introductory and follow-up letters, researching companies, interviews, handling job offers, and sample letters.

- ***Surfing for Success in Business: An Internet Guide*** is a brief, discipline-specific introduction to the Internet. In addition to addressing frequently asked questions, it offers advice on job searches, résumés, assistance in distance learning, and tips on navigating the information superhighway.
- ***The Business Student Writer's Manual*** is a separate book from Prentice Hall that teaches writing skills in the context of regular classes.
- ***The Prentice Hall Self-Assessment Library CD-ROM*** is an easy-to-use set of 45 exercises designed to give students insights into the skills they'll need in the business world. The CD-ROM is divided into three parts—"What about Me?" "Working with Others," and "Life in Organizations." Each exercise can be performed electronically and can be self-scored.
- ***Hot Topics in Business*** devotes separate chapters to the trends and practices that are currently fueling change in the dynamic world of business. Updated regularly to ensure current and exciting coverage, the *Hot Topics* guide includes not only background information and thorough discussions, but discussion questions and group and Internet exercises.

ACKNOWLEDGMENTS

Although only two names appear on the cover of this book, we could never have completed it without the participation of many fine individuals. First, we would like to thank the professionals who took time from their busy schedules to review materials for us:

Michael Baldigo
Sonoma State University

Harvey Bronstein
Oakland Community College

Gary Christiansen
North Iowa Area Community College

Pat Ellebracht
Northeast Missouri State University

John Gubbay
Moraine Valley Community College

Edward M. Henn
Broward Community College

Betty Ann Kirk
Tallahassee Community College

Sofia B. Klopp
Palm Beach Community College

Kenneth J. Lacho
University of New Orleans

Keith Leibham
Columbia Gorge Community College

John F. Mastriani
El Paso Community College

William E. Matthews
William Paterson College of New Jersey

Thomas J. Morrisey
Buffalo State College

David William Murphy
Madisonville Community College

Scott Norwood
San Jose State University

Joseph R. Novak
Blinn College

Constantine Petrides
Borough of Manhattan Community College

Roy R. Pipitone
Eric Community College

William D. Raffield
University of St. Thomas

Richard Randall
Nassau Community College

Betsy Ray
Indiana Business College

Richard Reed
Washington State University

Lewis Schlossinger
Community College of Aurora

Robert N. Stern
Cornell University

Arlene Strawn
Tallahassee Community College

Jane A. Treptow
Broward Community College

Janna P. Vice
Eastern Kentucky University

Philip A. Weatherford
Embry-Riddle Aeronautical University

Jerry E. Wheat
Indiana University Southeast

Pamela J. Winslow
Berkeley College of Business

Joseph Hecht of Montclair State University prepared the *Study Guide*, and Athena Miklos of Charles County Community College developed 100 acetate and 125 PowerPoint transparencies. The end-of-part video exercises on *Showtime* and *Small Business 2000* were written by Thomas E. Kaplan, of Farleigh Dickinson University, and John Bowdidge, of Southwest Missouri State University, respectively. Judy Block, president of JRB Communications Inc. of Westport, Connecticut, made substantive contributions to the text, ranging from resource materials to draft material on specialized topics and finished cases, boxes, and exercises. As always, she was inventive and indefatigible in her capacity as professional researcher and writer.

Authors, of course, typically get the credit when a book is successful, but the success of this book must be shared with an outstanding group of people at Prentice Hall, where a superb team of professionals made this book a pleasure to write. Our editor, Natalie Anderson, initiated this project and has contributed to the package in more ways than we can list. We are engaged in ongoing discussions with Natalie about the best possible positioning of both *Business* and *Business Essentials* and their future in both traditional and electronic formats. Michael Jennings, Carlisle Communications, Ltd. oversaw the production of the text, which was beautifully designed by Lorraine Castellano. Assistant Editor Kristen Imperatore managed the development of all the supplements. Melinda Reo, Melinda Alexander, and Zina Arabia handled photo research and permission. Marketing Manager Debbie Clare made numerous contributions to the product itself and has since been tireless in getting out the message about the result. Ron Librach, our Development Editor, inspired the overall tone for the revision, pored over the manuscript at every step of the process, provided truly innovative design ideas, and continually encouraged us to add value here, to update there, to clarify the discussion, and to meet our deadlines.

Also at Prentice Hall we would like to acknowledge the expertise and support of Director of Development Steve Deitmer, Director of Production and Manufacturing Michael Weinstein, Design Manager Pat Smythe, Associate Managing Editor Judith Leale, and Editorial Assistants Paula D'Introno and Susan Galle. On campus, Phyllis Washburn furnished timely and professional secretarial services.

Our colleagues at the University of Missouri and Texas A&M University also deserve recognition. We both have the good fortune to be a part of a community of scholars who enrich our lives and challenge our ideas. Without their intellectual stimulation and support, our work would suffer greatly.

Finally, our families. . . . We take pride in the accomplishments of our wives, Mary and Glenda, and draw strength from the knowledge that they are there for us to lean on. And we take great joy from our children, Matt, Kristen, Ashley, and Dustin. Sometimes in the late hours when we're ready for sleep but have to get one or two more pages written, looking at your pictures keeps us going. Thanks to all of you for making us what we are.

■ ABOUT THE AUTHORS

Ronald J. Ebert is Professor of Management at the University of Missouri–Columbia. He received his B.S. from The Ohio State University, his M.B.A. from the University of Dayton, and his D.B.A. from Indiana University. He is active in the Academy of Management and the Decision Sciences Institute (DSI). Dr. Ebert has also served as the editor of the *Journal of Operations Management,* as Chair of the Production and Operations Management Division of the Academy of Management, and is a Past-President and Fellow of DSI. In addition to *Business* and *Business Essentials,* he is the co-author of three books: *Organizational Decision Processes, Production and Operations Management* (published in English, Spanish and Chinese), and *Management.*

Dr. Ebert has held engineering and supervisory positions in quality management with the Frigidaire Division of General Motors Corp. He has also done consulting for the National Science Foundation, the United States Savings and Loan League, Kraft Foods, Oscar Mayer, Sola Optical USA Inc., and the American Public Power Association. His research interests include: production strategy, engineering design processes in product development, and strategy formulation.

Ricky W. Griffin was born and raised in Corsicana, Texas. He received his B.A. from North Texas State University and his M.B.A. and Ph.D. from the University of Houston. He served on the faculty of the University of Missouri–Columbia from 1978 until 1981, when he joined the faculty at Texas A&M. In 1990, he was named the university's Lawrence E. Fouraker Professor of Business Administration. He currently serves as Head of the Department of Management.

Dr. Griffin's research interests include: leadership, workplace violence, and international management. He has done consulting in the areas of task design, employee motivation, and quality circles for such organizations as Baker-Hughes, Texas Instruments, Six Flags Corp., Texas Commerce Bank, and AT&T. His research has won two Academy of Management Research Awards (both in the Organizational Behavior division) and one Texas A&M University Research Award.

In addition to *Business* and *Business Essentials,* Dr. Griffin is the author or co-author of five books and more than 40 journal articles and book chapters.

Introducing the Contemporary Business Environment

The Beanie Baby Business

Want to make some money fast? Drop everything and listen, because this is a deal you won't believe. No, we're not talking about a hot stock tip, an investment in commodities futures, or land in oil-well territory. This deal involves Bernie the St. Bernard, Nuts the Squirrel, Strut the Rooster, Web the Spider, and 141 more fist-size beanbags called Beanie Babies.

Manufactured by Ty Inc., a privately held company in Oakbrook, Illinois, that specializes in stuffed animals, Beanie Babies have earned a fortune for the company and made staggering profits for tens of thousands of children and adults who trade them in secondary markets via the Internet. How Ty Inc. made this happen and how company executives handled the inevitable business problems along the way is a story worth telling.

AN IDEA IS BORN

After graduating from college in 1962, future founder Ty Warner began working for Dakin Inc., an Illinois-based stuffed-animal manufacturer. He learned some important lessons during his 18 years with the company, especially in the marketing curriculum. "They taught me that it's better selling 40,000 accounts [to specialty gift shops] than it is five accounts" to mass-market retailers such as Toys "R" Us and Wal-Mart. "It's more difficult to do," Warner admits, "but for the longevity of the company and the profit margins, it's better. [Beanie Babies] could be around for years just as long as I don't take the easy road and sell it to a mass merchant who's going to put it in bins."

> "Beanie Babies could be around for years just as long as I don't take the easy road and sell it to a mass merchant who's going to put it in bins."
>
> —Ty Warner
> *Founder of Beanie Babies*

Warner learned that in the stuffed-animal business, affordable, high-quality merchandise is a must if you want children to spend their own money. Combining their allowances, earnings, and gifts, children under 14 spend about $20 billion a year and influence adult spending to the tune of another $200 billion. When Warner began manufacturing Beanie Babies in 1993, this was the market he decided to corner.

MAKING THE BUSINESS WORK

Warner's first task was manufacturing. To keep production costs down, he contracted with factories in China, where Beanie Babies were sewn and stuffed with polyvinyl chloride pellets. Then he began selling his product to independent gift shops for roughly $3 each. He already knew that an important benefit of working with such merchants as these was rapid cash flow: Small retailers usually pay cash on delivery or write checks within 15 days. "If we were to sell to Wal-Mart," advises Warner, "we wouldn't be paid for 30 days, and that would affect our financial situation."

When the Beanie Babies craze took off in December 1995, Warner and a staff of about 100 clerks handled orders and shipments on what was quickly becoming an obsolete computer system. With as many as 100,000 calls a day coming into the company, Ty Inc. faced a serious information system crisis. The original system was designed for about 100 order-entry clerks and took 2 to 4 weeks from order to shipment. It was also hard to use, requiring clerks to scroll through pages of forms for every customer and to enter every bit of information manually. Chris Johnson, Ty director of management information systems, was assigned to find a replacement system that could start work immediately. Money, he was told, was no obstacle—as long as he solved the problem as fast as humanly possible.

After compressing system planning time from 6 months to 2 months, Johnson chose a system designed for high-volume businesses. The new system cut the number of ordering steps, automated shipping information and billing, conducted credit checks, generated separate invoices, and balanced inventory with orders. It promised to halve the time spent on many operations and to enter large chunks of data automatically, and, oddly enough, it was also easy to use. Order clerks, explains Johnson, "have to be able to look up orders fast and click back and forth between windows. Customers need information on shipping fast, and the user interface needs to support that."

MARKETING GENIUS

The factor most responsible for turning Beanie Babies from a mere product to a craze was an innovative marketing strategy based on a deceptively simple three-step economic principle:

1. Provide stores with too few items to meet demand;
2. Stop production on individual items to induce permanent scarcity; and
3. Sit back and wait for demand to increase as word spreads.

By June 1997, Ty Inc. was limiting retailers to 36 pieces of each character per month. Only single monthly orders were accepted. The perception of scarcity and exclusivity was increased further by Warner's decision to forgo television advertising. The hardest part of the strategy was imposing production restraint while demand increased. Although it would have been profitable in the short term to boost production, Warner was convinced that Beanie Babies would last longer if there were a permanent scarcity. The plan worked. "I've been in the business 30 years," reports one toy store owner in Mamaroneck, New York, "and I've never seen an item like this."

To top off this strategy, Ty entered into a highly successful promotional relationship with McDonald's. The campaign broke all consumer-response records and increased Beanie Baby popularity immensely. Offering customers one of ten Teenie Beanie Babies with the purchase of a Happy Meal, McDonald's sold nearly 100 million meals in 10 days (instead of the 35 days originally anticipated). In the process, Ty received about $45 million worth of free advertising for its full-size product.

BIRTH OF A SECONDARY MARKET

With the Beanie Babies priced at only $5, young children fueled demand, both by making purchases with allowance money and convincing parents to buy on impulse. Children soon became avid collectors, and many owned the entire set. With some items out of production and others nearly impossible to find in retail stores, Beanie Babies soon became collectibles, and an active secondary market developed on the Internet. Ty Inc. encourages this market on its own Web site (*http://www.Ty.com*), which allows visitors to buy and sell and talk in chat rooms. Dozens of other Web sites have active marketplaces, where prices are set by supply and demand.

Prices, of course, started to increase, but as they did, adults became the primary collectors of the most valuable items, including Peanut the Elephant (in royal blue), which recently fetched $2,200, Rex the Tyrannosaurus ($1,750), and Peking the Panda ($1,295). Although children are priced out of this market, they congregate at Web sites with offerings that start at about $10.

WILL IT LAST?

Things look very good for Ty Inc., at least for now. Sales increased tenfold in 1997, up from about $26 million in 1996. Although there are cheaper competitors, none has achieved the levels of design and quality that make Beanie Babies such a hot collectible. Moreover, Warner promptly sues the makers of knockoffs that are too close to Ty's designs. So far, three companies have been forced to recall their products and hand over their profits to Warner.

As for Warner, he intends to stick with the strategy that's made his company a success. "Every time we make a shipment," he explains, "retailers want twice as many [Beanie Babies] as we can possibly get to them. And as long as kids keep fighting over them and retailers are angry at us because they can't get enough, I think those are good signs."

> "And as long as kids keep fighting over Beanie Babies and retailers are angry at us because they can't get enough, I think those are good signs."
>
> —Ty Warner
> *Founder of Beanie Babies*

WEB LINKS

Beanie Baby Web sites abound. The information in the following sites (and many others) will help you think about the questions at the end of this case:

- **Angel's Beanie Page** http://www.erols.com/angelisa/beanie.html
- **Barbies and Beanies:** Your Unofficial Link to the World of Vintage Barbie Dolls and Beanie Babies http://www.cyberstreet.com/users/coogan/main.html
- **Beanie Babies:** Buying Selling Trading http://beaniepost.com
- **Beanie Babies:** Collectible Exchange http:beaniex.com
- **Twohogwild for Beanies** http://members.ad.com/twohogwild/4beanies.html
- **Ty Inc.:** The Official Home of the Beanie Babies http://www.ty.com
- **Wild About Beanies** http//www.wildaboutbeanies.com

QUESTIONS FOR DISCUSSION

1. In what ways is Ty Inc.'s Beanie Baby business a good example of capitalism at work? Before you respond to this question, visit Ty.com to learn how the company increases market demand in ways left unmentioned in the case.
2. In what ways does the nature of the business conducted at various Web sites provide an example of capitalism at work? (Do *not* search Ty.com to answer this question.)
3. Warner's strategy calls for controlling supply to increase demand. The case explained the benefits of this strategy. Can you think of possible problems?
4. Ty Warner owns 100 percent of Ty Inc. Do you think that it is easier or harder for a privately controlled corporation to accomplish/conduct such a risky business strategy? Explain your answer.
5. As described in this case, Warner and his staff faced information system and legal problems as the Beanie Baby business grew. Based on what you know about business, why do you think problem solving is an important managerial skill? Do you agree or disagree with the following statement: *Success in business depends on your ability to turn problems into opportunities.*
6. Ty Inc. manufactures Beanie Babies in China. With product demand in primary and secondary markets linked to quality, what challenges does the practice of manufacturing abroad pose for the company? Have you noticed any comments on the Web expressing dissatisfaction with Beanie Baby quality?
7. Although Beanie Babies are toys for young children, prices on the secondary market are out of children's reach. How do you feel about this from a business ethics point of view? Do children in Web chat rooms express frustration at not being able to afford retired (out of production) or scarce Beanie Babies?

Understanding the U.S. Business System

Who Do You Think I Am, Your Concierge?

In her personal and professional life, Kelley Dunn had only one way to go—up. As a single mother and secretary living in Minneapolis, Dunn was overwhelmed by how much she had to do and how little time she had to do it. She was willing to pay someone to do certain personal chores—pick up and deliver the dry cleaning, buy gifts and cards, get her watch repaired—but there was no one to hire.

Then a lightbulb went on. Dunn had heard about corporate concierges—specialists who provide personalized services to companies and their employees—and so, she decided to attend a 1-day seminar on the business. Dunn quickly became convinced that the market was right for highly personalized concierge services. After all, Americans are working longer and harder. Research told Dunn that people are spending 163 hours more on the job than they did 20 years ago, which is the equivalent of an extra month a year. In two-career and single-parent families—the majority of American households—there is no one at home to shop, cook, plan for parties, order anniversary flowers, take clothes to the cleaners, and wait for furniture deliveries.

With $10,000 in the bank and a lot of hope, Dunn quit her secretarial job and began calling on office building managers for concierge work. Pillsbury hired her, and the assignment confirmed her market analysis. "We looked at [bringing on a concierge] as a good opportunity to help our employees balance their work with their home lives," explains Pillsbury Vice President Mike Nordstrom.

> **"We looked at bringing on a concierge as a good opportunity to help our employees balance their work with their home lives."**
>
> —Mike Nordstrom
> *Vice President, Pillsbury*

Pillsbury and other companies subsidize the cost of this service for employees because it is in their best interest. According to Harvard economist Juliet Schor, because corporations are "still vested in the model that minimizes the number of people you hire," they are offering an increasing number of perks that make it possible for their workforces to work at top efficiency.

Dunn's first priority was to find out what services Pillsbury employees needed. She began by sending out questionnaires to all 2,500 employees and then compiled responses in a database that enabled her to call people before birthdays and anniversaries and other occasions. Dunn's systems approach is not unique, confirms Mary Naylor, president of Capitol Concierge, the oldest and largest concierge service in Washington, D.C. Serving 80 commercial office buildings with 40,000 clients, Capitol learned early on that a centralized computer system for compiling and organizing data from marketing questionnaires, field interviews, and sales transactions was vital to success.

Market and data analysis has given Naylor the information she needs to define her market in terms of two distinct types of service: corporate and personal. On a corporate level, Naylor now caters to the property managers of office buildings with high vacancy rates. To help them attract new clients, her service arranges for catered business meetings and makes hotel, dinner, and transportation reservations for visiting executives. For the personal clients who work for these companies, Capitol runs the errands and generally helps them to keep their lives on track.

Both Dunn and Naylor have found that price competition in the concierge business is intense. To attract new clients, Dunn has so far found it necessary to charge about 30 percent less than her competitors. At one point, Naylor's four major competitors slashed prices so ruthlessly that she had to cut her building fees in half. Although her competitors ultimately went out of business, Naylor was left with bone-thin profit margins that forced her to focus

on greater ratios of personal business inside every corporate account.

To maximize profits, Naylor revamped her order and invoice systems, which centralized vendor billing and ensured that employees report every order to the home office. They now fax or e-mail orders to a central location, where they become part of the Capitol corporate data file. When confirmations for goods and services are faxed to vendors, orders become official while generating invoices. This accounting system not only permits Capitol to pay bills and receive payments more quickly, but also to match orders against costs of goods sold.

By 1998, Naylor was billing $6 million in sales. Her company made money not only from corporate and personal clients, but also as a commissioned broker of products and services: Film processors, dry cleaners, shoe repairmen, and other vendors pay Capitol an average of 15 percent of sales made to its clients. In turn, Capitol shares the revenue with the individual concierges in its employ. Kelley Dunn is also doing well, though on a smaller scale. Her 1998 gross profit reached $80,000 on revenues of $237,000, up from revenues of only $41,000 in 1997. How does the future look for both companies? Because more people are spending more time on the job, the market can only grow.

The challenge of building and sustaining a business to meet changing and newly emerging customer needs is as common to billion-dollar corporations as it is to small firms. A changing marketplace creates a need for the kind of innovative responses that have long characterized business in the United States. Such responses require vision, careful attention to quality and customer service, substantial financial commitment, internal accounting controls, and well-defined marketing strategies designed to help businesses grow over time.

These and a host of other forces provide the main themes for stories of success and failure that are told repeatedly in the annals of enterprise in the United States. As you will see in this chapter, these forces are also the key factors in the U.S. market economy. You will see, too, that although the world's economic systems differ markedly, standards for evaluating success or failure are linked to a system's capacity to achieve certain basic goals.

By focusing on the learning objectives of this chapter, you will better understand the U.S. business system and the mechanisms by which it not only pursues its goals but also permits businesses large and small to pursue theirs.

Our opening story is continued on page 25

After reading this chapter, you should be able to:

1. **Define the nature of U.S. *business* and identify its main goals.**
2. **Describe different types of *economic systems* according to the means by which they control the *factors of production.***
3. **Show how *demand* and *supply* affect resource distribution in the United States.**
4. **Identify the elements of *private enterprise* and explain the various *degrees of competition* in the U.S. economic system.**
5. **Explain the criteria for evaluating the success of an economic system in meeting its goals and show how the federal government attempts to manage the U.S. economy.**

THE CONCEPT OF BUSINESS AND THE CONCEPT OF PROFIT

business An organization that provides goods or services to earn profits

profits The difference between a business's revenues and its expenses

What do you think of when you hear the word *business*? Does your mind conjure up images of huge corporations such as General Motors and IBM? Are you reminded of smaller firms such as your local supermarket? Or do you think of even smaller one-person operations such as the barbershop around the corner? Each of these organizations, of course, is a **business**—an organization that provides goods or services to earn profits. Indeed, the prospect of earning **profits**—the difference between a business's revenues and its expenses—is what encourages people to open and expand businesses. After all, profits reward owners for taking the risks involved in investing their money and time.

Today, businesses produce most of the goods and services we consume. They also employ most of the working people in the United States. Moreover, new forms of technology, service businesses, and international opportunities promise to keep production, consumption, and employment growing indefinitely. In turn, profits from businesses are paid to millions of owners and stockholders. Taxes on business help support governments at all levels. In many cases, businesses also support charitable causes and provide community leadership.

In this chapter, we begin our introduction to business by looking at its role in both the U.S. economy and U.S. society. There are a variety of economic systems around the world. Once you understand something about the systems of most developed countries, you will better appreciate the workings of the U.S. system. As we will see, the effects of economic forces on businesses and the effects of businesses on the economy are dynamic—and, indeed, sometimes volatile.

ECONOMIC SYSTEMS AROUND THE WORLD

economic system A nation's system for allocating its resources among its citizens

Not surprisingly, a U.S. business operates differently from a business in, say, France or the People's Republic of China; and of course, businesses in these countries vary from those in Japan or Brazil. A major factor in these differences is the economic system of a firm's home country, in which it conducts most of its business. An **economic system** is a nation's system for allocating its resources among its citizens, both individuals and organizations. In this section we show how economic systems differ according to the ownership or control of these resources, which are often called factors of production. We will also describe several kinds of economic systems.

"Perhaps we could find a way to redefine 'profit.'"

Factors of Production

The key difference between economic systems is the way in which they manage the **factors of production**—the basic resources that a country's businesses use to produce goods and services. These resources include *labor, capital, entrepreneurs*, and *natural resources.*[1]

factors of production Resources used in the production of goods and services—natural resources, labor, capital, and entrepreneurs

LABOR The people who work for businesses provide labor. Sometimes called **human resources, labor** includes both the physical and mental contributions people make as they are engaged in economic production. For example, the forest-products firm Weyerhaeuser Co. employs about 40,000 people. Not surprisingly, the operations of such a huge company require a widely skilled labor force, ranging from financial planners to loggers to truck drivers.

labor (or **human resources**) The physical and mental capabilities of people as they contribute to economic production

CAPITAL Obtaining and using material resources and labor requires **capital**—the funds needed to operate an enterprise. Capital is needed both to start a business and to keep it operating and growing. Weyerhaeuser requires millions of dollars every year to run its mills, pay its workers, and ship its wood products to customers. A major source of capital for most smaller businesses is personal investment by owners. Personal investment can be made by the individual entrepreneurs, by partners who start businesses together, or by investors who buy stock. Revenue from the sale of products is another important ongoing source of capital. Finally, many firms borrow funds from banks and other lending institutions.

capital The funds needed to create and operate a business enterprise

ENTREPRENEURS Weyerhaeuser can trace its roots back to 1858, when a young German immigrant named Frederick Weyerhaeuser opened a lumberyard in Illinois. Over the years, his business prospered, and in 1900, he and 15 partners bought 900,000 acres of timbered land near Tacoma, Washington. Under Weyerhaeuser's leadership the firm grew and prospered and today is one of the largest forest-products companies in the world. Many economic systems need and encourage entrepreneurs like Frederick Weyerhaeuser, who start new businesses and who make the decisions that expand small businesses into larger ones. These people embrace the opportunities and accept the risks inherent in creating and operating businesses.

NATURAL RESOURCES Materials supplied by nature are **natural resources.** The most common natural resources are land, water, mineral deposits, and trees. For example, Weyerhaeuser obviously relies on land and trees. Even firms that do not directly use natural resources are still likely to depend on them indirectly. Chemicals, for example, are the basis for the plastic resins that computer manufacturers use for keyboards. All companies need land on which to build factories and office buildings and to generate the electric power they need to operate.

natural resources Materials supplied by nature—for example, land, water, mineral deposits, and trees

Types of Economic Systems

Different types of economic systems manage the factors of production in different ways. In some systems, ownership is private; in others, the factors of production are owned by the government. Economic systems also differ in the ways decisions are made about production and allocation. A **planned economy,** for example, relies on a centralized government to control all or most factors of production and to make all or most production and allocation decisions. In a **market economy,** individuals—producers and consumers—control production and allocation decisions through supply and demand. We will describe each of these economic types and then discuss the reality of the *mixed market economy*. We will also look closely at an important process in the development of the mixed market economy in more and more countries: *privatization*.

planned economy Economy that relies on a centralized government to control all or most factors of production and to make all or most production and allocation decisions

market economy Economy in which individuals control production and allocation decisions through supply and demand

PLANNED ECONOMIES The two most basic forms of planned economies are *communism* and *socialism*. As originally proposed by nineteenth-century German economist Karl Marx, *communism* is a system in which the government owns and operates all sources of production. Marx envisioned a society in which individuals would ultimately contribute according to their abilities and receive economic benefits according to their needs. He also expected government ownership of production factors to be only temporary: Once society had matured, government would "wither away" and the workers would gain direct ownership.

Most Eastern European countries and the former Soviet Union embraced communist systems until very recently. In the early 1990s, however, one country after another renounced communism as both an economic and a political system. The map in Figure 1.1 dramatizes the decline in the number of communist nations over the past decade. Today, Cuba, North Korea, Vietnam, and the People's Republic of China are among the few nations with avowedly communist systems. Even in these countries, however, planned economic systems are making room for features of the free enterprise system from the lowest to the highest levels.

market Mechanism for exchange between buyers and sellers of a particular good or service

MARKET ECONOMIES A **market** is a mechanism for exchange between the buyers and sellers of a particular good or service. To understand how a *market economy* works, consider what happens when a customer goes to a fruit market to buy apples. While one vendor is selling apples for $1 per pound, another is charging $1.50. Both vendors are free to charge what they want, and customers are free to buy what they choose. If both vendors' apples are of the same quality, the customer will buy the cheaper ones. If the $1.50 apples are fresher, the customer may buy them instead. In short, both buyers and sellers enjoy freedom of choice.

capitalism Market economy that provides for private ownership of production and encourages entrepreneurship by offering profits as an incentive

Capitalism. Market economies, which are based on the principles of capitalism, rely on markets, not governments, to decide what, when, and for whom to produce. **Capitalism** provides for the private ownership of the factors of production. It also encourages entrepreneurship by offering profits as an incentive. Businesses can provide whatever goods and services and charge whatever prices they choose. Similarly, customers can choose how and where to spend their money.

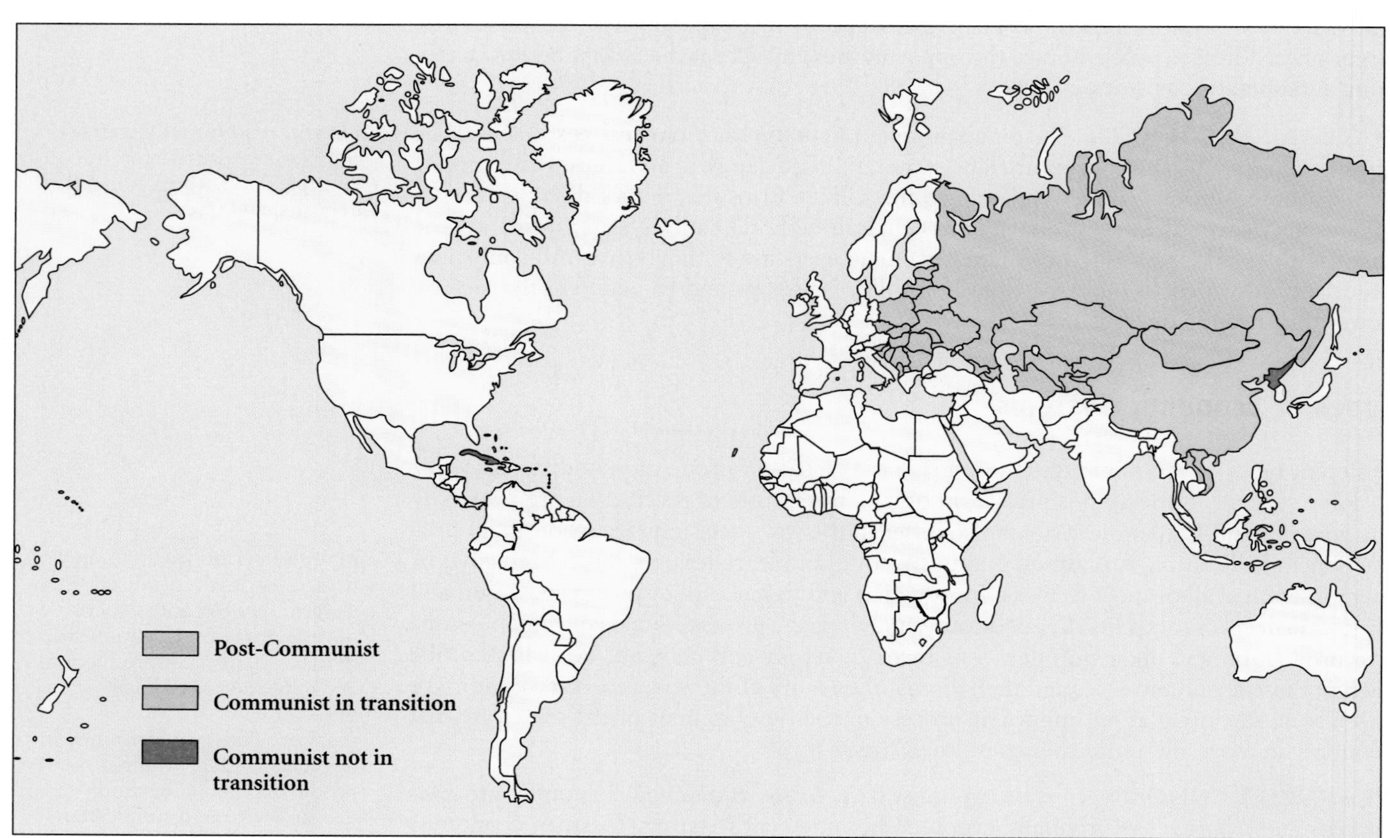

FIGURE 1.1 ◆ **Decline in Communist Governments**

MIXED MARKET ECONOMIES In their pure theoretical forms, planned and market economies are often seen as two extremes or opposites. In reality, however, most countries rely on some form of **mixed market economy**—a system featuring characteristics of both planned and market economies. For example, most countries of the former Eastern bloc are now adopting market mechanisms through a process called **privatization**—the process of converting government enterprises into privately owned companies.

mixed market economy Economic system featuring characteristics of both planned and market economies

privatization Process of converting government enterprises into privately owned companies

In Hungary, for instance, privatization is being used to help reduce the country's $22 billion national debt. Among the industries now being privatized are the state-owned oil and telephone companies, all major banks, and the entire electricity and gas distribution industry. Successful privatization often requires the ingenuity of creative capitalists such as Peter Rona, a Hungarian who is a major financial backer of North American Bus Industries Ltd., a Hungarian company that manufactures buses for U.S. mass-transit fleets in Miami, Baltimore, Buffalo, and Washington. After privatizing part of the state-owned bus company, Rona developed a plan to manufacture buses in both Hungary and Alabama, thereby meeting U.S. government requirements that 60 percent of the value of federally financed urban buses come from the United States. Although parts and partially assembled vehicle bodies are shipped back and forth from Budapest to Alabama, the company is more competitive than its U.S. business rivals, largely because of the low cost of Hungarian labor ($4 per hour) and Rona's perseverance. "I want to take a dying socialist company and save it," says Rona, who left his native country after the Soviet-crushed uprising in 1956 and did not return until 1989.[2]

> **"I want to take a dying socialist company and save it."**
>
> —Peter Rona
>
> *Financial backer of North American Bus Industries Ltd.*

In the partially planned system often called **socialism,** the government owns and operates selected major industries. In such mixed market economies, the government may control banking, communication, transportation, and industries that produce such basic goods as oil and steel. Smaller businesses, such as clothing stores and restaurants, are privately owned. For example, many Western European countries, including England and

socialism Planned economic system in which the government owns and operates only selected major sources of production

Global competitors can reach new U.S. markets as well, as did a Hungarian bus company whose vehicles now ply the streets of Portland, Oregon. This bus was made by a firm once owned by the communist government of Hungary. Now privatized, North American Bus Industries Ltd. makes vehicles in Alabama as well as Hungary.

France, allow free market operations in most economic areas but maintain government control in others, such as health care. Government planners in Japan give special centrally planned assistance to new industries that are expected to grow.

THE U.S. ECONOMIC SYSTEM

Understanding the complex nature of the U.S. economic system is essential to understanding the environment in which U.S. businesses operate. In this section, we describe the workings of the U.S. market economy in more detail. Specifically, we examine markets, the nature of demand and supply, private enterprise, and degrees of competition.

Markets, Demand, and Supply

A market economy consists of many different markets. For example, virtually every good or service has its own market. In each of these, businesses decide what to make, in what quantities, and what price to charge. Customers also make decisions: They decide what to buy and how much they are willing to pay. Billions of exchanges take place every day between businesses and individuals, between different businesses, and between individuals, businesses, and governments. Moreover, exchanges conducted under conditions in one place often have an impact on exchanges elsewhere.

Chocolate lovers, for example, should consider the story told by the three graphs in Figure 1.2. The graph in Figure 1.2(a) shows that, despite some ups and downs, worldwide consumption of cocoa, the principal ingredient in chocolate, has begun to outstrip production. Figure 1.2(b) shows that total worldwide reserves have consequently begun to fall. The pressure is being felt from both the demand side (consumption in such countries as Germany, Britain, France, Japan, and especially the United States has risen consistently over the past decade) and the supply side (disease and pests have plagued crops in such pro-

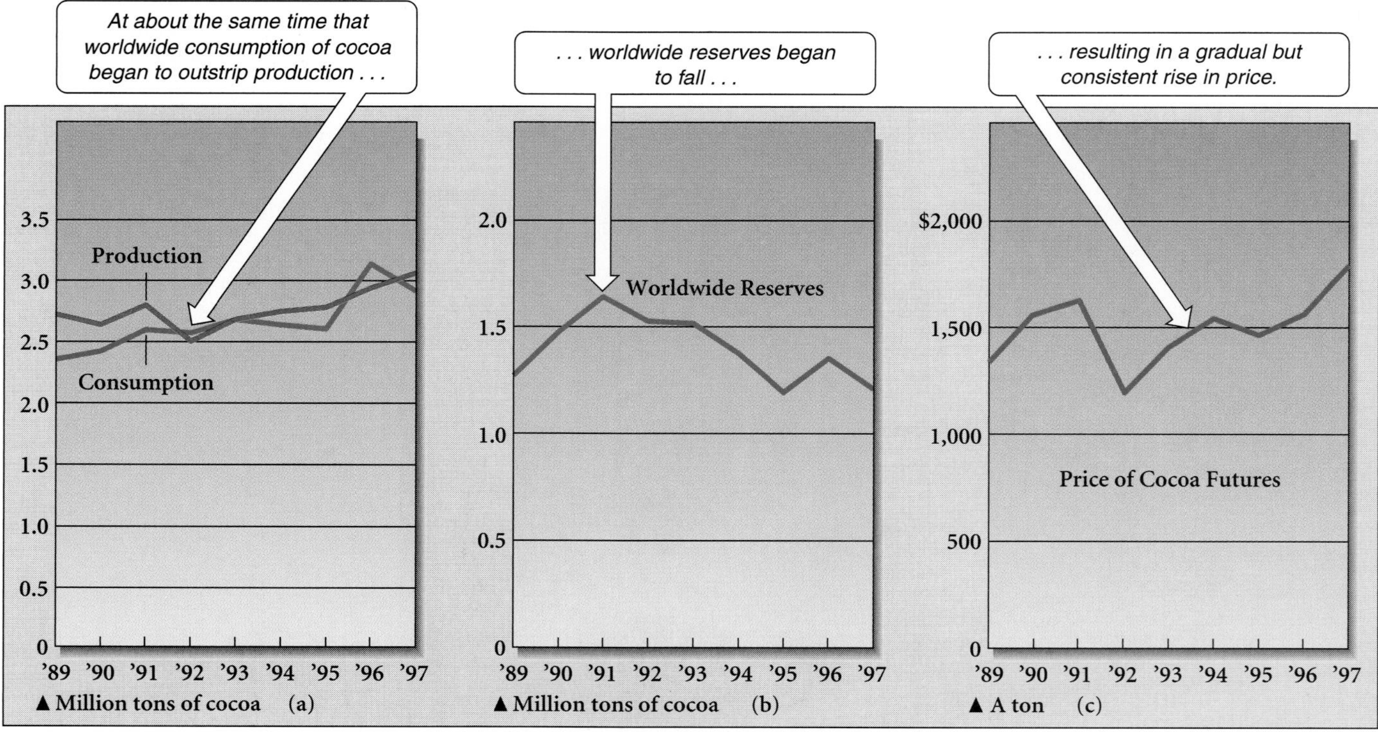

FIGURE 1.2 (a,b,c) ◆ **Cocoa Supply and Demand**

ducer countries as the Ivory Coast, Ghana, Indonesia, Brazil, Nigeria, and Malaysia). Figure 1.2(c) shows that the price of cocoa futures—agreements to buy cocoa at a future date—on the New York Coffee, Sugar and Cocoa Exchange has risen during the same period.[3]

THE LAWS OF DEMAND AND SUPPLY On all economic levels, decisions about what to buy and what to sell are determined primarily by the forces of demand and supply. **Demand** is the willingness and ability of buyers to purchase a product (a good or a service). **Supply** is the willingness and ability of producers to offer a good or service for sale. Generally speaking, demand and supply follow basic "laws":

- The **law of demand:** Buyers will purchase (*demand*) more of a product as its price drops and less of a product as its price increases.
- The **law of supply:** Producers will offer (*supply*) more of a product for sale as its price rises and less as its price drops.

The Demand and Supply Schedule. To appreciate these laws in action, consider the market for pizza in your town. If everyone in town is willing to pay $25 for a pizza (a high price), the town's only pizzeria will produce a large supply. If everyone is willing to pay only $5 (a low price), however, the restaurant will make fewer pizzas. Through careful analysis, we can determine how many pizzas will be sold at different prices. These results, called a **demand and supply schedule,** are obtained from marketing research and other systematic studies of the market. Properly applied, they help managers better understand the relationships among different levels of demand and supply at different price levels.

Demand and Supply Curves. The demand and supply schedule, for example, can be used to construct demand and supply curves for pizza in your town. A **demand curve** shows how many products—in this case, pizzas—will be **demanded** (bought) at different prices. A **supply curve** shows how many pizzas will be **supplied** (cooked) at different prices.

Figure 1.3 shows hypothetical demand and supply curves for pizzas. As you can see, demand increases as price decreases; supply increases as price increases. When the demand and supply curves are plotted on the same graph, the point at which they intersect is the **market price** or **equilibrium price**—the price at which the quantity of goods demanded and the quantity of goods supplied are equal. Note in Figure 1.3 that the equilibrium price for pizzas in our example is $10. At this point, the quantity of pizzas demanded and the quantity of pizzas supplied are the same: 1,000 pizzas per week.

Surpluses and Shortages. What if the restaurant chooses to make some other number of pizzas? For example, what would happen if the owner tried to increase profits by making more pizzas to sell? Or what if the owner wanted to reduce overhead, cut back on store hours, and reduce the number of pizzas offered for sale? In either case, the result would be an inefficient use of resources and lower profits. For instance, if the restaurant supplies 1,200 pizzas and tries to sell them for $10 each, 200 pizzas will not be purchased. The demand schedule clearly shows that only 1,000 pizzas will be demanded at this price. The pizza maker will thus have a **surplus**—a situation in which the quantity supplied exceeds the quantity demanded. The restaurant will lose the money it spent making those extra 200 pizzas.

Conversely, if the pizzeria supplies only 800 pizzas, a **shortage** will result: The quantity demanded will be greater than the quantity supplied. The pizzeria will lose the extra money it could have made by producing 200 more pizzas. Even though consumers may pay more for pizzas because of the shortage, the restaurant will still earn lower profits than if it had made 1,000 pizzas. In addition, it will risk angering customers who cannot buy pizzas. To maximize profits, therefore, all businesses must constantly seek the right combination of price charged and quantity supplied. This right combination is found at the equilibrium point.

Of course, this simple example involves only one company, one product, and a few buyers. Obviously, the U.S. economy is far more complex. Thousands of companies sell hundreds of thousands of products to millions of buyers every day. In the end, however, the result is much the same: Companies try to supply the quantity and selection of goods that will earn them the largest profits.

demand The willingness and ability of buyers to purchase a good or service

supply The willingness and ability of producers to offer a good or service for sale

law of demand Principle that buyers will purchase (demand) more of a product as its price drops and less as its price increases

law of supply Principle that producers will offer (supply) more of a product for sale as its price rises and less as its price drops

demand and supply schedule Assessment of the relationships between different levels of demand and supply at different price levels

demand curve Graph showing how many units of a product will be demanded (bought) at different prices

supply curve Graph showing how many units of a product will be supplied (offered for sale) at different prices

market price (or **equilibrium price**) Profit-maximizing price at which the quantity of goods demanded and the quantity of goods supplied are equal

surplus Situation in which quantity supplied exceeds quantity demanded

shortage Situation in which quantity demanded exceeds quantity supplied

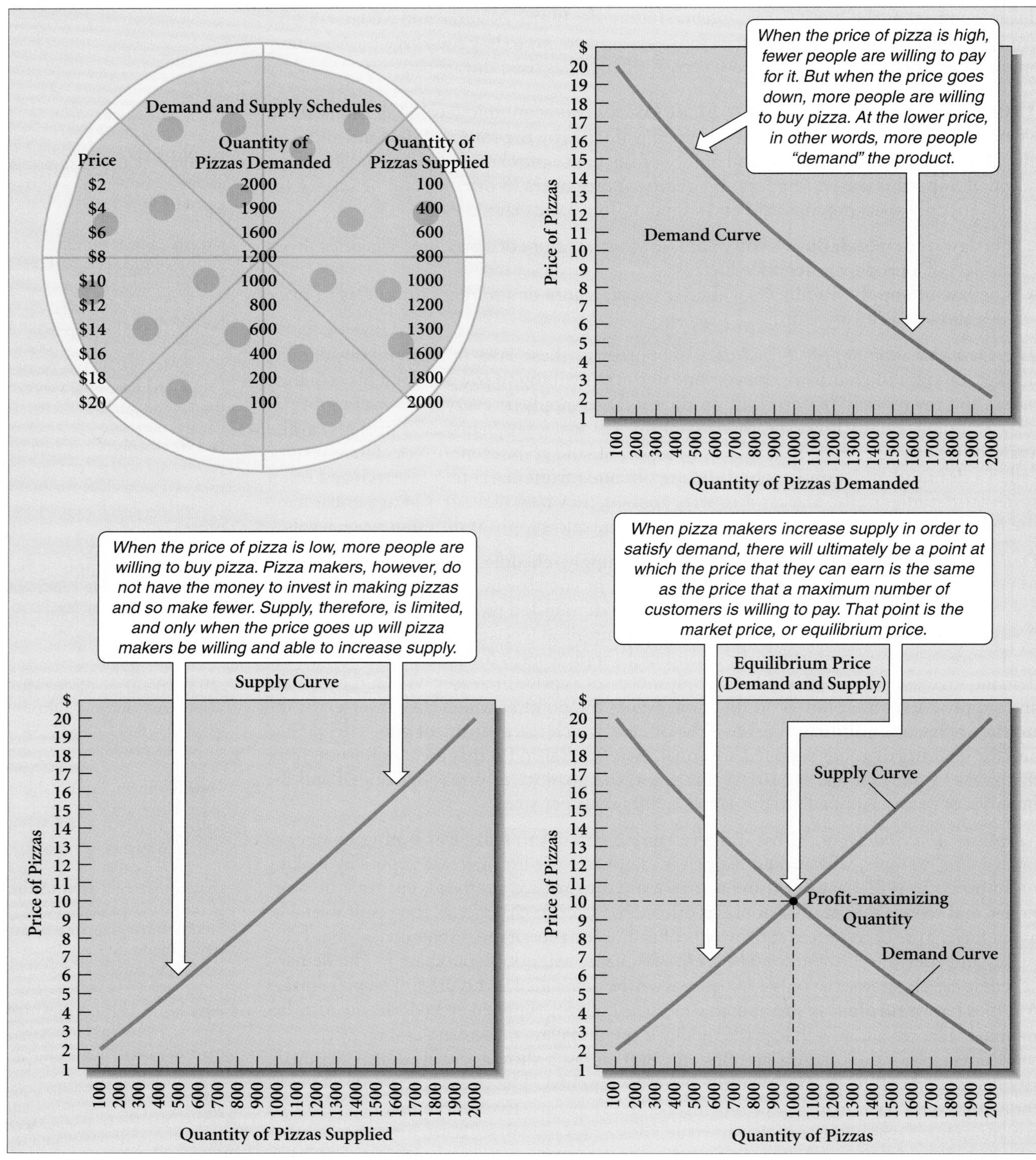

FIGURE 1.3 ◆ **Demand and Supply**

Private Enterprise

private enterprise Economic system that allows individuals to pursue their own interests without undue governmental restriction

In his book *The Wealth of Nations*, first published in 1776, Scottish economist Adam Smith argued that a society's interests are best served by **private enterprise**—a system that allows individuals to pursue their own interests without government restriction. Smith envisioned a system in which individual entrepreneurs sought their own self-interest. At the same time, the "invisible hand of competition" would lead businesses to produce the best products as efficiently as possible and to sell them at the lowest possible prices. After all, that strategy was the clearest route to successful profit making and fulfilled self-interest. In effect, then, each business would be working for the good of society as a whole. Society would benefit most from minimal interference with individuals' pursuit of economic self-interest.

Market economies are based on roughly the same concept of private enterprise. In both Smith's "pure" vision and the reality of contemporary practice, private enterprise requires the presence of four elements: *private property rights*, *freedom of choice*, *profits*, and *competition*.

PRIVATE PROPERTY RIGHTS Smith maintained that the creation of wealth should be the concern of individuals, not the government. Thus, he argued that the ownership of the resources used to create wealth must be in the hands of individuals. Of course, individual ownership of property is part of everyday life in the United States. No doubt you or someone you know has bought and owned automobiles, homes, land, or stock. The right to hold **private property**—to buy, own, use, and sell almost any form of property—is a fundamental right guaranteed by the U.S. Constitution.[4]

private property rights The right to buy, own, use, and sell almost any form of property

FREEDOM OF CHOICE A related right is *freedom of choice*. You enjoy the right to sell your labor to any employer you choose. You can also choose which products you want to buy. Finally, freedom of choice means that producers can usually choose whom to hire and what to produce. For example, the U.S. government normally does not tell Sears what it can and cannot sell.

PROFITS Naturally, a business that fails to make a profit will eventually close its doors, and many—in fact, most—small businesses fail within the first 6 years.[5] The lure of profits (and freedom), however, inevitably leads some people to abandon the security of working for someone else and to assume the risks of entrepreneurship. Obviously, anticipated profits also play a large part in individuals' choices of the goods or services they will produce.

COMPETITION If profits motivate individuals to start businesses, competition motivates them to operate their businesses efficiently. **Competition** occurs when two or more businesses vie for the same resources or customers. For example, if you decide to buy a new pair of athletic shoes, you have a choice of several different stores in which to shop. After selecting a store, you may then choose between brands (for example, Nike, Reebok, or Adidas). If you intend to buy only one pair of shoes, all these manufacturers are in competition with one another, as are all the shoe retailers in your area, from mass marketers such as Kmart to specialty outlets such as Foot Locker.

competition Vying among businesses for the same resources or customers

To gain an advantage over its competitors, a business must produce its goods or services efficiently and must be able to sell them for prices that earn reasonable profits. To achieve these goals, a business must convince customers that its products are either better or less expensive than those of competitors. In this sense, competition benefits society: It forces all competitive businesses to make their products better or cheaper. Naturally, a company that produces inferior, expensive products is sure to be forced out of business.

Degrees of Competition

Not all industries are equally competitive. Economists have identified four basic degrees of competition within a private enterprise system: pure competition, monopolistic competition, oligopoly, and monopoly. Table 1.1 summarizes the features of these four degrees of competition.

PURE COMPETITION For **pure competition** to exist, two conditions must prevail:

pure competition Market or industry characterized by numerous small firms producing an identical product

1. All firms in a given industry must be small.
2. The number of firms in the industry must be large.

TABLE 1.1 ◆ Degrees of Competition

CHARACTERISTIC	PURE COMPETITION	MONOPOLISTIC COMPETITION	OLIGOPOLY	MONOPOLY
Example	Local farmer	Stationery store	Steel industry	Public utility
Number of competitors	Many	Many, but fewer than in pure competition	Few	None
Ease of entry into industry	Easy	Fairly easy	Difficult	Regulated by government
Similarity of goods or services offered by competing firms	Identical	Similar	Can be similar or different	No directly competing goods or services
Level of control over price by individual firms	None	Some	Some	Considerable

Under such conditions, no single firm is powerful enough to influence the price of its product or service in the marketplace.

In turn, these conditions reflect four important principles:

1. The products offered by each firm are so similar that buyers view them as identical to those offered by other firms.
2. Both buyers and sellers know the prices that others are paying and receiving in the marketplace.
3. Because each firm is small, it is easy for any single firm to enter or leave the market.
4. Going prices are set exclusively by supply and demand and accepted by both sellers and buyers.

Despite government price support programs such as those described earlier, agriculture is a good example of pure competition in the U.S. economy. For example, the wheat produced on one farm is essentially the same as that produced on another. Producers and buyers both are well aware of prevailing market prices. Moreover, it is easy to start producing wheat and easy to stop when doing so is no longer profitable.

monopolistic competition Market or industry characterized by numerous buyers and relatively numerous sellers trying to differentiate their products from those of competitors

MONOPOLISTIC COMPETITION Fewer sellers are involved in **monopolistic competition** than in pure competition, but because there are still many buyers, sellers try to make their products at least appear to be different from those of competitors. Differentiating strategies include brand names (Tide and Cheer), design or styling (Ralph Lauren and Guess? jeans), and advertising (Coke and Pepsi). For example, in an effort to attract health-conscious consumers, the Kraft and General Foods divisions of Philip Morris are actively promoting such differentiated products as low-fat Breyers ice cream and Cool Whip, low-calorie Jell-O, and sugar-free Kool-Aid.

Monopolistically competitive businesses may be large or small, but still able to easily enter or leave the market. For example, many small clothing stores compete successfully with large apparel retailers such as Liz Claiborne and The Limited. Product differentiation also gives sellers some control over the prices they charge. For instance, even though Sears shirts may have similar styling and other features, Ralph Lauren Polo shirts can be priced with little regard for the lower price of Sears shirts.

oligopoly Market or industry characterized by a handful of (generally large) sellers with the power to influence the prices of their products

OLIGOPOLY When an industry has only a handful of sellers, an **oligopoly** exists. As a general rule, these sellers are quite large. The entry of new competitors is difficult because large capital investment is necessary. Consequently, oligopolistic industries (for example, the automobile, rubber, airline, and steel industries) tend to stay that way. Thus, only two companies, both among the biggest in the world, manufacture large commercial aircraft: Boeing (a U.S. company) and Airbus (a European consortium).

Not surprisingly, individual oligopolists have more control over their own strategies than monopolistically competitive firms. At the same time, however, the actions of any one firm can significantly affect the sales of every other firm. For example, when one firm reduces prices or offers incentives to increase sales, the others usually protect their sales by doing the same. Likewise, when one firm raises prices, the others generally follow suit. Therefore, the prices of comparable products are usually quite similar. When a major airline announces a new program of fare discounts, the others mimic its strategy almost immediately. Just as quickly, when the fare discounts end for one airline, they usually end for all the others at the same time.

MONOPOLY A **monopoly** exists when an industry or market has only one producer. Obviously, a sole supplier enjoys complete control over the prices of its products. Its only constraint is the fall of consumer demand in response to increased prices. In the United States, laws such as the Sherman Antitrust Act (1890) and the Clayton Act (1914) forbid many monopolies and regulate the prices charged by so-called **natural monopolies** (industries in which one company can most efficiently supply all the needed goods or services). For example, most local electric companies are natural monopolies because they can supply all the power needed in their local area. Duplicate facilities—such as two power plants, two sets of power lines, and so forth—would be wasteful.

monopoly Market or industry in which there is only one producer, which can therefore set the prices of its products

natural monopoly Industry in which one company can most efficiently supply all needed goods or services

A very high-profile legal battle began in 1998, when the U.S. government pursued a lawsuit against the software giant Microsoft, alleging practices designed to eliminate competition from such firms as Netscape and other software developers. The legal basis of this suit is the Clayton Act, which forbids certain types of *tying arrangements*, whereby a copyright holder issues a license only to buyers who also purchase other products. According to the government, Microsoft's so-called Enterprise agreements, which offer unlimited use of its Windows NT, Office, and BackOffice products at one price, constitute such an arrangement. Ken Wasch, president of the Software Publishers Assn., agrees: Microsoft's licensing agreements, he charges, "have an adverse impact on anyone competing with the Microsoft suite of products." Focusing on the company's practices in the markets for Internet-browsing and Web-navigation software, the government has charged that Microsoft's monopoly status (1) limits market entry for new competitors, (2) controls channels of distribution, (3) inflates prices and restricts product choices for consumers, and (4) privileges it as the sole supplier of software to major computer makers.[6]

> **"Microsoft's licensing agreements have an adverse impact on anyone competing with the Microsoft suite of products."**
>
> —Ken Wasch
> *President of the Software Publishers Assn.*

EVALUATING ECONOMIC SYSTEMS

Figures 1.4 through 1.8 display a variety of current economic indicators that can be used to highlight some key facts about the U.S. economy.[7] Using these data for reference points, we explain more fully the key goals of the U.S. economic system and measure the success of that system in achieving its goals. We conclude by describing government attempts to manage the U.S. economy in the interest of meeting national economic goals.

Economic Goals

Nearly every economic system has three broad goals: *stability*, *full employment*, and *growth*. Naturally, different systems place different emphasis on each of these goals and take different approaches to achieving them.

stability Condition in which the balance between the money available in an economy and the goods produced in it are growing at about the same rate

STABILITY In economic terms, **stability** is the condition in which the money available in an economy and the goods produced in that economy remain about the same. In other words, there are enough desirable products to satisfy consumer demand, and consumers have enough money, in the aggregate, to buy what they need and want. When conditions are stable, therefore, prices for consumer goods, interest rates, and wages paid to workers change very little. Stability helps maintain predictable conditions in which managers, consumers, and workers can analyze the business environment, project goals, and assess performance.

inflation Phenomenon of widespread price increases throughout an economic system

Inflation. The biggest threat to stability is **inflation**—a period of widespread price increases throughout an economic system. Typically, inflation has an impact on virtually all the goods and services that the system produces. For example, inflation explains why a pair of Levi's jeans that costs $35 today cost only $29 ten years ago and only $18 twenty years ago. For the last several years, inflation rates in the United States have been running below 3 percent. Recent annual rates have ranged from 2.6 to 2.9 percent, and this trend is expected to continue for at least the next few years.

Over the course of this century, inflation in the United States has varied dramatically. For example, prices rose sharply before the Great Depression and then plunged headlong. Immediately after the Depression, they began to rise steadily again, punctuated by brief periods of deflation. This same pattern characterized economic activity in the entire industrialized world in the years just before World War II. In the period immediately following the war, the United States experienced several decades of constant inflation, with steep increases often exceeding 10 percent per year in the late 1970s and early 1980s. Since then, however, inflation rates have declined.

Figure 1.4 shows inflation rates in the United States since 1960 by tracing the average annual increase in producer prices. At current levels, prices double approximately every 20 years. What does this figure mean in real terms for consumers? Among other things, if this trend remains constant, when they enter college, your children will pay about twice what you are now paying for tuition, fees, textbooks, clothing, and housing.

Inflation is not necessarily or entirely bad. Stability can degenerate into stagnation and contribute to a decline in the development and marketing of new products. After all, when the marketplace has enough products to buy at reasonable prices and consumers have enough money with which to buy the products, innovation and growth in new areas are not urgent business priorities. For the same reason, the onset of inflation is often a sign of economic growth. When businesses see that they can charge higher prices, they may hire

FIGURE 1.4 ◆ **U.S. Producer Price Index**

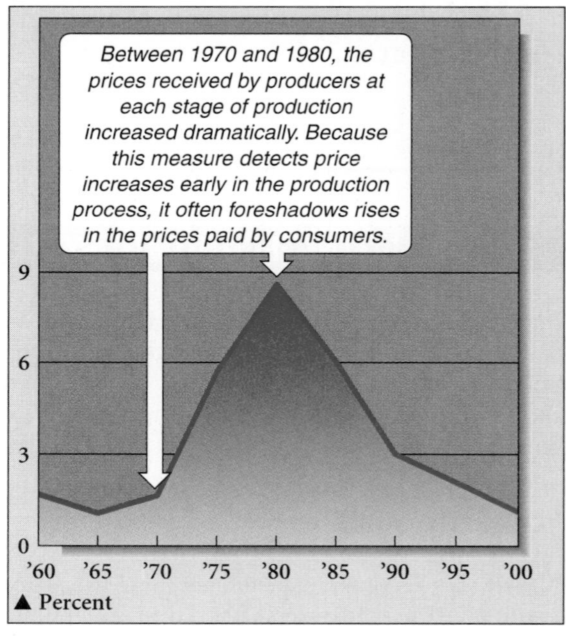

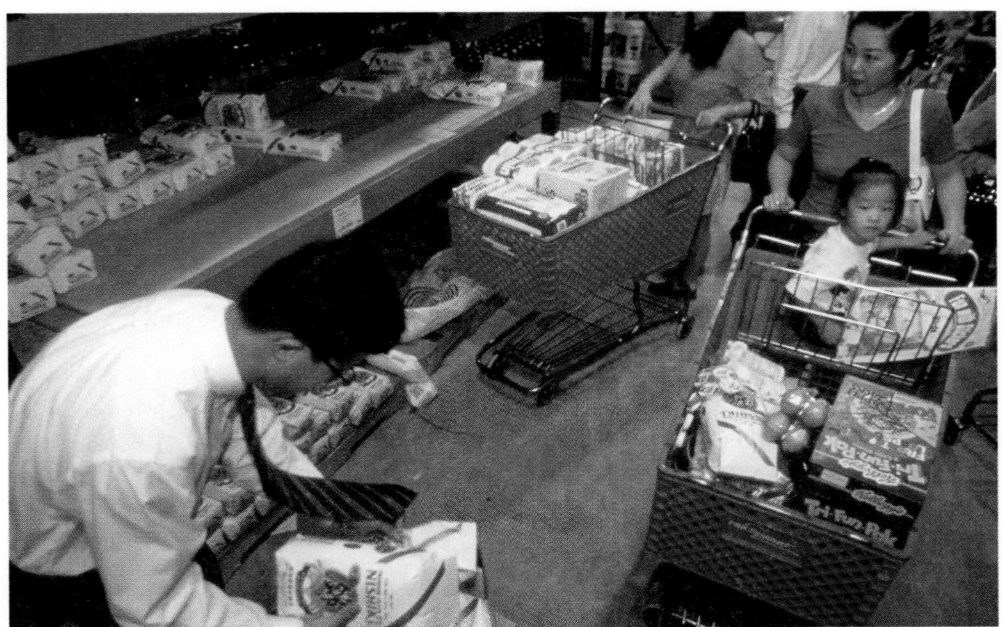

As the rupiah, the Indonesian unit of currency, falls in value, consumers can afford less and less. For Indonesian shoppers, therefore, buying now is better than buying later. When their governments proved unable to handle the foreign-debt loads they had taken on, foreign capital stopped coming, interest rates skyrocketed, and the national economies of Indonesia, Malaysia, South Korea, Russia, Brazil, and Mexico were among the hardest hit by the global economic crisis that struck in 1997–1998.

new workers, invest more money in advertising, and introduce new products. In addition, new businesses open to take advantage of perceived prosperity. At this point, of course, a damaging inflationary trend may set in: Workers may start demanding higher wages to pay for more expensive products, and because higher wages mean lower profits, sellers may raise prices even more. Inflation can be curtailed both naturally and artificially. For example, rates of increase may slow either because of an economic slump, such as the recession that hit the United States in the late 1980s, or because of government intervention.

Recession and Depression. Inflation is not the only threat to economic stability. Suppose that a major factory in your hometown closed. Hundreds or even thousands of workers would lose their jobs. If other companies in the area do not have jobs for them, these unemployed people will reduce their spending. Other local businesses will thus suffer drops in sales and perhaps cut their own workforces. The resulting **recession,** characterized by decreases in employment, income, and production, may spread across the city, the state, or even the nation. A particularly severe and long-lasting recession, such as the one that affected much of the world in the 1930s, is called a **depression.**

recession Period characterized by decreases in employment, income, and production

depression Particularly severe and long-lasting recession

FULL EMPLOYMENT Although there is some disagreement about the meaning of the term *full employment,* the concept remains a goal of most economic systems. Strictly speaking, full employment means that everyone who wants to work has an opportunity to do so. In reality, full employment is impossible: There will always be people looking for work.

Unemployment. The level of joblessness among people actively seeking work can define **unemployment.** Employment rates are an important element in the health of a nation's economy. For example, high unemployment suggests that businesses are performing poorly, whereas low unemployment suggests that business is better. The rate of unemployment in the United States has varied widely during the twentieth century. As with inflation, major fluctuations occurred during the Great Depression, which began in 1929 and lasted through most of the 1930s. Since the end of World War II, unemployment has generally varied between 5 and 10 percent.

unemployment Level of joblessness among people actively seeking work

In recent years, however, unemployment has dropped so low that many businesses have struggled to find enough qualified workers. Meanwhile, skilled workers have come to expect a growing array of incentives and benefits when they select employers. "A couple of years ago," recalls one ad company executive, "a guy came in and stenciled every square of toilet paper with the words, 'I'm willing to start at the bottom.' Today everyone thinks they're entitled to a job."[8]

> "A couple of years ago a guy came in and stenciled every square of toilet paper with the words, 'I'm willing to start at the bottom."
>
> —Ad company executive

growth Increase in the amount of goods and services produced by a nation's resources

GROWTH Perhaps the most fundamental goal of most economic systems is **growth**—an increase in the amount of goods and services produced by a nation's resources. In theory, we all want the whole system to expand and provide more businesses, more jobs, and more wealth for everyone. In practice, however, it is difficult to achieve growth without triggering inflation or other elements of instability. Conversely, an extended period without growth may eventually result in economic decline: business shutdowns, lost jobs, a decrease in overall wealth, and a lower standard of living for everyone.

Interestingly, some experts have recently expressed concern about the ability of the United States to sustain the 3 percent annual growth rate that it has enjoyed for the last several years. Troubling indicators include budget cuts for basic research, a decline in the number of students majoring in science and engineering, continuing debates about Internet regulation, visa quotas for high-tech workers, and encryption policies, all of which might adversely affect high-tech industries.[9]

Measuring Economic Performance

To judge the success of an economic system in meeting its goals, economists use one or more of five measures: *gross national* and *gross domestic product, productivity, balance of trade,* and *national debt.*

gross national product (GNP) The value of all goods and services produced by an economic system in a year regardless of where the factors of production are located

GROSS NATIONAL PRODUCT AND GROSS DOMESTIC PRODUCT If we add the total value of all the goods and services produced by an economic system in a 1-year period, the sum is that country's **gross national product,** or **GNP.** GNP is a useful indi-

TRENDS AND CHALLENGES

THE DEFLATION DILEMMA

At first glance, the news sounded good, even terrific: Japanese automaker Mazda was lowering the price of its 1999 Millenia S luxury car more than $5,500, and Acura was slashing the cost of its redesigned TL 3.2 by $5,200. These 15 percent reductions, especially when compared with prices posted a year earlier, promised to be a real boon to consumers; and competition being what it is, General Motors, Ford, and Chrysler announced significant price breaks of their own.

As American consumers cheered, economists worried—not that times were too good, but about the threat of deflation. In economic terms, *deflation* signals a period of falling prices brought about by production overcapacity. "If inflation is too much money chasing too few goods," explains one journalist, "deflation is too little money chasing too many goods. Prices rise when demand surges ahead of supply but fall when supply zooms ahead of demand."

> "If inflation is too much money chasing too few goods, deflation is too little money chasing too many goods."
>
> —James K. Glassman
> *Commentator, U.S. News & World Report*

Today, it seems as if there's a glut of everything on the world market, from oil to gold to computer chips, in large part because of the economic problems plaguing Thailand, South Korea, Indonesia, and other Asian economies. With the local demand for goods weak and their overbuilt manufacturing capacities linked to huge foreign investments, Asian companies have been forced to compete more fiercely than ever to sell their goods abroad. One way to compete, of course, is to lower prices, and a potent weapon in any export war is currency devaluation. "Goods invoiced in a devalued currency," explains economist John Makin of the American Enterprise Institute,

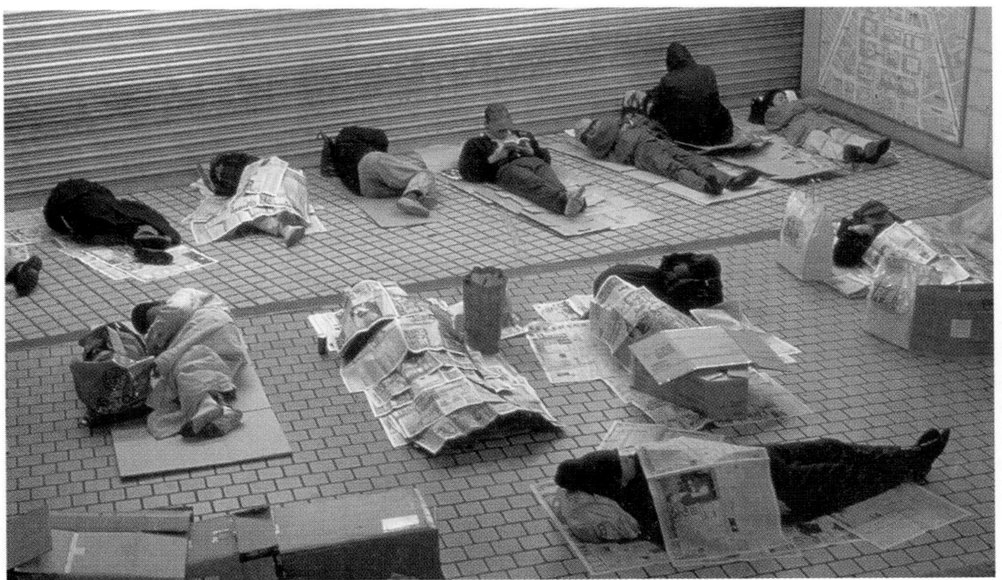

These homeless people sleeping in a Tokyo train station are one sign of the economic stress that Japan has suffered for most of the 1990s. Both the country's government and its banks made too many overly optimistic loans during the boom years from the 1950s through the 1980s, and in the 1990s the bad debt came back to haunt them. Fortunately, however, because Japan is owed more money than it owes, it has access to the resources it needs to take corrective measures. In addition, Japanese corporations tend to respond to hard times by cutting wages, not by laying off workers.

cator of economic growth because it allows us to track an economy's performance over time. The measure of an economy can be affected by inflation and other factors concerning the value of its currency. For example, if an economic system has a 5 percent decline in goods produced but experiences a 10 percent increase in inflation, its GNP will increase 5 percent. Changes in the value of a nation's currency relative to those of other countries also distort the value of imports and exports, and thus GNP. To control the effects of such factors, experts compare economies according to an adjusted figure called the **real gross national product** (real GNP)—the gross national product adjusted for inflation and changes in the value of a country's currency.

real gross national product (real GNP) Gross national product adjusted for inflation and changes in the value of a country's currency

The United States has the highest real GNP of any industrial nation in the world. For example, real GNP per capita in the United States is almost $21,000. By comparison, real GNP per capita in Japan is only slightly over $14,000. Other countries with high real GNP

"are less expensive for foreign buyers. This is called exporting deflation." There's no better way to lower prices in the global marketplace, adds Makin, than to devalue one's own currency.

Thus, American consumers could look forward to lower prices from America's big three carmakers: As export prices of Mazdas and Acuras dropped, U.S. companies were forced to lower their own prices to compete. This state of affairs squeezed corporate profits, especially in firms prevented from cutting labor costs because of a tight job market.

Deflation may sound like a new problem to generations of Americans raised on the maxim that inflation, rather than deflation, is the enemy of economic growth. Deflation, however, was largely responsible for the Great Depression of the 1930s. Between 1865 and 1900, economic recessions were consistently linked to falling, rather than rising, prices. Historically, moreover, inflation has been easier to cure than deflation. As you will see in Chapter 15, the U.S. Federal Reserve, the nation's central bank, typically drenches inflationary fires by raising interest rates: Companies that can no longer afford to borrow retrench and lower prices. Dealing with deflation is a little harder, but as governments struggled to get their economies back on track in 1998 and 1999, U.S. corporations made some important strategic moves to help themselves:

- Using careful purchasing to decrease costs faster than falling prices
- Cutting all unnecessary overhead
- Rapidly eliminating products that consumers no longer wanted
- Reallocating resources to the products and services that consumers were buying

Even with such steps, deflation is hard to stop: As prices fall, consumers postpone purchases in the expectation that the prices will drop even further. Until world markets stabilize, corporations must respond with flexibility and speed to survive the spiral of lowering prices.

This Subaru-Isuzu plant in Lafayette, Indiana, employs 1,700 local residents to make 60,000 cars and 60,000 trucks annually. The local payroll is $39 million per year. The plant's payroll, the value of the 120,000 vehicles manufactured there, and the profits earned by its Japanese owners are produced domestically and therefore counted in the U.S. gross domestic product.

per capita include Canada (almost $19,000), Norway (almost $17,000), and Germany (almost $15,000). The recent growth in international trade, however, has made GNP a less valid indicator of economic performance than was true in the past, mainly because GNP includes a nation's output regardless of where the factors of production are located.

gross domestic product (GDP) The value of all goods and services produced in a year by a nation's economy through domestic factors of production

To more accurately reflect economic performance in today's global environment, many experts prefer to use **gross domestic product,** or **GDP.** Like GNP, GDP measures a nation's annual output. However, the profits earned by a U.S. company abroad are only included in GNP, not GDP, because the output is not produced domestically (in the United States). Conversely, goods and services produced by foreign workers inside the United States, as well as profits earned by foreign companies operating here, are counted in the U.S. GDP because they are produced domestically.[10] Currently, U.S. GDP is about $6.7 trillion, about $12 billion higher than GNP.

productivity Measure of economic growth that compares how much a system produces with the resources needed to produce it

PRODUCTIVITY As a measure of economic growth, **productivity** compares what a system produces with the resources needed to produce it. The principle may be easier to understand if we apply the same measure on a smaller scale: If Xerox can produce a copier for $1,000 but Canon needs $1,200 to make a comparable product, Xerox is being more productive.

U.S. workers are among the most productive in the world. For instance, Figure 1.5 shows manufacturing productivity growth since 1960 in terms of annual average percentage of increase. As you can see, that growth slowed during the 1970s but began to rise again in the late 1980s. In recent years, however, other countries have made even greater strides in productivity growth. For example, annual increases in productivity in Taiwan have just about doubled gains made in the United States over the past 10 years.

Figure 1.6 shows another aspect of the U.S. economy that affects productivity. If we calculate output per dollar of equipment and plants, we see that U.S. businesses are investing their capital more and more efficiently; that is, they are buying new equipment and using it wisely. In theory these investments in better manufacturing technology will contribute to further increases in productivity. In Chapter 10, we take a more detailed look at the importance—and specific features—of productivity.

BALANCE OF TRADE *Balance of trade* is the difference between a country's *exports to* and *imports from* other countries. A *positive* balance of trade is generally considered favorable because new money flows into a country from the sales of its exports. A *negative* balance means that money is flowing out to pay for imports. During the 1980s, the United States suffered a large negative balance of trade. Things have improved during the 1990s, however, thanks largely to high foreign demand for U.S. services. For example, at the end of 1996 the United States had a negative balance of merchandise trade of $191.2 billion, but a positive balance of service trade of $80.2 billion. As Figure 1.7 shows, international trade is becoming an increasingly important part of the U.S. economy if we measure exports plus imports as a share

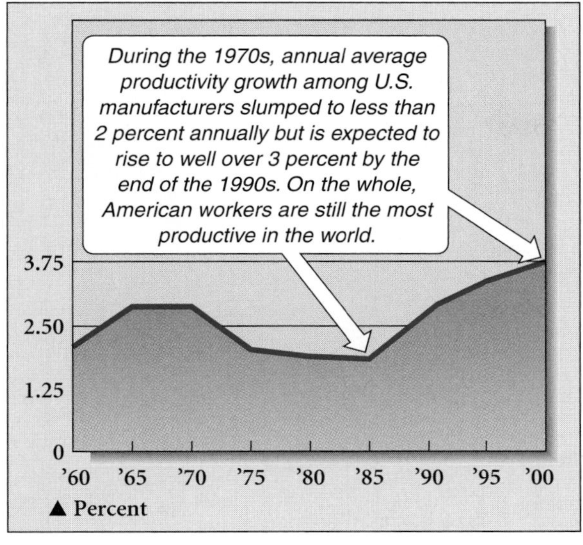

FIGURE 1.5 ◆ **Average Productivity Growth in the United States**

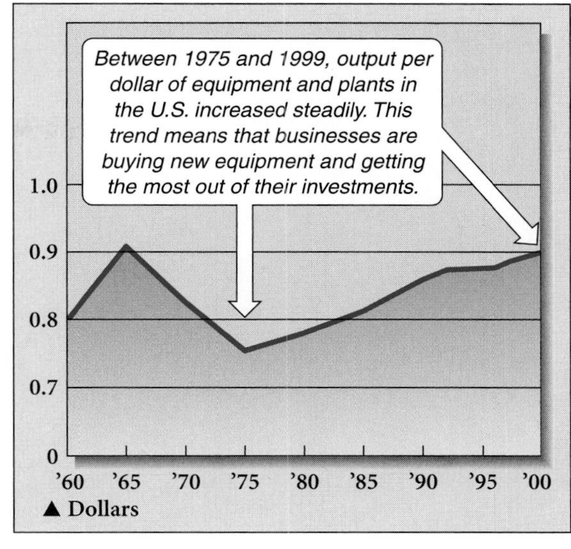

FIGURE 1.6 ◆ **Output per Dollar of Equipment and Plants**

of GDP. Thus, makers of economic and public policy pay closer attention to such economic indicators as balance of trade.

NATIONAL DEBT Like a business, the government takes in revenues (primarily in the form of taxes) and has expenses (military spending, social programs, and so forth). For the last several years, the United States has been running a **budget deficit:** It has been spending more money than it has been taking in. This deficit has created a huge **national debt**—the amount of money that the United States owes its creditors.

budget deficit Situation in which a government body spends more money than it takes in

national debt Total amount that a nation owes its creditors

The current national debt exceeds $5.5 *trillion.* Because this high level of debt results in higher interest rates throughout the economy, it limits growth. Unfortunately, reducing the size of the national debt has proven to be difficult. Obviously, the only two ways to reduce any budget deficit are to increase revenues (in this case, by raising taxes) and reduce spending. Unfortunately, neither of these is a popular option: No one is happy about the prospect of paying more taxes, and the prospect of spending cuts in virtually any area (the military, social programs, environmental protection, the prison system, education, or transportation) brings outcries from so many special-interest groups that policy makers have long been reluctant to take the political risks involved.

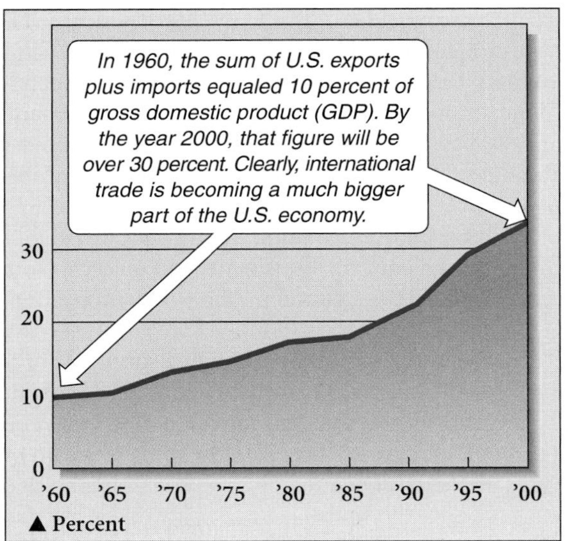

FIGURE 1.7 ◆ **Expanding International Trade in the United States**

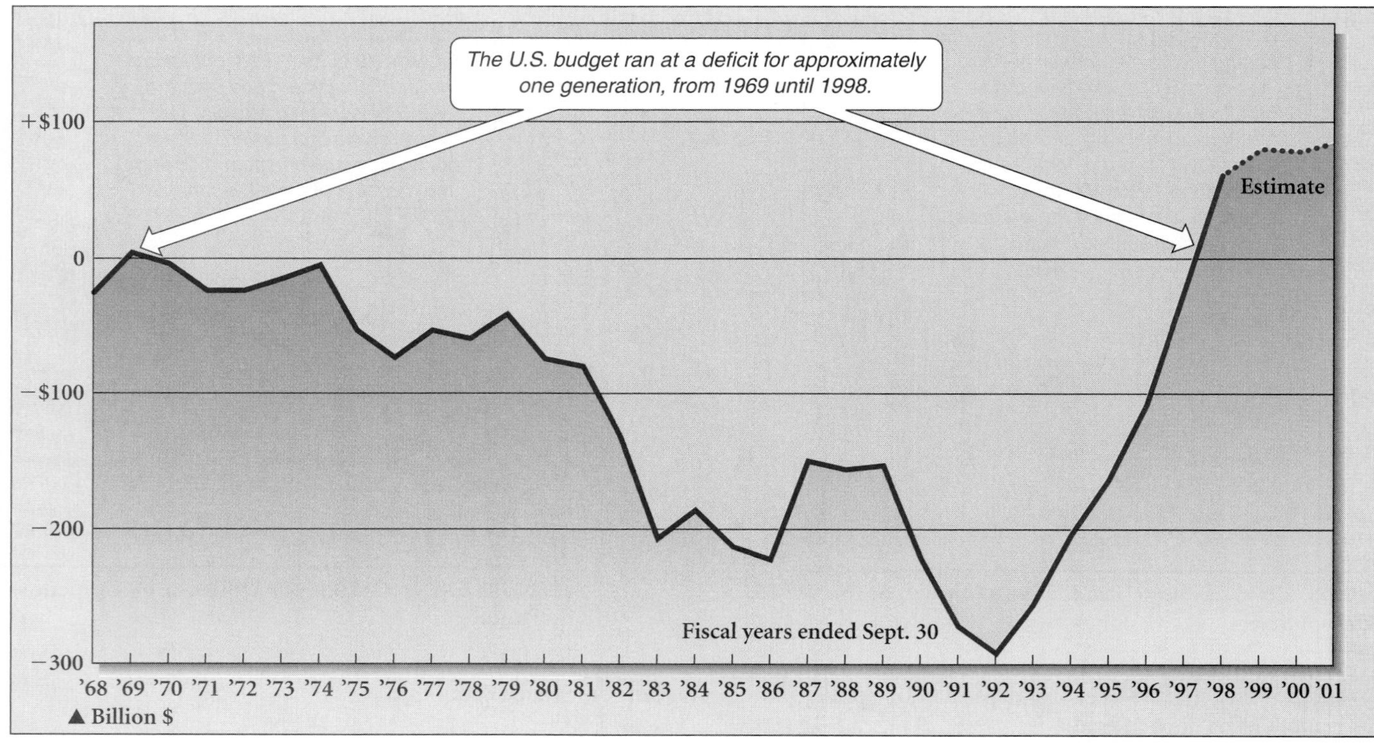

FIGURE 1.8 ◆ Trends in the U.S. Budget Deficit

The year 1998 saw the first U.S. budget surplus since 1969. Figure 1.8 shows what happened in between—continuous deficit spending leading to the huge total national debt facing us today. The surplus was primarily attributable to spending cuts and tax increases implemented during the Bush and Clinton presidencies. The Congressional Budget Office also forecasts continued surpluses for the next several years totaling perhaps as much as $1.55 trillion. Obviously, Congress will play a major role in determining how this surplus will be allocated according to pressures to lower taxes, increase spending, and/or reduce the debt.[11]

Managing the U.S. Economy

fiscal policies Government economic policies that determine how the government collects and spends its revenues

The government also acts to manage the U.S. economic system through two sets of policies. It manages the collection and spending of its revenues through **fiscal policies.** Tax increases, for instance, can function as fiscal policy to increase revenues. President Clinton's income tax increase in 1993, for example, generated an estimated $50 billion in additional revenues. Similarly, budget cuts (for example, closing military bases) function as fiscal policy when spending is decreased. Such policies can have a direct impact on inflation, growth, and employment.

An historically important example of a fiscal policy designed to boost employment was the Public Works Program following the Great Depression. The U.S. government employed tens of thousands of people to improve the nation's infrastructure by building roads, bridges, dams, post offices, schools, and hospitals. As a result, many people had jobs who would otherwise have had no income and the country itself benefited directly from the improvements. More recently, China announced a $1 trillion public works program to energize its own ailing economy.[12]

monetary policies Government economic policies that determine the size of a nation's money supply

Monetary policies focus on controlling the size of the nation's money supply. Working primarily through the Federal Reserve System (the nation's central bank), the government can influence the ability and willingness of banks throughout the country to lend money. It can also influence the supply of money by prompting interest rates to go up or down. A primary goal in recent years, for example, has been to adjust interest rates so that inflation is kept at a manageable level.

Continued from page 7

The Customized Concierge

The World Wide Web is creating electronic opportunities for corporate concierges to service customers throughout the country. The Capitol Concierge Web site (www.capitolconcierge.com) promises customers the convenience of having someone else take care of their "to do" lists. Mary Naylor, Capitol president, realizes that increasing customization is the key to success of this service. Using the company's customized "consider it done" service, therefore, customers can order flowers, gifts, event tickets, and more.

On a recent visit to its gift page, browsers discovered that Capitol was marketing customized picnic baskets, barbecue sets, and golf baskets, among other items. Prices ranged from $30 to $50, and senders could attach personalized gift cards to their orders. An 800 number and e-mail enable Capitol to offer specialized services to both individual and business Web clients.

Questions for Discussion

1. How are the concierge companies started by Kelley Dunn and Mary Naylor good examples of capitalism at work?
2. What role did changing market forces play in the development of the concierge business?
3. Why do you think the concierge business is priced so competitively? Why are small businesses that drastically undercut competitors' prices likely to fail in the long run?
4. Right now, the concierge business is characterized by pure competition. Do you see a shift to monopolistic competition, oligopoly, or monopoly?
5. Do you agree or disagree with the following statement: *Concierge companies would never have been created in a communist or socialist economy.* Support your answer with specific reasons.

SUMMARY

1. **Define the nature of U.S. *business* and identify its main goals.** *Businesses* are organizations that produce or sell goods or services to make a profit. *Profits* are the difference between a business's revenues and expenses. The prospect of earning profits encourages individuals and organizations to open and to expand businesses. The benefits of business activities also extend to wages paid to workers and to taxes that support government functions.
2. **Describe different types of *economic systems* according to the means by which they control the *factors of production*.** An *economic system* is a nation's system for allocating its resources among its citizens. Economic systems differ in terms of who owns or controls the four basic *factors of production:* labor, capital, entrepreneurs, and natural resources. In *planned economies*, the government controls all or most factors. In *market economies*, which are based on the principles of capitalism, individuals control the factors of production. Most countries today have *mixed market economies* that are dominated by one of these systems but include elements of the other. The process of *privatization* is an important means by which many of the world's planned economies are moving toward mixed market systems.
3. **Show how *demand* and *supply* affect resource distribution in the United States.** The U.S. economy is strongly influenced by markets, demand, and supply. *Demand* is the willingness and ability of buyers to purchase a good or service. *Supply* is the willingness and ability of producers to offer goods or services for sale. Demand and supply work together to set a *market* or *equilibrium price*—the price at which the quantity of goods demanded and the quantity of goods supplied are equal.
4. **Identify the elements of *private enterprise* and explain the various *degrees of competition* in the U.S. economic system.** The U.S. economy is founded on the principles of *private enterprise: private property rights*, *freedom of choice*, *profits*, and *competition*. Degrees of competition vary because not all industries are equally competitive. Under conditions of *pure competition*, numerous small firms compete in a market governed entirely by demand and supply. An *oligopoly* involves a handful of sellers only. A *monopoly* involves only one seller.
5. **Explain the criteria for evaluating the success of an economic system in meeting its goals and show how the federal government attempts to manage the U.S. economy.** The basic goals of an economic system are *stability*, *full employment*, and *growth*. Measures of

how well an economy has accomplished these goals include *gross national product*, *gross domestic product*, *productivity*, *balance of trade*, and *national debt*. The U.S. government uses *fiscal policies* to manage the effects of its spending and revenue collection, and *monetary policies* to control the size of the nation's money supply.

QUESTIONS AND EXERCISES

Questions for Review

1. What are the factors of production? Is one factor more important than the others? If so, which one? Why?
2. What is GDP? Real GDP? What does each measure?
3. Explain the differences between the four degrees of competition and give an example of each. (Do not use the examples given in the text.)
4. Why is inflation both good and bad? How does the government try to control it?

Questions for Analysis

5. Select a local business and show how it uses the basic factors of production. Now show how they are used by your college or university. What are the similarities and differences?
6. In recent years, many countries have moved from planned economies to market economies. Why do you think this has occurred? Can you envision a situation that would cause a resurgence of planned economies?
7. Identify a situation in which excess supply of a product led to decreased prices. Identify a situation in which a shortage led to increased prices. What eventually happened in each case? Why?

Application Exercises

8. Choose a locally owned and operated business. Interview the owner to find out how the business uses the factors of production and identify its sources for acquiring them.
9. Visit a local shopping mall or shopping area. List each store that you see and determine what degree of competition it faces in the immediate environment. For example, if there is only one store in the mall that sells shoes, that store represents a monopoly. Note the businesses with direct competitors (for example, two jewelry stores) and describe how they compete with one another.
10. Go to the library or on the Internet and research 10 different industries. Classify each according to degree of competition.

BUILDING YOUR BUSINESS SKILLS

TEACHING AN OLD DOG TO BYPASS LONG-DISTANCE CARRIERS

This exercise is designed to enhance the following SCANS workplace competencies: demonstrating basic skills, demonstrating thinking skills, exhibiting interpersonal skills, and working with information.

▼ Goal

To encourage students to understand how the changing competitive environment affects marketing and pricing.

▼ Background

Times have changed for AT&T. It wasn't that long ago that the company held a legal monopoly in the long-distance telephone market, which meant that nearly everyone was an

AT&T customer. Today, Sprint and MCI Worldcom are fierce competitors, and others are joining the fray.

Among the competitive upstarts are "dial-around" services, including those run by Sprint and MCI Worldcom. These services encourage consumers to use special access codes to bypass a phone's long-distance carrier in favor of one that offers a better deal. For example, no matter what long-distance service you're connected to, if you dial 10-10-321 before a long-distance phone number, your call will connect via MCI Worldcom.

Brand name isn't important to dial-around customers, and loyalty isn't in their vocabulary. They're interested in price, giveaways, and gimmicks and will abandon one service in favor of another in the time it takes to dial a new access code. In this hotly competitive environment, AT&T was losing customers and profits, and had to find a way to compete.

▼ Method

Join with three or four other classmates to investigate how AT&T now competes in the dial-around long-distance environment. Working as a team, research and analyze the following:

1. How dial-around long-distance services operate, including their pricing policies
2. The changing competitive environment for all long-distance services
3. The Lucky Dog Phone Company, AT&T's new dial-around service

The following sources provide helpful information:

- Lucky Dog's Web site: www.luckydog.com
- Stephanie N. Mehta, "Dog Teaches New Trick to AT&T," *The Wall Street Journal*, October 7, 1998, p. B1
- Seth Schiesel, "The Formerly Staid Ma Bell Hatches a Secret Offspring," *The New York Times*, October 7, 1998, p. A1.

▼ Follow-Up Questions

1. AT&T resisted entering the dial-around market, and even launched ads early in 1998 criticizing the pricing claims of other companies. Do you think AT&T's history as a monopoly affected the speed at which it entered this market? Explain your answer.
2. Are oligopolists likely to respond rapidly to new competitive threats? Is their response likely to be as rapid as companies in monopolistic-competition or pure-competition environments?
3. Do you agree that the consumption of long-distance telephone service is a price-sensitive behavior? Support your position with evidence from your own long-distance buying decisions and the decisions of your friends and family.
4. Lucky Dog's 10 cents a minute plus 10 cent connection fee is lower than most AT&T calling plans. If Lucky Dog successfully attracts new customers, is it reasonable for management to assume a cause-and-effect relationship between pricing and increased demand? If you were a brand manager, would you believe that no other factors contributed to the sales increase? Explain your answer.
5. Lucky Dog is also offering giveaways to service users, including airline tickets and cruises (see www.luckydog.com). How do you think these giveaways will affect long-term demand for the service in a price-sensitive environment?
6. It is difficult for consumers to compare the prices of dial-around price plans because of the complexity of these plans. How do you think lack of price clarity will affect the success of companies offering this service?
7. How often do you think Lucky Dog managers should reassess their company's pricing decisions? Why is regular reassessment especially important to oligopolistic firms? Does the need for reassessment differ according to the firm's competitive environment?

CRAFTING YOUR BUSINESS PLAN

FORMS OF COMPETITION AND FACTORS OF PRODUCTION

▼ THE PURPOSE OF THE ASSIGNMENT

1. To acquaint students with the process of navigating the Business PlanPro (BPP) software package.
2. To demonstrate how two chapter topics—forms of competition and factors of production—can be integrated as components in the BPP planning environment.
3. To acquaint students with different forms of competition and to show how factors of production differ in importance among various companies.

▼ ASSIGNMENT

After reading Chapter 1 in the textbook, open the BPP software and look around for information about types of competition and factors of production as it applies to two sample firms: Flower Importer (Fantastic Florals, Inc.) and Sports Medicine Manufacturing (Professional Athletic Equipment, Inc.). Then respond to the following questions:*

1. Describe the Flower Importer's product. [Sites to see in BPP (for this assignment): In the Task Manager screen, click on **What You're Selling.** Then click on **1. Summary and Introduction, 2. Detailed Description,** and **4. Sourcing and Fulfillment.**]
2. Describe the type of competition faced by the Flower Importer. [Sites to see in BPP: In the Task Manager screen, click on **The Business You're In.** Then click on **4. Factors of Competition** and **5. Main Competitors.**]
3. Repeat steps 1 and 2 (in this assignment) for the Sports Medicine Manufacturing company. [Sites to see in BPP: In the Task Manager screen, click on **What You're Selling.** Then click on **1. Summary and Introduction** to identify the product. For competition, in the Task Manager screen, click on **The Business You're In.** Then click on **4. Factors of Competition** and **5. Main Competitors.**]
4. Compare and contrast the kinds of competition faced by the two firms.
5. Choose one of the two companies and explore its business plan to see how many of its factors of production (labor, capital, entrepreneurs, and natural resources) you can find. Identify at least one example of each factor for the company you have chosen. [Sites to see in BPP: In the Task Manager screen, click on **Your Company,** then click on any of its categories. Now click on **Your Management Team,** then explore each of its item categories. Then click on **What You're Selling;** be sure to examine the categories **Sourcing and Fulfillment** and **Competitive Positioning.**]

▼ FOR YOUR OWN BUSINESS PLAN

6. Describe in detail the competition that your business will face. Include a description of the competing firms and competing products and identify geographic locations of main competitors. What factors of production do you expect to use in your business?

▼ *GENERAL TIPS FOR NAVIGATING IN BPP

1. Open the BPP program, examine the Welcome screen, and click on **Open a Sample Plan.**
2. From the **Open a Sample Plan** dialogue box, click on a sample company name; then click on **Open.**
3. On the Task Manager screen, click on any of the lines (for example, **Your Company**).

4. You can always return to the Task Manager screen by going to the bottom of the screen and clicking on the **Task Manager** icon.
5. When you are finished with a sample company, close its **Task Manager** screen.
6. After finishing with one sample company, you can get to the next one by going to the top of the screen and clicking on **File** (on the menu bar). Then beneath that, select **Open Sample Plan.** This will exit you from the current company file and send you to the **Open a Sample Plan** dialogue box, where you can select your next sample company.

EXPLORING THE NET

KNOWING THE DIFFERENCE BETWEEN RIGHT AND LEFT

◆ Yes, Virginia, there is a central planning support group. It even has a Web page. Review the Marxism Page at:

http://www.anu.edu.au/polsci/marx/

and then consider the following questions:

1. Note the use of the term *Marxism* throughout the contents of the home page. If you click to the Contemporary Marxist Material page, you'll note that the predominant term is *Socialism*. What do you think accounts for this difference in usage or emphasis?
2. Read *The Communist Manifesto* and play devil's advocate: Select two of the criticisms that Karl Marx and Frederich Engels leveled at capitalism in 1848 and defend the position that they are at least as applicable now as the authors believed them to be 150 years ago.

or

◆ At http://www.public-policy.org/~ncpa/pd/private/privat.html you will find the "Privatization" page of the National Center for Policy Analysis, a lobbying organization that seeks to shift control of key economic resources from the public to the private sector. Although we tend to think of privatization as an issue facing former communist and socialist nations, you can explore this site to learn about different facets of the privatization issue here in the United States. Examine several sections of this site, and then consider the following questions:

1. What does the Center mean by "Privatization Innovations"? Choose one of the examples given and summarize the Center's argument for privatizing it.
2. Identify two "Privatization Deterrents" and explain the Center's reasons for characterizing each as a barrier to privatization.
3. Identify five or six of the Center's "Candidates for Privatization." Then choose one or two about which you disagree and explain why.

Conducting Business in the United States

Fiddling around with Alliances

Robin Fiddle and her twin sister, Mandi Fiddle Bergenfeld, are pursuing a business strategy that's a little hard to understand. They want Twin Computer Training Inc., their 8-year-old New York City–based consulting firm, to stay small while it grows big. A contradiction? Not to the sisters, who are achieving their small-business goal through corporate alliances that, in a recent 6-month period, increased the firm's revenues by 30 percent.

These alliances take shape when Twin Computer Training teams up with strategic partners, who are recognized as the best in their fields, to provide clients with total systems solutions. Believing that specialization is inescapable in a technologically complex business world, Twin supplements its computer training services with the expertise of small companies in such specialties as systems integration, multimedia, Web design, networking, and other related computer services. "We provide our customers with a broad range of services," says Robin Fiddle, "but to succeed we have to remain focused on what we do best."

Twin's one-stop solution to serving small-business clients is catching on throughout the country. "Smart small businesses," says Daniel Nathanson, director of entrepreneurial programs at New York University's Stern School of Business, "are now creating alliances with people who offer complementary services and who have a similar client base, in order to compete against big companies." Forming alliances is so important to Twin that it is one of its four stated corporate goals.

Fiddle and Bergenfeld began building alliances when they started their company in 1991. Tired of working for large corporate bosses, the 27-year-old twins started working 7 days a week for clients in need of computer training, specialized manuals, and help in the middle of the night. They targeted corporate users in Manhattan and gave them the best service they could. By 1998, the firm was grossing $300,000 from a client roster that boasted such corporate all-stars as CBS, Chase Manhattan Bank, and Metropolitan Life.

Twin Computer's alliances take different forms, ranging from simple referrals to formal agreements involving joint bidding and revenue sharing. Of course, each arrangement comes with risks for Twin, which will be associated with the failure of any partner. But Fiddle and Bergenfeld believe that these risks are preferable to branching into areas beyond their expertise. Rather than expanding—adding facilities, equipment, and employees—Twin calls in specialists with immediate solutions. This approach also eliminates the need to keep searching for high-quality talent in a tight job market.

Granted, some companies are nervous about sharing clients, ideas, and employees with other firms in related fields. Admits Mark Voelpel, another small-business owner and alliance partner, "It's kind of a leap of faith to say that we have more to gain by opening up than we have to lose." Alliances become particularly complicated when competitors come together on a project. In these cases, the temporary partners usually sign formal legal contracts to safeguard proprietary information and guarantee confidentiality. Regardless of the internal arrangement between Twin and its partners, Fiddle and Bergenfeld always present a unified front to clients. Rather than separate statements from each alliance member, clients get a single proposal, a single schedule, and one bill.

Over the years, the sisters have also learned never to exchange money among alliance partners. "We don't want money to get in the way when we select our partners," explains Robin Fiddle. "We are basically trading services and referrals. It's a win-win situation for us, our clients, and our partners."

> "We don't want money to get in the way when we select our partners."
>
> —Robin Fiddle
> *Co-owner, Twin Computer Training*

As the owners of Twin Computer Training have learned, the structure of a business—how it organizes and relates to other companies—affects competitive and financial success. In this chapter, we examine the business structures and relationships that are open to both large and small companies. By focusing on the learning objectives of this chapter, you will better understand the options and the opportunities offered by different business structures.

Our opening story is continued on page 47

After reading this chapter, you should be able to:

1. **Trace the history of business in the United States.**
2. **Identify the major forms of business ownership.**
3. **Describe *sole proprietorships* and *partnerships* and explain the advantages and disadvantages of each.**
4. **Describe *corporations* and explain their advantages and disadvantages.**
5. **Describe the basic issues involved in creating and managing a corporation.**
6. **Identify recent trends and issues in corporate ownership.**

A SHORT HISTORY OF BUSINESS IN THE UNITED STATES

The contemporary landscape of U.S. business ownership has evolved over the course of many decades. Specifically, a look at the history of U.S. business shows a steady development from sole proprietorships to today's intricate corporate structures. We can gain a more detailed understanding of this development by tracing its history.

The Factory System and the Industrial Revolution

Industrial Revolution Major mid-eighteenth century change in production characterized by a shift to the factory system, mass production, and the specialization of labor.

With the coming of the **Industrial Revolution** in the middle of the eighteenth century, a manufacturing revolution was made possible by advances in technology and by the development of the factory system. Replacing hundreds of cottage workers who had turned out one item at a time, the factory system brought together in one place the materials and workers required to produce items in large quantities and the new machines needed for mass production.

In turn, mass production reduced duplication of equipment and allowed firms to purchase raw materials at better prices by buying in large lots. Even more important, it encouraged specialization of labor. Mass production replaced a system of highly skilled craftspeople who performed all the different tasks required to make a single item. Instead, a series of semiskilled workers, each trained to perform only one task and supported by specialized machines and tools, greatly increased output.

Laissez-Faire and the Entrepreneurial Era

Despite numerous early problems during the nineteenth century, the U.S. banking system began providing domestic businesses with some independence from European capital markets. In addition, improvements in transportation—the opening of the Erie Canal in the 1820s, steamboat navigation on major rivers, and the development of the railroads—soon made it not only possible but also economical to move products to distant markets.

Another significant feature of the times was the rise of the entrepreneur on a grand scale. Like businesses in many other nations in the nineteenth century, U.S. business embraced the philosophy of *laissez-faire*—the principle that the government should not in-

Founders and their guests celebrate the birth of United States Steel in 1901. When it was born out of a merger of competing steel companies, U.S. Steel inherited 65% of the nation's steel-producing capacity; a little over a decade later, the firm's gross income was greater than that of the U.S. Treasury. Today it is known as USX and is mainly in the oil business.

terfere in the economy but should instead let business function without regulation and according to its own "natural" laws. Risk taking and entrepreneurship became hallmarks of aggressive practices that created some of the biggest companies in the country and, ultimately, the world. During the last half of the 1800s, for instance, Andrew Carnegie founded U.S. Steel and Andrew Mellon created the Aluminum Company of America (Alcoa). At the same time, J. P. Morgan's Morgan Guarantee and Trust came to dominate the U.S. financial system, and John D. Rockefeller's Standard Oil controlled—in fact, monopolized—the petroleum industry.

The rise of such giant enterprises increased the national standard of living and made the United States a world power; but the size and economic power of such firms made it difficult, if not impossible, for competitors to enter their markets. Complete market control became a watchword in many industries, with many major corporations opting to collude rather than compete. Price fixing and other forms of market manipulation became common business practices, with captains of industry often behaving as robber barons. Reacting against unethical practices and the unregulated struggle for dominance, critics in many quarters began calling for corrective action and, ultimately, for antitrust laws and the breakup of monopolies.

Among other important laws, the Sherman Antitrust Act of 1890 and the Clayton Act of 1914 were passed specifically to limit the control a single business could gain in any given market. Other laws passed during this era sought to regulate a variety of employment and advertising practices, and still others attempted to regulate the ways in which businesses could handle their financial affairs. As discussed in Chapter 1, this antitrust legislation was the basis for the U.S. government's 1998 lawsuit against Microsoft Corp. (The appendix to this book provides more information about the legal environment of business, much of which has its roots in this era.)

The Production Era

The concepts of specialization and mass production that originated in the Industrial Revolution were further refined in the early twentieth century. At this time, many analysts of business organizations sought to focus management's attention on the production process. Especially among the theorists of so-called scientific management, increased efficiency through the "one best way" to accomplish production tasks became a major goal of management. Developed during the early 1900s, scientific management focused on maximizing

Lewis Hine, Carolina Cotton Mill, *1909. It is estimated that children once formed about one-third of the industrial workforce in the United States. Photos like those taken by Hine were enlisted in the efforts to limit child labor—efforts that led, in 1916, to the Keating-Owens Act, which sought to discourage child labor by prohibiting interstate commerce in any goods manufactured by children under 16 years of age. Progressive—and somewhat optimistic—opinion held that because very few producers could afford to limit sales to the confines of home-state markets, child labor would soon disappear altogether.*

output by developing the most efficient and productive ways for workers to perform carefully designed tasks.

production era Period during the early twentieth century in which U.S. business focused primarily on improving productivity and manufacturing efficiency

Scientific management was given further impetus when, in 1913, Henry Ford introduced the moving assembly line and ushered in the **production era.** The focus was largely on manufacturing efficiency: By adopting fixed workstations, increasing task specialization, and moving the work to the worker, Ford increased productivity and lowered prices. In so doing, he made the automobile affordable for the average person.

Both the growth of corporations and improved assembly-line output came at the expense of worker freedom. For one thing, the dominance of big firms made it harder for individuals to go into business for themselves. In some cases, employer-run company towns gave people little freedom of choice, either in selecting an employer or in choosing what products to buy. If some balance were to be restored in the overall system, two elements within it had to grow in power: government and organized labor. Thus, the production era saw the rise of labor unions and the practice of collective bargaining (see Chapter 9). In addition, the Great Depression of the 1930s and World War II prompted the government to intervene in the economic system on a previously unforeseen scale. Today, business, government, and labor are often referred to by economists and politicians as the three countervailing powers in society: Although all are big and all are strong, none completely dominates the others.

The Marketing Era

After World War II, the demand for consumer goods that had been frustrated by wartime shortages fueled the U.S. economy for some time. Despite brief periodic recessions, the 1950s and 1960s were prosperous times. Production continued to increase, technology advanced, and the standard of living rose. During this era, a new philosophy of business came of age—the marketing concept. Previously, business had been essentially production and sales oriented. Businesses tended to produce what other businesses produced, what they thought customers wanted, or simply what owners wanted to produce. Henry Ford, for example, is supposed to have said that his customers could buy his cars in whatever color they wanted—as long as it was black.

marketing concept Idea that a business must focus on identifying and satisfying consumer wants in order to be profitable

According to the **marketing concept,** however, business starts with the customer. Producers of goods and services begin by determining what customers want and then provide it.[1] The most successful practitioners of the marketing concept are companies such as Procter & Gamble and Anheuser-Busch. Such firms allow consumers to choose what best suits their needs by offering an array of products within a given market (toothpaste or beer, for example).

The Global Era

The 1980s saw the continuation of technological advances in production, computer technology, information systems, and communications capabilities. They also saw the emergence of a truly global economy. American consumers now drive cars made in Japan, wear sweaters made in Italy, and turn on CD players made in Taiwan. Elsewhere around the world, people drive Fords, drink Pepsi, wear Levi's jeans, use IBM computers, and watch Disney movies and television shows.

As we show in more detail in Chapter 3, globalization has become a fact of life for most businesses today. Improved communication and transportation, in addition to more efficient international methods for financing, producing, distributing, and marketing products and services, have combined to open distant marketplaces to businesses as never before.

Admittedly, many U.S. businesses have been hurt by foreign competition. Many others, however, have profited from new foreign markets. International competition also has forced many U.S. businesses to work harder than ever to cut costs, increase efficiency, and improve quality. A variety of important trends, opportunities, and challenges in the new global era are explored throughout this book.

TYPES OF BUSINESS ORGANIZATIONS

Whether they run small agricultural enterprises or large manufacturing concerns, all business owners must decide which form of legal organization best suits their goals: *sole proprietorship*, *partnership*, or *corporation*. Because this choice affects a host of managerial and financial issues, few decisions are more critical. In choosing a form of organization, entrepreneurs must consider their own preferences, their immediate and long-range needs, and the advantages and disadvantages of each form.

Sole Proprietorships

The very first legal form of business organization, the **sole proprietorship,** is owned and usually operated by one person who is responsible for its debts. Today, about 74 percent of all businesses in the United States are sole proprietorships; however, they account for only about 6 percent of the country's total business revenues.[2]

sole proprietorship Business owned and usually operated by one person who is responsible for all of its debts

Although a sole proprietorship is usually small, it may be as large as a steel mill or a department store. Moreover, many of today's largest companies started out as sole proprietorships. Sears, Roebuck and Co., for example, was originally a one-man enterprise owned and operated by Richard Sears, who had started the R.W. Sears Watch Co. in 1886. (Alvah Roebuck, who had answered an advertisement for a watchmaker in 1887, joined Sears to form a partnership in 1893.)

ADVANTAGES OF SOLE PROPRIETORSHIPS Freedom is perhaps the most important benefit of sole proprietorships. Because they own their businesses completely, sole proprietors answer to no one but themselves. Moreover, they enjoy a certain degree of privacy because they need not report information about their operations to anyone. Finally, they alone reap the rewards of success or suffer the penalties of failure.

Furthermore, sole proprietorships are simple to form. Sometimes a proprietor can go into business simply by putting a sign on the door. Naturally, the simplicity of legal setup procedures makes this form of organization appealing to self-starters and independent spirits. Sole proprietorships are also easy to dissolve. In fact, many proprietorships are organized for short life spans. For example, rock concerts and one-time athletic events are often organized as sole proprietorships and then dissolved when the events are over.

Betty Ford has set up shop on-line. Looking to tap into the market of men who buy in cyberspace, she's opened up City Boxers, a virtual retailer that markets hand-tailored boxer shorts. In addition to the many advantages that sole proprietorships already enjoy, consider how costs are trimmed by operating on-line. After all, it's cheaper to build a virtual place of business than it is to take hammer and nails to construct a physical storefront.

Low start-up costs also make sole proprietorships attractive. Because some sole proprietorships must register only with state governments (to ensure that no other business bears the same name), legal fees are usually low. Some proprietorships, however, such as restaurants, beauty salons, florist shops, and pet shops, must be licensed.

Finally, a particularly appealing feature of sole proprietorships is the tax benefits extended to new businesses that are likely to suffer losses in their early stages. Tax laws generally permit sole proprietors to treat sales revenues and operating expenses as part of their personal finances. They can thus cut their taxes by deducting business losses from income earned elsewhere (from personal sources other than the business). Because most new businesses lose money in the early stages of operation, tax incentives are quite helpful to entrepreneurs.

unlimited liability Legal principle holding owners responsible for paying off all debts of a business

DISADVANTAGES OF SOLE PROPRIETORSHIPS A major drawback of sole proprietorships is **unlimited liability:** A sole proprietor is personally liable for all debts incurred by the business. If the business fails to generate enough cash, bills must be paid out of the proprietor's own pocket. If bills are not paid, creditors can claim many of the proprietor's personal possessions, including home, furniture, and automobiles. Another disadvantage is lack of continuity: A sole proprietorship legally dissolves when the owner dies. Although the business can be reorganized if a successor is prepared to take over, executors or heirs must otherwise sell the assets of the business.

Finally, a sole proprietorship depends on the resources of a single individual. If the proprietor is a skillful manager with ample resources, this limitation is not a problem. In many cases, however, owners' managerial and financial limitations put limits on their organizations. Sole proprietors often find it hard to borrow money, not only to start up but also to expand. Many commercial bankers fear that they will not be able to recover loans when sole proprietors become disabled or insolvent. Often, therefore, would-be proprietors must rely for start-up funds on personal savings or family loans.

Partnerships

general partnership Business with two or more owners who share in both the operation of the firm and in financial responsibility for its debts

The most common type of partnership, the **general partnership,** is simply a sole proprietorship multiplied by the number of partner-owners. There is no legal limit to the number of parties who may form a general partnership. Moreover, partners may invest equal or unequal sums of money and may earn profits that bear no relation to their investments. Thus, a partner with no financial investment in a two-person partnership could receive 50 percent or more of the profits. Bill Trainer and Harvey Woodman, for example, opened an automatic car wash in Houston called Shinin' Bright. Woodman put up most of the funds, and Trainer provided the expertise needed to manage the business. They agreed to split the profits equally for the first 3 years. Trainer then had the option to invest some of his profits in return for a larger share.

Partnerships are often extensions of sole proprietorships. The original owner may want to expand, or the business may have grown too big for one person to handle. Richard Sears sold his watch business and, 2 years later, formed a mail-order catalog business. When his new business grew so large that he could no longer run it by himself, he invited former business associate Alvah Roebuck to join him as a partner. Many professional organizations, such as legal, architectural, and accounting firms, are also organized as partnerships.

ADVANTAGES OF PARTNERSHIPS The most striking advantage of general partnerships is their ability to grow with the addition of new talent and money. Because lending institutions prefer to make loans to enterprises that are not dependent on single individuals, partnerships also find it easier to borrow money than sole proprietorships. Moreover, most partnerships have access to the resources of more than one individual. Thus, when they needed money to fund an expansion program, Sears and Roebuck invited new partners to join them by investing in the company.

Like a sole proprietorship, a partnership can be organized by meeting only a few legal requirements. Even so, all partnerships must begin with an agreement of some kind. All but two states subscribe to the Revised Uniform Limited Partnership Act. This statute describes a written certificate that requires the filing of specific information about the business and its partners. Partners may also agree to bind themselves in ways not specified by the certificate.[3] In any case, a partnership agreement should answer questions such as the following:

- Who invested what sums of money?
- Who will receive what share of the profits?
- Who does what and who reports to whom?
- How may the partnership be dissolved? In the event of dissolution, how will assets be distributed?
- How will surviving partners be protected from claims made by a deceased partner's heirs?

Although it helps to clarify matters for the partners themselves, the partnership agreement is strictly a private document; no laws require partners to file their agreements with any government agency. Nor are partnerships regarded as legal entities; in the eyes of the law, a partnership is just two or more people working together. Because partnerships have no independent legal standing, the Internal Revenue Service taxes partners as individuals.

In 1995, Sunil Paul (left) and Mark Pincus started a partnership called FreeLoader, an off-line Internet browser that automatically downloaded information to computer desktops. In June 1996—that's just eight months after founding it—the partners sold FreeLoader for $38 million. Success resulted from a combination of shrewdness and good timing, but some observers wonder if, after a mere eight months, the partners qualify as "entrepreneurs." Says one investment banker familiar with the story: "Anyone smart enough to figure out that there's an opportunity, to start a company, and sell it fast—that's very *entrepreneurial."*

DISADVANTAGES OF PARTNERSHIPS For general partnerships, as for sole proprietorships, unlimited liability is the greatest drawback: By law, each partner may be liable for all debts incurred in the name of the partnership. If any partner incurs a business debt (with or without the knowledge of the other partners), all partners may still be held liable.

For example, shortly after Trainer and Woodman's car wash opened, their equipment severely damaged a customized van. The owner sued for damages. Because the business was just getting started and had no financial reserves, Trainer and Woodman were faced with the prospect of covering the costs from their own pockets. Unfortunately, Trainer lacked the personal funds to cover his share. To keep the business afloat, Woodman agreed to lend Trainer the money for his half of the business expense.

Partnerships also share with sole proprietorships the potential lack of continuity: When one partner dies or leaves it, the original partnership dissolves, even if one or more of the other partners want it to continue. The dissolving of a partnership need not cause a loss of sales revenues. Surviving partners may form a new partnership to retain the old firm's business.

A related disadvantage is the difficulty of transferring ownership. No partner may sell out without the consent of the others. Moreover, a partner who wants to retire or to transfer interest to a son or daughter must have the other partners' consent. Thus, the life of a partnership depends on the ability of retiring partners to find buyers who are compatible

"What happened to our working partnership?"

with current partners. Failure to do so may end a partnership. Of course, remaining partners may also buy out a retiring partner.

Finally, a partnership provides little or no guidance for resolving internal conflicts. Suppose that one partner wants to expand the business rapidly and the other wants it to grow cautiously. If the partnership agreement grants equal power, it may be difficult for the two partners to resolve the dispute. Conflicts can involve disagreements ranging from the company smoking policy to key managerial practices. Quite simply, it is sometimes impossible to resolve disagreements.

Corporations

There are about 3.1 million corporations in the United States. As you can see from Figure 2.1, although they account for about 19 percent of all U.S. businesses, they generate about 92 percent of all sales revenues.[4] Almost all larger businesses use this form, and corporations dominate the global business landscape. According to the most recent available data, for example, General Motors, the world's largest industrial firm, posted annual revenue of nearly $180 billion, with total profits of $6.6 billion. Even "smaller" large corporations post huge sales figures. Asarco Inc., a New York–based mining company that ranks 500th among U.S. corporations, posted a profit of $143 million on annual sales of $2.7 billion (three-fourths of which were made in Peru).[5] Given the size and influence of this form of ownership, we will devote a great deal of attention to various aspects of corporations.

THE CORPORATE ENTITY When you think of corporations, you probably think of giant businesses such as General Motors and IBM. Indeed, the very word *corporation* inspires images of size and power. In reality, however, the tiny corner newsstand has as much right to incorporate as a giant automaker. Moreover, the incorporated newsstand and GM would share the characteristics of all **corporations:** legal status as separate entities, property rights and obligations, and indefinite life spans.

corporation Business that is legally considered an entity separate from its owners and is liable for its own debts; owners' liability extends to the limits of their investments

In 1819, the U.S. Supreme Court defined a corporation as "an artificial being, invisible, intangible, and existing only in contemplation of the law." By these words, the Court defined the corporation as a legal person. Thus, corporations may perform the following activities:

- Sue and be sued
- Buy, hold, and sell property
- Make and sell products to consumers
- Commit crimes and be tried and punished for them

PUBLIC AND PRIVATE CORPORATIONS Corporations may be either public or private. The stock of a **public corporation** is widely held and available for sale to the general public. For example, anyone who has the money can buy shares of Caterpillar, Digital

public corporation Corporation whose stock is widely held and available for sale to the general public

FIGURE 2.1 ◆ **Proportions of U.S. Firms in Terms of Type of Business Organizational and Sales Revenue**

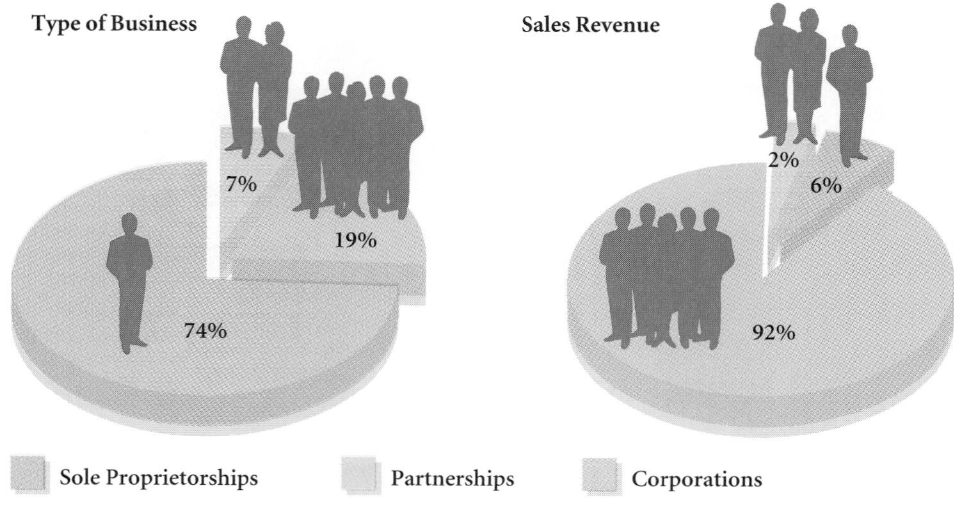

Equipment, or Time Warner. The stock of a **private corporation,** on the other hand, is held by only a few people and is not available for sale to the general public. The controlling group of stockholders may be a family, a management group, or even the firm's employees. Gallo Wine, Levi Strauss, and United Parcel Service are all private corporations. Because few investors will buy unknown stocks, most new corporations start out as private corporations. As the corporation grows and investors see evidence of success, it may issue shares to the public as a way to raise additional money. For example, Netscape Communications publicly issued stock for the first time in 1995. The firm quickly sold 81 million shares and raised over a billion dollars for new product development and expansion.

private corporation Corporation whose stock is held by only a few people and is not available for sale to the general public

ADVANTAGES OF INCORPORATION The biggest advantage of regular corporations is **limited liability:** The liability of investors is limited to their personal investments in the corporation. In the event of failure, the courts may seize and sell a corporation's assets but cannot touch the personal possessions of investors. For example, if you invest $1,000 in a corporation that goes bankrupt, you may lose your $1,000, but no more. In other words, $1,000 is the extent of your liability.

limited liability Legal principle holding investors liable for a firm's debts only to the limits of their personal investments in it

Another corporate advantage is continuity. Because it has a legal life independent of its founders and owners, a corporation can, at least in theory, continue forever. Shares of stock, for example, may be sold or passed on from generation to generation. Moreover, most corporations also benefit from the continuity provided by professional management.

Finally, corporations have advantages in raising money. By selling more stock, for instance, they can expand the number of investors and the amount of available funds. Continuity and the legal protections afforded to corporations also tend to make lenders more willing to grant loans.

DISADVANTAGES OF INCORPORATION One of the corporation's chief attractions is ease of transferring ownership; however, this same feature can also complicate the lives of managers. Figure 2.2, for example, outlines a basic **tender offer**—an offer to buy shares made by a prospective buyer directly to the target corporation's shareholders, who then make individual decisions about whether to sell. Now consider the recent travails of several California–based bank corporations. To begin, First Interstate tried to gain control of one of its largest competitors, Bank of America, through a tender offer—by buying its shares on the open market. First Interstate, however, could not acquire enough Bank of America shares to gain control and ended up having to sell those shares that it did buy at a big loss. In its weakened financial state, First Interstate then became a target itself and was purchased by a third bank corporation, Wells Fargo & Co. The corporate marriage paid few dividends for Wells Fargo because the cost of integrating the two companies was far greater than anticipated. Wells Fargo eventually merged with Norwest Bank.

tender offer Offer to buy shares made by a prospective buyer directly to a target corporation's shareholders, who then make individual decisions about whether to sell

Among other disadvantages of incorporation is the start-up cost. Not surprisingly, forming a corporation is more expensive than forming a sole proprietorship or a partnership. For one thing, corporations are heavily regulated, and incorporation entails meeting the complex legal requirements of the state in which the firm is chartered. Nonetheless, some states provide much better environments in which to charter corporations than others. For this reason, businesses often take out charters and maintain small headquarters facilities in one state while conducting most of their business in others. With its low corporate tax rate, for instance, Delaware is home to more corporations than any other state.

Double Taxation. The greatest potential drawback to corporate organization, however, is **double taxation.** First, a regular corporation must pay income taxes on company profits. In addition, stockholders must pay taxes on income returned by their investments in the corporation. Consider the case of Black & Decker Corp. In 1996, the firm had to pay federal income tax on $230 million in profits, and then a dividend of 48 cents per share. Each shareholder also had to pay personal income tax on the total dividend received from Black & Decker. Thus, the profits earned by Black & Decker are essentially taxed twice—once at the corporate level and again at the level of its individual owners. In contrast, because profits are treated as owners' personal income, sole proprietorships and partnerships are taxed only once.

double taxation Situation in which taxes may be payable both by a corporation on its profits and by shareholders on dividend incomes

Table 2.1 summarizes and compares the most important differences among three major business forms.

FIGURE 2.2 ◆ **Simple Tender Offer**

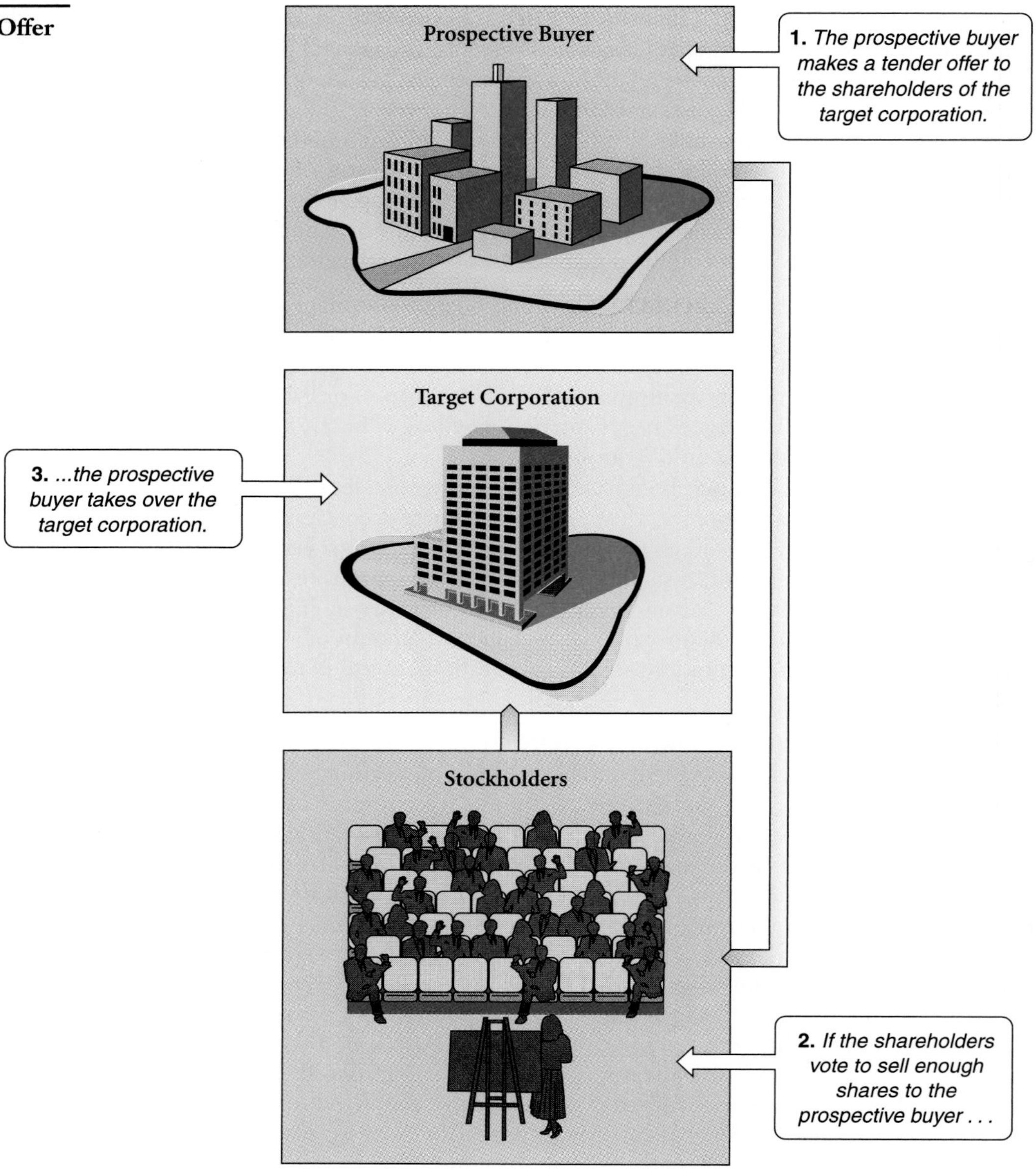

TABLE 2.1 ◆ **Comparative Summary: Three Forms of Business**

BUSINESS FORM	LIABILITY	CONTINUITY	MANAGEMENT	SOURCES OF INVESTMENT
Proprietorship	Personal, unlimited	Ends with death or decision of owner	Personal, unrestricted	Personal
General Partnership	Personal, unlimited	Ends with death or decision of any partner	Unrestricted or depends on partnership agreement	Personal by partner(s)
Corporation	Capital invested	As stated in charter, perpetual or for specified period of years	Under control of board of directors, which is selected by stockholders	Purchase of stock

■ CREATING AND MANAGING A CORPORATION

Not surprisingly, creating a corporation can be complicated. In addition, once the corporate entity has come into existence, it must be managed by people who understand the complex principles of **corporate governance**—the roles of shareholders, directors, and other managers in corporate decision making.

corporate governance Roles of shareholders, directors, and other managers in corporate decision making

In this section, we describe the steps in creating a corporation. We then discuss the principles of *stock ownership* and *stockholders' rights* and describe the role of *boards of directors*. Finally, we examine some of the most important trends in corporate ownership.

Creating a Corporation

In its simplest form, the process of creating a corporation consists of three basic steps:

1. *Consult an attorney.* Although it is possible to establish a corporation without legal guidance, most people soon realize that the process involves, among other things, satisfying various government rules and regulations.
2. *Select a state in which to incorporate.* As noted, many companies choose Delaware for tax purposes. It usually makes sense, however, for a smaller company to incorporate in the state in which it will conduct most of its business.
3. *File articles of incorporation and corporate bylaws.* **Articles of incorporation** specify such information as the firm's name and address, its purpose, the amount of stock it intends to issue, and other legally required information. **Bylaws** detail methods for electing directors and define terms and basic responsibilities. They also describe the process of issuing new stock and address such issues as stock ownership and stockholders' rights.

articles of incorporation Document detailing the corporate governance of a company, including its name and address, its purpose, and the amount of stock it intends to issue

bylaws Document detailing corporate rules and regulations, including election and responsibilities of directors and procedures for issuing new stock

Corporate Governance

Corporate governance, which is specified for each firm by its bylaws, involves three distinct bodies. **Stockholders** (or **shareholders**) are the real owners of a corporation—investors who buy shares of ownership. The *board of directors* is a group of people elected by stockholders to oversee the management of the corporation. Corporate *officers* are top managers hired by the board to run the corporation on a day-to-day basis.

stockholder (or **shareholder**) Owner of shares of stock in a corporation

STOCK OWNERSHIP AND STOCKHOLDERS' RIGHTS Corporations sell shares in the business, which is **stock,** to investors, who then become stockholders, or shareholders. Profits are distributed among stockholders in the form of dividends, and corporate managers serve at their discretion. Stockholders, then, are the owners of a corporation.

stock Share of ownership in a corporation

Preferred and Common Stock. Corporate stock may be either preferred or common. **Preferred stock** guarantees holders fixed dividends, much like the interest paid on savings accounts. Preferred stockholders are so called because they have preference, or priority, over common stockholders when dividends are distributed and, if a business liquidates, when the value of assets is distributed. Although many major corporations issue preferred stock, few small corporations do.

preferred stock Stock that guarantees its holders fixed dividends and priority claims over assets but no corporate voting rights

Common stock, however, must be issued by every corporation, big or small. It usually pays dividends only if the corporation makes a profit. Dividends on both common and preferred stock are paid on a per-share basis. Thus, a stockholder with 10 shares receives 10 times the dividend paid to a stockholder with 1 share. Holders of common stock have the last claims to any of the company's assets if it folds.

common stock Stock that pays dividends and guarantees corporate voting rights, but offers last claims over assets

Another difference involves voting rights. Preferred stockholders generally have no voting rights. Common stockholders always have voting rights, with each share of stock carrying one vote. Investors who cannot attend a stockholders' meeting may delegate their voting shares to someone who will attend. This procedure, called voting by **proxy,** is the way almost all individual investors vote.

proxy Authorization granted by a shareholder for someone else to vote his or her shares

Ownership of common stock does not automatically give an individual the right to act for the corporation or to share in its management. The only way that most stockholders can influence the running of a corporation is by casting their annual votes for the board of directors. In reality, however, any given individual usually has little influence over the affairs of a large corporation. For example, although General Motors boasts more than 1 million stockholders, only a handful have enough votes to affect the way GM is actually run. A few years ago, when many corporations were not only performing poorly but generally getting bad press about the high salaries of CEOs who were busy engineering layoffs, many annual shareholder meetings were downright nasty. For example, it was not uncommon for shareholders to picket meetings or even try to disrupt the proceedings. Not surprisingly, the more recent prosperity enjoyed by many U.S. corporations has resulted in happier shareholders.[6]

board of directors Governing body of a corporation that reports to its shareholders and delegates power to run its day-to-day operations, but remains responsible for sustaining its assets

BOARDS OF DIRECTORS By law, the governing body of a corporation is its **board of directors.** Boards communicate with stockholders and other potential investors through such channels as the annual report—a summary of the company's financial health. Directors also set policy on dividends, major spending, and executive salaries and benefits. They are legally responsible for corporate actions and are increasingly being held liable for them.

Board Makeup. Although requirements differ, most states require that there be at least 3 directors and one board meeting per year. Large corporations tend to have as many as 20 or 30 directors. Smaller corporations often have no more than 5 directors. Usually, directors are people with personal or professional ties to the corporation, such as family members, lawyers, and accountants.

Many boards have both outside and inside directors. Inside directors are top managers who have primary responsibility for the corporation. Outside directors are typically attorneys, accountants, university officials, and executives from other firms. However, all directors share the same basic responsibility: to ensure that the corporation is managed in the best interests of the stockholders. Traditionally, board members have been expected to keep a low profile, to avoid openly criticizing the firm or its executives, and to keep company activities and discussions confidential. Recently, however, some board members have begun to challenge these norms by making public statements, offering public criticisms of the firms they oversee, and openly describing what goes on at their meetings. For example, when Agnes Varis recently resigned from the board of Copley Pharmaceuticals, she sent a two-page letter of resignation to the press in which she broadly criticized the firm and its executives for mismanagement and failing to act in the best interests of its shareholders.[7]

chief executive officer (CEO) Top manager hired by the board of directors to run a corporation

OFFICERS Although board members oversee the corporation's operation, most of them do not participate in day-to-day management. Rather, they hire a team of managers to run the firm. As we have already seen, this team, called *officers*, is usually headed by the firm's **chief executive officer,** or **CEO,** who is responsible for the firm's overall performance. Other officers typically include a *president*, who is responsible for internal management, and *vice presidents*, who oversee various functional areas such as marketing and operations. Some officers may also be elected to serve on the board, and in some cases, a single person plays multiple roles. For example, one person might serve as board chairperson, CEO, and president. In most cases, however, a different person fills each slot.

Figure 2.3 summarizes the rights and responsibilities of each group in the corporate governance hierarchy.

Special Issues in Corporate Ownership

In recent years, several special issues have arisen or grown in importance in corporate ownership. The most important of these trends are *mergers* and *acquisitions* (including *corporate alliances*), *multinational corporations*, *joint ventures*, *divestitures and spin-offs*, *employee stock ownership plans*, and *institutional ownership*.

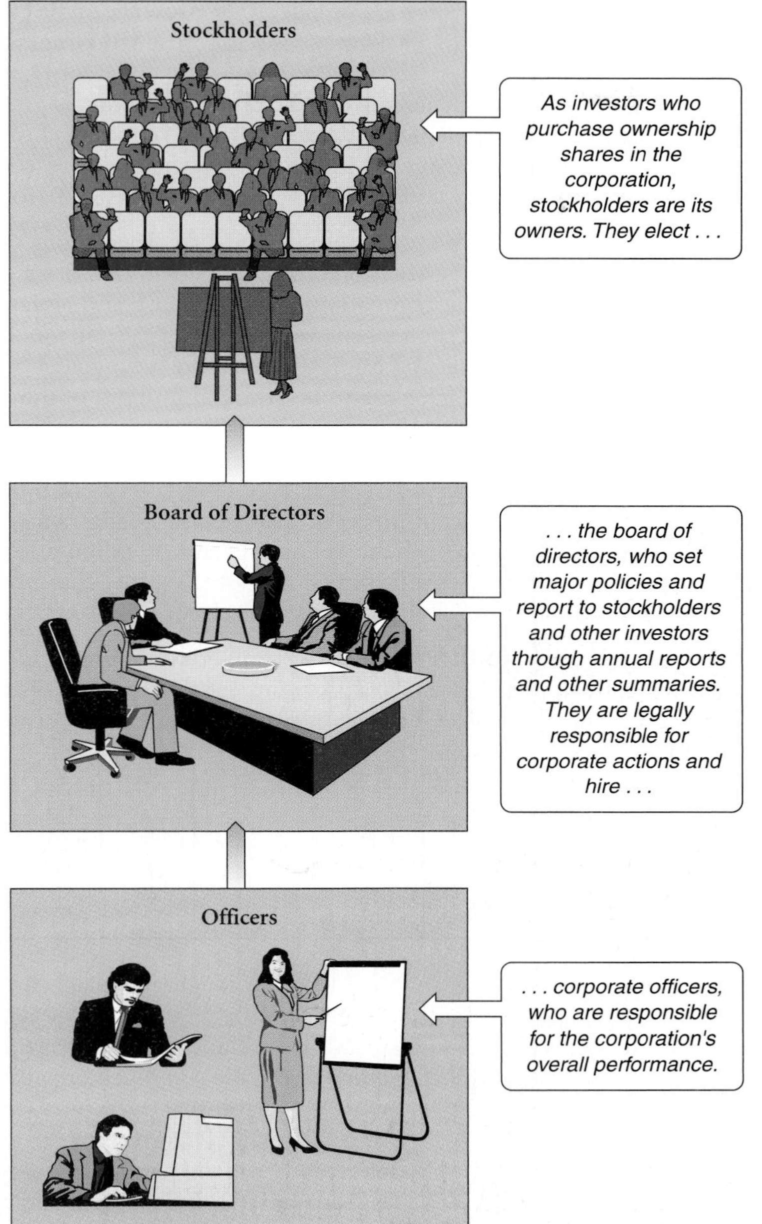

FIGURE 2.3 ◆ **Corporate Governance Hierarchy**

MERGERS AND ACQUISITIONS A **merger** occurs when two firms combine to create a new company. In an **acquisition,** one firm buys another outright. Although mergers and acquisitions are not new, they increased in both frequency and importance in the United States during the 1980s. In the 1990s, they remain an important form of corporate strategy. They allow firms to increase product lines, expand operations, go international, and create new enterprises in conjunction with other organizations. Mergers usually take one of three forms:

merger The union of two corporations to form a new corporation

acquisition The purchase of one company by another

- A *horizontal merger* occurs between two companies in the same industry. For example, Amoco, one of the largest petroleum companies in the United States, recently merged with British Petroleum to create the third largest oil company in the world. Other recent examples include the mergers of Daimler-Benz with Chrysler and Norwest Bank with Wells Fargo.

- When one of the companies is a supplier to or customer of the other, the venture is called a *vertical merger*. For example, Disney's acquisition of ABC/Capital Communications made sense because the network can serve as an effective outlet for Disney programming.
- Finally, when the companies are unrelated, the acquisition is called a *conglomerate merger*. For example, Gillette merged with Duracell in 1996 to capitalize on distribution-channel efficiencies; but the fundamental product lines of the two firms (personal care products and batteries) are essentially unrelated.

Takeover Tactics. A merger or acquisition can take place in one of several different ways. The process usually starts when one firm announces that it wants to buy another for a specified price. After some negotiation, the owners or board of the second company agrees to the sale and the firm is soon taken over by the buyer. Sometimes, a firm may realize that it is a likely takeover target and cannot forestall the inevitable. It may therefore seek out a favorable buyer and, in effect, ask to be acquired. In both of these two scenarios, the acquisition is called a *friendly takeover* because the acquired company welcomes the merger.

Sometimes, however, takeover targets resist. In such a case, a firm may wish to remain independent, or it may regard a purchase offer as too low or a potential buyer as a poor match. The would-be buyer, however, may persist. For instance, it may offer to buy the target firm's stock on the open market, usually at a premium price. If it can acquire a sufficient quantity of stock, it will gain control of the target company despite the resistance of the target firm's management. In this case, the acquisition is called a hostile takeover.

DIVESTITURES AND SPIN-OFFS Sometimes a corporation adopts the opposite strategy in that it decides to take a part of its existing business operations and either sell it to another corporation or set it up as a new independent corporation. Several reasons might motivate such a step.

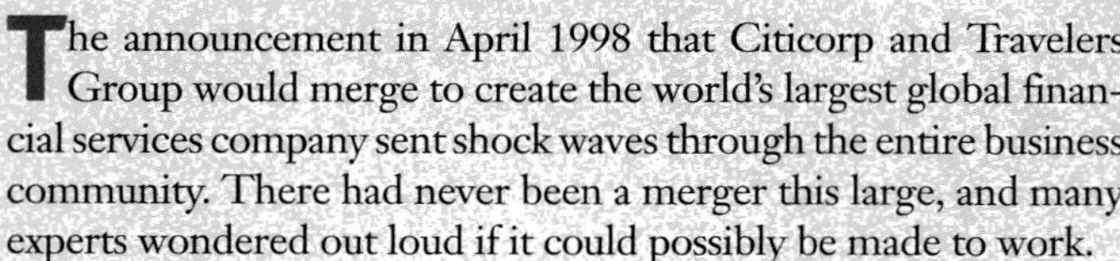

CAPITAL MAKES STRANGE BEDFELLOWS

The announcement in April 1998 that Citicorp and Travelers Group would merge to create the world's largest global financial services company sent shock waves through the entire business community. There had never been a merger this large, and many experts wondered out loud if it could possibly be made to work.

Citicorp CEO and Chairman John S. Reed and Sanford I. Weill, his Travelers counterpart, finalized the deal in just 6 months. Moving at lightning speed, they jumped legal and administrative hurdles that would have staggered less stouthearted corporate entities. Yet many of the same questions about the new organization remain as Citigroup, as the new company will be called, embarks on the challenge of combining leadership, organizations, technology, marketing, and cultures to form a unified company. The merger is receiving so much attention, in part, because of the following challenges:

- *The challenge of leadership.* Both Sandy Weill and John Reed are larger-than-life business leaders. Weill has a well-deserved reputation as the financial industry's consummate dealmaker, while Reed is known as a visionary in banking technology and an electronics-payment pioneer. How these men will work together as cochairmen and CEOs—how they will put egos aside—is the question on everyone's mind.

  Not only are their personal styles different (Reed is recognized as the more cerebral of the two, whereas Weill's element is the rough-and-tough interplay of the deal), but they also have different views about the relationships of people to machines. Both men are attracted to the scale and efficiency of the combined organization, but Weill focuses more on person-to-person interaction. Reed, observes one trade journalist, "has built Citi around credit cards and electronic banking and technological solutions. Weill's customers [at Travelers] demand a sometimes messy human interaction, usually because they're buying complex products."
- *The challenge of marketing.* The combined organization will be cross-selling a range of financial products, including banking, brokerage, insurance, and investment banking services to a customer base that approaches 100 million people. "It's about cross-marketing and providing better products to clients," says Weill, who adds that it's important to do these things in a disciplined way. A serious error would be to overwhelm customers with too many sales pitches that transform Citigroup into a financial bully.

  The marketing challenge becomes more difficult because of a potential clash of corporate cultures. "It would be very difficult," argues one industry analyst, "to convince [Weill's] brokers to sell [Citibank] car loans and credit cards. If you were ever to talk to a Dean Witter broker who was there [dur-

For example, a firm might decide that it needs to focus more specifically on its core businesses. Unilever, a large European consumer products company, recently did this. The firm makes such well-known products as Close-Up toothpaste, Dove soap, Vaseline lotions, and Q-tips. The company also owned several specialty chemical businesses which had been set up to make ingredients for its consumer products. The firm decided that it needed to focus more on the consumer products themselves and sold the chemical businesses to ICI, a European chemical giant. Such a sale is called a **divestiture.**

divestiture Selling of one or more corporate business units

In other cases a firm might decide to sell part of itself to raise capital. Kmart has had to resort to this strategy. It sold its profitable bookstore operations, including Borders and Waldenbooks, to raise money to expand its discount chain. The actual sale was a new stock offering in a newly created corporation comprising the bookstore chains. Such a sale is known as a **spin-off.**

spin-off Setting up one or more corporate units as new, independent corporations

JOINT VENTURES In a *strategic alliance,* two or more organizations collaborate on an enterprise. When the partners share ownership stakes in the enterprise, it is called a **joint venture.** The number of joint ventures has increased rapidly in recent years on both domestic and international fronts. For example, Disney and McDonald's recently announced an innovative marketing joint venture. McDonald's gets exclusive rights to sell Disney-licensed merchandise tied into new movie releases and to open restaurants in certain areas of Walt Disney World. In return, Disney receives licensing fees from both of these activities plus a guaranteed advertising budget from McDonald's, which is jointly promoting its movies and the restaurants.

joint venture Collaboration between two or more organizations on an enterprise

EMPLOYEE STOCK OWNERSHIP PROGRAMS Still another development in corporate ownership is the **employee stock ownership plan (ESOP).** As the term suggests, this plan allows employees to own a significant share of the corporation through what are

employee stock ownership plan (ESOP) Arrangement in which a corporation holds its own stock in trust for its employees, who gradually receive ownership of the stock and control its voting rights

ing the merger] with Sears, you won't find a Dean Witter broker who was happy to sit in a Sears store."

- *The challenge of technology.* In an industry as information-intensive as finance, Citigroup must combine its different technology systems rapidly and effectively. With bank and brokerage accounts, insurance policies, and business and personal loans at stake, there is little room for error.

  Technology must also move the organization where it wants to go. It must give managers mastery over data that will allow them to cross-market products and services, track trades, and stay well ahead of the personnel needs of its 160,000-member workforce. If Citigroup can do all this, says one observer at the MIT Media Lab, "technology becomes the single dominant driver of organizational consolidation and redesign for the next 20 years."
- *The challenge of convincing customers that the deal is good for them.* Citigroup must persuade customers that a financial services company which offers one-stop shopping is in their best interest. In an age where bigger is not always considered better, this is not an easy sell.

  In a survey of customers outside a Citibank branch just days after the merger announcement, customers talked about the importance of diversifying—of not putting all their money in one place. "If you have a problem with your heart," advised one customer, "you go to a cardiologist, not a general practitioner. I try to find the best out there." Individuals also expressed concern that small customers would be lost in the bureaucracy of such a massive company and that with fewer competitors, prices would rise.

"If you have a problem with your heart, you go to a cardiologist, not a general practitioner."

Citigroup customer on the importance of diversification in the banking industry

The business world will be watching to see how Citigroup manages these challenges in the years ahead. As for Weill and Reed, both men announced the deal with a sense of humor. "I know all about sharing challenges and responsibilities; I've been married for 43 years," said Weill. "Two people sharing a job is inherently difficult," agreed Reed. "I'm sure everyone will be measuring our office space to see who gets the prime location."

essentially trusts established on behalf of the employees. The company first secures a loan with which it buys shares of its own stock on the open market. A portion of future corporate profits is used to guarantee and eventually repay the loan. Employees gradually receive ownership of the stock, usually on the basis of seniority. Because the stock is being used to secure the original loan, they do not receive immediate possession of it, but they do take immediate control of its voting rights. Current estimates suggest that there are now almost 10,000 ESOPs in the United States. The growth rate in new ESOPs has slowed a bit in recent years, but they still are an important part of corporate ownership patterns in the United States.

institutional investors Large investors, such as mutual funds and pension funds, that purchase large blocks of corporate stock

INSTITUTIONAL OWNERSHIP Most individual investors do not own enough stock to exert any influence on the management of big corporations. In recent years, however, more and more stock has been purchased by **institutional investors.** Because they control enormous resources, these investors—especially mutual and pension funds—can buy huge blocks of stock. For example, the national teachers' retirement system (TIAA-CREF) has assets of over $95 billion and invests over one-third of that amount in stocks.

Indeed, institutional investors now own almost 40 percent of all the stock in the United States. An important trend in recent years is increased involvement by such investors in the companies that they partially own. TIAA-CREF, for example, now recommends standards for the makeup of company boards: They should have a majority of independent directors, and committees should be composed entirely of unaffiliated outsiders. Investor influence was important when PepsiCo decided to spin off its restaurant businesses—KFC, Taco Bell, and Pizza Hut—into a new corporation in 1997. Several large institutional investors had become unhappy with the firm's performance relative to Coca-Cola and pressured the board to take action. The board's response was to sell off these businesses to allow management to focus more attention on the firm's core soft drink business.

Continued from page 31

Alliance by Location

While the co-owners of Twin Computer Training search the canyons of New York City for alliances and client projects, the companies located in the Greenpoint Manufacturing and Design Center (GMDC) need to look no further than the neighbors in their own facility. Much as proximity—being physically close—affects our personal relationships, it also affects business alliances.

That's what Frank Lionti found after he moved his three-person operation, Distinction in Woods Ltd., into GMDC, which is located in Brooklyn, New York. Lionti was hired almost immediately by a larger woodworking company to do finishing work on its custom cabinetry jobs. "They don't have to do the finishing, and I don't have to do the woodworking," says Lionti. "It's much more to their advantage and much more to my advantage."

Business alliances are common among the 40 small woodworking companies located in GMDC. First created in 1992 by a government agency charged with keeping small woodworking companies in the local area, GMDC has a communal culture that stresses cooperation. Alliances breed because custom woodworking is a specialized business: Wood finishers need wood carvers who need cabinet designers and makers. With the advantage of a shared $350,000 wood shop, smaller tenants can take on bigger jobs. Working together, every firm thus adds capacity without adding to their fixed costs. "I'd like to say that's something that we brilliantly engineered," says GMDC CEO David Sweeney. "But this segment of the industry just seems to easily digest cooperation and competition in the same bite."

"I'd like to say that's something that we brilliantly engineered, but this segment of the industry just seems to easily digest cooperation and competition in the same bite."

—David Sweeney
CEO of GMDC

Questions for Discussion

1. What are the advantages of business alliances for small companies like Twin Computer Training?
2. Why are companies that offer complementary services more likely to join together than those with competing services? Do you think it's smart for potential competitors to join on a project basis?
3. Why is specialization so important in today's economy, and how do alliances help companies maintain their focus?
4. If you were a small-business owner, would you accept a loose arrangement (i.e., a handshake) to finalize the terms of the alliance, or would you be likely to seal the deal with signatures on legal contracts?
5. Why do you think it's smart for Twin Computer Training to present a unified front to its clients?
6. Why is the Greenpoint Manufacturing and Design Center a breeding ground for small-business alliances?

SUMMARY

1. **Trace the history of business in the United States.** Modern U.S. business structures reflect a pattern of development over centuries. Throughout much of the colonial period, sole proprietors supplied raw materials to English manufacturers. The rise of the factory system during the *Industrial Revolution* brought with it *mass production* and *specialization of labor*. During the *entrepreneurial era* in the nineteenth century, huge corporations—and monopolies—emerged. During the *production era* of the early twentieth century, companies grew by emphasizing output and production. During the *marketing era* of the mid-1900s, businesses began focusing on sales staff, advertising, and the need to produce what consumers wanted. The most recent development has been toward a global perspective.
2. **Identify the major forms of business ownership.** The most common forms of business ownership are the *sole proprietorship*, the *partnership*, the cooperative, and the regular *corporation*. Each form has several advantages and disadvantages. The form under which a business chooses to organize is crucial because it affects both long-term strategy and day-to-day

decision making. In addition to advantages and disadvantages, entrepreneurs must consider their preferences and long-range requirements.

3. **Describe *sole proprietorships* and *partnerships* and explain the advantages and disadvantages of each.** *Sole proprietorships*, the most common form of business, consist of one person doing business. Although sole proprietorships offer freedom and privacy and are easy to form, they lack continuity and present certain financial risks. For one thing, they feature *unlimited liability:* The sole proprietor is liable for all debts incurred by the business. *General partnerships* are proprietorships with multiple owners. *Limited partnerships* allow for limited partners who can invest without being liable for debts incurred by general or active partners. In master limited partnerships, master partners can sell shares and pay profits to investors. Partnerships have access to a larger talent pool and more investment money than sole proprietorships, but they may be dissolved if conflicts between partners cannot be settled.
4. **Describe *corporations* and explain their advantages and disadvantages.** *Corporations* are independent legal entities that are usually run by professional managers. The corporate form is used by most large businesses because it offers continuity and opportunities for raising money. It also features financial protection through *limited liability:* The liability of investors is limited to their personal investments. However, the corporation is a complex legal entity subject to double taxation. In addition to taxes paid on corporate profits, investors must pay taxes on earned income. The stock of *public corporations* is sold widely to the general public; the stock of *private corporations* is held by a few investors and is unavailable for sale to the public.
5. **Describe the basic issues involved in creating and managing a corporation.** Creating a corporation generally requires legal assistance to file *articles of incorporation* and corporate *bylaws* and to comply with government regulations. Managers must understand stockholders' rights as well as the rights and duties of the *board of directors.*
6. **Identify recent trends and issues in corporate ownership.** Recent trends in corporate ownership include *mergers* (when two companies combine to create a new one) and *acquisitions* (when one company buys another outright), *multinational corporations* (which conduct activities on an international scale), *joint ventures* or *strategic alliances* (in which two or more organizations collaborate on an enterprise), *employee stock ownership plans* (ESOPs by which employees buy large shares of their employer companies), and *institutional ownership* of corporations (by groups such as mutual and pension funds).

QUESTIONS AND EXERCISES

Questions for Review

1. Why is it important to understand the history of U.S. business?
2. Compare the advantages and disadvantages of the major forms of business ownership.
3. What are the primary benefits and drawbacks to serving as a general partner in a limited partnership?
4. Why might a corporation choose to remain private? Why might a private corporation choose to go public?
5. Why have joint ventures become more common in recent years?

Questions for Analysis

6. How can you, as a prospective manager, better prepare yourself now for the challenges you will face in the next 20 years?
7. What basic steps must be taken to incorporate a business in your state?
8. Go to the library or on the Internet and research a recent merger or acquisition. What factors led to the arrangement? What circumstances characterized the process of completing the arrangement? Were they friendly or unfriendly?

APPLICATION EXERCISES

9. Interview the owner-manager of a sole proprietorship or a general partnership. What characteristics of that business form led the owner to choose it? Does he or she ever contemplate changing the form of the business?

10. Interview the owner of or principal stockholder in a corporation. What characteristics of that business form led the individual to choose it?

BUILDING YOUR BUSINESS SKILLS

THE UPS AND DOWNS OF WIDGET OWNERSHIP

This exercise is designed to enhance the following SCANS workplace competencies: demonstrating basic skills, demonstrating thinking skills, exhibiting interpersonal skills, and working with information.

▼ GOAL

To help students analyze the implications of corporate acquisitions and mergers for individual stockholders.

▼ SITUATION

You own 500 shares of Widget International (WI). Although you like the company's products, you are disappointed with the current stock price. Analysts agree with you and warn that the company must drastically cut expenses or risk a takeover. Management begins to trim budgets, but its efforts are seen as too little too late. With the stock price continuing to drop, XYZ Corp. offers to buy WI. After successful negotiations, XYZ is set to acquire WI on January 1. When this happens, your 500 shares of WI will be converted into XYZ Corp. stock.

▼ METHOD

Working in groups of four or five, analyze the ways in which this acquisition may affect your stock holdings. Research a similar corporate merger that took place in the past year as you consider the following factors:

- The nature of the acquiring company
- The fit between the products or services offered by the two companies
- The fiscal health of the acquiring company, as reflected in its own stock price
- The stock market's long-term reaction to the acquisition. Does the market think it is a good move?
- Changes in corporate leadership as a result of the acquisition
- Changes in the way the acquired company's products are produced and marketed
- Announced budgetary changes

▼ FOLLOW-UP QUESTIONS

1. After one company acquires another, what factors are likely to push up the stock price of the acquired firm?
2. After one company acquires another, what factors are likely to push down the stock price of the acquired firm?
3. Did your research identify any factors that are likely to trigger a corporate takeover?
4. In an acquisition, who is likely to be named CEO (the person in charge of the acquired or acquiring company)? Who is likely to be named CEO in a merger of equals? What factors are likely to influence this decision?
5. How is the board of directors likely to change as a result of an acquisition? Of a merger?

CRAFTING YOUR BUSINESS PLAN

FORMS OF LEGAL ORGANIZATION

▼ The Purpose of the Assignment

1. To acquaint students with the process of navigating the *Business PlanPro* (BPP) software package.
2. To locate **Form of Ownership** and its information contents in *BPP.*
3. To introduce students to various forms of ownership for different companies.
4. To prepare students to enter a firm's form of ownership into *BPP.*

▼ Assignment

After reading Chapter 2 in the textbook, open the BPP *software* and search for information about forms of company ownership as it applies to these sample firms:* The Boulder Stop, Flower Importer, JavaNet Internet Cafe, *and* Ice Dreams Shaved Ice. *Also select a sample company yourself. Then respond to the following questions:*

1. Describe the steps that must be taken to find **Form of Ownership** information inside *BPP.* (Where in the *BPP* menu is that information located?)
2. When observing the sample companies' business plans, did you find any ownership information that was not covered in the textbook? If so, describe it.
3. Compare and contrast the different forms of ownership among the sample firms.
4. After exploring the form of ownership for one of the sample companies, go to the top of the screen and select **Instructions.** What information is given there? Next, select **Examples.** What information is given there?

▼ For Your Own Business Plan

5. Describe your intended form of ownership. Explain your choice, and indicate where in the BPP document (that is, in which section of the planning document) you will present your choice of ownership form and the rationale for your choice.

▼ *General Tips for Navigating in BPP

1. Open the *BPP* program, examine the Welcome screen, and click on **Open a Sample Plan.**
2. From the **Open a Sample Plan** dialogue box, click on a sample company name; then click on **Open.**
3. On the Task Manager screen, click on any of the lines (for example, **Your Company**).
4. You can always return to the Task Manager screen by going to the bottom of the screen and clicking on the **Task Manager** icon.
5. When you are finished with a sample company, close its Task Manager screen.
6. After finishing with one sample company, you can get to the next one by going to the top of the screen and clicking on **File** (on the menu bar). Then beneath that, select **Open Sample Plan.** This will exit you from the current company file and send you to the **Open a Sample Plan** dialogue box, where you can select your next sample company.

EXPLORING THE NET

OWNING A PIECE OF THE ACTION

To learn more about employee stock ownership plans, log on to the Web site maintained by the National Center for Employee Ownership (NCEO) at:

http://www.nceo.org:

Examine several sections of this site, especially those under "Library," "Training," "Columns," and "International." Then consider the following questions:

1. How effectively does the material in this Web site characterize the advantages and disadvantages of ESOPs?
2. What parts of the Web site do you find most informative? Least informative?
3. Note that you can perform your own searches from within this Web site. What, for example, can you find out about ESOPs in other countries? What sort of "Publications" does the NCEO offer? What sort of "Internet Resources" does it make available? What sort of ESOP-related "Events" are held, and what purposes are they designed to serve?
4. Do you think that you would want to work for a firm that offered an ESOP? Why or why not?
5. What factors do you think probably led to the creation of the National Center for Employee Ownership?
6. Specifically, what value can this Web site have for employees and managers at companies that already have ESOPs? At companies that do not?

UNDERSTANDING THE GLOBAL CONTEXT OF BUSINESS

Chrysler Gets Under the Hood with Daimler-Benz

Remember the "Big Three" U.S. automakers? General Motors, Ford, and Chrysler are about as American as apple pie, right? Well, that's the way it used to be. Flying the American flag over the corporate headquarters of the Big *Three* is no longer appropriate, because Chrysler is merging with Germany's Daimler-Benz to form DaimlerChrysler. The Big Three, it seems, are now the Big Two.

According to Juergen Schrempp, the Daimler-Benz chairman who will share the new reins of power with Chrysler chairman Robert Eaton, this $40 billion deal "will change the face of the industry forever." The effect of the merger on both the domestic and global auto industries will be watched carefully in the years ahead, as will the knocks and pings that are inevitable in a cross-cultural merger of this size.

Although it has been billed as a merger of equals, Daimler-Benz actually acquired Chrysler as part of a plan to form a transglobal company of Goliath proportions. Granted, as consolidation and intense competition promise to change the face of automaking in the decade ahead, the deal appears to be in the best interests of both companies. Combining operations will give Chrysler a major presence outside North America—a critical factor in its future profitability as U.S. market growth slows. It also will give Daimler access to vehicles at the low end of the market and open up the U.S. light-truck market, which includes minivans and sport-utility vehicles.

In the first year alone, the companies expect to realize $1.4 billion by combining supplier and logistics costs and product development operations and by increasing revenues through an improved sales-distribution system. Within 5 years they expect savings to climb to $3 billion, as DaimlerChrysler begins using the same under-the-hood components for different brands. Through economies of scale, predicts Schrempp, "we'll have the size, the profitability and the reach to take on everyone. Our efficiency and our bottom-line focus will make us the most profitable automotive company in the world."

> **"Our efficiency and our bottom-line focus will make us the most profitable automotive company in the world."**
>
> —Juergen Schrempp
> *Chairman of DaimlerChrysler*

Unfortunately, overcoming national and organizational culture clashes may be more difficult than achieving business efficiencies. Chrysler has a looser organizational style than Daimler, and its reporting relationships are often guided by a practical, if-it-works-use-it philosophy. In contrast, Daimler is formal and bureaucratic, with business associates rarely calling each other by their first names.

To see how well the organizations are coming together, observers will look at the signs coming from the office of the CEO, which Eaton and Schrempp will share for 3 years. After that, Schrempp will take charge—a move that does not necessarily mean that the next CEO

will be German. It will be, promises Schrempp, whoever "is best for the company." To promote the image of a global, rather than a German company, both Eaton and Schrempp have agreed to make English the company's official internal language.

In the climate of growing international activity, the study and practice of basic business management has in many ways become the study and practice of international business. When an all-American company such as Chrysler becomes a German company, it is easy to see how pervasive—and important—global business has become. By focusing on the learning objectives of this chapter, you will better understand the dynamics of international business management.

Our opening story is continued on page 71

After reading this chapter, you should be able to:

1. **Describe the rise of international business and identify the major world marketplaces.**
2. **Explain how different forms of *competitive advantage*, *import-export balances*, *exchange rates*, and *foreign competition* determine the ways in which countries and businesses respond to the international environment.**
3. **Discuss the factors involved in deciding to do business internationally and in selecting the appropriate levels of *international involvement* and *international organizational structure*.**
4. **Describe some of the ways in which *social*, *cultural*, *economic*, *legal*, and *political differences* among nations affect international business.**

■ THE RISE OF INTERNATIONAL BUSINESS

globalization Process by which the world economy is becoming a single interdependent system

import Product made or grown abroad but sold domestically

export Product made or grown domestically but shipped and sold abroad

The total volume of world trade today is immense—approximately $7 trillion each year. Foreign investment in the United States alone is approaching $1 trillion, and direct investment abroad by U.S. firms has already passed the $1 trillion mark. As more and more firms engage in international business, the world economy is fast becoming a single interdependent system—a process called **globalization.** We often take for granted the diversity of goods and services available today as a result of international trade. Your television set, your shoes, even your morning cup of coffee may be U.S. **imports**—products made or grown abroad and sold in the United States. At the same time, the success of many U.S. firms depends in large part on **exports**—products made or grown here and shipped for sale abroad.

The Contemporary Global Economy

MIT professor Paul Krugman argues that what we now regard as an extremely active "global economy" is not as unprecedented as we might think. Recall, for instance, our discussion of *gross domestic product (GDP),* which we defined in Chapter 1 as the value of all goods and services produced domestically by a nation each year. If an American firm imports foreign products to sell in this country, those imports are included in GDP. In 1880, Krugman points out, U.S. imports represented 8 percent of GDP. Today they are only 11 percent of GDP. Actual trade of products, therefore, is not much more active than it was in the nineteenth century. What about the movement of money from country to country—a phenomenon known as *capital mobility?* Except for some new forms of exchange, observes Krugman, capital mobility is about the same as it was in 1914. At that time, moreover, England's trade surplus—4 percent of GDP—was the same as the surplus enjoyed by Japan during the peak decade of the 1980s.

What factors, then, typify the global economy in the mid-1990s? Krugman points to vastly expanding growth in the exchange of information and the trade in services:

- In Cambridge, Massachusetts, for example, Montague Corp. designs a unique product—folding mountain bikes. Montague manufactures most of its bikes in Taiwan and sells them in Europe. A key facet of the company's operations is transmitting design specifications to three continents, sometimes on a daily basis. The process works—and the small firm survives—largely because fax machine technology is available.
- Molloy Electric is a small firm that services electric motors in Sioux Falls, South Dakota. Owner Garry Jacobson has observed that more and more customers are bringing in products powered by unreliable foreign-made motors. "Either they bring them in or they just throw them away, which costs us," says Jacobson, who thus acknowledges the impact of the global economy on his small part of the business world.

Note that Molloy Electric's service is not *tradable*—it cannot be directly exchanged for another product on the international market. In fact, this is the case with about 85 percent of all U.S. services—restaurants, retail sales, and the like. In effect, then, the shift to the service economy would seem to work against the development of a global economy. That situation will change, predicts Krugman; note the experience of Molloy Electric, which has already made contact with the manufacturing operations of China and other countries. The following conclusions can be drawn from the experiences of such firms as Molloy Electric and Montague Corp.: Information technology will be the centerpiece of the new global economy, and the growth in the service sector will help to fuel its development.[1]

In this section, we examine some key factors that have shaped—and are shaping—the global business environment of the 1990s and the dawn of the twenty-first century. To begin, we identify and describe the major world marketplaces. Then we discuss some important factors that determine the ways in which both nations and their businesses respond to the international environment: the roles of different forms of *competitive advantage,* of *import-export balances,* and *exchange rates.*

The Major World Marketplaces

The contemporary world economy revolves around three major marketplaces: North America, Western Europe, and Pacific Asia. Business, however, is not conducted solely in these markets. The World Bank notes, for example, that about 77 percent of the world's people live in so-called "developing" areas, and economies in those areas are expanding 5 to 6 percent annually. In a recent year, for example, the economies of all developing countries grew by an average of 5.8 percent, with the strongest growth coming in Asia (6.7 percent, though down from previous years because of the Asian currency crisis) and the smallest in Africa (3.2 percent).[2] There are 300 million consumers in Eastern Europe and another 300 million in South America. In India alone, estimates of the size of the middle class range from 150 million to 200 million.[3]

North America The United States dominates the North American business region. It is the single largest marketplace and enjoys the most stable economy in the world. Many U.S. firms, such as General Motors and Procter & Gamble, have had successful Canadian operations for years, and Canadian firms such as Northern Telecom and Alcan Aluminum are also major international competitors.

Mexico has also become a major manufacturing center, especially along the U.S. border, where cheap labor and low transportation costs have encouraged many firms, from the United States and other countries, to build plants in Mexico. Both Chrysler and General

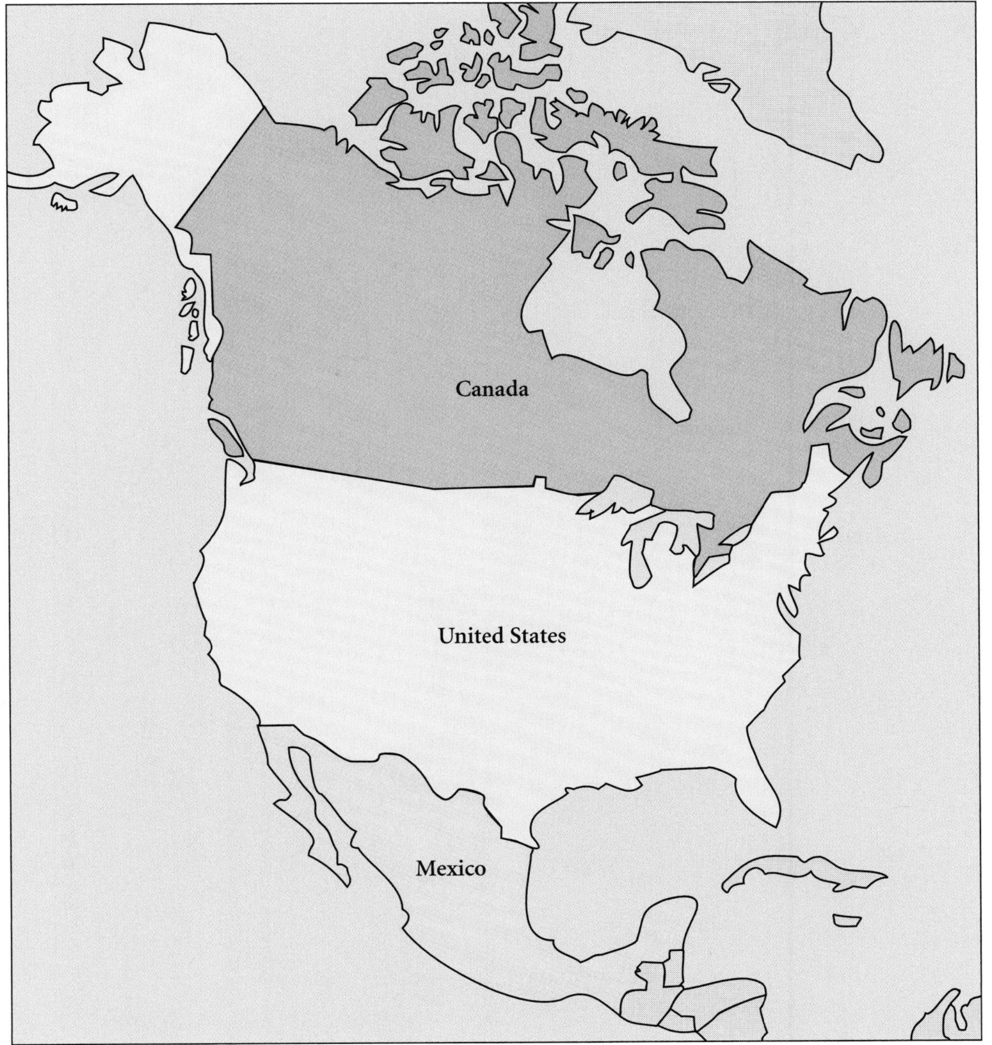

FIGURE 3.1 ◆ **The North American Marketplace and The Nations of NAFTA**

Motors, for instance, are building new assembly plants, as are suppliers such as Rockwell International Corp. Nissan opened an engine and transmission plant in 1983 and an automobile manufacturing plant in 1992. In addition to suppliers, Nissan has also attracted nonautomotive companies to the area, including Xerox and Texas Instruments. From 1993 to 1998, exports of automobiles and automobile parts from Mexico increased from only $7.2 billion to a stunning $19.2 billion, and the auto industry in Mexico employs 360,000 workers.[4]

Figure 3.1 on page 55 shows the three members of the North American Free Trade Agreement (NAFTA). According to this agreement, these three nations will gradually eliminate tariffs and all other trade barriers. Since its founding, NAFTA has added about 2.5 million U.S. jobs each year. Another 1.6 million jobs have been created in North America as total three-way trade among the three member countries has topped the $80 billion mark.[5]

EUROPE Europe has often been regarded as two regions—Western and Eastern Europe. Western Europe, dominated by Germany, the United Kingdom, France, and Italy, has long been a mature but fragmented marketplace. The transformation of the European Union in 1992 into a unified marketplace has further increased its importance (see Figure 3.2). Major international firms such as Unilever, Renault, Royal Dutch/Shell, Michelin, Siemens, and Nestlé are all headquartered in Western Europe.

Eastern Europe, which was primarily communist until recently, has also gained in importance, both as a marketplace and as a producer. Albania, for example, became the 197th

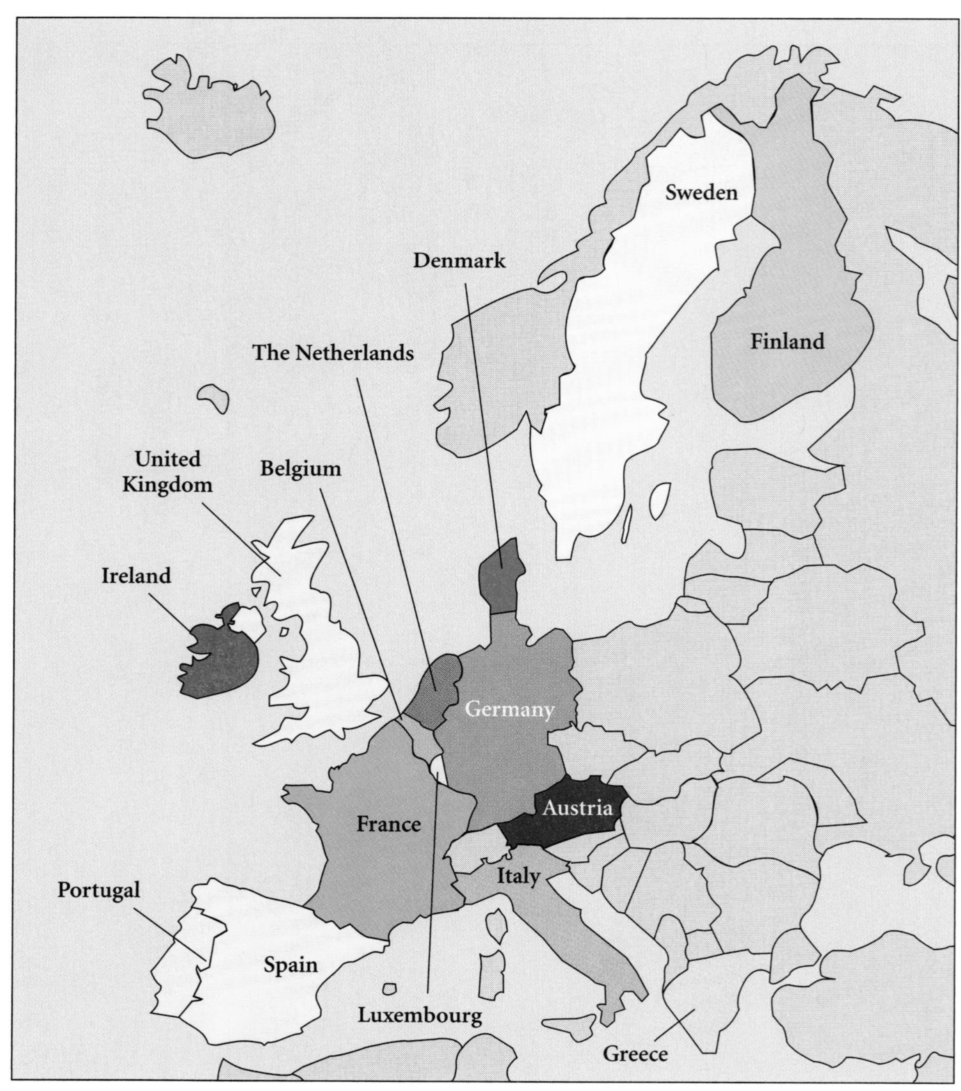

FIGURE 3.2 ◆ Europe and The Nations of the European Union

country in which Coca-Cola is produced when Coke opened a new $10 million bottling plant outside the capital city of Tirana. Over the last few years, foreign companies invested more than $8 billion in Poland, including $500 million from PepsiCo Inc., which is expanding its soft drink, restaurant, and snack food operations. The Korean automaker Daewoo has chosen Poland as the center of its new European operation, spending $1 billion for an existing auto plant near Warsaw.

PACIFIC ASIA Pacific Asia generally consists of Japan, China, Thailand, Malaysia, Singapore, Indonesia, South Korea, Taiwan, the Philippines, and Australia. Some experts still identify Hong Kong as a separate part of the region, but the former city-state is now actually part of China; Vietnam might also be thought of as part of this region. Fueled by strong entries in the automobile, electronics, and banking industries, the economies of these countries grew rapidly in the 1970s and 1980s. Experts expect them to spend nearly $2 trillion on energy, transportation, telecommunications, and office space by the year 2000. Unfortunately, however, a currency crisis in the late 1990s generally slowed growth in virtually every country of the region.

Pacific Asia is already an important force in the world economy and a major source of competition for North American firms. Led by Toyota, Toshiba, and Nippon Steel, Japan dominates the region. In addition, South Korea (with such firms as Samsung and Hyundai), Taiwan (owner of Chinese Petroleum and manufacturing home of many foreign firms), and Hong Kong (a major financial center) are also successful players in the international economy. China, the most densely populated country in the world, continues to emerge as an important market in its own right. In fact, most indicators suggest that the Chinese economy is now the world's third largest, behind the United States and only slightly behind Japan.

Figure 3.3 is a map of the Association of Southeast Asian Nations (ASEAN) countries of Pacific Asia. ASEAN (pronounced *OZZIE-on*) was founded in 1967 as an organization for economic, political, social, and cultural cooperation. In 1995, Vietnam became the group's first communist member. Today, the ASEAN group has a population of 400 million and a GNP of $350 billion. With two-way trade valued at over $80 billion, ASEAN is the sixth largest trading partner of the United States.[6]

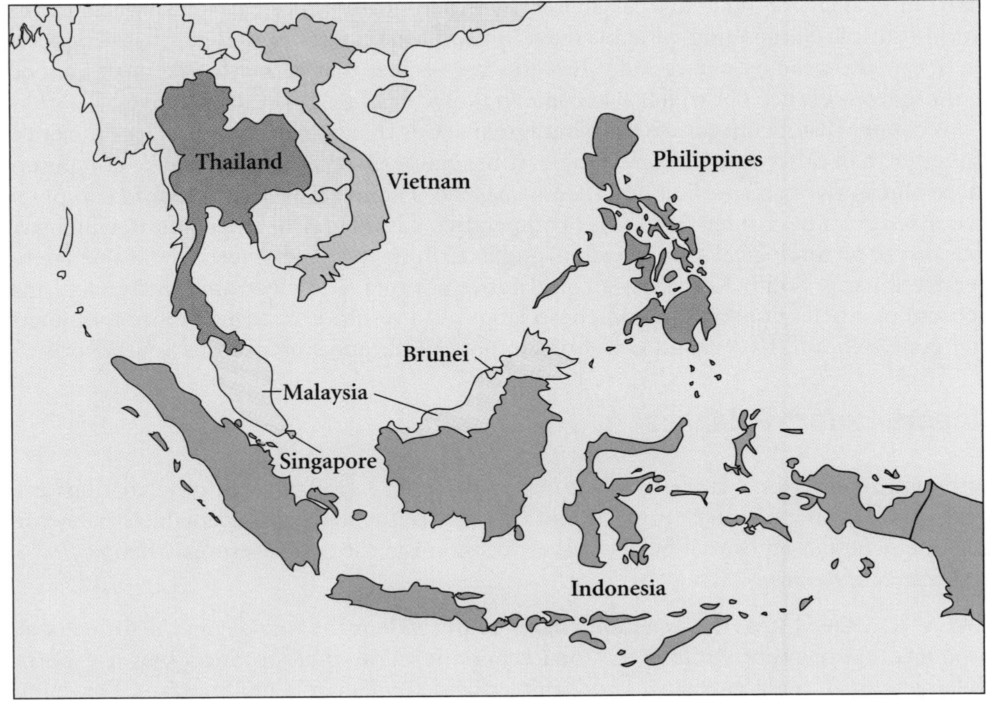

FIGURE 3.3 ◆ **The Nations of ASEAN**

Ashtech is leveraging the U.S. comparative advantage in the computer industry. This California business builds the circuits and chips that translate satellite signals into positional information. Surveyors, farmers, and others can find out where they are with nearly pinpoint accuracy using the U.S. government's Global Positioning System. Ashtech exports more than half of what it makes, with Japan its largest client.

Forms of Competitive Advantage

No country can produce all the goods and services that its people need. Thus, countries tend to export products they can produce better or less expensively than other countries and to use the proceeds to import products they cannot produce effectively. This principle does not fully explain why nations export and import what they do. Such decisions hinge partly on whether a country enjoys an *absolute* or a *comparative advantage* in the production of different goods and services.[7]

absolute advantage The ability to produce something more efficiently than any other country can

An **absolute advantage** exists when a country can produce something more cheaply and/or of higher quality than any other country. Saudi oil, Brazilian coffee beans, and Canadian timber approximate absolute advantage, but examples of true absolute advantage are rare. In reality, "absolute" advantages are always relative. For example, the vineyards of France are generally considered by experts to produce the finest wines in the world. But the burgeoning wine business in California attests to the fact that producers there can also produce very good values in wine—wines that are perhaps almost as good as those from France but which also come in more varieties and at lower prices.

comparative advantage The ability to produce some products more efficiently than others

A country has a **comparative advantage** in goods that it can produce more efficiently or better than other goods. For example, if businesses in a country can make computers more efficiently than automobiles, then firms have a comparative advantage in computer manufacture. The United States has comparative advantages in the computer industry (because of technological sophistication) and in farming (because of fertile land and a temperate climate). South Korea has a comparative advantage in electronics manufacturing because of efficient operations and cheap labor. As a result, U.S. firms export computers and grain to South Korea, and U.S. firms import VCRs and stereos from South Korea.

Import-Export Balances

Although international trade involves many advantages, trading with other nations can pose problems if a country's imports and exports do not strike an acceptable balance. In deciding whether an overall balance exists, economists use two measures: *balance of trade* and *balance of payments.*

balance of trade Economic value of all products a country imports minus the economic value of all products it exports

BALANCE OF TRADE A nation's **balance of trade** is the total economic value of all products that it imports minus the total economic value of all products that it exports. Relatively small trade imbalances are common and are generally unimportant. Large imbalances, however, are another matter. In 1997, for example, the United States had a negative balance of merchandise trade of $197.9 billion, but a positive balance of service trade of $87.7 billion. These figures combined to result in an overall negative trade balance of $110.2 billion. Although the U.S. trade imbalance has been negative for the last several years, strong increases in exports during the 1990s served to lower the imbalance substantially from previous years.

Trade Deficits and Surpluses. When a country's imports exceed its exports—that is, when it has a negative balance of trade—it suffers a **trade deficit.** In short, more money is flowing out of the country than flowing into the country. A positive balance of trade occurs when a country's exports exceed its imports and it enjoys a **trade surplus:** More money is flowing into the country than flowing out of the country. Trade deficits and surpluses are influenced by a wide array of factors, such as absolute or comparative advantages enjoyed by the relevant trading partners, the general economic conditions within various countries, trade agreements, and a host of other factors. For example, higher domestic costs in Japan combined with greater international competition have recently slowed that country's export growth. But rising prosperity in both China and India have resulted in strong increases in both exports from and imports to those countries.

trade deficit Situation in which a country's imports exceed its exports, creating a negative balance of trade

trade surplus Situation in which a country's exports exceed its imports, creating a positive balance of trade

In general, the United States suffers from fairly large trade deficits with Japan, China, Canada, Mexico, Germany, and Taiwan; in any given year, the United States may also have smaller trade deficits with any other given country. The most current U.S. trade deficit figures for its six major trading partners are $47.7 billion, $39.5 billion, $22.8 billion, $16.2 billion, $15.5 billion, and $11.5 billion, respectively. In contrast, U.S. trade deficits with Ireland and Bangladesh were only $1.1 billion each.

Conversely, the United States enjoys healthy trade surpluses with many countries. For example, the most current U.S. trade surplus figures are $10 billion with the Netherlands, $8.1 billion with Australia, $5.8 billion with Belgium-Luxembourg, $3.9 billion with Brazil and South Korea, and $2.5 billion with Egypt. At the lower end of the spectrum, U.S. surpluses in trade with Poland, Kuwait, and Haiti were $300 million each.[8]

BALANCE OF PAYMENTS The **balance of payments** refers to the flow of money into or out of a country.[9] The money that a nation pays for imports and receives for exports—that is, its balance of trade—comprises much of its balance of payments. Other financial exchanges also are factors. For example, money spent by tourists, money spent on foreign aid programs, and money spent and received in the buying and selling of currency in international money markets all affect the balance of payments.

balance of payments Flow of all money into or out of a country

For many years, the United States enjoyed a positive balance of payments (more inflows than outflows); more recently, the balance has been negative. That trend is gradually reversing itself, however, and many economists soon expect a positive balance of payments. Some U.S. industries have positive balances, whereas others have negative balances. U.S. firms such as Dow Chemical and Monsanto, for example, are among the world leaders in chemical exports. The cigarette, truck, and industrial machinery industries also enjoy positive balances. Conversely, the metalworking machinery, electrical generation, airplane parts, and auto industries suffer negative balances because the United States is importing more than it is exporting.

Exchange Rates

The balance of imports and exports between two countries is affected by the rate of exchange between their currencies. An **exchange rate** is the rate at which the currency of one nation can be exchanged for that of another.[10] Recently, for example, one U.S. dollar has been valued at about five French francs. The exchange rate, then, has been about 5 to 1.

exchange rate Rate at which the currency of one nation can be exchanged for the currency of another country

At the end of World War II, the major nations of the world agreed to establish *fixed* exchange rates. Under fixed exchange rates, the value of any country's currency relative to that of another country remains constant. Today, however, *floating* exchange rates are

Malaysian shoppers are spending their ringgit—the Malaysian unit of currency—to buy Procter & Gamble products. Many western nations, the United States among them, are looking to boost exports by tapping into Southeast Asia's huge customer base. Recently, because the ringgit has dropped in value, P&G profits have suffered (it can't buy as many dollars with the devalued ringgits used by Malaysian customers). Asia, however, remains the world's most populous continent, and as one American executive has put it, "Where multinationals used to see Asia as just a source of cheap labor, they now see it as a vast market."

the norm, and the value of one country's currency relative to that of another varies with market conditions. For example, when many French citizens want to spend francs to buy U.S. dollars (or goods), the value of the dollar relative to the franc increases, or gets "stronger"; *demand* for the dollar is high. The value of the dollar thus rises with the demand for U.S. goods. In reality, exchange rates fluctuate by very small degrees on a daily basis. More significant variations usually occur over a longer time.

Fluctuation in exchange rates can have an important impact on the balance of trade. Suppose that you want to buy some French wines priced at 50 francs per bottle. At an exchange rate of 10 francs to the dollar, a bottle will cost you $5 (50 ÷ 10 = 5). But what if the franc is stronger? At an exchange rate of only 5 francs to the dollar, that same bottle of wine would cost you $10 (50 ÷ 5 = 10).

Rate changes, of course, would affect more than wine. If the dollar were stronger in relation to the franc, the prices of all American-made products would rise in France and the prices of all French-made products would fall in the United States. As a result, the French would buy fewer American-made products, and Americans would be prompted to spend more on French-made products. The result could conceivably be a U.S. trade deficit with France.

EXCHANGE RATES AND COMPETITION Companies conducting international operations must watch exchange rate fluctuations closely because such changes affect overseas demand for their products and can be a major factor in international competition.

Case: Ups and Downs at Komatsu. Komatsu (a Japanese firm) and Caterpillar (a U.S. firm) are major competitors in the construction equipment market. In the 1980s, Komatsu enjoyed a competitive advantage over Caterpillar because of the exchange rate between Japanese yen and U.S. dollars. Komatsu used this advantage to gain a major share of the U.S. construction equipment market and to also eat into Caterpillar's market share in other countries.

The situation then changed dramatically, as the value of the dollar fell from 251 yen in 1984 to an all-time low of 80 yen in April 1995. Komatsu subsequently faced serious profit declines because each dollar of its sales in the United States produced far fewer yen to cover the Japanese production and transportation costs entailed in getting products to the United States. This situation forced Komatsu to keep its prices high while Caterpillar was able to lower prices and regain market share. In the summer of 1995, however, the dollar again started to rise relative to the yen, and by 1998, the exchange rate was 126 yen to 1 dollar. This situation eased the pressure on Komatsu's profits and allowed it to return to a more aggressive pricing strategy that resulted in regained market share.[11]

In general, when the value of a country's domestic currency rises, companies based there find it harder to export products to foreign markets and easier for foreign companies to enter local markets. It also makes it more cost-efficient for domestic companies to move production operations to lower-cost sites in foreign countries. When the value of a country's currency declines, just the opposite patterns occur. Thus, as the value of a country's currency falls, its balance of trade should improve because its domestic companies should experience a boost in exports, coupled with a corresponding decrease in the incentives for foreign companies to ship products into the domestic market.

THE U.S. ECONOMY AND FOREIGN TRADE Figures 3.4 and 3.5 highlight (1) recent trends in the U.S. trade deficit and (2) total U.S. exports and imports from January 1997 through September 1998. As you can see, the balance of trade remained consistently negative across this 20-month period, ranging from a high of $15.9 billion in May 1998 to a low of $8.2 billion in June 1997. Looking at Figure 3.5, you can also see that exports from the United States grew until early 1998 but then began to decline; meanwhile, imports into the United States continued to increase fairly steadily across the same period. By considering both sets of information, you can clearly see how changes in exports and imports combine to affect the balance of trade.

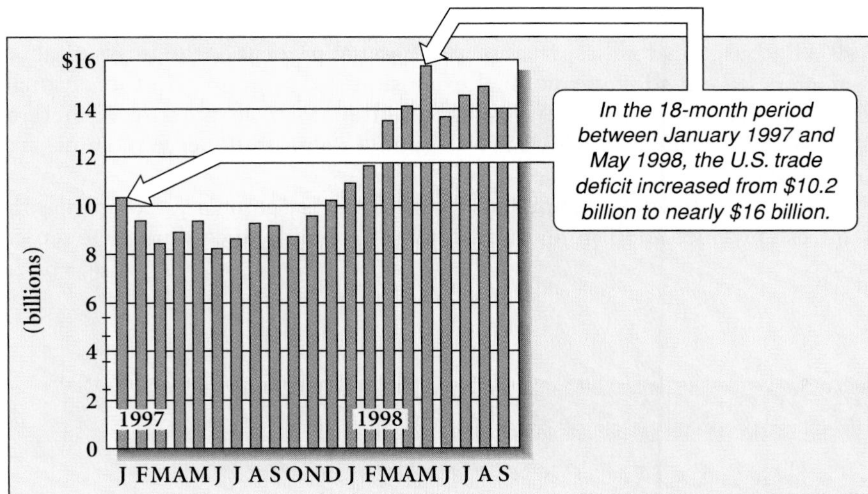

FIGURE 3.4 ◆ **U.S. Trade Deficit**

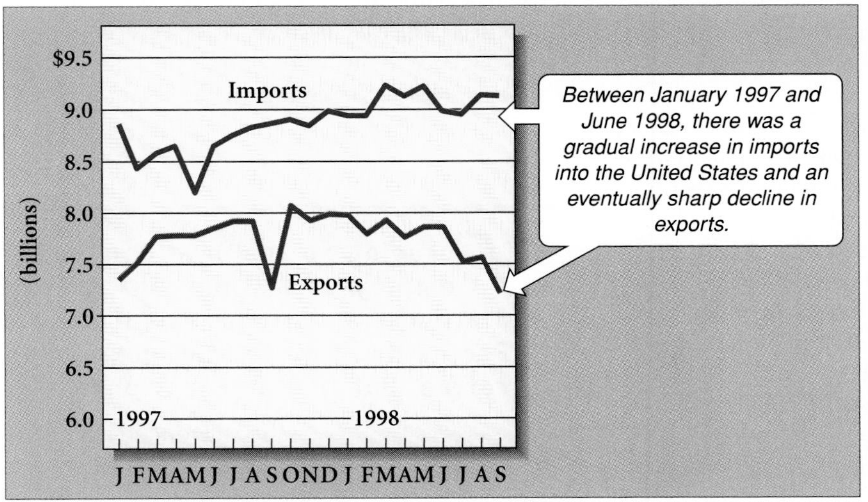

FIGURE 3.5 ◆ **U.S. Imports and Exports**

■ INTERNATIONAL BUSINESS MANAGEMENT

Wherever a firm is located, its success depends largely on how well it is managed. International business is so challenging because the basic management responsibilities—planning, organizing, directing, and controlling—are much more difficult to carry out when a business operates in several markets scattered around the globe.

Managing, of course, means making decisions. In this section, we examine in some depth the three most basic decisions that a company's management must make when faced with the prospect of globalization. The first decision is whether to "go international" at all. Once that decision has been made, managers must decide on the company's level of international involvement and on the organizational structure that will best meet its global needs.

Going International

The world economy is becoming globalized, and more and more firms are conducting international operations. Wal-Mart, for example, was once the quintessential U.S. growth company; but as managers perceived both fewer opportunities for expansion inside the United States and stronger competition from domestic competitors, they decided that foreign expansion was the key to future growth. By aggressively opening new stores abroad, Wal-Mart doubled its foreign sales to $7.5 billion between 1995 and 1997. Because this total represents only about 6 percent of the firm's total revenues, its managers have made international expansion and sales growth their primary goal for the future. All told, the 100 largest U.S. multinational corporations generate total sales of about $2.5 trillion, of which $960 billion, or almost 40 percent, comes from foreign operations.[12]

This route, however, is not appropriate for every company. Companies that buy and sell fresh produce and fish may find it most profitable to confine their activities to lim-

TRENDS AND CHALLENGES

IT CAN'T HURT TO SAY "SKINNY LATTE" IN CHINESE

Starbucks, the Seattle-based coffee retailer, was one of the entrepreneurial success stories of the 1990s. Under the leadership of CEO Howard Schultz, the company grew in the 1980s from a small Seattle coffee retailer to a nationwide chain of coffee bars specializing in custom-made specialty coffees with European flair. By the mid-1990s, Starbucks had transformed the common cup of coffee into a gourmet experience, and both sales and profits were growing by more than 50 percent a year.

By 1998, however, earnings growth had finally slowed and the stock price was dropping. With 1,800 outlets around the country—and markets in many areas increasingly crowded with new competitors—Schultz began to look abroad for opportunities. He targeted Europe and Asia with 500 stores that he hoped would contribute up to 25 percent of total earnings within 5 years. He had reason for optimism: The 23 Tokyo-based Starbucks outlets had lines out the door despite a local economy in deep recession.

Although he appreciated the challenge, Schultz was particularly interested in developing a presence for Starbucks in China. Convincing a nation of tea drinkers to switch to coffee would be hard enough, but finding and training local managers promised to be even harder.

Lawrence Maltz, who controls the Chinese Starbucks franchises, agrees with Schultz on the importance of committed,

> **"Focusing on the development of employees so they can deliver the Starbucks experience is our priority. People don't go to Starbucks for the coffee, but for the experience."**
>
> —Lawrence Maltz
> *Executive with Starbucks in China*

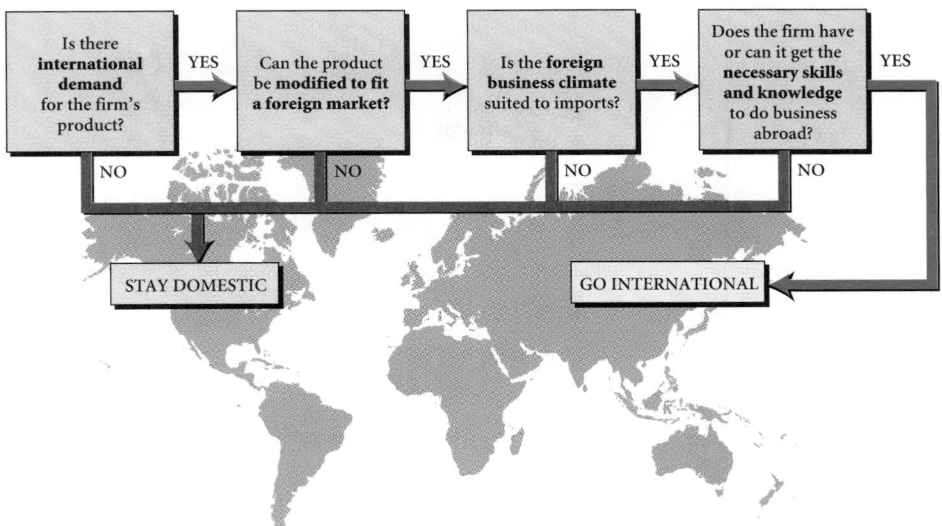

FIGURE 3.6 ◆ **Going International**

ited geographic areas: Storage and transport costs may be too high to make international operations worthwhile. As Figure 3.6 shows, several factors enter into the decision to go international. One overriding factor is the business climate in other nations. Even experienced firms have encountered cultural, legal, and economic roadblocks. (These problems are discussed in more detail later in this chapter.) In considering international expansion, a company should also consider at least two other questions: Is there a demand for its products abroad? If so, must those products be adapted for international consumption?

GAUGING INTERNATIONAL DEMAND Products that are successful in one country may be useless in another. Snowmobiles, for example, are popular for

well-trained employees. "Focusing on the development of employees so they can deliver the Starbucks experience is our priority," he says. "People don't go to Starbucks for the coffee, but for the experience."

Schultz and Maltz also agreed that the best way to teach Chinese management trainees about Starbucks was to have them live the Starbucks culture firsthand. Thus, Starbucks began bringing groups of trainees for 3-month stays in Tacoma, Washington, where they not only learned how to make cappuccinos, Frappuccinos, Tiazzis, and other Starbucks concoctions but also how to master Starbucks's unique vocabulary ("Triple grand latte, anyone?"). They also learned about the casual West Coast lifestyle that defines Starbucks—even in faraway China—as a "cool" brand. They saw how the corporate culture translates into respect for local employees. Although Starbucks veterans may find better pay elsewhere, they aren't likely to find an environment that fosters as much respect for the individual. "We can ask questions and feel free to discuss things," explains Jimmy Dong, a 32-year-old trainee. "Starbucks trusts us to contribute, which makes us want to stay."

This last policy may prove to be one of Starbucks's most important corporate ingredients in its expansion abroad. With few Chinese having experience in Western corporations, the demand for such workers is greater than the supply. The result is a Western-style marketplace in which employees jump into better jobs as soon as they see opportunity. Starbucks hopes to buck this trend by inducing employees to stay.

With his first stores scheduled to open in China before the millennium, Schultz is also betting that Chinese consumers will be willing to seek out a great cup of coffee at an all-American coffee bar. The Westernization of the Chinese consumer is all but inevitable as store managers introduce skinny lattes and Frappuccinos and tell tall tales of how they were treated in Tacoma, Washington.

"Look, everyone here loves vanilla, right? So let's start there."

transportation and recreation in Canada and the northern United States and actually revolutionized reindeer herding in Lapland. However, there is no demand for snowmobiles in Central America. Although this is an extreme example, the point is basic to the decision to go international: Foreign demand for a company's product may be greater than, the same as, or weaker than domestic demand. Market research and/or the prior market entry of competitors may indicate that there is an international demand for a firm's products.

One very large category of U.S. products that travels well is American popular culture. In one recent 12-month period, for instance, 88 of the world's 100 most popular movies were American (no foreign film placed higher than 27th). Billions of dollars are also involved in popular music, television shows, books, and even street fashions. Teenagers in Rome and Beirut, for instance, sport American baseball caps as part of their popular street dress; Super Mario Brothers is advertised on billboards in Bangkok, Thailand; and Bart Simpson piñatas are sold at bazaars in Mexico City. Vintage Levi's from the 1950s and 1960s sell for as much as $3,000 in countries such as Finland and Australia.

ADAPTING TO CUSTOMER NEEDS If there is international demand for its product, a firm must consider whether and how to adapt that product to meet the special demands of foreign customers. Consider the experience of General Motors in marketing the same product to buyers in two very different developing countries:

- In Mexico, GM's Chevrolet division sells a Spanish-made subcompact called the Joy. Chevy prices the Joy $1,500 to $2,000 higher than Volkswagen's old-fashioned Beetle, which still sells well in Mexico. GM upped its price because it has found that in a country where 60 percent of the population is under 25, there is a huge market of younger buyers who will pay for stylish, more powerful vehicles.
- In the Czech Republic, however, GM markets the same car—known as the Opel Corsa—to potential buyers in their thirties. "Here," says GM's director of sales for Central Europe, "younger buyers can't even afford bicycles."

> **"Here younger buyers can't even afford bicycles."**
> *GM's director of sales for Central Europe*

Levels of Involvement

After a firm decides to go international, it must decide on the level of its international involvement. At least three levels of involvement are possible. The firm may act as an *exporter* or *importer*, organize as an *international firm*, or operate as a *multinational firm*. Most of the world's largest industrial firms are multinationals.

exporter Firm that distributes and sells products to one or more foreign countries

importer Firm that buys products in foreign markets and then imports them for resale in its home country

EXPORTERS AND IMPORTERS An **exporter** is a firm that makes products in one country and then distributes and sells them in others. An **importer** buys products in foreign markets and then imports them for resale in its home country. Exporters and importers tend to conduct most of their business in their home nations. Both enterprises entail the lowest level of involvement in international operations and are excellent ways to learn the fine points of global business. Many large firms began international operations as exporters. IBM and Coca-Cola, among others, exported to Europe for several years before building manufacturing facilities there.

The Exporting Boom. In calendar year 1997, U.S. exports totaled $938 billion, representing a 10 percent increase from 1996 and a continuation of strong annual growth throughout the 1990s. Since 1986, U.S. exports have been growing four times as fast as the gross domestic product. At that rate, exports in two decades would equal 37 percent of GDP. Says one Wall Street economist, "We are now—far more than we ever have been—an export economy."

> **"We are now—far more than we ever have been—an export economy."**
>
> *Wall Street economist*

In 1997, for example, Boeing generated over $24 million in sales in the United States and another $21 million outside the country. Meanwhile, in the same year, Exxon earned over 56 percent of its revenues from foreign markets. The export boom, however, is by no means limited to large companies. Relatively small companies, so-called "mininationals," are increasingly visible in the global market. They can compete through the latest long-distance communications technology and the flexibility to enter numerous new markets.

international firm Firm that conducts a significant portion of its business in foreign countries

INTERNATIONAL FIRMS As firms gain experience and success as exporters and importers, they may move to the next level of involvement. An **international firm** conducts a significant portion of its business abroad. International firms also maintain manufacturing facilities overseas. Wal-Mart, for instance, is an international firm. Most of the retailer's stores are still in the United States, but as noted earlier, the company is rapidly expanding into such diverse markets as Mexico, Canada, South America, Indonesia, Europe, and China.

Although an international firm may be large and influential in the global economy, it remains basically a domestic firm with international operations: Its central concern is the domestic market in its home country. Wal-Mart, for example, still earns 94 percent of its revenues from U.S. sales. Product and manufacturing decisions typically reflect this concern. Burlington Industries, Toys "R" Us, and BMW are also international firms.

multinational firm Firm that designs, produces, and markets products in many nations

MULTINATIONAL FIRMS Most **multinational firms** do not ordinarily think of themselves as having domestic and international divisions. Instead, planning and decision making are geared to international markets. Headquarters locations are almost irrelevant. Royal Dutch/Shell, Nestlé, IBM, and Ford are well-known multinationals.

The economic importance of multinationals cannot be underestimated. From 1990 to 1996, for example, multinationals spearheaded $360 billion in investment by foreign com-

No global company enjoys greater profits than Royal Dutch/Shell. The giant multinational oil-and-gas business operates in 130 countries, with headquarters in both London and The Hague, Netherlands. This Shell sign stands next to a park in the Sudan.

panies in developing nations. China, India, and Vietnam are regarded as especially important emerging markets, as are most Latin American countries. In 1997, for instance, foreign firms invested $42.3 billion in China alone. East Asia and the Pacific Rim received another $53 billion, and Latin America $50 billion. There are several reasons for such large outlays, including the need to move closer to customers and the rapid growth of emerging markets. World Bank officials expect emerging nations to provide one-third of the growth in world trade between 1994 and 2005, and multinationals will account for a large part of that trade.[13]

International Organizational Structures

Different levels of involvement in international business require different kinds of organizational structure. For example, a structure that would help coordinate an exporter's activities would be inadequate for the activities of a multinational firm. In this section, we briefly consider the spectrum of international organizational strategies, including *independent agents, licensing arrangements, branch offices, strategic alliances,* and *direct investment.*

independent agent Foreign individual or organization that agrees to represent an exporter's interests

INDEPENDENT AGENTS An **independent agent** is a foreign individual or organization that agrees to represent an exporter's interests in foreign markets. Independent agents often act as sales representatives: They sell the exporter's products, collect payment, and make sure that customers are satisfied. Independent agents often represent several firms at once and usually do not specialize in a particular product or market. Levi Strauss uses agents to market clothing products in many small countries in Africa, Asia, and South America.

licensing arrangement Arrangement in which firms choose foreign individuals or organizations to manufacture or market their products in another country

royalty Payment made to a license holder in return for the right to market the licenser's product

LICENSING ARRANGEMENTS Companies seeking more substantial involvement in international business may opt for **licensing arrangements.** Firms give individuals or companies in a foreign country exclusive rights to manufacture or market their products in that market. In return, the exporter typically receives a fee plus ongoing payments called royalties. **Royalties** are usually calculated as a percentage of the license holder's sales.

BRANCH OFFICES Instead of developing relationships with foreign companies or independent agents, a firm may simply send some of its own managers to overseas **branch offices.** A company has more direct control over branch managers than over agents or license holders. Branch offices also give a company a more visible public presence in foreign countries. Potential customers tend to feel more secure when a business has branch offices in their country.

branch office Foreign office set up by an international or multinational firm

STRATEGIC ALLIANCES In a strategic alliance, a company finds a partner in the country in which it would like to conduct business. Each party agrees to invest roughly equal amounts of resources and capital into a new business. This new business—the alliance—is then owned by the partners, who divide its profits. Such alliances are sometimes called **joint ventures.** As we saw in Chapter 2, however, the term **strategic alliance** has arisen because of the increasingly important role that such partnerships play in the larger organizational strategies of many major companies.

strategic alliance (or joint venture) Arrangement in which a company finds a foreign partner to contribute approximately half of the resources needed to establish and operate a new business in the partner's country

The number of strategic alliances among major companies has increased significantly over the last decade and is likely to grow even more. In many countries, including Mexico, India, and China, laws make alliances virtually the only way to do international business within their borders. Mexico, for example, requires that all foreign firms investing there have local partners.

In addition to easing the way into new markets, alliances give firms greater control over their foreign activities than independent agents and licensing arrangements. (At the same time, of course, all partners in an alliance retain some say in its decisions.) Perhaps most important, alliances allow firms to benefit from the knowledge and expertise of their foreign partners. The importance of such knowledge in Japan, for instance, has prompted all but a handful of U.S. companies to do business there through alliances. For example, Petrofsky's International, a St. Louis maker of frozen bagel dough, encountered trouble with health officials when it first tried to market its product in Japan. Food inspectors objected to the fact that yeast—an essential ingredient—was an "active bacteria." Petrofsky entered an alliance with Itochu, a giant Japanese importer, who managed to get the product certified.

DIRECT INVESTMENT The term **direct investment** means buying or establishing tangible assets in another country. Mercedes-Benz and BMW, for example, have made significant investments by opening major manufacturing plants in the United States—BMW in Spartanburg, South Carolina, and Mercedes in Tuscaloosa, Alabama. Exxon has spent $1 billion to expand an oil refinery in Thailand, where it opens 40 new service stations every year. Texas Instruments invested $1.2 billion to build calculator and semiconductor plants in Italy. In China, drugmaker Merck has opened a new factory to manufacture a vaccine for hepatitis B, and AT&T has entered a joint venture to make fiber-optic cable with a Chinese partner. Daimler-Benz's acquisition of Chrysler and British Petroleum's acquisition of Amoco represent two of the most significant foreign direct investments ever made anywhere.

direct investment Arrangement in which a firm buys or establishes tangible assets in another country

MATCHING STRATEGIES AND OPPORTUNITIES Multinational firms often use whatever approach seems best suited to a particular situation in their search for worldwide business opportunities. In some cases, they opt for independent agents. In other cases, they prefer licensing arrangements, strategic alliances, or direct investments. For example, consider the case of ABB Asea Brown Boveri LTD, one of the world's most globally oriented businesses. Jointly owned by a Swedish firm and a Swiss firm, ABB is the world's largest electrical engineering company. It has 200,000 employees, of whom only 176 work at its headquarters in Zurich. ABB consists of 1,300 separate companies functioning in 140 countries. The CEO is Swedish, and other corporate officers are from Germany, France, Australia, and the United States.

BARRIERS TO INTERNATIONAL TRADE

Whether a business is truly multinational or sells to only a few foreign markets, several factors will affect its international operations. Its success in foreign markets is largely determined by the ways in which it responds to social, economic, and political barriers to international trade.

Social and Cultural Differences

Any firm planning to conduct business in another country must understand the social and cultural differences between the host country and the home country. Some differences, of course, are fairly obvious. Companies must take language factors into account when making adjustments in packaging, signs, and logos. Pepsi-Cola is exactly the same product whether it is sold in Seattle or Moscow—except for the lettering on the bottle. Less "universal" products, however, face a variety of conditions that require them to adjust their practices. In Thailand, for example, Kentucky Fried Chicken adjusted its menus, ingredients, and hours of operation to suit Thai culture.

Sometimes even the physical stature of the host country's population must be considered. Average Japanese and French consumers are slimmer and shorter than their U.S. counterparts—an important consideration if you intend to sell clothes in these markets. Differences in the average ages in the local population can also have ramifications. Countries with growing populations (such as South Korea) tend to have a high percentage of young people. As a result, electronics and fashionable clothing sell well. Countries with stable or declining populations (such as Sweden) tend to have more older people. Generic pharmaceuticals are successful in such markets.

A wide range of more subtle value differences can also affect international operations. For example, many Europeans shop daily. To U.S. consumers accustomed to weekly supermarket trips, the European pattern may seem like a waste of time. For many Europeans, however, shopping not only involves buying food, but it also is an outlet for meeting friends and exchanging political views. Consider the implications of this cultural difference for U.S. firms selling food products in European markets. First, large American supermarkets are not the norm in many parts of Europe. Second, people who shop daily do not need large refrigerators and freezers.

Economic Differences

Although cultural differences are often subtle, economic differences can be fairly pronounced. In dealing with mixed economies like those of France and Sweden, for example, firms must be aware of when, and to what extent, the government is involved in a given industry. The French government, for instance, is heavily involved in all aspects of airplane design and manufacturing.

Legal and Political Differences

Governments can affect international business activities in many ways. They can, for example, set conditions for doing business within their borders or even prohibit doing business altogether. They can control the flow of capital and use tax legislation to either discourage or encourage international activity in a given industry. In the extreme, they can even confiscate the property of foreign-owned companies. In this section, we discuss some of the more common legal and political issues in international business: *quotas, tariffs, and subsidies; local content laws;* and *business practice laws.*

QUOTAS, TARIFFS, AND SUBSIDIES Even free market economies often establish some system of quotas and/or tariffs. Both quotas and tariffs affect the prices and quanti-

In their efforts to punish certain regimes of the Middle East—Iran, Iraq, and Libya—U.S. policy makers are encountering some cold, hard economic facts. Iraq's oil reserves, for example, are second only to those of Saudi Arabia; oil fields like this one in Iran make it the world's third largest exporter. In addition, oil companies headquartered in other countries—notably Russia and France—are putting pressure on U.S. competitors by striking deals with Middle East producers. In 1995, for example, Conoco Inc. struck a $1-billion deal with Iran that it claims is legal despite U.S. government embargo.

ties of foreign-made products. A **quota** restricts the number of products of a certain type that can be imported into a country. By reducing supply, the quota raises the prices of those imports. For example, Belgian ice cream makers can ship no more than 922,315 kilograms of ice cream to the United States each year. Quotas are often determined by treaties. Moreover, better terms are often given to friendly trading partners, and quotas are typically adjusted to protect domestic producers.

quota Restriction on the number of products of a certain type that can be imported into a country

The ultimate form of quota is an **embargo:** a government order forbidding exportation and/or importation of a particular product—or even all the products—from a particular country. For example, many countries control bacteria and disease by banning certain agricultural products. The United States has embargoes against Cuba, Iraq, Libya, and Iran. Consequently, U.S. firms are forbidden from investing in these countries, and their products cannot be sold on American markets.

embargo Government order banning exportation and/or importation of a particular product or all products from a particular country

A **tariff** is a tax on imported products. Tariffs directly affect prices by raising the price of imports. Consumers pay not only for the products but also for tariff fees. Tariffs may take two forms. *Revenue tariffs* are imposed strictly to raise money for governments. Most tariffs, however, are *protectionist tariffs,* meant to discourage the import of particular products. For example, firms that import ironing board covers into the United States pay a tariff of 7 percent of the price of the product. Firms that import women's athletic shoes pay a flat rate of 90 cents per pair plus 20 percent of the price of the shoes. Each of these figures is set through a complicated process designed to put foreign and domestic firms on reasonably even competitive ground.

tariff Tax levied on imported products

A **subsidy** is a government payment to help a domestic business compete with foreign firms. Subsidies are actually indirect tariffs: They lower prices of domestic goods rather than raise prices of foreign goods. Many European governments subsidize farmers to help them compete with U.S. grain imports.

subsidy Government payment to help a domestic business compete with foreign firms

Quotas and tariffs are imposed for a variety of reasons. For example, the U.S. government aids domestic automakers by restricting the number of Japanese automobiles that can be *imported* into this country. National security concerns have prompted the United States to limit the extent to which certain forms of technology can be *exported* to other countries, for example, computer and nuclear technology exports to China.[14] The recent relaxation of controls on the licensing of technology has contributed to the export boom that we described earlier in this chapter. The United States is not the only country that uses tariffs and quotas. Italy, for example, imposes high tariffs on imported electronic goods to protect domestic firms. A Sony Walkman thus costs almost $150 in Italy, and CD players are prohibitively expensive.

protectionism Practice of protecting domestic business against foreign competition

The Protectionism Debate. In the United States as elsewhere, **protectionism**—the practice of protecting domestic business at the expense of free market competition—has long been controversial. Supporters argue, for example, that tariffs and quotas protect domestic firms and jobs and shelter new industries until they are able to compete internationally. They argue that the United States needs such measures to counter measures imposed by other nations. Other advocates justify protectionism in the name of national security. A nation, they argue, must be able to produce the goods needed for its survival in the event of war. Thus, the U.S. government requires the U.S. Air Force to buy all its planes from U.S. manufacturers.

Critics cite protectionism as a source of friction between nations. They also charge that it drives up prices by reducing competition. In addition, they maintain that although jobs in some industries would be lost as a result of free trade, jobs in other industries (for example, electronics and automobiles) would be created if all nations abandoned protectionist tactics.

local content law Law requiring that products sold in a particular country be at least partly made there

LOCAL CONTENT LAWS Many countries, including the United States, have **local content laws**—requirements that products sold in a particular country be at least partly made there. Typically, firms seeking to do business in a country must either invest there directly or take on a domestic partner. In this way, some of the profits from doing business in a foreign country stay there rather than flowing out to another nation. In some cases, the partnership arrangement is optional but wise. In Mexico, for instance, Radio Shack de Mexico is a joint venture owned by Tandy Corp. (49 percent) and Mexico's Grupo Gigante (51 percent). Both China and India currently require that foreign firms wishing to establish joint ventures with local firms to do business within their borders must hold less than 50 percent ownership in the venture, with the local partner having the controlling ownership stake.

BUSINESS PRACTICE LAWS Even with this arrangement, however, Tandy reports problems, especially in importing merchandise across the Mexican border. Consider, too, an experience of Wal-Mart officials in Mexico City:

- A few years ago government inspectors swooped down on Wal-Mart's newest Supercenter in Mexico City. Citing Mexican regulations, the inspectors reminded Wal-Mart managers that each of the store's 80,000 products must be labeled in Spanish. Labels must also indicate country of origin and provide instructions for use. Where necessary, they must display import permit numbers. Charging 11,700 violations, inspectors ordered the store closed for 72 hours while Wal-Mart rectified oversights. The store appealed to the U.S. ambassador, who managed to have the order lifted after only 24 hours.

business practice laws Laws or regulations governing business practices in given countries

cartel Association of producers whose purpose is to control supply and prices

Wal-Mart and other American companies that have recently entered Mexico have reported a host of problems in complying with stringent, and often changing, regulations and other bureaucratic obstacles. Such practices fall under the heading of the host country's **business practice laws.** Sometimes, a legal—even an accepted—business practice in one country is illegal in another. For example, in some South American countries, it is sometimes legal to bribe other businesses and government officials. The formation of **cartels**—associations of producers that control supply and prices—has given tremendous power to some nations, such as those belonging to the Organization of Petroleum Exporting Countries (OPEC). U.S. law forbids both bribery and cartels.

dumping Practice of selling a product abroad for less than the cost of production

Dumping. Many (but not all) countries forbid **dumping**—selling a product abroad for less than the cost of production. U.S. antidumping legislation is contained in the Trade Agreements Act of 1979. This statute sets tests for determining two conditions:

1. If products are being priced at "less than fair value."
2. If the result unfairly harms domestic industry.[15]

Continued from page 53

How Polo Shirts Came to Tuscaloosa

With the merger, the combined Chrysler Corp. and Daimler-Benz has more than 420,000 employees worldwide. To catch a glimpse of how this cross-cultural marriage might affect employees in American plants, experts are looking closely at the Mercedes-Benz plant in Tuscaloosa County, Alabama, where crews of 1,350 Americans and Germans have been churning out M-Class Mercedes vehicles since the early 1990s.

Described as a "melting pot of styles," the plant is headed by Andreas Renschler, a German national who chose a multinational facility-management team to address cultural differences. Before the plant opened, Renschler's six top managers spent a year at Daimler-Benz headquarters in Stuttgart, Germany, where they practiced dealing with potential cultural problems. They discussed everything from styles of decision making to building design to acceptable dress.

Although many of the Americans on the team were used to making rapid-fire decisions, Renschler tended to build understanding and consensus in extended meetings. "We spent hours and hours just talking about policy," reports American Emmett Meyer, the plant's director of human resources. But Meyer thinks the process was necessary: "We used the same words," he admits, "but they meant different things."

> **"We spent hours and hours just talking about policy. We used the same words, but they meant different things."**
>
> —Emmett Meyer
> *Director of Human Resources, DaimlerChrysler in Alabama*

German and American business cultures collided in a battle over building design. While German engineers pushed separate buildings for different assembly lines, the Americans argued for a single structure that would create a team feeling. "A family," argued Meyer, "lives under one roof." The American view prevailed and made a cultural statement: *The Wall Street Journal* has described the Alabama facility as "an operation that combines the precision of German industrial engineering with an American-style atmosphere of open communications between management and employees."

Open communication aside, laid-back southerners had to learn to cope with the direct bluntness of their German bosses on a person-to-person basis. Although sometimes painful, the adjustment has been largely successful. "When I got here," says Arthur Williams, an American-born supervisor on the chassis line, "I was taught you're going to know it if you do something wrong. Now I prefer that. You can learn that way."

And then there was the matter of acceptable dress. The Americans pushed for casual attire for all employees, including top executives. They favored "team wear"—casual shirts and sweaters emblazoned with the Mercedes logo—whereas the more formal Germans voted for suits and ties. Although everyone agreed on the casual look, acceptance took time. When executives from Germany visited the plant soon after it opened, facility managers quickly donned suits and ties. By 1998, however, even visiting German managers were opting for company polo shirts while they were on site.

Questions for Discussion

1. Why was expanding into the global marketplace important enough for Chrysler to consider a merger with Daimler-Benz? Why would international expansion have been more difficult for Chrysler acting alone?
2. Inasmuch as Daimler-Benz already had a presence in the United States (through its Alabama plant), why was it important for the company to acquire Chrysler? What strategic advantages would the merger provide?
3. Why do you think a merger—as opposed to, say, a strategic alliance—was preferable to both companies?
4. Robert Eaton leaves the company at the end of 3 years. Do you think that DaimlerChrysler will become a more German company with a German in sole charge?
5. Do you believe that Wall Street will accept the new company as American? Why is such acceptance important to investors and consumers?
6. Is too much being made over the national and organizational culture clash in the new company? Isn't it just about people getting along?

SUMMARY

1. **Describe the rise of international business and identify the major world marketplaces.** More and more firms are engaged in international business. The term *globalization* refers to the process by which the world economy is fast becoming a single interdependent system. According to some experts, the global economy of the mid-1990s is best typified by the rapid growth in two areas: exchange of information and trade in services. The three major marketplaces for international business are *North America* (the United States, Canada, and Mexico), *Western Europe* (which is dominated by Germany, the United Kingdom, France, and Italy), and the *Pacific Rim* (where the dominant country, Japan, is surrounded by such rapidly advancing nations as South Korea, Taiwan, Hong Kong, and China).

2. **Explain how different forms of *competitive advantage, import-export balances, exchange rates,* and *foreign competition* determine the ways in which countries and businesses respond to the international environment.** The different forms of *competitive advantage* are critical to international business. With an *absolute advantage,* a country engages in international trade because it can produce a product more efficiently than any other nation. But more often, countries trade because they enjoy *comparative advantages:* They can produce some items more efficiently than they can produce other items. The *import-export balance,* including the *balance of trade* and the *balance of payments,* and *exchange rate differences* in national currencies affect the international economic environment and are important elements of international business.

3. **Discuss the factors involved in deciding to do business internationally and in selecting the appropriate levels of *international involvement* and *international organizational structure.*** In deciding whether to do business internationally, a firm must determine whether a market for its product exists abroad, and if so, whether the firm has the skills and knowledge to manage such a business. It must also assess the business climates of other nations to make sure that they are conducive to international operations.

   A firm must also decide on its level of international involvement. It can choose to be an *exporter* or *importer;* to organize as an *international firm,* or to operate as a *multinational firm.* The choice will influence the organizational structure of its international operations, specifically, its use of *independent agents, licensing arrangements, branch offices, strategic alliances,* and *direct investment.*

4. **Describe some of the ways in which *social, cultural, economic, legal,* and *political differences* among nations affect international business.** *Social* and *cultural differences* that can serve as barriers to trade include language, social values, and traditional buying patterns. Differences in economic systems may force businesses to establish close relationships with foreign governments before they are permitted to do business abroad. *Quotas, tariffs, subsidies,* and *local content laws* offer protection to local industries. Differences in *business practice laws* can make standard business practices in one nation illegal in another.

QUESTIONS AND EXERCISES

QUESTIONS FOR REVIEW

1. How does the balance of trade differ from the balance of payments?
2. What are the three possible levels of involvement in international business? Give examples of each.

3. How does the economic system of a country affect the decisions of outside firms interested in doing business there?

4. What aspects of the culture in your state or region would be of particular interest to a foreign firm considering doing business there?

QUESTIONS FOR ANALYSIS

5. Make a list of all the major items in your bedroom, including furnishings. Try to identify the country in which each item was made. Offer possible reasons why a given nation might have a comparative advantage in producing a given good.

6. Suppose that you are the manager of a small firm seeking to enter the international arena. What basic information would you need about the market that you are thinking of entering?

7. Do you support protectionist tariffs for the United States? If so, in what instances and for what reasons? If not, why not?

8. Do you think that a firm operating internationally is better advised to adopt a single standard of ethical conduct or to adapt to local conditions? Under what kinds of conditions might each approach be preferable?

APPLICATION EXERCISES

9. Interview the manager of a local firm that does at least some business internationally. Identify reasons why the company decided to "go international." Describe the level of the firm's international involvement and the organizational structure(s) it uses for its international operations.

10. Select a product familiar to you. Using library reference works to gain some insight into the culture of India, identify the problems that might arise in trying to market this product to Indian consumers.

BUILDING YOUR BUSINESS SKILLS

"I INTEND TO BE A GLOBAL COMPANY"

This exercise enhances the following SCANS workplace competencies: demonstrating basic skills, demonstrating thinking skills, exhibiting interpersonal skills, and working with information.

▼ GOAL

To encourage students to apply global business strategies to a small-business situation.

▼ BACKGROUND

Some people might say that Yolanda Lang is a bit too confident. Others might say that she needs confidence—and more—to succeed in the business she's chosen. But one thing is certain: Lang is determined to grow INDE, her handbag design company, into a global enterprise. At only 28 years of age, she has time on her side—if she makes the right business moves now.

These days, Lang spends most of her time in Milan, Italy. Backed by $50,000 of her parents' personal savings, she is trying to compete with Gucci, Fendi, and other high-end handbag makers. Her target market: American women who are willing to spend $200 and more on a purse. Ironically, Lang was forced to set up shop in Italy because of the snobbishness of these

(continued)

Yolanda Lang's company, INDE, makes high-end handbags that compete with firms like Gucci and Fendi. Much of the year finds Lang, an American, operating out of Milan, Italy. Why? Because U.S. retailers will pay top prices for high-quality accessories only if they're made overseas. "Strangely enough," reports Lang, "to compete I need to be in Europe to sell America."

same customers, who only buy high-end bags if they are European-made. "Strangely enough," she muses, "I need to be in Europe to sell America."

To succeed, she must first find ways to keep production costs down, which is a tough task for a woman working in a male-dominated business culture. Her fluent Italian is an important advantage, but she often turns down inappropriate dinner invitations. She also has to figure out how to get her 22-bag collection into stores worldwide. So far, although retailers are showing her bags in Italy and Japan, she's had little luck in the United States.

"I intend to be a global company," says Lang. The question is how to succeed first as a small business.

▼ METHOD

STEP 1

Join together with three or four other students to discuss the steps that Lang has taken so far to break into the U.S. retail market. These steps include:

- Buying a mailing list of 5,000 shoppers from Neiman Marcus, a high-end department store, and selling directly to these customers.
- Linking with a manufacturer's representative to sell her line in major U.S. cities while she herself concentrates on Europe.

STEP 2

Based on what you learned in this chapter, suggest other strategies that might help Lang grow her business. Working with group members, consider whether the following options would help or hurt Lang's business. Explain why a strategy would be likely to work or why it would be likely to fail.

- Lang could relocate back in the United States and sell her goods abroad through an independent agent.
- Lang could relocate back in the United States and set up a branch office in Italy.
- Lang could find a partner in Italy and form a strategic alliance that would allow her to build her business on both continents.

STEP 3

Working alone, create a written marketing plan for INDE. What steps would you recommend Lang take to reach her goal of becoming a global company? Compare your written response with those of other group members.

▼ Follow-Up

1. What are the most promising steps that Lang can take to grow her business? What are the least promising?
2. Lang thinks that her trouble breaking into the U.S. retail market stems from the fact that her company is unknown. How would this circumstance affect the strategies suggested in Steps 1 and 2?
3. When Lang deals with Italian manufacturers, she is a young, attractive woman in a man's world. Often, she must convince men that her purpose is business and nothing else. How should Lang handle personal invitations that get in the way of business? How can she say no while still maintaining business relationships? Why is it often difficult for American women to do business in male-dominated cultures?
4. The American consulate has given Lang little business help because her products are made in Italy. Do you think the consulate's treatment of an American businessperson is fair or unfair? Explain your answer.
5. Do you think Lang's relocation to Italy will pay off? Why or why not?
6. With Lang's goals of creating a global company, can INDE continue to be a one-person operation?

CRAFTING YOUR BUSINESS PLAN

GOING GLOBAL

▼ Purpose of Assignment

1. To acquaint students with the process of navigating through the *Business PlanPro (BPP)* software package.
2. To familiarize students with issues faced by a firm that has decided to go global.
3. To determine where, in the framework of the *BPP* business plan, global issues might appropriately be presented.
4. To prepare students to enter international business considerations into a firm's business plan through *BPP.*

▼ Assignment

After reading Chapter 3 in the textbook, open the *BPP* software* and examine the information dealing with the types of global business considerations that would be of concern to the sample firm of *Acme Consulting*. Then respond to the following questions:

1. What products does Acme plan to offer and in which international markets will they be competing? [Sites to see in *BPP* (for this assignment): In the Task Manager screen,

(*continued*)

click on **Initial Assessment;** then click on **2. Mission** and then **6. Potential Customers.** Next, still in the Task Manager screen, click on **Your Company** and then on **1. Company Summary.** Finally, in the Task Manager screen, click on **Your Market** and then **1. Summary and Introduction.**]

2. In Acme's business plan, see if you can find any discussion of the international organizational structures used by Acme's competitors. Assess the adequacy of the available information. [Sites to see in *BPP:* In the Task Manager screen, first click on **The Business You're In** and then **5. Main Competitors.**]

3. What is the planned organization structure for Acme's international activities? Would you categorize Acme's relationship to its Paris partner as that of a branch office or that of a strategic alliance? [Sites to see in *BPP:* In the Task Manager screen, click on **Your Management Team** and then on **2. Organizational Structure.**]

4. Figure 3.6 in the textbook indicates that going international requires "necessary skills and knowledge." Does Acme's business plan indicate that the company possesses the skills and knowledge to succeed internationally? [Sites to see in *BPP:* In the Task Manager screen, click on **Your Management Team** and then on **3. Management Team.** Next, in the Task Manager screen, click on **What You're Selling** and then click on **3. Competitive Positioning.**]

▼ For Your Own Business Plan

5. In what ways will international considerations affect your business—say, competing companies or products from other countries, foreign sources of supply, customers in other countries, international laws, international finance, and so forth? If such considerations are not relevant now, might they become so in the future? Where in your business planning document would you include international factors?

▼ * Tips for Navigating in *BPP:*

1. Open the *BPP* program, observe the Welcome screen, and click on **Open a Sample Plan.**
2. From the Open a Sample Plan dialogue box, click on a sample company name and then click on **Open.**
3. On the Task Manager screen, click onto any of the lines, such as the **Your Company** line.
4. You can always return to the Task Manager screen by going to the bottom of the screen and clicking on the **Task Manager** icon.
5. When you are finished with a sample company, close its Task Manager screen.
6. You can get to the next sample company by going to the top of the screen and clicking on **File** (on the menu bar) and then, beneath it, on **Open Sample Plan.** This process will exit you from the current company file and send you to the Open a Sample Plan dialogue box, where you can select your next sample company.

EXPLORING THE WEB

TAPPING INTO THE CIA

One of the best sources of information about foreign countries is the CIA's *World Factbook*. Visit its Web site at and then consider the following questions.

http://www.odci.gov/cia/publications/factbook/index.html

1. Assume that you are a manager interested in learning more about the market potential for your firm's products in a certain foreign country. What information from this site might be most helpful?
2. How accurate and reliable would you expect this information to be? Why?
3. What additional information do you think you might need? How and where might you go to look for it?

Conducting Business Ethically and Responsibly

The Side Effects of Power Stats

It's been called the greatest baseball season in history. In 1998, the St. Louis Cardinals' Mark McGwire and the Chicago Cubs' Sammy Sosa both shattered Roger Maris's single-season record of 61 home runs. McGwire did it with 70 homers and Sosa with 66. Maris's mark had stood for 37 years.

Fans fell in love with McGwire. At 6′ 5″ and 250 pounds, he is an imposing athlete. He's also a devoted father and a genuinely nice man. "He's Middle America," says Bill Mullon, president of Florida-based ProSports Marketing Inc., and as such he sounds like the perfect corporate pitchman.

But there was one potential flaw in the image. As McGwire pounded away at Maris's record in late August, an Associated Press sportswriter observed that McGwire used androstenedione, which increases the male sex hormone testosterone for several hours after it is taken. With an elevated testosterone level, muscles build more rapidly during exercise; an athlete can thus train harder and recover faster. McGwire admitted to taking the supplement for more than a year. "Andro," as the drug is known, is a perfectly legal substance sold as an over-the-counter diet supplement.

It may also be dangerous. The governing bodies of many governing sports groups—including the National Football League, the National Collegiate Athletic Association, and the International Olympic Committee—ban andro. Some medical experts fear that like anabolic steroids, which also increase testosterone, andro may contribute to an array of health problems running the gamut from liver and heart disease, to sterility and fits of rage, to acne and baldness. Particularly troubling is the fact that no one knows the supplement's long-term effects on high school athletes, many of whom consider McGwire a role model. "You don't know what you're getting in the future," warns Dr. Gary Wadler of the New York University School of Medicine. Wadler and others suspect permanently stunted growth and disruptions in puberty. A day after the story broke, the all-sports TV network ESPN pulled all ads for andro.

Despite the controversy, andro can be found on store shelves throughout the country. Wal-Mart carries it, and books promoting it are stacked high at Barnes & Noble. Its makers downplay its side effects and point to the absence of any Food and Drug Administration studies proving its dangers. Such claims are accurate. FDA control over andro ended in 1994, when the Dietary Supplement Health and Education Act prohibited the FDA from ruling on the safety of dietary supplements. Today, the only message that the FDA can send to consumers is a generic "Buyer Beware."

But as sales piled up with Mark McGwire's home runs, it quickly became apparent that few buyers were exercising caution. Len Moskovits, CEO of andro manufacturer MET-Rx Engineered Nutrition, projected industry sales of $100 million in 1998—up from $5 million a year earlier. "The last time I saw publicity like this was when Viagra hit the market," quipped Moskovits, referring to the drug for male impotence. Adds Kevin Murphy of Osmo, another andro manufacturer: "We have distributors all over the country asking us to overnight it." At Great Earth Vitamin's 138 stores, sales jumped 30 percent. At one New York outlet, a single customer bought every bottle in the store.

> **"The last time I saw publicity like this was when Viagra hit the market."**
>
> —Len Moskovits
> *CEO of MET-Rx Engineered Nutrition*

But not every retailer of dietary supplements agrees that selling andro is the right thing to do. Pennsylvania-based General Nutrition Companies, the country's largest supplement chain with 3,700 stores nationwide, turned its back on andro because it didn't meet companywide scientific and safety standards. "There's no clear data that the product is safe," says GNC vice president of scientific affairs John Troup, "and no clear demonstration that it enhances performance. Clearly, no kids under 18 should be ingesting this hormone at all." When GNC learned that one franchisee continued to sell andro in violation of company policy, it issued a strong warning to all franchise owners.

As producers and retailers weigh potential profits against concerns for public health, they are also dealing with the issue of fairness. Says Steve Wilstein, the reporter who first uncovered the story: "Mark McGwire is a good man, a good father, a good ballplayer. He works out every day and he is not hitting home runs because of this drug. On the other hand, [Olympic shot-putter] Randy Barnes is also a good man who won a gold medal for this country. He also works out every day. Yet because he used androstenedione he is banned for life. . . . Where's the fairness in that?"

Issues of fairness and ethics are becoming increasingly important as companies around the world enter an era of intense competition, not only for public and consumer support, but also for the support of employees and stockholders. By focusing on the learning objectives of this chapter, you will see that many firms establish policies on business ethics and social responsibility to stipulate exactly how managers and employees should act with regard to the environment, customers, fellow employees, and investors.

Our opening story is continued on page 94

After reading this chapter, you should be able to:

1. **Explain how individuals develop their personal *codes of ethics* and why ethics are important in the workplace.**
2. **Distinguish *social responsibility* from *ethics* and trace the evolution of social responsibility in U.S. business.**
3. **Show how the concept of social responsibility applies both to environmental issues and to a firm's relationships with customers, employees, and investors.**
4. **Identify three general *approaches to social responsibility* and describe the four steps that a firm must take to implement a *social responsibility program.***
5. **Explain how issues of social responsibility and ethics affect small business.**

In this chapter, we look at the issues of individual ethics in business and the social responsibility of business as a whole. Remember that these issues were not always considered important in business philosophy or practice. Today, however, the ethical implications of business practices are very much in the spotlight. Managers must confront a variety of ethical problems, and companies must address many issues of social responsibility.

■ ETHICS IN THE WORKPLACE

ethics Beliefs about what is right and wrong or good and bad in actions that affect others

ethical behavior Behavior conforming to generally accepted social norms concerning beneficial and harmful actions

unethical behavior Behavior which does not conform to generally accepted social norms concerning beneficial and harmful actions

business ethics Ethical or unethical behaviors by a manager or employer of an organization

Just what is *ethical behavior?* **Ethics** are beliefs about what is right and wrong or good and bad. An individual's personal values and morals and the social context in which it occurs determine whether a particular behavior is seen as being ethical or unethical. In other words, **ethical behavior** is behavior that conforms to individual beliefs and social norms about what is right and good. **Unethical behavior** is behavior that individual beliefs and social norms define as being wrong and bad. **Business ethics** is a term often used to refer to ethical or unethical behaviors by a manager or employee of an organization.

Because ethics are based on both individual beliefs and social concepts, they vary from person to person, from situation to situation, and from culture to culture. Social standards, for example, tend to be broad enough to support certain differences in beliefs. Without violating the general standards of the culture, therefore, individuals may develop personal codes of ethics that reflect a fairly wide range of attitudes and beliefs. Thus, what constitutes ethical and unethical behavior is determined partly by the individual and partly by culture.

Figure 4.1 presents a simplified—and deceptively simple—three-step model for applying ethical judgments to situations that may arise during the course of business activities:

1. Gather the relevant factual information.
2. Determine the most appropriate moral values.
3. Make an ethical judgment based on the rightness or wrongness of the proposed activity or policy.

Unfortunately, the process does not always work as smoothly as the scheme in Figure 4.1 suggests. What if the facts are not clear-cut? What if there are no agreed-upon moral values? Nevertheless, a judgment and a decision must be made. Experts point out that,

FIGURE 4.1 ◆ Steps in Making Ethical Judgments

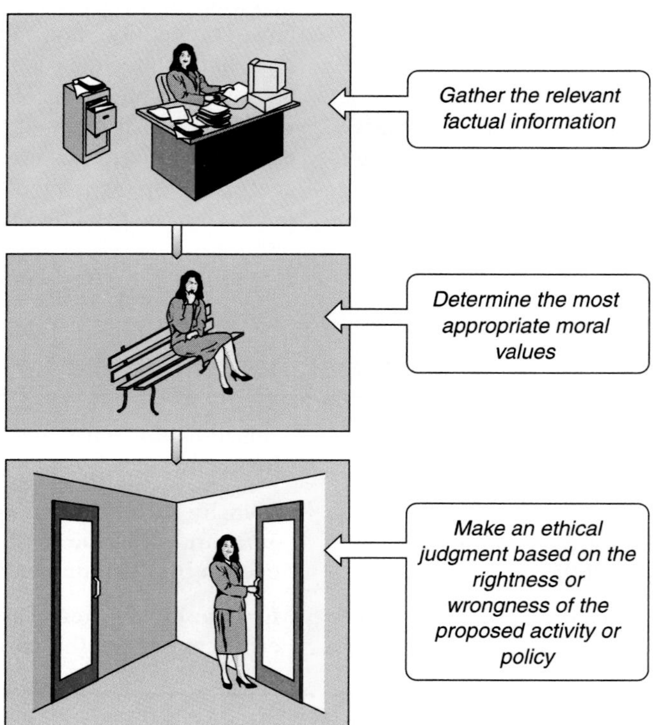

otherwise, trust is impossible; and trust, they add, is indispensable to any business transaction. Not surprisingly, therefore, many businesses are concerned about the various influences on the ethical behavior of their personnel.[1]

Company Policies and Business Ethics

Within the workplace, of course, the company itself influences individual ethical behavior. As unethical and even illegal activities by both managers and employees have plagued more and more companies, many firms have taken steps to encourage ethical behavior in the workplace. Many firms, for example, establish codes of conduct and develop clear ethical positions on how the firm and its employees will conduct its business.

Perhaps the single most effective step that a company can take is to demonstrate top management support. When United Technologies, a Connecticut-based industrial conglomerate, published its 21-page code of ethics, it also named a vice president for business practices. In contrast, the management of Astra USA, a subsidiary of a large Swedish drug manufacturer, has been criticized for ethically questionable leadership. Among other things, former CEO Lars Bildman was charged in 1996 with several counts of sexual harassment, using company funds to remodel his home, and taking frequent company-paid private cruises with crews of company executives and prostitutes. Although only Bildman was charged with legal wrongdoing, apparently dozens of other senior managers were aware of Bildman's activities and either ignored the problem or began taking similar liberties. As part of his legal defense, Bildman has subsequently claimed that his actions were actually consistent with the way Astra and its sister companies routinely operated.[2]

Demonstrating Commitment An excellent, and now classic, illustration of the power of ethical commitment involves Johnson & Johnson. In 1982, capsules of the company's Tylenol pain reliever were found to be laced with cyanide. Managers at J&J quickly recalled all Tylenol bottles still on retailers' shelves and then went public with candid information throughout the crisis. Its ethical choices proved to be a crucial factor in J&J's campaign to rescue its product: Both the firm and the brand bounced back much more quickly than most observers had thought possible. A more recent example took place in England. Government reports linking beef products tainted by "mad cow disease" and fatal illnesses prompted fast-food giants such as McDonald's and Burger King to suspend sales of all British beef products. In addition to demonstrating an attitude of honesty and openness, firms can take specific steps to formalize the commitment to ethical practices. Two options are *adopting written codes* and *instituting ethics programs.*

Peter W. England, left, CEO of the cosmetics company Elizabeth Arden, listens to a plan presented by employees of Vogue, *a magazine that carries a lot of cosmetics advertising.* Vogue *is making the pitch that Elizabeth Arden and* Vogue *become marketing partners. In the past, magazines have only carried ads, not worked with the advertiser to shape a marketing message. Might a magazine lose its editorial independence if it joined forces with an advertiser? Would the magazine's business ethics in some way be compromised?*

After an outpouring of anger about Nike's overseas factory policies, the company pumped up wages of Indonesian workers by 22 percent. But Nike is hardly alone in taking advantage of overseas sweatshops, where laborers work for painfully low wages. A presidential task force is ready to put together guidelines for overseas businesses to use in monitoring the conditions that their workers face. If that effort comes up short, the extent of negative publicity on sweatshops may force factories to regulate themselves.

Adopting Written Codes. Many companies, including J&J, McDonald's, and Burger King, have adopted written codes of ethics that formally acknowledge their intent to do business in an ethical manner. Indeed, the number of such companies has risen dramatically in the last three decades. In 1968, 32 percent of companies surveyed maintained ethical codes. A mere 2 years later, the number was 75 percent. Today more than 90 percent of all Fortune 500 firms have such codes.

Many experts attribute J&J's successful response to the Tylenol-tampering scare to the ethical anchor provided by its written code. Called "Our Credo," J&J's written code was first published in 1948. The code is revised as new issues arise, but its explicit purpose is to furnish a set of *core* values that is as consistent as possible over time. Most such codes are designed to perform one or more of these four functions:

- To increase public confidence in a firm or its industry
- To stem the tide of government regulation—that is, to aid in self-regulation
- To improve internal operations by providing consistent standards of both ethical and legal conduct
- To respond to problems that arise as a result of unethical or illegal behavior

Instituting Ethics Programs. Instances like the Tylenol case suggest that ethical responses can be learned through experience. But can business ethics be "taught," either in the workplace or in schools? Not surprisingly, business schools have become important players in the debate about ethics education. Most analysts agree that even though business schools must address the issue of ethics in the workplace, companies must take the chief responsibility for educating employees. In fact, more and more firms are doing so.

It is not hard to figure out where Levi Strauss & Co. stands with regard to ethical issues—just check the company's "Aspiration Statement." Forged by top management and printed on recycled denim, the statement is a real document that hangs on office and factory

TRENDS AND CHALLENGES

NIKE SWEATS SOME UNPLEASANT DETAILS

For years, nearly one of every two pairs of sneakers bought in the United States bore the famous Nike swoosh. For years, Nike was the epitome of cool. And for years, Nike was unstoppable in manufacturing and marketing.

Then, in the mid-1990s, sales began to slump. Maybe it was the advent of the so-called "brown shoe" revolution, as hiking boots became the footwear of choice for younger buyers. Maybe it was the aggressiveness of competitors such as Reebok and Adidas. It might even have had something to do with the 2 years of scathing publicity about Nike's infamous sneaker and apparel sweatshops.

In the mid-1990s, human rights groups around the world began criticizing Nike for subjecting more than 500,000 workers in 35 countries to abusive conditions. The publicity sparked anti-Nike protests on college campuses, inspired an International Nike Day of Protest in 28 states and 12 countries, and spawned product boycotts.

Nike was an easy target, largely because the company was apparently guilty on many counts. Protesters pointed to underage workers, poor air quality and working conditions, the lack of educational programs for child laborers, and substandard wages. Nike's position as a market leader also made it the perfect target. "Nike," explains Kim Miyoshi of Global Exchange, a human rights organization based in San Francisco, "is one of the few companies that has great influence over the entire industry. If they changed and raised their human rights standards, it could set a precedent for the entire apparel and garment industries."

"Nike is one of the few companies that has great influence over the entire industry. If they changed and raised their human rights standards it could set a precedent for the entire apparel and garment industries."

—Kim Miyoshi
Global Exchange

After considerable soul-searching and internal investigation, Nike made some important changes. In a May 1998 speech before the National Press Club in Washington, chairman and CEO Phil Knight outlined six anti-sweatshop initiatives that Nike would take in dealing with contractors worldwide:

1. An expanded independent monitoring program to include nongovernment organizations, foundations, and educational institutions. The program would make inspection reports available to the public.

walls. It spells out Levi's unusual values-based formula for simultaneously earning profits and making the world a better place. It addresses several issues, including workforce diversity, employee empowerment and recognition, honest communication, and ethical management practices. It declares, for example, that management will set an example for ethical behavior that others in the company must follow. "We must," says the statement, "provide clarity about our expectations and must enforce these standards throughout the corporation." In addition to encouraging teamwork and open communication, top management works to see that Levi's offers attractive career opportunities for minorities and women.[3]

Management also believes that special responsibilities go hand in hand with the image that Levi's wants to project, both in the United States and elsewhere. For example, about half of the apparel sold by the company is manufactured in low-wage countries such as Bangladesh, Indonesia, and Malaysia. Throughout the world, Levi's is strict about enforcing International Labor Organization standards on child labor. In Bangladesh, for instance, Levi's learned that many underage employees were the sole breadwinners in their families. Instead of firing the children, Levi's agreed to pay their wages while the children returned to school and to hire back the youths when they come of age. Says marketing executive David Schmidt: "When ethical issues collide with commercial appeal, we try to ensure ethics as the trump card."

■ SOCIAL RESPONSIBILITY

Ethics affect individual behavior in the workplace. **Social responsibility,** however, refers to the way in which a business tries to balance its commitments to groups and individuals in its social environment: customers, other businesses, employees, and investors. In effect, social responsibility is an attempt to balance different commitments. For example, to behave responsibly toward investors, a company must try to maximize profits. But it

social responsibility The attempt of a business to balance its commitments to groups and individuals in its environment, including customers, other businesses, employees, and investors

2. Universal minimum working-age standards: 18 for footwear-factory workers and 16 for apparel, accessory, and equipment workers.
3. Adherence to standards set by the U.S. Occupational Safety and Health Administration for indoor air quality at all footwear plants.
4. Expanded educational equivalency courses for middle and high school students.
5. Corporate support for microenterprise loan programs to fund small businesses run by women in Vietnam, Indonesia, Pakistan, and Thailand.
6. Support for research exploring issues in social responsibility in global manufacturing.

According to a company spokeswoman, Knight's address was a "watershed speech for Nike. It's about Nike's responsibility to consumers and shareholders. It's gone way beyond making the best product. We want to be more than just a sportswear company. We want to be a socially responsible company, which we've been addressing, and now we're going to do more."

Critics, however, would still like to see more from Nike, especially in the area of wages. The Interfaith Center on Corporate Responsibility, a religious coalition of institutional investors, is calling on Nike to raise factory workers' wages in China, Vietnam, and Indonesia, arguing that current wages are below subsistence level. "For religious investors," points out Rev. David Schilling, director of ICCR's Global Corporate Accountability Programs, "there's a real question of a fair distribution of profits. If you're an export company, you have a greater ability to reap profits. It's a question of fairness and a question of human dignity."

Although Nike has changed many of its basic manufacturing practices as a result of the anti-sweatshop protests, CEO Knight still believes that the attack on his company was not completely fair. "It has been said," he complained to the National Press Corps, "that Nike has single-handedly lowered the human rights standards for the sole purpose of maximizing profits; that Nike products have become synonymous with slave wages, forced overtime and arbitrary abuse. One columnist said Nike represents not only everything that's wrong with sports but everything that is wrong with the world."

In an industry in which the perception of its cool is as important as its products, the perception of corporate social responsibility toward factory workers may be as important as what is said about a company—perhaps even as important as what it actually does. Nike is smart enough to realize this fact of commercial life as it tries to reverse its sales decline. Although no one is stating outright that the sweatshop controversy caused Nike's sales slump, few experts doubt that it was a contributing factor.

also has a responsibility toward its customers to market safe products—a commitment that may raise production costs and lower profits. Not surprisingly, then, firms sometimes act irresponsibly toward customers because of their zeal to please investors. For example, AT&T, General Signal Corporation, Citicorp, Eastman Kodak, and IBM have all been criticized in recent years because of certain accounting practices they employ which may appear to inflate their projections for their future earnings.[4]

Like an individual's personal code of ethics, an organization's sense of social responsibility is influenced by many factors. To a large extent, of course, social responsibility reflects the ethics of the individuals employed by a firm, especially its top management. But social responsibility can also be encouraged—even enforced—from outside, whether by government agencies or by consumers. A firm's behavior is also shaped by the demands of investors and by the behavior of other firms in the same country and same industry.

Contemporary Social Consciousness

Social consciousness and views toward social responsibility continue to evolve. Today's views seem to be moving toward an enlightened view stressing the need for a greater social role for business. Some observers suggest that an increased awareness of the global economy and heightened campaigning on the part of environmentalists and other activists have combined to make many businesses more sensitive to their social responsibilities.

For example, retailers such as Sears and Target have policies against selling handguns and other weapons. Likewise, national toy retailers KayBee and Toys "R" Us refuse to sell toy guns that look too realistic. Firms in numerous other industries have also integrated socially conscious thinking into their production plans and marketing efforts. The production of environmentally safe products, for example, has become a potential boom area, as many companies introduce products designed to be "environmentally friendly." Sales of vegetable-based cleaning products, recycled-paper products, and all-natural toiletries are on the rise. Procter & Gamble's Downy fabric softener concentrate is sold in paper packages and reconstituted in plastic bottles already owned by consumers. Papermaker Union Camp Corp. now removes the ink from discarded paper so that recycled fibers can go into new paper; the company has also replaced chlorine (a toxic water pollutant) with ozone in the bleaching line at its riverside plant in Franklin, Virginia. Volkswagen and BMW are designing cars whose parts will be completely recyclable. Several small businesses have found a profitable niche in recycling laser printer ink cartridges, computer keyboards and monitors, and other computer-related equipment which seems to become outdated and tossed aside at an ever-faster pace.

■ AREAS OF SOCIAL RESPONSIBILITY

When defining its sense of social responsibility, a firm typically confronts four areas of concern: responsibilities toward the *environment*, its *customers*, its *employees*, and its *investors*.

Responsibility toward the Environment

Figure 4.2 tells a troubling story. The chart shows two trends in atmospheric carbon dioxide (CO_2) levels between the years 1750 and 2100:

1. Levels calculated for the past 250 years
2. Three scenarios for the future as levels increase under different sets of conditions

The three projections—lowest, middle, highest—were developed by the Intergovernmental Panel on Climate Change, which calculated likely changes in the atmosphere over the next century if no efforts were made to reduce so-called greenhouse emissions—waste industrial gases that trap heat in the atmosphere. The criteria for estimating changes are population, economic growth, energy supplies, and technologies: The less pressure exerted by these conditions, the less the increase in CO_2 levels. Energy supplies are mea-

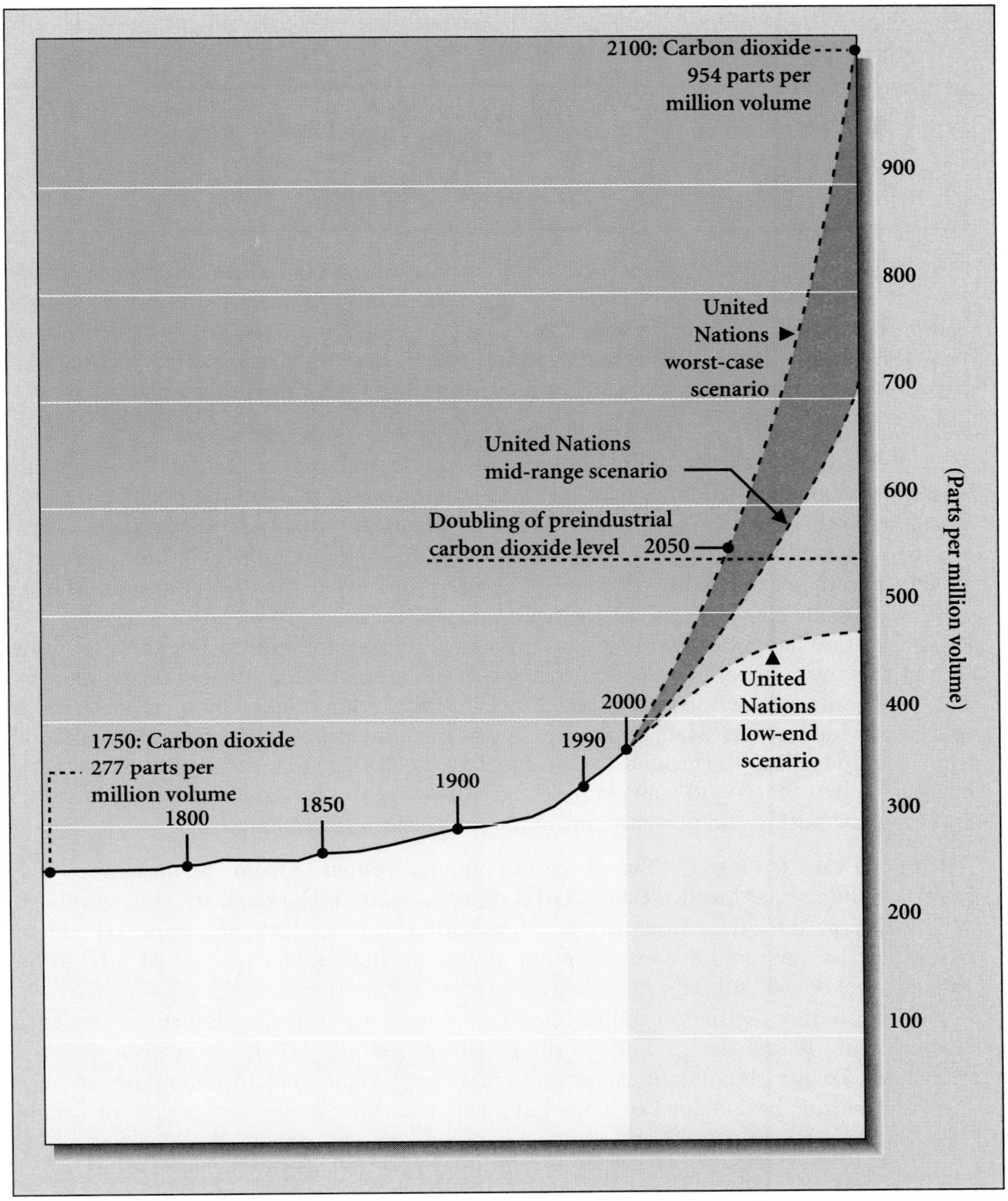

FIGURE 4.2 ◆ CO_2 Emissions, Past and Future

sured in *exajoules*—roughly the annual energy consumption of the New York Metropolitan area. Under the lowest, or "best-case," scenario, the following would happen:

- Population would grow to 6.4 billion.
- Economic growth would occur at a rate of 1.2 to 2.0 percent.
- Energy supplies would require 8,000 exajoules of conventional oil.

Under the highest, or "worst-case," scenario, the following numbers would prevail:

- Population would increase to 11.3 billion.
- Economic growth would be between 3.0 and 3.5 percent.
- Energy supplies would require 18,400 exajoules of conventional oil.

The resulting changes in climate would be relatively mild; we would hardly experience any day-to-day changes in the weather. We would, however, increase the likelihood of having troublesome weather all around the globe: droughts, hurricanes, winter sieges, and so forth. The charges leveled against greenhouse emissions are disputed, but as one researcher puts it, "The only way to prove them for sure is hang around 10, 20, or 30 more years, when the evidence would be overwhelming. But in the meantime, we're conducting a global experiment. And we're all in the test tube."[5]

> **"We're conducting a global experiment. And we're all in the test tube."**
>
> *Researcher on greenhouse emissions*

Controlling *pollution*—the injection of harmful substances into the environment—is a significant challenge to contemporary business. Although noise pollution is now attracting increased concern, air, water, and land pollution remain the greatest problems in need of solutions from governments and businesses alike. In the following sections, we focus on the nature of the problems in these areas and on some of the current efforts to address them.[6]

AIR POLLUTION Air pollution results when several factors combine to lower air quality. Carbon monoxide emitted by automobiles contributes to air pollution, as do smoke and other chemicals from manufacturing plants. Air quality is usually worst in certain geographic locations, such as the Denver area and the Los Angeles basin, where pollutants tend to get trapped in the atmosphere. For this very reason the air around Mexico City is generally considered to be the most polluted in the entire world.

Legislation has gone a long way toward controlling air pollution. Under new laws, for example, many companies must now install special devices to limit the pollutants they expel into the air. Such efforts are costly. Air pollution is compounded by such problems as *acid rain*, which occurs when sulfur is pumped into the atmosphere, mixes with natural moisture, and falls to the ground as rain. Much of the damage to forests and streams in the eastern United States and Canada has been attributed to acid rain originating in sulfur from manufacturing and power plants in the midwestern United States.

WATER POLLUTION Water becomes polluted primarily from chemical and waste dumping. For years, businesses and cities dumped waste into rivers, streams, and lakes with little regard for the consequences. Cleveland's Cuyahoga River was once so polluted that it literally burst into flames one hot summer day. After an oil spill in 1994, a Houston ship channel burned for days.

Thanks to new legislation and increased awareness, water quality in many areas of the United States is improving. The Cuyahoga River now boasts fish and is even used for recreation. Laws forbidding phosphates (an ingredient found in many detergents) in New York and Florida have helped to make Lake Erie and other major waters safe for fishing

With India's population growing by 20 million people every year and city traffic doubling every five years, Indian cities—like New Delhi, pictured here—are facing increasingly high levels of air pollution. As bad as urban air is in New Delhi, Bombay, and Calcutta, five countries actually produce more carbon gases. From the top down, they are the United States, the former Soviet Union, China, Japan, and Germany.

and swimming again. Both the Passaic River in New Jersey and the Hudson River in New York are much cleaner now than they were just a few years ago.

LAND POLLUTION There are two key issues in land pollution. The first is how to restore the quality of land that has already been damaged. Land and water damaged by toxic waste, for example, must be cleaned up for the simple reason that people still need to use them. The second problem, of course, concerns how to prevent future contamination. New forms of solid waste disposal constitute one response to these problems. Combustible wastes can be separated and used as fuels in industrial boilers, and decomposition can be accelerated by exposing waste matter to certain microorganisms.

Toxic Waste Disposal. An especially controversial problem in land pollution is toxic waste disposal. *Toxic wastes* are dangerous chemical and/or radioactive by-products of manufacturing processes. U.S. manufacturers produce between 40 and 60 *million tons* of such material each year. As a rule, toxic waste must be stored; it cannot be destroyed or processed into harmless material. However, very few people want toxic waste storage sites in their backyards.

Recycling. At least one new industry has arisen from increased consciousness about land pollution. *Recycling*, the reconversion of waste materials into useful products, has become a priority not only for municipal and state governments but also for many companies engaged in high-waste activities. At Union Camp's Virginia paper plant, for example, one executive explains the firm's commitment to recycling as a market-oriented strategy: "Customers," he says, "want recycled products. There is a growing awareness that waste is a form of pollution, and that will keep demand for recycled paper high."

> **"Customers want recycled products. There is a growing awareness that waste is a form of pollution, and that will keep demand for recycled paper high."**
>
> —Executive
> *Union Camp*

Case: The Pallet Problem. A growing problem today involving both waste disposal and recycling is the proliferation of wooden pallets—those splintery wooden platforms used to store and transport consumer goods. Pallets are popular because they provide an efficient method for stacking and moving large quantities of smaller items. Boxes of canned goods, batteries, or hair dryers, cans of paint, bags of fertilizer, and bundles of roofing shingles can all be stacked on pallets and wrapped with plastic or other binding material. Pallets of merchandise can be easily and efficiently forklifted from factories to trucks, from trucks to warehouses, from warehouses on to more trucks, and, finally, into Wal-Mart, Home Depot, and Kroger storerooms.

Unfortunately, we cut down about a million acres of forest to make new pallets every year. Indeed, about 40 percent of the hardwood harvested annually in the United States goes into pallets. In one recent year, for example, over 400 million pallets were made. The total number of pallets in this country is estimated to exceed 1.5 billion—about 6 for every man, woman, and child in America. Granted, pallets are eminently recyclable, but the cost of new ones is still generally lower than the cost of returning and/or redistributing used ones. As a result, many companies just toss used pallets aside and collect more.

One firm in Ohio, for example, has over 10,000 pallets stacked behind its factory, simply because they are hard to dispose of. Some entrepreneurs have tried to sell them for firewood, but because the wood is thin and tends to be quite dry, it burns both too quickly and too hot for most applications. Because they are both heavy and prone to dangerous splintering, pallets are also hard to handle without a forklift. Thus, many landfills refuse to take them, and others assess surcharges for recycling them. They eventually biodegrade, of course, after several decades. Ironically, some environmentalists argue that abandoned pallets actually serve a useful purpose: In urban areas, they often become refuge for such animals as raccoons, rats, and abandoned pets.[7]

Responsibility toward Customers

A company that does not act responsibly toward its customers will ultimately lose its business. Moreover, the government controls what businesses can and cannot do regarding consumers.[8] The Federal Trade Commission (FTC), for example, regulates advertising and pricing practices. The Food and Drug Administration (FDA) enforces guidelines for labeling food products.

Unethical and irresponsible business practices toward customers can result in government-imposed penalties and expensive civil litigation. For example, SmithKline Beecham PLC, the maker of Orafix denture adhesive, has been charged with using benzine, a proven carcinogen, in the product. The FDA forced a recall in 1990, and by 1996, several lawsuits—including one for $30 million—had been filed against the company. SmithKline Beecham eventually settled out of court, but incurred over $1 million in legal fees and undisclosed costs in conjunction with the actual settlement itself.[9]

Social responsibility toward customers generally falls into two categories:

- Providing quality products
- Pricing products fairly

Naturally, firms differ as much in their level of concern about customer responsibility as in their approaches to environmental responsibility. Yet unlike environmental problems, many customer problems do not require expensive solutions. In fact, most problems can be avoided if companies simply heed laws regarding consumer rights and regulated practices.

consumerism Form of social activism dedicated to protecting the rights of consumers in their dealings with businesses

CONSUMER RIGHTS Much of the current interest in business responsibility toward customers can be traced to the rise of **consumerism:** social activism dedicated to protecting the rights of consumers in their dealings with businesses. The first formal declaration of consumer rights protection came in the early 1960s, when President John F. Kennedy identified four basic consumer rights. These rights are now backed by numerous federal and state laws:

1. Consumers have a right to safe products.
2. Consumers have a right to be informed about all relevant aspects of a product.
3. Consumers have a right to be heard.
4. Consumers have a right to choose what they buy.

collusion Illegal agreement between two or more companies to commit a wrongful act

UNFAIR PRICING Interfering with competition can take the form of illegal pricing practices. **Collusion** occurs when two or more firms agree to collaborate on such wrongful acts as *price fixing*. The Federal Trade Commission (FTC), for example, recently launched an investigation into practices at Toys "R" Us, the largest toy retailer in the country. Investigators charge that Toys "R" Us routinely pressures major suppliers to limit quantities or delay shipments of hot-selling toys to warehouse clubs such as Sam's Club or Costco. Although Toys "R" Us denies the charges, the firm also contends that it has the right to tell suppliers that it may choose to not stock toys that are sold to warehouse clubs. Although the case will probably take years to resolve, it nevertheless highlights the scrutiny under which many business practices may be examined.[10]

Under some circumstances, firms can also come under attack for *price gouging*—responding to increased demand with overly steep (and often unwarranted) price increases. For example, when BMW launched its Z3 Roadsters, demand for the car was so strong that some dealers sold Z3s only to customers willing to pay thousands of dollars over sticker prices. A similar practice was adopted by Volkswagen dealers when the new Beetle was launched.

ETHICS IN ADVERTISING In recent years, increased attention has been given to ethics in advertising and product information. In the early 1970s, for example, many firms began promoting food products touted as "light," suggesting that the products were low in calories and/or saturated fat. The FDA confirmed that although many such products were in fact lower in fat than the same products in their regular versions, they still contained fairly high levels of fat and calories and certainly did not qualify as health food. As a result, many products were forced to drop "light" labeling; others added notices to the consumer that they were not truly low-fat products. Food producers are now required to use a standardized format for listing ingredients on product packages.

Another issue concerns advertising that some consumers consider morally objectionable. Recent examples have involved controversial television ads by Victoria's Secret showing models wearing skimpy underwear, and advertising campaigns by tobacco and alcohol companies that apparently target young people. For instance, although R. J. Reynold's was recently forced to retire Joe Camel, many beer commercials still feature animated frogs and lizards and other child-friendly characters.

Responsibility toward Employees

In Chapter 8, we will see how a number of human resource management activities are essential to a smoothly functioning business. These activities—recruiting, hiring, training, promoting, and compensating—are also the basis for social responsibility toward employees. A company that provides its employees with equal opportunities for rewards and advancement without regard to race, sex, or other irrelevant factors is meeting its social responsibilities. Firms that ignore these responsibilities run the risk of losing productive, highly motivated employees. They also leave themselves open to lawsuits.[11]

In addition to their responsibility to employees as company resources, firms have a responsibility to employees as people who are more productive when their needs are met. Firms that accept this responsibility ensure that the workplace is safe, both physically and socially.

ETHICAL COMMITMENTS: THE CASE OF WHISTLEBLOWERS Respecting employees as people means respecting their behavior as ethically responsible individuals. Too often, however, individuals who try to act ethically on the job find themselves in trouble with their employers. This problem is especially true for **whistleblowers**—employees who detect and try to put an end to a company's unethical, illegal, and/or socially irresponsible actions by publicizing them.

whistleblower Employee who detects and tries to put an end to a company's unethical, illegal, or socially irresponsible actions by publicizing them

In a socially responsible company, whistleblowers can confidently report findings to higher-level managers who can be expected to take action. In fact, many whistleblowers find management unwilling to listen, or worse: Whistleblowers at Beech-Nut, Citicorp, Prudential Insurance, General Dynamics, and Archer-Daniels Midland have all reported a lack of interest by managers about charges of company misconduct.

In extreme circumstances, whistleblowers may find themselves demoted or fired. The law does offer some recourse to employees who take action. The current whistleblower law stems from the False Claims Act of 1863, which was designed to prevent contractors from selling defective supplies to the Union Army during the Civil War. With 1986 revisions to the law, the government can recover triple damages from fraudulent contractors. Since 1986, over 700 suits have been filed. The government has intervened to prosecute in about 100 of those cases and collected $750 million in damages. With more cases being filed and larger amounts of fraudulent funds coming to light, that figure will soon top $1 billion. Whistleblowers receive 15 to 25 percent of what the government collects. If the Justice Department does not intervene, a whistleblower can proceed with a civil suit. In that case, the whistleblower receives 25 to 30 percent of any money recovered. In one of the largest judgments to date, a former testing supervisor at FMC Corp. recently won a whistleblowing case in U.S. District Court. Because he considered it inaccurate, he had refused to sign a report regarding a troop carrier being sold to the U.S. military. When FMC fired him, he filed suit against his former employer. The court awarded him $100 million.[12]

Responsibility toward Investors

Because shareholders are the owners of a company, it may sound odd to say that a firm can act irresponsibly toward its investors. Managers can abuse their responsibilities to investors in several ways. As a rule, irresponsible behavior toward shareholders means abuse of a firm's financial resources. In such cases, the ultimate losers are indeed the shareholder-owners who do not receive their due earnings or dividends. Companies can also act irresponsibly toward shareholder-owners by misrepresenting company resources.

IMPROPER FINANCIAL MANAGEMENT Occasionally, organizations or their officers are guilty of blatant financial mismanagement—offenses that are unethical but not

"But won't absconding with the company's funds cast the board in a bad light?"

necessarily illegal. For example, some firms have been accused of paying excessive salaries to senior managers, of sending them on extravagant "retreats" to exotic and expensive resorts, and of providing frivolous "perks," including ready access to corporate jets, lavish expense accounts, and memberships at plush country clubs.

In such situations, creditors can often do little, and stockholders have few options. Trying to force a management changeover, for example, is a difficult process that can drive down stock prices, a penalty that shareholders are usually unwilling to impose on themselves.

check kiting Illegal practice of writing checks against money that has not yet been credited at the bank on which the checks are drawn

CHECK KITING Other unethical practices are illegal. **Check kiting,** for instance, involves writing a check against money that has not yet arrived at the bank on which it is drawn. In a typical scheme, managers deposit customer checks totaling, say, $1 million into the company account. Knowing that the bank will not collect all of the total deposit for several days, they proceed to write checks against the total amount deposited, knowing that their account is so important to the bank that the checks will be covered until the full deposits have been collected.

INSIDER TRADING When someone uses confidential information to gain from the purchase or sale of stocks, that person is practicing *insider trading.* Several years ago, a highly publicized case featuring Wall Street trader Ivan Boesky and investment banker Dennis Levine substantially reduced the practice. But the recent surge in mergers and acquisitions seems to have made insider trading popular again. In 1998, for example, a former junior market analyst at investment banker Salomon Smith Barney was charged with conspiring to trade stock illegally ahead of a merger involving two large public utilities. Another investment banker at the same firm was charged with allegedly reaping $1.8 million in illegal profits ahead of six pending mergers.[13]

MISREPRESENTATION OF FINANCES Certain behavior regarding financial representation is also illegal. In maintaining and reporting its financial status, every corporation must conform to *generally accepted accounting practices (GAAP)* (see Chapter 11). Sometimes, however, managers project profits far in excess of what they actually expect to earn. When the truth comes out, investors are disappointed.

IMPLEMENTING SOCIAL RESPONSIBILITY PROGRAMS

Thus far, we have discussed social responsibility as if there were some agreement on how organizations should behave. In fact, dramatic differences of opinion exist concerning the role of social responsibility as a business goal. Some people oppose any business activity that threatens profits. Others argue that social responsibility must take precedence over profits.

Even businesspeople who agree on the importance of social responsibility will cite different reasons for their views. Some skeptics of business-sponsored social projects fear that if businesses become too active, they will gain too much control over the ways in which those projects are addressed by society as a whole. These critics point to the influence that many businesses have been able to exert on the government agencies that are supposed to regulate their industries. Other critics claim that business organizations lack the expertise needed to address social issues. They argue, for instance, that technical experts, not businesses, should decide how to clean up polluted rivers.

Proponents of socially responsible business believe that corporations are citizens and should therefore help to improve the lives of fellow citizens. Still others point to the vast resources controlled by businesses and note that they help to create many of the problems social programs are designed to alleviate.

Approaches to Social Responsibility

Given these differences of opinion, it is little wonder that corporations have adopted a variety of approaches to social responsibility. In this section, we describe the three most common approaches: the *social obligation*, *social reaction*, and *social response approaches*.

SOCIAL OBLIGATION APPROACH The **social obligation approach,** a fairly conservative concept, is consistent with the argument that profits should not be spent on social programs. Companies adopting this approach tend to meet the minimum requirements of government regulation and standard business practices.

Tobacco companies can be said to exemplify this approach. They attached health warnings on cigarette packages and stopped advertising on television in the United States only when forced to do so by the government. In countries that lack such controls, U.S. tobacco companies advertise heavily and make no mention of the negative effects of smoking.

social obligation approach
Approach to social responsibility by which a company meets only minimum legal requirements in its commitments to groups and individuals in its social environment

SOCIAL REACTION APPROACH An intermediate level of social responsibility is found in the **social reaction approach.** Firms taking this stance go beyond the bare minimum if they are specifically asked to do so. Many companies, for example, match employee contributions to company-approved causes. Others sponsor community activities. As a rule, however, someone must first ask for this support.

social reaction approach
Approach to social responsibility by which a company, if specifically asked to do so, exceeds legal minimums in its commitments to groups and individuals in its social environment

SOCIAL RESPONSE APPROACH Firms that adopt the most liberal approach to social responsibility, the **social response approach,** actively seek opportunities to contribute to social projects. McDonald's, for example, established Ronald McDonald Houses to provide lodging for families of children hospitalized away from home. Sears and General Electric support artists and performers. Such efforts go beyond the normal response to requests for contributions. Table 4.1 lists the fifteen top corporate givers.

social response approach
Approach to social responsibility by which a company actively seeks opportunities to contribute to the well-being of groups and individuals in its social environment

TABLE 4.1 ◆ **Top Corporate Givers (in Millions)**

RANK	NAME/(STATE)	TOTAL GRANTS
1.	AT&T Foundation (NY)	$37,738,769
2.	Wal-Mart Foundation (AR)	32,571,556
3.	Ford Motor Company Fund (MI)	28,948,869
4.	GE Fund (CT)	28,637,618
5.	Procter & Gamble Fund (OH)	27,341,322
6.	General Motors Foundation (MI)	27,041,994
7.	GTE Foundation (CT)	23,558,526
8.	General Mills Foundation (MN)	23,000,048
9.	Chrysler Corporation Fund (MI)	22,701,371
10.	SBC Foundation (TX)	21,261,053
11.	US West Foundation (CO)	20,896,047
12.	Exxon Education Foundation (TX)	18,843,153
13.	Prudential Foundation	18,712,354
14.	Bank America Foundation (CA)	18,633,872
15.	Shell Oil Company Foundation (TX)	18,055,890

FIGURE 4.3 ◆ **Establishing a Social Responsibility Program**

Managing Social Responsibility Programs

Making a company socially responsible in the full sense of the social response approach takes a carefully organized and managed program. In particular, managers must take steps to foster a companywide sense of social responsibility. Figure 4.3 summarizes those steps.

1. *Social responsibility must start at the top.* Without the support of top management, no program can succeed. Thus, top management must embrace a strong stand on social responsibility and develop a policy statement outlining that commitment.
2. *A committee of top managers must develop a plan detailing the level of management support.* Some companies set aside percentages of profits for social programs. Levi Strauss, for example, earmarks 2.4 percent of pretax earnings for worthy projects. Managers must also set specific priorities. For instance, should the firm train the hard-core unemployed or support the arts?
3. *One executive must be put in charge of the firm's agenda.* Whether the role is created as a separate job or added to an existing one, the selected individual must monitor the program and ensure that its implementation is consistent with the firm's policy statement and strategic plan.
4. *The organization must conduct occasional* ***social audits:*** *systematic analyses of its success in using funds earmarked for its social responsibility goals.* Consider the case of a company whose strategic plan calls for spending $100,000 to train 200 hard-core unemployed people and to place 180 of them in jobs. If at the end of a year the firm has spent $98,000, trained 210 people, and filled 175 jobs, a social audit will confirm the program's success. But if the program has cost $150,000, trained only 90 people, and placed only 10 of them, the audit will reveal the program's failure. Such failure should prompt a rethinking of the program's implementation and/or its priorities.

social audit Systematic analysis of a firm's success in using funds earmarked for meeting its social responsibility goals

Social Responsibility and the Small Business

As the owner of a garden supply store, how would you respond to a building inspector's suggestion that a cash payment will speed your application for a building permit? As the manager of a liquor store, would you call the police, refuse to sell, or sell to a customer whose identification card looks forged? As the owner of a small laboratory, would you call the state board of health to make sure that it has licensed the company with whom you want to contract to dispose of medical waste? Who will really be harmed if a small firm pads its income statement to help it get a much-needed bank loan?

Most of the examples in this chapter illustrate big-business responses to ethical and social responsibility issues. Such examples, however, show quite clearly that small businesses must answer many of the same questions. Differences are primarily differences of scale.

At the same time, these are largely questions of *individual* ethics. What about questions of *social* responsibility? Can a small business, for example, afford a social agenda? Should it sponsor Little League baseball teams, make donations to the United Fund, and buy lightbulbs from the Lion's Club? Do joining the Chamber of Commerce and supporting the Better Business Bureau cost too much? Clearly, ethics and social responsibility are decisions faced by all managers in all organizations, regardless of rank or size. One key to business success is to decide in advance how to respond to the issues that underlie all questions of ethical and social responsibility.

Continued from page 79

Are There Big Bucks in Big Mac's Future?

Observers still don't know whether Mark McGwire's use of androstenedione will affect his appeal to either fans or marketers. Having set a new single-season home run record at the seemingly impossible mark of 70, he could earn more than $25 million in single-season endorsements in 1999 if he chooses to plug everything from soft drinks, fast food, and sneakers to cars and vacation packages.

Meanwhile, the Association of Professional Team Physicians has urged that andro be removed from the market, especially because of its potential danger to teenage athletes. An association spokesman also derided manufacturers' claims that andro is "natural." "L-tryptophan supplements were natural, too, but they killed people," said San Francisco Giants' chief physician Dr. William Straw, referring to the death of 35 people who had taken another supplement in the 1980s.

> **"Too many athletes decide to use supplements until they are proven dangerous, when they should be holding off until they are proven safe."**
>
> —Dr. William Straw
> *San Francisco Giants' chief physician*

Straw warns that current law, giving the FDA power to ban dietary supplements only after illnesses or deaths, has created a false sense of safety among those willing to take *any* substance that remains legal. "Too many athletes," chides Straw, "decide to use supplements until they are proven dangerous, when they should be holding off until they are proven safe."

Questions for Discussion

1. Do you think that warning labels on andro bottles fulfill manufacturers' and retailers' responsibilities to customers?
2. Explain why you agree or disagree with the following statement: *Companies have a greater responsibility to safeguard the health of underage consumers than they do adult consumers.*
3. Do you think that the FDA should have the same regulatory control over dietary supplements as it has over prescription drugs and medical devices? Or should the dietary-supplement industry regulate itself?
4. Would you describe General Nutrition Companies as a more socially responsible firm than MET-Rx Engineered Nutrition? Explain your answer in terms of both law and ethics.
5. Based on this case, do you believe that legality and ethics are always the same for a company? Explain your answer.
6. If you were the marketing manager of a consumer products company, would you consider using Mark McGwire as a spokesman? Why or why not?

SUMMARY

1. **Explain how individuals develop their personal *codes of ethics* and why ethics are important in the workplace.** Individual *codes of ethics* are derived from social standards of right and wrong. *Ethical behavior* is behavior that conforms to generally accepted social norms concerning beneficial and harmful actions. Because ethics affect the behavior of individuals on behalf of the companies that employ them, many firms are adopting formal statements of ethics. Unethical behavior can result in loss of business, fines, and even *imprisonment.*
2. **Distinguish *social responsibility* from *ethics* and trace the evolution of social responsibility in U.S. business.** *Social responsibility* refers to an organization's response to social needs. Until the second half of the nineteenth century, businesses often paid little attention to these needs. Since then, however, both public pressure and government regulation, especially as a result of the Great Depression of the 1930s and the social activism of the 1960s and 1970s, have forced businesses to consider the public welfare, at least to some degree. A trend toward increased social consciousness, including a heightened sense of environmental activism, has recently emerged.
3. **Show how the concept of social responsibility applies both to environmental issues and to a firm's relationships with customers, employees, and investors.** Social re-

sponsibility toward the environment requires firms to minimize pollution of air, water, and land. Social responsibility toward customers requires firms to provide products of acceptable quality, to price products fairly, and to respect consumers' rights. Social responsibility toward employees requires firms to respect workers both as resources and as people who are more productive when their needs are met. Social responsibility toward investors requires firms to manage their resources and to represent their financial status honestly.

4. **Identify three general *approaches to social responsibility* and describe the four steps a firm must take to implement a *social responsibility program*.** The *social obligation approach* emphasizes compliance with legal minimum requirements. Companies adopting the *social reaction approach* go beyond minimum activities, if asked. The *social response approach* commits a company to actively seeking to contribute to social projects. Implementing a social responsibility program entails four steps: (1) drafting a policy statement with the support of top management, (2) developing a detailed plan, (3) appointing a director to implement the plan, and (4) conducting *social audits* to monitor results.

QUESTIONS AND EXERCISES

5. **Explain how issues of social responsibility and ethics affect small businesses.** Managers and employees of small businesses face many of the same ethical questions as their counterparts at larger firms. Small businesses face the same issues of social responsibility and the same need to decide on an approach to social responsibility. The differences are primarily differences of scale.

QUESTIONS FOR REVIEW

1. What basic factors should be considered in any ethical decision?
2. What are the major areas of social responsibility with which businesses should be concerned?
3. List the four rights of consumers that were proposed during the Kennedy administration and eventually formalized by state and federal law.
4. What are the three basic approaches to social responsibility?
5. In what ways do you think your personal code of ethics might clash with the operations of some companies? How might you try to resolve these differences?

QUESTIONS FOR ANALYSIS

6. What kind of wrongdoing would most likely prompt you to be a whistleblower? What kind of wrongdoing would be least likely? Why?
7. In your opinion, which area of social responsibility is most important? Why? Are there areas other than those noted in the chapter that you consider important?
8. Identify some specific ethical or social responsibility issues that might be faced by small-business managers and employees in each of the following areas: environment, customers, employees, and investors.

APPLICATION EXERCISES

9. Develop and put in writing a code of ethics for use in the classroom. Your document should include guidelines for students, instructors, and administrators.
10. Using newspapers, magazines, and other business references, identify and describe at least three companies that take a social obligation approach to social responsibility, three companies that take a social reaction approach, and three companies that take a social response approach.

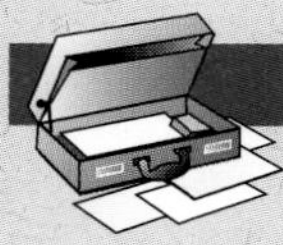

BUILDING YOUR BUSINESS SKILLS

TO LIE OR NOT TO LIE: THAT IS THE QUESTION

This exercise enhances the following SCANS workplace competencies: demonstrating basic skills, demonstrating thinking skills, exhibiting interpersonal skills, and working with information.

▼ GOAL

To encourage students to apply general concepts of business ethics to specific situations.

▼ BACKGROUND

Even before President Bill Clinton's public acknowledgment of an inappropriate relationship with White House intern Monica S. Lewinsky, and well before his secretary was forced to testify about the affair before a federal grand jury, the issue of workplace lying was front-page news.

Why? Perhaps because lying is so common. According to one survey, a quarter of working American adults said that they had been asked to do something illegal or unethical on the job. Four in 10 did what they were told. Another survey of more than 2,000 secretaries showed that many employees face ethical dilemmas in their day-to-day work.

▼ METHOD

STEP 1

Working with four other students, discuss ways in which you would respond to the following ethical dilemmas. When there is a difference of opinion among group members, try to determine the specific factors that influence different responses:

- Would you lie about your supervisor's whereabouts to someone on the phone?
- Would you lie about who was responsible for a business decision that cost your company thousands of dollars to protect your own or your supervisor's job?
- Would you inflate sales and revenue data on official company accounting statements to increase stock value?
- Would you say that you witnessed a signature when you did not if you were acting in the role of a notary?
- Would you keep silent if you knew that the official minutes of a corporate meeting had been changed?
- Would you destroy or remove information that could hurt your company if it fell into the "wrong" hands?

STEP 2

Research the commitment to business ethics at Johnson & Johnson (http://www.johnsonandjohnson.com) and Texas Instruments (http://www.ti.com/corp/docs/ethics/home.htm) by clicking on their respective Web sites. As a group, discuss ways in which these statements are likely to affect the specific behaviors mentioned in Step 1.

STEP 3

Working with group members, draft a corporate code of ethics that would discourage the specific behaviors mentioned in Step 1. Limit your code to a single, typewritten page, but make it sufficiently broad to cover different ethical dilemmas.

▼ FOLLOW-UP

1. What personal, workplace, and cultural factors do you think contribute to lying in the workplace?

2. Do you agree or disagree with the following statement? *The term* business ethics *is an oxymoron.* Support your answer with examples from your own work experience or that of a family member.
3. If you were your company's director of human resources, how would you make your code of ethics a "living document"?
4. If you were faced with any of the ethical dilemmas described in Step 1, how would you handle them? How far would you go to maintain your personal ethical standards?

CRAFTING YOUR BUSINESS PLAN

ETHICAL AND SOCIALLY RESPONSIBLE CONDUCT

▼ Purpose of the Assignment

1. To acquaint students with the process of navigating the *Business PlanPro (BPP)* software package.
2. To familiarize students with some of the ethical and social responsibility considerations faced by businesses and to show where the topic can be found in different sections of the *BPP* business plan.
3. To prepare students for entering social responsibility considerations into a firm's business plan through *BPP.*

▼ Assignment

After reading Chapter 4 in the textbook, open the BPP software* and look around for information about the types of ethical considerations and social responsibility factors that would be of concern to the sample firm of Southeast Health Services (Southeast Health Plans, Inc.). Then respond to the following questions:

1. Do you think a company in Southeast's line of business should have a code of ethics? Call up Southeast's Business Plan Outline [click on the **Plan Outline** at the bottom of the screen]. In which sections of Southeast's business plan would you expect to find their code of ethics? Go into those sections from the Task Manager and identify information about their code of ethics. What did you find?
2. The textbook states that a firm's social responsibility includes providing quality products for its customers. Explore Southeast's business plan and describe its position on providing quality products. [Sites to see in BPP (for this assignment): In the Task Manager screen, click on **Initial Assessment;** then click on **2. Mission** and then **3. Keys to Success.**]
3. Another dimension of social responsibility is pricing products fairly. Search through Southeast's plan to identify information about the fairness of pricing for services they offer. Does Southeast's planned gross margin reflect "fair pricing"? Why or why not? [Sites to see in BPP: In the Task Manager screen, click on **What You're Selling,** then **3. Competitive Positioning,** then **4. Sourcing and Fulfillment.** After returning to the Task Manager screen, click on **Finish and Polish** and then **6. Executive Summary.**]

▼ For Your Own Business Plan

4. To what extent will your business plan deal with your business's social responsibilities to customers? To the local community? To employees? In what section(s) of the BPP document should social responsibility matters be presented? What purpose do you think they would serve?

(continued)

▼ *Tips for Navigating in BPP

1. Open the *BPP* program, observe the Welcome screen, and click on **Open a Sample Plan.**
2. From the Open a Sample Plan dialogue box, click on a sample company name, then click on **Open.**
3. On the Task Manager screen, click on any of the lines, such as the **Your Company** line.
4. You can always return to the Task Manager screen by going to the bottom of the screen and clicking on the **Task Manager** icon.
5. When you are finished with an example company, close its Task Manager screen.
6. After finishing with an example company, to get to the next one, go to the top of the screen and click on **File** (on the menu bar) and select **Open Sample Plan.** This will exit you from the current company file and send you to the Open a Sample Plan dialogue box, where you can select your next example company.

EXPLORING THE NET

JUDGING ETHICALLY

Texas Instruments was a pioneer in the area of business ethics. Indeed, TI was one of the very first corporations in the United States to create and publish a code of ethics for managers and employees. To learn more about ethics at TI, visit the company Web site and then answer the questions that follow:

http://www.ti.com/corp/docs/ethics/home.htm

1. Overall, how beneficial do you think this Web site would be for a Texas Instruments employee interested in corporate ethics?
2. Visit the area in the Web site and review the information dealing with ethics across the organization. How useful do you find this information to be?
3. Visit the area in the site about ethics in the global market. What are the strengths and weaknesses of this area?
4. One area of the Web site features an ethics quiz designed to help employees get a sense of the ethics of a particular action. How practical is this section?
5. If you were developing an ethics Web site for another company, would you pattern it after the TI site? Why or why not?
6. Why don't more companies have Web sites like this one?

VIDEO EXERCISE 1.1

Rewrapping the Entertainment Package

Learning Objectives

The purpose of this video is to help you

1. Understand the ways in which businesses differ across various industries.
2. Appreciate the dynamics of change in our current business environment.
3. Understand how social and cultural differences affect the practice of business.

Background Information

Showtime exemplifies the contemporary business environment, evolving to meet changing entertainment needs throughout the world. Showtime's initial role was to broaden the movie market by making movies available to cable television companies, which reach home audiences. Showtime then moved beyond the role of distributor and began producing its own programs. From sporting events to original movies to its new network, Showtime Extreme, Showtime has adopted a broad view of its market. With high doses of action Showtime Extreme hopes to succeed throughout Europe.

The Video

While Part One presents an introduction to Showtime, it can also illustrate ways in which businesses differ. Showtime's adaptation over the years can be a framework for discussing the changes that have occurred in other industries. The issues of ethics and social responsibility can also be addressed by discussing the pressure put on the entertainment industry to limit or filter its content, particularly for children. Because Showtime does business throughout the world, it is greatly affected by social and cultural differences. Other issues discussed in Part One include diversity and ways in which policies and procedures help shape the company's culture.

Discussion Questions

1. Which stakeholder groups are most important—internal or external?
2. What activities fall under the heading "market research," and how should this information be used?
3. What do people mean when they talk about the era of social responsibility?
4. What are some of the keys to an effective ethics policy?

Follow-Up Assignment

Using whatever sources of information you choose, identify three instances when a company has acted in a socially responsible manner. In each instance, assess whether you think the company's leaders acted for the right reasons. How have their efforts in social responsibility affected other areas of their business?

For Further Exploration

Sometimes one employee commits an unethical act, which can significantly hurt the company. Other times, unethical behavior is more widespread, sometimes involving a company's top management. Go to the Internet and search for an article about company or employee unethical behavior. Then go to the company's Web site and evaluate how it has responded. How has the company suffered because of this behavior? Have they taken any actions to prevent future violations?

VIDEO EXERCISE 1.2

The Tile Connection

Learning Objectives

The purpose of this video exercise is to help you

1. Realize that a new business often starts because existing businesses in the industry are not fully meeting the needs of consumers.
2. Understand that the selection of *suppliers* is a critical decision for a firm, especially when the suppliers are located in distant nations.
3. Realize how important it is for a firm to maintain an excellent credit record.

Background Information

We meet Jimmy and Maria Fand, the owners and operators of The Tile Connection in Tampa, Florida. Most of the interviewing time is devoted to Jimmy, a man with an interesting background. He dropped out of school in his native Colombia at age 14 and wanted to travel all over the Western Hemisphere. He landed in New York and quickly realized that if the American Dream was to be his, he would need an education. He graduated from college with teaching credentials. As he and Maria started their family, they soon decided that they wanted to raise their children in Florida. As a part of developing a new home down South, Jimmy happened into a tile store in Clearwater. He thought the prices there were too high and the selection was too small. Why not become a tile importer?

The Tile Connection imports tile from firms in Spain, Portugal, Colombia, Brazil, Argentina, Japan, and Turkey. The company offers a much broader selection of tiles than other American tile firms, and at lower prices. At the time this video was taped, The Tile Connection was the largest tile importer in America. Wholesale tile salespeople from The Tile Connection cover all Florida, and providing high-quality service for the customers is extremely important to The Tile Connection. But concern for quality also goes in another direction—toward the suppliers. It is terribly important to weed out firms known for poor quality and for unreliability. Of the world's suppliers of tile, Jimmy deals with only 10 percent, and these 10 percent are makers superb of tiles. Jimmy tells us that a new importer should not be nervous about the new undertaking, but should be very cautious about choosing companies to form working relationships.

Once the firm locates a highly reliable tile supplier, The Tile Connection strives to maintain an exemplary credit record. Jimmy explains that the international department of his bank makes required payment to the supplier on the exact date established for payment. And Jimmy has a customs broker in Tampa who helps to keep smooth the flow of tile.

The Video

Small Business 2000 Master Class, SB2000 Program #405. A major reason behind the success of **The Tile Connection** is that it imports high-quality goods at affordable prices. Learning what firms to work with can be a difficult task, though. When you find those reliable suppliers, work hard to maintain good relationships with them.

Discussion Questions

1. How did Jimmy notice that there was a *need* for his importing business?
2. Can you determine what role Jimmy's wife, Maria, plays in **The Tile Connection?** Do you get the impression that she can take decisive actions in his absence?

3. Provide a biographical sketch on Jimmy.
4. Has this highly successful entrepreneur had some failures in small business? If so, explain what the problems were.
5. How important does Jimmy find a trade show to be?
6. An old saying in finance is "pay slowly, collect quickly." What would Jimmy say about this advice? Does he follow it?
7. What are the reasons Jimmy gives for importing tile?
8. In which aspect of business does Jimmy caution us to do lots of homework?
9. Jimmy refers to the American Dream. Do you feel that he has lived that dream? Why or why not?

Follow-Up Assignment

To better understand the nature of the industry and how The Tile Connection operates, familiarize yourself with the following concepts in the textbook:

- Dealing in the global market (Chapter 3)
- The small business (Chapter 7)
- Staffing, not overstaffing (Chapter 9)
- Importing and producing quality goods (Chapter 13)
- Knowing your customers (Chapter 10)
- Importance of pricing (Chapter 11)
- Help from banks (Chapter 15)

The Internet Connection and One Last Thing to Remember

As we went to press, The Tile Connection was in the process of developing a totally new Web site. To find out when it is ready, you can call 813-886-0576.

As you know, this is the frustrating age of the automated telephone response in which the caller yearns to talk to a human being—a human being who can answer a question. At The Tile Connection, when the boss, Jimmy, is not available to help a customer, Maria can take charge. The company wants to prevent that major business roadblock that comes up when there's no one at the company who can give the customer the needed information.

UNDERSTANDING THE BUSINESS OF MANAGING

Cape Cod Revival

Songwriters tell us that love is better the second time around, but they don't say a word about business ownership. Is success sweeter, more satisfying, more ego-boosting when you build a company, sell it, and then buy it back in order to rebuild? There aren't many people with the firsthand experience to answer this question, but entrepreneur Stephen Bernard can. In a period of 17 years, Bernard founded, sold, and repurchased Massachusetts-based Cape Cod Potato Chips. His story is one of an unsinkable entrepreneurial spirit and keen management know-how.

STEP 1: BUILD THE BUSINESS

Ever since he was a kid, Bernard had dreamed of running an innovative food company, and potato chips seemed like a product in search of innovation. No matter who made them, all chips tasted the same to Bernard. Whether plain, ruffled, or coated with sour cream or barbecue seasoning, they all had that same mass-produced taste, look, and feel. Sensing opportunity, Bernard began experimenting with a dough fryer and potato slices until he hit on an all-natural chip that looked homemade and tasted rich—and thereby differed from everything else on the market. "Most commercial potato chips," explains Bernard, "are continuously processed so the temperature and other conditions remain constant. What we figured out is that doing them as a batch in a single container causes the temperature to drop as soon as they go into the oil, and then it comes back up slowly. This gives the chips their unique texture."

Convinced that his chips would create a new premium-quality marketing niche, Bernard and his wife mortgaged their home and invested about $25,000 to start the Cape Cod Potato Chip Co. Working out of a tiny storefront in Hyannis, Massachusetts, they ran a 100-hour-a-week mom-and-pop operation, making, packaging, and selling chips to local retailers. Tourists who sampled the brand were immediately hooked and urged local retailers to stock the Bernards' product.

> "There are damn few products that have that kind of discernible difference."
>
> —Gus Lordi
> *Boston food broker*

New retailers tried, liked, and stocked Cape Cod chips, and "we never looked back." By 1985, the company was at home in a new 20,000-square-foot plant and had grown into a profitable $10 million enterprise.

Believing that his chips were good enough to speak for themselves, Bernard chose sampling over advertising as his chief marketing tool. Cape Cod's distinctive quality created immediate consumer loyalty and even convinced retailers to waive shelf space stocking fees. Boston food broker Gus Lordi agrees with Bernard's strategy: "There are damn few products that have that kind of discernible difference," he says. Just about everything else needs advertising.

Bernard priced Cape Cod Chips at 20 to 30 cents more than other brands, but consumers were willing to pay more for a specialty product with a uniquely good taste. Instead of competing head-to-head with industry giant Frito-Lay, Bernard worked to carve out a business niche in which he could give consumers the quality they wanted without having to capture a large market share. Like the microbrewers who would later redefine the beer-making industry, Bernard took a premium-product approach that identified and depended on a small but profitable market segment. Bernard, contends Harvard Business School professor Ray A. Goldberg, "was catering to individual tastes long before beer companies were talking about micromanaging and micromarketing. He woke up a sleepy industry where people weren't being as creative as they could be, because they didn't feel they had to be."

STEP 2: SELL THE BUSINESS

Cape Cod's extraordinary success forced Bernard to think about expanding into other states—a risky move that would require an infusion of capital. Before he could make up his mind, he received a call from Anheuser-Busch. A company known almost exclusively for its beer, Anheuser was in the process of launching a new snack division, Eagle Snacks, to compete with PepsiCo's Frito-Lay. Anheuser's strategy called for developing a line of premium niche products by purchasing regional snack companies with excellent track records. Cape Cod seemed a natural fit.

> "Bernard was catering to individual tastes long before beer companies were talking about micromanaging and micromarketing. He woke up a sleepy industry where people weren't being as creative as they could be, because they didn't feel they had to be."
>
> —Ray A. Goldberg
> *Harvard Business School professor*

Bernard received an offer he couldn't refuse and sold his company for a reported $7 million. As part of the deal, he agreed to stay on as president. Within 5 years, sales hit $40 million, and Cape Cod Chips could be found throughout the United States and Canada. Despite this success, however, Cape Cod's status as a "specialty" product didn't fit well with Anheuser-Busch's broader-based marketing goals. "It became just another part of a much bigger effort," says Bernard, "and they lost focus on Cape Cod."

In fact, Anheuser's commitment to Eagle waned as the parent corporation came to a painful realization: Frito-Lay's grip on the $5 billion salty-snack market was *very* tight. While Eagle enjoyed a mere 10 percent of the market, Frito-Lay commanded 50 percent. Such realities convinced Anheuser to pull back on its support for Cape Cod, and by 1995, annual sales had dropped to $12 million. By early 1996, the product capacity of Eagle Snacks had been sold to Frito-Lay. Cape Cod Potato Chips no longer existed.

STEP 3: BUY BACK THE BUSINESS

Bernard could have walked away. He had already started another food-related company and had profited handsomely from the original Cape Cod sale. Cape Cod, however, meant more to him than dollars and cents: It was the company that he and his wife had created and nurtured; it was their business home. So, with the help of venture capitalists, he bought back the company—for considerably less than he had originally received from Anheuser-Busch. It was "an emotional experience," recalls Bernard. "When I entered the factory and told 100 employees that we were back and their jobs were safe, they began to cheer and my knees began to shake."

His next job, of course, was rebuilding. To maintain his base of consumer loyalty, he had to get Cape Cod Potato Chips back on store shelves as soon as possible. With this priority in mind, Bernard's marketing team connected first with New England retailers, who had supported the brand from the beginning. They were "tremendously supportive upon hearing that the brand was coming back," reports Cape Cod vice president for sales Tony Cusano. Within 3 months, Cape Cod Chips were back in 3,000 stores throughout New England.

The right marketing strategy was critical to a successful comeback, but lacking Anheuser-Busch's deep pockets, the reborn company had limited resources for advertising. Marketing director Nicole Bernard, the boss's daughter, went back to her father's original strategy—product sampling. In 1996 alone, she gave away 400,000 1-ounce bags to consumers all over New England. "We really believe in our product," explains Nicole. "Once we can get a customer to try it, the retention rate is high. We look at sampling as a way to create a purchase."

With success assured in New England, Cape Cod looked toward sales opportunities up and down the East Coast, across the Midwest, and in California. The shelf space formerly occupied by Eagle Snack products was up for grabs, and Bernard's management team was confident that a premium potato chip would attract reasonably broad interest. Within months, Cape Cod had aligned itself with 60 master distributors who were able to place its product in 5,000 supermarket outlets. In addition, three new products, all introduced in 1997, helped to fuel the comeback: Golden Chips, Dark Russet Chips, and 40 percent Reduced Fat Chips. Each product is cooked in Cape Cod's small-batch method to maximize quality. According to Bernard, this method enables him "to closely monitor the individual needs of each type of potato chip."

The year 1997 was good for Cape Cod Potato Chips. Through entrepreneurial pluck and management skill, Stephen Bernard turned his company around, moving from $6 million in sales in 1996 to nearly $30 million in 1997. "Our focus," he says, "is to get about 3 percent of the [overall] business, wherever the business is. Potato chips are a multibillion-dollar market, so 3 percent would be terrific."

WEB LINKS

Snack-food, small-business, and management Web sites abound, including the following. The information in these and other sites will help you answer the questions that follow.

- **American Management Association**
  http://www.amanet.org/
- **Cape Cod Potato Chips**
  http://www.capecodchips.com
- **Dun & Bradstreet's Small Business Services**
  http://www.dnb.com/sbs/hmenu.htm
- **Entrepreneur Magazine: The Online Small Business Authority**
  http://www.entrepreneurmag.com
- **Frito-Lay**
  http://www.fritolay.com
- **Hopnotes.com: Home of Anheuser-Busch's Specialty Beers**
  http://www.hopnotes.com/
- **Online Women's Business Center: Finance Center**
  http://www.onlinewbc.org/docs/finance/index.html
- **Small Business Administration**
  http://www.sba.gov/

QUESTIONS FOR DISCUSSION

1. Imagine that Stephen Bernard is about to write a mission statement for Cape Cod Potato Chips and that you are his advisor. Draft a statement that reflects the company's product and marketing objectives.
2. Which of Stephen Bernard's management skills do you think contribute most to his success? Why?
3. Does it surprise you that Cape Cod, rather than Frito-Lay, developed the batch-processing method that makes Cape Cod Chips distinctive? Link your answer to the role that small businesses play in creating innovative products. (Visit the Cape Cod, Frito-Lay, and Entrepreneur Magazine Web sites for helpful information.)
4. Does it surprise you that Bernard's start-up company needed the insurance money from an automobile accident to make ends meet? Support your answer with information that you gather from the Online Women's Business Center and SBA Web sites.
5. Would you characterize Stephen Bernard as a small-business owner or an entrepreneur? Explain your answer by searching the Web site of Entrepreneur Magazine for other businesspeople with Bernard's characteristics.
6. Analyze Hopnotes.com: Home of Anheuser Busch's Specialty Beers. Why do you think Anheuser-Busch is able to market specialty beers but not specialty potato chips?
7. What kind of SBA assistance would have helped Stephen Bernard when he first opened his company? What kind of SBA assistance did he need when he bought it back? Search the SBA Web site for information.
8. Although Bernard is operating a small company, he has built a business organization around employees who perform specialized functions. Why is departmentalization crucial to the success of a small company such as Cape Cod?

Chapter 5: Managing the Business Enterprise

The Management Equivalent of Juggling

What looked like a superb business opportunity for 3Com Corp. turned into a painful—almost disastrous—business experience. Led by Chairman and CEO Eric Benhamou, 3Com, a California-based telecommunications company and the world's second largest maker of computer networking products, acquired rival U.S. Robotics, the world's largest modem maker, in 1997 and embarked on a plan of rapid expansion. The acquisition, admits Benhamou, "stressed the innards of the company to its limits," in part because of U.S. Robotics's poor inventory control. An inventory buildup clogged the combined company's distribution channel for a year after the merger and tied up needed capital. The acquisition also doubled the size of 3Com's workforce, compounding the personnel pressures exerted by greater numbers and greater diversity. Worse, the market's initial response to U.S. Robotics's new 56K standard modems was poor, with consumers complaining about the need for yet another hardware upgrade, especially at a time when satellite dishes and cable modems were promising faster connections.

> **"The acquisition stressed the innards of the company to its limits."**
>
> —Eric Benhamou
> *CEO of 3Com*

External troubles were also mounting. As the economies of Japan, Korea, and other Asian countries soured in 1997 and 1998, 3Com lost its fastest-growing market for networking products. According to one observer, the Asian market "practically vanished from 3Com's radar screen from one day to the next." When 3Com's earnings sank 91 percent in the second quarter of 1998 and operating income fell 10 cents a share below expectations, Benhamou was pressured to redefine the company's underlying business strategy and change its direction.

Instead, he dug in his heels and pledged to take 3Com back to business basics. Known as a deliberative manager who carefully weighs every decision, Benhamou decided to refocus the corporation's energy on what 3Com did best in the networking market and to develop and sell the Palm Pilot, its handheld computer.

Moreover, Benhamou saw expanded opportunity in the networking industry. In addition to the large, conventional markets, two new market segments—one for small and medium-size businesses and consumers and another for small and home offices—held tremendous potential. For Benhamou, taking advantage of these opportunities meant introducing a range of new products while, simultaneously, coping with the continuing upheaval resulting from the purchase of U.S. Robotics.

By the end of 1998, quarterly earnings had jumped 52 percent, exceeding analysts' expectations. "We turned a corner," said Benhamou modestly, but industry observers likened his management feat to a juggling act in which he had developed a leaner inventory system, managed product development, dealt with workforce issues, and convinced shareholders to hold on for better times.

Benhamou also understands that a large part of 3Com's success comes from strategic alliances with companies that connect end users to networks. When Microsoft rolls out a new product such as NT 5, for instance, 3Com—at least according to Benhamou—"has

more expertise than any other company" to make it work. The company's high-speed connections, service, and network management make it a natural partner in an expanding industry. In all probability, with collaboration in everyone's best interest, such relationships will continue to grow.

All corporations depend on effective management. Whether managers are involved in running a small business or a stable corporation or, like Eric Benhamou, are trying to deal with the fallout from a corporate merger, they must set goals and strategies to grow their specific business. The work of all managers involves developing strategic and tactical plans. They must analyze their competitive environments and organize, direct, and control day-to-day operations. In Benhamou's case, we also have a manager who must function effectively in both global and technological environments.

By focusing on the learning objectives of this chapter, you will better understand the nature of managing, the meaning of corporate culture, and the range of skills that managers like Eric Benhamou need if they are to work effectively.

Our opening story is continued on p. 123

After reading this chapter, you should be able to:

1. **Explain the importance of setting *goals* and formulating *strategies* as the starting points of effective management.**
2. **Describe the four activities that constitute the *management process.***
3. **Identify *types of managers* by level and area.**
4. **Describe the five basic *management skills.***
5. **Explain the importance of *corporate culture.***

Although our focus here is on managers in *business* settings, remember that the principles of *management* apply to all kinds of organizations. Managers work in charities, churches, social organizations, educational institutions, and government agencies. The Prime Minister of Canada, curators at the Museum of Modern Art, the dean of your college, and the chief administrator of your local hospital are all managers. Remember, too, that managers bring to small organizations much the same kinds of skills—the ability to make decisions and respond to a variety of challenges—as they bring to large ones.

Regardless of the nature and size of an organization, managers are among its most important resources. Consider, for example, the cases of these three managers:

- Jack Harnett is president of D.L. Rogers Corp., a Texas-based company that owns 54 Sonic Drive-In franchises. At Sonic restaurants, which are located primarily in the South, customers order hamburgers and malts from their cars and wait for roller-skating carhops to deliver the order directly to the car window. With 1997 revenues topping $44 million, D.L. Rogers is no small operation, and Harnett gets much of the credit for the company's success. He prides himself on being direct and honest with his employees. He also knows who's the boss and insists that everyone at D.L. Rogers do things his way. Fortunately, Harnett's way has so far been the best way.[1]
- Sherry Lansing is the chairman (and yes, that's her real title) at Paramount Pictures. Before she joined the firm in 1992, Paramount consistently performed about average for its industry and was generally viewed as a good buy, though not a great company. Lansing, however, has changed all that. Through an astute combination of acumen, ability, and the powers of persuasion, Lansing has steadily guided Paramount to consistent growth, profitability, and increasing market share. Among the firm's most recent successes under Lansing's leadership have been *Titanic*, *The Truman Show*, and *Saving Private Ryan*.[2]
- Timothy Koogle is the CEO of Yahoo!, one of the most successful technology-based companies in history and a leader in the burgeoning industry of Internet-oriented enterprises. Yahoo! started out as your basic search engine—a vehicle for locating Web sites about specific topics—but it's grown dramatically by integrating into a single Internet portal virtually every form of information source that an inquisitive individual might need. Over 40 million users a month log onto Yahoo!, compared with about 30 million who tune into the highest-rated TV program, *ER*. Actually, Koogle didn't found Yahoo!. He was hired to run it when it became apparent to its founders that it was headed for big things and today gets most of the credit for leading the firm to its current Internet prominence.[3]

Although Jack Harnett, Sherry Lansing, and Timothy Koogle are clearly very different people, work in very different kinds of organizations, and have different approaches to what they do, they also share one fundamental commonality—they are managers responsible for the performance and effectiveness of business enterprises and are thus accountable to shareholders, employees, customers, and other key constituents. In this chapter, we describe the management process and the skills that managers must develop to perform their functions in organizations. Perhaps you will then have a better feel for the reasons why organizations value good managers so highly.

■ SETTING GOALS AND FORMULATING STRATEGY

goal Objective that a business hopes and plans to achieve

The starting point in effective management is setting **goals**—objectives that a business hopes (and plans) to achieve. Every business needs goals. We begin by discussing the basic aspects of organizational goal setting. Remember, however, that deciding what it *intends* to do is only the first step for an organization. Managers must also make decisions about *actions* that will and will not achieve company goals. Decisions cannot be made on a problem-by-problem basis or merely to meet needs as they arise. In most companies, a broad program underlies those decisions. That program is called a *strategy*, and we will complete this section by detailing the basic steps in strategy formulation.

Setting Business Goals

Goals are performance targets—the means by which organizations and their managers measure success or failure at every level. Jack Harnett, for example, wants his Sonic restaurants to be run as efficiently as possible and to earn strong profits for the company. Sherry Lansing wants Paramount to make high-quality movies that attract a large paying audience and that are well received by the critics. Timothy Koogle wants Yahoo! to be the most widely used search engine on the Internet.

PURPOSES OF GOAL SETTING An organization functions systematically because it sets goals and plans accordingly. An organization commits its resources on all levels to achieving its goals. Specifically, we can identify four main purposes in organizational goal setting:

1. *Goal setting provides direction and guidance for managers at all levels.* If managers know precisely where the company is headed, there is less potential for error in the different units of the company. For example, 3M Corp. has a stated goal of earning 30 percent of its profits from sales of products less than 4 years old. 3M managers know that they must emphasize research and development and promote creativity and innovation.
2. *Goal setting helps firms allocate resources.* Areas that are expected to grow, for example, will get first priority. The company allocates more resources to new projects with large sales potential than it allocates to mature products with established but stagnant sales potential.
3. *Goal setting helps to define corporate culture.* General Electric's goal is to push each of its divisions to first or second in its industry. The result is a competitive (and often stressful) environment and a culture that rewards success and has little tolerance for failure.
4. *Goal setting helps managers assess performance.* If a unit sets a goal of increasing sales by 10 percent in a given year, managers in that unit who attain or exceed the goal can be rewarded. Units failing to reach the goal will also be compensated accordingly.

KINDS OF GOALS Goals differ from company to company, depending on the firm's purpose and mission. Every enterprise has a *purpose*, or a reason for being. Businesses seek profits, universities seek to discover and transmit new knowledge, and government agencies seek to set and enforce public policy. Many enterprises also have missions and **mission statements**—statements of *how* they will achieve their purposes in the environments in which they conduct their business.

mission statement Organization's statement of how it will achieve its purpose in the environment in which it conducts its business

A company's purpose is usually easy to identify. Reebok, for example, attempts to make a profit by manufacturing and selling athletic shoes and related merchandise. IBM has the same purpose in selling computers and computer technology. The demands of change force many companies to rethink their missions, and thus to revise their statements of what they are and what they do. (We discuss more fully the problems in managing change, and some solutions, later in this chapter.)

At many companies, top management drafts and circulates detailed mission statements. Because such a statement reflects a company's understanding of its activities as a *marketer*, it is not easily described. For example, consider the similarities and differences between Timex and Rolex. Although both firms share a common purpose—to sell watches at a profit—they have very different missions. Timex sells low-cost, reliable watches in outlets ranging from department stores to corner drugstores. Rolex sells high-quality, high-priced watches through selected jewelry stores.

Regardless of a company's purpose and mission, however, every firm has long-term, intermediate, and short-term goals:

- **Long-term goals** relate to extended periods of time, typically 5 years or more. For example, American Express might set a long-term goal of doubling the number of participating merchants during the next 10 years. Kodak might adopt a long-term goal of increasing its share of the 35mm film market by 10 percent during the next 8 years.
- **Intermediate goals** are set for a period of 1 to 5 years. Companies usually set intermediate goals in several areas. For example, the marketing department's goal might be to increase

long-term goals Goals set for an extended time, typically 5 years or more into the future

intermediate goals Goals set for a period of 1 to 5 years into the future sales by 3 percent in 2 years. The production department might want to reduce expenses by 6 percent in 4 years. Human resources might seek to cut turnover by 10 percent in 2 years. Finance might aim for a 3 percent increase in return on investment in 3 years.

short-term goals Goals set for the very near future, typically less than 1 year

- **Short-term goals** are set for perhaps 1 year and are developed for several different areas. Increasing sales by 2 percent this year, cutting costs by 1 percent next quarter, and reducing turnover by 4 percent over the next 6 months are examples of short-term goals.

Formulating Strategy

Planning, then, is often concerned with the nuts and bolts of setting goals, choosing tactics, and establishing schedules. In contrast, strategy tends to have a wider scope. It is by definition a "broad program" that describes an organization's intentions. A business strategy outlines how it intends to meet its goals, and includes the organization's responsiveness to new challenges and new needs.

Until a few years ago, for example, Carson Inc. was a modestly performing, privately held company producing personal-care products for African Americans. The firm's white management team, however, did not fully understand the firm's customer base and had no clear vision or strategy for the future. As a result, Carson basically muddled along, earning decent profits but falling short of its real potential. Then in 1995, Leroy Keith, outgoing president of Morehouse College, put together a consortium of black investors and bought Carson for $96 million.

Keith began by formulating a new strategy designed to take the firm to the head of its industry. First, he assembled a team of experienced black executives. Then he took the firm public to raise additional capital to fuel expansion and growth. To boost efficiency and profitability, he focused his efforts on the firm's operations—those activities directly related to the production of its product line. Finally, he embarked on an aggressive plan of product and market expansion. Carson, for example, has rapidly expanded its product line to target other ethnic groups. In addition, it is moving into more and more foreign markets, such as South Africa, Brazil, and several Caribbean nations.

Keith has also set the ambitious goal of increasing Carson's revenue each year by 20 to 25 percent. Recognizing that such growth cannot come from product extension alone (that is, marketing unmodified products to untapped groups of consumers), Carson management has opted to acquire firms that produce products that complement its own. Thus, Carson recently bought Cutex, the largest producer of nail-polish removing products in the United States. Clearly, then, the strategy that Keith has formulated for Carson has put the firm on the road toward becoming a major player in the global market for personal-care products.[4]

strategy formulation Creation of a broad program for defining and meeting an organization's goals

Because a well-formulated strategy is so vital to a business's success, most top managers devote much attention (and creativity) to this process. **Strategy formulation** involves three basic steps summarized in Figure 5.1.

FIGURE 5.1 ◆ **Strategy Formulation**

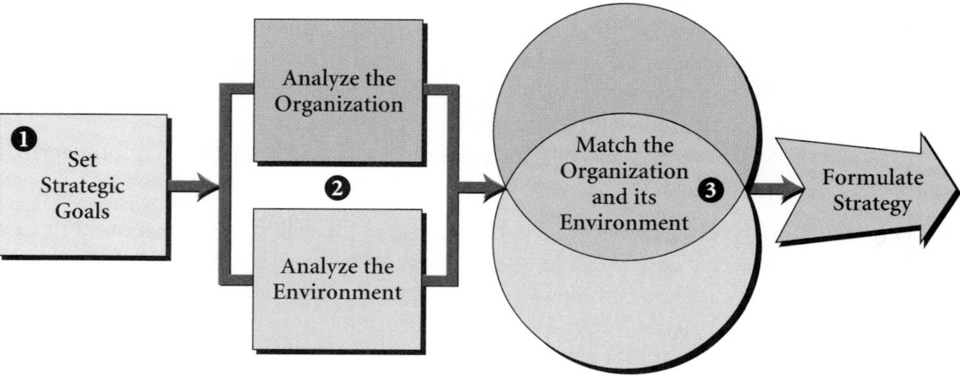

It is interesting to note at least one change in contemporary thinking about the role of strategy. Once the responsibility of top management, strategy made its way into the everyday world of setting and implementing goals (planning) by means of a fairly rigid top-down process. Today, however, strategy formulation is often a much more "democratic" process.[5]

strategic goals Long-term goals derived directly from a firm's mission statement

SETTING STRATEGIC GOALS Described as long-term goals, **strategic goals** are derived directly from a firm's mission statement. At Carson Inc., Leroy Keith's goal of annual revenue growth of 20 to 25 percent is clearly a strategic goal. Moreover, it provides clear direction: It conveys to everyone in the firm management's commitment to aggressive growth and underscores the importance of both expanding existing products and acquiring new ones.

Similarly, Nike CEO Philip Knight recently announced a new strategic goal for his well-known company. For years, Nike has relied on athletic shoe sales in the United States for the bulk of its revenues. Now, however, top managers have decided that they can achieve significant new growth only by pursuing a twofold strategy of expanding Nike's various product lines into more sports fields and entering more and more foreign markets. To reinforce management's commitment to this strategy, Knight announced that Nike would double its revenues—from $6 billion to $12 billion a year—by the year 2001. Nike also announced that it intended to become the world's top supplier of soccer footwear, apparel, and equipment in time for the World Cup playoffs in 2002.[6]

environmental analysis Process of scanning the business environment for threats and opportunities

ANALYZING THE ORGANIZATION AND ITS ENVIRONMENT The term **environmental analysis** involves scanning the environment for threats and opportunities. Changing consumer tastes and hostile takeover offers are *threats*, as are new government regulations. Even more important threats come from new products and new competitors. Opportunities, meanwhile, are areas in which the firm can potentially expand, grow, or take advantage of existing strengths.

Managers at Nike, for example, saw their well-known brand name as a strength. In other words, because so many consumers associated the Nike name with athletic shoes, they would probably be comfortable buying such other sports-related merchandise as Nike sunglasses, ski equipment, and baseball gloves. A major threat, on the other hand, is the established strength of the German shoe manufacturer Adidas among soccer enthusiasts.

organizational analysis Process of analyzing a firm's strengths and weaknesses

In addition to performing environmental analysis, which is analysis of *external* factors, managers must also examine *internal* factors. The purpose of **organizational analysis** is to better understand a company's strengths and weaknesses. Strengths might include surplus cash, a dedicated workforce, an ample supply of managerial talent, technical expertise, or little competition. The absence of any of these strengths could represent an important weakness.

The Walt Disney Co., for instance, continues to exploit its internal strengths by opening new theme parks, producing new animated movies, and expanding its chain of resorts in Florida, California, France, and Japan. Unfortunately, the mediocre ratings of Disney's ABC television network is a major weakness in the firm's plans to expand its TV-programming operations and is limiting the revenues that the parent company would like to earn from the sale of commercial advertising time.

MATCHING THE ORGANIZATION AND ITS ENVIRONMENT The final step in strategy formulation is matching environmental threats and opportunities against corporate strengths and weaknesses. The matching process is the heart of strategy formulation. More than any other facet of strategy, matching companies with their environments lays the foundation for successfully planning and conducting business. This is almost exactly the perspective adopted by Leroy Keith and his managers at Carson Inc. They recognized immediately, for instance, that their own familiarity with the personal-care products and preferences of ethnic minorities constituted a distinctive strength. Moreover, they knew that the market for ethnic hair-care products alone is over $1.2 billion a year; that African American women spend about three times as much per year on personal-care products and services as white American women; and that there are over 900 million people of African descent in the world today. Because few other firms were aggressively pursuing this market, Carson managers rightly regarded this untapped potential as a major opportunity.

Over the long term, this process may also determine whether a firm typically takes risks or behaves more conservatively. Either strategy can be successful. For example, Blue Bell is one of the most profitable ice cream makers in the world, even though it sells its products in only five states. Based in Brenham, Texas, Blue Bell controls more than 50 percent of the market in each state in which it does business. The firm has resisted the temptation to expand too quickly. Its success is based on product freshness and frequent deliveries—strengths that may suffer if the company grows too large.

A Hierarchy of Plans Plans can be viewed on three levels: strategic, tactical, and operational. Managerial responsibilities are defined at each level. The levels constitute a hierarchy because implementing plans is practical only when there is a logical flow from one level to the next.

strategic plans Plans reflecting decisions about resource allocations, company priorities, and steps needed to meet strategic goals

tactical plans Generally short-range plans concerned with implementing specific aspects of a company's strategic plans

operational plans Plans setting short-term targets for daily, weekly, or monthly performance

- **Strategic plans** reflect decisions about resource allocations, company priorities, and the steps needed to meet strategic goals. They are usually determined by the board of directors and top management. Procter & Gamble's decision that viable products must rank first or second within their respective categories is a matter of strategic planning.
- **Tactical plans** are shorter-range plans for implementing specific aspects of the company's strategic plans. They typically involve upper and middle management. Coca-Cola's decision to increase sales in Europe by building European bottling facilities is an example of tactical planning.
- **Operational plans,** which are developed by mid- and lower-level managers, set short-term targets for daily, weekly, or monthly performance. McDonald's, for example, establishes operational plans when it explains to franchisees precisely how Big Macs are to be cooked, warmed, and served.

THE MANAGEMENT PROCESS

management Process of planning, organizing, directing, and controlling an organization's resources to achieve its goals

Management is the process of planning, organizing, directing, and controlling an organization's financial, physical, human, and information resources to achieve its goals. As managers, Jack Harnett, Sherry Lansing, and Timothy Koogle oversee the use of all these resources in their respective firms. All aspects of a manager's job are interrelated. In fact, any given manager is likely to be engaged in each of these activities during the course of any given day.

Planning

planning Management process of determining what an organization needs to do and how best to get it done

Determining what the organization needs to do and how best to get it done requires **planning.** Planning has three main components. As we have seen, it begins when managers determine the firm's goals. Next, they develop a comprehensive strategy for achieving those goals. After a strategy is developed, they design tactical and operational plans for implementing the strategy.

As we noted earlier, for example, when Timothy Koogle joined Yahoo!, he and the firm's other top managers set a strategic goal of becoming a top firm in the emerging market for Internet search engines. Next, of course, Koogle and his team then had to decide how to achieve this strategic goal. They started by assessing the ways in which people actually use the Web. They also studied ways in which they would probably use it in the future, analyzed the successful strategies of other growing firms, and assessed the ways in which big companies were using the Internet. They concluded that people wanted an easy-to-understand Web interface. They also wanted to be able to satisfy a wide array of needs, preferences, and priorities by going to as few sites as possible.

One key component of Yahoo!'s strategy, therefore, was to foster partnerships and relationships with other companies so that potential Web surfers could draw upon several sources through a single portal—which would, of course, be Yahoo!. Thus, the goal of partnering emerged as one set of tactical plans for moving forward.

Koogle then began fashioning alliances with such diverse partners as Reuters, Standard & Poor's, and the Associated Press (for news coverage), RE/Max (for real estate information), and a wide array of information providers specializing in sports, weather, entertainment, shopping, travel, and so forth. The creation of individual partnership agreements with each of these partners represents a form of operational planning.

Organizing

Several years ago, the board of directors of Compaq Computer became concerned about the firm's lethargic growth and performance and named a new CEO, Eckhard Pfeiffer, to reenergize the company and boost its growth. Pfeiffer quickly concluded that part of the problem was Compaq's development into a slow-moving, bureaucratic organization that stifled innovation and made it difficult to respond to rapid changes in the information technology market. One of his first priorities, therefore, was to make the firm more responsive to changing technology and competition.

Under Compaq's former management, research and development, manufacturing, and marketing had all been run as large, centralized groups. As the firm grew from a fledging start-up to a Fortune 500 giant in less than a decade, these departments also grew—to the point that it took too long to make decisions and take action. Pfeiffer segmented the company into several small units, each of which is now assigned responsibility for its own R&D, manufacturing, and marketing. Unfortunately for Pfeiffer, however, the "new" Compaq fell victim to the same lethargy as the "old" Compaq. The board of directors forced him out in 1999, citing the firm's inability to compete with more nimble Dell and Gateway.

This process—determining the best way to arrange a business's resources and activities into a coherent structure—is called **organizing.** (We explore this topic further in Chapter 6.)

organizing Management process of determining how best to arrange an organization's resources and activities into a coherent structure

Directing

Managers have the power to give orders and demand results. Directing, however, involves more complex activities. When **directing,** a manager works to guide and motivate employees to meet the firm's objectives. Shortly after reorganizing Compaq, for instance, Eckhard Pfeiffer informed his engineers that he wanted them to cut product costs, shorten the lead time required to get new products to market, and boost product quality—all simultaneously. They were also informed that how they managed to meet these goals was up to them. Pfeiffer's emphasis on speed, responsiveness, and autonomy continues to be the hallmarks of Compaq today, and the firm remains one of the top performers in the computer industry.

directing Management process of guiding and motivating employees to meet an organization's objectives

Controlling

Controlling is the process of monitoring a firm's performance to make sure that it is meeting its goals. All CEOs must pay close attention to costs and performance. When a firm is small, monitoring costs is especially important. Jack Harnett, for example, closely monitors expenses, revenues, and profits at each Sonic restaurant in his company to ensure that expenses remain low and revenues and profits remain high. At the very first sign of trouble, such as an increase in expenses at one or more outlets, Harnett quickly moves to discover the source of the change. Indeed, he regularly visits various restaurants, often

controlling Management process of monitoring an organization's performance to ensure that it is meeting its goals

FIGURE 5.2 ◆ The Control Process

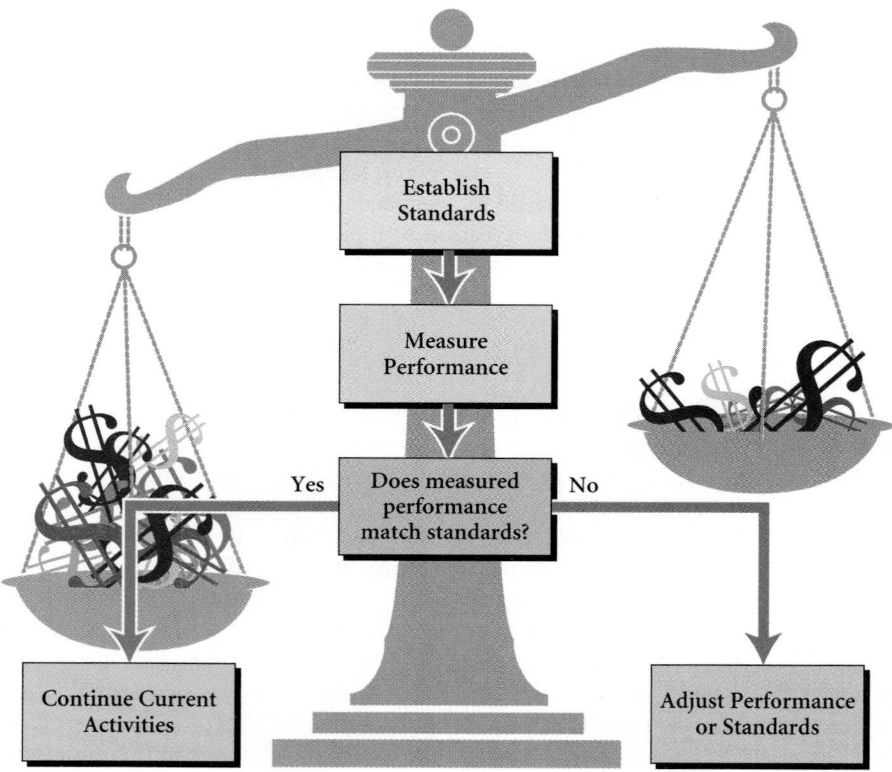

giving managers no advance notice. He tours the facility, talks to employees, and helps serve customers. At every juncture, however, he is looking for things that need to be corrected, be it a sign that needs to be replaced, a tree that needs to be trimmed, or a loyal and hard-working employee who desires higher pay.

The same task, however, faces managers at the largest firms. For example, when Sherry Lansing took over at Paramount, she saw that the firm was paying too little attention to controlling costs and perhaps giving too much autonomy to the individual producers of various projects. As a result, she implemented a new financial control system that better allows top-level managers to monitor costs. In addition, she implemented a new review system under which an additional group of managers helps assess the potential attractiveness of various movie projects.

Figure 5.2 illustrates the control process that begins when management establishes standards, often for financial performance. If, for example, a company wants to increase sales by 20 percent over the next 10 years, then an appropriate standard might be an increase of about 2 percent a year.

Managers then measure actual performance against standards. If the two amounts agree, the organization continues along its present course. If they vary significantly, however, one or the other needs adjustment. For instance, if sales have increased 2.1 percent by the end of the first year, things are probably fine. If sales have dropped 1 percent, some revision in plans may be needed. Perhaps the original goal should be lowered or more money should be spent on advertising. (We discuss the control process in more detail in Chapter 6.)

TYPES OF MANAGERS

Although all managers plan, organize, direct, and control, not all managers have the same degree of responsibility for these activities. Thus, it is helpful to classify managers according to levels and areas of responsibility.

DILBERT reprinted by permission of United Features Syndicate, Inc.

Levels of Management

The three basic levels of management are *top*, *middle*, and *first-line* management. Not surprisingly, most firms have more middle managers than top managers, and more first-line managers than middle managers. Both the power of managers and the complexity of their duties increase as they move up the ladder.

TOP MANAGERS Like Jack Harnett, Sherry Lansing, and Timothy Koogle, the fairly small number of executives who guide the fortunes of most companies are **top managers.** Common titles include *president, vice president, treasurer, chief executive officer (CEO),* and *chief financial officer (CFO).* Top managers are responsible for the overall performance and effectiveness of the firm. They set general policies, formulate strategies, approve all significant decisions, and represent the company in dealings with other firms and with government bodies.

top managers Managers responsible to the board of directors and stockholders for a firm's overall performance and effectiveness

MIDDLE MANAGERS Those who occupy positions of considerable autonomy and importance are **middle managers.** Titles such as *plant manager, operations manager,* and *division manager* designate middle-management slots. In general, middle managers are responsible for implementing the strategies, policies, and decisions made by top managers. For example, if top management decides to introduce a new product in 12 months or to cut costs by 5 percent in the next quarter, middle management must decide how to meet these goals. The manager of a Compaq factory, Mattel warehouse, or Continental hub operation will likely be a middle manager.

middle managers Managers responsible for implementing the strategies, policies, and decisions made by top managers

FIRST-LINE MANAGERS Those who hold such titles as *supervisor, office manager,* and *group leader* are **first-line managers.** Although they spend most of their time working with and supervising the employees who report to them, first-line managers' activities are not limited to that arena. At a building site, for example, the *project manager* not only ensures that workers are carrying out construction as specified by the architect, but also interacts extensively with materials suppliers, community officials, and middle- and upper-level managers at the home office.

first-line managers Managers responsible for supervising the work of employees

Areas of Management

In any large company, top, middle, and first-line managers work in a variety of areas, including *human resources, operations, marketing, information,* and *finance.* For the most part, these areas correspond to the types of managerial skills described later in this chapter and to the wide range of business principles and activities discussed in the rest of this book.

HUMAN RESOURCE MANAGERS Most companies have *human resource managers* who hire and train employees, who evaluate performance, and who determine compensation. At large firms, separate departments deal with recruiting and hiring, wage and salary levels, and labor relations. A smaller firm may have a single department—or a single person—responsible for all human resource activities. (Some key issues in human resource management are discussed in Part 3.)

OPERATIONS MANAGERS As we will see in Chapter 13, the term *operations* refers to the systems by which a firm produces goods and services. Among other duties, operations managers are responsible for production, inventory, and quality control. Manufacturing companies such as Texas Instruments, Ford, and Caterpillar have a strong need for operations managers at many levels. Such firms typically have a *vice president for operations* (top), *plant managers* (middle), and *production supervisors* (first-line managers). In recent years, sound operations management practices have become increasingly important to a variety of service organizations. (Operations management is examined more fully in Part 5.)

MARKETING MANAGERS As we will see in Chapter 10, *marketing* encompasses the development, pricing, promotion, and distribution of goods and services. *Marketing managers* are responsible for getting products from producers to consumers. Marketing is especially important for firms that manufacture consumer products, such as Procter & Gamble, Coca-Cola, and Levi Strauss. Such firms often have large numbers of marketing managers at several levels. For example, a large consumer products firm is likely to have a *vice president for marketing* (top), several *regional marketing managers* (middle), and several *district sales managers* (first-line managers). (The different areas of marketing are discussed in Part 4.)

INFORMATION MANAGERS Occupying a fairly new managerial position in many firms, information managers design and implement systems to gather, organize, and distribute information. Huge increases in both the sheer volume of information and the ability to manage it have led to the emergence of this important function.

Although relatively few in number, the ranks of *information managers* are growing at all levels. Some firms have a top-management position called a *chief information officer*. Middle managers help design information systems for divisions or plants. Computer systems managers within smaller businesses are usually first-line managers. (Information management is discussed in more detail in Chapter 14.)

FINANCIAL MANAGERS Nearly every company has *financial managers* to plan and oversee its accounting functions and financial resources. Levels of financial management may include *chief financial officer (CFO)* or *vice president for finance* (top), a *division controller* (middle), and an *accounting supervisor* (first-line manager). Some institutions—NationsBank and Prudential, for example—have even made effective financial manage-

Operations managers organize work, design jobs, measure performance, control quality, and schedule work. At Boeing, the result is a tangible product, such as a 777 jet aircraft. This 14,000-pound section, which houses the lower cargo hold and the economy passenger section, is the product of coordinated operations processes being carried out in more than a dozen countries.

ment the company's reason for being. (Financial management is treated in more detail in Part 6.)

OTHER MANAGERS Some firms also employ other specialized managers. Many companies, for example, have public relations managers. Chemical and pharmaceutical companies such as Monsanto and Merck have research and development managers. The range of possibilities is wide, and the areas of management are limited only by the needs and imagination of the firm.

BASIC MANAGEMENT SKILLS

Although the range of managerial positions is almost limitless, the success that people enjoy in those positions is often limited by their skills and abilities. Effective managers must develop *technical*, *human relations*, *conceptual*, *decision-making*, and *time management skills*.

Technical Skills

The skills needed to perform specialized tasks are called **technical skills.** A secretary's ability to type, an animator's ability to draw, and an accountant's ability to audit a company's records are all examples of technical skills. People develop technical skills through a combination of education and experience. Technical skills are especially important for first-line managers. Most of these managers spend considerable time helping employees solve work-related problems, training them in more efficient procedures, and monitoring performance.

technical skills Skills needed to perform specialized tasks

Human Relations Skills

A few years ago, Hyatt Hotels checked 379 corporate employees into the chain's 98 hotels. They were not, however, treated as guests. Rather, they were asked to make beds, carry luggage, and perform the other tasks necessary to make a big hotel function. Top management at Hyatt believes that learning more about the work of lower-level employees will allow executives to understand them better as human beings (and coworkers).

The Hyatt experiment was designed to test and improve the **human relations skills** of upper-level managers, specifically, skills in understanding and getting along with other people. A manager with poor human relations skills may have trouble getting along with subordinates, cause valuable employees to quit or transfer, and contribute to poor morale.

human relations skills Skills in understanding and getting along with people

Although human relations skills are important at all levels, they are probably most important for middle managers, who must often act as bridges between top managers, first-line managers, and managers from other areas of the organization. Managers should possess good communication skills. Many managers have found that being able to understand others, and to get them to understand, can go far toward maintaining good relations in an organization.

Conceptual Skills

Conceptual skills refer to a person's ability to think in the abstract, to diagnose and analyze different situations, and to see beyond the present situation. Conceptual skills help managers recognize new market opportunities (and threats). They can also help managers analyze the probable outcomes of their decisions. The need for conceptual skills differs at various management levels: Top managers depend most on conceptual skills, first-line managers least. Although the purposes and everyday needs of various jobs differ, conceptual skills are needed in almost any job-related activity.

conceptual skills Abilities to think in the abstract, diagnose and analyze different situations, and see beyond the present situation

FIGURE 5.3 ◆ **The Decision-Making Process**

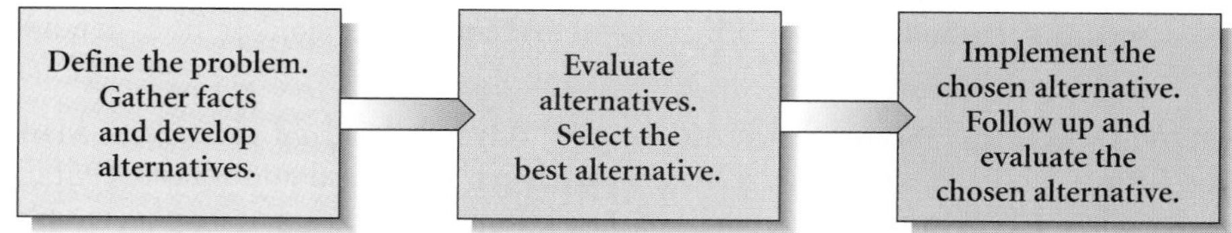

Decision-Making Skills

decision-making skills Skills in defining problems and selecting the best courses of action

Decision-making skills include the ability to define problems and select the best course of action. Figure 5.3 illustrates the basic steps in decision making.

1. *Define the problem, gather facts, and identify alternative solutions.* Current managers at bicycle maker Schwinn, for instance, realized that their predecessors had made some serious errors in assuming that mountain bikes were just a fad. The opposite had proved to be true, and Schwinn's share of the bicycle market had dropped dramatically.
2. *Evaluate each alternative and select the best one.* Managers at Schwinn acknowledged that they had to take corrective action. They discussed such alternatives as buying a mountain bike maker, launching their own line of mountain bikes, or refocusing on other product lines. They chose to develop their own line of mountain bikes and did so in 1994.
3. *Implement the chosen alternative, periodically following up and evaluating the effectiveness of that choice.* Schwinn's actions turned out to be right on track—the firm's revenues began to increase steadily after its first mountain bikes went on the market. At first, true mountain bike enthusiasts were wary of the new products because they still associated Schwinn with recreational bicycles for casual or occasional riders; but after

TRENDS AND CHALLENGES

WHAT'S YOUR EMOTIONAL INTELLIGENCE QUOTIENT?

The stock price was rising, but not quite fast enough for impatient investors. Unfortunately, although financial analysts *liked* the company, they didn't *love* it. There was too much fat in the operation, analysts told the CEO. If investors wanted a spectacular run-up, expenses would have to be slashed.

The CEO had the man for the job. As president of a Midwest subsidiary, Tim Jones had managed to submit bare-bones budgets and record-stunning profits year after year. Within months of arriving at headquarters, he had become cost-cutter par excellence for the whole company. Analysts took notice, and the stock price climbed to a new high.

Unfortunately, Jones's "financial miracle" took a severe organizational toll. Pursuing a ruthless, take-no-prisoners battle plan, he yelled at subordinates in front of others, refused to listen to dissenting views, disdained teamwork, and made few allies and no friends. No one wanted to work for him, and valued employees left in droves.

Within a year, Jones himself was asked to leave despite his extraordinary performance and the expectation that he would be the next CEO. He would go no further, he was informed, because of his poor "people skills." In the process of improving the numbers, he had devastated the workforce.

To psychologist Daniel Goleman, author of *Working with Emotional Intelligence*, Jones failed because he lacked *emotional intelligence (EI)*—the ability to master your own emotions and handle relationships. EI is demonstrated through such competencies as adaptability, self-control, empathy, effective communication and conflict management, cooperation, and teamwork. IQ, argues Goleman, "does not determine who succeeds and who fails" in business. It is emotional intelligence that makes the difference. Goleman points out that when IQ test scores are correlated with career performance, clearly technical skill is necessary to get a job, but not sufficient to propel you up the management ladder. EI, Goleman concludes, "carries much more weight than IQ" in predicting the most effective and successful managers.

Of course, people with limited emotional intelligence are part of every organization. Consider the following examples.

a few professional mountain bike racers started using Schwinn bikes, these concerns evaporated. Today Schwinn is once again a preeminent company in every market where it competes.

time management skills Skills associated with the productive use of time

Time Management Skills

Time management skills refer to the productive use that managers make of their time. In one recent year, for example, General Electric CEO Jack Welch was paid $6.3 million in salary. Assuming that he worked 50 hours a week and took 2 weeks' vacation, Welch earned $2,520 an hour—about $42 per minute. Any amount of time that Welch wastes clearly represents a large cost to GE and its stockholders. Most managers, of course, receive much smaller salaries than Welch. Their time, however, is valuable, and poor use of it still translates into costs and wasted productivity.

To manage time effectively, managers must address four leading causes of wasted time:

- *Paperwork.* Some managers spend too much time deciding what to do with letters and reports. Most documents of this sort are routine and can be handled quickly. Managers must learn to recognize those documents that require more attention.
- *The telephone.* Experts estimate that managers get interrupted by the telephone every 5 minutes. To manage this time more effectively, they suggest having a secretary screen all calls and setting aside a certain block of time each day to return the important ones.
- *Meetings.* Many managers spend as much as 4 hours a day in meetings. To help keep this time productive, the person handling the meeting should specify a clear agenda, start on time, keep everyone focused on the agenda, and end on time.
- *E-mail.* Increasingly, of course, more and more managers are also relying heavily on e-mail and other forms of electronic communication. Like memos and telephone calls, many e-mail messages are not particularly important; some are even trivial. As a result,

Decision making can be an expensive proposition. What manager wouldn't like to test the impact of a decision before bringing it to the real world? Enter virtual management. The Emergent Solutions Group, a part of PricewaterhouseCoopers, is building a computer program that can model certain aspects of consumer behavior. Macy's, the retailing giant, is one client looking to test the virtual waters before diving into the real decision making. Among the key questions that Macy's wants the software to help answer: How do we turn browsers into shoppers?

- A computer programmer who focuses on manipulating software and machines rather than giving clients what they want and need
- An account executive who is reluctant to delegate responsibility to his assistant, thereby making her question whether she's good enough for the job
- An accountant who prefers to work alone rather than as part of a team

> "**Emotional intelligence is the underlying premise for all management training.**"
>
> —Linda Keegan
> *VP for Executive Development, Citibank*

EI, Goleman contends, is more important today than ever before. "In the new, stripped-down every-job-counts business climate, human realities will matter more than ever. Massive change is a constant; technological innovations, global competition, and the pressures of institutional investors are ever-escalating forces for flux. People desperately [feel] the need for connection, for empathy, for open communication." Those who master EI are better managers and, thus, better at generating profits. That's why, says Linda Keegan, VP for executive development, "emotional intelligence is the underlying premise for all management training" at Citibank.

Unlike IQ, which changes little after adolescence, EI can be learned. "It continues to develop as we go through life and learn from our experiences," explains Goleman. "People get better and better in these capabilities as they grow more adept at handling their own emotions and impulses, at motivating themselves, and at honing their empathy and social adroitness." But EI, warns Goleman, is not the same thing as "being nice" all the time. Nor does it require an I-feel-your-pain management style. At times, direct, hard-nosed confrontations are necessary and no alternative is available but to demand results.

time is wasted when managers have to sort through a variety of electronic folders, in baskets, and archives. As the average number of electronic messages grows, the potential time wasted also increases.

Plugged in and ready to travel, Shelly Shope, who works for a pharmaceutical company, waits at Chicago's O'Hare airport for her flight to England. With the rapid growth of communications tools—modems, e-mail, faxes—global businesspeople don't miss a beat. Time zones and national boundaries don't slow down business anymore.

Management Skills for the Twenty-First Century

Although the skills discussed in this chapter have long been an important part of every successful manager's career, new skill requirements continue to emerge. As we enter the twenty-first century, most experts point to the growing importance of skills involving *global management* and *technology*.

GLOBAL MANAGEMENT SKILLS Tomorrow's managers must equip themselves with the special tools, techniques, and skills necessary to compete in a global environment. They will need to understand foreign markets, cultural differences, and the motives and practices of foreign rivals.

On a more practical level, businesses will need managers who are capable of understanding international operations. In the past, most U.S. businesses hired local managers to run their operations in the various countries in which they operated. More recently, however, the trend has been to transfer U.S. managers to foreign locations. This practice helps firms better transfer their corporate cultures to foreign operations. In addition, foreign assignments help managers become better prepared for international competition as they advance within the organization. General Motors now has almost 500 U.S. managers in foreign posts.

MANAGEMENT AND TECHNOLOGY SKILLS Another significant issue facing tomorrow's managers is technology, especially as it relates to communication. Managers have always had to deal with information. In today's world, however, the amount of information has reached staggering proportions. In the United States alone, for example, there are already 28 million electronic mailboxes. New forms of technology have added to a manager's ability to process information while simultaneously making it even more important to organize and interpret an ever-increasing wealth of input.

Technology has also begun to change the way the interaction of managers shapes corporate structures. Computer networking, for example, exists because it is no longer too expensive to put a computer on virtually every desk in the company. In turn, this elaborate network controls the flow of the firm's lifeblood—information. This information no longer flows strictly up and down through hierarchies. It now flows to everyone simultaneously. As a result, decisions are made more quickly, and more people are directly involved. With e-mail, teleconferencing, and other forms of communication, neither time nor distance—nor such corporate "boundaries" as departments and divisions—can prevent people from working more closely together. More than ever, bureaucracies are breaking down, while planning, decision making, and other activities are beginning to benefit from group building and teamwork.

Bill Raduchel, chief information officer of Sun Microsystems, goes so far as to say that "e-mail is a major cultural event—it changes the way you run the organization." But of course, as noted earlier, managers must also work to use information technology wisely and efficiently.

> **"E-mail is a major cultural event—it changes the way you run the organization."**
>
> —Bill Raduchel
> *Chief Information Officer of Sun Microsystems*

■ MANAGEMENT AND THE CORPORATE CULTURE

Consider the following story about the way in which one company set about creating a unique working environment for its employees.

Empower Training & Consultants is a computer training, applications development, and Internet instruction firm based in Kansas City. It has been highly successful, growing rapidly in recent years and returning significant profits to its owners. One key to Empower's success is its unique and off-the-wall work environment. CEO Michael May, for example, stresses that a key business goal is for all Empower associates to have fun at what they do. May himself has a fun-loving attitude and a personality that allows him to be highly motivated and goal oriented, but to never be *too* serious about himself or anyone else. He encourages his training director to dress up as the "Sparkle Fairy" and remind everyone else that top performers sparkle by anointing them with glitter. When he takes prospective employees out to dinner, May tends to be suspicious of those who decline to order dessert—he sees eating dessert as fun and values those who enjoy it. He plays Frank Sinatra's "Young at Heart" at meetings, and the firm's official "Cookie and Bagel/Doughnut Policy" is three times longer than its mission statement; anyone uttering the words *employee, boss,* or *manager* is fined $5. Empower associates are paid above-average salaries, and virtually everyone gets stock options and bonuses tied to the firm's performance. They all believe that they are on the same team and that they are all working for the same things.[7]

Not surprisingly, this setting contrasts starkly with that of, say, Exxon, the nation's largest oil company. Employees at Exxon work in relatively austere surroundings, wear formal business attire, and maintain fairly regimented work schedules. Both Empower and Exxon are each quite successful in their respective industries, but they differ significantly in at least one obvious respect. Just as every individual has a unique personality, so every company has a unique identity, called **corporate culture:** the shared experiences, stories, beliefs, and norms that characterize an organization.

corporate culture The shared experiences, stories, beliefs, and norms that characterize an organization

A strong corporate culture serves several purposes:

- It directs employees' efforts and helps everyone work toward the same goals.
- It helps newcomers learn accepted behaviors.
- It gives each organization its own identity, much as personalities give identity to people.

Communicating the Culture and Managing Change

Corporate culture influences management philosophy, style, and behavior. Managers, therefore, must carefully consider the kind of culture they want for their organization, then work to nourish that culture by communicating with everyone who works there. Wal-Mart, for example, is acutely conscious of the need to spread the message of its culture as it opens new stores in new areas. One of the company's methods is to regularly assign veteran managers to lead employees in new territories.

COMMUNICATING THE CULTURE To use its culture to a firm's advantage, managers must accomplish several tasks, all of which hinge on effective communication:

- Managers must have a clear understanding of the culture.
- Managers must transmit the culture to others in the organization. Communication is thus one aim in training and orienting newcomers. A clear and meaningful statement of the organization's mission is also a valuable communication tool.
- Managers can maintain the culture by rewarding and promoting those who understand it and work toward maintaining it.

MANAGING CHANGE Not surprisingly, organizations must sometimes change their cultures. In such cases, they must also communicate the nature of the change to both employees and customers. According to the CEOs of several companies that have undergone radical change in the last decade or so, the process usually goes through three stages:

1. *At the highest level, analysis of the company's environment highlights extensive change as the most effective response to its problems.* This period is typically characterized by conflict and resistance.
2. *Top management begins to formulate a vision of a new company.* Whatever that vision, it must include renewed focus on the activities of competitors and the needs of customers.
3. *The firm sets up new systems for appraising and compensating employees that enforce its new values.* The purpose is to give the new culture solid shape from within the firm.

Continued from page 107

Management by Posting Pictures

When 3Com Corp. acquired U.S. Robotics, it became a more diverse company—one with all the advantages and problems that diversity brings. Management's success in handling the diversity of nearly 13,000 employees, many of whom worked in fast moving, complex factory environments, would affect productivity.

At 3Com's Morton Grove, Illinois, modem plant, 1,200 people claim 65 different nationalities and speak more than 20 languages. The vast majority are immigrants who speak little English and know almost nothing about American culture. Saying "please," for example, especially to a subordinate, is something many workers simply do not do.

More importantly, operations managers teach job specifics by relying on the universal language of pictures to explain the work. At one workstation, a drawing shows a 23-year-old Philippine worker how to connect a printed circuit board that will eventually plug into a computer. Clear diagrams break the task into manageable steps. According to Mary Ellen Smith, 3Com director of manufacturing, "we keep as much simplicity in the process that we can. The key is that anyone can come in and do that job."

Although 3Com helps employees master their jobs, the company accommodates few cultural idiosyncrasies and expects everyone to learn. "They're here because they want to be here," says Tom Werner, manufacturing VP at 3Com's two Chicago-area plants. Because we all "start from that assumption, we can get things done."

"We keep as much simplicity in the process that we can. The key is that anyone can come in and do that job."

—Mary Ellen Smith
Director of Manufacturing, 3Com

Questions for Discussion

1. Identify Eric Benhamou's strategic goals for 3Com.
2. In the CEO's attempt to turn the company around, how would you describe the internal and external environmental threats that he faced? Which do you think posed the greatest challenge to the company's survival?
3. How would you evaluate Benhamou's decision-making ability?
4. In a tight job environment, why are operations managers in many firms likely to encounter language and cultural problems such as those faced by the managers at 3Com's Morton Grove plant? How would you evaluate the way Morton Grove managers are handling these problems?
5. Why is any corporate merger, such as the one between 3Com and U.S. Robotics, likely to disrupt the corporate culture?

SUMMARY

1. **Explain the importance of setting *goals* and formulating *strategies* as the starting points of effective management.** *Goals*—the performance targets of an organization—can be *long term, intermediate*, or *short term.* They provide direction for managers, help managers decide how to allocate limited resources, define the corporate culture, and help managers assess performance. Strategies—the methods that a company uses to meet its stated goals—involve three major activities: setting strategic goals, analyzing the organization and its environment, and matching the organization and its environment. These strategies are translated into *strategic, tactical,* and *operational* plans.

2. **Describe the four activities that constitute the *management process.*** *Management* is the process of planning, organizing, directing, and controlling an organization's financial, physical, human, and information resources to achieve the organization's goals. *Planning* means determining what the company needs to do and how best to get it done. *Organizing* means determining how best to arrange a business's resources and the necessary jobs into an overall structure. *Directing* means guiding and motivating employees to meet the firm's objectives. *Controlling* means monitoring the firm's performance to ensure that it is meeting its goals.

3. **Identify *types of managers* by level and area.** Managers can be differentiated in two ways: by level and by area. By level, *top managers* set policies, formulate strategies, and approve decisions. *Middle managers* implement strategies, policies, and decisions. *First-line managers* usually work with and directly supervise employees. Areas of management include human resources, operations, marketing, information, and finance. Managers at all levels may be found in every area of a company.

4. **Describe the five basic *management skills*.** Most managers agree that five basic management skills are necessary for success. *Technical skills* are associated with performing specialized tasks. *Human relations skills* are associated with understanding and getting along with other people. *Conceptual skills* are the abilities to think in the abstract, to diagnose and analyze different situations, and to see beyond present circumstances. *Decision-making skills* allow managers to define problems and to select the best course of action. *Time management skills* refer to the productive use that managers make of their time.

5. **Explain the importance of *corporate culture*.** A strong, well-defined culture can help a business reach its goals and can influence management styles. In addition to having a clear understanding of *corporate culture*, managers must be able to communicate it effectively to others. Communication is especially important when organizations find it necessary to make changes in the culture. Top management must establish new values that reflect a vision of a new company, and these values must play a role in appraising and compensating employee performance.

QUESTIONS AND EXERCISES

Questions for Review

1. What are the four main purposes of setting goals in an organization?
2. Identify and explain the three basic steps in strategy formulation.
3. Relate the five basic management skills to the four activities in the management process. For example, which skills are most important in leading?
4. What is corporate culture? How is it formed? How is it sustained?

Questions for Analysis

5. Select any group of which you are a member (your company, your family, or a club or organization, for example). Explain how planning, organizing, directing, and controlling are practiced in that group.
6. Identify managers by level and area at your school, college, or university.
7. In what kind of company would the technical skills of top managers be more important than human relations or conceptual skills? Are there organizations in which conceptual skills are not important?
8. How well do you manage your own time? What activities or habits waste your time?

Application Exercises

9. Interview the manager at any level of a local company. Identify that manager's job according to level and area. Show how planning, organizing, directing, and controlling are part of this person's job. Inquire about the manager's education and work experience. Which management skills are most important for this manager's job?
10. Compare and contrast the corporate cultures of two companies that do business in most communities. Be sure to choose two companies in the same industry—for example, a Sears department store and a Wal-Mart discount store.

BUILDING YOUR BUSINESS SKILLS

SKILLFUL TALKING

This exercise enhances the following SCANS workplace competencies: demonstrating basic skills, demonstrating thinking skills, exhibiting interpersonal skills, and working with information.

▼ GOAL

To encourage students to appreciate effective speaking as a critical human relations skill.

▼ BACKGROUND

A manager's ability to understand and get along with supervisors, peers, and subordinates is a critical human relations skill. At the heart of this skill, says Harvard University professor of education Sarah McGinty, is the ability to speak with power and control. McGinty defines "powerful speech" in terms of the following characteristics:

- The ability to speak at length and in complete sentences
- The ability to set a conversational agenda
- The ability to deter interruptions
- The ability to argue openly and to express strong opinions about ideas, not people
- The ability to make statements that offer solutions rather than pose questions
- The ability to express humor

Taken together, says McGinty, "all this creates a sense of confidence in listeners."

▼ METHOD

STEP 1

Working alone, compare your own personal speaking style with McGinty's description of powerful speech by taping yourself as you speak during a meeting with classmates or during a phone conversation. (Tape both sides of the conversation only if the person to whom you are speaking gives permission.) Listen for the following problems:

- Unfinished sentences
- An absence of solutions
- Too many disclaimers ("I'm not sure I have enough information to say this, but . . .")
- The habit of seeking support from others instead of making definitive statements of personal conviction (saying, "I recommend consolidating the medical and fitness functions," instead of, "As Emily stated in her report, I recommend consolidating the medical and fitness functions")
- Language fillers (saying, "you know," "like," and "um" when you are unsure of your facts or uneasy about expressing your opinion)

STEP 2

Join with three or four other classmates to evaluate each other's speaking styles. Finally:

- Have a 10-minute group discussion on the importance of human relations skills in business.
- Listen to other group members and take notes on the "power" content of what you hear.
- Offer constructive criticism by focusing on what speakers say rather than on personal characteristics (say, "Bob, you sympathized with Paul's position, but I still don't know what *you* think," instead of, "Bob, you sounded like a weakling").

▼ FOLLOW-UP

1. How do you think the power content of speech affects a manager's ability to communicate? Evaluate some of the ways in which effects may differ among supervisors, peers, and subordinates.

(continued)

2. How do you evaluate yourself and group members in terms of powerful and powerless speech? List the strengths and weaknesses of the group.
3. Do you agree or disagree with McGinty that business success depends on gaining insight into your own language habits? Explain your answer.
4. In our age of computers and e-mail, why do you think personal presentation continues to be important in management?
5. McGinty believes that power language differs from company to company and that it is linked to the corporate culture. Do you agree, or do you believe that people express themselves in similar ways no matter where they are?

CRAFTING YOUR BUSINESS PLAN

MANAGING THE BUSINESS ENTERPRISE

▼ THE PURPOSE OF THE ASSIGNMENT

1. To acquaint students with the process of navigating the *Business PlanPro* (BPP) software package.
2. To familiarize students with management-related issues that a firm must address in developing its business plan.
3. To demonstrate how three chapter topics—business goals, business strategies, and management skills—can be integrated as components in the *BPP* planning environment.

▼ ASSIGNMENT

After reading Chapter 5 in the textbook, open the *BPP* software* and look around for information about business goals, business strategies, and management skills as they apply to a sample firm: *Furniture Manufacturer* (Willamette Furniture). Then respond to the following questions:

1. Evaluate Willamette's business objectives. Are they clearly stated? Are they measurable? [Sites to see in *BPP* (for this assignment): In the Task Manager screen, click on **Initial Assessment.** Then click on **1. Objectives.**]
2. Evaluate Willamette's mission and strategy statements. Do they state clearly how Willamette intends to achieve its purposes? [Sites to see in *BPP:* In the Task Manager screen, click on **Initial Assessment.** Then click on **2. Mission.** Next click on **Finish and Polish** and then on **1. Strategy and Implementation** and **2. Strategy Pyramids.]**
3. In what areas of the business does each of Willamette's top managers work? [Sites to see in *BPP:* In the Task Manager screen, click on **Your Management Team.** Now click on **2. Organizational Structure** and then on **3. Management Team.**]
4. What management skills areas are lacking in Willamette's management team? Would you classify the missing skills as technical, human resources, conceptual, or decision-making skills? [Sites to see in *BPP:* In the Task Manager screen, click on **Your Management Team.** Then click on **4. Gaps.**]

▼ For Your Own Business Plan

5. Suppose you are ready to develop a "statement of mission" for your firm and to formulate its objectives and strategy. To what extent do you first need a clear picture of your firm's products and customers? In developing your business plan, which will you clarify first—mission/objectives/strategy or products/customers? Explain how your answer will affect your business planning process.

▼ * General Tips for Navigating in BPP

1. Open the *BPP* program, examine the Welcome screen, and click on **Open a Sample Plan.**
2. From the Open a Sample Plan dialogue box, click on a sample company name. Then click on **Open.**
3. On the Task Manager screen, click onto any of the lines (for example, **Your Company**).
4. You can always return to the Task Manager screen by going to the bottom of the screen and clicking on the **Task Manager** icon.
5. When you are finished with a sample company, close its Task Manager screen.
6. After finishing with one sample company, you can get to the next one by going to the top of the screen and clicking on **File** (on the menu bar). Then beneath that, select **Open Sample Plan,** which will exit you from the current company file and send you to the Open a Sample Plan dialogue box, where you can select your next sample company.

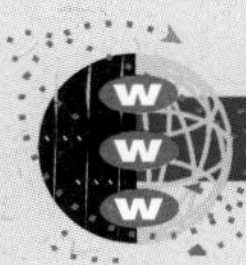

EXPLORING THE NET

DO YOU YAHOO!?

Yahoo! is featured prominently as a running example in this chapter. Visit the Yahoo! Web site at

http://www.yahoo.com

and then consider the following questions:

1. From the standpoint of you as an individual surfing the Internet in your leisure time, which parts of Yahoo! are most and least interesting and relevant to you?
2. Now put yourself in the shoes of the owner–top manager of a relatively small but rapidly growing retail company catering to college-age customers. Which parts of Yahoo! are the most and least interesting and relevant to you?
3. Assume that you are a middle manager at a major corporation such as General Motors. Again, which parts of Yahoo! are the most and least interesting and relevant to you?
4. If you were giving Timothy Koogle suggestions for improving Yahoo!, what would you advise?
5. Managers at Yahoo! are now expanding the company site to countries outside the United States. What changes would be necessary to make Yahoo! popular in, say, Australia? China? Italy?

Organizing the Business Enterprise

The Agony and Ecstasy of Delegating

> **"I was so desperate to sustain the head rush of start-up chaos that I made all the final decisions and didn't let the managers do their jobs."**
>
> —Norm Brodsky
> *Owner of a messenger service*

Imagine that you are a successful small-business owner. After 3 years of working 16 hours a day, you have built your company into a highly profitable entrepreneurial powerhouse. You did everything yourself and did it well—from production to marketing to keeping the books to hiring and firing. Now that the company has grown in sales, profits, and payroll, you have to learn to let go: You must delegate authority and responsibility to top managers that you personally hired.

Easier said than done—or so Richard Louis learned. Although Louis, founder of a growing Internet service business, hired a staff to help him run his company, he insisted on maintaining control over every detail. Unfortunately, he left himself little time for such strategic tasks as analyzing his market. Only after he heard himself asking a competitor for industry news did he realize that he was focusing on the details of day-to-day operations at the expense of effective leadership. "Now," says Louis, "I teach my employees how to do something and let them do it themselves. That way they learn to do it, and I can concentrate on running the business."

Norm Brodsky, a small-business owner who built six successful companies, learned firsthand what happens when the CEO cannot let go. It took Brodsky 7 years to build a messenger service into a $120 million operation—and just 14 months to go from $120 million into bankruptcy. "Where did I go wrong?" he asks rhetorically and provides his own answer: "The company needed management, stability, and structure, and I kept it from getting them. I was so desperate to sustain the head rush of start-up chaos that I made all the final decisions and didn't let the managers do their jobs. In the end I paid a steep price."

Delegating responsibility has been especially difficult for Rene Reiser, owner of Paradise Candles, a three-employee candle manufacturer in Idaho. Reiser believes that it was her personal creative style that built her company. It took her years to develop a specialized production process, and she has found it hard to let others take charge of it. "Eventually," she concedes, "I'll have to teach someone else to do it. It makes me nervous, and I wonder, 'Will they do it in my style?' "

Louis, Brodsky, and Reiser had to change their organizational behavior (and their own) as their companies grew. First, however, they had to admit that they had become *micromanagers*—top managers who cannot seem to share power or control. Experts pinpoint certain symptoms of micromanagement:

- The feeling that employees can never do anything as well as you can
- The fear that something will go wrong if someone else takes over a job
- The lack of time for long-range planning because you are bogged down in day-to-day operations
- The sense of being in the dark about industry trends and competitive products because of the time you devote to day-to-day operations

To overcome the micromanagement compulsion, small-business owners must begin by admitting that they can never go back to running the entire show and that they can in fact prosper—with the help of their employees—if they learn to let go.

For small companies, the organizational issues involved in delegating authority can affect operations and profits in dramatic ways. Whether a company employs 5 people or 50,000, these and other organizational issues determine how—and how well—it will function. In this chapter, we consider the elements of business organization and the basic structures that firms typically use.

By focusing on the learning objectives of this chapter, you will better understand the importance of business organization and the ways in which both formal and informal aspects of its structure affect the decisions that a business makes.

Our opening story is continued on page 143

After reading this chapter, you should be able to:

1. **Discuss the elements that influence a firm's *organizational structure.***
2. **Describe *specialization* and *departmentalization* as the building blocks of organizational structure.**
3. **Distinguish between *responsibility, authority, delegation,* and *accountability,* and explain the differences between decision making in *centralized* and *decentralized organizations.***
4. **Explain the differences between *functional, divisional, matrix,* and *international organizational structures.***
5. **Describe the *informal organization* and discuss *intrapreneuring.***

WHAT IS ORGANIZATIONAL STRUCTURE?

What do we mean by the term *organizational structure?* Consider a simple analogy. In some ways, a business is like an automobile. All cars have engines, four wheels, fenders, and other structural components. They all have passenger compartments, storage areas, and various operating systems (fuel, braking, climate control). Although each component has a distinct purpose, it must also work in accord with the others. In addition, although the ways they look and fit may vary widely, all automobiles have the same basic components. Similarly, all businesses have common structural and operating components, each composed of a series of *jobs to be done* and each with a *specific overall purpose.* From company to company, these components look different and fit together differently, but in every organization, components have the same fundamental purpose—each must perform its own function while working in concert with the others.

Although all organizations feature the same basic elements, each must develop the structure that is most appropriate for it. What works for Texas Instruments will not work for Exxon or the U.S. Department of Justice. The structure of the American Red Cross will probably not work for Union Carbide or the University of Minnesota. We define **organizational structure** as the specification of the jobs to be done within an organization and the ways in which those jobs relate to one another.

organizational structure
Specification of the jobs to be done within an organization and the ways in which they relate to one another

Determinants of Organization

How is an organization's structure determined? Does it happen by chance, or is there some logic that managers use to create structure? Does it develop by some combination of circumstance and strategy? Ideally, managers carefully assess a variety of important factors as they plan for and then create a structure that will allow their organization to function efficiently.

Indeed, many elements work together to determine an organization's structure. Chief among these are the organization's *purpose*, *mission*, and *strategy*. A dynamic and rapidly growing enterprise, for example, achieved that position because of its purpose and successful strategies for achieving it. Such a firm will need a structure that contributes to flexibility and growth. A stable organization with only modest growth will function best with a different structure.

Size, technology, and changes in environmental circumstances also affect structure. A large manufacturer operating in a strongly competitive environment—say, Boeing or Hewlett-Packard—requires a different structure than a local barbershop or video store. Moreover, even after a structure has been created, it is rarely free from tinkering—or even outright re-creation. Indeed, most organizations change their structures on an almost continuing basis.

As we saw in Chapter 5, organizing is a function of managerial planning. As such, it is conducted with an equal awareness of both a firm's external and internal environments. For example, since it was first incorporated in 1903, Ford Motor Co. has undergone literally dozens of major structural changes, hundreds of moderate changes, and thousands of minor changes. In the last decade alone, Ford has initiated several major structural changes. In 1994, the firm announced a major restructuring plan called Ford 2000, which was intended to integrate all of Ford's vast international operations into a single and unified structure by the year 2000. By 1998, however, midway through implementation of the grand plan, top Ford executives announced major modifications, indicating that (1) additional changes would be made, (2) some previously planned changes would not be made, and (3) some recently realigned operations would be changed again. In early 1999, managers announced yet another sweeping set of changes intended to eliminate corporate bureaucracy, speed decision making, and improve communication and working relationships among people at different levels of the organization.[1]

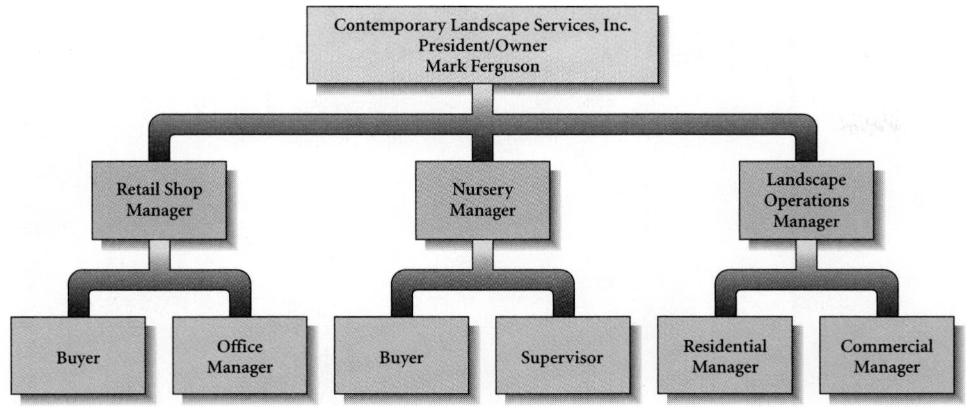

FIGURE 6.1 ◆ **The Organization Chart**

Chain of Command

Most businesses prepare **organization charts** to clarify structure and to show employees where they fit into a firm's operations. Figure 6.1 is an organization chart for Contemporary Landscape Services Inc., a small but thriving business in Bryan, Texas. Each box in the chart represents a job. The solid lines define the **chain of command,** or *reporting relationships*, within the company. For example, the retail shop, nursery, and landscape operations managers all report to the owner and president, Mark Ferguson. Within the landscape operation is one manager for residential accounts and another for commercial accounts. Similarly, there are other managers in the retail shop and the nursery.[2]

organization chart Diagram depicting a company's structure and showing employees where they fit into its operations

chain of command Reporting relationships within a company

The organization charts of large firms are far more complex and include individuals at many more levels than those shown in Figure 6.1. Indeed, size prevents many large firms from drawing charts that include all their managers. Typically, they create one organization chart showing overall corporate structure and separate charts for each division.

THE BUILDING BLOCKS OF ORGANIZATIONAL STRUCTURE

The first step in developing the structure of any business, large or small, involves two activities:

- *Specialization:* determining who will do what
- *Departmentalization:* determining how people performing certain tasks can best be grouped together

These two activities are the building blocks of all business organizations.[3]

Specialization

The process of identifying the specific jobs that need to be done and designating the people who will perform them leads to **job specialization.** In a sense, all organizations have only one major "job," such as making cars (like Ford), selling finished goods to consumers (like Wal-Mart), or providing telecommunications services (like AT&T). Usually, of course, the "job" is more complex in nature; for example, the "job" of Chaparral Steel is converting scrap steel, such as wrecked automobiles, into finished steel products such as beams and reinforcement bars. But to perform this one overall "job," managers actually break it down, or *specialize* it, into several smaller jobs. Thus, some workers transport the scrap steel to the company's mill in Midlothian, Texas. Others operate shredding equipment before turning raw materials over to the workers who then melt them into liquid form. Other specialists oversee the flow of the liquid into molding equipment in which it is transformed into new products. Finally, other workers are responsible for moving finished

job specialization The process of identifying the specific jobs that need to be done and designating the people who will perform them

Whether they are produced manually or digitally, the drawings that comprise a full-length cartoon such as Antz *are the result of highly coordinated job specialization. A lead animator, for example, may provide a rough pencil sketch that is then refined by one or more artists. Other teams scan clean drawings into a computer and color them according to a plan devised by the art director. The process is a far cry from the one pioneered by Walt and Roy Disney, who did virtually everything themselves in the 1930s.*

products to a holding area before they are shipped out to customers. When the overall "job" of the organization is thus broken down, each worker can develop real expertise in his or her job, and employees can better coordinate their work with that done by others.[4]

SPECIALIZATION AND GROWTH In a very small organization, the owner may perform every job. As the firm grows, however, so does the need to specialize jobs so that others can perform them. To see how specialization can evolve in an organization, consider the case of the Walt Disney Co. When Walt Disney first opened his studio, he and his brother Roy did everything. For example, when they created the very first animated feature, *Steamboat Willy*, they wrote the story, drew the pictures, transferred the pictures to film, provided the voices, and then went out and sold the cartoon to theater operators. Today, by sharp contrast, a Disney animated feature is made possible only through the efforts of hundreds of creators. The job of one cartoonist, for example, may be to draw the face of a single character throughout an entire feature. Another artist may be charged with erasing stray pencil marks inadvertently made by other illustrators. People other than artists are responsible for the subsequent operations that turn individual animated cells into a moving picture or for the marketing of the finished product.

Job specialization, then, is a natural part of organizational growth. It also has certain advantages. For example, specialized jobs are learned more easily and can be performed more efficiently than nonspecialized jobs, and it is also easier to replace people who leave an organization. However, jobs at lower levels of the organization are especially susceptible to overspecialization. If such jobs become too narrowly defined, employees may become bored and careless, derive less satisfaction from their jobs, and lose sight of their roles in the organization.

Departmentalization

departmentalization Process of grouping jobs into logical units

profit center Separate company unit responsible for its own costs and profits

After jobs are specialized, they must be grouped into logical units, which is the process of **departmentalization.** Departmentalized companies benefit from the division of activities. Control and coordination are narrowed and made easier, and top managers can see more easily how various units are performing.

For example, departmentalization allows the firm to treat a department as a **profit center**—a separate unit responsible for its own costs and profits. Thus, Sears can calculate the profits it generates from men's clothing, appliances, home furnishings, and every other department within a given store. Managers can then use this information in making decisions about advertising and promotional events, space allocation, and so forth.

The Boeing Co. has recently been obliged to face the fact that its organizational structure in general, and its approach to departmentalization in particular, was hindering its effectiveness. A long and bitter strike by the firm's machinists, for example, exposed a deep rift between the firm and its employees at the same time that its biggest customers were complaining about slow delivery schedules and high prices. Boeing CEO Philip M. Condit concluded that the firm could address such fundamental problems—which, like those of Ford, are both internal and external—only by reorganizing. As a result of restructuring initiatives, Boeing now makes greater use of work teams and gives more authority to workers to make their own decisions for themselves. The giant aircraft maker has also improved communication both up and down the organization and across different areas within it.[5]

Obviously, managers do not departmentalize jobs randomly. They group them logically, according to some common thread or purpose. In general, departmentalization may occur along *customer, product, process, geographic,* or *functional* lines (or any combination of these).

CUSTOMER DEPARTMENTALIZATION Stores such as Sears and Macy's are divided into departments—a men's department, a women's department, a luggage department, and so on. Each department targets a specific customer category (men, women, people who want to buy luggage). **Customer departmentalization** makes shopping easier by providing identifiable store segments. Thus, a customer shopping for a baby's playpen can bypass Lawn and Garden Supplies and head straight for Children's Furniture. Stores can also group products in locations designated for deliveries, special sales, and other service-oriented purposes. In general, the store is more efficient and customers get better service, in part because salespeople tend to specialize and gain expertise in their departments.

customer departmentalization
Departmentalization according to types of customers likely to buy a given product

PRODUCT DEPARTMENTALIZATION Manufacturers and service providers often opt for **product departmentalization**—dividing an organization according to the specific product or service being created. A bank, for example, may handle consumer loans in one department and commercial loans in another. On a larger scale, 3M Corp., which makes both consumer and industrial products, operates different divisions for Post-It tape flags, Scotch-Brite scrub sponges, and the Sarns 9000 perfusion system for open-heart surgery.

product departmentalization
Departmentalization according to specific products being created

PROCESS DEPARTMENTALIZATION Other manufacturers favor **process departmentalization,** in which the organization is divided according to production processes. This principle, for example, is logical for the pickle maker Vlasic, which has separate departments to transform cucumbers into fresh-packed pickles, pickles cured in brine, and relishes. Cucumbers destined to become fresh-packed pickles must be packed into jars immediately, covered with a solution of water and vinegar, and prepared for sale. Those slated for brined pickles must be aged in brine solution before packing. Relish cucumbers must be minced and combined with a host of other ingredients. Each process requires different equipment and worker skills.

process departmentalization
Departmentalization according to production processes used to create a good or service

GEOGRAPHIC DEPARTMENTALIZATION Some firms are divided according to the areas of the country, or the world, that they serve. Levi Strauss, for instance, has one division for the United States, one for Europe, and another for the rest of the world. Within the United States, **geographic departmentalization** is common among utilities. Thus, Pacific Power and Light is organized as four geographic departments—Southwestern, Columbia Basin, Mid-Oregon, and Wyoming.

geographic departmentalization
Departmentalization according to areas served by a business

FUNCTIONAL DEPARTMENTALIZATION Many service and manufacturing companies develop departments according to a group's functions or activities—a form of organization known as **functional departmentalization.** Such firms typically have production, marketing and sales, human resource, and accounting and finance departments. Departments may be further subdivided. For example, the marketing department might be divided geographically or into separate staffs for market research and advertising.

functional departmentalization
Departmentalization according to groups' functions or activities

Because different forms of departmentalization have different advantages, larger companies tend to adopt different types of departmentalization for various levels. For example,

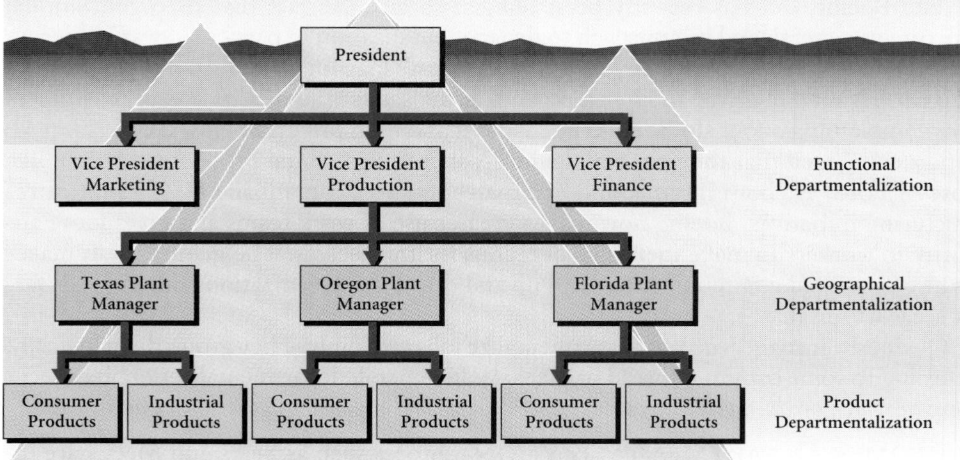

FIGURE 6.2 ◆ Multiple Forms of Departmentalization

the company illustrated in Figure 6.2 uses functional departmentalization at the top level. At the middle level, production is divided along geographic lines. At a lower level, marketing is departmentalized by product group.

Process Organization

In recent years, many companies have begun to realize that functional organization often lends itself to a sharper focus on customer needs. In May 1994, for example, CEO Lou Gerstner announced a sweeping reorganization of IBM's marketing and sales structure. The changes achieved a shift from geographic departmentalization to an organization based on customer industries. Previously, top sales managers reported to the heads of regional areas (say, New England) or countries (IBM Germany). Under the reorganization they report to the heads of 14 newly formed industry groups—groups focused on customers engaged in banking, retailing, insurance, and so forth. Gerstner's foremost goal is to make top sales executives more customer oriented by making them more knowledgeable about the industries they serve. So far, Gerstner's efforts have paid off handsomely. Restructuring has led to substantially lower costs, a smaller and trimmer workforce, a shake-up in the firm's entrenched corporate mindset, a new focus on innovation, and a big boost in customer service. Since the new plan was announced in 1994, IBM's revenues have increased from just over $64 billion to almost $79 billion, and profits have more than doubled.[6]

IBM's reorganization plan has other advantages. Several management layers, for example, have been eliminated. Moreover, less power is vested with top executives in far-flung countries and more power centralized at U.S. headquarters. In similar efforts to streamline decision making and to work more directly with customers, more companies have begun to use variations of functional organization. One variation is organizing according to units, or teams, responsible for *all* the various *processes* involved in getting products to consumers. The most important feature of this system is its marketing and customer orientation.

■ ESTABLISHING THE DECISION-MAKING HIERARCHY

Like most Japanese organizations, Toyota has a long history of maintaining a tall, hierarchical, and mechanistic organization structure. Much of what managers did in the firm was governed by detailed rules, regulations, and procedures. Almost every decision had to follow a rigid chain of command up and down the organization. Indeed, taking a problem to someone higher up than one's immediate supervisor was grounds for dismissal. Although this structure kept the firm efficient and its costs low, it also resulted in snail's-pace decision making and stifled individual creativity and initiative.

When Hiroshi Okuda was appointed president, he decided to shake things up. Specifically, he decided that if Toyota was to remain competitive in the global automobile industry, it needed to make decisions more quickly and to operate with more flexibility. Accordingly, he eliminated several layers of managerial bureaucracy, discarded volumes of antiquated rules and regulations, and gave more decision-making authority to operations managers on the front lines. The message at Toyota, reports one upper-level manager, "is speed, speed, speed." (Okuda did add one rule: It is now okay to discuss problems with anyone in the organization who might be able to help solve it.)[7]

> "The message is speed, speed, speed."
> —*Upper-level manager at Toyota*

Although Hiroshi Okuda actually addressed several different issues at Toyota, perhaps the most fundamental issue involved decision making. Specifically, he was focusing on a major question that must be asked about any organization: *Who makes which decisions?* The answer almost never focuses on an individual or even on a small group. The more accurate answer usually refers to the decision-making hierarchy. The development of this hierarchy generally results from a three-step process:

1. *Assigning tasks:* determining who can make decisions and specifying how they should be made
2. *Performing tasks:* implementing decisions that have been made
3. *Distributing authority:* determining whether the organization is to be centralized or decentralized

Assigning Tasks: Responsibility and Authority

The question of who is *supposed* to do what and who is *entitled* to do what in an organization is complex. In any company with more than one person, individuals must work out agreements about responsibilities and authority. **Responsibility** is the duty to perform an assigned task. **Authority** is the power to make the decisions necessary to complete the task.

responsibility Duty to perform an assigned task

authority Power to make the decisions necessary to complete a task

For example, imagine a mid-level buyer for Macy's department store who encounters an unexpected opportunity to make a large purchase at an extremely good price. Assume that an immediate decision is absolutely necessary—a decision that this buyer has no authority to make without confirmation from above. The company's policies on delegation and authority are inconsistent, because the buyer is *responsible* for purchasing the clothes that will be sold in the upcoming season but lacks the *authority* to make the needed purchases.

Performing Tasks: Delegation and Accountability

Trouble occurs when appropriate levels of responsibility and authority are not clearly delineated in the working relationships between managers and subordinates. Here, the issues become delegation and accountability. **Delegation** begins when a manager assigns a task to a subordinate. **Accountability** falls to the subordinate, who must then complete the task. If the subordinate does not perform the assigned task properly and promptly, he or she may be reprimanded or punished, possibly even dismissed.

delegation Assignment of a task, responsibility, or authority by a manager to a subordinate

accountability Liability of subordinates for accomplishing tasks assigned by managers

Distributing Authority: Centralization and Decentralization

Delegation involves a specific relationship between managers and subordinates. Most businesses must also make decisions about general patterns of authority throughout the company. This pattern may be largely centralized or decentralized (or, usually, somewhere in between).

centralized organization Organization in which most decision-making authority is held by upper-level management

In a **centralized organization,** most decision-making authority is held by upper-level managers. Most lower-level decisions must be approved by upper management before they can be implemented. McDonald's, for example, practices centralization as a way to maintain standardization. At Dillard's department stores, a $2.7 billion family-run chain based in Little Rock, Arkansas, family management still insists on tight cost controls and the centralized administration of everything from payroll to buying. Indeed, owner-operated companies frequently have presidents or CEOs who make most of their decisions. Centralized authority is also typical of small businesses.

decentralized organization Organization in which a great deal of decision-making authority is delegated to levels of management at points below the top

As a company gets larger, increasingly more decisions must be made; thus, the company tends to adopt a more decentralized pattern. In a **decentralized organization,** much decision-making authority is delegated to levels of management at various points below the top. The purpose of decentralization is to make a company more responsive to its environment by breaking it into more manageable units, ranging from product lines to independent businesses. Reducing top-heavy bureaucracies is also a common goal.

span of control Number of people supervised by one manager

SPAN OF CONTROL The distribution of authority in an organization also affects the number of people who work for any individual manager. The number of people managed by one supervisor is called the manager's **span of control** and depends on many factors. Employees' abilities and the supervisor's managerial skills help determine whether span of control is wide or narrow, as do the similarity and simplicity of tasks performed under the manager's supervision and the extent to which they are interrelated.[8]

In general, span of control and decentralization are often interrelated. For example, if lower-level managers are given *more* decision-making authority, their supervisors will thus have *less* work to do because some of the decisions they previously made will be transferred to their subordinates. By the same token, these managers may then be able to oversee and coordinate the work of more subordinates, resulting in an increased span of control. When the changes previously described were implemented at Toyota, senior managers saw their spans of control increase from between 5 and 7 to 10 and 12 employees each.

TRENDS AND CHALLENGES

STAR TRACKING: THE NEXT GENERATION

Who will take over when the CEO retires? Top executives and corporate boards often spend months or sometimes years deciding who's going to be the next boss. No one is arguing the wisdom and importance of this decision, because every company needs a qualified leader with future vision. Some experts, however, think too many search committees set themselves targets that are too narrow. They maintain that focusing the succession decision on the CEO alone overlooks the critical fact that corporate success depends on succession planning for a management *team.*

Broad-based succession planning starts with asking hard questions. Who will take charge of developing new technologies if the head of management information systems leaves the company? What will happen to advertising and promotion strategies if the head of marketing gets a better offer somewhere else? Who will be responsible for compensation and benefits management if the department's senior vice president takes early retirement? When high-level people leave companies unexpectedly, there may be no one in the wings to fill their shoes.

According to John Beeson, a principal of Korn Beeson Consulting in Overland Park, Kansas, the situation has gotten worse in the last decade. He contends that "downsizing, reengineering, reduced organizational levels, broadened spans of managerial control are challenging the traditional succession planning and executive development practices" that have been in place since the mid-1970s. Downsizing has thinned managerial ranks and forced companies to slot key people in narrow positions that limit their experience. With fewer organizational levels and broader spans of control, it is safer to assign "up-and-coming" talent to a single organizational area rather than challenge their abilities in a succession of new areas. "The risks of non-performance," concludes Beeson, "have become too high for the firm and the individual."

Companies that have recognized the hazards of this practice are now rotating high-potential people across various functions. "Context is the most important thing" during these rotations, says Morgan W. McCall, an authority on corporate leadership development. "Training has to be relevant, and you have to stay there long enough to live with the consequences of your actions.

Similarly, when several employees perform either the same simple task or a group of interrelated tasks, a wide span of control is possible and often desirable. For instance, because all the jobs are routine, one supervisor may well control an entire assembly line. Moreover, each task depends on another. If one station stops, everyone stops. Having one supervisor ensures that all stations receive equal attention and function equally well.

In contrast, when jobs are more diversified or prone to change, a narrow span of control is preferable. For example, the fully automated Kellogg plant in Battle Creek, Michigan, produces breakfast cereals. Some machines process and mix ingredients, others sort and package. Although workers are highly skilled operators of their particular machines, each machine is different. In this kind of setup, the complexities of each machine and the advanced skills needed by each operator mean that one supervisor can oversee only a small number of employees.

Three Forms of Authority

Whatever type of structure a company develops it must decide who will have authority over whom. As individuals are delegated responsibility and authority in a firm, a complex web of interactions develops. These interactions may take one of three forms of authority: *line*, *staff*, or *committee* and *team*. In reality, like departmentalization, all three forms may be found in a given company, especially a large one.

LINE AUTHORITY The type of authority that flows up and down the chain of command is **line authority.** Most companies rely heavily on **line departments**—those directly linked to the production and sales of specific products. For example, Clark Equipment Corp. has a division that produces forklifts and small earthmovers. In this division, line departments include purchasing, materials handling, fabrication, painting, and assembly (all of which are directly linked to production) along with sales and distribution (both of which are directly linked to sales).

Each line department is essential to an organization's success. Line employees are the doers and producers in a company. If any line department fails to complete its task, the

line authority Organizational structure in which authority flows in a direct chain of command from the top of the company to the bottom

line department Department directly linked to the production and sales of a specific product

> **"The risks of non-performance have become too high for the firm and the individual."**
>
> —John Beeson
> *Principal of Korn Beeson Consulting*

Spending six months in England on a staff assignment is a far cry from doing a three-year start-up in China."

What else can a company do to increase the number of managers who are ultimately qualified for top jobs? Among the best practices used by companies that are known for the depth of their management teams are the following:

- Early identification and monitoring of promising talent throughout the company. "Stars" receive assignments that develop their skills and are mentored by high-level managers.
- Careful planning of developmental assignments entailing profit-and-loss responsibility and start-up and cross-functional team leadership experience.
- Frequent, high-level executive talent reviews that examine performance, potential, and developmental needs of key employees.

In addition, as the internal and external environments of corporations change, succession planning must shift its focus from current to future needs. For example, if a company decentralizes, it needs more people with broad, general management skills than it did when it maintained a centralized organizational structure. In this situation, explains Beeson, "an overemphasis on creating candidate slates for existing positions can divert attention from the rapid ramp up in the number of potential general managers required."

Finally, successful succession planning requires a commitment from the CEO and the corporate board of directors to develop talent. It also requires mechanisms for bringing people along through formative experiences as well as the flexibility to change these mechanisms as the organization evolves.

The 1996 merger of the Union Pacific (UP) and Southern Pacific (SP) railroads should have produced a very efficient company. By 1998, however, the new railroad was losing $150 million a quarter. The problem, it seems, was poorly managed centralization. Instead of taking advantage of SP managers' expertise in compensating for the inadequacies of the smaller company's Houston-based operations, UP tried to impose its own procedures on them. Before long, shipments promised in 4 days were taking 45, and some (in the words of one disgruntled customer) were even lost "in orbit somewhere around Houston."

company cannot sell and deliver finished goods. Thus, the authority delegated to line departments is important. A bad decision by the manager in one department can hold up production for an entire plant. For example, say that the painting department manager at Clark Equipment changes a paint application on a batch of forklifts, which then show signs of peeling paint. The batch will have to be repainted (and perhaps partially reassembled) before the machines can be shipped.

staff authority Authority based on expertise that usually involves advising line managers

staff members Advisors and counselors who aid line departments in making decisions but do not have the authority to make final decisions

STAFF AUTHORITY Most companies also rely on **staff authority,** which is based on special expertise and usually involves counseling and advising line managers. Common **staff members** include specialists in areas such as law, accounting, and human resource management. A corporate attorney, for example, may be asked to advise the marketing department as it prepares a new contract with the firm's advertising agency. Legal staff, however, do not actually make decisions that affect how the marketing department does its job. Staff members, therefore, aid line departments in making decisions but do not have the authority to make final decisions.

Suppose, for example, that the fabrication department at Clark Equipment has an employee with a drinking problem. The manager of the department could consult a human resource staff expert for advice on handling the situation. The staff expert might suggest that the worker stay on the job but enter a counseling program. If the line manager decides that the job is too dangerous to be handled by a person whose judgment is often impaired by alcohol, then the line manager's decision will most likely prevail.

Typically, the separation between line authority and staff responsibility is clearly delineated. As Figure 6.3 shows, this separation is usually shown in organization charts by solid lines (line authority) and dotted lines (staff responsibility). It may help to understand this separation by remembering that whereas staff members generally provide services to management, line managers are directly involved in producing the firm's products.

committee and team authority Authority granted to committees or work teams involved in a firm's daily operations

COMMITTEE AND TEAM AUTHORITY Recently, more and more organizations have started to use **committee and team authority**—authority granted to committees or work teams that play central roles in the firm's daily operations. A committee, for example, may consist of top managers from several major areas. If the work of the committee is especially important, and if the committee will be working together for an extended time, the organization may even grant it special authority as a decision-making body that goes beyond the individual authority possessed by each of its members.

At the operating level, many firms today are also using *work teams*—groups of operating employees who are empowered to plan and organize their own work and to perform that work with a minimum of supervision. As with permanent committees, the organization will usually find it beneficial to grant special authority to work teams so that they may function more effectively.

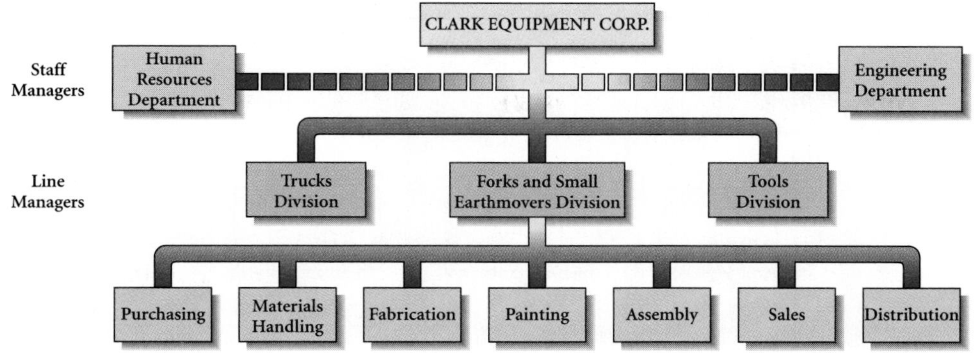

FIGURE 6.3 ◆ Line and Staff Organization

■ BASIC FORMS OF ORGANIZATIONAL STRUCTURE

Organizations can structure themselves in almost an infinite number of ways—according to specialization, for example, or departmentalization or the decision-making hierarchy. Nevertheless, it is possible to identify four basic forms of organizational structure that reflect the general trends followed by most firms: *functional*, *divisional*, *matrix*, and *international*.

Functional Organization

Functional organization is the approach to organizational structure used by most small to medium-size firms. Such organizations are usually structured around basic business functions (marketing, operations, finance, and so forth). Thus, within the company there is a marketing department, an operations department, and a finance department. The benefits of this approach include specialization within functional areas and smoother coordination among them. Experts with specialized training, for example, are hired to work in the marketing department, which handles all marketing for the firm.

functional organization Form of business organization in which authority is determined by the relationships between group functions and activities

In large firms, coordination across functional departments becomes more complicated. Functional organization also fosters centralization (which may possibly be desirable) and makes accountability more difficult. As organizations grow, therefore, they tend to shed this form and move toward one of the other three structures.

Divisional Organization

A **divisional organization** relies on product departmentalization. The firm creates product-based divisions, each of which may then be managed as a separate enterprise. Organizations using this approach are typically structured around several **divisions**—departments that resemble separate businesses in that they produce and market their own products. The head of each division may be a corporate vice president or, if the organization is large, a divisional president. In addition, each division usually has its own identity and operates as a relatively autonomous business under the larger corporate umbrella.

divisional organization Organizational structure in which corporate divisions operate as autonomous businesses under the larger corporate umbrella

division Department that resembles a separate business in producing and marketing its own products

H.J. Heinz, for example, is one of the world's largest food-processing companies. Heinz makes literally thousands of different products and markets them around the world. The firm is organized into six basic divisions: the food service division (selling small packaged products such as mustard and relish to restaurants), the infant foods division, the condiments divisions, the Star-Kist tuna division, the pet foods division, and the Weight Watchers division. Because of its divisional structure, Heinz can evaluate the performance of each division independently. Weight Watchers, for instance, has been performing below expectations. In 1999 Heinz announced plans to sell this under-performing division to another company. Because each division is relatively autonomous, a firm can take such action with minimal disruption to its remaining business operations.

Like Heinz, other divisionalized companies are free to buy, sell, create, and disband divisions without disrupting the rest of their operations. Divisions can maintain healthy

FIGURE 6.4 ◆ **A Matrix Organization**

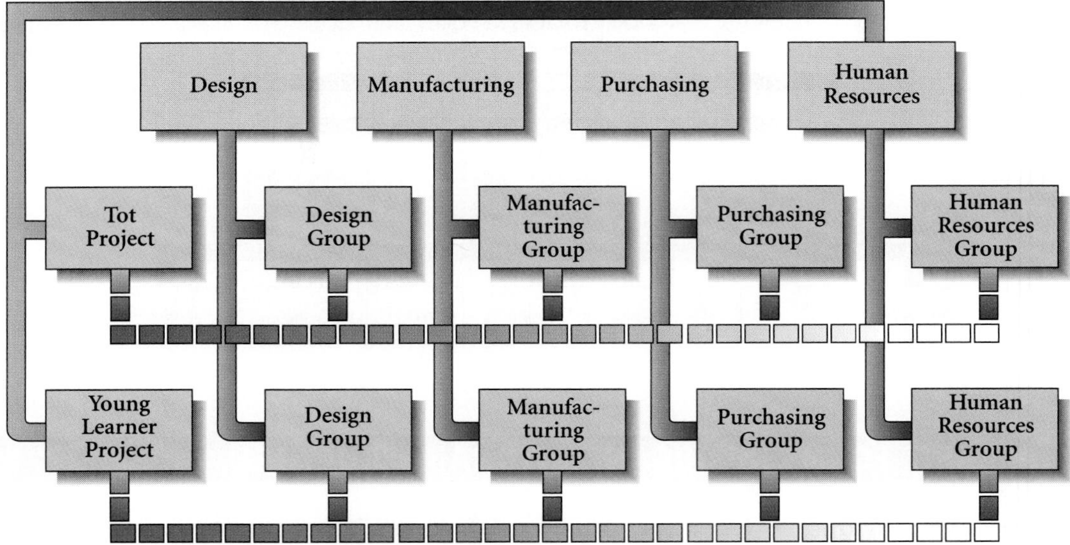

competition among themselves by sponsoring separate advertising campaigns, fostering different corporate identities, and so forth. They can also share certain corporate-level resources (such as market research data). Of course, if too much control is delegated to divisional managers, corporate managers may lose touch with daily operations. Competition between divisions has also been known to become disruptive, and efforts in one division may be duplicated by those of another.

Matrix Organization

matrix structure Organizational structure in which teams are formed and team members report to two or more managers

In a **matrix structure,** teams are formed in which individuals report to two or more managers, usually including a line manager and a staff manager. This structure was pioneered by the National Aeronautics and Space Administration (NASA) for use in developing specific programs. It is a highly flexible form that is readily adaptable to changing circumstances. Matrix structures rely heavily on committee and team authority.

Figure 6.4 shows a matrix organization for a hypothetical manufacturer of educational toys. Along the top, you see some familiar organizational functions: design, manufacturing, purchasing, and human resources. This firm, however, is also working on two special projects: Tot (for preschoolers) and Young Learner (for older children). These have been added to the organizational chart by means of the vertical column on the far left. Each project is headed by a manager who draws upon each of the functional groups for his or her personnel. Such an organization is characterized as a *matrix* because the two special projects add a vertical dimension to a traditional horizontal structure. Note, too, that the matrix entails the addition of a second chain of command.[9]

In some companies, matrix organization is a temporary measure, installed to complete a specific project and affecting only one part of the firm. In these firms, the end of the project usually means the end of the matrix—either a breakup of the team or a restructuring to fit it into the company's existing line-and-staff structure. For example, IBM used a matrix organization to put together the original PC, but then disbanded the team and returned members to the line-and-staff structure once the PC was created. Elsewhere the matrix organization is a semipermanent fixture.

International Organization

international organizational structures Approaches to organizational structure developed in response to the need to manufacture, purchase, and sell in global markets

As discussed in Chapter 3, many businesses today manufacture, purchase, and sell in the world market. Thus, several different **international organizational structures** have emerged. Moreover, as competition on a global scale becomes more complex, companies often find that they must experiment with the ways in which they respond.

FIGURE 6.5 ◆ International Division Structure

For example, when Wal-Mart opened its first store outside the United States in 1992, it set up a special projects team to handle the logistics. As more stores were opened abroad in the mid-1990s, the firm created a small international department to handle overseas expansion. By 1999, however, international sales and expansion had become such a major part of Wal-Mart's operations that the firm created a separate international division headed up by a senior vice president. Interestingly, Wal-Mart now envisions the day when this separate division may no longer be needed, simply because international operations will have become so thoroughly integrated in the firm's overall business.

Wal-Mart typifies the form of organization outlined in Figure 6.5. Other firms have also developed a wide range of approaches to international organizational structure. Whirlpool, for example, purchased the appliance division of the Dutch electronics giant, N.V. Philips, and as part of its international organizational structure now makes the cooling coils for its refrigerators at its new plant in Trento, Italy. Other companies, such as Levi Strauss, handle all international operations through separate international divisions. Still others concentrate production in low-cost areas and then distribute and market globally. Some firms, such as Britain's Pearson PLC (which runs such diverse businesses as publishing, investment banking, and Madame Tussaud's Wax Museum), allow each of their businesses to function autonomously within local markets.

Finally, some companies adopt a truly global structure in which they acquire resources (including capital), produce goods and services, engage in research and development, and sell products in whatever local market is appropriate, without any consideration of national boundaries. General Electric uses a global structure for many of its businesses and has also managed to graft other forms of organization onto its global operations. For its $3 billion lighting business, for example, GE has created a matrix-type team of 9 to 12 senior managers. Team members have "multiple competencies" rather than narrow specialties, and the team itself is multidisciplinary, that is, it cuts across functions. From new product design to equipment redesign, the matrix team oversees about 100 programs and processes located all around the world.

INFORMAL ORGANIZATION

Much of our discussion has focused on the organization's *formal* structure—its "official" arrangement of jobs and job relationships. In reality, however, all organizations also have another dimension—an *informal* organization within which people do their jobs in different ways and interact with other people in ways that do not follow formal lines of communication.

Formal versus Informal Organizational Systems

The formal organization of a business is the part that can be seen and represented in chart form. The structure of a company, however, is by no means limited to the organization chart and the formal assignment of authority. Frequently, the **informal organization**—

informal organization
Network, unrelated to the firm's formal authority structure, of everyday social interactions among company employees

everyday social interactions among employees that transcend formal jobs and job interrelationships—effectively alters a company's formal structure. Indeed, this level of organization is sometimes just as powerful, if not more powerful, than the formal structure.

In their milestone book, *In Search of Excellence*, Thomas Peters and Robert Waterman report that many successful companies support and encourage informal organization just as much as they support formal structure.[10] For example, 3M sponsors clubs for 12 or more employees to enhance communication and interaction across departments. Other companies have rearranged offices and other facilities to make them more conducive to informal interaction. Citibank, for instance, once moved two departments to the same floor to encourage intermingling of employees. MCI still has no doors on its offices—the better to grease the flow of ideas. These and other companies believe that informal interaction among employees stimulates the kind of discussions and group processes that can help solve organizational problems.

On the negative side, the informal organization can reinforce office politics that put the interests of individuals ahead of those of the firm. Likewise, a great deal of harm can be caused by distorted or inaccurate information communicated without management input or review. For example, if the informal organization is highlighting false information about impending layoffs, valuable employees may act quickly (and unnecessarily) to seek other employment.

intrapreneuring Process of creating and maintaining the innovation and flexibility of a small-business environment within the confines of a large organization

Intrapreneuring

Sometimes organizations actually take steps to encourage the informal organization. They do so for a variety of reasons, two of which we have already discussed. First, most experienced managers recognize that the informal organization exists whether they want it or not. Second, many managers know how to use the informal organization to reinforce the formal organization. Perhaps more important, however, the energy of the informal organization can be harnessed to improve productivity.

Many firms, including Compaq Computer, Rubbermaid, 3M, and Xerox, are supporting a process called **intrapreneuring:** creating and maintaining the innovation and flexibility of a small-business environment within the confines of a large, bureaucratic structure. The concept is basically sound. Historically, most innovations have come from individuals in small businesses (see Chapter 7). As businesses increase in size, however, innovation and creativity tend to become casualties in the battle for more sales and profits. In some large companies, new ideas are even discouraged, and champions of innovation have been stalled in mid-career. Compaq is an excellent example of how intrapreneuring works to counteract this trend. The firm has one major division called the New Business Group. When a manager or engineer has an idea for a new product or product application, he or she takes it to the New Business Group and "sells" it. The managers in the group itself are then encouraged to help the innovator develop the idea for field testing. If the product takes off and does well, it is then spun off into its own new business group or division. If it doesn't do as well, it may still be maintained as part of the New Business Group, or it will be phased out.

Continued from page 129

My Name is Anita, and I'm a Micromanager

There are ways to overcome micromanagement, but often they involve learning some hard lessons and taking some difficult steps. Like Richard Louis, Norm Brodsky, and Rene Reiser, Anita Brattina, founder and president of Pittsburgh-based Direct Response Marketing, experienced some tough times before learning to delegate. "A lack of confidence," she warns, "makes you want to check and recheck. [Unfortunately] when you're critical and keep checking your employees' work, they quit."

Fortunately, however, Brattina had some good reasons for sharing control. She first recognized them when she began to picture her company's future. "You need to have a clear picture of what the company will look like so many years from now," she says. "How many employees and what kind? How many customers, and where are they? What kind of equipment and space, and what are you doing in that space? This makes it easier to delegate. When you're clear about where the company is going and the right people are hired . . . it's a nice feeling to be with a team that's heading in the same direction."

"When you're clear about where the company is going and the right people are hired . . . it's a nice feeling to be with a team that's heading in the same direction."

—Anita Brattina
Founder and President of Direct Response Marketing

As for Norm Brodsky, once he gave up tending to every detail, he had to redefine his personal mission. To find out what that mission was, he reminded himself of what it was that he loved doing—selling, negotiating deals, and overseeing projects. "I have my work cut out for me," he admits. "For the next two years, I'm going to divide my time between making sales calls and supervising the construction of a new building. Those two jobs will keep me involved with the business—and out of everybody's hair."

Questions for Discussion

1. Why is the boss's willingness to delegate so important to growing a small business?
2. What signs tell a CEO that his or her span of control is too wide?
3. How does a business owner's willingness to delegate affect the responsibility and authority of company employees?
4. Why is micromanagement difficult in a decentralized organization?
5. Describe three situations in which delegating would be the wrong choice for a small-business owner.

SUMMARY

1. **Discuss the elements that influence a firm's *organizational structure*.** Every business needs structure to operate. *Organizational structure* varies according to a firm's mission, purpose, and strategy. Size, technology, and changes in environmental circumstances also influence structure. In general, although all organizations have the same basic elements, each develops the structure that contributes to the most efficient operations.

2. **Describe *specialization* and *departmentalization* as the building blocks of organizational structure.** The building blocks of organizational structure are *job specialization* and *departmentalization*. As a firm grows, it usually has a greater need for people to perform specialized tasks (specialization). It also has a greater need to group types of work into logical units (departmentalization). Common forms of departmentalization are *customer*, *product*, *process*, *geographic*, and *functional*. Large businesses often use more than one form of departmentalization. *Process organization* (as opposed to process departmentalization) means organizing according to units or teams responsible for all the various processes involved in getting products to consumers.

3. **Distinguish between *responsibility, authority, delegation,* and *accountability,* and explain the differences between decision making in *centralized* and *decentralized organizations.*** *Responsibility* is the duty to perform a task; *authority* is the power to make the decisions necessary to complete tasks. *Delegation* begins when a manager assigns a task to a subordinate; *accountability* means that the subordinate must complete the task. *Span of control* refers to the number of people who work for any individual manager. The more people supervised, the wider the span of control. Wide spans are usually desirable when employees perform simple or unrelated tasks. When jobs are diversified or prone to change, a narrower span is generally preferable.

   In a *centralized organization,* only a few individuals in top management have real decision-making authority. In a *decentralized organization,* much authority is delegated to lower-level management. When both *line* and *line-and-staff systems* are involved, *line departments* generally have authority to make decisions whereas *staff departments* have a responsibility to advise. A relatively new concept, *committee and team authority,* empowers committees or work teams involved in a firm's daily operations.

4. **Explain the differences between *functional, divisional, matrix,* and *international organizational structures.*** In a *functional organization,* authority is usually distributed among such basic functions as marketing and finance. In a *divisional organization,* the various divisions of a larger company, which may be related or unrelated, operate in a relatively autonomous fashion. In *matrix organizations,* in which individuals report to more than one manager, a company creates teams to address specific problems or to conduct specific projects. A company that has divisions in many countries may require an additional level of *international organization* to coordinate those operations.

5. **Describe the *informal organization* and discuss *intrapreneuring.*** The informal organization consists of the everyday social interactions among employees that transcend formal jobs and job interrelationships. To foster the innovation and flexibility of a small business within the big-business environment, some large companies encourage *intrapreneuring*—creating and maintaining the innovation and flexibility of a small-business environment within the confines of a large bureaucratic structure.

QUESTIONS AND EXERCISES

Questions for Review

1. What is an organization chart? What purpose does it serve?
2. Explain the significance of size as it relates to organizational structure. Describe the changes that are likely to occur as an organization grows.
3. What is the difference between responsibility and authority?
4. Why is process organization an innovative approach to organizational structure?
5. Why is a company's informal organization important?

Questions for Analysis

6. Draw up an organization chart for your college or university.
7. Describe a hypothetical organizational structure for a small printing firm. Describe changes that might be necessary as the business grows.
8. Compare and contrast the matrix and divisional approaches to organizational structure.

Application Exercises

9. Interview the manager of a local service business—say, a fast-food restaurant. What types of tasks does this manager typically delegate? Is the appropriate authority also delegated in each case?

10. Using books, magazines, or personal interviews, identify a person who has succeeded as an intrapreneur. In what ways did the structure of the intrapreneur's company help this individual succeed? In what ways did the structure pose problems?

BUILDING YOUR BUSINESS SKILLS

HOLDING ON TO QUALIFIED COMPUTER PROGRAMMERS

This exercise enhances the following SCANS workplace competencies: demonstrating basic skills, demonstrating thinking skills, exhibiting interpersonal skills, and working with information.

▼ Goal

To encourage students to understand the relationship between organizational structure and a company's ability to attract and keep valued employees.

▼ Situation

You are the founder of a small but growing high-technology company that develops new computer software. With your current workload and new contracts in the pipeline, your business is thriving except for one problem: You cannot find computer programmers for product development. Worse yet, current staff members are being lured away by other high-tech firms. After suffering a particularly discouraging personnel raid in which competitors captured three of your most valued employees, you schedule a meeting with your director of human resources to plan organizational changes designed to encourage worker loyalty. You already pay top dollar, but the continuing exodus tells you that programmers are looking for something more.

▼ Method

Working with three or four classmates, identify some ways in which specific organizational changes might improve the working environment and encourage employee loyalty. As you analyze the following factors, ask yourself the obvious question: *If I were a programmer, what organizational changes would encourage me to stay?*

- *Level of job specialization.* With many programmers describing their jobs as tedious because of the focus on detail in a narrow work area, what changes, if any, would you make in job specialization? Right now, for instance, few of your programmers have any say in product design.
- *Decision-making hierarchy.* What decision-making authority would encourage people to stay? Is expanding worker authority likely to work better in a centralized or decentralized organization?
- *Team authority.* Can team empowerment make a difference? Taking the point of view of the worker, describe the ideal team.
- *Intrapreneuring.* What can your company do to encourage and reward innovation?

(continued)

▼ FOLLOW-UP QUESTIONS

1. With the average computer programmer earning nearly $70,000, and with all competitive firms paying top dollar, why might organizational issues be critical in determining employee loyalty?
2. If you were a programmer, what organizational factors would make a difference to you? Why?
3. As the company founder, how willing would you be to make major organizational changes in light of the shortage of qualified programmers?

CRAFTING YOUR BUSINESS PLAN

ORGANIZING THE BUSINESS ENTERPRISE

▼ THE PURPOSE OF THE ASSIGNMENT

1. To acquaint students with the process of navigating the *Business PlanPro* (BPP) software package.
2. To provide an example that illustrates ways in which organizational options can be presented in a business plan.
3. To demonstrate how three chapter topics—organization structure, departmentalization, and authority and responsibility—can be integrated as components in the *BPP* planning environment.

▼ ASSIGNMENT

After reading Chapter 6 in the textbook, open the *BPP* software* and look around for information about organizational structure, departmentalization, and authority and responsibility as it applies to a sample firm: *Medical Equipment Development* (Medquip, Inc.). Then respond to the following questions:

1. Construct an organization chart for Medquip, Inc. [Sites to see in BPP (for this assignment): In the Task Manager screen, click on **Your Management Team.** Then click on each of the following: **1. Management Summary; 2. Organizational Structure; 3. Management Team;** and **5. Personnel Table.**]
2. Explain how Medquip's organization structure is set up to take advantage of its competitor's weakness in product innovation. [Sites to see in BPP: In the Task Manager screen, click on **The Business You're In.** Then click on **5. Main Competitors.**]
3. Which type of departmentalization—customer, product, functional, or process—does Medquip use? Give examples from Medquip's business plan to support your answer.
4. For each job position at Medquip, how clearly are its authority and responsibility delineated in the business plan?

▼ For Your Own Business Plan

5. Describe the composition of your firm's management team. Explain the responsibilities of each position in the firm and identify its organizational structure. Do you plan to modify that organizational structure as the firm and its managers gain experience? Explain in your plan why you expect the company's structure either to remain constant or to change.

*▼ General Tips for Navigating in *BPP*

1. Open the BPP program, examine the Welcome screen, and click on **Open a Sample Plan.**
2. From the Open a Sample Plan dialogue box, click on a sample company name; then click on **Open.**
3. On the Task Manager screen, click onto any of the lines (for example, **Your Company**).
4. You can always return to the Task Manager screen by going to the bottom of the screen and clicking on the **Task Manager** icon.
5. When you are finished with a sample company, close its Task Manager screen.
6. After finishing with a sample company, get to the next one by going to the top of the screen and clicking on **File** (on the menu bar). Then beneath that, select **Open Sample Plan.** This will exit you from the current company file and send you to the Open a Sample Plan dialogue box, where you can select your next sample company.

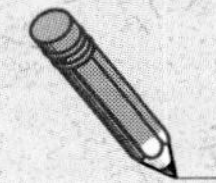

EXPLORING THE NET

HOW TO ORGANIZE AN EMPIRE

This chapter alludes to the years when Walt Disney and his brother Roy first opened their studio. To introduce the concept of job specialization, we describe the opposite practice—a few people doing just about everything. As their jobs grew more complex, of course, the Disney brothers found it increasingly necessary to assign facets of them to other people. Today, of course, the Walt Disney Co. is a multinational entertainment empire. The company's Web site can be found at

http://www.disney.com/.

Browse this Web site and then consider the following questions and activities:

1. Using the Disney Web site as a guide, diagram an organization structure that might make sense for the firm. Make your diagram as detailed as possible.
2. What base of departmentalization does Disney apparently use?
3. Disney has a history of being relatively centralized. What impact would this practice likely have on the firm's current structure?
4. Can you draw any implications from your diagram about the firm's span of control?
5. Disney employs people it calls "Imagineers." See what you can learn about the jobs performed by these people, and compare them with the various roles played by intrapreneurs.
6. Research Disney's "real" organizational structure. Compare and contrast it with the one you diagrammed. What basic factors might account for major differences?

Understanding Entrepreneurship and the Small Business

Please Turn to Chapter 11

Few small-business retailers have the nerve to go head-to-head with giant megastores. As the record shows, even fewer know the secret of emerging with a profit (or even intact). But competing with Goliaths is exactly what Barbara Babbit Kaufman is doing with the small chain of Atlanta-based independent bookstores that she calls Chapter 11. Moreover, Kaufman is succeeding as a small-business owner because of entrepreneurial drive, market savvy, and strategic acumen that have grown the chain from 1 to 13 locations and pushed annual revenues to nearly $10 million in just 8 years. Granted, Kaufman is not a typical small bookstore owner. "A lot of people," she explains, "open bookstores because books are their passion. Retail is my passion."

> **"A lot of people open bookstores because books are their passion. Retail is my passion."**
>
> —Barbara Babbit Kaufman
> *Small bookstore owner*

Kaufman helped start Chapter 11 in 1990 with a $200,000 investment from family and friends. Rather than try to compete with the likes of Borders and Barnes & Noble through superior service, wide selection, or literary allure, Kaufman chose the brash, aggressive style of a David fighting Goliath on the battlefield of price. The company's slogan says it all: "Prices So Low, You'd Think We Were Going Bankrupt," which is a playful reference to both the chain's name and the federal bankruptcy code.

Chapter 11 offers a 30 percent discount on a typical best-seller (the same as the superstores) and discounts all books at least 11 percent—a slightly better deal than that offered by the superstores. What Chapter 11 does a *lot* better is promote its *image* as a rock-bottom pricer. In 1997, for example, Chapter 11 not only advertised John Grisham's novel, *The Partner*, at $14.99 but focused its message on the difference between that price and those being charged elsewhere (the highest price was $26.95). Not only is the price good, but, more importantly, the strategy also has convinced consumers that Chapter 11 prices can't be beat. "I assume I get the best price here," says a typically loyal Atlanta customer.

How does Kaufman manage to offer the prices that back up her strategy? Basically, she keeps overhead low. Each Chapter 11 store has only 3,000 to 6,000 square feet, compared with at least 20,000 square feet for a Barnes & Noble or Borders outlet. Relying on using instinct rather than research to choose sites, Kaufman also locates her stores in low-cost strip malls that offer the kind of fast access that customers want. Of her second location, Kaufman recalls, "I lived nearby, and I knew it was a power center with great traffic and that spaces didn't come available often. Even though I wasn't ready to open a second store, I knew I had to. . . . When you've lived in a market all your life, you know the habits of its shoppers." Admittedly, Kaufman often follows the lead of Wolf Camera, another Atlanta-based small business, in choosing store sites. "Out of our 13 locations," she acknowledges, "all but three are close to Wolf. Our customer demographics are the same. Why do market research twice?"

Although Kaufman takes a mass-market approach to bookselling, aiming for the majority of readers rather than specialty markets, she gives managers the freedom to customize the look and feel of each store for its neighborhood. Managers order, display, and promote books according to what they think will sell. With limited space, of course, Chapter 11 stores lack the amenities and ambiance of the superstores, and customers looking for coffee bars and couches won't find them. But to customers who know exactly what they want, who want to shop quickly, and who

have little interest in the superstore "experience," smallness is an advantage.

So far, Kaufman's personal drive and business good sense have created one of the few independent booksellers in the nation that competes successfully with the megastores. She plans to build on Chapter 11's accomplishments, but like many small-business owners, she first must find the capital to move ahead.

In many ways, Chapter 11 is no different from thousands of small companies trying to succeed in a competitive marketplace. Like Chapter 11, small companies face the challenge of defining a market niche and developing strategies to survive and thrive, often in the face of daunting competition. They also face obstacles that threaten their very existence and are responsible for the failure of millions of small businesses a year. Nevertheless, small-business ownership remains a prominent feature of the American dream. In this chapter, we consider what small businesses are and why they are so important to the U.S. economy.

Our opening story is continued on page 167

After reading this chapter, you should be able to:

1. **Define *small business* and explain its importance to the U.S. economy.**
2. **Explain which *types of small business* best lend themselves to success.**
3. **Define *entrepreneurship* and describe some basic *entrepreneurial characteristics*.**
4. **Describe the *start-up decisions* made by small businesses and identify sources of *financial aid* and *management advice* available to such enterprises.**
5. **Identify the advantages and disadvantages of *franchising*.**

■ WHAT IS A SMALL BUSINESS?

Small Business Administration (SBA) Federal agency charged with assisting small businesses

small business Independently owned and managed business that does not dominate its market

The term *small business* defies easy definition. Clearly, locally owned and operated groceries, video stores, and restaurants are small businesses, and giant corporations such as Sony, Caterpillar, and Eastman Kodak are big businesses. Between these two extremes fall thousands of companies that cannot be easily categorized.

The U.S. Department of Commerce considers a business "small" if it has fewer than 500 employees; but the U.S. **Small Business Administration (SBA),** a government assistance agency for small businesses, regards some companies with 1,500 employees as small. The SBA bases its definition on two factors: *number of employees* and *total annual sales.* For example, manufacturers are defined as "small" according to the first criterion and grocery stores according to the second. Thus, although an independent grocery store with $13 million in sales may sound large, the SBA still sees it as a small business when its revenues are compared with those of truly large food retailers.

Because it is difficult to define a small business in numerical terms, we define a **small business** as one that is independently owned and managed and does not dominate its market. A small business, then, cannot be part of another business: Operators must be their own bosses, free to run their businesses as they please. In addition, the small business must have little influence in its market. For example, although Compaq Computer and Dell Computer were both certainly small businesses when they were founded in 1984, they are now among the dominant companies in the personal computer market.

The federal government plays a significant role in the formation and operation of small business in the United States. On the whole, this interest in the role and well-being of small business derives from the importance of such businesses to the overall economy. (As we will see later in this chapter, the U.S. government sponsors numerous assistance programs for small businesses.) In this section, we discuss the role and importance of small business in the U.S. economy and then describe the major types of small businesses in the United States.

The Importance of Small Business in the U.S. Economy

As Figure 7.1 shows, most U.S. businesses employ fewer than 100 people, and most U.S. workers are employed by small firms. For example, Figure 7.1(a) shows that 87.09 percent of all U.S. businesses employ 20 or fewer people; another 10.74 percent employ between 20 and 99 people. Figure 7.1(b) shows that 26.62 percent of all U.S. workers are employed by firms with fewer than 20 people; another 28.95 percent work in firms that employ between 20 and 99 people. The vast majority of these companies are owner operated.[1]

On the basis of numbers alone, then, small business is a strong presence in the economy, which is true in virtually all the world's mature economies. In Germany, for example, companies with fewer than 500 employees produce two-thirds of the nation's gross national product, train 9 of 10 apprentices, and employ four of every five workers. Small businesses also play major roles in the economies of Italy, France, and Brazil. In addition, experts agree that small businesses will be quite important in the emerging economies of countries such as Russia and Vietnam. The contribution of small business can be measured in terms of its effects on key aspects of an economic system. In the United States, these aspects include *job creation*, *innovation*, and *importance to big business.*

JOB CREATION In the early 1980s, a widely circulated study proposed that small businesses create 8 of every 10 new jobs in the United States. This contention touched off considerable interest in the fostering of small business as a matter of public policy. As we will see, relative job growth among businesses of different sizes is not easy to determine. It is clear, however, that small business—especially in certain industries—is an important source of new (and often well-paid) jobs in this country. Between 1992 and 1996, for example, businesses employing fewer than 500 people created 11,827,000 new jobs, whereas businesses employing 500 or more people eliminated 625,000 jobs.[2]

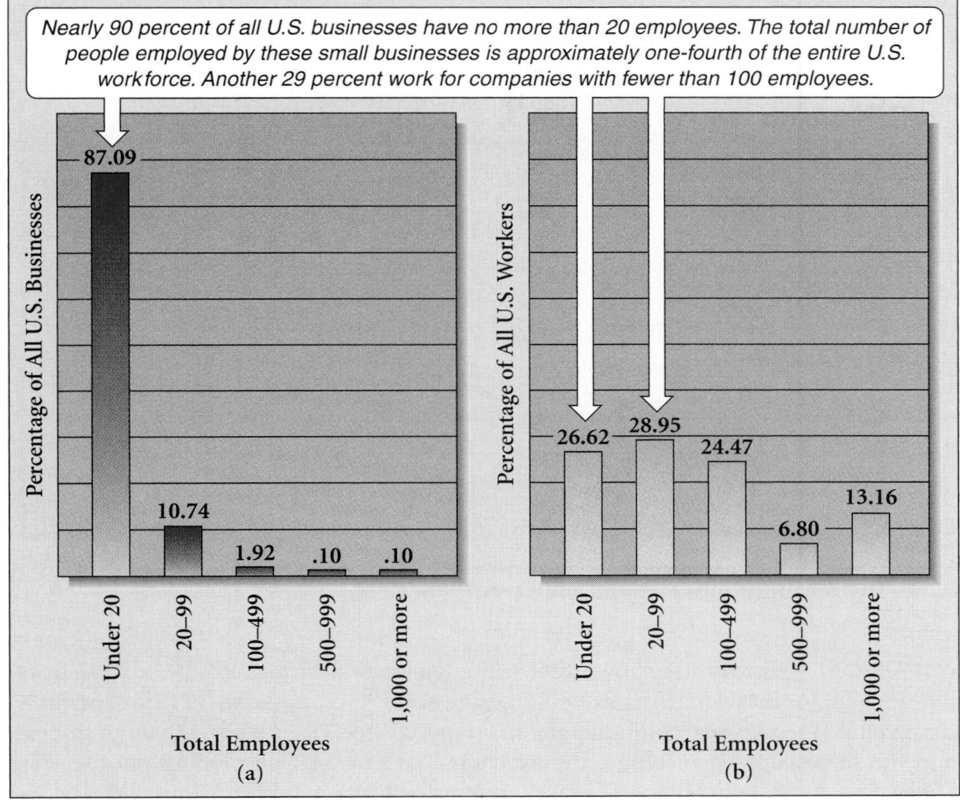

FIGURE 7.1 ◆ **The Importance of Small Business in the United States**

Note that new jobs are also being created by small firms specializing in international business. For example, Bob Knosp operates a small business in Bellevue, Washington, that makes computerized sign-making systems. Knosp gets over half his sales from abroad and has dedicated almost 75 percent of his workforce to handling international sales. According to the SBA, small businesses account for 96 percent of all U.S. exporters.[3]

Adjusting the Myth: The Big-Business Job Machine. Although small businesses certainly create many new jobs each year, the importance of big businesses in job creation should not be overlooked. The large-scale layoffs and cutbacks of the late 1980s and early 1990s contributed to an impression that jobs in all big businesses were on the decline. In reality, however, many large businesses have also been creating thousands of new jobs every year. Figure 7.2 details the changes in the number of jobs at 16 large U.S. companies during the 10-year period between 1988 and 1998. As you can see, both General Motors and Sears eliminated more than 160,000 jobs each. Wal-Mart alone, however, created over 500,000 new jobs during the period, PepsiCo more than 250,000.

At least one message is clear: Business success, more than business size, accounts for most new job creation. Whereas successful retailers such as Wal-Mart and The Limited have been adding thousands of new jobs, struggling chains such as Sears and Woolworth have been eliminating thousands. At the same time, flourishing high-tech giants such as Dell, Compaq, Intel, and Microsoft continue to add jobs at a constant pace. It is also essential to take a long-term view when analyzing job growth. In 1988, for example, Boeing had 143,100 jobs. During the next decade, that number increased and decreased several times, achieving the highest total (163,000) in 1989 and falling to the lowest total (50,000) in 1995. The total in 1997 was 143,000—a difference of 100 from the total of 10 years earlier!

The reality, then, is that jobs are created by companies of all sizes, all of which hire workers and all of which lay them off. Although small firms often hire at a faster rate than large ones, they are also likely to eliminate jobs at a far higher rate. Small firms are also the first to hire in times of economic recovery, large firms the last. Conversely, however, big companies are also the last to lay off workers during economic downswings.

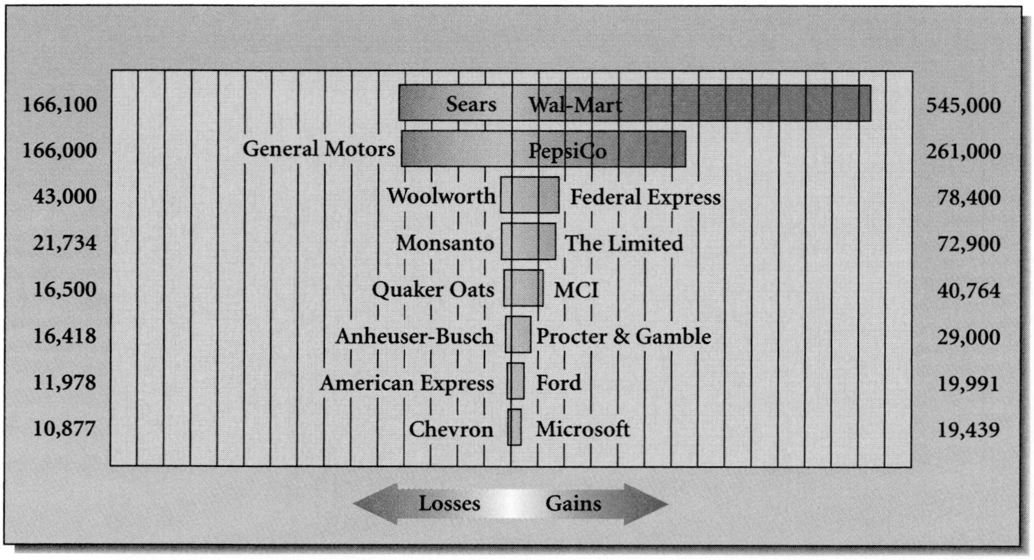

Losses		Gains	
166,100	Sears	Wal-Mart	545,000
166,000	General Motors	PepsiCo	261,000
43,000	Woolworth	Federal Express	78,400
21,734	Monsanto	The Limited	72,900
16,500	Quaker Oats	MCI	40,764
16,418	Anheuser-Busch	Procter & Gamble	29,000
11,978	American Express	Ford	19,991
10,877	Chevron	Microsoft	19,439

Losses Gains

FIGURE 7.2 ◆ **Big Business: Jobs Created and Lost, 1988–1998**

INNOVATION History has shown that major innovations are as likely to come from small businesses (or individuals) as from big businesses. For example, small firms and individuals invented the personal computer and the stainless-steel razor blade, the transistor radio and the photocopying machine, the jet engine and the self-developing photograph. They also gave us the helicopter and power steering, automatic transmissions and air conditioning, cellophane, and the 19-cent ballpoint pen. Today, says the SBA, small businesses supply 55 percent of all "innovations" introduced into the American marketplace.[4]

Not surprisingly, history is repeating itself infinitely more rapidly in the age of computers and high-tech communication. For example, much of today's most innovative software is being written at new start-up companies such as Trilogy Software Inc., an Austin-based company started by Stanford dropout Joe Liemandt. Trilogy's products help optimize and streamline complicated sales and marketing processes for big-business customers such as IBM and Whirlpool.[5] Yahoo! and Netscape brought the Internet into the average American living room, and on-line companies such as amazon.com are using it to redefine our shopping habits. Even today, however, entrepreneurial innovation can still have a decidedly low-tech flavor. For example, drywall installer Jerry Free was frustrated by conventional methods of joining angled wallboards. In his spare time, he developed a simple, handheld device that makes it easier and faster to perform this common task. He eventually licensed his invention to United States Gypsum, and it is now widely used throughout the construction industry. As for Free, the experience convinced him that "the cliché about invention being 1 percent inspiration and 99 percent perspiration is true."[6]

> **"The cliché about invention being 1 percent inspiration and 99 percent perspiration is true."**
>
> —Jerry Free
> *Drywall installer and inventor*

IMPORTANCE TO BIG BUSINESS Most of the products made by big manufacturers are sold to consumers by small businesses. For example, the majority of dealerships selling Fords, Chevrolets, Toyotas, and Volvos are independently owned and operated.

Moreover, small businesses provide big businesses with many of the services, supplies, and raw materials they need. As noted, for example, Trilogy Software has become an important supplier to big businesses. Likewise, McDonald's relies heavily on small agricultural distributors, bakeries, and wholesalers to supply many of the ingredients that it needs to make Big Macs. It also hires local maintenance contractors to clean its parking lights and service its electrical signs. Although airlines use large catering companies such as Marriott Hosts to supply in-flight meals, those caterers routinely subcontract preparation to small local businesses in each city they serve.

Popular Forms of Small-Business Enterprise

Not surprisingly, small businesses are more common in some industries than in others. The five major small-business industry groups are *services, retailing, wholesaling, agriculture,* and *manufacturing*. Obviously, each group differs in its requirements for employees, money, materials, and machines. Remember: The more resources an industry requires, the harder it is to start a business and the less likely that the industry is dominated by small firms. Remember, too, that *small* is a relative term: The criteria (number of employees and total annual sales) differ from industry to industry and are often meaningful only when compared with businesses that are truly large.

Finally, as a general rule, manufacturing businesses are the hardest to start, and service businesses are the easiest to start. To make sewing machines, for example, a manufacturer must invest not only in people but also in raw materials and machines. It must also develop a distribution network and advertise heavily. To prepare tax forms, however, an entrepreneur need invest only in an education and a few office supplies and reference books. The business can be run out of a storefront or a home.

SERVICES Partly because they require few resources, service businesses are the fastest-growing segment of small-business enterprise. In addition, no other industry group offers a higher return on time invested. Finally, services appeal to the talent for innovation typified by many small enterprises.

Small-business services range from shoeshine parlors to car rental agencies, from marriage counseling to computer software, from accounting and management consulting to professional dog walking. In Dallas, for example, Jani-King has prospered by selling commercial cleaning services to local companies. In Virginia Beach, Virginia, Jackson Hewitt Tax Service has found a profitable niche in providing computerized tax preparation and electronic tax filing services. Great Clips Inc. is a fast-growing family-run hair salon in Minneapolis.[7]

RETAILING A *retail business* sells directly to consumers products manufactured by other firms. There are hundreds of different kinds of retailers, ranging from wig shops and frozen yogurt stands to automobile dealerships and department stores. Usually, however, people who start small businesses favor specialty shops—for example, big men's clothing or gourmet coffees—that let them focus limited resources on narrow market segments.

For example, John Mackey launched Whole Foods out of his own frustration at being unable to find a full range of natural foods at other stores. He soon found, however, that he had tapped a lucrative market and started an ambitious expansion program. Today, with 87 outlets nationwide, Whole Foods is the largest natural foods retailer in the United States, three times larger than its biggest competitor.[8] Likewise, when Olga Tereshko found it difficult to locate just the right cloth diapers and breast-feeding supplies for her newborn son, she decided to start selling them herself. Instead of taking the conventional retailing route, however, Tereshko set up shop on the Internet. Her business, called Little Koala, has continued to expand at a rate of about 10 percent a month, and she has established a customer base of 8,000 to 9,000 loyal customers.[9]

"The online business," says Tereshko, "is growing each month. More people are getting used to computers and going online. The Web increases your visibility, and business

Small businesses often do very well in retailing. For example, Starbucks started as a small-time operation, but today it has grown into an internationally recognized brand with dozens of new stores opening every year. The firm's commitment to quality and keen understanding of its customers have made Starbucks the dominant firm in its market.

grows faster." Jeff Levy, an Atlanta-based consultant who tracks Web usage agrees but cautions that "very few brands . . . have been built solely on the Web. You can market solely on the Web if you are only trying to reach people online."[10]

> **"Very few brands have been built solely on the Web. You can market solely on the Web if you are only trying to reach people online."**
>
> —Jeff Levy
> *Atlanta-based consultant*

WHOLESALING As with services and retailing, small business owners dominate wholesaling. A *wholesale business* buys products from manufacturers or other producers and then sells them to retailers. Wholesalers usually buy goods in bulk and store them in quantities and places that are convenient for retailers. For a given volume of business, therefore, they need fewer employees than manufacturers, retailers, or service providers.

They also serve fewer customers than other providers—usually those who repeatedly order large volumes of goods. For example, wholesalers in the grocery industry buy packaged food in bulk from companies such as Del Monte and Campbell's and then sell it to both large grocery chains and smaller independent grocers. Like retailing, the wholesaling industry has also been affected by the increase in consumer demand for specialty products, a trend that has fueled the growth of firms such as Central Garden & Pet, a warehousing firm located in Lafayette, California. Central began by stocking and distributing garden and pool supplies made by firms such as Ortho and Monsanto. It subsequently bought out a distributor of pet supplies and diversified. Now, in addition to pesticides, gopher traps, and garden hoses, Central stocks shelves and manages inventory for pet supply retailers, the fastest-growing facet of its business.

MANUFACTURING More than any other industry group, manufacturing lends itself to big business, and for good reason. Because of the investment normally required in equipment, energy, and raw materials, a good deal of money is usually needed to start a manufacturing business. Automobile manufacturing, for example, calls for billions of dollars of investment and thousands of workers before the first automobile rolls off the assembly line. Obviously, such requirements shut out most individuals. Although Henry Ford began with $28,000, it has been a long time since anyone started a U.S. car company from scratch.

This is not to say that there are no small business owners who do well in manufacturing. Indeed, it is not uncommon for them to outdo big business in such innovative industries as chemistry, electronics, toys, and computer software. At other times, small manufacturers prosper by locating interesting niches. Peter Johnstone, for example, has formed a small company called Escape Sailboats. The firm makes small, inexpensive boats from plastics and sells them to beginning sailors for substantially less than the prices charged by larger, more conventional manufacturers such as Hobie.[11]

■ ENTREPRENEURSHIP

In the previous section, we discussed each of the popular forms of small business. We also described a couple of firms that started small and grew larger (sometimes much larger). In each of these cases, growth was spurred by the imagination and skill of the entrepreneurs who operated those companies. Although the concepts of *entrepreneurship* and *small business* are closely related, in this section we begin by discussing some important, though often subtle, differences between them. Then we describe some key characteristics of entrepreneurial personalities and activities.

The Distinction between Entrepreneurship and Small Business

Many small business owners like to think of themselves as **entrepreneurs**—people who assume the risk of business ownership with a primary goal of growth and expansion. In reality, however, a person may be a small business owner only, an entrepreneur only, or both. Consider a person who starts a small pizza parlor with no plans other than to earn enough money from the restaurant to lead a comfortable life. That person is clearly a small business owner. With no plans to grow and expand, he or she is not really an entrepreneur. Conversely, an entrepreneur starts with one pizza parlor and fulfills the ambition of turning it into a national chain to rival Domino's or Little Caesar's. Although this person may have started as a small business owner, the growth of the firm resulted from entrepreneurial vision and activity.[12]

entrepreneur Businessperson who accepts both the risks and the opportunities involved in creating and operating a new business venture

Entrepreneurial Characteristics

In general, most successful entrepreneurs have characteristics that set them apart from most other business owners (for example, resourcefulness and a concern for good, often personal, customer relations). Most successful entrepreneurs also have a strong desire to be their own bosses. Many express a need to "gain control over my life" or "build for the family" and believe that building successful businesses will help them do it. They can also handle ambiguity, not knowing what tomorrow holds.

■ SUCCESS AND FAILURE IN SMALL BUSINESS

For every Henry Ford, Walt Disney, Mary Kay Ash, or Bill Gates—people who transformed small businesses into major corporations—there are many small business owners and entrepreneurs who fail. Figure 7.3 illustrates recent trends in new business start-ups and failures. As you can see, over the last 10 years new business start-ups have generally run between 150,000 and 200,000 per year, with 166,740 new businesses being launched in 1997. Over this same period, business failures have generally been between 50,000 and

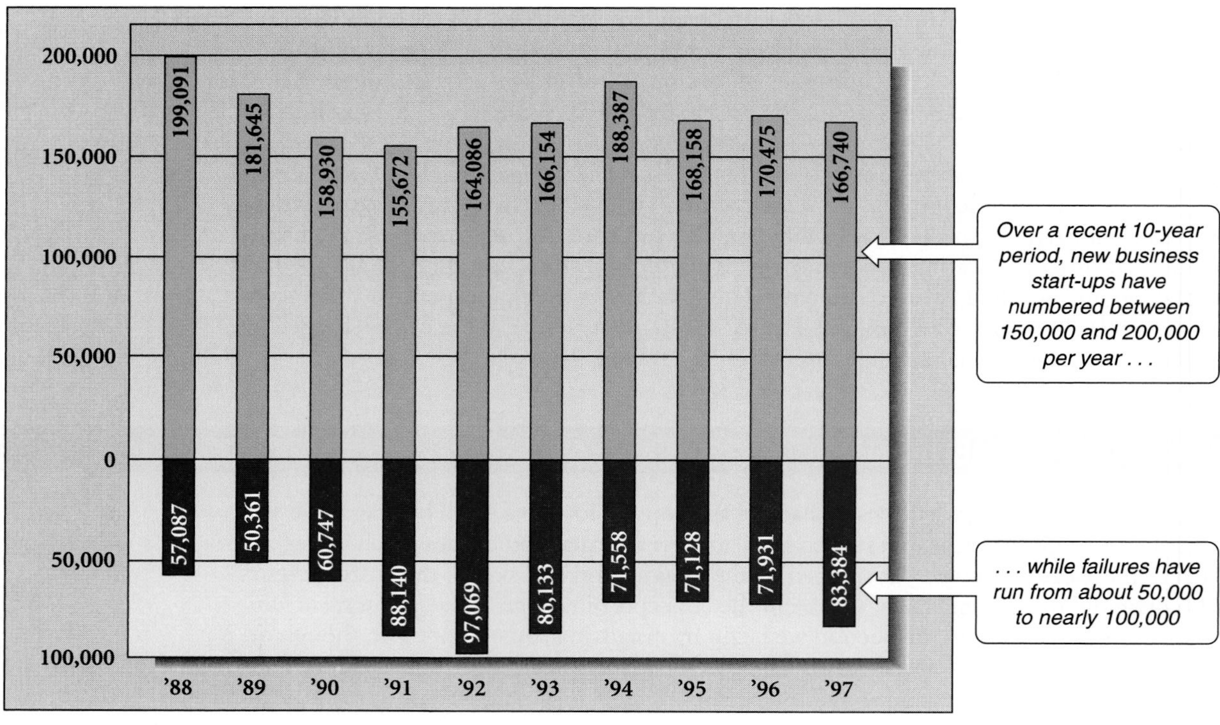

FIGURE 7.3 ◆ **Start-Ups: Success and Failure**

100,000, with a total of 83,384 failing in 1997. In this section, we look first at a few key trends in small-business start-ups. Then we examine some of the main reasons for success and failure in small-business undertakings.

Trends in Small-Business Start-Ups

Thousands of new businesses are started in the United States every year. Several factors account for this trend, and in this section we focus on four of them: entrepreneurs who cross over from big business, increased opportunities for minorities and women, new opportunities in global enterprise, and improved rates of survival among small businesses.

Crossovers from Big Business It is interesting to note that increasingly more businesses are being started by people who have opted to leave big corporations and put their experience and know-how to work for themselves.

For example, Doug Hyde spent most of his career working in large public-utility companies and had become CEO of Green Mountain Power in Vermont. Seeing the growing trend toward deregulation of public utilities as a great opportunity, Hyde left Green Mountain Power and launched his own business called Green Mountain Energy Resources (GMER). Hyde and GMER buy electricity at wholesale prices from generators that produce the electricity from such ecologically friendly sources as wind, water, and geothermal energy. Hyde then sells branded renewable energy to environmentally conscious customers. As for Hyde himself, his main job is no longer controlling costs and catering to regulators, but rather finding and keeping customers. He admits that "It took some adjusting to the notion that, at the end of the day, the results and value of your work could not be observed in the same way that wires, transformers, and hydroelectric facilities can be."[13]

> **"It took some adjusting to the notion that, at the end of the day, the results and value of your work could not be observed in the same way that wires, transformers, and hydroelectric facilities can be."**
>
> —Doug Hyde
> *Founder, Green Mountain Energy Resources*

OPPORTUNITIES FOR MINORITIES AND WOMEN In addition to big-business expatriates, more small businesses are being started by minorities and women. For example, the number of black-owned businesses has increased by 46 percent during the most recent 5-year period for which data are available and now number about 621,000. Chicago's Gardner family is just one of thousands of examples illustrating this trend. The Gardners are the founders of Soft Sheen Products Inc., a firm specializing in ethnic hair products. Soft Sheen attained sales of $80 million in the year before the Gardners sold it to France's L'Oréal S.A. for more than $160 million. The emergence of such opportunities is hardly surprising, either to black entrepreneurs or to the corporate marketers who have taken an interest in their companies. Black purchasing power topped $530 billion in 1999. Up from just over $300 billion in 1990, that increase of 73 percent far outstrips the 57 percent increase experienced by all Americans.[14]

Hispanic-owned businesses have grown at the even faster rate of 76 percent and now number about 862,000. Other ethnic groups also are making their presence felt among U.S. business owners. For instance, business ownership among Asian and Pacific Islanders has increased 56 percent, to over 600,000. Although the number of businesses owned by American Indians and Alaska Natives is still somewhat small, at slightly over 100,000, this total nevertheless represents a 5-year increase of 93 percent.[15]

The number of women entrepreneurs is also growing rapidly. Celeste Johnson, for example, left a management position at Pitney Bowes to launch Obex Inc., which makes gardening and landscaping products from mixed recycled plastics. Katrina Garnett gave up a lucrative job at Oracle to start her own software company, Crossworlds Software Inc. Laila Rubenstein closed her management consulting practice to create Greeting Cards.com Inc., an Internet-based business selling customizable electronic greetings. "Women-owned business," says Teresa Cavanaugh, director of the Women Entrepreneur's Connection at BankBoston, "is the largest emerging segment of the small-business market. Women-owned businesses are an economic force that no bank can afford to overlook."[16]

> **"Women-owned business is the largest emerging segment of the small-business market. Women-owned businesses are an economic force that no bank can afford to overlook."**
>
> —Teresa Cavanaugh
> *Director of the Women Entrepreneur's Connection at BankBoston*

Likewise, the number of women-owned businesses is also growing rapidly. The total has risen from 2.78 million in 1981 to more than 6.4 million, and projections indicate that by the year 2000, almost half of the country's businesses will be owned by women. According to the National Foundation for Women Business Owners, almost a third of all U.S. firms with fewer than 500 employees—some 7.7 million enterprises—are now owned or controlled by women. Figure 7.4 shows rates of increase in various industries between 1987 and 1996; as you can see, the increase in the number of women-owned companies cuts across the business spectrum.

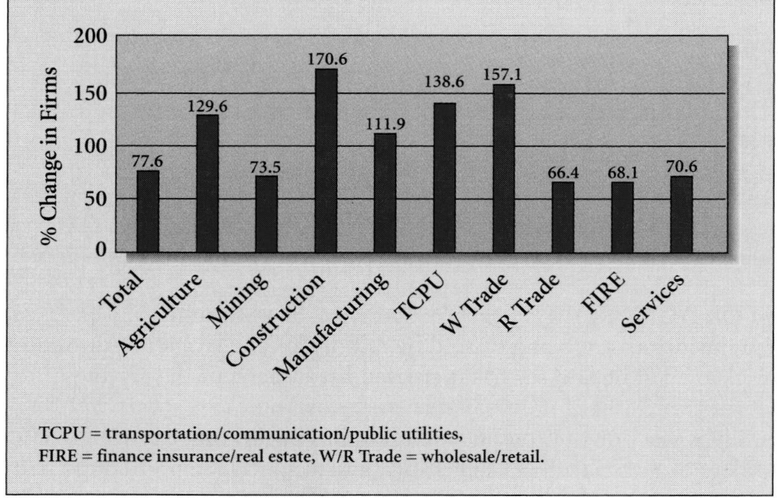

FIGURE 7.4 ◆ **Growth among Women-Owned Firms in the United States**

GLOBAL OPPORTUNITIES In addition, many entrepreneurs today are also finding new opportunities in foreign markets. For example, Doug Mellinger is founder and CEO of PRT Group Inc., a software development company. One of Mellinger's biggest problems was finding enough trained programmers: There are not enough American programmers to go around, and foreign-born programmers face strict immigration quotas. Consequently, Mellinger set up shop on Barbados, a Caribbean island eager for economic development. The local government helps him attract foreign programmers and has gone to great lengths to make it easy for him to do business. Today, Mellinger has both customers and suppliers from dozens of nations around the world.[17]

BETTER SURVIVAL RATES Finally, more people are encouraged to test their skills as entrepreneurs because the failure rate among small businesses has been declining in recent years. During the 1960s and 1970s, for example, less than half of all new start-ups survived more than 18 months; only one in five lasted 10 years. Now, however, new businesses have a better chance of surviving. Of new businesses started in the 1980s, for instance, over 77 percent remained in operation for at least 3 years. Today, the SBA estimates that at least 40 percent of all new businesses can expect to survive for 6 years. As you can see from Figure 7.5, which shows the small-business survival rate over a 10-year period, the key is longevity. For the reasons discussed in the next section, small businesses suffer a higher mortality rate than larger concerns. Among those, however, that manage to stay in business for 6 to 10 years, the survival rate levels off.

Reasons for Failure

Unfortunately, 60 percent of all new businesses will not celebrate a sixth anniversary. Why do some succeed and others fail? Although no set pattern has been established, four general factors contribute to small-business failure:

- *Managerial incompetence or inexperience.* If managers do not know how to make basic business decisions, they are unlikely to be successful in the long run.
- *Neglect.* Starting a small business requires an overwhelming time commitment.
- *Weak control systems.* If control systems do not signal impending problems, managers may be in serious trouble before more visible difficulties alert them.
- *Insufficient capital.* A new business should have enough capital to operate at least 6 months without earning a profit.[18]

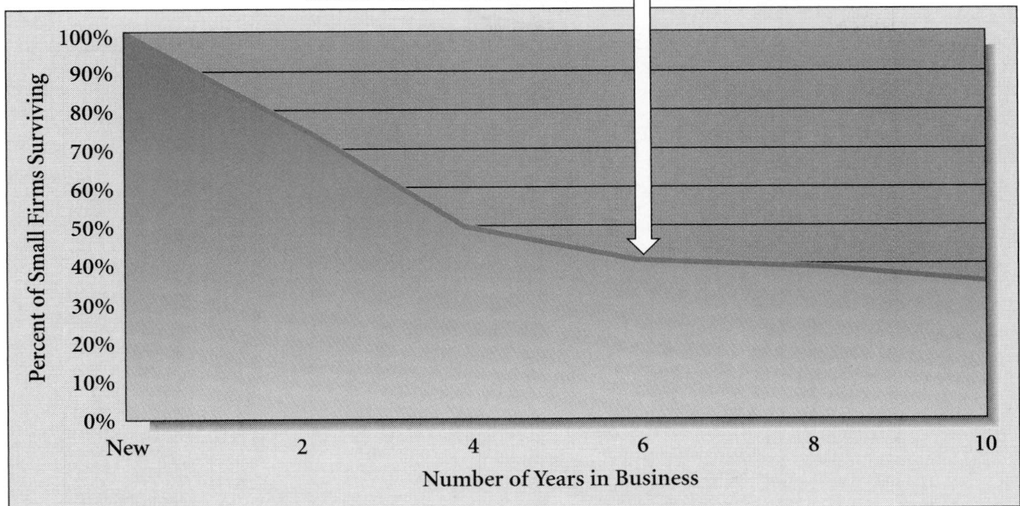

FIGURE 7.5 ◆ **Small-Business Survival Rate**

Reasons for Success

Similarly, four basic factors are typically cited to explain small-business success:

- *Hard work, drive, and dedication.* Small-business owners must be committed to succeeding and be willing to put in the time and effort to make it happen.
- *Market demand for the products or services being provided.* Careful analysis of market conditions can help small business owners assess the probable reception of their products in the marketplace.
- *Managerial competence.* Successful small business owners may acquire competence through training or experience, or by using the expertise of others.
- *Luck.* Lady Luck also plays a role in the success of some firms. For example, after Alan McKim started Clean Harbors, an environmental cleanup firm based in New England, he struggled to keep his business afloat. Then the U.S. government committed $1.6 billion to toxic waste cleanup—McKim's specialty. He was able to get several large government contracts and put his business on solid financial footing. Had the government fund not been created at just the right time, McKim may have failed.

STARTING AND OPERATING THE SMALL BUSINESS

Several other factors contribute to the success of a small business. In particular, most successful entrepreneurs make the right decisions when they start their businesses. For example, they must decide precisely *how* to get into business. Should they buy an existing business or build from the ground up? In addition, would-be entrepreneurs must find appropriate sources of financing and decide when to seek the advice of experts.

Starting the Small Business

An old Chinese saying notes that a journey of a thousand miles begins with a single step. This is also true of a new business. The first step is the individual's commitment to becoming a small business owner. Next is choosing the good or service to be offered, a process that means investigating one's chosen industry and market. Making this choice also requires would-be

"If I heard it once, I heard it a thousand times. 'Margie,' he'd say, 'when I die, the business dies with me.'"

TRENDS AND CHALLENGES

CASHING IN ON CUBAN NOSTALGIA

Small-business owners need an angle—something that makes them stand out from the competition. This is especially true in the restaurant and nightclub business, where owners search for that something special that will attract the crowds. No one knows *exactly* what packs in the customers, but generally speaking, it's ambiance and entertainment—and, oh yes, the food.

No matter where you look today, from Connecticut to Florida to New York City to Chicago, the latest angle in ambiance seems to be Cuba—not the poverty and oppression that is Cuba today, but the idealized image of the island in the 1940s and 1950s, before Fidel Castro. It is an image of merriment and escapism, of a tropical island paradise, of Cuban cigars and Cuban rum, of Latin romance and live Cuban jazz, of Ernest Hemingway and hotels with beachfront verandas.

In South Norwalk, Connecticut, for example, Mario Fontana decided to open a Cuban restaurant when he realized that, at least in the world of nightspots, Cuba is the latest thing in ambiance. "We needed to have something very of-the-moment," explains Fontana, "and nothing is more of-the-moment than Cuba." Decorated with real banana trees, his restaurant, Habana, serves 20 different varieties of rum and features the band Mambo Combo. How's the place doing? It's "ridiculously busy," says the owner.

About 1,500 miles down the East Coast is Cafe Nostalgia, the hottest Cuban-music dance club in Miami. The crowd is filled not only with Cuban exiles who want to relive a little of the past, but also with their children and other non-Cubans who want a taste of what the island was like in its legendary heyday. Cafe Nostalgia owner Pepe Horta, who understands that the legend revolves around mystery, inaccessibility, and romance, has created an ambiance to reflect these elements. With plans to open clubs in Miami Beach, Paris, and Madrid, Horta is proba-

entrepreneurs to assess not only industry trends but also their own skills. Like the managers of big businesses, small-business owners must also be sure that they understand the true nature of their businesses.

BUYING OUT AN EXISTING BUSINESS After choosing a product and making sure that the choice fits their own skills and interests, entrepreneurs must decide whether to buy an existing business or to start from scratch. Consultants often recommend the first approach. Quite simply, the odds are better: If successful, an existing business has already proved its ability to draw customers at a profit. It has established working relationships with lenders, suppliers, and the community. Moreover, the track record of an existing business gives potential buyers a much clearer picture of what to expect than any estimate of a new business's prospects. Around 30 percent of the new businesses started in the past decade were bought from someone else.

STARTING FROM SCRATCH Some people seek the satisfaction that comes from planting an idea, nurturing it, and making it grow into a strong and sturdy business. There are also practical reasons to start a business from scratch. A new business does not suffer the ill effects of a prior owner's errors. The start-up owner is also free to choose lenders, equipment, inventories, locations, suppliers, and workers, unbound by a predecessor's commitments and policies. Of the new businesses begun in the past decade, 64 percent were started from scratch.

Not surprisingly, the risks of starting a business from scratch are greater than those of buying an existing firm. Founders of new businesses can only make predictions and projections about their prospects. Success or failure thus depends heavily on identifying a genuine business opportunity—a product for which many customers will pay well that is currently unavailable to them. To find openings, entrepreneurs must study their markets and answer the following questions:

- Who are my customers?
- Where are they?
- At what price will they buy my product?

bly the first entrepreneur to market Cuban nostalgia throughout the world.

In Miami, small-business owners have in fact understood the marketing potential for Cuban nostalgia ever since Cubans started fleeing the Castro regime in the early 1960s. Retail shops, restaurants, and bookstores opened throughout the city almost immediately and, at first, attracted Cuban customers who wanted to recapture what they had lost. Many of these small businesses kept the same names they had in Havana: La Gran Via (a bakery) and El Centro Vasco (a restaurant) were successful in part because they reminded people of home.

But how did the interest in Cuba spread to such far-off spots as Norwalk, Connecticut? Ironically, the Pope's 1998 visit to Cuba was certainly a factor, as television, magazines, and newspapers ran specials on Cuban history and culture. A more powerful factor, however, is the dramatic increase in the number of cigar-smoking Americans who long to savor legendary Cuban brands that have been banned from the United States for almost 40 years. Cuban cigars have long been regarded as the best in the world, and in this case, too, image plays a role: "Clearly," says a spokesman for Zagat restaurant guides, "there's a romance between the slicked-back-hair cigar aficionado and Cuban atmosphere."

Another small-business owner to benefit from Cuban nostalgia is Mark PoKempner, a Chicago-based photographer who has traveled back and forth to the island since 1981. With the new interest in just about anything Cuban, PoKempner is selling more and more of his island photographs. He thus has enough money to enjoy all the Cuban restaurants which have opened in Chicago and which, he maintains, are "much better than they are in Cuba." Apparently, American small-business ingenuity is doing Cuba better than Cuba did itself.

After selling her first start-up at age 23, Melissa Bradley founded the Entrepreneurial Development Institute (TEDI), a nonprofit company devoted to teaching at-risk children in Washington, DC. To finance her enterprise, Bradley borrowed a page from the for-profit sector—she sold "community stock" to interested shareholders. TEDI is thus independent from government and financial grants and works to build the confidence of shareholders and clients rather than to generate sympathy and charity.

- In what quantities will they buy?
- Who are my competitors?
- How will my product differ from those of my competitors?

Finding answers to these questions is a difficult task even for large, well-established firms. Where can the small business owner get the necessary information? Other sources of assistance are discussed later in this chapter, but we briefly describe three of the most accessible here:

- The best way to gain knowledge about a market is to work in it before going into business in it. For example, if you once worked in a bookstore and now plan to open one of your own, you probably already have some idea about the kinds of books people request and buy.
- A quick scan of the Yellow Pages will reveal many potential competitors, as will advertisements in trade journals. Personal visits to these establishments can give you insights into their strengths and weaknesses.
- Studying magazines and books aimed specifically at small businesses can also be of help, as can hiring professionals to survey the market for you.

Financing the Small Business

Although the choice of how to start is obviously important, it is meaningless unless a small business owner can obtain the money to set up shop. As Figure 7.6 shows, a wide variety of monetary resources, ranging from private to government sources, is available. Notice that lending institutions are more likely to help finance the purchase of an existing business than a new business because the risks are better understood. Individuals starting up new businesses must rely more on their personal resources.

According to a study by the National Federation of Independent Business, an owner's personal resources, not loans, are the most important source of money. Including money borrowed from friends and relatives, personal resources account for over two-thirds of all money invested in new small businesses and one-half of that invested in the purchase of existing businesses.

Although banks, independent investors, and government loans all provide much smaller portions of start-up funds than the personal resources of owners, they are important in many cases. Getting money from these sources, however, requires some extra ef-

FIGURE 7.6 ◆ Financing the Small Business

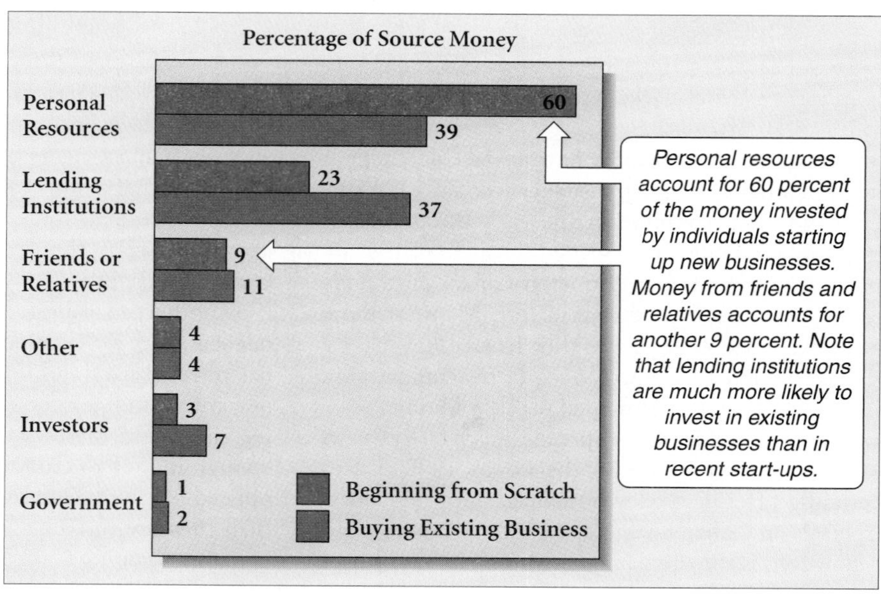

fort. Banks and private investors usually want to see formal business plans—detailed outlines of proposed businesses and markets, owners' backgrounds, and other sources of funding. Government loans have strict eligibility guidelines.

OTHER SOURCES OF INVESTMENT Two other sources of start-up funds are *venture capital companies* and *small-business investment companies.*

Venture Capital Companies. To define, **venture capital companies** are groups of small investors seeking to make profits on companies with rapid growth potential. Most of these firms do not lend money, but rather, they *invest* it, supplying capital in return for stock. The venture capital company may also demand a representative on the board of directors. In some cases, managers may even need approval from the venture capital company before making major decisions. In 1997, there were a total of 1,800 new businesses launched in the United States with the assistance of venture capital; the total investment of this capital was about $11.5 billion.[19]

venture capital company Group of small investors that invest money in companies with rapid growth potential

Small-Business Investment Companies. Taking a more balanced approach in their choices than venture capital companies, **small-business investment companies (SBICs)** seek profits from investments in companies with potential for rapid growth. Created by the Small Business Investment Act of 1958, SBICs are federally licensed to borrow money from the SBA and to invest it in or lend it to small businesses. They are themselves investments for their shareholders. Past beneficiaries of SBIC capital include Apple Computer, Intel, and Federal Express. In addition, the government has recently begun to sponsor **minority enterprise small-business investment companies (MESBICs).** As the name suggests, MESBICs specialize in financing businesses that are owned and operated by minorities.

small-business investment company (SBIC) A government-regulated investment company that borrows money from the SBA to invest in or lend to a small business

minority enterprise small-business investment company (MESBIC) Federally sponsored company that specializes in financing businesses that are owned and operated by minorities

SBA FINANCIAL PROGRAMS Since its founding in 1953, the SBA has offered more than 20 financing programs to small businesses that meet standards in size and independence. Eligible firms must also be unable to get private financing at reasonable terms. Because of these and other restrictions, SBA loans have never been a major source of small-business financing. In addition, budget cutbacks at the SBA have reduced the number of firms benefiting from loans. Several SBA programs currently offer funds to qualified applicants:

- Under the SBA's **guaranteed loans program,** small businesses can borrow from commercial lenders. The SBA guarantees to repay 75 to 85 percent of the loan amount, not to exceed $750,000. Under a related program, companies engaged in international trade can borrow up to $1.25 million. Such loans may be made for as long as 15 years. Most SBA lending activity flows through this program.
- Sometimes both the desired bank and SBA-guaranteed loans are unavailable (perhaps because the business cannot meet stringent requirements). In such cases, the SBA may help finance the entrepreneur through its **immediate participation loans program.** Under this arrangement, the SBA and the bank each put up a share of the money, with the SBA's share not to exceed $150,000.
- Under the **local development companies (LDCs) program,** the SBA works with a corporation (either for-profit or nonprofit) founded by local citizens who want to boost the local economy. The SBA can lend up to $500,000 for each small business to be helped by an LDC.

guaranteed loans program Program in which the SBA guarantees to repay 75 to 85 percent of small-business commercial loans up to $750,000

immediate participation loans program Program in which small businesses are loaned funds put up jointly by banks and the SBA

local development companies (LDCs) program Program in which the SBA works with local for-profit or nonprofit organizations seeking to boost a community's economy

Sources of Management Advice

Financing is not the only area in which small businesses need help. Until World War II, for example, the business world involved few regulations, few taxes, few records, few big competitors, and no computers. Since then, simplicity has given way to complexity: Today, few entrepreneurs are equipped with all the business skills they need to survive. Small business owners can no longer be their own troubleshooters, lawyers, bookkeepers, financiers, and tax experts. For these jobs, they rely on professional help. To survive and grow, however, small businesses also need advice regarding management. This advice is usually available from four sources: *advisory boards, management consultants, the SBA,* and a process called *networking.*

ADVISORY BOARDS All companies, even those that do not legally need boards of directors, can benefit from the problem-solving abilities of advisory boards. Thus, some small businesses create boards to provide advice and assistance. For example, an advisory board might help an entrepreneur determine the best way to finance a plant expansion or to start exporting products to foreign markets.

management consultant Independent outside specialist hired to help managers solve business problems

MANAGEMENT CONSULTANTS Opinions vary widely about the value of **management consultants**—experts who charge fees to help managers solve problems. They often specialize in one area, such as international business, small business, or manufacturing. Thus, they can bring an objective and trained outlook to problems and provide logical recommendations. They can be quite expensive, however, as some consultants charge $1,000 or more for a day of assistance.

Like other professionals, consultants should be chosen with care. They can be found through major corporations who have used their services and who can provide references and reports on their work. Not surprisingly, they are most effective when the client helps (for instance, by providing schedules and written proposals for work to be done).

THE SMALL BUSINESS ADMINISTRATION Even more important than its financing role is the SBA's role in helping small business owners improve their management skills. It is easy for entrepreneurs to spend money; SBA programs are designed to show them how to spend it wisely. The SBA offers small businesses four major management counseling programs at virtually no cost:

Service Corps of Retired Executives (SCORE) SBA program in which retired executives work with small businesses on a volunteer basis

Active Corps of Executives (ACE) SBA program in which currently employed executives work with small businesses on a volunteer basis

Small Business Institute (SBI) SBA program in which college and university students and instructors work with small-business owners to help solve specific problems

Small Business Development Center (SBDC) SBA program designed to consolidate information from various disciplines and make it available to small businesses

networking Interactions among businesspeople for the purpose of discussing mutual problems and opportunities and perhaps pooling resources

- A small business owner who needs help in starting a new business can get it free through the **Service Corps of Retired Executives (SCORE).** All SCORE members are retired executives, and all are volunteers. Under this program, the SBA tries to match the expert to the need. For example, if a small business owner needs help putting together a marketing plan, the SBA will send a SCORE counselor with marketing expertise.
- Like SCORE, the **Active Corps of Executives (ACE)** program is designed to help small businesses that cannot afford consultants. The SBA recruits ACE volunteers from virtually every industry. All ACE volunteers are currently involved in successful activities, mostly as small business owners themselves. Together, SCORE and ACE have more than 12,000 counselors working out of 350 chapters throughout the United States. They provide assistance to some 140,000 small businesses each year.
- The talents and skills of students and instructors at colleges and universities are fundamental to the **Small Business Institute (SBI).** Under the guidance of seasoned professors of business administration, students seeking advanced degrees work closely with small business owners to help solve specific problems, such as sagging sales or rising costs. Students earn credit toward their degrees, with their grades depending on how well they handle a client's problems. Several hundred colleges and universities counsel thousands of small-business owners through this program every year.
- The newest of the SBA's management counseling projects is its **Small Business Development Center (SBDC)** program. Begun in 1976, SBDCs are designed to consolidate information from various disciplines and institutions, including technical and professional schools. Then they make this knowledge available to new and existing small businesses. In 1995, universities in 45 states took part in the program.

NETWORKING More and more, small-business owners are discovering the value of **networking**—meeting regularly with one another to discuss common problems and opportunities and, perhaps most important, pool resources. Businesspeople have long joined organizations such as the local chamber of commerce and the National Federation of Independent Businesses (NFIB) to make such contacts.

Today, organizations are springing up all over the United States to facilitate small-business networking. One such organization, the Council of Smaller Enterprises of Cleveland, boasts a total membership of more than 9,000 small business owners, the largest number in the country. This organization offers its members not only networking possibilities but also educational programs and services tailored to their needs. In a typical year, its 85 educational programs draw more than 8,500 small business owners.

In particular, women and minorities have found networking to be an effective problem-solving tool. The National Association of Women Business Owners (NAWBO), for example, provides a variety of networking forums. The NAWBO also has chapters in most major cities where its members can meet regularly. Increasingly, women are relying more on other women to help locate venture capital, establish relationships with customers, and provide such essential services as accounting and legal advice. According to Patty Abramson of the Women's Growth Capital Fund, all of these tasks have traditionally been harder for women because, until now, they've never had friends in the right places. "I wouldn't say this is about discrimination," adds Abramson. "It's about not having the relationships, and business is about relationships."[20]

> **"I wouldn't say this is about discrimination. It's about not having the relationships, and business is about relationships."**
>
> —Patty Abramson
> *Women's Growth Capital Fund*

FRANCHISING

The next time you drive or walk around town, be on the alert for a McDonald's, Taco Bell, Subway, Denny's, or KFC restaurant, a 7-Eleven or Circle K convenience store, a RE/Max or Coldwell Banker real estate office, a Super 8 or Ramada motel, a Blockbuster Video store, a Sylvan Learning Center educational center, an Express Oil Change or Precision Auto Wash car-service center, or a Supercuts hair salon. What do these businesses have in common? In most cases, they will be franchised operations, operating under licenses issued by parent companies to local entrepreneurs who own and manage them.

As many would-be businesspeople have discovered, franchising agreements are an accessible doorway to entrepreneurship. A **franchise** is an arrangement that permits the *franchisee* (buyer) to sell the product of the *franchiser* (seller, or parent company). Franchisees can thus benefit from the selling corporation's experience and expertise. They can also consult the franchiser for managerial and financial help.

franchise Arrangement in which a buyer (franchisee) purchases the right to sell the good or service of the seller (franchiser)

For example, the franchiser may supply financing. It may pick the store location, negotiate the lease, design the store, and purchase necessary equipment. It may train the first set of employees and managers and provide standardized policies and procedures. Once the business is open, the franchiser may offer savings by allowing it to purchase from a central location. Marketing strategy (especially advertising) may also be handled by the franchiser. Finally, franchisees may benefit from continued management counseling. In short, franchisees receive—that is, invest in—not only their own ready-made businesses but also expert help in running them.

With more than 13,000 outlets in 64 countries, Subway is second only to McDonald's in the fast-food franchising business. Subway's royalty fee of 8% of gross sales is the highest in the industry, but the company's complicated franchise agreement is cluttered with clauses that are unenforceable in several states. "I've seen over 300 franchise agreements," says one attorney who chaired a national commission on franchising standards, "and Subway's is the worst." There are currently 160 pending legal suits filed by agents, salespeople, and store owners against Subway, more than the combined total of its seven largest competitors. However, claims one company franchisee trainer, fewer than 10% of Subway franchisees ever read the franchise agreement.

Advantages and Disadvantages of Franchising

Franchises offer many advantages to both sellers and buyers. For example, franchisers benefit from the ability to grow rapidly by using the investment money provided by franchisees. This strategy has enabled giant franchisers such as McDonald's and Baskin-Robbins to mushroom into billion-dollar concerns in a brief time.

For the franchisee, the arrangement combines the incentive of owning a business with the advantage of access to big-business management skills. Unlike the person who starts from scratch, the franchisee does not have to build a business step by step. Instead, the business is established virtually overnight. Moreover, because each franchise outlet is probably a carbon copy of every other outlet, the chances of failure are reduced. According to the U.S. Department of Commerce, only 5 percent of all franchises in the country were discontinued in 1990.

Of course owning a franchise also involves certain disadvantages. Perhaps the most significant is the start-up cost. Franchise prices vary widely. Fantastic Sam's hair salon franchise fees are $25,000, but a Gingiss Formalwear franchise can run as high as $100,000. Extremely profitable or hard-to-get franchises are even more expensive. A McDonald's franchise costs $650,000 to $750,000, and a professional sports team can cost several hundred million dollars. Franchisees may also have continued obligations to contribute percentages of sales to parent corporations.

Buying a franchise also entails less tangible costs. For one thing, the small business owner sacrifices some independence. A McDonald's franchisee cannot change the way hamburgers or milkshakes are made. Nor can franchisees create individual identities in their communities; for all practical purposes, the McDonald's owner is anonymous. In addition, many franchise agreements are difficult to terminate.

Finally, although franchises minimize risks, they do not guarantee success. Many franchisees have seen their investments—and their dreams—disappear because of poor locations, rising costs, or lack of continued franchiser commitment. Moreover, figures on failure rates are artificially low because they do not include failing franchisees bought out by their franchising parent companies. An additional risk is that the chain itself could collapse. In any given year, dozens—sometimes hundreds—of franchisers close shop or stop selling franchises.

Continued from page 149

The Next Installment

Barbara Babbit Kaufman is not likely to rest on the success of Chapter 11. Having carved out a retailing niche that emphasizes discount prices and shopping convenience, she has already expanded beyond familiar business territory by acquiring Onyx Entertainment, a book and music store based in Gainesville, Georgia. The acquisition not only moves Chapter 11 into the music business but also widens its geographic reach as a bookseller.

Kaufman's expansion plans are just beginning. She is planning to open another 15 stores in the Atlanta area and is trying to attract outside funding for expansion into another Southeastern city. Her ultimate goal is to go national.

Questions for Discussion

1. Do you consider Barbara Babbit Kaufman a successful entrepreneur? Why?
2. Why is it important for a small company to find a marketing niche? Why is this particularly important when small companies compete directly with big businesses for the same customers?
3. Why was choosing locations in low-cost strip malls a smart business strategy? Would it be feasible for Borders or Barnes & Noble to use the same strategy?
4. What risks does Kaufman run in acquiring Onyx Entertainment? What are the risks of expanding to another city? What are the risks of becoming a national chain? Why do you think that many small businesses fail when they expand too rapidly or with too little capital?

SUMMARY

1. **Define *small business* and explain its importance to the U.S. economy.** A *small business* is independently owned and managed and does not dominate its market. Small businesses are crucial to the economy because they create new jobs, foster *entrepreneurship* and *innovation*, and supply goods and services needed by larger businesses.

2. **Explain which *types of small business* best lend themselves to success.** Services are the easiest operations for small business owners to start because they require low levels of resources. They also offer high returns on investment and tend to foster innovation. Retailing and wholesaling are more difficult because they usually require some experience, but they are still attractive to many entrepreneurs. New technology and management techniques are making agriculture profitable once again for small farmers. As the most resource-intensive area of the economy, manufacturing is the area least dominated by small firms.

3. **Define *entrepreneurship* and describe some basic *entrepreneurial characteristics*.** *Entrepreneurs* are small business owners who assume the risk of business ownership. Unlike many business owners, they seek growth and expansion as their primary goal. Most successful entrepreneurs share a strong desire to be their own bosses and believe that building businesses will help them gain control over their lives and build for their families. Many also enjoy taking risks and committing themselves to the necessary time and work. Finally, most report that freedom and creative expression are important factors in the decision to own and operate their own businesses.

4. **Describe the *start-up decisions* made by small businesses and identify sources of *financial aid* and *management advice* available to such enterprises.** In deciding to go into business, the entrepreneur must choose between buying an existing business and starting

from scratch. Both approaches involve practical advantages and disadvantages. A successful existing business has working relationships with other businesses and has already proved its ability to make a profit. New businesses, on the other hand, allow owners to plan and work with clean slates, but it is hard to make projections about the business's prospects.

Although small business owners generally draw heavily on their own resources for financing, they can get financial aid from venture capital firms, which seek profits from investments in companies with rapid growth potential. The Small Business Administration (SBA) also sponsors a variety of loan programs, including small-business investment companies. Finally, foreign firms and other nonbank lenders make funds available under various circumstances. Management advice is available from *advisory boards*, *management consultants*, *the SBA*, and the practice of *networking* (meeting regularly with people in related businesses to discuss problems and opportunities).

5. **Identify the advantages and disadvantages of *franchising*.** *Franchising* has become a popular form of small-business ownership because the *franchiser* (parent company) supplies financial, managerial, and marketing assistance to the *franchisee*, who buys the right to sell the franchiser's product. Franchising also enables small businesses to grow rapidly. Finally, the risks in franchising are lower than those in starting a new business from scratch. The costs of purchasing a franchise can be quite high, however, and the franchisee sacrifices independence and creativity. In addition, owning franchises provides no guarantee of success.

QUESTIONS AND EXERCISES

Questions for Review

1. Why are small businesses important to the U.S. economy?
2. What key factors typically contribute to the success and failure of small businesses?
3. Identify the primary sources of funding for small businesses and rank them in order of importance.
4. From the standpoint of the franchisee, what are the primary advantages and disadvantages of most franchise arrangements?

Questions for Analysis

5. If you were going to open a small business, what type would it be? Why?
6. Do you think you would be a successful entrepreneur? Why or why not?
7. Would you prefer to buy an existing business or start your own business from scratch? Why?
8. Would you prefer to open an independent business or enter a franchise agreement? Why?

Application Exercises

9. Select a small local firm that has gone out of business recently. Identify as many factors as you can that led to the company's failure.
10. At the library, research the role of small business in another country.

BUILDING YOUR BUSINESS SKILLS

WORKING THE INTERNET

This exercise enhances the following SCANS workplace competencies: demonstrating basic skills, demonstrating thinking skills, exhibiting interpersonal skills, and working with information.

▼ Goal

To encourage students to define the opportunities and problems for small companies doing business on the Internet.

▼ Situation

Suppose you and two partners own a gift basket store, specializing in special occasion baskets for individual and corporate clients. Your business is doing well in your community, but you believe there may be opportunity for growth through a virtual storefront on the Internet.

▼ Method

STEP 1

Join with two other students and assume the role of business partners. Start by researching Internet businesses. Look at books and articles at the library and contact the following Web sites for help:

- Small Business Administration: <http://www.sba.gov/>
- IBM Small Business Center: <http://www.businesscenter.ibm.com/>
- Apple Small Business Home Page: <http://www.smallbusiness.apple.com/>

These sites may lead you to other sites, so keep an open mind.

STEP 2

Based on your research, determine the importance of the following small-business issues:

- An analysis of changing company finances as a result of expansion onto the Internet
- An analysis of your new competitive marketplace (the world) and how it affects your current marketing approach, which focuses on your local community
- Identification of sources of management advice as the expansion proceeds
- The role of technology consultants in launching and maintaining the Web site
- Customer service policies in your virtual environment

▼ Follow-Up Questions

1. Do you think your business would be successful on the Internet? Why or why not?
2. Based on your analysis, how will Internet expansion affect your current business practices? What specific changes are you likely to make?
3. Do you think that operating a virtual storefront will be harder or easier than doing business in your local community? Explain your answer.

CRAFTING YOUR BUSINESS PLAN

FITTING INTO THE ENTREPRENEURIAL MOLD

▼ The Purpose of the Assignment

1. To acquaint students with the process of navigating the Business PlanPro (BPP) software package.
2. To familiarize students with the ways in which entrepreneurship and small-business considerations enter into the business planning framework of BPP.
3. To encourage students to apply their textbook information on entrepreneurship to the preparation of their BPP small-business plans.

▼ Assignment

After reading Chapter 7 in the textbook, open the BPP software* and look around for information about planning a new start-up company called Corporate Fitness. In the Task Manager screen, click on **Finish and Polish;** then click on **6. Executive Summary** to familiarize yourself with an overview of this firm. Next respond to the following questions:

1. Which industry category for small businesses—wholesaling, retailing, services, or manufacturing—best describes Corporate Fitness's line of business?
2. The textbook identifies several characteristics of successful entrepreneurs. Judging by its business plan, do you think the management team of Corporate Fitness has an "entrepreneurial" orientation? [Sites to see in *BPP* (for this assignment): In the Task Manager screen, click on **Your Management Team.** Then click on each of the following: **1. Management Summary, 3. Management Team,** and **4. Gaps.**]
3. Look at Corporate Fitness's planned sales growth and the firm's plans for promoting its business during the coming years. Do you have confidence in the projected growth figures? Why or why not? [Sites to see in *BPP:* In the Task Manager screen, click on **The Bottom Line.** Then click on **3. Profit and Loss Table.** In the Task Manager screen, click on **Your Sales Forecast.** Next click on each of the following in turn: **4. Sales Forecast** and **3. Promotion Strategy.** After returning to the Task Manager screen, click on **Your Marketing Plan.** Then click on **3. Marketing Strategy Summary.**]
4. Your textbook identifies several sources of advice for starting and running small businesses. Judging from its business plan, do you think that Corporate Fitness is planning to seek advice from any of those sources in getting started? Do you think it is a good idea to discuss the planned use of such sources in the business plan? Explain why or why not.

▼ For Your Own Plan

5. What sources of advice and assistance do you plan to tap in getting your firm off the ground? What kinds of advice—that is, in which areas and for what kinds of activities—will you need most at specific stages in the future development of your firm? Identify in your business plan your plans for seeking advice, the specific value that you expect to gain from each of your sources, and the points in time when you expect to tap different sources.

▼ *General Tips for Navigating in BPP

1. Open the BPP program, examine the Welcome screen, and click on **Open a Sample Plan.**
2. From the Open a Sample Plan dialogue box, click on a sample company name; then click on **Open.**

3. On the Task Manager screen, click onto any of the lines, such as **Your Company.**
4. You can always return to the Task Manager screen by going to the bottom of the screen and clicking on the **Task Manager** icon.
5. When you are finished with a sample company, close its Task Manager screen.
6. After finishing with one sample company, you can get to the next one by going to the top of the screen and clicking on **File** (on the menu bar). Then beneath that, select **Open Sample Plan.** This will exit you from the current company file and send you to the Open a Sample Plan dialogue box, where you can select your next sample company.

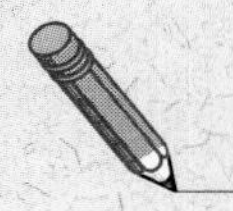

EXPLORING THE NET

FIELD TRIP TO THE SBA

One of the most important contacts for most small business owners is the Small Business Administration (SBA). You can reach the SBA's Website at the following address:

http://www.sbaonline.sba.gov/textonly/.

Begin by examining the sections on "Starting Your Business," "Financing Your Business," and "Expanding Your Business." After you have examined these features, consider the following questions:

1. Assume that you are planning to purchase an existing small business. In the previous areas, what was the most important information that you could find? Identify other sections of the SBA site that might be relevant to you. What useful information did you find by browsing a few of these additional areas?
2. Assume that you are planning to start a new small business from scratch. Again, review the sections of the SBA site that might be most relevant, and report on the available information.
3. Assume that you are already operating a small business but are concerned about increasing competition. In what sections of its Web site does the SBA offer material that might be helpful to you?
4. Use the SBA links to visit the Web sites maintained by your U.S. representative and/or senator. What specific information on these sites, if any, might be most helpful to a small business owner?
5. Overall, do you think the SBA site is likely to be more helpful for an existing business or for a new business just starting out? Why?

VIDEO EXERCISE 2.1

Playing One Team In Diverse Markets

Learning Objectives

The purpose of this video is to help you

1. Understand the many roles managers must play.
2. Recognize the different management needs for various types of businesses.
3. Appreciate how performance evaluation fits into the management process.

Background Information

Managing encompasses a wide variety of activities ranging from evaluating the business environment, to setting goals for the organization, to strategizing, to leading employees. The management process becomes more complex in businesses such as Showtime, where areas of the organization often have different objectives and stakeholders. Showtime's market—its six companies serve 70 percent of U.S. cable television subscribers—is also diverse. Strategies and approaches that work in one area of the U.S. market may not be effective in another area, and American-based programming is not always best suited for some foreign markets.

This diversity places several demands on Showtime's management. Top managers must operate as "one team" while allowing lower-level managers to adapt to the specific needs of their employees and markets. As employees and managers develop and advance, they may need to change their approach from what worked in their previous environment. This demands human relations, conceptual, and problem-solving skills. Showtime's managers must also make sure their employees keep up with the constant advances in entertainment technology. Although Showtime is organized by functional areas, many employees share responsibilities.

The Video

Part Two of the Showtime video highlights the different management needs for various types of businesses at different times. The video also shows the process Showtime uses to evaluate employee performance. See if you can assess how effective this process is based on what you have seen.

Discussion Questions

1. What do people mean by strategic planning horizon and strategic priorities?
2. What are some of the strategies managers in a large corporation can use to create an entrepreneurial culture?
3. What is the parent company's role in a large, multidimensional organization?

Follow-Up Assignment

Part Two of the video discusses the management process at Showtime, but how might this process differ in other types of businesses? Obtain the annual reports for a large consulting firm (such as McKinsey & Co.) and a manufacturer of computer chips (such as Intel Corp.). From reading these annual reports, what are your thoughts on how the management process differs at these firms?

For Further Exploration

Go to Intel's Web site at

http://www.intel.com/intel/museum/25anniv/index.html

Click on the links provided on this Web page to learn about Intel's history. How has the company changed over the past 25 years? How have management's needs changed at Intel over that time? What have been the keys to Intel's success? What management issues do you believe will be the most critical at Intel in the next 5 to 10 years?

Tires Plus

"I've had a spiritual teacher, an intellectual teacher, then why not an emotional-psychological teacher?"

—*Tires Plus cofounder*

Learning Objectives

The purpose of this video exercise is to help you

1. Become better acquainted with a specific, highly successful American company that was born when two enterprising young men decided to start from scratch.
2. Understand what is meant by the terms *teammates* and *guests* and how these terms give a different meaning to a day's work at Tires Plus.
3. Grasp the Tires Plus approach to training employees.

Background Information

Hattie Bryant, accompanied by her commentator, Jim Shell, talks with the cofounders of **Tires Plus,** which has nearly 70 stores nationwide and sales of $100 million annually. Of the two founders, Hattie says that Tom is the people person and Don is the operations person. At the beginning, we see "head coach" Tom speaking to a training session at *Tires Plus University.* With genuine earnestness, he is telling these future *teammates* (employees) that making money for the company is **not** the object of **Tires Plus.** Rather, the object is to properly serve the *guests* (customers), and then the money will follow. This point seems like a modern-day application of Adam Smith's *invisible hand,* which dictates that an entrepreneur must serve society if a profit is to be made. Tom tells us that when he and Don left Shell Oil Company to start their own firm, they had to go to 10 banks before finding someone to lend to them.

Tires Plus establishments feature speed. Installing tires should take no more than 30 to 60 minutes. If they can't make it within 58 minutes, you receive a coupon for a free oil change whenever you want it. And the firm keeps track of quality matters. How a *teammate* answers the phone is important, and after a *guest* has come and gone, there is a follow-up call to be sure that the customer is satisfied with **Tires Plus** service.

To ensure a uniform level of quality service at all the firm's stores, **Tires Plus** must train its personnel. Commentator Jim Shell is brought on to treat the area of training. Although Jim Shell is an enthusiastic supporter of the small-business sector of the American economy, he admits that large corporations far outdo the small enterprises in training. Training, Shell says, is a significant expense, and so small firms often neglect it. Almost without exception, as a firm grows, its training just does not keep up. The consequences can be inefficient and unenlightened personnel clumsily plodding toward the goals of the firm. Shell says that some entrepreneurs think it is bad business to train personnel only to have them leave. Far worse, says Shell, is to **not** train them and have them *stay.*

As this firm has grown, it has been tempted to expand further by going public—selling stock in the company. So far, founder Tom tells us, the firm is juggling just two balls in the air—*guests* and *teammates.* Bringing in *stockholders* as a third ball to juggle is not what **Tires Plus** wants right now. You can shop for tires from **Tires Plus** on the Internet, and Hattie gets one of the employees to show us the electronic catalog available to net surfers.

The Video

SMALL BUSINESS 2000 MASTER CLASS, SB2000 SHOW #103.
In your search for information about a successful company you will rarely encounter a founder willing to take a half hour to explain the firm's philosophy and/or corporate culture. This video provides such an opportunity, as one of the founders takes the time to show you how he cares about his company.

Discussion Questions

1. You've seen Tom interviewed throughout the videotape and heard him talking to a *Tires Plus University* class. How would you like to work for him? Which seems to be his most outstanding quality?
2. What is your reaction to Tom being the *coach* managing the *teammates*, all in an effort to keep the *guests* happy? What kind of corporate culture is being nurtured here?
3. Have Tom's emotional problems, referred to on the videotape, made him a better manager at **Tires Plus?** Why or why not?
4. Based on what you know about computers and the Internet, is it a special claim today to indicate that your firm's products can be ordered on the Internet?
5. What is the main reason that small businesses, according to Jim Shell, do not devote enough attention to *training?*
6. What are retained earnings, which are mentioned on the videotape?
7. Did you catch Tom talking about retained earnings? What role have retained earnings played in the firm's growth?

Follow-Up Assignment

The **Tires Plus** video informs us that Tom and Don left Shell Oil Company to start their own firm. Your assignment is to locate an entrepreneur who has the time to talk to you, and then ask that entrepreneur some questions. Sometimes when sharp young people like Tom and Don leave a secure firm to start their own business, they hear these parting words: "Remember, if things don't work out, there will always be a job for you here." Ask your entrepreneur interviewee if he or she heard a similar parting statement. Then ask if the entrepreneur, in a low moment, ever seriously considered going back to that secure position with the old firm. Or perhaps the entrepreneur left the secure position on a less-than-friendly basis. Why? Or maybe he or she left because of a human resources cutback. Would your interviewee consider going back to the old firm if the right job opened up?

The Internet Connection and One Last Thing to Remember

You can contact **Tires Plus** on the Internet at

http://www.tiresplus.com

At one point, Tom says: "I've had a spiritual teacher, an intellectual teacher, then why not have an emotional-psychological teacher?" Video host Hattie then says that it sounds as if Tom has had some therapy. He admits to a "wake-up call" some 6 years ago as a result of going through a divorce and having cancer for a time. That call convinced Tom that to run the firm effectively, he would have to manage himself, too. With the help of other people who could be called *mentors*, Tom feels now more capable of heading the firm. Tom indicates that despite his devotion to his partner and the other *teammates* and to the firm, he does take time now and then to be good to himself. Such rest and relaxation make him more effective for the firm.

UNDERSTANDING PEOPLE IN ORGANIZATIONS

The Wacky World of Southwest Airlines

What could be more serious than running an airline? Meeting schedules, maintaining equipment, tracking baggage, training staff, dealing with federal and state regulations, and keeping customers happy—could there be a better recipe for stress? So why does Herb Kelleher, cofounder and chief executive of Southwest Airlines, encourage his 25,000 employees to outsmile and outjoke the competition? Kelleher believes that a fun workplace is also a productive workplace; and a productive workplace can earn more while charging less.

As a rule, figures don't lie: Operating costs at Southwest are 7.5 cents per seat per mile—2 cents lower than the average of other airlines. Southwest's profit margin is more than 6 percent—a third more than those of other airlines. The result: Southwest is the most consistently profitable, rapidly growing airline in the United States.

FUN + EMPOWERMENT + RESPECT = HIGH PRODUCTIVITY

The employee productivity that made Southwest the nation's fifth-largest airline is one of the wonders of the aviation world: Whereas it takes another airline a full 45 minutes to service arriving planes and get them back in the air, Southwest does it in 20 minutes. In what can best be described as a whirlwind of activity, employees fuel the plane, load and unload passengers and bags, and restock refreshments (Southwest doesn't serve meals). Everyone pitches in, including pilots, who can be seen working with the ground crew to pick up trash. These break-the-sound-barrier turnaround times enable Southwest's fleet of 250 planes to do the job of 300.

Employees work their tails off largely because of the corporate culture that Herb Kelleher has fostered—a culture based on empowerment, respect for the individual, and just plain fun. A case in point is Marilyn, a flight attendant who takes the mike as her plane backs away from the Houston terminal.

"Could y'all lean in a little toward the center aisle, please?" she chirps in an irresistible Southern drawl. "Just a bit, please. That's it. No, the other way, sir. Thanks."

Baffled passengers comply even though they have no idea why.

"You see," says Marilyn at last, "the pilot has to pull out of this space here, and he needs to be able to check the rearview mirrors."

Only when the laughter subsides does Marilyn launch into the standard aircraft safety speech. An environment that respects individuals enough to encourage this kind of unique self-expression has made Southwest the top-rated company on *Fortune* magazine's list of the 100 best companies to work for in America.

EMPLOYEES COME FIRST

Kelleher believes that his employees constitute his prime business advantage. Competitors, he argues, "can imitate the airplanes. They can imitate our ticket counters and all the other hardware. But they can't duplicate the people of Southwest and their attitudes. . . . It used to be a business conundrum: 'Who comes first? The employees, customers, or shareholders?' That's never been an issue to me. The employees come first. If they're happy, satisfied, dedicated, and energetic, they'll take real good care of the customers. When the customers are happy, they come back. And that makes the shareholders happy."

> **"If employees are happy, satisfied, dedicated, and energetic, they'll take real good care of the customers. When the customers are happy, they come back. And that makes the shareholders happy."**
>
> —Herb Kelleher
> *Cofounder and Chief Executive of Southwest Airlines*

Not surprisingly, a lot of people want to work at Southwest, but of the 150,000 résumés the airline receives each year, it hires just 5,000 people. Those who make the cut are chosen mainly for their can-do attitude, their desire to color outside the lines, and their sense of humor. New employees are trained at Southwest's University for People, where they are encouraged to strive for their personal best by doing whatever they do better, faster, and more cheaply.

They are rewarded for taking initiative and making sound situational decisions. In a cross-training program that paints the big picture of company operations, they are taught to look beyond the obvious. When pilots help skycaps and reservationists work with baggage handlers, everyone begins to take ownership of overall operations and looks for ways to make a difference. Kelleher realizes that mistakes are inevitable when people take responsibility, but punishment has no part in his human resources plan. His focus is on learning and doing better the next time.

In return for dedicated service, employees receive impressive benefits:

- *Job security.* In 27 years, Southwest has never furloughed anyone.
- *Opportunities for personal career growth.* Stability brings steady promotions based on skill, experience, and attitude.
- *Perks.* Employees with perfect attendance for 3 months receive two free space-available tickets to anywhere Southwest travels.
- *Compensation.* Southwest is a union company. More than 8 of 10 employees are union members, and they receive union wages negotiated for the entire airline industry. Kelleher sweetens the compensation pot through a generous profit-sharing plan that invests in Southwest stock—stock whose market performance has made millionaires out of many long-time employees.
- *Social fulfillment.* Motivation in the form of fun is administered at Christmas parties (in July), chili cook-offs, and outlandish Halloween bashes.

"IT ALL STARTS WITH HERB"

Obviously, Herb Kelleher's leadership style has a lot to do with the success of Southwest. "It all starts with Herb," says pilot Sonny Childers. "I've seen Herb hand out peanuts on flights. He'll go out the Wednesday before Thanksgiving and load bags onto planes. We know he'd never ask us to do anything he wouldn't do himself."

And then there's his legendary leadership in the area of fun. "He is a true party animal who is always the last one standing," reports director of employment Sherry Phelps. Kelleher takes several trips a month and can be found handing out peanuts and cracking jokes with passengers and crew. He has also been known to visit night-shift mechanics wearing a feather boa and floppy hat.

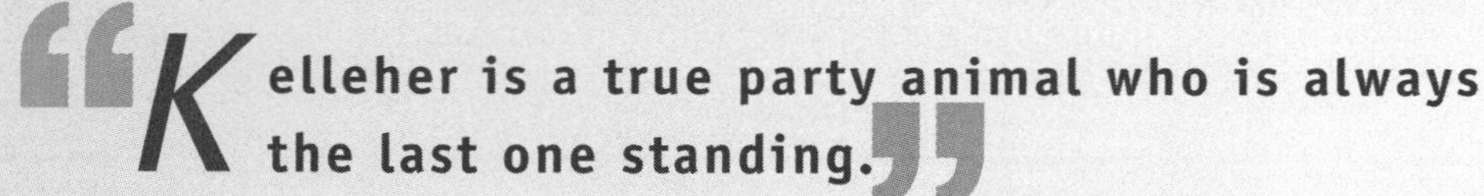

—Sherry Phelps
Director of Employment, Southwest Airlines

Is Kelleher's leadership style important to productivity and profits? Absolutely, says Robert Levering, coauthor of *The 100 Best Companies to Work for in America.* "The fact is," says Levering, "that in companies that are truly fun, [fun] is a separate objective. People explicitly say this is what we want to do here: We want to have fun. After all, what's life for and what's work for?"

THE CHALLENGE AHEAD

Since its first flight in June 1971, Southwest Airlines has expanded from its home base in Dallas to Louisiana, New Mexico, Oklahoma, Arizona, California, the Midwest,

Florida, Rhode Island, Alabama, and Maryland. Now it flies coast-to-coast with one stopover. Kelleher's next expansion target is the New York region. Thus far, as Southwest has expanded, passengers have followed in search of efficient low-cost transportation.

Perhaps the greatest challenge facing Kelleher is maintaining the corporate culture as the company grows. Can Southwest recruit employees in the Northeast who will embrace the company's core values? "There are people everywhere who fit into the Southwest culture," says Kelleher.

He also believes that from management's point of view, bigger does not necessarily mean better—or even different. "You should not get yourself into a rigid frame of mind where you say, 'By virtue of the fact that we're bigger, we have to function differently,' and give up all the advantages that the smaller, more entrepreneurial company has. We've tried to reduce the bureaucracy and avoid the hierarchy as much as we can," explains Kelleher, who wants employees to "deal with each other person-to-person and informally instead of through a formalized network of communication." As managers, he adds, we must never "get too big to have a personal relationship with the people of Southwest Airlines."

WEB LINKS

Along with Southwest Airlines, the January 12, 1998, issue of *Fortune* magazine lists the following companies as among the 100 best companies to work for in the United States. Visit their Web sites and see what you learn about their attitudes toward their employees. The information in these sites will help you answer the questions that follow.

- **Corning**
  http://www.corning.com/
- **Deloitte & Touche**
  http://www.dttus.com/us/home.htm
- **Microsoft Job Search**
  http://www.microsoft.com/jobs/visit.htm
- **Smucker's**
  http://www.smucker.com/
- **Southwest Airlines**
  http://www.southwest.com/
- **TDIndustries**
  http://www.tdindustries.com/

QUESTIONS FOR DISCUSSION

1. As a motivational factor, how important is fun likely to be in your personal job choice? Do you think that it will be more or less important than good pay and benefits?
2. Why is Southwest's no-furlough policy so important to employee morale?
3. Do you think that Herb Kelleher practices Theory X or Theory Y? Explain your answer. In your opinion, why should Corning, Deloitte & Touche, Microsoft, Smucker's, and TDIndustries be considered Theory Y organizations?
4. Judging from the information that you have gathered, both in this case and from Southwest Airlines' Web site, how would you apply Herzberg's two-factor theory to the practice of employee motivation at Southwest?
5. Why is empowerment such an important motivational factor at Southwest? What evidence do you see at the other Web sites that employees have a voice in the management of their jobs and their companies?
6. How would you describe Herb Kelleher's leadership style? Do you consider Kelleher a year-2000 leader? Explain your answer.

MOTIVATING, SATISFYING, AND LEADING EMPLOYEES

Do Stock Options Make it Happen?

In 1995, Chemical Banking Corp. joined with Chase Manhattan Bank to form what was then the largest bank in the United States. The merger, needless to say, was complex and exhausting for the thousands of employees in both organizations who were told to "make it happen." Toiling round the clock, an army of employees combined and re-created whole departments, joined internal and external computer systems, reconfigured office space, combined and closed neighborhood branches, redesigned health insurance plans, initiated marketing and advertising programs, hired vendors, and more—much, much more.

Their accomplishments were remarkable, and the board of directors wanted to recognize them in a concrete way. So in 1996, Chase Manhattan Bank, as the new company is known, issued stock options to 67,000 full- and part-time employees. It was management's way of thanking employees for their hard work—and, of course, motivating them to do more. Chairman and CEO Walter V. Shipley told employees in his announcement letter that the new company wanted them to "continue your very best work so that we can indeed achieve our mission of becoming the world's premier financial services company, a goal well within our grasp."

Chase is not alone in using stock options to reward and motivate workers. In fact, it is just one of a rapidly expanding number of organizations in such industries as high technology, telecommunications, pharmaceuticals, and financial services. Indeed, employees in these industries have come to expect options as part of their compensation packages; but do stock options really motivate employees to work harder and smarter by aligning their interests with those of managers and shareholders? Or do they also have a darker side? The answer to both questions, it seems, is yes, and therein lies the problem.

First of all, to explain, stock options give employees the right to purchase a certain number of shares at a so-called *strike price*—say, $10 a share—for a given period of time. This offer is a valuable asset if the share price rises to, say, $15. At that point, employees can exercise their options to buy at the strike price ($10 per share) and sell at the market price ($15). The gain, of course, is the difference between the strike price and the market prices—in this case, $5 a share. At companies such as Microsoft, Dell, Intel, and Chase Manhattan, employees at all organizational levels have actually become millionaires by exercising options for hundreds, and sometimes thousands, of shares. Of course, if the market value falls, the story has a different ending.

In theory, stock options create a culture of ownership—a climate in which effort and results translate for the employee into the possibility of earning a personal fortune. In theory, then, they raise morale and encourage people to stay on board to collect on options, all the while helping to mold a pay-for-performance culture. Options, says stock analyst Ronald Mandle, "give employees a bigger stake" in the company, its activities, and its performance. They give people the incentive to focus on the company's long-term goals.

And what about the downside? Although options often spur expectations of wealth, there is no guarantee that employees will ever collect, especially if company earnings fall short or the stock market itself slumps. At highest risk are employees who cash out as soon as they are in the money, thereby eliminating the value of their options as long-term incentives. Typically, explains Mark Lang, a researcher who has studied worker reactions to option programs, many employees "are willing to give up a lot of the option's theoretical value in exchange for getting rid of the risk." They are willing to forgo the long-term value of the offer to eliminate the risk of sinking market prices. "Market volatility," notes Lang, "spooks most people," especially if they need money to pay bills.

Likewise, instead of motivating people to stay with employers for the long haul, stock options can have the opposite effect if employees believe that they can find other jobs

right away. This is particularly true of mid- and upper-level employees in high-technology companies. In a so-called game of "stock-option roulette," an employee joins a start-up company, takes the options, and then sells the shares as soon as they gain substantial value (which, in Silicon Valley, can be a fairly short time). Then the employee finds another job that includes options as part of the deal.

This game is becoming so popular that it has begun to change the way companies are built. "In the entrepreneurial world of the '80s," reports business writer Edward O. Welles, "people got rich through logical means: starting companies, working hard, and hoping their efforts would build value. People like Steve Jobs, Bill Gates, and Michael Dell did so, becoming cultural heroes and creating value along the way. Now it seems that the mindset has shifted. Join the right company, hitch your wagon to the star of the next Jobs, Gates, or Dell, and the payoff is yours. Getting rich used to first require the creation of wealth. Now it seems possible—via options—that getting rich can be disconnected from that process, not unlike waking up one morning to find yourself holding the right lottery ticket."

With more than 40 percent of U.S. companies now offering some sort of stock-based compensation, the link between options and motivation will continue to be explored, as will the role of job satisfaction as a motivating force in employee productivity. The wild card, of course, is the stock market. If the market plunges and money is the *only* reason people have for working, what will happen to employee morale then?

As you will see in this chapter, people work hard for reasons other than money. They want interesting work which makes them feel part of a team and which satisfies their intellectual, social, and emotional needs. They also want the ability to create work schedules that fit in with the rest of their lives. By focusing on the learning objectives of this chapter, you will better understand why employee morale and job satisfaction are important to all types of business organizations. You will also understand the role of leadership in motivating employees—or team members—to high levels of achievement.

Our opening story is continued on page 200

After reading this chapter, you should be able to:

1. **Discuss the importance of *job satisfaction* and *employee morale* and summarize their roles in *human relations* in the workplace.**
2. **Identify and summarize the most important theories of *employee motivation*.**
3. **Describe some of the strategies used by organizations to improve job satisfaction and employee motivation.**
4. **Discuss different managerial styles of *leadership* and their impact on human relations in the workplace.**

human relations Interactions between employers and employees and their attitudes toward one another

The foundation of good **human relations**—the interactions between employers and employees and their attitudes toward one another—is a satisfied workforce. Although most people have a general idea what "job satisfaction" is, both job satisfaction and high morale can be elusive in the workplace. Because they are critical to an organization's success, we begin our discussion by explaining their importance.

■ THE IMPORTANCE OF SATISFACTION AND MORALE

job satisfaction Degree of enjoyment that people derive from performing their jobs

morale Overall attitude that employees have toward their workplace

Broadly speaking, **job satisfaction** is the degree of enjoyment that people derive from performing their jobs. If people enjoy their work, they are relatively satisfied; if they do not enjoy their work, they are relatively dissatisfied. In turn, satisfied employees are likely to have high **morale**—the overall attitude that employees have toward their workplace. Morale reflects the degree to which they perceive that their needs are being met by their jobs. It is determined by a variety of factors, including job satisfaction and satisfaction with such things as pay, benefits, coworkers, and promotion opportunities.[1]

Companies can improve employee morale and job satisfaction in a variety of ways. Some large firms, for example, have instituted companywide programs designed specifically to address employees' needs. Employees at SAS Institute, a large software development company in North Carolina, enjoy private offices, a free health clinic, two on-site day-care centers, flexible work hours with 35-hour work weeks, a company-subsidized cafeteria, and year-end bonuses and profit sharing.[2] Managers at Hyatt Hotels report that conducting frequent surveys of employee attitudes, soliciting employee input, and—most important—acting on that input give their company an edge in recruiting and retaining productive workers. Managers of smaller businesses realize that the personal touch can reap big benefits in employee morale and even devotion. For example, First Tennessee, a midsize regional bank, believes that work and family are so closely related that family considerations should enter into job design. Thus, it offers such benefits as on-site child care.

When workers are satisfied and morale is high, the organization benefits in many ways. Compared with dissatisfied workers, for example, satisfied employees are more committed and loyal. Such employees are more likely to work hard and to make useful contributions to the organization. In addition, they tend to have fewer grievances and engage in fewer negative behaviors (complaining, deliberately slowing their work pace, and so forth) than dissatisfied counterparts. Finally, satisfied workers tend not only to come to work every day but also to remain with the organization. By promoting satisfaction and morale, then, management is working to ensure more efficient operations.

Jackie Demo works at Baxter Export Corp., helping the health care products maker get its catheters, intravenous tubes, and the like to a growing international market. And she does this with flexible hours and at least one day a week of telecommuting. Demo starts her day at 6:30 in the morning, which gets her home in time to pick her daughter up from day care and look in on her terminally ill mother-in-law. Demo's manager, John Lindner, believes that people are up to 10% more productive when they telecommute, though the company does limit telecommuting to 2 days a week maximum. In return for its flexibility—30% of Baxter employees telecommute, work part-time, or share jobs—the company gets greater commitment from its employees.

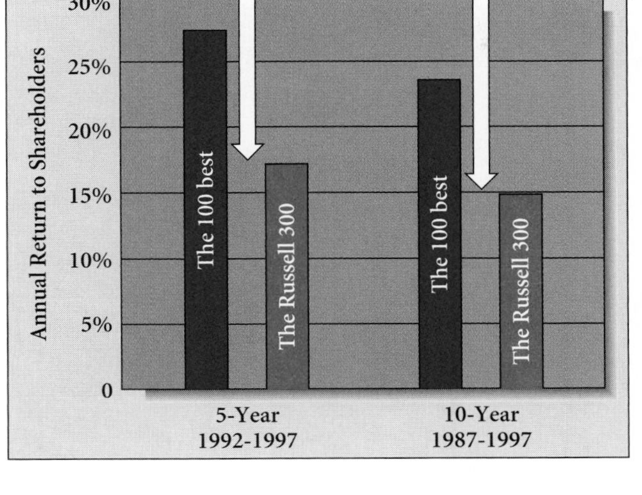

FIGURE 8.1 ◆ Satisfaction and Return to Shareholders

Conversely, the costs of dissatisfaction and poor morale are high. Dissatisfied workers are far more likely to be absent for minor illnesses, personal reasons, or a general disinclination to go to work. Low morale may also result in high *turnover*—the ratio of newly hired to currently employed workers. High levels of turnover have many negative consequences, including the disruption of production schedules, high retraining costs, and decreased productivity.

In fact, evidence suggests that job satisfaction and employee morale may directly affect a company's performance. The results of one recent study are highlighted in Figure 8.1. The study focused on the businesses identified as the 100 best companies to work for in America. It then compared the average annual return to shareholders (a major indicator of company performance) for those firms against the 3,000 U.S. largest companies. As you can see, the sample of 100 companies with the highest levels of satisfaction and morale significantly outperformed the larger sample over both 5 and 10 years. Of course, many other factors contributed to the performance of both sets of companies, but these differences nevertheless cannot be ignored.[3]

Recent Trends in Managing Satisfaction and Morale

Achieving high levels of job satisfaction and morale seems like a reasonable organizational goal, especially in light of findings such as those noted. From the late 1980s through the mid-1990s, many major companies went through periods of massive layoffs and cutbacks. AT&T, for example, eliminated 40,000 jobs. Although this case is extreme, such firms as Nabisco, Apple Computer, Conagra, Exxon, and Delta Airlines also cut thousands of jobs. Not surprisingly, then, satisfaction and morale plummeted in many companies. Workers feared for their job security, and even those who kept their jobs were unhappy about their less fortunate colleagues and friends.

In the late 1990s, however, things changed dramatically. A booming economy and the creation of thousands of new jobs led to low unemployment in most industries and regions. As a result, companies suddenly found themselves having to work harder not only to retain current employees who were being courted by other employers, but also to offer creative incentives to secure new employees, many of whom had multiple job opportunities to consider.

In the process, many leading firms came up with innovative benefits and "perks" designed to keep employees happy, boost satisfaction, and enhance morale. Figure 8.2 shows some recent trends in the area of benefits. In 1994, for example, no major employer reported offering employees group homeowner's insurance. By 1997, 12 percent had such

FIGURE 8.2 ◆ **Expansion of Benefits**

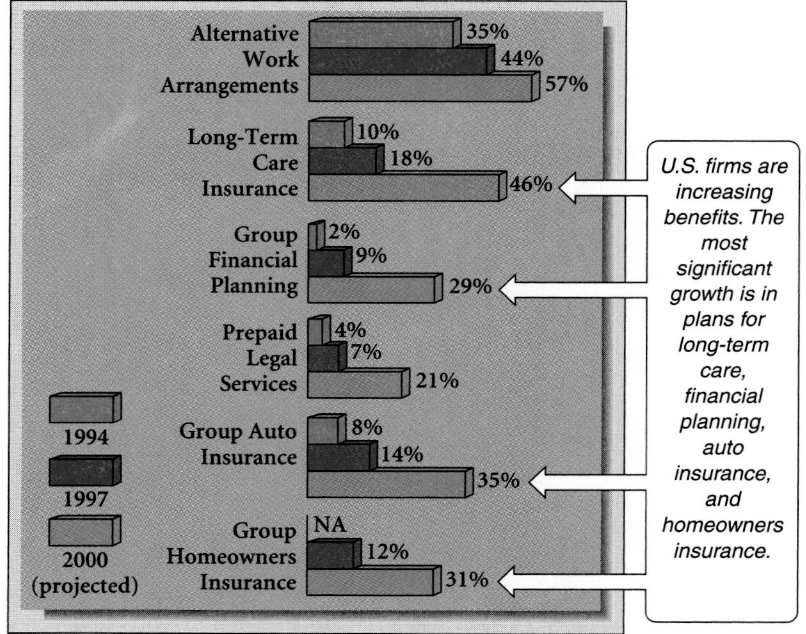

plans, with 31 percent expecting to have them in place by the year 2000. Virtually all of this expansion in benefits and perks results from the desire of businesses to make themselves more attractive workplaces by maintaining job satisfaction and employee morale.[4]

MOTIVATION IN THE WORKPLACE

motivation The set of forces that cause people to behave in certain ways

Although job satisfaction and morale are important, employee motivation is even more critical to a firm's success. As discussed in Chapter 5, motivation is one part of the managerial function of directing. Broadly defined, **motivation** is the set of forces that cause people to behave in certain ways. One worker may be motivated to work hard to produce as much as possible, whereas another may be motivated to do just enough to survive. Managers must understand these differences in behavior and the reasons for them.

Over the years, a steady progression of theories and studies has attempted to address these issues. In this section, we survey the major studies and theories of employee motivation. In particular, we focus on three approaches to human relations in the workplace that reflect a basic chronology of thinking in the area: classical theory and scientific management, behavior theory, and contemporary motivational theories.[5]

Classical Theory

classical theory of motivation Theory holding that workers are motivated solely by money

According to the so-called **classical theory of motivation,** workers are motivated solely by money. In his seminal book, *The Principles of Scientific Management*, industrial engineer Frederick Taylor (1911) proposed a way for both companies and workers to benefit from this widely accepted view of life in the workplace. If workers are motivated by money, Taylor reasoned, then paying them more should prompt them to produce more. Meanwhile, the firm that analyzed jobs and found better ways to perform them would be able to produce goods more cheaply, make higher profits, and thus pay and motivate workers better than its competitors.

Behavior Theory: The Hawthorne Studies

In 1925, a group of Harvard researchers began a study at the Hawthorne Works of Western Electric outside Chicago. With an eye to increasing productivity, they wanted to examine the relationship between changes in the physical environment and worker output.

The results of the experiment were unexpected, even confusing. Not surprisingly, for example, increased lighting levels improved productivity. For some reason, however, so did lower lighting levels. Moreover, against all expectations, increased pay *failed* to increase productivity. Gradually, the researchers pieced together the puzzle. The explanation lay in the workers' response to the *attention* that they were receiving. The researchers concluded that productivity rose in response to almost any management action that workers interpreted as special attention. This finding, known widely today as the **Hawthorne effect,** had a major influence on human relations theory, although in many cases it amounted simply to convincing managers that they should pay more attention to employees.

Hawthorne effect Tendency for productivity to increase when workers believe they are receiving special attention from management

Contemporary Motivational Theories

Following the Hawthorne studies, managers and researchers alike focused more attention on the importance of good human relations in motivating employee performance. Stressing the factors that cause, focus, and sustain workers' behavior, most motivation theorists are concerned with the ways in which management thinks about and treats employees. The major motivation theories include the *human resources model*, the *hierarchy of needs model*, *two-factor theory*, *expectancy theory*, *equity theory*, and *goal-setting theory*.

HUMAN RESOURCES MODEL: THEORIES X AND Y In an important study, behavioral scientist Douglas McGregor concluded that managers had radically different beliefs about how best to use the human resources at a firm's disposal. He classified these beliefs into sets of assumptions that he labeled "Theory X" and "Theory Y." The basic differences between these two theories are highlighted in Table 8.1.

Managers who subscribe to **Theory X** tend to believe that people are naturally lazy and uncooperative and must therefore be either punished or rewarded to be made productive. Managers who incline to **Theory Y** tend to believe that people are naturally energetic, growth oriented, self-motivated, and interested in being productive.

Theory X Theory of motivation holding that people are naturally irresponsible and uncooperative

McGregor generally favored Theory Y beliefs. Thus, he argued that Theory Y managers are more likely to have satisfied, motivated employees. Of course, Theory X and Y distinctions are somewhat simplistic and offer little concrete basis for action. Their value lies primarily in their ability to highlight and classify the behavior of managers in light of their attitudes toward employees.

Theory Y Theory of motivation holding that people are naturally responsible, growth oriented, self-motivated, and interested in being productive

MASLOW'S HIERARCHY OF NEEDS MODEL Psychologist Abraham Maslow's **hierarchy of human needs model** proposed that people have several different needs that they attempt to satisfy in their work. He classified these needs into five basic types and suggested that they be arranged in the hierarchy of importance as shown in Figure 8.3. According to Maslow, needs are hierarchical because lower-level needs must be met before a person will try to satisfy higher-level needs.

hierarchy of human needs model Theory of motivation describing five levels of human needs and arguing that basic needs must be fulfilled before people work to satisfy higher-level needs

Once a set of needs has been satisfied, it ceases to motivate behavior. This is the sense in which the hierarchical nature of lower- and higher-level needs affects employee motivation and satisfaction. For example, if you feel secure in your job, a new pension plan will

TABLE 8.1 ◆ **Theory X and Theory Y**

THEORY X	THEORY Y
People are lazy.	People are energetic.
People lack ambition and dislike responsibility.	People are ambitious and seek responsibility.
People are self-centered.	People can be selfless.
People resist change.	People want to contribute to business growth and change.
People are gullible and not very bright.	People are intelligent.

FIGURE 8.3 ◆ Maslow's Hierarchy of Needs

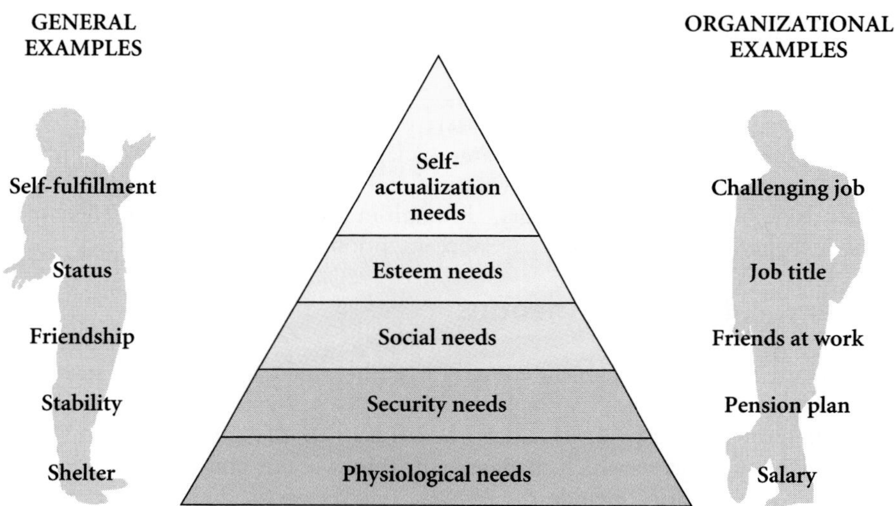

probably be less important to you than the chance to make new friends and join an informal network among your coworkers. If, however, a lower-level need suddenly becomes unfulfilled, most people immediately refocus on that lower level. Suppose, for example, that you are seeking to meet your self-esteem needs by working as a divisional manager at a major company. If you learn that your division, and consequently your job, may be eliminated, you might very well find the promise of job security at a new firm as motivating as a promotion once would have been at your old company.

Maslow's theory recognizes that because different people have different needs, they are motivated by different things. Unfortunately, it provides few specific guidelines for action in the workplace. Furthermore, research has found that the hierarchy varies widely, not only for different people but across different cultures.

TWO-FACTOR THEORY After studying a group of accountants and engineers, psychologist Frederick Herzberg concluded that job satisfaction and dissatisfaction depend on two factors: *hygiene factors*, such as working conditions, and *motivation factors*, such as recognition for a job well done.

two-factor theory Theory of motivation holding that job satisfaction depends on two types of factors, hygiene and motivation

According to the **two-factor theory,** hygiene factors affect motivation and satisfaction only if they are absent or fail to meet expectations. For example, workers will be dissatisfied if they believe that they have poor working conditions. If working conditions are improved, however, they will not necessarily become satisfied; they will simply be not dissatisfied. If workers receive no recognition for successful work, they may be neither dissatisfied nor satisfied. If recognition is provided, they will likely become more satisfied.

Figure 8.4 illustrates the two-factor theory. Note that motivation factors lie along a continuum from *satisfaction* to *no satisfaction.* Hygiene factors, in contrast, are likely to produce feelings that lie on a continuum from *dissatisfaction* to *no dissatisfaction.* Whereas motivation factors are directly related to the work that employees actually perform, hygiene factors refer to the environment in which they perform it.

This theory thus suggests that managers should follow a two-step approach to enhancing motivation. First, they must ensure that hygiene factors—working conditions, clearly stated policies—are acceptable. This practice will result in an absence of dissatisfaction. Then they must offer motivation factors—recognition, added responsibility—as means of improving satisfaction and motivation.

Research suggests that although two-factor theory works in some professional settings, it is less effective in clerical and manufacturing settings. (Herzberg's research was limited to accountants and engineers.) In addition, one person's hygiene factor may be another person's

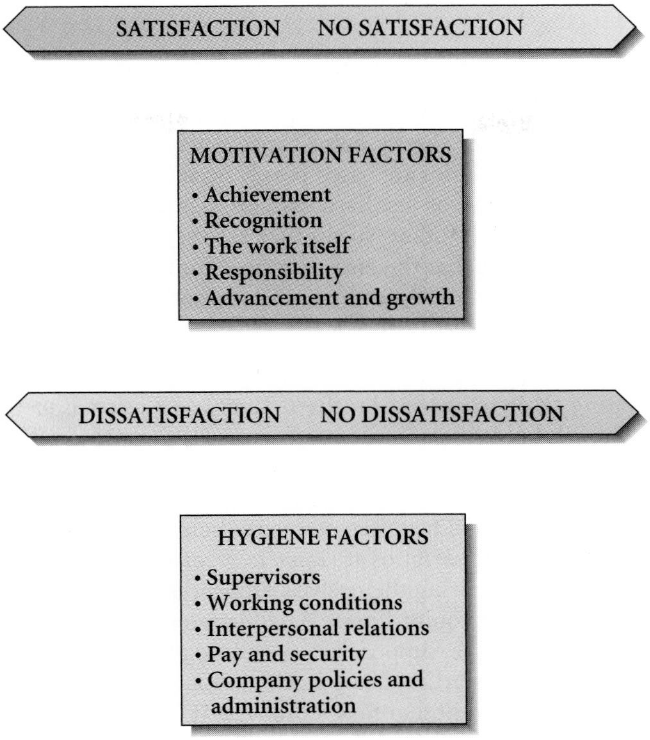

SATISFACTION — NO SATISFACTION

MOTIVATION FACTORS

- Achievement
- Recognition
- The work itself
- Responsibility
- Advancement and growth

DISSATISFACTION — NO DISSATISFACTION

HYGIENE FACTORS

- Supervisors
- Working conditions
- Interpersonal relations
- Pay and security
- Company policies and administration

FIGURE 8.4 ◆ Two-Factor Theory of Motivation

motivation factor. For example, if money represents nothing more than pay for time worked, it may be a hygiene factor for one person. For another person, however, money may be a motivation factor because it represents recognition and achievement.

expectancy theory Theory of motivation holding that people are motivated to work toward rewards that they want and that they believe they have a reasonable chance of obtaining

EXPECTANCY THEORY The **expectancy theory** suggests that people are motivated to work toward rewards that they want *and* that they believe they have a reasonable chance—or expectancy—of obtaining. A reward that seems out of reach is likely to be undesirable even if it is intrinsically positive. Figure 8.5 illustrates expectancy theory in terms of issues that are likely to be considered by an individual employee. Consider the case of an assistant department manager who learns that her firm needs to replace a retiring division manager two levels above her in the organization. Even though she wants the job, she does not apply because she doubts that she will be selected. In this case, she raises the *performance-reward issue:* for some reason, she believes that her performance will not get her the position. Note that she may think that her performance merits the new job but that performance alone will not be enough; perhaps she expects the reward to go to someone with more seniority.

Assume that our employee also learns that the firm is looking for a production manager on a later shift. She thinks that she could get this job but does not apply because she does not want to change shifts. In this instance, she raises the *rewards-personal goals issue.*

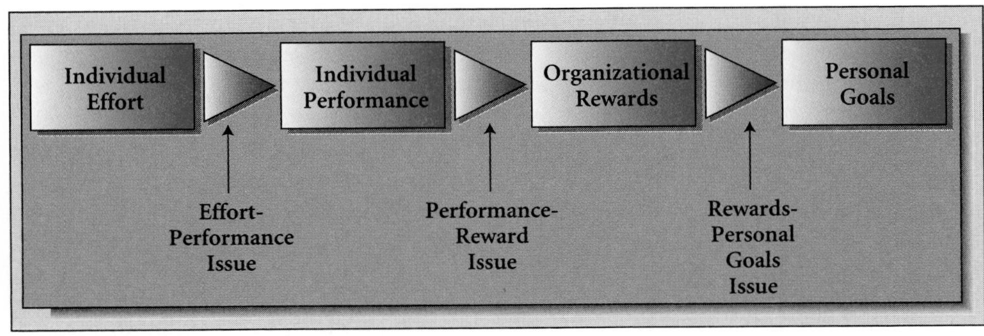

FIGURE 8.5 ◆ Expectancy Theory Model

Finally, she learns of an opening one level higher—department manager—in her own division. She may well apply for this job because she both wants it and thinks that she has a good chance of getting it. In this case, her consideration of all the issues has led to an expectancy that she can reach a given goal.

Expectancy theory helps explain why some people do not work as hard as they can when their salaries are based purely on seniority. Paying employees the same whether they work very hard or just hard enough to get by removes the financial incentive for them to work harder. In other words, they ask themselves, "If I work harder, will I get a pay raise?" and conclude that the answer is no. Similarly, if hard work will result in one or more *undesirable* outcomes—say, a transfer to another location or a promotion to a job that requires travel—employees will not be motivated to work hard.

equity theory Theory of motivation holding that people evaluate their treatment by employers relative to the treatment of others

EQUITY THEORY The **equity theory** focuses on social comparisons—people evaluating their treatment by the organization relative to the treatment of others. This approach holds that people begin by analyzing *inputs* (what they contribute to their jobs in terms of time, effort, education, experience, and so forth) relative to *outputs* (what they receive in return—salary, benefits, recognition, security). The result is a ratio of contribution to return. They then compare their own ratios with those of other employees: They ask whether their ratios are *equal to*, *greater than*, or *less than* those of the people with whom they are comparing themselves. Depending on their assessments, they experience feelings of equity or inequity. Figure 8.6 illustrates the three possible results of such an assessment.

For example, suppose a new college graduate gets a starting job at a large manufacturing firm. His starting salary is $25,000 a year, he gets a compact company car, and he shares an office with another new employee. If he later learns that another new employee has received the same salary, car, and office arrangement, he will feel equitably treated. If the other newcomer, however, has received $30,000, a full-size company car, and a private office, he may feel inequity (see Result 2 in Figure 8.6).

Note, however, that for an individual to feel equitably treated, the two ratios do not have to be the same, only *fair*. Assume, for instance, that our new employee has a bachelor's degree and 2 years of work experience. Perhaps he learns subsequently that the other new employee has an advanced degree and 10 years of experience. After first feeling inequity, the new employee may conclude that the person with whom he compared him-

TRENDS AND CHALLENGES

HOW TO ENERGIZE A GLOBAL MANAGER

Global managers are a lot like the Energizer Rabbit: To get the job done, they keep going and going and going—across countries, continents, time zones, languages, and cultures. Richard Rawlinson may not be a typical global manager, but he's not unusual either. It's not out of the question for his schedule to put him in 13 countries in as many days. Depending on where he is, he gives out one of 14 contact phone numbers on three continents. Last year, he crossed international boundaries 139 times and racked up enough frequent-flyer miles to transport his wife around the world every month of the year at no charge. Barry Salzman, president of DoubleClick International, a division of a New York–based Internet advertising company, travels 75 percent of his working life to 13 offices worldwide. On call day and night, he carries two cell phones and four battery packs for his laptop. On average, he receives 200 e-mail messages a day.

Now consider the fact that as Rawlinson and Salzman deal with their own grueling schedules, they must also manage and motivate global employee networks. Although high-technology equipment helps them meet the challenge, both men repeatedly turn to basic management techniques to get the job done.

Effective communication is especially important when it's necessary to connect employees in remote offices to headquarters. It's the personal relationship that matters, says Salzman, who conducts a regular Monday morning conference call for managers in Canada, Europe, and Asia. "We try to maintain voice contact," he explains. "We lose that with computers and e-mail." Salzman also makes a special effort to recognize employee achievements. A shattered sales record earns a case of champagne for every office around the world, compliments of headquarters.

Motivating overseas employees often means empowering them to operate autonomously. On a practical level, it is virtually

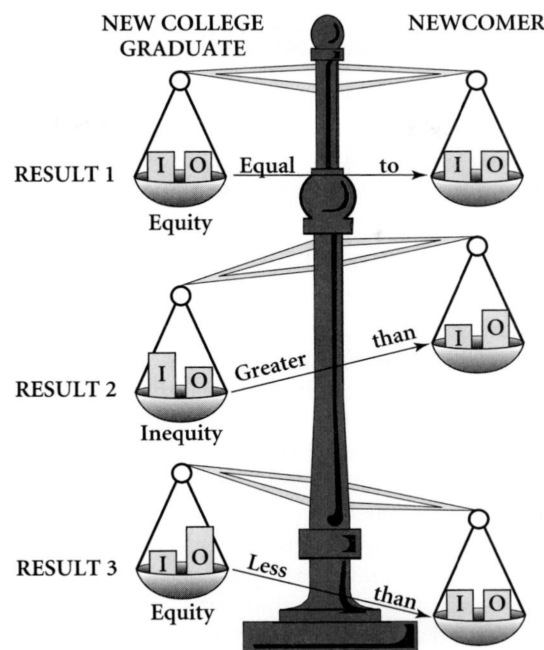

FIGURE 8.6 ◆ Equity Theory: Possible Assessments

self is actually contributing more to the organization. That employee is equitably entitled, therefore, to receive more in return (Result 3).

When people feel they are being inequitably treated, they may do various things to restore fairness. For example, they may ask for raises, reduce their efforts, work shorter hours, or just complain to their bosses. They may also rationalize ("Management succumbed to pressure to promote a woman/Asian American"), find different people with whom to compare themselves, or leave their jobs.

Virtually perfect examples of equity theory at work can be found in professional sports. Each year, for example, rookies, sometimes fresh out of college, are often signed to lucrative contracts. No sooner than the ink is dry do veteran players start grumbling about raises or revised contracts.

---

impossible for top managers with offices in different time zones, countries, and cultures to keep every ball in the air. They need local help who can make decisions. "The control style is archaic," admits Christine Hughes, an executive at Secure Computing, a California software developer who does business in North and South America, Asia, and Australia. "You have to be more of an adviser."

> **"The control style is archaic. You have to be more of an adviser."**
>
> —Christine Hughes
> *Executive at Secure Computing*

Management-at-a-distance makes every hiring choice crucial. Alan Naumann, president and CEO of Calico Technology, another California software company, looks for self-motivators with enough experience to take charge when the boss can't be reached. He gives local managers the support they need to learn the company by assigning veterans to work with them. Veterans, he advises, "have connections to the right people, know the decision-making process and the best people for certain jobs. It greatly short-circuits the learning curve."

Even with a network of experienced, motivated employees in place, the global manager—the person in charge—usually gets little rest. After a long workday in Australia, Christine Hughes usually returns to her hotel room and begins a round of calls to the home office. "I'm on the phone until two in the morning," she reports. "You just have to accept that."

STRATEGIES FOR ENHANCING JOB SATISFACTION AND MOTIVATION

Deciding what provides job satisfaction and motivates workers is only one part of human resource management. The other part is applying that knowledge. Experts have suggested—and many companies have implemented—a range of programs designed to make jobs more interesting and rewarding and to make the work environment more pleasant.

Reinforcement/Behavior Modification Theory

Many companies try to control, and even alter or modify, workers' behavior through systematic rewards and punishments for specific behaviors. In other words, they first try to define the specific behaviors that they want their employees to exhibit (working hard, being courteous to customers, stressing quality) and the specific behaviors they want to eliminate (wasting time, being rude to customers, ignoring quality). Then they try to shape employee behavior by linking reinforcement with desired behaviors and punishment with undesired behaviors.

reinforcement Theory that behavior can be encouraged or discouraged by means of rewards or punishments

Reinforcement is used, for instance, when a company pays *piecework* rewards—when workers are paid for each piece or product completed. In reinforcement strategies, *rewards* refer to all the positive things that people get for working (pay, praise, promotions, job security, and so forth). When rewards are tied directly to performance, they serve as *positive reinforcement.* For example, paying large cash bonuses to salespeople who exceed quotas prompts them to work even harder during the next selling period. John Deere has recently adopted a new reward system based on positive reinforcement. The firm now gives pay increases when its workers complete college courses and demonstrate mastery of new job skills.

Punishment is designed to change behavior by presenting people with unpleasant consequences if they fail to change in desirable ways. Employees who are repeatedly late to work, for example, may be suspended or have their pay docked. Similarly, when the National Football League or Major League Baseball fines or suspends players found guilty of substance abuse, the organization is seeking to change players' behavior.

Extensive rewards work best when people are learning new behavior, new skills, or new jobs. As workers become more adept, rewards can be used less frequently. Because such actions contribute to positive employer—employee relationships, managers generally prefer giving rewards and placing positive value on performance. Conversely, most managers dislike doling out punishment, partly because workers may respond with anger, resentment, hostility, or even retaliation. To reduce this risk, many managers couple punishment with reward for good behavior.

Management by Objectives

management by objectives (MBO) Set of procedures involving both managers and subordinates in setting goals and evaluating progress

Management by objectives (MBO) is a system of collaborative goal setting that extends from the top of an organization to the bottom. As a technique for managing the planning process, MBO is concerned mainly with helping managers implement and carry out their plans. As you can see from Figure 8.7, however, MBO involves managers and subordinates in setting goals and evaluating progress. Once the program is set up, the first step is establishing overall organizational goals. It is also these goals that will ultimately be evaluated to determine the success of the program. At the same time, however, collaborative activity—communicating, meeting, controlling, and so forth—is the key to MBO. Therefore, it can also serve as a program for improving satisfaction and motivation. (Note, too, that MBO represents an effort to apply throughout an entire organization the goal-setting theory of motivation that we discussed earlier.)

Indeed, according to many experts, motivational impact is the biggest advantage of MBO. When employees sit down with managers to set upcoming goals, they learn more about companywide objectives, come to feel that they are an important part of a team, and see how they can improve companywide performance by reaching their own goals. If an

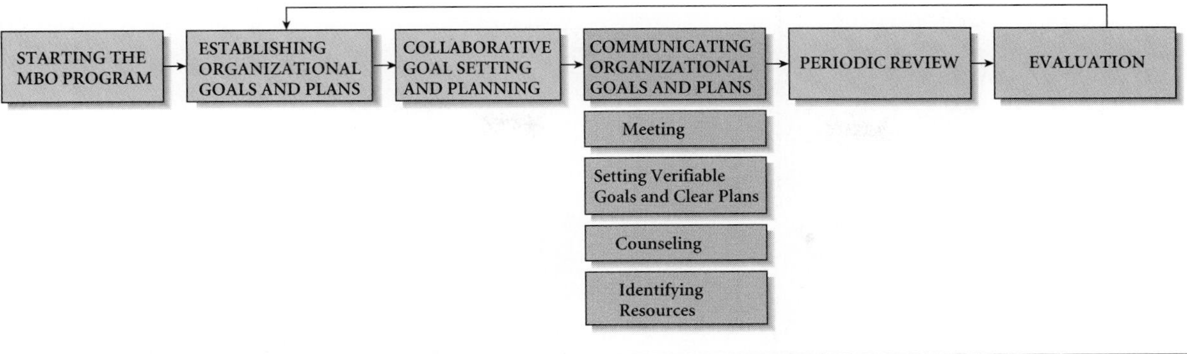

FIGURE 8.7 ◆ **Managing by Objectives**

MBO system is used properly, employees should leave meetings not only with an understanding of the value of their contributions, but also with fair rewards for their performances. They should also accept and be committed to the moderately difficult and specific goals they have helped set for themselves.

Participative Management and Empowerment

In **participative management and empowerment,** employees are given a voice in how they do their jobs and how the company is managed—they become *empowered* to take greater responsibility for their own performance. Not surprisingly, participation and empowerment make employees feel more committed to organizational goals they have helped to shape.[6]

participative management and empowerment Method of increasing job satisfaction by giving employees a voice in the management of their jobs and the company

Participation and empowerment can be used in large firms or small firms, both with managers and operating employees. For example, managers at General Electric who once needed higher-level approval for any expenditure over $5,000 now have the autonomy to make their own expense decisions up to as much as $50,000. At Adam Hat Co., a small firm that makes men's dress, military, and cowboy hats, workers who previously had to report all product defects to supervisors now have the freedom to correct problems themselves or even return products to the workers who are responsible for them.

TEAM MANAGEMENT At one level, employees may be given decision-making responsibility for certain narrow activities, such as when to take lunch breaks or how to divide assignments with coworkers. On a broader level, employees are also being consulted on such decisions as production scheduling, work procedures and schedules, and the hiring of new employees.[7] Among the many organizations actively using teams today are Texas Instruments, AT&T, and Shell Oil.

Although some employees thrive in participative programs, such programs are not for everyone. Many people will be frustrated by responsibilities they are not equipped to handle. Moreover, participative programs may actually result in dissatisfied employees if workers see the invitation to participate as more symbolic than substantive. One key, say most experts, is to invite participation only to the extent that employees want to have input and only if participation will have real value for an organization.

Managers, therefore, should remember that teams are not for everyone. Levi Strauss, for example, has encountered major problems in its efforts to use teams. Previously, individual workers performed repetitive, highly specialized tasks, such as sewing zippers into jeans, and were paid according to the number of jobs they completed each day. In an attempt to boost productivity, company management reorganized everyone into teams of 10 to 35 workers and assigned tasks to the entire group. Each team member's pay was determined by the team's level of productivity. In practice, however, faster workers became resentful of slower workers because they reduced the group's total output. Slower workers, meanwhile, resented the pressure put on them by faster-working coworkers. As a result,

Fastenal sells nuts and bolts to North America. Over the past five years, profits have skyrocketed 38.1% annually. At 39.3% annually, total return to Fastenal stockholders has outstripped even Coca-Cola. How? The company will tell you that Fastenal empowers its employees. Even entry-level positions make decisions. When Fastenal's New Jersey branches were getting shipments from the company's distribution hub in Scranton only twice a week, inventory was running out. The New Jersey staff employees made the decision to drive to Scranton themselves to stock their shelves. One staffer made the trip at 2 a.m. The result of such quick decision making is that Fastenal customers can count on getting what they need on time, and they're willing to pay a higher price than Fastenal's competitors for that service.

motivation, satisfaction, and morale all dropped, and Levi's eventually abandoned the teamwork plan altogether.[8]

By and large, however, participation and empowerment in general, and team management in particular, continue to be widely used as enhancers of employee motivation and company performance. Although teams are not often less effective in traditional and rigidly structured bureaucratic organizations, they often help smaller, more flexible organizations make decisions more quickly and effectively, enhance companywide communication, and encourage organizational members to feel more like a part of an organization. In turn, these attitudes usually lead to higher levels of both employee motivation and job satisfaction.[9]

Job Enrichment and Job Redesign

While MBO programs and empowerment can work in a variety of settings, *job enrichment* and *job redesign* programs are generally used to increase satisfaction in jobs significantly lacking in motivating factors.[10]

job enrichment Method of increasing job satisfaction by adding one or more motivating factors to job activities

JOB ENRICHMENT PROGRAMS **Job enrichment** is designed to add one or more motivating factors to job activities. For example, *job rotation programs* expand growth opportunities by rotating employees through various positions in the same firm. Workers thus gain not only new skills but also broader overviews of their work and their organization. Other programs focus on increasing responsibility or recognition. At Continental Airlines, for example, flight attendants now have more control over their own scheduling. The jobs of flight service managers were enriched when they were given more responsibility and authority for assigning tasks to flight crew members.

job redesign Method of increasing job satisfaction by designing a more satisfactory fit between workers and their jobs

JOB REDESIGN PROGRAMS Job redesign acknowledges that different people want different things from their jobs. By restructuring work to achieve a more satisfactory fit between workers and their jobs, **job redesign** can motivate individuals with strong needs for career growth or achievement. Job redesign is usually implemented in one of three ways: through *combining tasks*, *forming natural work groups*, or *establishing client relationships*.

Combining Tasks. The job of combining tasks involves enlarging jobs and increasing their variety to make employees feel that their work is more meaningful. In turn, employees become more motivated. For example, the job done by a programmer who maintains computer systems might be redesigned to include some system design and system development work. While developing additional skills, then, the programmer also gets involved in the overall system package.

Forming Natural Work Groups. People who do different jobs on the same projects are candidates for natural work groups. These groups are formed to help employees see the place and importance of their jobs in the total structure of the firm. They are valuable to management because the people working on a project are usually the most knowledgeable about it, and thus the most capable problem solvers.

Establishing Client Relationships. Establishing client relationships means letting employees interact with customers. This approach increases job variety. It gives workers both a greater sense of control and more feedback about performance than they get when their jobs are not highly interactive.

For example, software writers at Microsoft watch test users work with programs and discuss problems with them directly rather than receive feedback from third-party researchers. In Fargo, North Dakota, Great Plains Software has employee turnover of less than 7 percent, compared with an average of 15 to 20 percent in the software industry. The company recruits and rewards in large part according to candidates' customer service skills and their experience with customer needs and complaints.

Modified Work Schedules

As another way of increasing job satisfaction, many companies are experimenting with *modified work schedules*—different approaches to working hours and the workweek. The two most common forms of modified scheduling are *work-share programs* and *flextime programs*, including *alternative workplace strategies.*[11]

WORK-SHARE PROGRAMS At Steelcase Inc., the country's largest maker of office furnishings, two very talented women in the marketing division both wanted to work only part time. The solution: They now share a single full-time job. With each working 2.5 days a week, both got their wishes and the job gets done—and done well. In another situation, one person might work mornings and the other afternoons. The practice, known as **work sharing** (or **job sharing**), has "brought sanity back to our lives," according to at least one Steelcase employee.

work sharing (or job sharing) Method of increasing job satisfaction by allowing two or more people to share a single full-time job

"Work sharing brought sanity back to our lives."

—Employee at Steelcase

Job sharing usually benefits both employees and employers. Employees, for instance, tend to appreciate the organization's attention to their personal needs. At the same time, the company can reduce turnover and save on the cost of benefits. On the negative side, job-share employees generally receive fewer benefits than their full-time counterparts and may be the first to be laid off when cutbacks are necessary.

FLEXTIME PROGRAMS AND ALTERNATIVE WORKPLACE STRATEGIES **Flextime programs** allow people to choose their working hours by adjusting a standard work schedule on a daily or weekly basis. There are, of course, limits. The Steelcase program, for instance, requires all employees to work certain core hours. This practice allows everyone to reach coworkers at a specified time of day. Employees can then decide whether to make up the rest of the standard 8-hour day by coming in and leaving early (say, by working 6:00 A.M. to 2:00 P.M. or 7:00 A.M. to 3:00 P.M.) or late (9:00 A.M. to 5:00 P.M. or 10:00 A.M. to 6:00 P.M.).

flextime programs Method of increasing job satisfaction by allowing workers to adjust work schedules on a daily or weekly basis

Figure 8.8 shows a hypothetical flextime system that could be used by three different people. The office is open from 6:00 A.M. until 7:00 P.M. Core time is 9:00 A.M. to 11:00 A.M. and 1:00 P.M. to 3:00 P.M. Joe, an early riser, comes in at 6:00, takes an hour for lunch between 11:00 and noon, and finishes his day by 3:00. Sue, a working mother, prefers a later day. She comes in at 9:00, takes a long lunch from 11:00 to 1:00, and then works until 7:00. Pat works a more traditional 8-to-5 schedule.

In one variation, companies may also allow employees to choose 4, 5, or 6 days on which to work each week. Some, for instance, may choose Monday through Thursday, others Tuesday through Friday. Still others may work Monday–Tuesday and Thursday–Friday and take Wednesday off. By working 10 hours over 4 workdays, employees still complete 40-hour weeks.

Telecommuting and Virtual Offices. Tammy Aultman sells computer systems for Hewlett-Packard, which is located in Mountain View, California. Aultman accepted the job even though she lives in Laguna Hills, 350 miles away. Her solution: She outfitted a room in her home with a modem-equipped personal computer and a fax machine and now works comfortably out of Laguna Hills. Aultman is one of a rapidly growing number of U.S. workers who do a significant portion of their work by a relatively new version of flextime known as **telecommuting**—performing some or all of a job away from standard office settings. Among salaried employees, the telecommuter workforce grew by 21.5 percent in 1994, to 7.6 million. By the year 2000, that number may reach 25 million.[12] The key to telecommuting is technology. The availability of networked computers, fax machines, cellular telephones, and overnight-delivery services makes it possible for many professionals to work at home or while traveling.

telecommuting Form of flextime that allows people to perform some or all of a job away from standard office settings

Other companies have experimented with so-called virtual offices. They have redesigned conventional office space to accommodate jobs and schedules that are far less dependent on assigned spaces and personal apparatus. At the advertising firm of Chiat Day Mojo in Venice, California, only about a third of the salaried workforce is in the office on any given day. The office building features informal work carrels or nooks and open areas available to every employee. "The work environment," explains Director of Operations Adelaide Horton, "was designed around the concept that one's best thinking isn't necessarily done at a desk or in an office. Sometimes it's done in a conference room with other people. Other times it's done on a ski slope or driving to a client's office."

FIGURE 8.8 ◆ **Sample Flextime Schedule**

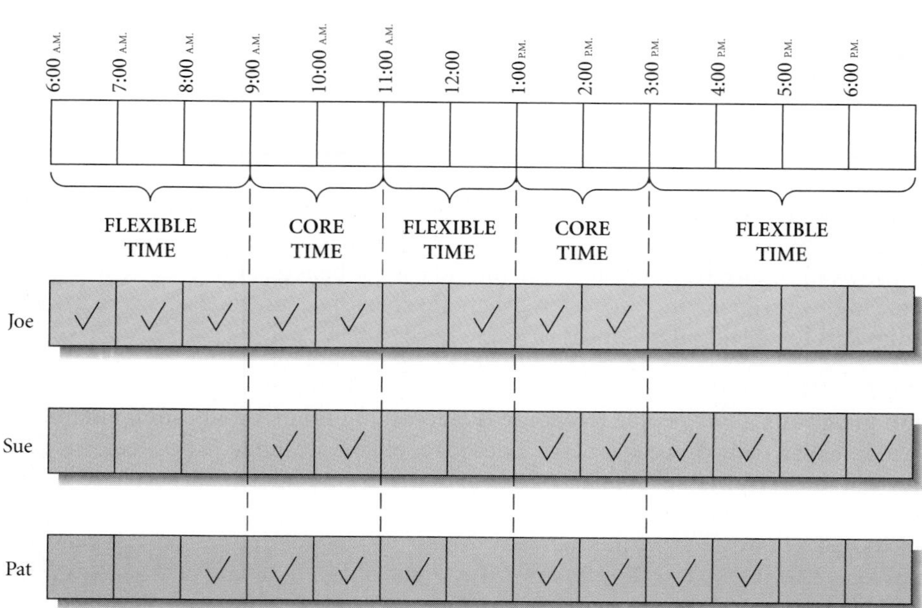

> **"The work environment was designed around the concept that one's best thinking isn't necessarily done at a desk or in an office. Sometimes it's done in a conference room with other people. Other times it's done on a ski slope or driving to a client's office."**
>
> —Adelaide Horton
> *Director of Operations, Chiat Day Mojo advertising firm*

ADVANTAGES AND DISADVANTAGES OF MODIFIED SCHEDULES AND ALTERNATIVE WORKPLACES Flextime gives employees more freedom in their professional and personal lives. It allows workers to plan around the work schedules of spouses and the school schedules of young children. Studies show that the increased sense of freedom and control reduces stress and thus improves individual productivity.

Companies also benefit in other ways. In urban areas, for example, such programs can reduce traffic congestion and similar problems that contribute to stress and lost work time. Furthermore, employers benefit from higher levels of commitment and job satisfaction. John Hancock Insurance, Atlantic Richfield, and Metropolitan Life are among the major American corporations that have successfully adopted some form of flextime.

Conversely, flextime sometimes complicates coordination because people are working different schedules. In the schedules shown in Figure 8.8, for instance, Sue may need some important information from Joe at 4:30 P.M., but because Joe is working an earlier schedule, he leaves for the day at 3:00. In addition, if workers are paid by the hour, flextime may make it difficult for employers to keep accurate records of when they are actually working.

As for telecommuting and virtual offices, although they may be the wave of the future, they may not be for everyone. For example, consultant Gil Gordon points out that telecommuters are attracted to the ideas of "not having to shave and put on make-up or go through traffic, and sitting in their blue jeans all day." However, he suggests that would-be telecommuters ask themselves several other questions: "Can I manage deadlines? What will it be like to be away from the social context of the office five days

Alcoa Aluminum chairman Paul H. O'Neill has an office much like those of everyone else in the company's new Pittsburgh headquarters. In fact, it's exactly like everyone else's: it's 9 feet by 9 feet and no more than 45 feet from a window. "A lot of buildings put people in their place, and I think that's a mistake," says O'Neill, who ordered the building constructed so that people were encouraged to interact. There are no hallways or private offices; there are escalators instead of elevators, and meeting rooms are walled in glass. And everyone has a parking space.

a week? Can I renegotiate the rules of the family, so my spouse doesn't come home every night expecting me to have a four-course meal on the table?" One study has shown that even though telecommuters may be producing results, those with strong advancement ambitions may miss networking and rubbing elbows with management on a day-to-day basis.

Another obstacle to establishing a telecommuting program is convincing management that it can be beneficial for all involved. Telecommuters may have to fight the perception, from both bosses and coworkers, that if they are not being supervised, they are not working. Managers, admits one experienced consultant, "usually have to be dragged kicking and screaming into this. They always ask, 'How can I tell if someone is working when I can't see them?' " By the same token, he adds, "that's based on the erroneous assumption that if you can see them they are working." Most experts agree that reeducation and constant communication are requirements of a successful telecommuting arrangement. Both managers and employees must determine expectations in advance.

MANAGERIAL STYLES AND LEADERSHIP

leadership Process of motivating others to work to meet specific objectives

In trying to enhance morale, job satisfaction, and motivation, managers can use many different styles of leadership. **Leadership** is the process of motivating others to work to meet specific objectives. Leading is also one of the key aspects of a manager's job and an important component of the directing function.

Joe Liemandt dropped out of Stanford in 1990 to start a software company in Austin, Texas. As part of his strategy, he was determined to develop and maintain a workforce of creative people who worked well in teams, adapted to rapid change, and felt comfortable taking risks. A decade later, people with these qualities—now numbering nearly 1,000—have helped build Liemandt's company, Trilogy Software Inc., into a rapidly growing maker of industry-leading software for managing product pricing, sales plans, and commissions.

When Trilogy hires a new group of employees, Liemandt himself oversees their training. He sees himself as the firm's leader and believes that, as such, it is his responsibility to ensure that every employee shares his vision and understands his way of doing business. Training takes several weeks, starting with a series of classes devoted to the technical aspects of Trilogy's products and methods of software development. Then recruits move into areas in which Liemandt truly believes they make a real difference—developing risk-taking skills and the ability to recognize new opportunities.

Recruits are formed into teams, and each team is given 3 weeks to complete various projects, ranging from the creating of new products to the developing of marketing campaigns for existing products. Teams actually compete with one another and are scored on such criteria as risk and innovation, goal setting, and goal accomplishment. Evaluations are completed by Liemandt, other Trilogy managers, and some of the firm's venture capital backers. Winners get free trips to Las Vegas. Losers go straight to work.

Liemandt's leadership doesn't stop there, even for those who go to Las Vegas, where Liemandt challenges everyone to place a $2,000 bet at the roulette wheel. He argues that $2,000 is a meaningful sum, and one that can cause real pain, but not so much that it will cause financial disaster for anyone. Actually, Liemandt puts up the money, which losers pay back through payroll deductions of $400 over 5 months. Not everyone, of course, decides to take the chance, but enough do to make the message clear: Liemandt aims to succeed by taking chances, and he expects employees to share the risks. Those who do stand to earn bigger returns on more intrepid investments.[13]

In this section, we begin by describing some of the basic features of and differences in managerial styles and then focus on an approach to managing and leading that, like Joe Liemandt's, understands those jobs as responses to a variety of complex situations.

Managerial Styles

Early theories of leadership tried to identify specific traits associated with strong leaders. For example, physical appearance, intelligence, and public speaking skills were once thought to be "leadership traits." Indeed, it was once believed that taller people made better leaders than shorter people. The trait approach, however, proved to be a poor predictor of leadership potential. Ultimately, attention shifted from managers' traits to their behaviors, or **managerial styles**—patterns of behavior that a manager exhibits in dealing with subordinates. Managerial styles run the gamut from autocratic to democratic to free rein. Naturally, most managers do not clearly conform to any one style, but these three major types of styles involve very different kinds of responses to human relations problems. Under different circumstances, any given style or combination of styles may prove appropriate.

managerial style Pattern of behavior that a manager exhibits in dealing with subordinates

- Managers who adopt an **autocratic style** generally issue orders and expect them to be obeyed without question. The military commander prefers and usually needs the autocratic style on the battlefield. Because no one else is consulted, the autocratic style allows for rapid decision making. It may, therefore, be useful in situations testing a firm's effectiveness as a time-based competitor.
- Managers who adopt a **democratic style** generally ask for input from subordinates before making decisions but retain final decision-making power. For example, the manager of a technical group may ask other group members to interview and offer opinions about job applicants. The manager, however, will ultimately make the hiring decision.
- Managers who adopt a **free-rein style** typically serve as advisers to subordinates who are allowed to make decisions. The chairperson of a volunteer committee to raise funds for a new library may find a free-rein style most effective.

autocratic style Managerial style in which managers generally issue orders and expect them to be obeyed without question

democratic style Managerial style in which managers generally ask for input from subordinates but retain final decision-making power

free-rein style Managerial style in which managers typically serve as advisers to subordinates who are allowed to make decisions

According to many observers, the free-rein style of leadership is currently giving rise to an approach that emphasizes broad-based employee input into decision making and the fostering of workplace environments in which employees increasingly determine what needs to be done and how.

Regardless of theories about the ways in which leaders ought to lead, the relative effectiveness of any leadership style depends largely on the desire of subordinates to share input or to exercise creativity. Whereas some people, for example, are frustrated, others prefer autocratic managers because they do not want a voice in making decisions. The democratic approach, meanwhile, can be disconcerting both to people who want decision-making responsibility and to those who do not. A free-rein style lends itself to employee creativity, and thus to creative solutions to pressing problems. This style also appeals to

"It's a vice-president thing, Berger. You wouldn't understand."

Southwest Airlines' cofounder and chief executive Herb Kelleher passes out snacks to passengers in another light-hearted moment. He also joked around with employees at Nerd Day at the Southwest Airlines center in Albuquerque. His loose management style motivates his employees, who in turn make their customers smile. The management strategy works. Southwest Airlines is the fastest growing airline, and its profit margins are about 150 percent above competitors.

employees who like to plan their own work. Not all subordinates, however, have the necessary background or skills to make creative decisions. Others are not sufficiently self-motivated to work without supervision.

The Contingency Approach to Leadership

Because each managerial style has both strengths and weaknesses, most managers vary their responses to different situations. Flexibility, however, has not always characterized managerial style or responsiveness. For most of the twentieth century, in fact, managers tended to believe that all problems yielded to preconceived, pretested solutions. If raising pay reduced turnover in one plant, for example, it followed that the same tactic would work equally well in another.

contingency approach
Approach to managerial style holding that the appropriate behavior in any situation is dependent (contingent) on the unique elements of that situation

More recently, however, managers have begun to adopt a **contingency approach** to managerial style. They have started to view appropriate managerial behavior in any situation as dependent, or contingent, on the elements unique to that situation. This change in outlook has resulted largely from an increasing appreciation of the complexity of managerial problems and solutions. For example, pay raises may reduce turnover when workers have been badly underpaid. The contingency approach, however, recognizes that raises will have little effect when workers feel adequately paid but ill-treated by management. This approach also recommends that training managers in human relations skills may be crucial to solving the problem in the second case.[14]

The contingency approach also acknowledges that people in different cultures behave differently and expect different things from their managers. A certain managerial style, therefore, is more likely to be successful in some countries than in others. Japanese workers, for example, generally expect managers to be highly participative and to give them input in decision making. In contrast, many South American workers actually balk at participation and want take-charge leaders. The basic idea, then, is that managers will be more effective when they adapt their styles to the contingencies of the situations they face.[15]

Motivation and Leadership in the Twenty-First Century

Motivation and leadership remain critically important areas of organizational behavior. As times change, however, so do the ways managers motivate and lead their employees. From the motivational side, today's employees want rewards that are often very different from those that earlier generations desired. Money, for example, is no longer the prime motivator for most people. In addition, because businesses today cannot offer the degree of job security that many workers want, motivating employees to strive toward higher levels of performance requires skillful attention from managers.

Finally, as we will see in Chapter 9, the diversity inherent in today's workforce also makes motivating behavior more complex for managers. The reasons why people work reflect more goals than ever before, and the varying lifestyles of diverse workers mean that managers must first pay closer attention to what their employees expect to get for their efforts and then try to link rewards with job performance.

Today's leaders are also finding it necessary to change their own behavior. As organizations become flatter and workers more empowered, managers naturally find it less acceptable to use the autocratic approach to leadership. Instead, many are becoming more democratic—functioning more as "coaches" than "bosses." Just as an athletic coach teaches athletes how to play and then steps back to let them take the field, many leaders now try to provide workers with the skills and resources to perform at their best before backing off to let them do their work with less supervision.

Continued from page 181

The Price of Repricing

In studies linking stock options to excesses that discourage performance at the very top of an organization, the main culprit to emerge is a practice known as *repricing*. When the price of a stock collapses—as a result, say, of declining sales or profit margins—companies lower the strike prices of options that they have already awarded. Why? They want to discourage employees from joining with competitors who may be enjoying better performances.

According to critics, however, repricing undermines the very reason that stock options are granted in the first place: to motivate employees to achieve higher performance levels at the company that is already rewarding their contributions. In fact, repricing may even reward poor performance by offering the same incentive at a cut-rate price. Nevertheless, it is a common practice in high-tech companies that are going through rough times.

Dennis Beresford, former chairman of the Financial Accounting Standards Board, has another serious problem with the practice of repricing: "I can't think of anything more irritating from an ethical standpoint," he says, "than when companies reprice options." What is the ethical angle? When the stock price drops, Beresford points out, outside investors lose money—real money. Option holders, meanwhile, get a second chance to buy equally valuable stock at lower prices.

Finally, many observers criticize corporations that refuse to link the stock options granted CEOs to specific or meaningful performance targets. As a result, CEOs who fail to get the job done often leave with nicely lined pockets. Consider the case of Gilbert Amelio, who was hired in 1996 to turn Apple Computer around. Seventeen months later, Apple was not exactly turned around and Amelio was out of a job. At the same time, however, the Apple board gave him options on nearly 131,000 shares for meeting minimal performance targets. Ironically, the news of Amelio's firing and the rehiring of company cofounder Steve Jobs sent the value of the company's stock—and Amelio's performance options—skyrocketing. The ex-CEO cashed in $3.2 million worth of stock options that, arguably, he had "earned" by performing poorly enough to get fired.

Questions for Discussion

1. Explain the success of and problems with stock option programs in terms of the following theories: classical theory, human resources model (Theory X and Theory Y), Maslow's hierarchy of needs, two-factor theory, expectancy theory, and equity theory.
2. Why is the success of stock option programs as employee motivators linked to the rise of the stock market?
3. Why do you think that the popular and business press has paid so much attention to stock options and so little to such motivational factors as achievement, recognition, the nature of work, responsibility, and advancement?
4. Do you think stock options should be used primarily to reward employees for work well done or to give them an incentive to work for future gain? Explain your answer.
5. What is the motivational value of a "culture of ownership"?
6. How do you think "stock-option roulette" will ultimately affect employee-players who continue to jump from company to company?
7. How do you think repricing affects the motivation of employees who do not benefit from the practice?

SUMMARY

1. **Discuss the importance of *job satisfaction* and *employee morale* and summarize their roles in *human relations* in the workplace.** Good human relations—the interactions between employers and employees and their attitudes toward one another—are important to business because they lead to high levels of job satisfaction (the degree of enjoyment that workers derive from their jobs) and morale (workers' overall attitude toward their workplace). Satisfied employees generally exhibit lower levels of absenteeism and turnover. They also have fewer grievances and engage in fewer negative behaviors.
2. **Identify and summarize the most important theories of *employee motivation*.** Views of employee motivation have changed dramatically over the years. The classical theory holds

that people are motivated solely by money. Scientific management tried to analyze jobs and increase production by finding better ways to perform tasks. The Hawthorne studies were the first to demonstrate the importance of making workers feel that their needs were being considered. The human resources model identifies two kinds of managers—Theory X managers, who believe that people are inherently uncooperative and must be constantly punished or rewarded, and Theory Y managers, who believe that people are naturally responsible and self-motivated to be productive.

Maslow's hierarchy of needs model proposes that people have several different needs (ranging from physiological to self-actualization), which they attempt to satisfy in their work. People must fulfill lower-level needs before seeking to fulfill higher-level needs. The two-factor theory suggests that if basic hygiene factors are not met, workers will be dissatisfied. Only by increasing more complex motivation factors can companies increase employees' performance.

Expectancy theory holds that people will work hard if they believe that their efforts will lead to desired rewards. Equity theory says that motivation depends on the way employees evaluate their treatment by an organization relative to its treatment of other workers.

3. **Describe some of the strategies used by organizations to improve job satisfaction and employee motivation.** Managers can use several strategies to increase employee satisfaction and motivation. The principle of reinforcement, or behavior modification theory, holds that reward and punishment can control behavior. Rewards, for example, are positive reinforcement when they are tied directly to desired or improved performance. Punishment (using unpleasant consequences to change undesirable behavior) is generally less effective.

   Management by objectives (a system of collaborative goal setting) and participative management and empowerment (techniques for giving employees a voice in management decisions) can improve human relations by making employees feel like part of a team. Job enrichment, job redesign, and modified work schedules (including work-share programs, flextime, and alternative workplace strategies) can enhance job satisfaction by adding motivation factors to jobs in which they are normally lacking.

4. **Discuss different managerial styles of *leadership* and their impact on human relations in the workplace.** Effective leadership—the process of motivating others to meet specific objectives—is an important determinant of employee satisfaction and motivation. Generally speaking, managers practice one of three basic managerial styles. Autocratic managers generally issue orders that they expect to be obeyed. Democratic managers generally seek subordinates' input into decisions. Free-rein managers are more likely to advise than to make decisions. The contingency approach to leadership views appropriate managerial behavior in any situation as dependent on the elements of that situation. Managers thus need to assess situations carefully, especially to determine the desire of subordinates to share input or exercise creativity.

QUESTIONS AND EXERCISES

Questions for Review

1. Do you think most people are relatively satisfied or dissatisfied with their work? Why are they mainly satisfied or dissatisfied?
2. Compare and contrast Maslow's hierarchy of needs with the two-factor theory of motivation.
3. How can participative management programs enhance employee satisfaction and motivation?

Questions for Analysis

4. What managerial style do you think best describes your own approach to leadership?
5. Some evidence suggests that recent college graduates show high levels of job satisfaction. Levels then drop dramatically as they reach their late twenties, only to increase gradually once they get older. What might account for this pattern?

6. As a manager, under what sort of circumstances might you apply each of the theories of motivation discussed in this chapter? Which would be easiest to use? Which would be hardest? Why?
7. Suppose you realize one day that you are dissatisfied with your job. Short of quitting, what might you do to improve your situation?
8. List five U.S. managers who you think would also qualify as great leaders.

APPLICATION EXERCISES

9. At the library, research the manager or owner of a company in the early twentieth century and the manager or owner of a company in the 1990s. Compare and contrast the two in terms of their times, leadership styles, and views of employee motivation.
10. Interview the manager of a local manufacturing company. Identify as many different strategies for enhancing job satisfaction at that company as you can.

BUILDING YOUR BUSINESS SKILLS

TOO MUCH OF A GOOD THING

This exercise enhances the following SCANS workplace competencies: demonstrating basic skills, demonstrating thinking skills, exhibiting interpersonal skills, working with information, and applying systems knowledge.

▼ GOAL

To encourage students to apply different motivational theories to a workplace problem involving poor productivity.

▼ BACKGROUND

For years, working for the George Uhe Co., a small chemicals broker in Paramus, New Jersey, made employees feel as if they were members of a big family. Unfortunately, this family was going broke because too few members were working hard enough to make money for it. They were happy, comfortable, complacent—and lazy.

With sales dropping in the pharmaceutical and specialty-chemicals division, Uhe brought in management consultants to analyze the situation and make recommendations. The outsiders quickly identified a motivational problem affecting the sales force: Reps were paid a handsome salary and received automatic, year-end bonuses regardless of performance. They were also treated to bagels every Friday and regular group birthday lunches that cost as much as $200. Employees felt satisfied, but had little incentive to work very hard.

Eager to return to profitability, Uhe's owners waited to hear the consultants' recommendations.

▼ METHOD

STEP 1

In groups of four, step into the role of Uhe's management consultants. Start by analyzing your client's workforce-motivation problems from the following perspectives (our questions focus on key motivational issues):

- *Job satisfaction and morale.* As part of a 77-year-old family-owned business, Uhe employees were happy and loyal, in part, because they were treated so well. Can high morale have a downside? How can it breed stagnation, and what can managers do to prevent stagnation from taking hold?

- *Theory X versus Theory Y.* Although the behavior of these workers seems to make a case for Theory X, why is it difficult to draw this conclusion about a company that focuses more on satisfaction than on sales and profits?
- *Two-factor theory.* Analyze the various ways in which improving such motivational factors as recognition, added responsibility, advancement, and growth might reduce the importance of hygiene factors, including pay and security.
- *Expectancy theory.* Analyze the effect on productivity of redesigning the company's sales force compensation structure: namely, by paying lower base salaries while offering greater earnings potential through a sales-based incentive system. Why would linking performance with increased pay that is achievable through hard work motivate employees? Why would the threat of a job loss also motivate greater effort?

STEP 2

Writing a short report based on your analysis, make recommendations to Uhe's owners. The goal of your report is to change the working environment in ways that will motivate greater effort and generate greater productivity.

▼ Follow-Up

1. What is your group's most important recommendation? Why do you think it is likely to succeed?
2. Changing the corporate culture to make it less paternalistic may reduce employees' sense of belonging to a family. If you were an employee, would you consider a greater focus on profits to be an improvement or a problem? How would it affect your motivation and productivity?
3. What steps would you take to improve the attitude and productivity of longtime employees who resist change?

CRAFTING YOUR BUSINESS PLAN

Business PlanPro

MAKING RESERVATIONS AND OTHER PLANS

▼ The Purpose of the Assignment

1. To acquaint students with the process of navigating the Business PlanPro (BPP) software package.
2. To familiarize students with the ways in which employee considerations (morale, motivation, and job satisfaction) enter into the development of a business plan.
3. To stimulate students' thinking about the application of textbook information on employee morale, motivation, and job satisfaction to the preparation of a BPP business plan.

▼ Assignment

After reading Chapter 8 in the textbook, open the BPP software and look around for information about the plans being made by a sample firm: Puddle Jumpers Airline. In the Task Manager screen, click on* ***Finish and Polish.*** *Next, familiarize yourself with this firm by clicking on* ***6. Executive Summary.*** *Then respond to the following questions:*

1. Consider Puddle Jumpers' plans to lower costs by using its flight crews more effectively than its competition. If implemented, how might these plans affect

(*continued*)

employee morale? Job satisfaction? [Sites to see in *BPP* (for this assignment): In the Task Manager screen, click on **Initial Assessment.** Then click on **2. Mission.** After returning to the Task Manager screen, click on **What You're Selling,** and then on **3. Competitive Positioning.** Finally, return to the Task Manager screen and explore any listed categories in which you would expect to find information about employee motivation and job satisfaction.]

2. Consider both Puddle Jumpers' plans for dealing with the high turnover among airline reservationists and its plans for training reservationists. Do you think the planned redesign will enrich the reservationist's job? Will it affect job satisfaction? [Sites to see in *BPP:* In the Task Manager screen, click on **What You're Selling.** Then click, in turn, on **3. Competitive Positioning** and **5. Technology.** After returning to the Task Manager screen, click on **Finish and Polish.** Then click on **1. Strategy and Implementation.**]
3. Consider the qualifications of Judy Land, director of reservations. Based on her background, would you say that she is qualified to lead and motivate employees under the new reservations system? [Sites to see in *BPP:* In the Task Manager screen, click first on **Your Management Team** and then on **3. Management Team.**]
4. How will employees be affected by Puddle Jumpers' plans to acquire additional aircraft and offer expanded routes? What kinds of motivational considerations would you anticipate when Puddle Jumpers implements its expansion plans? [Sites to see in BPP: In the Task Manager screen, click first on **Finish and Polish** and then on **6. Executive Summary.**]

▼ For Your Own Business Plan

5. Implementation of your business plan depends on leadership. Identify those individuals in your planned organization who will provide leadership in implementing each of your organization's activity areas. Describe specific leadership activities that you expected to rely upon at various times from each of the key personnel in your organization.

▼ *General Tips for Navigating in BPP

1. Open the BPP program, examine the Welcome screen, and click on **Open a Sample Plan.**
2. From the Open a Sample Plan dialogue box, click on a sample company name; then click on **Open.**
3. On the Task Manager screen, click on any of the lines (for example, **Your Company**).
4. You can always return to the Task Manager screen by going to the bottom of the screen and clicking on the **Task Manager** icon.
5. When you are finished with a sample company, close its Task Manager screen.
6. After finishing with one sample company, you can get to the next one by going to the top of the screen and clicking on **File** (on the menu bar). Then beneath that, select **Open Sample Plan.** This will exit you from the current company file and send you to the Open a Sample Plan dialogue box, where you can select your next sample company.

EXPLORING THE NET

A SATISFACTION SURVEY

This chapter stresses the fact that employee satisfaction and morale are important to any organization. However, it is also quite difficult for managers to know for sure just how satisfied and motivated their employees actually are. In most cases, managers interested in assessing satisfaction and/or morale do so with surveys. Employees are asked to respond to various questions about how they feel about their work, and their responses are scored to provide an indication of their satisfaction and morale. To examine such a survey, visit the Web site at:

http://www.fdgroup.co.uk/neo/djassoc/dj_jdq.html

After you have examined the satisfaction questionnaire at this site, consider the following questions:

1. For whose use is this questionnaire geared? After studying the explanatory headnote, can you identify two or three key principles of instruments like this one?
2. At face value, how valid does this survey instrument seem to be? Is it likely to meet the objectives outlined in the headnote?
3. Fill out the survey yourself, and then analyze your responses.
4. What appear to be the biggest strengths and weaknesses of this particular survey? Assuming this questionnaire to be typical, what would you judge to be the strengths and weaknesses of job satisfaction surveys in general?
5. Try writing a survey yourself. Focus it on job satisfaction in your present job, in a previous job, or in this class. What information do you most want to elicit? What aspect of this information is hardest to elicit? Why?

Managing Human Resources and Labor Relations

Labor Rolls the Dice in Las Vegas

They worked hard all day as hotel waiters and waitresses, cooks, and housekeepers, but when they get to the union hall, they're filled with energy. "Unions, yes," they chant as they listen to stories of recruiting successes at the MGM Grand, the world's largest hotel, and New York New York, one of the area's newest hotels. All told, local union membership has doubled in the past decade to 40,000 members. At the Grand alone, Local 226 of the Hotel Employees & Restaurant Employees Union signed up 2,700 new members.

Where is this hotbed of union activism? Not in any traditional labor stronghold, such as Detroit or Chicago, but in Las Vegas, which, along with its casinos, is fast becoming known as a proving ground for organized labor. "Las Vegas," reports one labor historian, "is where the future of the union movement is being hammered out."

The AFL-CIO, the umbrella organization for the union movement, chose to test its recruiting power in Las Vegas for a good reason: It's a boomtown with a burgeoning population and an abundance of jobs. When labor leaders look at all the under-construction casinos, hotels, and houses, they see opportunity to nourish the movement and add to the ranks. The Venetian is just one example of the fertile field that labor is tilling in Vegas. With its gaming palaces, 6,000 hotel rooms, and "authentic" Italian touches (including canals), building costs will top $2 billion, and the project will employ thousands of construction and service workers.

In targeting these workers in its latest membership push, the AFL-CIO is promising improved wages and benefits. This message may be traditional, but the approach is not. Sidestepping union elections administered by the National Labor Relations Board (NLRB), organizers are instead showing employers rosters of recruited workers and petitioning for voluntary union recognition. "Card signing," as this tactic is known, has worked in casinos, and it increased membership in the building-trades and hotel-workers unions by 20 percent in a year.

Union organizers are workers themselves—people like Edelisa Wolf, an $11.25-an-hour waitress at the MGM Grand who signs up recruits as they walk out of the New York New York hiring office. "I spend a day a week volunteering for the union," says Wolf, "because otherwise, we would earn $7.50 an hour and no benefits." Charley Phillips, a construction worker with years of experience in Las Vegas, takes jobs in nonunion companies for the sole purpose of recruiting new members. When he was fired by one company for his pro-union activities, he was quickly rehired on the order of the NLRB. He stayed on that job for 6 more weeks and, his union work done, headed for another company.

> **"I spend a day a week volunteering for the union because otherwise, we would earn $7.50 an hour and no benefits."**
>
> —Edelisa Wolf
> *MGM Grand waitress*

Las Vegas is so important to the union movement because it represents a challenge in nonmanufacturing industries. With fewer and fewer factory jobs being created in the United States, organized labor can ensure its own survival only by convincing service and construction workers to embrace the movement. Obviously, the job won't be an easy one. New York New York has already thwarted unionization attempts by hiring nonunion catering companies to run its restaurants. It's a first for Las Vegas and a new move for unions to contemplate.

The union movement is only one part of the human resources and labor relations environment in which businesses operate. Whether or not a company is unionized, it must deal with staffing and promotions, worker training, compensation and benefits, and such legal and ethical issues as equal employment opportunity, equal pay, and occupational safety and health. Companies must also deal with workforce diversity, which is increasing the number and complexity of labor-management issues.

By focusing on the learning objectives of this chapter, you will better understand some of the formal systems that companies use to manage their employees, as well as some of the key issues in contemporary labor relations.

Our opening story is continued on page 230

After reading this chapter, you should be able to:

1. **Define *human resource management* and explain how managers plan for human resources.**
2. **Identify the steps involved in *staffing* a company.**
3. **Explain how organizations can develop workers' skills and manage workers who do not perform well.**
4. **Discuss the importance of *wages* and *salaries, incentives,* and *benefits programs* in attracting and keeping skilled workers.**
5. **Describe some of the key legal and ethical issues involved in hiring, compensating, and managing workers in today's workplace.**
6. **Discuss *workforce diversity* and the *contingent workforce* as important changes in the contemporary workplace.**
7. **Describe the *major laws governing labor-management relations* and identify the steps in the *collective bargaining process.***

■ THE FOUNDATIONS OF HUMAN RESOURCE MANAGEMENT

human resource management Development and administration of programs to enhance the quality and performance of a company's workforce

human resource managers Managers responsible for hiring, training, evaluating, and compensating employees

Human resource management is the development and administration of programs to enhance the quality and performance of people working in an organization. **Human resource managers,** sometimes called *personnel managers,* are employed by all but the smallest firms. They recruit, train, and develop employees and set up evaluation, compensation, and benefit programs. In reality, however, all managers deal with human resources: Managers of accounting, finance, and marketing departments, for example, help select and train workers and evaluate their performance. In this respect, two main concerns of all managers are *job relatedness* and *person-job matching.*

Job Relatedness and Person-Job Matching

job relatedness Principle that all employment decisions should be based on the requirements of the jobs in question

Job relatedness—the foundation of effective human resource management—requires that all employment decisions be based on the requirements of a position. The criteria used in hiring, evaluating, promoting, and rewarding people must be tied directly to the jobs being performed. For example, a policy that all office managers must be female would violate job relatedness because gender is irrelevant to the job. Conversely, hiring only young females to model clothing designed for teenage girls is a job-related practice and thus reflects sound human resource management.

person-job matching Process of matching the right person to the right job

Central to the principle of job relatedness is **person-job matching:** the process of matching the right person to the right job. Good human resource managers match people's skills, interests, and temperaments with the requirements of their jobs. When people and jobs are well matched, the company benefits from high performance and employee satisfaction, high retention of effective workers, and low absenteeism.

PLANNING FOR HUMAN RESOURCES Like planning for future equipment, planning for future human resource needs is crucial in any organization. The basis for human resource planning, in turn, is job analysis.[1]

job analysis Evaluation of the duties and qualities required by a job

Job Analysis. Evaluating the duties required by a particular job and the qualities required to perform it is called **job analysis.** For simple, repetitive jobs, managers may ask workers to create checklists of all the duties they perform and the importance of each. In analyzing more complex jobs, they may also hold interviews to determine jobholders' exact duties. Managers may also observe workers to record the nature of their duties.

job description Outline of the objectives, tasks, and responsibilities of a job

job specifications Description of the skills, education, and experience required by a job

From the job analysis, a manager develops a **job description,** which is a statement outlining the objectives, tasks, and responsibilities of a job. It also describes the conditions under which the job will be done, the ways in which it relates to other positions, and the skills needed to perform it. Managers also draw up **job specifications,** which describe the skills, education, and experience required by a job. Together, job analyses and descriptions serve as tools for filling specific positions, as guides in establishing training programs, and as comparative guidelines for setting wages. Most importantly, by objectively defining requirements, they allow managers to make employment decisions based on job relatedness.

■ STAFFING THE ORGANIZATION

Once managers have decided what positions they need to fill, they must find and hire qualified people. Staffing the organization is one of the most complex and important tasks of good human resource management. In this section we describe both the process of acquiring staff from outside the company (*external staffing*) and the process of promoting staff from within the company (*internal staffing*).[2]

External Staffing

A new firm has little choice but to hire people from outside the company. Established firms may also hire outsiders for a variety of reasons: to fill positions for which there are no good internal candidates, to accommodate growth, or to attract fresh ideas. External staffing involves recruitment and selection.

RECRUITMENT The first step in hiring new workers is to recruit a pool of applicants who are interested in and qualified for available positions. Successful recruiting focuses only on the most basic qualifications of a job. For example, a recruitment ad for a financial analyst might specify applicants with degrees in finance. Requiring a degree from a particular school, however, would unduly restrict applicants.

Recruiters often visit high schools, vocational schools, colleges, and universities. In some cases, labor agreements stipulate that new employees be hired from union membership rolls. Many companies advertise in newspapers or trade publications or seek the help of employment agencies. In addition, unsolicited letters and resumés from job seekers can help identify the right person for a job.

Recruiters have faced a difficult job in recent years as unemployment has continued to drop. Indeed, in early 1998 unemployment had dropped to a 23-year low of 4.6 percent. As a result, recruiters at firms such as Sprint, PeopleSoft, and Cognex had started to stress how much fun it was to work at their companies and to reinforce this message with ice cream socials, karaoke contests, softball leagues, and free movie nights.[3]

SELECTION Once recruiting efforts have attracted job applicants, managers must evaluate each individual and select the best candidate. Figure 9.1 places testing procedures among the stages and possible outcomes of a typical selection process: applications or resumés, screening interviews, ability and aptitude tests, on-site interviews, reference checks, and medical and drug tests. Each organization develops its own mix of selection techniques and may use them in any order.

Michael Pehl, CEO of i-Cube, an IT-consulting-services company, needs employees—good employees—in the worst way. He's willing to pay $15,000 for billboards touting i-Cube as "An Incredible Place to Work," and he has launched a variety of incentives to motivate current employees as recruiters. Anyone making a successful referral may get $2,000, a 32-inch TV, and, depending on when the new recruit starts, a VCR to go with the TV. Eight successful referrals in a calendar year can be worth as much as a Jeep Wrangler.

FIGURE 9.1 ◆ Sample Selection System

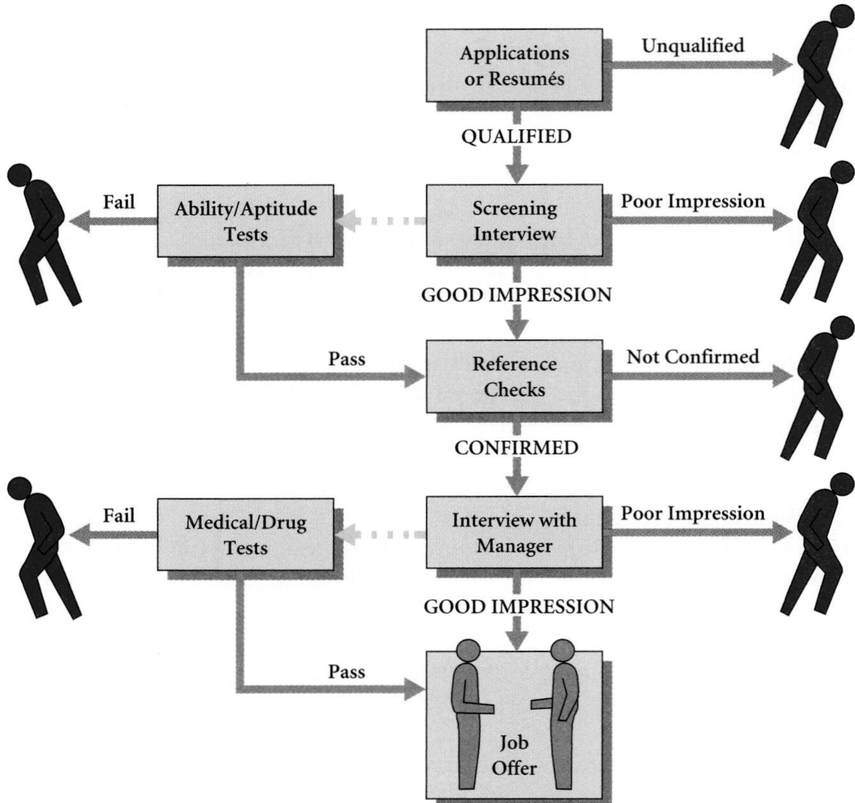

1. *Applications or resumés.* A job application is a standardized form that asks the applicant for such information as background, experience, and education. A resumé is a prepared statement of the applicant's qualifications and career goals.
2. *Screening interviews.* Companies often find themselves with several applications or resumés for every job opening. Managers thus narrow the field, first on the basis of applications and then by holding screening interviews to eliminate clearly unqualified applicants. Then managers interview qualified applicants in greater depth.
3. *Ability and aptitude tests.* For some positions, ability or aptitude tests may be given. Such tests must meet two conditions. First, they must be job related, and second, the test must indicate clearly that top scorers are more likely to perform well in the specified job.

Teamwork Criteria. Increasingly, many firms are also stressing skills related to teamwork in selecting new employees. Southwest Airlines, Procter & Gamble, and Merck, for example, use current employees, in addition to managers, to interview applicants. These employees strive to determine how well applicants will fit into the company's culture and how well they will get along with other people in the firm.[4]

Internal Staffing: Promotions

Many organizations prefer to hire from within. Thus, they prefer when possible to promote or transfer existing employees to fill openings. Systems for promoting employees usually take one of two forms:

- In **closed promotion systems,** managers decide which workers will be considered for promotions. Decisions are usually made informally (and often subjectively) and tend to rely on the recommendations of immediate supervisors.
- In **open promotion systems,** available jobs and requirements are posted. Employees who feel that they have the necessary qualifications fill out applications, take tests, and interview with managers.

closed promotion system System by which managers decide, often informally, which workers are considered for promotions

open promotion system System by which employees apply, test, and interview for available jobs, requirements of which are posted

Seniority. Some promotions are determined, at least in part, by seniority: Employees with more years of service receive priority in promotions. This pattern is a standard feature of many union contracts and ensures that experienced employees are promoted. Of course, it does not guarantee that they will be the most competent candidates.

DEVELOPING THE WORKFORCE

After a company has hired new employees, it must acquaint them with the firm and their new jobs. Managers also take steps to train employees and further develop necessary job skills. In addition, every firm has some system for performance appraisal and feedback. Unfortunately, the results of these assessments sometimes require procedures for demoting or terminating employees.[5]

Training

As its name suggests, **on-the-job training** occurs while the employee is at work. Much of this training is informal, as when one employee shows another how to use the photocopier. In other cases, it is quite formal. For example, a trainer may teach secretaries how to operate a new e-mail system from their workstations.

on-the-job training Training, sometimes informal, conducted while an employee is at work

Off-the-job training takes place at locations away from the work site. This approach offers a controlled environment and allows focused study without interruptions. For example, the petroleum equipment manufacturer Baker-Hughes uses classroom-based programs to teach new methods of quality control. Chaparral Steel's training program includes 4 hours a week of classroom training in areas such as basic math and grammar. Other firms use **vestibule training,** in simulated work environments, to make off-the-job training more realistic. American Airlines, for example, trains flight attendants through vestibule training, and AT&T uses it to train telephone operators.

off-the-job training Training conducted in a controlled environment away from the work site

vestibule training Off-the-job training conducted in a simulated environment

Performance Appraisal

In some small companies, **performance appraisal** takes place when the owner tells an employee, "You're doing a good job." In larger firms, performance appraisals are designed to show more precisely how well workers are doing their jobs. Typically, the appraisal process involves a written assessment issued on a regular basis. As a rule, however, the written evaluation is only one part of a multistep process.

performance appraisal Evaluation, often in writing, of an employee's job performance

The appraisal process begins when a manager defines performance standards for an employee. The manager then observes the employee's performance. If the standards are clear, the manager should have little difficulty comparing expectations with performance. For some jobs, a rating scale like the abbreviated one in Figure 9.2 is useful in providing a basis for comparisons. In addition to scales for initiative, punctuality, and cleanliness, a complete form will include several other scales directly related to performance. Comparisons drawn from such scales form the basis for written appraisals and for decisions about raises, promotions, demotions, and firings. The process is completed when manager and employee meet to discuss the appraisal.

FIGURE 9.2 ◆ Performance Rating Scale

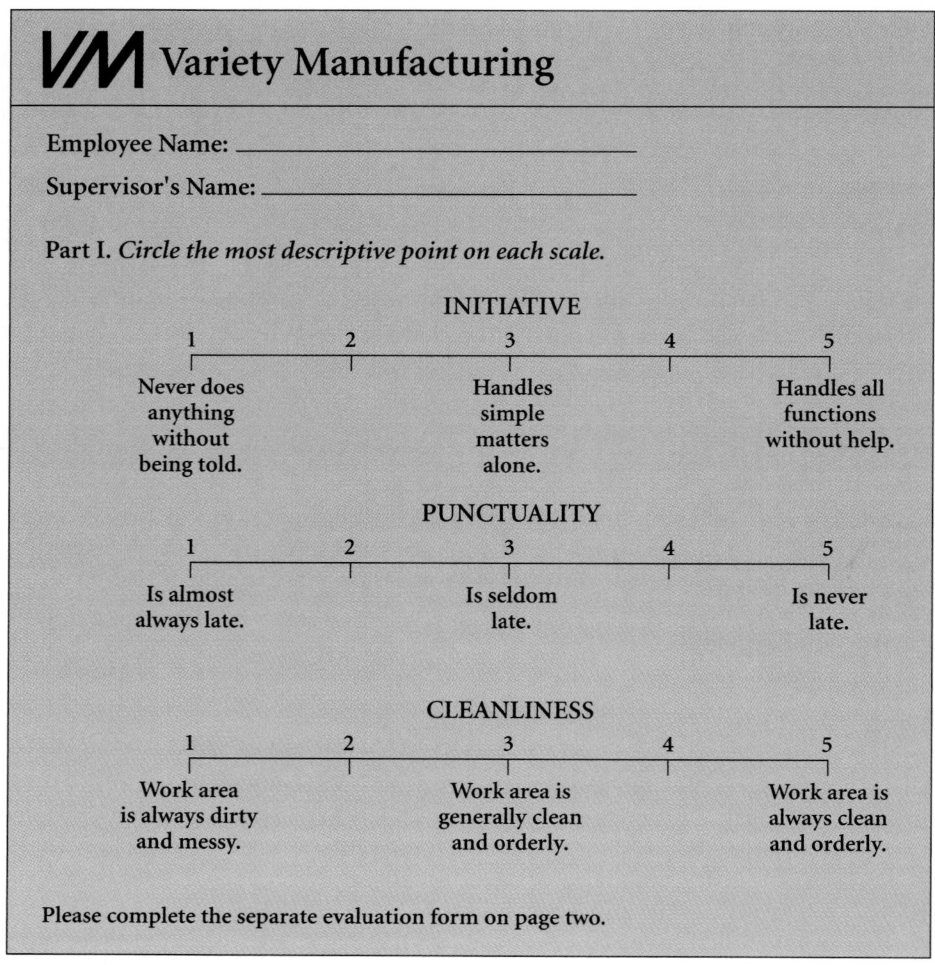

VM Variety Manufacturing

Employee Name: ______________________

Supervisor's Name: ______________________

Part I. *Circle the most descriptive point on each scale.*

INITIATIVE

1	2	3	4	5
Never does anything without being told.		Handles simple matters alone.		Handles all functions without help.

PUNCTUALITY

1	2	3	4	5
Is almost always late.		Is seldom late.		Is never late.

CLEANLINESS

1	2	3	4	5
Work area is always dirty and messy.		Work area is generally clean and orderly.		Work area is always clean and orderly.

Please complete the separate evaluation form on page two.

COMPENSATION AND BENEFITS

compensation system Total package offered by a company to employees in return for their labor

Most workers today also expect certain benefits from their employers. Indeed, a major factor in retaining skilled workers is a company's **compensation system**—the total package that it offers employees in return for their labor.

Although wages and salaries are key parts of all compensation systems, most also include *incentives* and *employee benefits programs.* We discuss these and other types of employee benefits in this section. Remember, however, that finding the right combination of compensation elements is always complicated by the need to make employees feel valued while holding down company costs. Thus, compensation systems differ widely, depending on the nature of the industry, the company, and the types of workers involved.

Wages and Salaries

wages Compensation in the form of money paid for time worked

salary Compensation in the form of money paid for discharging the responsibilities of a job

Wages and salaries are the dollar amounts paid to employees for their labor. **Wages** are paid for time worked. For example, workers who are paid by the hour receive wages. A **salary** is paid for discharging the responsibilities of a job. A salaried executive earning $100,000 per year is paid to achieve results even if that means working 5 hours one day and 15 the next. Salaries are usually expressed as an amount paid per year.

In setting wage and salary levels, a company may start by looking at its competitors' levels. A firm that pays less than its rivals knows that it runs the risk of losing valuable per-

"It appears, Fredrick, since we instituted the merit system you owe us twenty-five-hundred dollars."

sonnel. Conversely, to attract top employees, some companies pay more than their rivals. M&M/Mars, for example, pays managerial salaries about 10 percent above the average in the candy and snack food industry.

A firm must also decide how its internal wage and salary levels will compare for different jobs. For example, Sears must determine the relative salaries of store managers, buyers, and advertising managers. In turn, managers must decide how much to pay individual workers within the company's wage and salary structure. Although two employees may do exactly the same job, the employee with more experience may earn more. Moreover, some union contracts specify differential wages based on experience.

Incentive Programs

Naturally, employees feel better about their companies when they believe that they are being fairly compensated; however, studies and experience have shown that beyond a certain point, more money will not produce better performance. Indeed, neither across-the-board nor cost-of-living wage increases cause people to work harder. Money motivates employees only if it is tied directly to performance. The most common method of establishing this link is the use of **incentive programs**—special pay programs designed to motivate high performance. Some programs are available to individuals, whereas others are distributed on a companywide basis.

incentive program Special compensation program designed to motivate high performance

INDIVIDUAL INCENTIVES A sales bonus is a typical incentive: Employees receive **bonuses**—special payments above their salaries—when they sell a certain number or certain dollar amount of goods for the year. Employees who fail to reach this goal earn no bonuses. **Merit salary systems** link raises to performance levels in nonsales jobs. For example, many baseball players have contract clauses that pay them bonuses for hitting over .300, making the All-Star team, or being named Most Valuable Player.

bonus Individual performance incentive in the form of a special payment made over and above the employee's salary

merit salary system Incentive program linking compensation to performance in nonsales jobs

Executives commonly receive stock options as incentives. Disney CEO Michael Eisner, for example, can buy several thousand shares of company stock each year at a predetermined price. If his managerial talent leads to higher profits and stock prices, he can buy the stock at a price lower than the market value for which, in theory, he is largely responsible. He is then free to sell them at market price, keeping the profits for himself.

pay-for-performance (or variable pay) Individual incentive that rewards a manager for especially productive output

A newer incentive plan is called **pay for performance,** or **variable pay.** In essence, middle managers are rewarded for especially productive output—for producing earnings that significantly exceed the cost of bonuses. Such incentives have long been common among top-level executives and factory workers, but variable pay goes to middle managers on the basis of companywide performance, business unit performance, personal record, or all three factors.

The number of variable pay programs in the United States has been growing consistently for the last decade, and most experts predict that they will continue to grow in popularity.[6] Eligible managers must often forgo merit or "entitlement" raises (increases for staying on and reporting to work every day), but many firms say that variable pay is a better motivator because the range between generous and mediocre merit raises is usually quite small anyway. Merit raises also increase fixed costs: They are added to base pay and increase the base pay used to determine the retirement benefits that the company must pay out.

profit-sharing plan Incentive program for distributing bonuses to employees for company profits above a certain level

gain-sharing plan Incentive program for distributing bonuses to employees whose performances improve productivity

pay-for-knowledge plan Incentive program to encourage employees to learn new skills or become proficient at different jobs

COMPANYWIDE INCENTIVES Some incentive programs apply to all the employees in a firm. Under **profit-sharing plans,** for example, profits earned above a certain level are distributed to employees. Conversely, **gain-sharing plans** distribute bonuses to employees when a company's costs are reduced through greater work efficiency. **Pay-for-knowledge plans** encourage workers to learn new skills and to become proficient at different jobs. They receive additional pay for each new skill or job that they master.

Benefits Programs

benefits Compensation other than wages and salaries

workers' compensation insurance Legally required insurance for compensating workers injured on the job

A growing part of nearly every firm's compensation system is its benefits program. **Benefits**—compensation other than wages and salaries offered by a firm to its workers—comprise a large percentage of most compensation budgets. Most companies are required by law to provide social security retirement benefits and **workers' compensation insurance** (insurance for compensating workers injured on the job). Most businesses also voluntarily provide health, life, and disability insurance. Many also allow employees to use payroll deductions to buy stock at discounted prices. Another common benefit is paid time off for vacations and holidays. Counseling services for employees with alcohol, drug, or emotional problems are also becoming more common.

RETIREMENT PLANS Retirement plans are also an important, and sometimes controversial, benefit that is available to many employees. Most company-sponsored retirement plans are set up to pay pensions to workers when they retire. In some cases, the company contributes all the money to the pension fund. In others, contributions are made by both the company and employees. Currently, about 60 percent of U.S. workers are covered by pension plans of some kind.

cafeteria benefits plan Benefits plan that establishes dollar amount of benefits per employee and allows employees to choose from a variety of alternative benefits

CONTAINING THE COSTS OF BENEFITS As the range of benefits has grown, so has concern about containing their costs. Many companies are experimenting with cost-cutting plans under which they can still attract and retain valuable employees. One approach is the **cafeteria benefits plan:** A certain dollar amount of benefits per employee is set aside so that each employee can choose from a variety of alternatives.

Another area of increasing concern is health care costs. Medical procedures that once cost several hundred dollars now cost several thousand dollars. Medical expenses have increased insurance premiums, which in turn have increased the cost to employers of maintaining benefits plans.

Many employers are looking for new ways to cut those costs. One increasingly popular approach is for organizations to create their own networks of health care providers. These providers agree to charge lower fees for services rendered to employees of member organizations. In return, they enjoy established relationships with large employers, and thus more clients and patients. Because they must make lower reimbursement payments, insurers also charge less to cover the employees of network members.

■ LEGAL AND ETHICAL ISSUES IN MANAGING PEOPLE

In the course of performing their jobs, human resource managers are confronted by numerous legal issues, which often have ethical implications as well. In this section, we discuss some of the basic principles that underlie human resource policies in U.S. business: *equal employment opportunity*, *equal pay* and *comparable worth*, and *occupational safety and health*.

Equal Employment Opportunity

For many years, white males dominated U.S. business, especially at the managerial and professional levels. In recent years, however, this situation has begun to change, partly as a result of changes in the legal environment. Title VII of the 1964 Civil Rights Act was the first major law to prohibit discrimination and paved the way for over three decades of change. This act also created the Equal Employment Opportunity Commission (EEOC), which is responsible for enforcing its provisions. Today, numerous federal and state laws, federal guidelines, presidential executive orders, and judicial decisions mandate **equal employment opportunity**—nondiscrimination in employment on the basis of race, color, creed, sex, or national origin.

equal employment opportunity Legally mandated nondiscrimination in employment on the basis of race, creed, sex, or national origin

Under the Equal Employment Opportunity Act of 1992, the EEOC can file civil suits in federal court on behalf of individuals who claim that their rights have been violated. Remedies include reinstatement, back pay, and compensation for the victim's suffering. Because litigation can last for years, settlements can be huge. Recent awards include $2.3 million in back pay to three older employees of Federated Department Stores, $42.5 million to female and minority employees at General Motors, and $52.5 million to female employees at Northwest Airlines.

SEXUAL HARASSMENT Sexual harassment is a form of employer or management behavior that falls under the category of employment discrimination.[7] Under the terms of the Equal Opportunity Act, the behaviors previously listed are forms of sexual harassment. In fact, any " 'unwelcome' sexual attention, whether verbal or physical, that affects an employee's job conditions or creates a 'hostile' working environment" constitutes sexual harassment. When does acceptable behavior become unacceptable? The U.S. Supreme Court ruled in 1986 that behavior may be judged on the basis of what would offend a "reasonable woman."

Alicia Edwards is a 1998 graduate of Florida A&M University's School of Business and Industry, one of the most aggressive recruiters of talented African American students. Edwards, who is now a Bell Atlantic marketing manager in Manhattan, believes that American companies are committed to diversity for different reasons: while some want minority employees who can help them identify with minority customers, others want mainly to avoid EEOC scrutiny. Among Edwards' graduating class, 40% believe that corporate America is still doing a "poor" job when it comes to promoting African Americans on an equitable basis.

In November 1993, the Court expanded its 1986 ruling and issued an even broader definition of sexual harassment in the workplace: The law is violated when "the environment would be reasonably perceived, and is perceived, as hostile or abusive."

Today, most large corporations provide their employees with detailed information regarding what kinds of behavior are and are not acceptable. They also publish standard procedures for receiving and investigating reports of harassment. Others, such as Du Pont and Corning, go even further. Both of these firms require all employees to attend seminars in which participants role-play potential harassment situations.

A newly emerging emphasis on a harassment-free workplace, plus the willingness to discipline offenders, reflects several trends in modern business. For example, growing public outrage over sexual harassment, coupled with rising numbers of women in the workforce, has had a significant impact. Any company that does not vigorously pursue all employee complaints of harassment may find itself being sued and paying huge settlements.

At the same time, however, confusing legislation and judicial decisions often make it difficult for managers to know where to start. A headline-grabbing verdict stemming from what the media dubbed the "Seinfeld" case clearly illustrates this point. A male executive for Miller Brewing Co. was charged with sexual harassment by a female coworker. The incident revolved around the male executive's insistence upon repeating, over his coworker's protests, certain off-color details from an episode of the television program *Seinfeld.* Miller fired the executive, in part because he was allegedly already on "probation" because of an earlier incident. The fired executive then sued Miller not simply because of his termination, but because he had never been informed that such action had been taken against him. The courts awarded him $24.7 million (although the case is currently under appeal).[8]

affirmative action program
Legally mandated program for recruiting qualified employees belonging to racial, gender, or ethnic groups that are underrepresented in an organization

Affirmative Action Various executive orders spanning more than two decades have also required many organizations to engage in affirmative action. Executive Order 11246, for example, mandates **affirmative action programs** to recruit qualified or qualifiable employees from racial, gender, and ethnic groups that are underrepresented in an organization. All organizations receiving over $100,000 per year in government contracts

TRENDS AND CHALLENGES

CONDUCTING ROMANCE IN PARALLEL UNIVERSES (AND OTHER PLACES)

An attorney in the nation's largest employment law firm recently got a call from the chief counsel at one of his client companies. The nervous caller explained that the president of his company was "planning to have a consensual affair with one of his employees." Before proceeding, however, "he wanted to draft a written agreement" stating that the affair was voluntary and involved no sexual harassment. "You won't believe it," replied the attorney, "but we've already drafted a standard form [for cases like this]."

This story makes two very important points about the murky world of gender relationships in the business world. First, workplace romances between higher- and lower-level employees are common. Second, top executives recognize the risks entailed by such affairs, both to themselves and to their companies.

The stakes, advises Elizabeth J. du Fresne, an attorney specializing in sexual harassment lawsuits, are high. du Fresne settles more than a dozen cases a year for more than $500,000 a case and several for more than $1 million. Money aside, top executives are also losing their jobs over office affairs. "In the last three years," reports employment law attorney Garry G. Mathiason, "I've been involved in more terminations of CEOs due to claims of sex harassment [than for anything else]."

Although office romances have always been a feature of the business landscape, they are more common today simply because of the increased number of working women. Women now represent nearly 27 percent of all middle and senior managers—a fact that makes male-female working relationships and emotional entanglements much more likely. As Eric Greenberg, director of management studies at the American Management Association, puts it, "No company is going to stop Cupid at the front door." Especially on business trips, adds one executive who chose to remain anonymous. "Just imagine what it's like to be somewhere where nobody knows you. It's like a parallel universe."

must have written affirmative action plans. Many other businesses practice affirmative action on a voluntary basis. Legislation passed in 1991 reinforces the legal basis of affirmative action but specifically forbids organizations to set hiring quotas that might result in **reverse discrimination.** This practice can occur when an organization concentrates so much on hiring from some groups that others suffer discrimination.

reverse discrimination
Practice of discriminating against well-represented groups by overhiring members of underrepresented groups

Equal Pay and Comparable Worth

A special area of equal employment, employment opportunities for women, has given rise to one of the most controversial issues in compensation today. The Equal Pay Act of 1963 specifically forbids sex discrimination in pay: No company can legally pay men and women of equal experience differently for work performed under similar conditions that requires equal skill, effort, and responsibility. Differing job titles alone cannot justify pay differences. Thus, if a woman whose job title is *senior secretary* performs essentially the same job as a man whose title is *administrative assistant,* the two must have the same pay scale. As a result of the Equal Pay Act, many women have sued and received back pay and other adjustments from employers who have discriminated on the basis of pay.[9]

THE GLASS CEILING Despite the Equal Pay Act, however, statistics show that women still earn less than men for performing similar jobs. Only in the last 25 to 30 or so years have large numbers of women sought professional careers. Thus, most women typically have less work experience than men of the same age. A related issue is the glass ceiling phenomenon, so called because there still seems to be an invisible but very real barrier over their heads that keeps not only women but also minorities from advancing to higher levels in U.S. organizations.

In a series of hearings held between 1991 and 1994, a congressional panel, called the Glass Ceiling Commission, gathered information and opinions for a report on the lack of progress in advancement by women and minorities. Findings show that despite the Civil Rights Act and women's rights activism, women at that time made up one-half the nation's workforce but only 3 to 6 percent of its corporate officials. Minorities made up

> **"No company is going to stop Cupid at the front door."**
>
> —Eric Greenberg
> *Director of Management Studies at the American Management Association*

Although they can't stop it, many companies try to discourage dating between superiors and subordinates. Intel has a "non-fraternization" policy that threatens any supervisor who dates a subordinate with termination. A kinder, gentler policy at General Motors requires managers to report romantic attachments so that the company can reassign the parties involved.

For all the concern over office romances, however, a survey of 2,800 human resources professionals conducted by the Society for Human Resource Management reports that only 13 percent of companies have written policies on the subject. Given the fact that 6 of 10 respondents reported that the number of workplace romances had either increased or stayed the same over the past 5 years, this number is surprisingly small. The survey also showed some unexpected effects of office romances, including complaints of favoritism from coworkers (28 percent), decreased productivity by those involved (24 percent), complaints of retaliation after breakups (17 percent), and decreased morale among coworkers (16 percent).

Despite the controversy, there are some happy endings. Microsoft CEO Bill Gates met his wife, Melinda, while she was working at the company as a product manager. General Motors Chairman John F. Smith Jr. met his wife, Lydia, when she worked briefly for him in the 1980s. Neither woman is currently working for her husband.

only 1 percent. Robert B. Reich, who was then secretary of labor, revealed that the federal government's managerial structure was also seriously skewed. Although minorities filled 28 percent of all federal jobs, they occupied only 8 percent of upper-level positions. Women made up 44 percent of the workforce but held only 13 percent of the top jobs. "In Washington sometimes," concluded Reich, "the only architectural feature as prominent as the Capitol Dome is the glass ceiling." Most analysts cite lack of resources and unaggressive enforcement of existing laws as primary reasons why so little progress has been made in the years since passage of the Civil Rights Act of 1964.

> **"In Washington sometimes the only architectural feature as prominent as the Capital Dome is the glass ceiling."**
>
> —Robert B. Reich
> *Former Secretary of Labor*

During the years since the original Glass Ceiling Commission reports, things have continued to improve for women and minorities. The pace, however, has been disappointingly slow. As of 1999, for example, there were still only two female CEOs among the 500 largest corporations in the United States. At the same time, women's presence among the ranks of managers in general has improved. In 1983, for instance, women comprised 43.7 percent of the overall workforce, but held only 32.4 percent of the executive, administrative, and managerial positions. By 1997 these numbers had grown to 46.2 percent and 44.3 percent, respectively—a much smaller gap. The gains for blacks and Hispanics have been smaller, but gains nevertheless have been made.[10]

comparable worth Principle that women should receive the same pay for traditionally "female" jobs of the same worth to a company as traditionally "male" jobs

PROGRESS TOWARD "COMPARABLE WORTH" Many experts agree that subtle and perhaps even unconscious discrimination still exists in many organizations. To combat this discrimination, some analysts have called for a policy of **comparable worth:** Women would receive the same wage for traditionally "female" jobs (such as secretary) as men do for traditional "male" jobs of the same worth to the company (say, mechanic).

At chemical giant Hoechst Celanese, Linda J. Welty is global business director for superabsorbent materials. She started out in sales before taking advantage of a mentoring program that fast-tracks women and minorities by pairing them with senior male executives. Based on the gender and ethnic breakdown of students graduating in fields in which it recruits, Hoechst intends to raise the proportion of women and minorities in entry-level management posts from 37% to 43%.

TABLE 9.1 ◆ Gender and Earnings by Occupation (median weekly earnings of full-time workers)

OCCUPATION	MEN	WOMEN
Executive, administrative, and managerial	$868	$605
Administrators and officials, public administration	876	653
Financial managers	991	660
Managers, marketing, advertising, and public relations	1,059	736
Accountants and auditors	791	590
Professional specialty	883	662
Engineers	994	837
Mathematical and computer scientists	994	837
Physicians	1,220	946
Registered nurses	778	705
Pharmacists	1,129	907
Social, recreation, and religious workers	558	502
Lawyers	1,267	959
Designers	792	514
Editors and reporters	769	606
Health technologists and technicians	553	466
Computer programmers	869	742
Sales occupations	603	352
Real estate sales	685	523
Securities and financial services sales	858	550
Sales workers, retail and personal services	392	266
Administrative support, including clerical	514	403
Computer equipment operators	526	422
Bookkeepers, accounting and auditing clerks	446	418
Mail carriers, postal service	691	610
Insurance adjusters, examiners, and investigators	655	473
Police and detectives	628	547
Waiters and waitresses	328	268
Cooks, except short order	300	245
Janitors and cleaners	330	275
Mechanics and repairers, except supervisors	570	475
Construction trades	538	445
Precision metalworking occupations	597	399
Machine operators, assemblers, and inspectors	449	313
Truck drivers	509	399
Farm workers	276	247

Government statistics and working women both confirm the suspicions of experts about lingering discrimination. For instance, figures show that women still earn substantially less than men. Part of this differential results from the fact that women are still concentrated in occupational categories that are traditionally low paying, especially nursing, teaching, secretarial, and retail sales. As Table 9.1 clearly indicates, however, differences in median weekly earnings still exist across the board, across an array of occupations.

Occupational Safety and Health

Occupational Safety and Health Administration (OSHA) Federal agency that sets and enforces guidelines for protecting workers from unsafe conditions and potential health hazards in the workplace

Issues of worker safety on the job have also been addressed through legislation. The Occupational Safety and Health Act of 1970, which created the **Occupational Safety and Health Administration (OSHA),** is the most far-reaching piece of legislation in this area. The act covers all firms with one or more employees.

OSHA sets numerous guidelines in two general areas. First, it protects employee safety by eliminating unsafe working conditions, such as dangerous machinery and unsafe ladders and scaffolding, that might lead to accidents. Second, it protects the health of workers from long-term exposure to health hazards ranging from excessive noise to cancer-causing chemicals. OSHA inspectors can investigate any complaint filed by a worker. They also spot-check companies in particularly hazardous industries. Plants failing to meet safety or health standards can be fined.

■ NEW CHALLENGES IN THE CHANGING WORKPLACE

As we have seen throughout this chapter, human resource managers face several ongoing challenges in their efforts to keep their organizations staffed with effective workforces. To complicate matters, new challenges arise as the economic and social environments of business change. More specifically, today's human resource managers must deal with workforces that are increasingly *diverse* and *contingent.*

Managing Workforce Diversity

workforce diversity Range of workers' attitudes, values, and behaviors that differ by gender, race, and ethnicity

An extremely important set of human resource challenges centers on **workforce diversity**—the range of workers' attitudes, values, beliefs, and behaviors that differ by gender, race, and ethnicity. The diverse workforce is also characterized by individuals of different ages and physical abilities. In the past, organizations tended to work toward *homogenizing* their workforces, getting everyone to think and behave in similar ways. Partly as a result of affirmative action efforts, however, many U.S. organizations are now creating workforces that are more diverse, thus embracing more women, more ethnic minorities, and more foreign-born employees than ever before.

Figures 9.3 and 9.4 help put the changing U.S. workforce into perspective. Figure 9.3 shows changes in the percentages of different groups of workers—white males, white females, blacks, Hispanics, and Asians and others—in the total workforce in the years 1980, 1993, and (as projected) 2005. Figure 9.4 shows changes among managerial and professional workers for blacks and Hispanics between 1983 and 1997. The first picture is one of increasing diversity over the past decade. The second is one of a slower but steady trend toward diversity: By 2005, says the Labor Department, half of all workers entering the labor force will be women and more than one-third will be blacks, Hispanics, Asian Americans, and others.

DIVERSITY AS A COMPETITIVE ADVANTAGE Today, organizations are recognizing not only that they should treat everyone equitably, but also that they should acknowledge the individuality of each person they employ. They are also recognizing that diversity can be a competitive advantage. For example, by hiring the best people available from every single group rather than hiring from just one or a few groups, a firm can develop a higher-

FIGURE 9.3 ◆ **Diversity: Total Workforce**

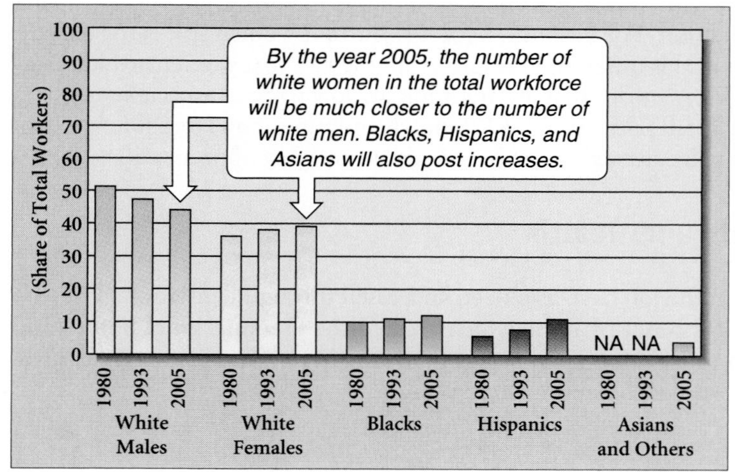

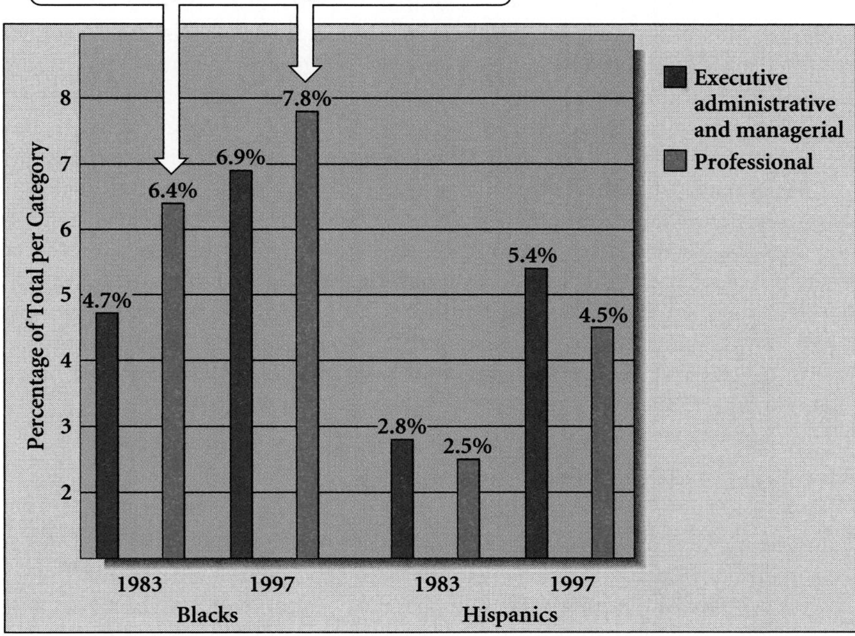

FIGURE 9.4 ◆ Diversity: Managerial and Professional

quality labor force. Similarly, a diverse workforce can bring a wider array of information to bear on problems and can provide insights on marketing products to a wider range of consumers. Says the head of workforce diversity at IBM: "We think it is important for our customers to look inside and see people like them. If they can't . . . the prospect of them becoming or staying our customers declines."

> **"We think it is important for our customers to look inside and see people like them. If they can't . . . the prospect of them becoming or staying our customers declines."**
>
> *Head of workforce diversity at IBM*

Admittedly, not all U.S. companies have worked equally hard to adjust their thinking and diversify their workforces. In fact, experts estimate that only a handful of U.S. corporations are diversifying with any effect. Even among those making progress, it has nevertheless been slow.[11] In a recent survey of executives at 1,405 participating firms, only 5 percent believed that they were doing a "very good job" of diversifying their human resources. Many others, however, have instituted—and, more importantly, maintained—diversity programs. The experience of these companies (including IBM, Xerox, Avon, AT&T, Burger King, Levi Strauss, and Hoechst Celanese) has made it possible to draw up some general guidelines for a successful workforce diversity program:

- *Make diversity a specific management goal.*
- *Analyze compensation scales and be scrupulously fair in tracking individual careers.*
- *Continue to focus on diversity in the midst of downsizing.*
- *Contribute to the supply of diverse workers.*
- *Celebrate diversity.*
- *Respond to the concerns of white males.*

diversity training Programs designed to improve employee awareness of differences in attitudes and behaviors of coworkers from different racial, ethnic, or gender groups

DIVERSITY TRAINING Another guideline calls for companies to use **diversity training**—programs designed to improve employees' understanding of differences in attitudes and behavior patterns among their coworkers. However, there is no consensus yet on how to *conduct* such programs—on exactly what to teach and how to do it.

Not surprisingly, there are sometimes repercussions to such an approach. Indeed, some recent studies have shown that focusing strictly on such issues as race and gender can arouse deep feelings and be almost as divisive as ignoring negative stereotyping in the first place. Other studies suggest that too many training programs are limited to correcting affirmative action problems: Backlash occurs when participants appear to be either "winners" (say, black women) or "losers" (white men) as a result of the process.

Many companies therefore try to go beyond mere awareness training. Du Pont, for example, offers a course for managers on how to seek and use more diverse input before making decisions. Sears offers what it calls diversity-friendly programs: bus service for workers who must commute from the inner city to the suburbs and leaves of absence for foreign-born employees to visit families still living overseas. Finally, one consultant emphasizes that it is extremely important to integrate training into daily routines: "Diversity training," he says, "is like hearing a good sermon on Sunday. You must practice what you heard during the week."

The Contingency Workforce

Can you identify the largest private employer in the United States? Is it General Motors? Exxon? IBM? Actually, it is not a manufacturing company at all. Manpower Inc., the nation's largest supplier of temporary workers, has a payroll of over 2 million (which happens to be more than 3 times the number of employees at General Motors!). Firms such as Manpower are products of some fairly dramatic changes in the U.S. workforce. For decades, businesses in all industries added new employees with regularity. In the 1980s and 1990s, however, cutbacks and retrenchments caused many human resource managers to rethink their staffing philosophies. Rather than hiring permanent employees to fill all new jobs, many firms now use **contingent workers**—employees hired to supplement an organization's permanent workforce. They include part-time employees, freelancers, subcontractors, and temporary workers. Figure 9.5 illustrates recent trends among contingent workers.

contingent worker Temporary employee hired to supplement an organization's permanent workforce

By most accounts, the number of contingent workers is on the rise. Figure 9.5 shows the increase in daily temporary workers, or temps, between 1990 and 1996. According to

FIGURE 9.5 ◆ **The Contingent Workforce**

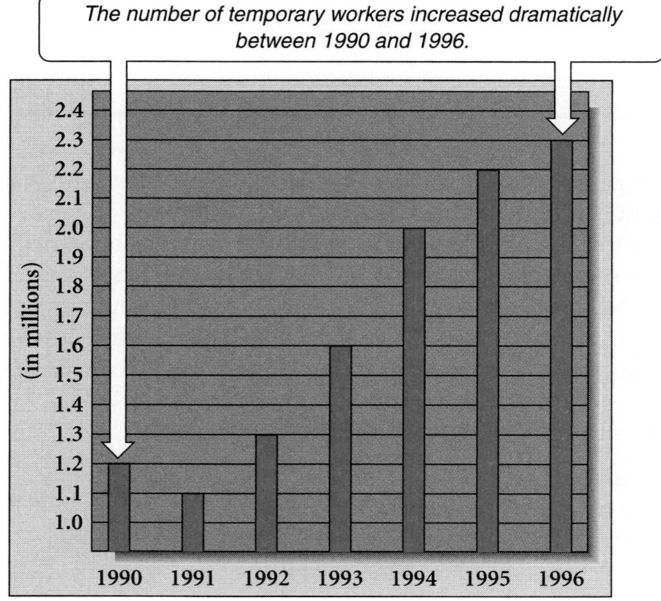

This young woman is one of 1,500 temporary workers at Sola Optical, one of the country's biggest makers of eyeglasses. Sola keeps at least 100 temps working at all times, because human resources managers like both the scheduling flexibility and the opportunity to try potential permanent employees. Pointing to the army of temp workers in U.S. factories—anywhere from 400,000 to 840,000—some analysts argue that the manufacturing sector is actually generating more jobs than such industries as communications and financial services. On the other hand, of course, temps earn about one-third less and usually get no benefits, such as health care.

a poll conducted by the research firm Clark Martire & Bartolomeo, 44 percent of Fortune 500 CEOs said that they use more temps than they did 5 years ago; only 13 percent said they used fewer. Moreover, 44 percent indicated that they would be using more in the future. "Any worker still expecting to hold one job from cradle to grave," says Sara Lee CEO John Bryan, "will need to adjust his thinking."

> **"Any worker still expecting to hold one job from cradle to grave will need to adjust his thinking."**
>
> —John Bryan
> *CEO at Sara Lee*

DEALING WITH ORGANIZED LABOR

Over 2,000 years ago, the Greek poet Homer wrote, "There is a strength in the union even of very sorry men." There were no labor unions in Homer's time, but his comment is a particularly effective expression of the rationale for unions. A **labor union** is a group of individuals working together to achieve shared job-related goals, such as higher pay, shorter working hours, greater benefits, or better working conditions.

labor union Group of individuals working together formally to achieve shared job-related goals

Collective Bargaining

Unions appeared and ultimately prospered because they constituted a solution to the worker's most serious problem: They forced management to listen to the complaints of all their workers rather than to just the few who were brave (or foolish) enough to speak out. The power of unions, then, comes from collective action. **Collective bargaining** is the process by which union leaders and managers negotiate common terms and conditions of employment for the workers represented by unions. Although collective bargaining does not often occur in small businesses, many midsize and larger businesses must engage in the process, which we will discuss in more detail in this chapter.

collective bargaining Process by which labor and management negotiate conditions of employment for workers represented by the union

Unionism Today

Figure 9.6 shows trends in union membership as a percentage of the workforce between 1983 and 1997. Since the mid-1950s, unions have experienced increasing difficulties in attracting members. Even as late as 1977, however, over 26 percent of U.S. wage and salary employees (both private and public) still belonged to unions. Today, as you can see, less than 15 percent of those workers are union members. If government employees are not counted, unions represent only about 11 percent of private industry employees, and some experts suggest that this figure could drop to 4 or 5 percent by the turn of the century.[12]

FACTORS IN DECLINING UNION POWER Despite occasional successes, union fortunes have been in decline for the past 40 years. In this section, we first survey some key factors that have contributed to this reduction of union power. Then we will take a brief look at the future of American labor unions. Finally, to better explain the role of unions not only in such processes as collective bargaining but also in the daily life of the unionized workforce, we describe the typical structure of the contemporary labor union.

Several factors have contributed to the downward slide in union fortunes. Following are three of the most important:

- *Composition of the workforce.* Traditionally, union members have been white men in blue-collar jobs. Today's workforce, however, is increasingly made up of women and minorities. With a much weaker tradition of union affiliation, members of those groups are less likely to join unions when they enter the workforce.
- *Antiunionization strategies.* Many nonunionized industries have developed strategies for avoiding unionization. For example, some companies have introduced new employee relations programs to keep facilities union free. Other employers have launched carefully managed campaigns to persuade workers to reject unions. Some firms have even relocated to states or countries in which unions are unpopular or difficult to install.
- *Negotiated concessions.* Growing international competition in certain industries has led employers to demand unprecedented concessions. As a result, givebacks, or sacrifices of previously won rights and terms, have become common.

As a result of such trends, many experts have observed that in the 1980s and 1990s, unions have altered the focus of the demands that they make at the bargaining table. In recent talks, for example, the United Automobile Workers has shifted its emphasis away from higher wages. Instead, the union now is fighting to prevent wage cuts, preserve health benefits, improve job security, and secure larger pensions.

THE FUTURE OF UNIONS Despite setbacks, however, labor unions remain a major factor in the U.S. business world. The 86 labor organizations in the AFL-CIO, as well

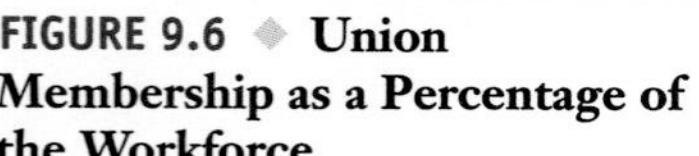

FIGURE 9.6 ◆ Union Membership as a Percentage of the Workforce

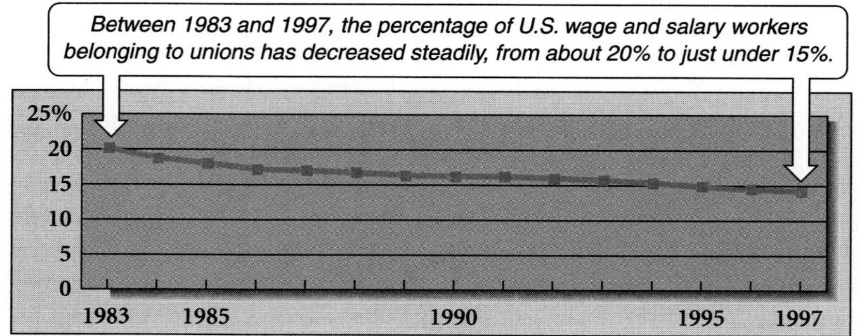

as independent major unions such as the Teamsters and the National Education Association, still play a major role in U.S. business.

Moreover, some unions still wield considerable power, especially in traditional strongholds in goods-producing industries, but also in certain service industries. In February 1999, for example, American Airlines was forced to cancel hundreds of flights due to a union action. In late 1998, American had purchased another airline, Reno Air, but failed to boost the pay of the newly acquired airline's pilots to levels dictated by American's contract with its own pilots' union. Although American pilots could not legally go out on strike, they did engage in an organized action, either calling in sick or refusing to accept overtime assignments. American suffered significant financial losses because of the canceled flights.

Labor and management in some industries, notably airlines and steel, are beginning to favor contracts that establish formal mechanisms for greater worker input into management decisions. Inland Steel, for instance, recently granted its major union the right to name a member to the board of directors; union officers can also attend executive meetings.

The big question, however, remains: Will unions dwindle in power and perhaps disappear, or can they evolve, survive to face new challenges, and play a new role in U.S. business? They will probably evolve to take on new roles and responsibilities. As we have already seen, more and more unions are asking for—and often getting—voices in management. In 1980, for example, as a part of the Chrysler bailout, UAW president Douglas Fraser became the first labor official appointed to the board of directors of a major corporation. Several other companies have since followed suit.

By the same token, unions are increasingly aware that they must cooperate with employers if both are to survive. Critics of unions contend that excessive wage rates won through years of strikes and hard-nosed negotiation are partly to blame for the demise of large employers such as Eastern Airlines. Others argue that excessively tight work rules limit the productivity of businesses in many industries. More often, however, unions are working with organizations to create effective partnerships in which managers and workers share the same goals: profitability, growth, and effectiveness with equitable rewards for everyone.

LAWS GOVERNING LABOR-MANAGEMENT RELATIONS

Like almost every other aspect of labor-management relations today, the process of unionizing workers is governed by numerous laws, administrative interpretations, and judicial decisions. In fact, the growth and decline of unionism in the United States can be traced by following the history of labor laws.[13]

For the first 150 years of U.S. independence, workers were judged to have little legal right to organize. Indeed, interpretation of the 1890 Sherman Antitrust Act classified labor unions as monopolies, thus making them illegal. During the first 30 years of the twentieth century, however, social activism and turmoil in the labor force changed the landscape of U.S. labor relations.

The Major Labor Laws

Five major federal laws, all enacted between 1932 and 1959, lay the groundwork for all the rules, regulations, and judicial decisions governing union activity in the United States. Several more recent laws have dealt with specific groups and specific issues.

Norris-LaGuardia Act (1932) Federal law limiting the ability of courts to issue injunctions prohibiting certain union activities

NORRIS-LAGUARDIA ACT During the 1930s, labor leaders finally persuaded lawmakers that the legal environment discriminated against the collective efforts of workers to improve working conditions. Legislators responded with the **Norris-LaGuardia Act** in 1932. This act imposed severe limitations on the ability of the courts to issue injunctions prohibiting certain union activities, including strikes. Norris-LaGuardia also

yellow-dog contracts Requirements that workers state that they did not belong to and would not join a union

National Labor Relations Act (Wagner Act) (1935) Federal law protecting the rights of workers to form unions, bargain collectively, and engage in strikes to achieve their goals

outlawed **yellow-dog contracts,** which are requirements that workers state that they did not belong to and would not join a union.

NATIONAL LABOR RELATIONS (WAGNER) ACT

In 1935 Congress passed the **National Labor Relations Act** (also called the **Wagner Act**), which is the cornerstone of contemporary labor relations law. This act put labor unions on a more equal footing with management in terms of the rights of employees to organize and bargain. For example,

- It gave most workers the right to form unions, bargain collectively, and engage in group activities (such as strikes) to reach their goals.
- It forced employers to bargain with duly elected union leaders and prohibited employer practices that unjustly restrict employees' rights (for example, discriminating against union members in hiring, promoting, and firing).

National Labor Relations Board (NLRB) Federal agency established by the National Labor Relations Act to enforce its provisions

Fair Labor Standards Act (1938) Federal law setting minimum wage and maximum number of hours in the workweek

The Wagner Act also established the **National Labor Relations Board (NLRB)** to administer its provisions. Today, the NLRB administers virtually all labor law in this country.

FAIR LABOR STANDARDS ACT

Enacted in 1938, the **Fair Labor Standards Act** addressed issues of minimum wages and maximum work hours:

- It set a minimum wage (originally $0.25 an hour) to be paid to workers. The minimum wage has been increased many times since 1938 and now stands at $5.15 per hour.
- It set a maximum number of hours for the workweek, initially 44 hours per week, later 40 hours.
- It mandated time-and-a-half pay for those who worked beyond the legally stipulated number of hours.
- It outlawed child labor.

Labor-Management Relations Act (Taft-Hartley Act) (1947) Federal law defining certain union practices as unfair and illegal

closed shop Workplace in which an employer may hire only workers already belonging to a union

TAFT-HARTLEY ACT

Supported by the Norris-LaGuardia, Wagner, and Fair Labor Standards Acts, organized labor eventually grew into a powerful political and economic force; but a series of disruptive strikes in the immediate post–World War II years turned public opinion against unions. Inconvenienced by strikes and the resulting shortages of goods and services, the public became openly critical of unions and pressured the government to take action. Congress responded by passing the **Labor-Management Relations Act** (more commonly known as the **Taft-Hartley Act**) in 1947.

Unfair and Illegal Union Practices. The Taft-Hartley Act defined certain union practices as unfair and illegal. For example, it prohibited such practices as featherbedding (requiring extra workers solely to provide more jobs) and refusing to bargain in good faith. It also generally forbade the **closed shop**—a workplace in which only workers already belonging to a union may be hired by an employer.

Injunctions and Cooling-Off Periods. Passed in the wake of crippling strikes in the steel industry, the Taft-Hartley Act also established procedures for resolving any strike deemed to pose a national emergency. Initially, the concept of national emergency was broadly interpreted. For example, virtually any large company could claim that a strike was doing irreparable harm to its financial base and that the nation's economy would be harmed if workers were not forced back to their jobs.

Enforced Resolution. If differences are not resolved during the cooling-off period, the injunction may be extended for another 20 days. During this period, employees must vote, in a secret ballot election, on whether to accept or reject the employer's latest offer. If they accept the offer, the threat of strike is ended and the contract is signed. If they do not accept the offer, the president reports to Congress, and the workers may either be forced back to work under threat of criminal action or fired and replaced by nonunion employees. Presidential intervention has been invoked only 35 times since Taft-Hartley was passed.

LANDRUM-GRIFFIN ACT The National Labor Relations Act was further amended by the **Landrum-Griffin Act** in 1959. Officially titled the **Labor-Management Reporting and Disclosure Act,** this law resulted from congressional hearings that revealed unethical, illegal, and undemocratic union practices. The act thus imposed regulations on internal union procedures:

- It required the election of national union leaders at least once every 5 years.
- It gave union members the right to participate in various union affairs.
- It required unions to file annual financial disclosure statements with the Department of Labor.

Labor-Management Reporting and Disclosure Act (Landrum-Griffin Act) (1959) Federal law imposing regulations on internal union procedures, including elections of national leaders and filing of financial disclosure statements

THE COLLECTIVE BARGAINING PROCESS

When a union has been legally certified, it assumes the role of official bargaining agent for the workers whom it represents. Collective bargaining is an ongoing process involving both the drafting and the administering of the terms of a labor contract.[14]

Reaching Agreement on Contract Terms

The collective bargaining process begins when the union is recognized as the exclusive negotiator for its members. The bargaining cycle itself begins when union leaders meet with management representatives to agree on a contract. By law, both parties must sit at the bargaining table and negotiate in good faith.

Sometimes this process goes quite smoothly. At other times, however, the two sides cannot, or will not, agree. The speed and ease with which such an impasse is resolved depend in part on the nature of the contract issues, the willingness of each side to use certain tactics, and the prospects for mediation or arbitration.

Although only about 15% of U.S. wage and salary employees now belong to such unions as the United Steelworkers of America, it is worth noting that union retirement funds hold about 14% of all outstanding stock in the country—$1.4 trillion worth. Many labor leaders, particularly those at the AFL-CIO, would like unions to unite in wielding what could be an extremely powerful weapon in the ongoing battle with corporate America. Unions could easily become the largest bloc of organized shareholders in the nation. "Our goal," says AFL-CIO Secretary-Treasurer Richard L. Trumka, "is to make worker capital serve workers." Opponents argue that the strategy is just "a new form of union blackmail against companies."

Contract Issues

The labor contract itself can address an array of different issues. Most of these concern demands that unions make on behalf of their members. In this section we survey the categories of issues that are typically most important to union negotiators: compensation, benefits, and job security. Although few issues covered in a labor contract are company sponsored, we also describe the kinds of management rights that are negotiated in most bargaining agreements.

First, note that bargaining items generally fall into two categories:

- *Mandatory items* are matters over which both parties must negotiate if either desires it. This category includes wages, working hours, and benefits.
- *Permissive items* may be negotiated if both parties agree. A union demand for veto power over the promotion of managerial personnel would be a permissive bargaining item.

Illegal items may not be brought to the table by either party. A management demand for a nonstrike clause would be an illegal item.

Other possible issues include working hours, overtime policies, rest period arrangements, differential pay plans for shift employees, the use of temporary workers, grievance procedures, and allowable union activities (dues collection, union bulletin boards, and so forth).

MANAGEMENT RIGHTS Management wants to retain as much control as possible over hiring policies, work assignments, and so forth, while unions often try to limit management rights by specifying hiring, assignment, and other policies. At a Chrysler plant in Detroit, for example, the contract stipulates that three workers are needed to change fuses in robots: a machinist to open the robot, an electrician to change the fuse, and a supervisor to oversee the process. As in this case, contracts often bar workers in one job category from performing work that falls in the domain of another. Unions try to secure jobs by defining as many different categories as possible (the Chrysler plant has more than 100 categories). Management resists the practice, which limits flexibility and makes it difficult to reassign workers.

When Bargaining Fails

An impasse occurs when, after a series of bargaining sessions, management and labor have failed to agree on a new contract or a contract to replace an agreement that is about to expire. Although it is generally agreed that both parties suffer when an impasse is reached and action is taken, each side can use several tactics to support its cause until the impasse is resolved.

Union Tactics When their demands are not met, unions may bring a variety of tactics to the bargaining table. Chief among these is the strike, which may be supported by *pickets*, *boycotts*, or both.

strike Labor action in which employees temporarily walk off the job and refuse to work

economic strike Strike usually triggered by stalemate over one or more mandatory bargaining items

The Strike. A **strike** occurs when employees temporarily walk off the job and refuse to work. Most strikes in the United States are **economic strikes,** triggered by stalemates over mandatory bargaining items, including such noneconomic issues as working hours and job security. In mid-1998, for example, employees at General Motors went out on a bitter 7-week strike that shut down virtually all the firm's U.S. production. The basic issue was one of job security: GM wanted to cut jobs and move more operations overseas, but workers wanted jobs maintained at existing U.S. plants. Only after both sides made major concessions over job security did production resume. All told, however, GM estimated that it lost $2.2 billion due to lost production.

Not all strikes are legal. Sympathy strikes (also called secondary strikes), which occur when one union strikes in sympathy with action initiated by another, may violate the sympathetic union's contract. Wildcat strikes—strikes unauthorized by the union that occur during the life of a contract—deprive strikers of their status as employees and thus of the protection of national labor law.

Other Labor Actions. To support a strike, a union faced with an impasse has recourse to additional legal activities:

picketing Labor action in which workers publicize their grievances at the entrance to an employer's facility

boycott Labor action in which workers refuse to buy the products of a targeted employer

lockout Management tactic whereby workers are denied access to their workplace

- In **picketing,** workers march at the entrance to the employer's facility with signs explaining their reasons for striking.
- A **boycott** occurs when union members agree to not buy the products of a targeted employer. Workers may also urge consumers to boycott the firm's products.

Management Tactics Like workers, management can respond forcefully to an impasse:

- **Lockouts** occur when employers deny employees access to the workplace. Lockouts are illegal if they are used as offensive weapons to give management a bargaining advantage. They are legal if management has a legitimate business need (for instance, avoiding a buildup of perishable inventory). Although rare today, lockouts were used in two very different cases in 1998 to 1999, one involving the National Basketball Association and its players and the other ABC and its off-camera technical employees. In the case of the NBA, the league was forced to cancel half its season and play did not resume until February 1999. ABC's actions were prompted by a surprise 1-day strike by a union during an especially hectic time—coverage of the November 1998 elections and a Monday-night football game. ABC indicated that it expected the union to give advance notice of future strikes.

- A firm can also hire temporary or permanent replacements called **strikebreakers.** However, the law forbids the permanent replacement of workers who strike because of unfair practices. In some cases, an employer can also obtain legal injunctions that either prohibit workers from striking or prohibit a union from interfering with its efforts to use replacement workers.

strikebreaker Worker hired as permanent or temporary replacement for a striking employee

MEDIATION AND ARBITRATION Rather than wield these often unpleasant weapons against one another, labor and management can agree to call in a third party to help resolve the dispute:

- In **mediation,** the neutral third party (the mediator) can advise, but cannot impose a settlement on the other parties.
- In **voluntary arbitration,** the neutral third party (the arbitrator) dictates a settlement between the two sides, who have agreed to submit to outside judgment.
- In some cases, arbitration is legally required to settle bargaining disputes. **Compulsory arbitration** is used to settle disputes between the government and public employees such as firefighters and police officers.

mediation Method of resolving a labor dispute in which a third party advises on, but does not impose, a settlement

voluntary arbitration Method of resolving a labor dispute in which both parties agree to submit to the judgment of a neutral party

compulsory arbitration Method of resolving a labor dispute in which both parties are legally required to accept the judgment of a neutral party

Continued from page 207

Membership Is Job #1

To AFL-CIO President John J. Sweeney, every union win in Las Vegas is a win for the union movement throughout the country. With Las Vegas as a model, Sweeney has focused union activities on recruiting new members instead of defending the jobs, pay, and benefits of current members. His chief targets are the women and minorities who comprise the majority of the country's low-wage service workers.

With the union movement still hemorrhaging members (AFL-CIO membership dropped by 100,000 in 1996 alone), how will Sweeney turn things around? He'll start by increasing the money spent on recruitment, which has languished for decades at a mere 3 percent of unions' annual budgets. The strategy seems promising: In a period during which the United Farm Workers earmarked 40 percent of its resources for recruiting, it won 13 straight certification elections. Likewise, once the Teamsters had begun to recruit more aggressively, they were able to unionize such long elusive targets as the Overnite Transportation Co. With the annual income of unions estimated to be about $5 billion, unions could dramatically shift the employer-employee power relationship by spending approximately a third of that sum—$1.65 billion—on recruitment. Currently, they spend only about $200 million a year on membership drives.

To free resources for organizing, union leaders are also cleaning house. Like big business, they are restructuring and insisting on layoffs, when necessary, and performance standards for staff workers. "We have a product to deliver," says United Brotherhood of Carpenters President Douglas J. McCarron, "and we have to do it more efficiently. Who says you're entitled to a lifetime job just because you work at a union?" At UNITE, the needle-trades union, 25 percent of the staff was let go as 20 percent more money was channeled into recruitment. Receiving the first pink slips were those with no recruiting skills.

"We have a product to deliver, and we have to do it more efficiently. Who says you're entitled to a lifetime job just because you work at a union?"

—Douglas J. McCarron
President of United Brotherhood of Carpenters

Questions for Discussion

1. Why is Las Vegas such an important battleground for the union movement?
2. Why do low-paid service workers provide a promising opportunity for the expansion of the movement?
3. How has the change in leadership at the top of the AFL-CIO refocused the union movement? Do you agree with John J. Sweeney that it is smarter to focus the union movement on recruiting new members than on defending the jobs, pay, and benefits of current members?
4. In what ways might a shift from a nonunion to a union company affect staffing, promotion, training, compensation, and benefits decisions?
5. Why do you think that "card signing" has been more successful in unionizing companies than NLRB elections?
6. In what ways are unions like any other business organization in terms of human resources and labor relations?

SUMMARY

1. **Define *human resource management* and explain how managers plan for human resources.** *Human resource management* is the development, administration, and evaluation of programs to acquire new employees and enhance the quality and performance of people working in an organization. Planning for human resource needs entails several steps. Conducting a *job analysis* enables managers to create detailed, accurate *job descriptions* and *specifications.*
2. **Identify the steps involved in *staffing* a company.** *External staffing*—hiring from outside the company—requires that a firm *recruit* applicants and then *select* from among the applicants. The selection phase may include *interviewing* and *testing.* When possible, however, many companies prefer the practice of *internal staffing*—filling positions by promoting existing personnel.

3. **Explain how organizations can develop workers' skills and manage workers who do not perform well.** If a company is to get the most out of its workers, it must develop those workers and their skills. Nearly all employees undergo some initial orientation process that introduces them to the company and to their new jobs. Many employees are given the opportunity to acquire new skills through *on-the-job* or *off-the-job training programs. Performance appraisals* help managers decide who needs training and who should be promoted. Appraisals also tell employees how well they are meeting expectations.

4. **Discuss the importance of *wages* and *salaries, incentives,* and *benefits programs* in attracting and keeping skilled workers.** Wages and salaries, incentives, and benefit packages may all be parts of a company's *compensation program.* By paying its workers as well as or better than competitors do, a business can attract and keep qualified personnel. Incentive programs (for example, *bonuses, gain sharing, profit sharing,* and *pay for knowledge*) can also motivate personnel to work more productively. Although *benefits programs* may increase employee satisfaction, they are a major expense to business today.

5. **Describe some of the key legal and ethical issues involved in hiring, compensating, and managing workers in today's workplace.** In hiring, compensating, and managing workers, managers must obey a variety of federal laws. *Equal employment opportunity* and *equal pay laws* forbid discrimination other than action based on legitimate job requirements. The concept of *comparable worth* holds that different jobs requiring equal levels of training and skill should pay the same. Firms are also required to provide employees with safe working environments, as set down by the guidelines of the *Occupational Safety and Health Administration.*

6. **Discuss *workforce diversity* and the *contingent workforce* as important changes in the contemporary workplace.** *Workforce diversity* refers to the range of workers' attitudes, values, beliefs, and behaviors that differ by gender, race, ethnicity, age, and physical ability. Today, many U.S. businesses are working to create workforces that reflect the growing diversity of the population as it enters the labor pool. Although many firms see the diverse workforce as a competitive advantage, not all are equally successful in or eager about implementing diversity programs. *Diversity training* consists of programs to improve employees' understanding of differences among their coworkers.

   Contingent workers are temporary and part-time employees hired to supplement an organization's permanent workforce. Their numbers have grown significantly since the early 1980s and are expected to rise further. The practice of hiring contingent workers is gaining in popularity because it gives managers more flexibility and because temps are usually not covered by employers' benefit programs.

7. **Describe the *major laws governing labor-management relations* and identify the steps in the *collective bargaining process.*** Several significant laws affect labor-management relations. The *Norris-LaGuardia Act* and the *National Labor Relations (Wagner) Act* limited the ability of employers to keep unions out of the workplace. The *Fair Labor Standards Act* established a minimum wage and outlawed child labor. The *Taft-Hartley Act* and the *Landrum-Griffin Act* limited the power of unions and provided for the settlement of strikes in key industries.

   Once certified, the union engages in *collective bargaining* with the organization. The initial step in collective bargaining is reaching agreement on a *labor contract.* Contract demands usually involve wages, job security, or management rights. Both labor and management have several tactics that can be used against the other if negotiations break down. Unions may attempt a *strike* or a *boycott* of the firm or may engage in a slowdown. Companies may hire replacement workers (*strikebreakers*) or lock out all workers. In extreme cases, *mediation* or *arbitration* may be used to settle disputes.

QUESTIONS AND EXERCISES

Questions for Review

1. What are the advantages and disadvantages of both internal and external staffing? Under what circumstances is each appropriate?

2. Why is the formal training of workers so important to most employers? Why don't most employers just let employees learn about their jobs as they perform them?
3. What are the different forms of compensation that firms typically use to attract and retain productive workers?
4. What is a cafeteria benefits plan? Compared with conventional plans, what are its advantages and disadvantages?

QUESTIONS FOR ANALYSIS

5. Recall the most recent instance in which you applied for a job. Which selection techniques did the employer use to assess your qualifications? How well do you think each technique predicted your potential as an employee?
6. Have you or anyone you know ever suffered discrimination in a hiring decision? Did you or that person do anything about it?
7. Suppose that someone you know is interested in a career in human resources management. What advice might you give that person about applicable experience and preparation?
8. How much will benefit considerations affect your choice of an employer after graduation?

APPLICATION EXERCISES

9. Interview a human resource manager at a local company. Focus on a position for which the firm is currently recruiting applicants and identify the steps in the selection process.
10. Identify some journals in your library that might be useful to a human resource manager. What topics have been covered in recent features and cover stories?

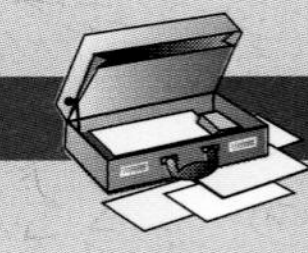

BUILDING YOUR BUSINESS SKILLS

GETTING ON-LINE FOR A JOB

This exercise enhances the following SCANS workplace competencies: demonstrating basic skills, demonstrating thinking skills, exhibiting interpersonal skills, working with information, applying systems knowledge, and using technology.

▼ GOAL

To introduce students to career-search resources available on the Internet.

▼ BACKGROUND

If companies are on one side of the external staffing process, people looking for work are on the other. Companies need qualified candidates to fill job openings and candidates need jobs that are right for them. The challenge, of course, is to make successful matches. Increasingly, this matchmaking is being conducted on the Internet. Companies are posting jobs in cyberspace, and job seekers are posting resumés in response.

The number of job postings has grown dramatically in recent years. On a typical Sunday, you might find as many as 50,000 postings on the Monster Board, a leading job site. That's about five times the number that you'd find in the national edition of *The New York Times.* With so many companies looking for qualified candidates on-line, it makes good business sense to learn how to use the system.

▼ METHOD

Using Internet career-resources means locating job databases and preparing and posting a resumé. (You will therefore need access to the Internet to complete this exercise.)

STEP 1

Team up with three classmates to investigate and analyze specific job databases. In each case, write a short report describing the database (which you and other group members may use during an actual job search). Summarize the site and its features as well as advantages, disadvantages, and costs.

Start with the following sites, and add others that you find on your own:

- The Monster Board http://www.monster.com
- CareerMosaic http://www.careermosaic.com
- College Grad Job Hunter http://www.collegegrad.com
- HRS Federal Job Search http://www.hrsjobs.com
- America's Job Bank http://www.ajb.dni.us/

STEP 2

Investigate the job opportunities listed on the home pages of various companies. Among the companies you can try, consider the following:

- AT&T http://www.att.com
- IBM http://www.ibm.com
- Chase Manhattan Bank http://www.chasemanhattan.com
- JCPenney http://www.jcpenney.com
- McDonald's http://www.mcdonalds.com
- General Electric http://ge.com

Write a summary of the specific career-related information you find on each site.

STEP 3

Working with group members, research strategies for composing effective cyber resumés. The following Web sites provide some helpful information on formats and personal and job-related information that should be included in your resumé. They also offer hints on the art of creating a scannable resumé:

- E-Span http://www.espan.com
- JobSource http://www.jobsource.com
- Career Magazine http://www.careermag.com

Two books by Joyce Lain Kennedy, *Electronic Job Search Revolution* and *Electronic Resumé Revolution*, also contain valuable information.

STEP 4

Working as a group, create an effective electronic resumé for a fictitious college graduate looking for a first job. Pay attention to format, language, style, and the effective communication of background and goals.

STEP 5

Working as a group, learn how to post your resumé on-line. (Do not submit the resumé you created for this exercise, which is, after all, fictitious.) The databases provided will guide you in this process.

▼ Follow-Up

1. Why is it necessary to learn how to conduct an electronic job search? Do you think it will be more or less necessary in the years ahead?
2. Why do you think more computer-related jobs than nontechnical jobs are posted on-line? Do you think this situation will change?
3. Why is it a waste of time to stylize your resumé with different fonts, point sizes, and centered headings?
4. What is the advantage of e-mailing your resumé directly to a company rather than applying for the same job through an on-line databank?

CRAFTING YOUR BUSINESS PLAN

KEEPING YOUR BUSINESS HEALTHY

▼ THE PURPOSE OF THE ASSIGNMENT

1. To acquaint students with the process of navigating the Business PlanPro (BPP) software package.
2. To familiarize students with the human resources and labor relations issues faced by a sample firm as it develops its business plan.
3. To demonstrate how four chapter topics—external versus internal staffing, financial incentives programs, hiring and training employees, and management-union agreements—can be integrated as components in the BPP planning environment.

▼ ASSIGNMENT

After reading Chapter 9 in the textbook, open the BPP software and look around for information about human resources management as it applies to a sample firm: Southwest Health Plans, Inc. Then respond to the following questions:*

1. Explore the business plan for this company, paying special attention to its product line and the types of clients that will be buying its products. Do you suspect that there will be union members among the employees of some Southwest customers? Explain why some experience with labor laws and management-union contract issues would be valuable for Southwest salespeople. [Sites to see in *BPP* (for this assignment): In the Task Manager screen, click on **What You're Selling.** Then click on **1. Summary and Introduction** and **4. Sourcing and Fulfillment.** After returning to the Task Manager screen, click on **The Business You're In.** Then click on **2. Industry Participants.** After returning once again to the Task Manager screen, click on **Initial Assessment.** Finally, click on **3. Keys to Success.**]
2. Judging from both the company's growth expectations and contents of its business plan, describe Southwest's plans for hiring and training its sales staff. [Sites to see in *BPP*: In the Task Manager screen, click on **Initial Assessment.** Then click on **1. Objectives.** After returning to Initial Assessment, click on each of the following in turn: **2. Mission** and **3. Keys to Success.** Finally, examine any other windows whose titles suggest staffing-related material.]
3. Considering Southwest's growth projections, what type of incentives program would you recommend that it use for its sales staff? Individual merit pay? Individual bonuses? Companywide profit sharing? Explain the reasons for your recommendation. [Sites to see in *BPP:* In the Task Manager screen, click on **Your Market.** Then click on **1. Summary and Introduction.** After returning to the Task Manager screen, click on **Your Sales Forecast.** From there, click on each of the following: **2. Pricing Strategy** and **3. Sales Forecast.**]
4. Judging from the contents of its business plan, do you think Southwest intends to rely on external or internal staffing for future management personnel? In what ways might the internal versus external choice affect Southwest's performance? [Sites to see in *BPP:* In the Task Manager screen, click on **Your Management Team.** Then click on each of the following in turn: **1. Management Summary, 3. Management Team,** and **5. Personnel Table.**]

▼ FOR YOUR OWN BUSINESS PLAN

5. Analyzing your own plan, would you consider hiring Southwest Health Plans Inc. to administer your firm's benefits package? Identify which services Southwest would provide and which you would otherwise have to provide yourself. How would you

estimate the costs of obtaining these services? [Sites to see in *BPP:* To learn about Southwest's experience with benefits planning, go to the Task Manager screen and click on **Your Management Team.** Then click on each of the following: **3. Management Team** and **5. Personnel Table.**]

▼ *General Tips for Navigating in BPP

1. Open the BPP program, examine the Welcome screen, and click on **Open a Sample Plan.**
2. From the Open a Sample Plan dialogue box, click on a sample company name; then click on **Open.**
3. On the Task Manager screen, click on any of the lines (for example, **Your Company**).
4. You can always return to the Task Manager screen by going to the bottom of the screen and clicking on the **Task Manager** icon.
5. When you are finished with a sample company, close its Task Manager screen.
6. After finishing with one sample company, you can get to the next one by going to the top of the screen and clicking on **File** (on the menu bar). Then beneath that, select **Open Sample Plan.** This will exit you from the current company file and send you to the Open a Sample Plan dialogue box, where you can select your next sample company.

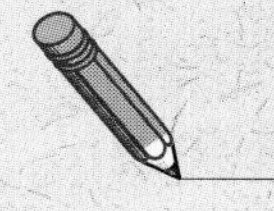

EXPLORING THE NET

KEEPING THE INTERNET ON RETAINER

One of the most important issues facing managers today is compliance with various legal regulations. The following Web site summarizes many current legal cases involving discrimination claims of various forms:

http://www.nyper.com

Visit the site and select any two categories of pending lawsuits. Then visit those locations and review some of the cases. Choose two lawsuits from each area that seem interesting to you (for a total of four). Write a brief description of each case. Describe the potential implications for human resource managers and, finally, respond to the following questions:

1. How useful is the Internet in keeping human resource managers informed about legal actions that may affect them?
2. Does relying on the Internet for legal information pose any risks?
3. What other legal information about human resource management might be useful to have on the Internet?

VIDEO EXERCISE 3.1

The Business of Managing in Showbiz

Learning Objectives

The purpose of this video is to help you

1. Understand how managers and employees view the management process differently.
2. Appreciate how different management styles can fit specific employee and situational needs.
3. Understand how evaluation and rewards systems shape employee behavior.

Background Information

Large companies like Showtime sometimes struggle to find suitable employees. The company has learned that referrals from satisfied and competent employees are one of the best methods of recruitment. Showtime offers performance-based incentives to employees along with consistent growth opportunities. Although leadership styles vary from individual to individual, Showtime's managers tend to be collaborative, inviting employee participation in the management process. Managers achieve this collaboration by delegating responsibilities and empowering subordinates with decision-making authority. This process plays a large role in establishing the culture that exists at Showtime—a strong, positive culture that is essential in helping Showtime consistently retain its employees.

The Video

Part Three of this video shows how management styles shape work environments. In some cases, the type of business may determine which styles are most effective. In many organizations, employee development is a major management concern. This video also shows how management can use different evaluation and reward mechanisms to motivate employees. Showtime's efforts in this area are an example of what one firm has done.

Discussion Questions

1. What are some of the most significant issues human resource managers face?
2. What can top management do to foster leadership at all levels of the firm?
3. How can a business create opportunities for employee growth?
4. What are some traits of effective top managers?

Follow-Up Assignment

A company's management style is something you learn quickly in any job. Identify one manager from your work experience, and describe his or her management style. How did the management style mesh with what you expected or desired as an employee? How did this manager's style affect the unit's performance?

For Further Exploration

Go to the Web site, Management By Strengths

http://www.strengths.com

Explore the information provided on the 4 High Traits framework: directness, extroversion, pace, and structure. How would you describe yourself using this framework? Apply this framework to the manager you described in the follow-up assignment.

VIDEO EXERCISE 3.2

Buckeye Beans & Herbs

SMALL BUSINESS 2000

> "Nobody really wants this kind of item right now!"
>
> —*Sad, but sometimes wise, conclusion*

Learning Objectives

The purpose of this video exercise is to help you

1. See that confidence is a key ingredient for an entrepreneur, perhaps even the most important ingredient!
2. Learn about a firm where the work seems to be fun and where the firm tries to make the product fun for the consumers.
3. Investigate the matter of integrating family and friends into the firm.

Background Information

Hattie Bryant introduces us to Jill and Doug Smith, founders of Buckeye Beans & Herbs in Spokane, Washington. In addition to beans and herbs, the firm packages spices and pasta. We pick up right away that the firm fosters an upbeat atmosphere, and departments carry such names as *Bean Boss*, *Bean Queen*, *Bean Counters*, and *Human Beans*, to name but a few. The firm produces sacks of dry food products that when added to a pot of boiling water turn into a delicious meal. Jill, who does much of the talking on the videotape, believes that cooking can be a good experience, and Buckeye Beans & Herbs is standing by to make meal preparation easy and even entertaining. Consider Aunt Patsy's Pantry, a sack of exciting culinary ingredients with enough instructions that even a totally inept cook could make a delicious meal out of it. Simplicity and fun are the hallmarks, and supper does not have to be drudgery. Doug states that the firm pledges allegiance to the HEHE principle, which stands for humor, education, health, and the environment.

Always looking for a new way to insert *fun* into their product, the firm came up with pasta in strange shapes—Christmas trees, baseballs, baseball bats, gloves, and so on. Jill says she received a lot of help with the funny shapes by listening to customers at a trade show. This innovation has been a tremendous hit in stores. Buckeye Beans & Herbs also markets its products through its cute catalog. A clever little story goes along with each product, and Hattie's marketing specialist contends that the catalog "creates the company personality" for the person flipping through its pages.

Hattie's strategist says a firm should identify its unique gift and then go international, but Doug warns that marketing abroad may take time. To prove it, he relates all the steps the firm went through to eventually do business in Japan. And Doug warns that many small businesses are just not ready to take on such a prolonged series of negotiations to get into another country's markets.

Hattie and Jill point out that Buckeye Beans & Herbs is "not selling a product but a concept." Those words sound good, but what do they mean? Hattie explains that a sack of beans is not what the firm sells. Rather, the firm is selling the whole idea that putting those beans into boiling water is a quick and fun way to get supper ready for your family. Speaking of family, the firm has brought into its workforce many friends and family. The Smiths readily admit that such a close-knit arrangement will not work for every company, but folks at **Buckeye Beans & Herbs** seem to be quite happy.

The Video

SMALL BUSINESS 2000 MASTER CLASS, SB2000 SERIES 2, SHOW #3. Many business theorists will tell you that confidence and enthusiasm are very important for a person wanting to become a successful entrepreneur. Well, Jill Smith has both in large supply. Having fun with the whole enterprise seems very important, and **Buckeye Beans and Herbs** conveys as much of that fun as possible through its catalog.

Discussion Questions

1. In building a business with family and friends, can **Buckeye Beans & Herbs** call itself an equal opportunity employer? Why or why not? Suggestion: Recall the camera shot showing the entire staff sitting in one room.
2. What do you think of the happy atmosphere that seems to exist at **Buckeye Beans & Herbs?** How important is it there to get along with your peers?
3. What do you think would happen to a new person who had great new ideas but who did not get along well with everyone?
4. It is stated on the videotape that a "business runs on relationships." What does this statement mean?
5. Explain what the statement "We're not selling a product, but a concept" means.
6. How does **Buckeye Beans & Herbs** use its catalog to convey its ideas about conducting business?
7. What would be the major advantage of having a board of advisors rather than bringing in a partner? Can you offer some arguments in support of bringing in a partner?
8. Recap briefly the long series of steps **Buckeye Beans & Herbs** went through to market its products in Japan. Has all this trouble been worth it for the firm?

Follow-Up Assignment

The video on **Buckeye Beans & Herbs** conveys an atmosphere of *fun*. As we watch, we discover *fun* with the product, *fun* with the catalog, and *fun* for the employees (management included). Your textbook first treats **corporate culture** in Chapter 5, Managing the Business Enterprise. However, you already know that not every firm has such a pleasant corporate culture. Your assignment is to ask several employed people—friends, fellow students, people with whom you do business—what the atmosphere at their job is like. No doubt about it, some will say it's bad. When you locate a person who feels there is a happy atmosphere at work, make an appointment to see the manager of that firm and ask what he or she is doing to establish a corporate culture that encourages employee happiness. Caution: Keep in mind that corporate culture means far more than just employees' attitudes.

The Internet Connection and One Last Thing to Remember

You can contact **Buckeye Beans & Herbs** on the Internet at

http://www.buckeyeranch.com

For small business operators, confidence is an important product. Clearly, Jill Smith has it. She is to be admired for such a positive approach. However, persons considering opening their own business need to hear from a pessimist every now and then. Statistics gathered over many decades show that not every attempt at entrepreneurship meets with success. (The preceding sentence is perhaps the understatement of the year!)

*U*NDERSTANDING *P*RINCIPLES OF *M*ARKETING

Off to the Races

There's nothing subtle about the kind of auto racing that takes place on the NASCAR circuit. It's fast and furious and makes extreme demands on drivers, cars, and the products that racing teams depend on. Speeds topping 200 miles an hour, daredevil maneuvers with little margin for error, and grueling conditions attract fans and consumers for the products that can be the difference between winning and losing.

When a car wins an important race, its corporate sponsors are winners, too, because all America is watching—or so it seems. With an astounding 25 percent of the American public describing themselves as enthusiasts, auto racing is America's top spectator sport. It's not surprising, therefore, that companies as diverse as Kellogg, Kodak, Texaco, and even the Cartoon Network have made motorsport sponsorship an important element in their marketing plans. The NASCAR (National Association for Stock Car Auto Racing) circuit alone attracts more than one-third of the nation's 100 leading advertisers. In 1997, corporate sponsorships totaled $441 million, up from $405 million in 1996.

THE VALUE OF MAKING IMPRESSIONS

Underpinning the success of motorsport sponsorships is advertising value. This kind of value is based on repeated brand impressions: If you put a recognizable corporate or product emblem in front of consumers again and again, and if you do it in a compelling environment like auto racing, consumers will remember your company and your products in a positive way.

Every time a Texaco/Havoline Motor Oil–sponsored car hits the straightaway at a major NASCAR race, the Texaco star is seen by millions of fans, both those in the stadium and those who are watching on televisions around the world. These repeated impressions have measurable marketing value. Likewise, every time the Texaco/Havoline brand is mentioned on radio, in newspaper and magazine articles, in track signage, and even on the clothing worn by drivers and fans, the impact translates into advertising value. And every time Michael Andretti, Shelly Anderson, and other drivers make public appearances on behalf of Texaco/Havoline, the result is still more positive impressions.

Marketers determine the value of these impressions by calculating the number of times that viewers get a 1-second impression of a specific brand name. The aggregate number of these impressions is calculated to have one-half the advertising value of commercial spots, which tell a brand's story. Impact results from the fact that impressions are so numerous. Thus, when Valvoline motor oil writes a $6 million check to sponsor a NASCAR team, it can expect more than $30 million in impression-based advertising.

TARGETING KEY AUDIENCES

Participating companies target their marketing efforts at racing enthusiasts, who are renowned for their brand loyalty. Research shows that more than 70 percent of NASCAR fans make a conscious effort to buy sponsors' products, as compared with only 36 percent of pro football fans. In other words, when the Goodyear logo appears on a car, Goodyear stands a good chance of selling tires to the fans who see it.

Who are these fans? Research also shows that more than 7 of 10 NASCAR fans are between 25 and 54 years old (the prime buying years), have full-time jobs, and own their own homes. Nearly 50 percent earn more than $40,000 annually, and nearly 30 percent are professionals and managers. Moreover, despite the sport's reputation as a male bastion, nearly 4 of 10 fans are women.

Combined with the factor of brand loyalty, these demographics are luring new sponsors to auto racing. Although the sport has traditionally attracted oil companies (Texaco), tire makers (Goodyear), auto parts manufacturers (Raybestos brakes), cigarette makers (Winston), and beer manufacturers (Budweiser), today's cars are also emblazoned with the logos of such companies as McDonald's, Procter & Gamble's, The Family Channel, and Coca-Cola. All of them want the stadium and media exposure and increasing brand awareness that comes with auto racing. Many complement their motorsport connections with promotions on the World Wide Web.

THE PUBLICITY VALUE OF AUTO RACING

Racing also generates millions of dollars in free publicity. As droves of reporters from around the world cover major races, sponsor names are mentioned again and again. The resulting broadcast and print coverage brings a sponsor's message to millions of consumers worldwide. Even though there may be *only* 60,000 people at the track, there are millions more watching at home in real time and during rebroadcasts. The impression value of this coverage adds up to millions of dollars in advertising benefits. Print coverage also reaches millions. A single article in *Sports Illustrated* might reach nearly 8 million readers.

FORGING BUSINESS ALLIANCES

Motorsport programs also target trade customers, including wholesalers and the general public. To influence this audience, companies run hospitality programs in which trade customers are escorted to and from the track, treated to pre-race meals, and introduced to drivers. The VIP treatment builds relationships that lead to sales. Rather than spending 15 minutes making a sales presentation in a purchasing agent's office, sales personnel can spend a few hours with a purchasing agent before the race. By the end of the day, trade customers feel as if they're part of a team and, ideally, leave the track infected with the sponsor's esprit de corps.

Trade customers are particularly impressed by racing's demanding product-testing environment. Says Steve Myers, director of racing tire sales and marketing for Goodyear: "There's no environment that tests [products better] than racing. If you can develop a product that will withstand the racing environment and is successful in it, it is very easy to transfer information and produce a better passenger tire for a sedan, a sports car, a luxury vehicle, or a sports utility vehicle."

Finally, the success of many motorsport programs is also linked to business alliances forged with other companies who have mutual marketing interests. Texaco, for example, maintains alliances with such retailing giants as Target, Kmart, and Western Auto. By virtue of these partnerships, Texaco lubricant products get preferred treatment on store shelves. In the case of Western Auto and Western Auto's Parts America, both subsidiaries of Sears, this distribution link has opened nearly 1,500 stores nationwide to Texaco brands. Like other motorsport marketers, major retailers are convinced that appealing to racing enthusiasts makes good business sense.

The most effective motorsport marketing programs connect all the pieces of the promotional puzzle so that the message, impact, and timing of every piece support the message, impact, and timing of every other piece. Sponsors of winning teams follow up big victories with advertising, publicity, sales promotions, and even clothing lines that showcase products. "Race on Sunday. Sell on Monday" is a time-honored slogan among motorsport sponsors. With annual sponsorships expected to grow as much as 10 percent a year, the marketing formula seems to be catching on.

WEB LINKS

Among the companies and products mentioned in this case, the following maintain Web sites highlighting motorsports programs. The information in these sites will help you answer the questions that follow.

- **Budweiser**
  http://www.budweiser.com/comp.html
- **Goodyear Racing**
  http://www.goodyear.com/aboutracing/index.html
- **Kodak: NASCAR Section**
  http://www.kodak.com/ciHome/nascar/nascar.shtml
- **McDonald's Motor Sports**
  http://www.mcdonalds.com/a_sports/motor_sports/
- **NASCAR Online: Home Page**
  http://www.nascar.com/
- **People Who Know Use Valvoline**
  http://www.valvoline.com/
- **Raybestos Racing**
  http://www.raybestosracing.com/index.html
- **Texaco/Havoline: Racing Guide**
  http://www.texaco.com/tic/racing.html
- **Tide Racing**
  http://www.tide.com/tideRacing/index.html
- **Welcome to Kellogg's Racing**
  http://www.kelloggs.com/nascar/njs/index.html
- **Welcome to Target Team**
  http://beepbeep.target.com/
- **Western Auto: Motorsports WAPA Racing**
  http://www.westernauto.com/motorsports/

QUESTIONS FOR DISCUSSION

1. Imagine that you are a member of the marketing team at a company specializing in auto supplies. What are the primary goals of your motorsports program? (See Web sites for Texaco, Valvoline, Goodyear, Raybestos, and other auto-related companies.)
2. Imagine that you are a member of the marketing team at a consumer products company (nonautomotive). What are the primary goals of your motorsports program? (See Web sites for McDonald's, Kellogg's, Tide, and other consumer products companies.)
3. Why is targeting motorsport enthusiasts such a natural marketing fit for companies such as Valvoline, Goodyear, McDonald's, and Kodak? In your answer, refer to the demographic, psychographic, and product use variables that make racing enthusiasts an ideal market.
4. What is the role of brand loyalty in this market? By what different means are marketers trying to take advantage of it in their motorsports programs? Be specific in your answer by referring to company Web sites.
5. Why are Texaco's alliances with retailers such a vital part of its marketing strategy? How do these alliances support Texaco's need for an effective distribution network?
6. Sponsors place a great deal of emphasis on impression value. How do impressions affect advertising, sales promotion, publicity, and distribution?
7. Many companies sell racing-related products, including clothing and toys (see Web sites for specific offerings). What role do such products play in different marketing programs?

Understanding Marketing Processes and Consumer Behavior

Baggy Brands and Deep Pockets

Adults don't know how to pronounce "JNCO" jeans, and, more importantly, they have no idea why teenagers like to wear them. With billowing 40-inch bottoms and cavernous 17-inch-deep pockets, JNCO has made wide legs fashionable, albeit no easier to wear. Ever try climbing stairs with pants that wide? And what about the dirt and chewing gum that collect at the cuff? Most adults won't even think about walking in the rain.

Nevertheless, JNCO was recently rated the sixth "coolest brand" by boys aged 12 to 15, right behind Tommy Hilfiger and Adidas. Strength in this market translates into millions of consumer dollars. According to *Tactical Retail Monitor*, a New York–based market report, the market for wide-leg jeans grew 30 percent in 1997, to $900 million, compared with only 5.9 percent growth for the entire men's-jean category. That's why Revatex, the Los Angeles firm that manufactures JNCO, pays serious attention to marketing research that tells them what teenagers want and how they are likely to spend their consumer dollars.

Conscious of the independent, rebellious spirit of their target audience, Revatex marketers take a stealth approach to cultivating JNCO's cool image. No billboards or GAP-type ads in popular magazines. Instead, Revatex supplies free clothes to trendsetting DJs and band members who play the all-night techno-dance parties known as "raves." They advertise in such magazines as *Electric Ink* and *Thrasher*, which target skateboarders and extreme rollerbladers.

With wholesale revenues somewhere between $100 million and $200 million, Revatex is hitting Levi Strauss and other mainstream less-than-cool jeans makers where it hurts—in the wallet. Nicholas Lynch, who owns 11 pairs of JNCOs, says you'll never find a pair of Levi's in his closet: "Levi's came out with wide jeans," he admits, "but it just isn't the same because of who wears them." Translation: Baby boomers (also known as losers) wear Levi's, but those on the cutting edge wear JNCOs.

> **"Levi's came out with wide jeans, but it just isn't the same because of who wears them."**
>
> —Nicholas Lynch
> *JNCO wearer*

Finding and defining the cutting edge in teen taste is the work of marketing researchers who specialize in the teen market. Companies pay a high price for this research to attract a share of the roughly $4 billion that teens spend every year on clothes, cosmetics, CDs, and other personal and fashion items. According to Teen-Age Research Unlimited, one of the most respected marketing research firms in the segment, figuring out teen buying behavior means identifying and targeting the teen decision makers known as "influencers." Marketers' dreams-come-true influencers spend money on fashion trends before they are popular and then influence "conformers" to follow suit. Conformers, explains one researcher, "make up the bulk of the teenage population. They're looking for brands and badges to . . . get them to the next level."

With 30 million teenagers currently living in the United States and 35 million projected in 2010, the importance of the teen market is self-evident. What may not be so obvious is the fact that this group has more money in

its pocket and more control over spending than any teen generation before it. With both parents working and their spending habits learned at the knees of self-gratifying baby-boomer parents, teens are worth studying.

Identifying a market segment and targeting messages to its members are among the crucial marketing activities that you will learn about in this chapter. As you will see, business success depends on these activities in what has increasingly become a market-oriented environment. By focusing on the learning objectives of this chapter, you will gain a better understanding of marketing activities and the ways in which marketing influences consumer purchases.

Our opening story is continued on p. 264

After reading this chapter, you should be able to:

1. **Define *marketing*.**
2. **Describe the five forces that constitute the *external marketing environment*.**
3. **Explain *market segmentation* and show how it is used in *target marketing*.**
4. **Describe the key factors that influence the *consumer buying process*.**
5. **Discuss the three categories of *organizational markets* and explain how *organizational buying behavior* differs from consumer buying behavior.**

■ WHAT IS MARKETING?

What comes to mind when you think of *marketing?* Most people usually think of advertising for products such as detergent or soft drinks; but marketing encompasses a much wider range of activities. The American Marketing Association has formally defined **marketing** as "the process of planning and executing the conception, pricing, promotion, and distribution of ideas, goods, and services to create exchanges that satisfy individual and organizational objectives." In this section, we discuss the multifaceted activity of marketing by exploring this definition. We then explore the marketing environment and the development of marketing strategy. We focus on the four activities—developing, pricing, promoting, and placing products—that comprise the *marketing mix.*

marketing The process of planning and executing the conception, pricing, promotion, and distribution of ideas, goods, and services to create exchanges that satisfy individual and organizational objectives

consumer goods Products purchased by consumers for personal use

industrial goods Products purchased by companies to produce other products

services Intangible products, such as time, expertise, or an activity, that can be purchased

Marketing: Goods, Services, and Ideas

The marketing of tangible goods is obvious in everyday life. You walk into a department store and a woman with a clipboard asks if you would like to try a new cologne. A pharmaceutical company proclaims the virtues of its new cold medicine. Your local auto dealer offers an economy car at an economy price. These products—the cologne, the cold medicine, and the car—are all **consumer goods:** products that you, the consumer, may buy for personal use. Firms that sell products to consumers for personal consumption are engaged in *consumer marketing.*

Marketing also applies to **industrial goods:** products used by companies to produce other products. Conveyors, surgical instruments, and earthmovers are industrial goods, as are components and raw materials such as transistors, integrated circuits, coal, steel, and unformed plastic. Firms that sell their products to other manufacturers are engaged in *industrial marketing.*

Marketing techniques can also be applied to **services:** intangible products such as time, expertise, or an activity that can be purchased. Service marketing has become a major area of growth in the United States. Insurance companies, airlines, investment counselors, health clinics, and public accountants all engage in service marketing, either to individuals or to other companies.

Marketing is relevant to the promotion of ideas. For example, television advertising and other promotional activities have made the cartoon dog McGruff a symbol of crime prevention. Other advertisements stress the importance of driving only when sober and the advantages of not smoking.

Each of the advertisements in Figures 10.1 A, B, and C provides information about specific goods, services, or ideas—and, in some cases, combinations of all three. The Omron ad, for example, actually combines consumer and industrial products: The company reminds readers that it makes not only equipment that is used by workers who make cars (vision-protection gear), but also equipment that an autoworker might want to purchase for her own car (a keyless entry system). UPS markets its expertise in providing business-to-business delivery service on a global scale. Finally, the ad for the Tampa Bay, Florida, area turns place advertising into idea advertising by promoting the idea of an area especially suited to attract and service both new businesses and their customers.

FIGURE 10.1A ◆ **Marketing Types**

RELATIONSHIP MARKETING Although marketing often focuses on single transactions for products, services, or ideas, a longer-term perspective has become equally important

FIGURE 10.1 B and C ◆ **Marketing Types**

for successful marketing. Rather than emphasizing a single transaction, **relationship marketing** emphasizes lasting relationships with customers and suppliers. Not surprisingly, stronger relationships—including stronger economic and social ties—can result in greater long-term satisfaction and retention of customers. Commercial banks, for example, feature "loyalty banking" programs that offer *economic* incentives to encourage longer-lasting relationships. Customers who purchase more of the bank's products (for example, checking accounts, savings accounts, and loans) accumulate credits toward free or reduced-price services, such as free travelers checks or lower interest rates. Harley-Davidson offers *social* incentives through the Harley Owners Group (H.O.G.)—the largest motorcycle club in the world, with nearly 300,000 members and approximately 900 dealer-sponsored chapters worldwide. H.O.G., explain Harley marketers, "is dedicated to building customers for life. H.O.G. fosters long-term commitments to the sport of motorcycling by providing opportunities for our customers to bond with other riders and develop long-term friendships."[1]

relationship marketing Marketing strategy that emphasizes lasting relationships with customers and suppliers

The Marketing Environment

Marketing plans, decisions, and strategies are not determined unilaterally by any business, not even by marketers as experienced and influential as Coca-Cola and Procter & Gamble. Rather, they are strongly influenced by powerful outside forces. As you can see in Figure 10.2, any marketing program must recognize the outside factors that comprise a company's **external environment.** In this section, we describe five of these environmental factors: the *political-legal, social-cultural, technological, economic,* and *competitive environments.*

external environment Outside factors that influence marketing programs by posing opportunities or threats

FIGURE 10.2 ◆ The External Marketing Environment

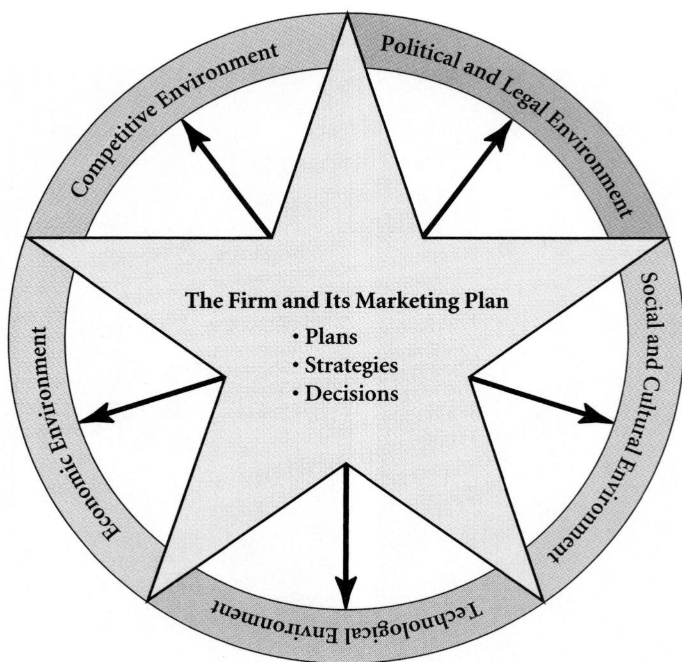

POLITICAL AND LEGAL ENVIRONMENT Political activities, both foreign and domestic, have profound effects on business. For example, congressional hearings on tobacco, budgetary decisions on national defense expenditures, and enactment of the Clean Air Act have substantially determined the destinies of entire industries.

To help shape their companies' futures, marketing managers try to maintain favorable political-legal environments in several ways. For example, to gain public support for their products and activities, marketing uses advertising campaigns for public awareness on issues of local, regional, or national import. They also contribute to political candidates (although there are legal restrictions on how much they can contribute). Frequently, they support the activities of political action committees (PACs) maintained by their respective industries. Such activities sometimes result in favorable laws and regulations and may even open up new international business opportunities.

SOCIAL AND CULTURAL ENVIRONMENT More women are entering the workforce, the number of single-parent families is increasing, food preferences and physical activities reflect the growing concern for healthful lifestyles, violent crimes are on the decrease, and the growing recognition of cultural diversity continues. These and other issues reflect the values, beliefs, and ideas that form the fabric of U.S. society today.

The need to recognize social values stimulates marketers to take fresh looks at the ways they conduct their business, by developing and promoting new products for both consumers and industrial customers. For example, there are now more than 5 million female golfers spending nearly $170 million on equipment, most of which, up to now, has been modeled after men's gear. Responding to the growth in the number of female golfers, Spalding has introduced a line of golf gear designed specifically for women. Such equipment has entailed new methods for advertising, promoting, and distributing products to meet the emerging preferences of women golfers.

TECHNOLOGICAL ENVIRONMENT New technologies affect marketing in several ways. They create new goods (the satellite dish) and services (home television shopping). New products, of course, make some existing products obsolete (compact discs are replacing audio tapes), and many of them change our values and lifestyles. In turn, they often stimulate new goods and services not directly related to the new technology itself. Cellular phones, for example, not only facilitate business communication but free up time for recreation and leisure. New communications technologies, which we discuss in Chapter 14, have blazed entirely new paths for marketers to travel. Internet accessibility,

In most years, 90 percent of the grain grown in the Pacific Northwest of the United States is sold to countries in Asia. But the Asian economic crisis has cut deeply into sales, even though the price per bushel of wheat has dropped over 2 years from a high of $5.20 to a low of $2.24. Sales of computers, apples, software, and other products have also plummeted. Meanwhile, U.S. goods pile up. The economic connection of one region of the world on another is as real as this mountain of unsold wheat.

for example, provides a new medium for selling, buying, and even distributing products from your own home to customers around the world.

ECONOMIC ENVIRONMENT Economic conditions determine spending patterns by consumers, businesses, and governments. They thus influence every marketer's plans for product offerings, pricing, and promotional strategies. Among the more significant economic variables, marketers are concerned with inflation, interest rates, recession, and recovery. In other words, they must monitor the general business cycle, which typically features a pattern of transition from periods of prosperity to recession to recovery (return to prosperity). Not surprisingly, consumer spending increases as "consumer confidence" in economic conditions grows during periods of prosperity. Spending decreases during low-growth periods, when unemployment rises and purchasing power declines.

Traditionally, analysis of economic conditions focused on the national economy and the government's policies for controlling or moderating it. Increasingly, however, as nations form more and more economic connections, the "global economy" is becoming more prominent in the thinking of marketers everywhere. New trading partnerships have led to greater economic dependence among both firms and nations. As discussed in Chapter 3, global economic conditions—indeed, conditions from nation to nation—are directly influencing the economic fortunes of all trading partners. Gillette and Coca-Cola, for example, profited handsomely from strong international growth until the 1998 financial crisis in Asia and Latin America disrupted growing sectors of their respective markets. Meanwhile, two companies whose growth relies less on international sales—Pepsi and Wal-Mart—suffered less severely during the economic crisis. Certainly, marketers must now consider this new and perhaps unpredictable economic variable in developing both domestic and foreign marketing strategies.

COMPETITIVE ENVIRONMENT In a competitive environment, marketers must convince buyers that they should purchase their products rather than those of some other seller. Because both consumers and commercial buyers have limited resources, every dollar spent on one product is no longer available for other purchases. Each marketing program, therefore, seeks to make its product the most attractive. Theoretically, a failed program loses the buyer's dollar forever (or at least until it is time for the next purchase decision).

By studying the competition, marketers determine how best to position their own products for three specific types of competition:

- **Substitute products** are dissimilar from those of competitors but can fulfill the same need. For example, your cholesterol level may be controlled with either a physical fitness program or a drug regimen. The fitness program and the drugs compete as substitute products.
- **Brand competition** occurs between similar products, such as the auditing services provided by the large accounting firms of Ernst & Young and KPMG Peat Marwick. The

substitute product Product that is dissimilar to those of competitors but that can fulfill the same need

brand competition Competitive marketing that appeals to consumer perceptions of similar products competition is based on buyers' perceptions of the benefits of products offered by particular companies.

- **International competition** matches the products of domestic marketers against those of foreign competitors—a flight on Swissair versus Delta Airlines. The intensity of international competition has of course been heightened by the formation of alliances such as the European Community and NAFTA.

international competition Competitive marketing of domestic products against foreign products

marketing mix The combination of product, pricing, promotion, and distribution strategies used to market products

product Good, service, or idea that is marketed to fill consumer needs and wants

product differentiation Creation of a product or product image that differs enough from existing products to attract consumers

The Marketing Mix

In planning and implementing strategies, marketing managers rely on four basic components. These elements, often called the "Four P's" of marketing, constitute the **marketing mix.** In this section, we describe each of the following activities:

- Product
- Pricing
- Promotion
- Place

PRODUCT Marketing begins with a **product—**a good, a service, or an idea designed to fill a consumer need. Conceiving and developing new products is a constant challenge for marketers, who must always consider the factor of change. Marketers, for example, must consider changing technology, changing consumer wants and needs, and changing economic conditions.

Meeting consumer needs, then, often means changing existing products. In the clothing industry, for example, manufacturers must be alert to changes in fashion, which often occur rapidly and unpredictably. This need to change is also true in electronics technology, where there are virtually constant advances.

Zebra Technologies Corp., for example, long enjoyed a reputation for manufacturing high-quality, top-of-the-line bar code printers. Zebra also saw sales potential in the low-end market but did not want to market a product that would tarnish its reputation or cannibalize sales from existing printers. Zebra thus developed a no-frills version, the new Stripes printer, to complement its faster, more versatile, more expensive model. Stripes was an immediate success in its own right—boosting sales by 47 percent the first year—and did not compete with Zebra's own high-end model.

This employee is examining printouts from Zebra Technologies' production line. In developing a new bar code printer, Zebra had to stress two elements of the marketing mix. First, because its main goal was a larger share of the lower end of the market, Zebra had to build a machine that would price for $500 less than its high-end model. Second, the new product had to be differentiated from the faster, more flexible model, without sacrificing the company's widely recognized level of quality. The result: The new Stripes printer is a high-quality printer minus a few top-of-the-line features. Moreover, because it cannot be upgraded, it cannot compete with Zebra's existing product.

Companies may also develop new products and enter markets in which they have not previously competed. For example, the German company SAP AG has created a winner with its new R/3 business software system. This so-called "enterprise software" manages all of a company's internal operations in a single powerful network. It ties together the basic processes of taking customer orders, checking credit, ordering materials, distributing products, verifying payments, and balancing the books. With nearly 8,500 customers, including Microsoft, Chevron, and Nestlé, SAP's annual software revenues have grown more than 30 percent, reaching more than $3 billion per year.[2]

Product Differentiation. Often producers develop new or "improved" products for the sake of distinguishing them on the marketplace. **Product differentiation** is the creation of a product or product image that differs enough from existing products to attract consumers. For example, the popularity of Campbell's Soups is based, in part, on successful differentiation. The distinctive beauty of its time-honored label inspired Andy Warhol to paint his masterpiece, *Campbell's Soup Cans.* In 1995, the company changed the packaging and ingredient mix for some of its classic soup lines, updating the red-and-white label with color pictures of the contents. The label for condensed chicken noodle soup added a prominent announcement: "Now! 33% more chicken meat." In an even riskier move, Campbell's famous slogan was changed from "M'm-m'm good" to "M'm-m'm better." The reasoning behind these changes? According to Marty Thrasher, the president of Campbell's U.S. soup business, "We needed to get noticed in a new way, and we needed to break through." Renewing the emphasis on the company's differentiated product line seemed to be the most logical strategy. Sales of Campbell's red and white brands continued to show strong growth through the end of 1998.[3]

> **"We needed to get noticed in a new way, and we needed to break through."**
>
> —Marty Thrasher
> *President, Campbell's U.S. soup business*

Services can also be sources of differentiation. For example, Weyerhauser Co. developed a computer system that allows customers at retail home centers and lumber yards to custom-design decks and shelving. As a result, the company has differentiated its commodity two-by-fours by turning them into premium products.

PRICING *Pricing* a product—selecting the most appropriate price at which to sell it—is often a balancing act. On the one hand, prices must support a variety of costs—the organization's operating, administrative, and research costs as well as marketing costs such as advertising and sales salaries. On the other hand, prices cannot be so high that consumers turn to competitors. Successful pricing means finding a profitable middle ground between these two requirements. An appliance retailer, for instance, sells refrigerators and washing machines at prices that are both profitable and attractive to customers. The same products, however, are priced lower when customers buy sets of kitchen or laundry appliances to furnish new homes. The retailers' lower transaction costs enable them to reduce their selling prices.

Whereas some firms succeed by offering lower prices than competitors, others price successfully on the high side. Both low- and high-price strategies can be effective in different situations. Low prices, for example, generally lead to larger sales volumes. High prices usually limit market size but increase profits per unit. High prices may also attract customers by implying that a product is of especially high quality. We discuss pricing in more detail in Chapter 11.

PROMOTION The most highly visible component of the marketing mix is no doubt *promotion*, which refers to techniques for communicating information about products. We describe promotional activities more fully in Chapter 12. Here we briefly describe the most important promotional tools:

Advertising. Advertising is any form of paid nonpersonal communication used by an identified sponsor to persuade or inform potential buyers about a product. For example, NationsBank, a financial adviser to corporations, reaches its customer audience by advertising its services in *Fortune* magazine.

Personal Selling. Many products (for example, insurance, clothing, and stereo equipment) are best promoted through personal selling, or person-to-person sales. Industrial goods, however, receive the bulk of personal selling. When companies buy from other companies, purchasing agents and others who need technical and detailed information are usually referred to the selling company's sales representatives.

Sales Promotions. Relatively inexpensive items are often marketed through sales promotions, which involve one-time direct inducements to buyers. Premiums (usually free gifts), coupons, and package inserts are all sales promotions meant to tempt consumers to buy products.

Public Relations. Public relations includes all communication efforts directed at building goodwill. It seeks to build favorable attitudes toward the organization and its products. Ronald McDonald Houses are a famous example of public relations. *Publicity* also refers to a firm's efforts to communicate to the public, usually through mass media. Publicity, however, is not paid for by the firm, nor does the firm control its content. Publicity, therefore, can sometimes hurt a business.

distribution Part of the marketing mix concerned with getting products from producers to consumers

PLACE (DISTRIBUTION) In the marketing mix, *place* refers to **distribution.** Placing a product in the proper outlet—say, a retail store—requires decisions about several distribution activities, all of which are concerned with getting the product from the producer to the consumer. For example, transportation options include railroad, truck, air freight, and pipelines. Decisions about warehousing and inventory control are also distribution decisions.

Firms must also make decisions about the *channels* through which they distribute their products. Many manufacturers, for instance, sell to other companies that, in turn, distribute the goods to retailers. Del Monte, for example, produces canned foods that it sells to Evco Wholesale Foods and other distributors, who then sell the food to grocery stores. Other companies sell directly to major retailers such as Sears, Wal-Mart, Kmart, and Safeway. Still others sell directly to final consumers. We explain distribution decisions further in Chapter 12.

■ TARGET MARKETING AND MARKET SEGMENTATION

target market Group of people that has similar wants and needs and that can be expected to show interest in the same products

market segmentation Process of dividing a market into categories of customer types

Marketers recognized long ago that products and services cannot be "all things to all people." Buyers have different tastes, interests, goals, lifestyles, and so on. Among other things, the emergence of the marketing concept and the recognition of consumer needs and wants led marketers to think in terms of *target marketing.* **Target markets** are groups of people with similar wants and needs. For most companies, selecting target markets is the first step in the marketing strategy.

Target marketing clearly requires **market segmentation**—dividing a market into categories of customer types or "segments." Once they have identified market segments, companies may adopt a variety of strategies. Some firms try to market products to more than one segment of the population. For example, General Motors offers compact cars, vans, trucks, luxury cars, and sports cars with various features and at various price levels. GM's strategy is to provide an automobile for nearly every segment of the market.

In contrast, some businesses appeal to the optimal number of market segments by offering fewer products, each aimed toward a specific market segment. Table 10.1, for example, shows how the radio market might be segmented by a marketer of home electronics equipment. Note that segmentation is a strategy for analyzing consumers, not products. The analysis in Table 10.1 identifies consumer users (joggers, commuters, travelers). Only

TABLE 10.1 ◆ **Possible Segmentation of the Radio Market**

SEGMENTATION BY	PRODUCT/TARGET MARKET
Age	Inexpensive, unbreakable, portable models for young children
	Inexpensive equipment, possibly portable, for teens
	Moderate to expensive equipment for adults
Consumer attitude	Sophisticated components for audio buffs
	All-in-one units in furniture cabinets for those concerned with room appearance
Product use	Miniature models for joggers and commuters
	Boom box portables for taking outdoors
	Car stereo systems for traveling
	Components and all-in-one units for home use
Location	Battery-powered models for use where electricity is unavailable
	110-volt current for North American users
	220-volt current for other users

indirectly, then, does it focus on the uses of the product itself. In marketing, the process of fixing, adapting, and communicating the nature of the product itself is called *positioning*.

Identifying Market Segments

By definition, the members of a market segment must share some common traits that will affect their purchasing decisions. In identifying market segments, researchers look at several different influences on consumer behavior. Four of the most important are *geographic, demographic, psychographic*, and *product use variables*.

GEOGRAPHIC VARIABLES In many cases, buying decisions are affected by the places that people call home. The heavy rainfall in Washington State, for instance, means that inhabitants purchase more umbrellas than people living in the Sun Belt. Urban residents have little need for four-wheel-drive vehicles, and sailboats sell better along the coasts than in the Great Plains. **Geographic variables** are the geographical units, from countries to neighborhoods, that may be considered in developing a segmentation strategy.

geographic variables
Geographical units that may be considered in developing a segmentation strategy

These patterns affect decisions about the marketing mix for a huge range of products. For example, consider a project to market down-filled parkas in rural Minnesota. Demand will be high and price competition intense. Local newspaper advertising may be very effective, and the best retail location may be one that is easily reached from several small towns. Marketing the same parkas in downtown Honolulu would be considerably more challenging.

Although the marketability of some products is geographically sensitive, others benefit from nearly universal acceptance. Coca-Cola, for example, derives more than 80 percent of its income from international sales. Coke is the market leader in Great Britain, Germany, Japan, Brazil, and Spain. Pepsi's international sales equal only about 5 percent of Coke's. In fact, Coke's chief competitor in most countries is some local soft drink, not Pepsi, which earns 80 percent of its income at home.[4]

DEMOGRAPHIC VARIABLES The **demographic variables** describe populations by identifying such traits as age, income, gender, ethnic background, marital status, race, religion, and social class. Table 10.2 lists some possible demographic breakdowns. Depending on the marketer's purpose, a segment could be a single classification *(aged 20–34)* or a combination of *categories (aged 20–34, married with children, earning $25,000–$34,999)*. For example, in its attempts to reach younger readers (the median age of its readers was 47 in 1996),

demographic variables
Characteristics of populations that may be considered in developing a segmentation strategy

TABLE 10.2 ◆ **Demographic Variables**

Variable	Breakdowns
Age	Under 5, 5–11, 12–19, 20–34, 35–49, 50–64, 65+
Education	Grade school or less, some high school, graduated high school, some college, college degree, advanced degree
Family life cycle	Young single, young married without children, young married with children, older married with children under 18, older married without children under 18, older single, other
Family size	1, 2–3, 4–5, 6+
Income	Under $9,000, $9,000–14,999, $15,000–24,999, $25,000–34,999, $35,000–45,000, over $45,000
Nationality	Including African, American, Asian, British, Eastern European, French, German, Irish, Italian, Latin American, Middle Eastern, and Scandinavian
Race	Including American Indian, Asian, black, and white
Religion	Including Buddhist, Catholic, Hindu, Jewish, Muslim, and Protestant
Sex	Male, female

Reader's Digest targets advertising at specific demographic groups, especially families with parents under the age of 50 who have children at home and households with incomes of more than $75,000.

Naturally, demographics affect marketing decisions. For example, several general consumption characteristics can be attributed to certain age groups (*18–25*, *26–35*, *36–45*, and so on). Marketers can thus divide markets into age groups as they develop specific marketing plans.

In addition, marketers can use demographics to identify trends that might shape future spending patterns. Nursing care and funeral service companies, for example, are expanding offerings in response to projected changes in the U.S. population in the years 1995 to 2005. Those changes are shown in Figure 10.3. As you can see, the number of people between ages 60 and 89—and even the number of those in their 90s—is expected to rise. So-called "death care" companies, such as Stewart Enterprises and Service Corp. International, are preparing for the upturn by acquiring additional cemetery and funeral homes that give customers one-stop shopping.

TRENDS AND CHALLENGES

HOW TO TELL A FAST FORWARD FROM A HAND-SHAKER

As the consumer market for technology has exploded in recent years, so have marketers' efforts to target the people most likely to buy. They have discovered that selling computers, software, Internet services, and cellular phones is quite different from selling dishwashers, cosmetics, or dining tables. They've also discovered that although traditional marketing research provides some broad consumer-identification information, it offers little insight into what makes technology buyers tick.

Enter Forrester Research Inc., a Cambridge, Massachusetts, marketing research firm that specializes in helping companies assess the effects of technology on their businesses. Forrester has developed a new marketing research tool, called Technographics, to help companies predict specific buying behaviors. The company defines Technographics as "the science of segmenting consumers according to their motivation, desire, and ability to invest in technology products."

To learn how technology consumers behave, Forrester surveys approximately 131,000 consumers annually for their thoughts on everything from new media to networking to buying products on the World Wide Web. Among the companies that pay substantial sums to plug into the results are Sprint, Visa, and Ford. Technology, explains an executive of one client company, "is not just changing the way consumers spend time. It's also changing the way nearly every company is making, selling, and delivering products. We've got to understand that."

Technographics analyzes consumer behavior in terms of three variables: (1) why people purchase technology, (2) how they feel about it, and (3) how much money they can spend on it. Using these variables, Forrester then devised 10 categories (see Figure 10.4) to help marketers promote products among specific target groups.

Note that the table divides consumers into *optimists* and *pessimists*—those who look to technology for career, family, and entertainment solutions and those who resist or reject its role in their lives. Thus, whereas "Fast Forwards" are fanatics who are first in line to buy the latest products, "Hand-Shakers" resist all forms of electronic communication in favor of personal relationships.

To see how companies use this information to increase sales, let us look at Cindy and Gary Williams, a middle-income couple in their 40s with two pre-teen sons and a 3-year-old computer with no Internet connection. Although conventional marketing research might regard Cindy and Gary as prime targets because of income and family profile, a Technographics analysis would advise marketers to steer clear. As "Traditionalists" satisfied with what technogeeks consider an "ancient" computer, the Williamses may take years to upgrade. According to Forrester analyst Josh Bernoff, people like Cindy and Gary Williams are "not a very fertile part of the online market."

Delta Airlines is using Technographics to target "Fast Forwards" and "New Age Nurturers" who are likely to buy tickets on-line. Delta is also using it to avoid trying to sell technology pessimists, regardless of income or any other criterion.

> **"Traditional marketing research gives you a picture of the universe but doesn't focus on the people more likely to book online."**
>
> —Paul Lai
> *Marketing Research Manager, Delta*

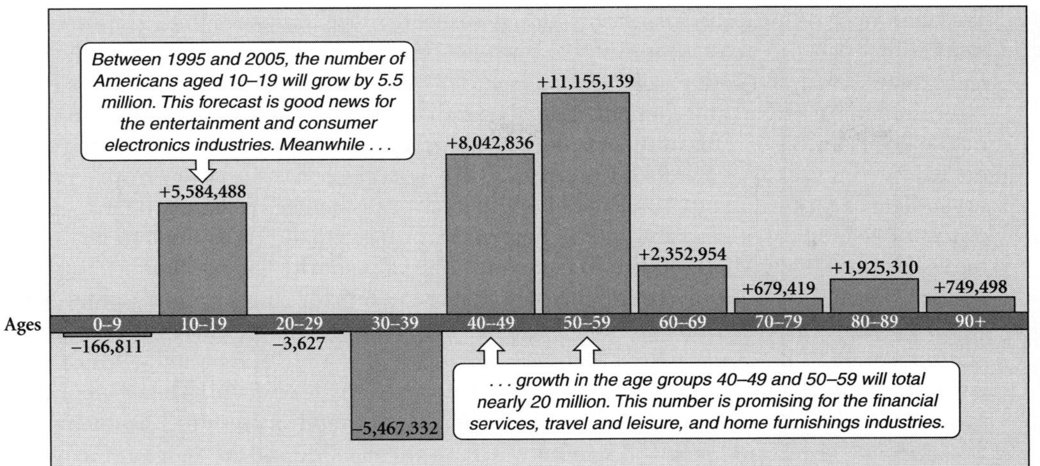

FIGURE 10.3 ◆ **Changes in the U.S. Population**

"Traditional marketing research," explains Delta marketing research manager Paul Lai, "gives you a picture of the universe but doesn't focus on the people more likely to book online."

Although Forrester's model is a giant step forward in targeting technology consumers, it may not help companies reach the country's largest consumer group. About 70 million strong, "Sidelined Citizens" have no interest in technology and no money to spend on it. Reaching them may take something broader and more visionary than a state-of-the-art marketing effort.

	CAREER	FAMILY	ENTERTAINMENT
OPTIMISTS	**FAST FORWARDS** These consumers are the biggest spenders, and they're early adopters of new technology for home, office, and personal use.	**NEW AGE NURTURERS** Also big spenders, but focused on technology for home uses, such as a family PC.	**MOUSE POTATOES** They like the on-line world for entertainment and are willing to spend for the latest in technotainment
OPTIMISTS	**TECHNO-STRIVERS** Use technology from cell phones and pagers to on-line services primarily to gain a career edge.	**DIGITAL HOPEFULS** Families with a limited budget but still interested in new technology. Good candidates for the under-$1,000 PC.	**GADGET-GRABBERS** They also favor on-line entertainment but have less cash to spend on it.
PESSIMISTS	**HAND-SHAKERS** Older consumers—typically managers—who don't touch their computers at work. They leave that to younger assistants.	**TRADITIONALISTS** Willing to use technology but slow to upgrade. Not convinced upgrades and other add-ons are worth paying for.	**MEDIA JUNKIES** Seek entertainment and can't find much of it on-line. Prefer TV and other older media.
PESSIMISTS	**SIDELINED CITIZENS** Not interested in technology		

MORE AFFLUENT | LESS AFFLUENT

FIGURE 10.4 **Technographics Variables**

These kids are holding out the welcome sign for the musical group Hanson. Whatever the latest teenage entertainment draw—in music, sports, movies, TV—smart marketers pay attention. This particular segment of the population—teenage girls—spent about $84 million of their own money in 1997. And more teenagers are coming. By 2006 the number of teens will crest at about 30 million.

Like most other industries, professional baseball tracks demographics trends to set marketing goals for its $4 billion-a-year business. Two decades ago, for instance, the typical fan was a kid, but today's average fan is a 37.5-year-old white male. With teens more interested in basketball and football, many baseball executives are worried about the aging of the core fan base. The numbers (demographics), gathered by market research conducted by Major League Baseball Enterprises (MLB), support the shift away from a youthful audience: Among 12- to 18-year-olds, 67 percent call themselves baseball fans, but 78 percent declare football loyalty, and 82 percent favor basketball. "We'd love to get in the high seventies," says MLB VP Jim Masterson. "The value of the young fan is . . . very important, because it not only represents fans for today but for thirty to forty years from now." By the same token, former major leaguer John Young sees the current downturn as an opportunity: "Baseball's got a great chance to turn it around. Kids watch a lot of television and now they're seeing Ken [Griffey, Jr.], and Sammy [Sosa], and Mark [McGwire] instead of lockouts and strikes." Unfortunately, the demographics point to a problem with TV as well: Viewers under age 18 seldom watch an entire game and are more apt to watch highlights recaps.[5]

> **"The value of the young fan is . . . very important, because it not only represents fans for today but for thirty to forty years from now."**
>
> —Jim Masterson
> *Vice-President, Major League Baseball*

psychographic variables Consumer characteristics, such as lifestyles, opinions, interests, and attitudes, that may be considered in developing a segmentation strategy

PSYCHOGRAPHIC VARIABLES Members of a market can also be segmented according to such **psychographic variables** as lifestyles, opinions, interests, and attitudes. One company that is using psychographic variables to revive its brand is Burberry, whose plaid-lined gabardine raincoats have been a symbol of British tradition since 1856. With a downturn in sales, Burberry is repositioning itself as a global luxury brand, such as Gucci and Louis Vuitton. The strategy calls for luring a different type of customer—the top-of-the-line fashion conscious—who shop at such stores as Neiman Marcus and Bergdorf Goodman. Burberry pictures today's luxury product shopper as a world traveler who identifies with prestige fashion brands and watches social and fashion trends in *Harper's Bazaar.*[6]

"Apparently the fastest-growing market segment in the country is grungy little insecure losers."

Psychographics are particularly important to marketers because, unlike demographics and geographics, they can sometimes be changed by marketing efforts. For example, many companies have succeeded in changing at least some consumers' opinions by running ads highlighting products that have been improved directly in response to consumer desires. Many companies in Poland have succeeded in overcoming consumer resistance by promoting the safety and desirability of using credit rather than depending solely on cash for family purchases. One product of such changing attitudes is a booming economy and the emergence of a growing and robust middle class. The increasing number of Polish households owning televisions, appliances, automobiles, and houses is fueling the status of Poland's middle class as the most stable in the former Soviet bloc.[7]

PRODUCT USE VARIABLES The term **product use variables** includes the ways in which consumers use a product, their brand loyalty to it, and their reasons for purchasing it. A women's shoemaker, for example, might identify three segments—wearers of athletic, casual, and dress shoes. Each market segment is looking for different benefits in a shoe. A woman buying an athletic shoe, for instance, may not care much about its appearance but cares a great deal about arch support, sturdiness, and traction in the sole. A woman buying a casual shoe, however, will want it to look good and feel comfortable. A woman buying a dress shoe may require a specific color or style and may even accept some discomfort.

product use variables Consumer characteristics based on the ways in which a product is used, the brand loyalty it enjoys, and the reasons for which it is purchased

UNDERSTANDING CONSUMER BEHAVIOR

Although marketing managers can tell us what qualities people want in a new VCR, they cannot tell us *why* people buy VCRs. What desire are they fulfilling? Is there a psychological or sociological explanation for why consumers purchase one product and not another? These questions and many others are addressed in the area of marketing known as **consumer behavior**—the study of the decision process by which customers come to purchase and consume products.[8]

consumer behavior Various facets of the decision process by which customers come to purchase and consume products

Influences on Consumer Behavior

According to the title of one classic study, we are "social animals." To understand consumer behavior, marketers draw heavily on the fields of psychology and sociology. The result is a focus on four major influences on consumer behavior: *psychological, personal, social,* and *cultural.* By identifying the four influences that are most active, marketers try to explain consumer choices and predict future purchasing behavior:

- *Psychological influences* include an individual's motivations, perceptions, ability to learn, and attitudes.
- *Personal influences* include lifestyle, personality, and economic status.
- *Social influences* include family, opinion leaders (people whose opinions are sought by others), and such reference groups as friends, coworkers, and professional associates.
- *Cultural influences* include culture (the "way of living" that distinguishes one large group from another), subculture (smaller groups, such as ethnic groups, with shared values), and social class (the cultural ranking of groups according to such criteria as background, occupation, and income).

Although these factors can have a strong impact on consumers' choices, their impact on the actual purchase of some products is either very weak or negligible. Some consumers, for example, exhibit high **brand loyalty,** which means they regularly purchase products because they are satisfied with their performance. Such people (say, users of Maytag appliances) are generally less subject to typical influences and stick with preferred brands. Closer to home, however, the clothes you wear and the food you eat often reflect social and psychological influences on your consuming behavior.

brand loyalty Pattern of regular consumer purchasing based on satisfaction with a product

The Consumer Buying Process

Students of consumer behavior have constructed various models to help marketers understand how consumers come to purchase products. Figure 10.5 presents one such model. At the core of this and similar models is an awareness of the psychosocial influences that lead to consumption. Ultimately, marketers use this information to develop marketing plans.

PROBLEM/NEED RECOGNITION The buying process begins when the consumer recognizes a problem or need. After strenuous exercise, for example, you may realize that you are thirsty. After the birth of twins, you may find your one-bedroom apartment too small for comfort.

Need recognition also occurs when you have a chance to change your purchasing habits. For example, when you obtain your first job after graduation, your new income may let you purchase items that were once too expensive for you. You may also discover a need for professional clothing, apartment furnishings, and a car. American Express and Sears recognize this shift in typical needs when they market credit cards to college seniors.

INFORMATION SEEKING Once they have recognized a need, consumers often seek information. This search is not always extensive. If you are thirsty, for instance, you may simply ask someone to point you to a soft drink machine. At other times, you may simply rely on your memory for information.

Before making major purchases, however, most people seek information from personal sources, marketing sources, public sources, and experience. For example, if you move to a new town, you will want to identify the best dentist, physician, hair stylist, butcher, or pizza maker in your area. To get this information, you may check with personal sources, such as acquaintances, coworkers, and relatives. Before buying an exercise bike, you may go to the library and read the relevant issue of *Consumer Reports*. You may also question market sources such as sales clerks or rely on direct experience by test-riding several bikes before you buy.

By the same token, some sellers thus treat information as a value to be added to their products. For example, Glaxo Wellcome has prepared a Web site (www.zyban.com) dedicated to patient information about Zyban, the first nicotine-free pill for helping people quit smoking. One page at the site introduces nicotine replacement methods, discussing patches, gum, and nasal sprays and including information on the advantages and side effects of each method. The site provides a range of additional information such as the availability of patient support programs such as that of the American Lung Association. It also

FIGURE 10.5 ◆ **The Consumer Buying Process**

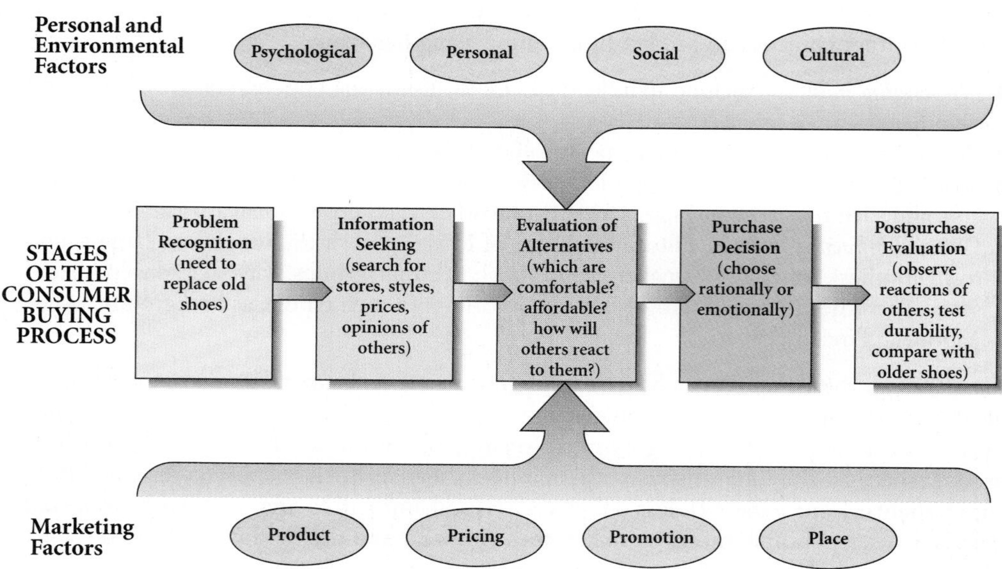

provides postings on upcoming events such as the Glaxo Wellcome–sponsored live educational satellite broadcast, *Stop Smoking: Get Ready for Success.*

EVALUATION OF ALTERNATIVES If you are in the market for a set of skis, you probably have some idea of who makes skis and how they differ. You may have accumulated some of this knowledge during the information-seeking stage and combined it with what you knew previously. By analyzing the product attributes that apply to a given product (color, taste, price, prestige, quality, service record) you will consider your choices and decide which product best meets your needs.

PURCHASE DECISION Ultimately, consumers must make purchase decisions. They may decide to defer a purchase until a later time or they may decide to buy now. "Buy" decisions are based on rational motives, emotional motives, or both. **Rational motives** involve the logical evaluation of product attributes: cost, quality, and usefulness. **Emotional motives** involve nonobjective factors and lead to irrational decisions. Although not all irrational decisions are sudden, many spur-of-the-moment decisions are emotionally driven. Emotional motives include sociability, imitation of others, and aesthetics—motives that are common. For example, you might buy the same brand of jeans as your friends to feel comfortable among that group, not because your friends happen to have the good sense to prefer durable, comfortably priced jeans.

rational motives Reasons for purchasing a product that are based on a logical evaluation of product attributes

emotional motives Reasons for purchasing a product that are based on nonobjective factors

Irrational, therefore, does not mean wrong. It merely refers to a decision based on nonobjective factors. Such decisions can be either satisfying or, largely because they were not based on objective criteria, ill considered. We have all purchased items, taken them home, and then wondered, "Why in the world did I spend good money on this thing?"

POSTPURCHASE EVALUATIONS Marketing does not stop with the sale of a product. It includes the process of consumption. What happens *after* the sale is important. Marketers want consumers to be happy after the consumption of products so that they are more likely to buy them again. Because consumers do not want to go through a complex decision process for every purchase, they often repurchase products they have used and liked.

Not all consumers are satisfied with their purchases, of course. Dissatisfied consumers may complain to sellers, criticize products publicly, or even file lawsuits. Dissatisfied consumers are not likely to purchase the same products again. Moreover, dissatisfied customers are much more likely to broadcast their experiences than are satisfied customers.

■ ORGANIZATIONAL MARKETING AND BUYING BEHAVIOR

Buying behavior is observable daily in the consumer market, where marketing activities, including buying and selling transactions, are visible to the public. Equally important, however, but far less visible, are *organizational* (or *commercial*) *markets.* Some 23 million organizations in the United States buy goods and services to be used in creating and delivering consumer products. As we will see in the following sections, marketing to these buyers must deal with different kinds of organizational markets and with buying behaviors that are different from those found in consumer markets.

Organizational Markets

Organizational or commercial markets fall into three categories—*industrial, reseller,* and *government/institutional markets.* Taken together, these three markets do about $7 *trillion* in business annually, approximately three times the business done in the consumer market.

industrial market Organizational market consisting of firms that buy goods that are either converted into products or used during production

INDUSTRIAL MARKET The **industrial market** includes businesses that buy goods to be converted into other products and goods that are used up during production. This market includes farmers, manufacturers, and some retailers. For example, Seth Thomas purchases electronics, metal components, and glass to make clocks for the consumer market. The company also buys office supplies, tools, and factory equipment—items never seen by clock buyers—to be used during production. Baskin-Robbins buys not only ingredients for ice cream but also paper bags and wrappers to package products for customers and freezer cabinets for storage.

reseller market Organizational market consisting of intermediaries who buy and resell finished goods

RESELLER MARKET Before products reach consumers, they pass through a **reseller market** consisting of intermediaries, including wholesalers and retailers, who buy the finished goods and resell them (wholesalers and retailers are discussed in detail in Chapter 12). The Coast Distribution System, for example, is a leading distributor of parts and accessories for the pleasure boat market. It buys items such as lights, steering wheels, and propellers and resells them to marinas and boat repair shops. On the products resold to their customers, 750,000 U.S. wholesalers have annual sales of $2.4 trillion. Some 2.4 million U.S. retailers purchase merchandise which, when resold to consumers, is valued at $2.4 trillion per year. Retailers also buy such services as maintenance, housekeeping, and communications.[9]

GOVERNMENT AND INSTITUTIONAL MARKET In addition to federal and state governments, more than 87,000 local governments (municipalities, counties, townships, and school districts) are in the United States. State and local governments alone make annual purchases of $1 trillion for durable goods, nondurables, purchased services, and construction. Note that, after a 10-year reduction, spending for military procurement is down 69 percent—from $97 billion to $44 billion—since 1985.[10]

institutional market Organizational market consisting of such nongovernmental buyers of goods and services as hospitals, churches, museums, and charitable organizations

The **institutional market** consists of nongovernment organizations, such as hospitals, churches, museums, and charitable organizations, that also comprise a substantial market for goods and services. Like organizations in other commercial markets, these institutions use supplies and equipment, as well as legal, accounting, and transportation services.

Organizational Buying Behavior

In many respects, organizational buying behavior bears little resemblance to consumer buying practices. Industrial product demand is stimulated by demand for consumer products and is less sensitive to price changes. Other differences include the buyers' purchasing skills and buyer-seller relationships.[11]

DIFFERENCES IN DEMAND Recall our definition of *demand* in Chapter 1—the willingness and ability of buyers to purchase a good or service. The two major differences in demand between consumer and industrial products are *derived demand* and *inelasticity of demand.*

derived demand Demand for industrial products that results from demand for consumer products

Derived Demand. The term **derived demand** refers to the fact that demand for industrial products often results from demand for related consumer products (that is, industrial demand is frequently *derived from* consumer demand).

Consider the chain of industrial demand that was ignited when 3M realized how many consumers wanted the new Scotch-Brite Never Rust soap pads that it had launched in 1993. First, construction had already started on a new plant in Prairie Du Chien, Wisconsin. This project required an array of services and such materials as structural steel, windows, bathroom fixtures, heating apparatus, and production equipment. In turn, these needs stimulated demand back through the supply chain. For example, to make the materials for the plant's construction, the steel supplier had to buy more scrap steel, carbon, and other raw materials from its suppliers. Once the 3M plant was complete, there were new purchases of raw materials for production, including used plastic bottles and abrasives for coating the pads.

inelastic demand Demand for industrial products that is not largely affected by price changes

Inelasticity of Demand. The term **inelastic demand** is when a price change for a product does not have much effect on demand. Take, for instance, the demand for cardboard used to package products such as file cabinets. Because cardboard packaging is such a small part of the manufacturer's overall cabinet cost, an increase in cardboard prices will not lessen the demand for cardboard. In turn, because cabinet buyers will see little price increase, demand for filing cabinets, and for their accompanying cardboard packaging, will remain at about the same level.

DIFFERENCES IN BUYERS Unlike most consumers, organizational buyers are professional, specialized, and expert (or at least well informed):

- As *professionals*, organizational buyers are trained in arranging buyer-seller relationships and in methods for negotiating purchase terms. Once buyer-seller agreements have been reached, industrial buyers also arrange for formal contracts.
- As a rule, industrial buyers are company *specialists* in a line of items. As one of several buyers for a large bakery, for example, you may specialize in food ingredients such as flour, yeast, butter, and so on. Another buyer may specialize in baking equipment (industrial ovens and mixers), whereas a third may purchase office equipment and supplies.
- Industrial buyers are often *experts* about the products they are buying. On a regular basis, organizational buyers learn about competing products and alternative suppliers by attending trade shows, reading trade magazines, and conducting technical discussions with sellers' representatives.

DIFFERENCES IN THE BUYER-SELLER RELATIONSHIP Consumer-seller relationships are often impersonal and fleeting; they are often short-lived, one-time interactions. In contrast, industrial situations often involve frequent, enduring buyer-seller relationships. Accordingly, industrial sellers emphasize personal selling by trained representatives who can better understand the needs of each customer.

■ THE INTERNATIONAL MARKETING MIX

Marketing products internationally means mounting a strategy to support global business operations, which is no easy task. Foreign customers, for example, differ from domestic buyers in language, customs, business practices, and consumer behavior. When they decide to go global, marketers must thus reconsider each element of the marketing mix—product, pricing, promotion, and place.[12]

INTERNATIONAL PRODUCTS Some products can be sold abroad with virtually no changes. Budweiser, Coca-Cola, and Marlboros are exactly the same in Peoria and Paris. In other cases, U.S. firms have been obliged to create products with built-in flexibility, for instance, electric shavers that adapt to either 115- or 230-volt outlets.

Cosmetics are among those products that travel well internationally. They can sell in almost any country in the world with few or no changes. The Estée Lauder fragrances on sale at this Japanese counter smell just the same as Estée Lauder products sold in Milan, Italy, or Little Rock, Arkansas.

As noted earlier, however, sometimes only a redesigned or completely different product will meet the needs of foreign buyers. To sell the Macintosh in Japan, for example, Apple had to develop a Japanese-language operating system. Nevertheless, more companies are designing products for universal application. Whether designed for unique or universal markets, the branding and labeling of products are especially important for communicating global messages about them. For example, KFC (formerly Kentucky Fried Chicken) boxes and Pepsi-Cola cans display universal logos that are instantly recognizable in many nations.

INTERNATIONAL PRICING When pricing for international markets, marketers must handle all the considerations of domestic pricing while also considering the higher costs of transporting and selling products abroad. Bass Pro Shops, for example, sells outdoor sports equipment to customers in Europe at higher prices that cover the added costs of delivery. In contrast, major products such as jet airplanes are priced the same worldwide, because delivery costs are incidental; huge development and production costs are the major considerations regardless of customer location. Meanwhile, because of the higher costs of buildings, rent, equipment, and imported meat, a McDonald's Big Mac that sells for $2.42 in the United States has a price tag of more than $4 in Switzerland.

INTERNATIONAL PROMOTION Occasionally, a good advertising campaign here is a good advertising campaign just about everywhere else—it can be transported to another country virtually intact. Quite often, however, standard U.S. promotional devices do not succeed in other countries. In fact, many Europeans believe that a product must be inherently shoddy if a company resorts to *any* advertising, particularly the American hard-sell variety.

International marketers must also be aware that cultural differences can cause negative reactions to products that are advertised improperly. Some Europeans, for example, are offended by television commercials that show weapons or violence. Advertising practices are regulated accordingly. Consequently, Dutch commercials for toys do not feature the guns and combat scenes that are commonplace on Saturday morning U.S. television. Meanwhile, liquor and cigarette commercials that are banned from U.S. television are thriving in many Asian and European markets. Product promotions must be carefully matched to the customs and cultural values of each country.

INTERNATIONAL DISTRIBUTION International distribution presents several problems. In some industries, delays in starting new distribution networks can be costly. Therefore, companies with existing distribution systems often enjoy an advantage over new businesses. Similarly, several companies have gained advantages in time-based competition by buying existing businesses. Procter & Gamble, for example, saved 3 years of start-up time by buying Revlon's Max Factor and Betrix cosmetics, both of which are well established in foreign markets. P&G can thus immediately use these companies' distribution and marketing networks for selling its own U.S. brands in the United Kingdom, Germany, and Japan.

Given the need to adjust the marketing mix, success in international markets is hard won. Even experienced firms can err in marketing to other countries. International success requires flexibility and a willingness to adapt to the nuances of other cultures. Whether a firm markets in domestic or international markets, however, the basic principles of marketing still apply. It is only the implementation of those principles that changes.

SMALL BUSINESS AND THE MARKETING MIX

As noted in Chapter 7, far more small businesses fail than succeed. Yet many of today's largest firms were yesterday's small businesses. McDonald's began with one restaurant, a concept, and one individual (Ray Kroc) who had foresight. Behind the success of many small firms lies a skillful application of the marketing concept and careful consideration of each element in the marketing mix.[13]

SMALL-BUSINESS PRODUCTS Some new products and firms are doomed at the start simply because few consumers want or need what they have to offer. Too often, enthusiastic entrepreneurs introduce products that they and their friends like but fail to estimate realistic market potential. Other small businesses offer new products before they have clear pictures of their target segments and how to reach them. They try to be everything to everyone, and they end up serving no one well.

In contrast, a thorough understanding of what customers want has paid off for many small firms. "Keep it simple" is a familiar key to success: Fulfill a specific need and do it efficiently. In 1996, for example, entrepreneur Marsha Serlin was named National Small Business Subcontractor of the Year by the U.S. Small Business Administration. Her recycling business, United Scrap Metal Inc., purchases scrap metal, paper, and plastic from other companies, then sorts, cleans, chops, bales, and resells it to customers such as U.S. Steel and Alcoa to be remade into other products. United Scrap's success, Serlin says, is due primarily to concentrating on what customers want; she learned the business and her customers' needs by asking questions: "My customer is the No. 1 person . . . I do everything as though it were for me. I put myself into the shoes of the customer, and I say, 'If I were him, what would I want from me?' " The result of this focused approach is United's annual revenues of $40 million and 120 employees.

Mike (left) and Brendan Moylan founded Sports Endeavors Inc. to sell soccer and lacrosse equipment in 1984. In 1994, they began building an increasingly sophisticated database-marketing system—the kind that, typically, only very large companies use to amass information and target customers. The falling cost of hardware and software made it possible for the Moylans to achieve what has long been the small competitor's advantage: a closer, more informed relationship with customers. "We're now able to anticipate what customers want," says Brendan, "and give it to them."

> **"My customer is the No. 1 person. I do everything as though it were for me."**
>
> —Marsha Serlin
> *Owner, United Scrap Metal*

SMALL-BUSINESS PRICING Haphazard pricing that is often little more than guesswork can sink even a firm with a good product. Most often, small-business pricing errors result from a failure to project operating expenses accurately. Owners of failing businesses have often been heard to say, "I didn't realize how much it costs to run the business!" and "If I price the product high enough to cover my expenses, no one will buy it!" But when small businesses set prices by carefully assessing costs, many earn very satisfactory profits—sometimes enough to expand or diversify.

SMALL-BUSINESS PROMOTION Many small businesses are also ignorant when it comes to the methods and costs of promotion. To save expenses, for example, they may avoid advertising and rely instead on personal selling. As a result, too many potential customers remain unaware of their products.

Successful small businesses plan for promotional expenses as part of start-up costs. Some hold down costs by taking advantage of less-expensive promotional methods. Local newspapers, for example, are sources of publicity when they publish articles about new or unique businesses. Other small businesses have succeeded by identifying themselves and their products with associated groups, organizations, and events. Thus, a custom crafts gallery might join with a local art league and local artists to organize public showings of their combined products.

SMALL-BUSINESS DISTRIBUTION Problems in arranging distribution can also make or break small businesses. Perhaps the most critical aspect of distribution is facility location, especially for new service businesses. The ability of many small businesses (retailers, veterinary clinics, and gourmet coffee shops) to attract and retain customers depends partly on the choice of location.

In distribution, as in other aspects of the marketing mix, smaller companies may have advantages over larger competitors, even in highly complex industries. They may be quicker in applying service technologies. Everex Systems Inc. of Fremont, California, sells personal computers to wholesalers and dealers through a system the company calls zero response time: Because the company is small and flexible, phone orders can be reviewed every 2 hours and factory assembly adjusted to match demand.

Continued from page 245

Between the Barbie Doll and the Driver's License

Remember the days when teenagers had all the discretionary cash and 4- to 12-year-olds only had change for a pack of gum? To the delight of marketers, those days are long gone, as is the distinction between what young kids and teenagers want to buy. Today's 4- to 12-year-olds now spend more than $24 billion a year (of their parents' money) on food and drink, clothes, movies, games, and toys—an amount that tripled in the 1990s.

Both this surge in children's spending power and their maturing tastes are linked to the ways in which dual-career parents raise their kids. "The style of child rearing today," suggests one child psychologist, "is to empower very young children and give them choices about everything. When you give small children power, they act like adolescents."

With newfound maturity and anchored buying decisions, children are now viewed as a prime marketing target. It's no coincidence that retail stores for sophisticated tikes are opening in malls throughout the country. The Limited Too, Abercrombie & Fitch, Gap Kids, and Gymboree are stocking clothes and gear for 6- to 12-year-olds and doing land-office business.

Even when parents make the final buying decision, marketers now realize the influence exerted by kids. That's why Ford's Lincoln Mercury division launched its new Mercury Villager minivan with the 1998 premier of the Rugrats movie. That's why Liberty Financial Companies is pitching a mutual fund to children. The fund controls $725 million in assets from investors whose average age is 9 years.

While some marketers are thriving because of the maturity shift, others are being forced to rethink long-standing strategies. Mattel Inc., manufacturer of the Barbie Doll, can no longer count on 7- to 8-year-old buyers. "We're losing them sooner," laments Mattel president Bruce Stein, whose core Barbie market has been trimmed to 2- to 6-year-olds. "They're in sensory overload. . . . There are too many things competing for their interests."

Other marketers have decided to cater to the special needs of the youngest sophisticates. When the Limited Too opened in 1991, it targeted girls aged 2 to 16. Six years later, it narrowed its focus to 6- to 14-year-olds, because it recognized preteens as a special market segment. The preteen girl, explains the chain's VP of marketing, is "moving out of the fantasy play world. She's kind of caught between Barbie and a driver's license."

Questions for Discussion

1. What social and cultural factors have influenced the growth of the teen and preteen markets?
2. How would you define the teenage target market? Why is it growing in importance?
3. What characteristics would you include in a psychographic profile of teenagers and preteenagers?
4. Do you agree or disagree with Revatex's stealth marketing tactics to reach teenage influencers? How do influencers affect consumer buying behavior?
5. If you worked in the marketing department of Mattel, what would you do to reattract 7- to 8-year-old buyers? Can you think of any spin-off Barbie products that might interest this market segment?

SUMMARY

1. **Define *marketing*.** According to the American Marketing Association, *marketing* is "the process of planning and executing the conception, pricing, promotion, and distribution of ideas, goods, and services to create exchanges that satisfy individual and organizational objectives."

2. **Describe the five forces that constitute the *external marketing environment*.** *The external environment* consists of the outside forces that influence marketing strategy and decision making. The *political-legal environment* includes laws and regulations, both domestic and foreign, that may define or constrain business activities. The *social-cultural environment* is the context within which people's values, beliefs, and ideas affect marketing decisions. The *technological environment* includes the technological developments that affect existing and new products. The *economic environment* consists of the factors, such as inflation, recession, and interest rates, that influence both consumer and organizational spending patterns. The

competitive environment is the environment in which marketers must persuade buyers to purchase their products rather than their competitors' products.

3. **Explain *market segmentation* and show how it is used in *target marketing*.** *Market segmentation* is the process of dividing markets into categories of customers. Businesses have learned that marketing is more successful when it is aimed at specific *target markets*—groups of consumers with similar wants and needs. Markets may be segmented by *geographic, demographic, psychographic,* or *product use variables.*

4. **Describe the key factors that influence the *consumer buying process*.** A number of personal and psychological considerations, along with various social and cultural influences, affect consumer behavior. When making buying decisions, consumers first determine or respond to a problem or need and then collect as much information as they think necessary before making a purchase. *Postpurchase evaluations* are also important to marketers because they influence future buying patterns.

5. **Discuss the three categories of *organizational markets* and explain how *organizational buying behavior* differs from consumer buying behavior.** The *industrial market* includes firms that buy (1) goods to be converted into other products and (2) goods that are used up during production. Farmers and manufacturers are members of the industrial market. Members of the *reseller market* (mostly wholesalers) are intermediaries who buy and resell finished goods. *The government and institutional market* includes governments and agencies at all levels, and nongovernment organizations such as hospitals, museums, and charities.

   There are three main differences between consumer and organizational buying behavior. First, the nature of *demand* is different in organizational demands. It is often *derived* (resulting from related consumer demand), *inelastic* (largely unaffected by price changes), or both. Second, organizational buyers are typically professionals, specialists, or experts. Third, they often develop enduring buyer-seller relationships.

QUESTIONS AND EXERCISES

Questions for Review

1. What are the key similarities and differences between consumer buying behavior and organizational buying behavior?
2. Why and how is market segmentation used in target marketing?
3. What elements of the marketing mix may need to be adjusted to market a product internationally? Why?
4. How do the needs of organizations differ according to the different organizational markets of which they are members?

Questions for Analysis

5. Using examples of everyday products, explain why marketing plans must consider both the external marketing environment and the marketing mix.
6. Select an everyday product (books, dog food, or shoes, for example). Show how different versions of your chosen product are aimed toward different market segments. Explain how the marketing mix differs for each segment.
7. Select a second everyday product and describe the consumer buying process that typically goes into its purchase.
8. If you were starting your own small business—say, marketing a consumer good that you already know something about—then which of the forces in the external marketing environment would you believe to have the greatest potential impact on your success?

APPLICATION EXERCISES

9. Interview the marketing manager of a local business. Identify the degree to which this person's job is oriented toward each element in the marketing mix.
10. Select a product made by a foreign company and sold in the United States. Compare it with a similar domestically made product in terms of product features, price, promotion, and distribution. Which of the two products do you believe is more successful with U.S. buyers? Why?

EXTRA EXERCISE

Break the class into small groups and assign each group a specific industry. Have each group discuss the marketing strategies that they believe important to the effective marketing of products in that industry.

BUILDING YOUR BUSINESS SKILLS

DEALING IN SEGMENTS AND VARIABLES

This exercise enhances the following SCANS workplace competencies: demonstrating basic skills, demonstrating thinking skills, exhibiting interpersonal skills, and working with information.

▼ GOAL

To encourage students to analyze the ways in which various market segmentation variables affect business success.

▼ SITUATION

You and four partners are thinking of purchasing an automobile dealership that specializes in four-wheel-drive vehicles priced between $30,000 and $40,000. You are now in the process of deciding where that dealership should be. You are considering four locations: Miami, Florida; Westport, Connecticut; Dallas, Texas; and Spokane, Washington.

▼ METHOD

STEP 1

Working with four classmates (your partnership group), do library research to learn how automakers market four-wheel-drive vehicles. Check for articles in *The Wall Street Journal*, *Business Week*, *Fortune*, and other business publications.

STEP 2

Continue your research. This time, focus on the specific marketing variables that define each prospective location. Check Census Bureau and Department of Labor data at your library and on the Internet and contact local chambers of commerce (by phone and via the Internet) to learn about the following factors for each location:

- Geography
- Demography (especially age, income, gender, family status, and social class)
- Psychographic factors (lifestyles, interests, and attitudes)

STEP 3

Come together with group members to analyze which location holds the greatest promise as a dealership site. Base your decision on your analysis of market segment variables and their effects on car sales.

▼ Follow-Up Questions

1. Which location did you choose? Describe the market segmentation factors that influenced your decision.
2. Identify the two most important variables that you believe will have the greatest impact on the dealership's success. Why are these factors so important?
3. Which factors were least important in your decision? Why?
4. When automakers advertise four-wheel-drive vehicles, they often show them in precarious situations (on mountaintops, for example, or climbing the sides of buildings). Which market segments are these ads targeting? Describe these segments in terms of demographic and psychographic characteristics.

CRAFTING YOUR BUSINESS PLAN

MARKETING PROCESSES

▼ The Purpose of the Assignment

1. To acquaint students with the process of navigating the *Business PlanPro* (BPP) software package.
2. To familiarize students with various marketing issues that a sample firm faces in developing its business plan.
3. To demonstrate how four chapter topics—the definition of marketing, relationship marketing, market segmentation, and product differentiation—can be integrated as components in the *BPP* planning environment.

▼ Assignment

After reading Chapter 10 in the textbook, open the *BPP* software* and look around for information about the marketing plans for a sample firm: *Elseware Products* (Elseware Promotional Products & Packaging). Then respond to the following questions:

1. Is Elseware involved in *consumer marketing* or *organizational marketing?* Is its product a *good* or a *service* or an *idea?* Explain. [Sites to see in ***BPP*** (for this assignment): In the Task Manager screen, click on Initial Assessment, then click on each of **1. Objectives, 2. Mission,** and **3. Keys to Success.** Return to the Task Manager and click on Finish and Polish, then click on **6. Executive Summary.**]
2. Identify Elseware's strategy and methods for building *relationships with its customers.* [Sites to see in *BPP:* In the Task Manager screen, click on Finish and Polish, then click on each of **1. Strategy and Implementation,** and **6. Executive Summary.** Return to the Task Manager and click on Initial Assessment, then click on **3. Keys to Success.**]

(*continued*)

3. What basis—demographic, psychographic, geographic, or product use—does Elseware plan to use for its *market segmentation?* [Sites to see in *BPP:* In the Task Manager screen, click on Your Market, then click on **2. Market Segmentation.**]

4. Describe Elseware's plans for *differentiating* its product. Do you believe that the plan is clear enough on this matter? Why or why not? [Sites to see in *BPP:* In the Task Manager screen, click on Your Marketing Plan, then explore throughout that section.]

▼ For Your Own Business Plan

5. Consider market segmentation—demographic, geographic, or product use—as it relates to the business plan that you are developing. Where in the BPP framework is (are) the most appropriate location(s) for your presentation on segmentation? How do you intend to explain the segmentation choices in your plan?

▼ *General Tips for Navigating in BPP

1. Open the BPP program, examine the Welcome screen, and click on **Open a Sample Plan.**

2. From the Open a Sample Plan dialogue box, click on a sample company name; then click on **Open.**

3. On the Task Manager screen, click onto any of the lines (for example, **Your Company**).

4. You can always return to the Task Manager screen by going to the bottom of the screen and clicking on the **Task Manager** icon.

5. When you are finished with a sample company, close its Task Manager screen.

6. After finishing with one sample company, you can get to the next one by going to the top of the screen and clicking on **File** (on the menu bar). Then beneath that, select **Open Sample Plan.** This will exit you from the current company file and send you to the Open a Sample Plan dialogue box, where you can select your next sample company.

EXPLORING THE NET

DEALING IN SEGMENTS AND VARIABLES

To find out about some of the marketing methods used by a world-class company, log on to the Marriott Hotels Web site at

http://www.mariott.com/

In the left column of the Marriott home page, click on **Site Map.** Now select **Marriott International** and, from there, **Marriott at a Glance.** Next, return to the Site Map: Now click on **Marriott Lodging** and read the general description of the company's lodging business. Finally, go to the category **Our Hotels** and, one at a time, look into each of Marriott's various hotel brands. Consider the following issues, all of which pertain to the company's marketing processes:

1. Identify a Marriott product that seems oriented toward the *consumer market* and one that is directed more at the *commercial market.* What are some specific services that you found that are different for the two product markets?
2. Consider the way in which Marriott has identified market segments for five brands: Marriott Hotels, Resorts, and Suites; Courtyard Hotels; Residence Inn; Fairfield Inn & Suites; and Towneplace Suites. Can you find an example of *segmentation by geographic variables?* By *demographic* variables? By *psychographic* variables? By *product use* variables?
3. Cite examples of incentives that Marriott uses and services that it offers to *build relationships* with its clients.

Developing and Pricing Products

Everybody Has a Price

In issuing U.S. patent number 5,794,207 to Walker Digital, a Connecticut-based intellectual property laboratory, the U.S. Patent and Trademark Office (PTO) acknowledged that unique approaches to Internet retailing are inventions in their own right. The acknowledgment was good news for Walker, which had invested millions of dollars and years of effort to develop, fine-tune, and implement priceline.com—the world's first buyer-driven electronic commerce system.

Led by founder and CEO Jay Walker, the company observed an unfilled "open" consumer demand for such "perishable" products as airline tickets at prices below retail. "That demand creates a 'catch-22' for sellers," explains a Walker spokesperson. "On the one hand, sellers want the increased sales revenue. However, if they publicly discount their retail prices, or sell their products through a liquidator, sellers risk harming their retail channels and profitability." In other words, otherwise unsold tickets could be sold at discount prices, but sellers needed a channel that did not disrupt those through which they did the great majority of their business at regular retail prices.

Walker's answer was priceline.com, a brand-name system that allows individual consumers to submit their own prices for products or services to various sellers via the World Wide Web or toll-free phones. Every electronic offer is privately presented to sellers, who then decide if it is worth accepting. The transaction is confidential—no other retail customer knows about any offer or deal—and costs nothing unless the seller accepts the buyer's offer in writing.

In 1998, priceline.com launched its "name your own price" service in the leisure airline ticket market. Fifteen major domestic and international carriers signed up in an effort to fill some of the 500,000 seats that fly empty each day. This is how the system works: Customers submit the prices that they are willing to pay, guaranteeing offers with credit cards. Priceline.com then finds an airline that is interested in each potential deal and informs all buyers, within 1 hour for domestic flights and 24 hours for international flights, that they have purchased a nonrefundable ticket. Buyers with Internet access are notified electronically. Others call a toll-free number to find out if their offers have been accepted. "Priceline.com," says Walker, "lets consumers communicate the price they want with potential sellers in a quick and powerful way."

The idea caught on quickly, thanks to an aggressive advertising campaign featuring former *Star Trek* captain William Shatner that turned priceline.com into a national brand. Within months, the company had sold 60,000 tickets (that's a ticket every 70 seconds) and emerged as one of the Internet's 10 leading sellers of leisure airline tickets. According to Nicole Vanderbilt, director of digital commerce at New York–based Jupiter Communications, the success of priceline.com resides in the pricing advantages that it gives both buyers and sellers. "A buyer-driven commerce model," says Vanderbilt, "will be very attractive to consumers who want more control over their purchases and to sellers as they continue to look for alternative means to sell their inventory."

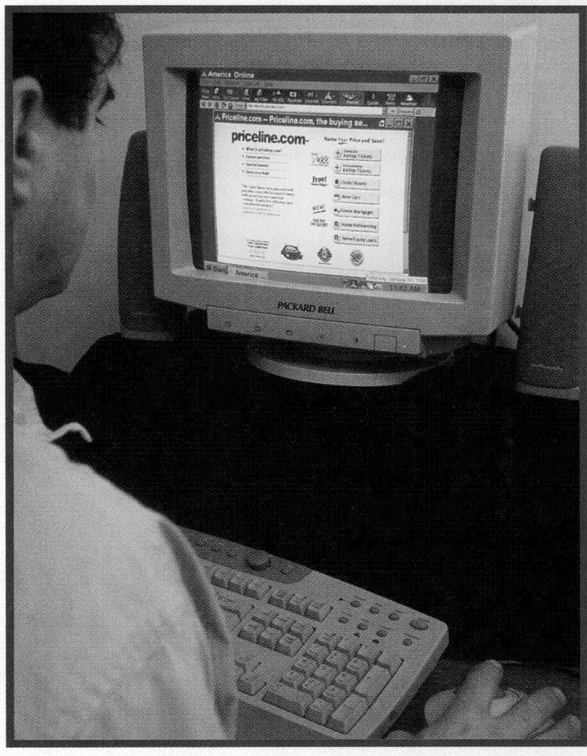

"A buyer-driven commerce model will be very attractive to consumers who want more control over their purchases and to sellers as they continue to look for alternative means to sell their inventory."

—Nicole Vanderbilt
Director of digital commerce, Jupiter Communications

The story of priceline.com demonstrates the willingness of companies to explore different pricing alternatives as they open new marketing channels in electronic commerce. It also illustrates the process by which an idea is developed and branded at the start of the product life cycle. As you will see in this chapter, it is the challenge of all marketers to meet their strategic goals by making the right development and pricing choices. By focusing on the learning objectives of this chapter, you will better understand how product development and pricing fit into the marketing mix.

Our opening story is continued on page 287

After reading this chapter, you should be able to:

1. **Identify a *product* and distinguish between *consumer* and *industrial products*.**
2. **Trace the stages of the *product life cycle*.**
3. **Explain the importance of *branding* and *packaging*.**
4. **Identify the various *pricing objectives* that govern *pricing decisions* and describe the *price-setting tools* used in making these decisions.**
5. **Discuss *pricing strategies* and *tactics* for both existing and new products.**

WHAT IS A PRODUCT?

In developing the marketing mix for any products, whether ideas, goods, or services, marketers must consider what consumers really buy when they purchase products. Only then can they plan their strategies effectively. We begin this section where product strategy begins: with an understanding of product *features* and *benefits*. Next, we describe the major *classifications of products*, both consumer and industrial. Finally, we discuss the most important component in the offerings of any business: its *product mix*.

Features and Benefits

feature Tangible quality that a company builds into a product

Customers do not buy products simply because they like the products themselves: They buy products because they like what the products can do for them, either physically or emotionally. To succeed, then, a product must include the right features and offer the right benefits. Product **features** are the qualities, tangible and intangible, that a company builds into its products, such as a 12-horsepower motor on a lawn mower. To be saleable, a product's features also must provide *benefits:* The mower must provide an attractive lawn.

Obviously, features and benefits play extremely important roles in the pricing of products. If you look carefully at the Price Waterhouse ad in Figure 11.1, you will realize that products are much more than just visible features and benefits. In buying a product, customers are also buying an image and a reputation. The marketers of the consulting services advertised here are well aware that brand name, labeling, and after-purchase satisfaction are indispensable facets of their product. The ad is designed to remind business customers that such features as practical ideas, results, and a global perspective go hand-in-hand with PW's commitment to integrity and trustworthiness.

Classifying Goods and Services

One way to classify a product is according to expected buyers. Buyers fall into two groups: buyers of *consumer* products and buyers of *industrial* products. As we saw in Chapter 10, the consumer and industrial buying processes differ significantly. Not surprisingly, then, marketing products to consumers is vastly different from marketing them to other companies.

FIGURE 11.1 ◆ The Product: Features and Benefits

CLASSIFYING CONSUMER PRODUCTS Consumer products are commonly divided into three categories that reflect buyer behavior:

- **Convenience goods** (such as milk and newspapers) and **convenience services** (such as those offered by fast-food restaurants) are consumed rapidly and regularly. They are inexpensive and are purchased often and with little expenditure of time and effort.
- **Shopping goods** (such as stereos and tires) and **shopping services** (such as insurance) are more expensive and are purchased less often than convenience products. Consumers often compare brands, sometimes in different stores. They may also evaluate alternatives in terms of style, performance, color, price, and other criteria.
- **Specialty goods** (such as wedding gowns) and **specialty services** (such as catering for wedding receptions) are extremely important and expensive purchases. Consumers usually decide on precisely what they want and will accept no substitutes. They will often go from store to store, sometimes spending a great deal of money and time to get a specific product.

convenience good/service Inexpensive product purchased and consumed rapidly and regularly

shopping good/service Moderately expensive, infrequently purchased product

specialty good/service Expensive, rarely purchased product

CLASSIFYING INDUSTRIAL PRODUCTS Depending on how much they cost and how they will be used, industrial products can be divided into two categories:

- **Expense items.** Expense items are any materials and services that are consumed within a year by firms producing other goods or supplying other services. The most obvious expense items are industrial goods used directly in the production process (for example, bulkloads of tea processed into tea bags).
- **Capital items.** Capital items are permanent (that is, expensive and long lasting) goods and services. All these items have expected lives of more than a year, and typically up to several years. Expensive buildings (offices, factories), fixed equipment (water towers, baking ovens), and accessory equipment (computers, airplanes) are capital goods. Capital services are those for which long-term commitments are made. These may include purchases for employee food services, building and equipment maintenance, or legal services. Because capital items are expensive and purchased infrequently, they often involve decisions by high-level managers.

expense item Industrial product purchased and consumed rapidly and regularly for daily operations

capital item Expensive, long-lasting, infrequently purchased industrial product such as a building

The Product Mix

The group of products that a company makes available for sale, whether consumer, industrial, or both, is its **product mix.**[1] Black & Decker, for example, makes toasters, vacuum cleaners, electric drills, and a variety of other appliances and tools. 3M Corp. makes everything from Post-It notes to laser optics.

product mix Group of products that a firm makes available for sale

PRODUCT LINES Many companies begin with a single product. Over time, however, they find that their initial products fail to suit all the consumers shopping for the product type. To meet market demand, therefore, they often introduce similar products designed to reach other consumers. ServiceMaster, for example, was among the first successful home services, offering mothproofing and carpet cleaning. Then the company expanded into lawn care (TruGreen, ChemLawn), pest control (Terminix), cleaning (Merry Maids), and home warranty services (American Home Shield) for various residential services applications. A group of similar products intended for similar but not identical buyers who will use them in similar ways is a **product line.**

product line Group of similar products intended for a similar group of buyers who will use them in similar ways

Companies may also extend their horizons and identify opportunities outside existing product lines. The result—*multiple* (or *diversified*) *product lines*—is evident at firms such as ServiceMaster. After years of serving residential customers, ServiceMaster has added product lines for business and industry called Commercial Services (landscaping and janitorial), Management Services (management of schools and institutions, including physical facilities and financial and personnel resources), and Healthcare Management Services (management of support services—plant operations, asset management, laundry/linen, clinical equipment maintenance—for long-term care facilities). Multiple product lines allow a company to grow more rapidly and can help to offset the consequences of slow sales in any one product line.

DEVELOPING NEW PRODUCTS AND MANAGING THE PRODUCT LIFE CYCLE

To expand or diversify product lines—indeed, just to survive—firms must develop and successfully introduce streams of new products. Faced with competition and shifting consumer preferences, no firm can count on a single successful product to carry it forever. Even basic products that have been widely purchased for decades require nearly constant renewal. Consider the unassuming facial tissue. The white tissue in the low rectangular box has been joined (if not replaced) by tissues of many different colors and patterns. They arrive in boxes shaped and decorated for nearly every room in the house, and they are made to be placed or carried not only in the bathroom but in the purse, the briefcase, and the car. In this section, we focus on the process by which companies develop the new goods and services that allow them to survive.

The New Product Development Process

The demand for food and beverage ingredients will grow more than 6 percent per year, reaching $5 billion by the year 2000. Flavors and flavor enhancers will be the biggest part of that growth, especially artificial sweeteners. However, companies that develop and sell these products face a big problem: It costs between $30 million and $50 million and can take as long as 8 to 10 years to get a new product through the approval process at the Food and Drug Administration. Testing, both for FDA approval and for marketing, can be the most time-consuming stage of development. For example, Hoechst Celanese Corp.'s acesulfame K sweetener has been through more than 90 safety studies and 1,000 technical studies to see how it performs in various kinds of beverages. After testing, additional stages include advertising and demonstration to food producers at the right time (namely, when they are ready to reformulate their products with new ingredients). In short, cashing in on the growth of the food and beverage-ingredients market requires an immense amount of time, patience, and money.[2]

Like Hoechst Celanese Corp., many firms maintain research and development departments or divisions for exploring new product possibilities. Why do they devote so many resources to thinking about products and exploring their possibilities, rejecting many seemingly good ideas along the way?

According to George Milne, head of research at drugmaker Pfizer, speed is of the essence in getting products to market. These days, it is too easy for competitors to duplicate successful products and inundate the market. Diversity counts, too. Because only one out of about 7 million tested compounds makes it to market, companies like Pfizer must make quick work of the testing process, and they must test drugs for just about every known disease. At any given time, Pfizer has about 60 drugs, for conditions ranging from diabetes to anxiety, in early stages of development.

"We're looking for the kind of bad taste that will grab—but not appall."

We address these questions in this section. We see, for instance, that the high mortality rate for new ideas means that only a few new products eventually reach the market. Moreover, for many companies, speed to market with a product is often as important as care in developing it. Finally, product development is a long, complex, and expensive process. Companies do not dream up new products one day and ship them to retailers the next. In fact, new products usually involve carefully planned and sometimes risky commitments of time and resources.

PRODUCT MORTALITY RATES It is estimated that it takes 50 new product ideas to generate one product that finally reaches the market. Even then, only a few of those survivors become successful products. Many seemingly great ideas have failed as products. Indeed, creating a successful new product has become increasingly more difficult, even for the most experienced marketers. For one thing, the number of new products hitting the market each year has increased dramatically. More than 25,000 new household, grocery, and drugstore items are introduced annually. In 1997, the beverage industry alone launched more than 3,400 new products (including Coca-Cola's Surge and Citra). At any given time, however, the average supermarket carries a total of only 20,000 to 25,000 different items. Because of lack of space and customer demand, about 9 of 10 new products will fail.[3] Products with the best chances for success are the ones that are innovative and deliver unique benefits.

SPEED TO MARKET A product's chances for success are also better if it beats its competition to market. Consider the following scenario.

Sinanet is a Web site that functions as an on-line service provider in much the same way as America Online (AOL). Sinanet, however, is in Chinese instead of English. There are in fact more than twice as many Chinese speakers as English speakers in the world, and yet there are few Web sites for them. Sinanet.com began life in Cupertino, California, in 1995 as a casual experiment by Stanford University students Jack Hong, Benjamin Tsiang, and Hurst Lin. The site began getting so many hits that angry university officials ordered them to relocate. Although its growth has continued—each month, 600,000 people visit for free e-mail and real-time news—Sinanet still was operating at a financial loss as of 1998. Its founders estimate, however, that by the year 2001, more than 19 million people will be surfing the Web in Chinese, and Sinanet will be the first site to have established a loyal following. And they'll need that advantage to offset some fearsome competition: Yahoo! and AOL are already launching Chinese-language Internet services.[4]

The principle reflected in this case is actually quite simple and applies to all industries: The more rapidly a product moves from the laboratory to the marketplace, the more likely

At ChemStation, a small industrial-detergent maker based in Dayton, Ohio, the computer database is called the Tank Management System (TMS) because it controls a network of vats for mixing formulas customized to fit the cleaning needs of client firms. This, however, is not the TMS: This is a real tank, in which chemist Kathy Hansen and CEO George Homan are developing a new product. "The money we've been able to save by doing things this way is mind-boggling," reports Homan, whose company has brought mass customization to the business-to-business market.

speed to market Strategy of introducing new products to respond quickly to customer or market changes

it is to survive. By introducing new products ahead of competitors, companies quickly establish market leadership. They become entrenched in the market before being challenged by late-arriving competitors. How important is **speed to market**—that is, a firm's success in responding to customer demand or market changes? One study has estimated that any product that is only 3 months late to market (3 months behind the leader) sacrifices 12 percent of its lifetime profit potential. A product that is 6 months late will lose 33 percent.[5]

The Product Life Cycle

product life cycle (PLC) Series of stages in a product's profit-producing life

A product that reaches the market enters the **product life cycle (PLC):** a series of stages through which it passes during its profit-producing life. Depending on the product's ability to attract and keep customers over time, its PLC may be a matter of months, years, or decades. Strong products (Kellogg's Corn Flakes, Maxwell House coffee, H&R Block tax preparation) have had extremely long, productive lives.

STAGES IN THE PRODUCT LIFE CYCLE The life cycle for both goods and services is a natural process in which products are born, grow in stature, mature, and finally decline and die.[6] Look, for example, at the two graphics in Figure 11.2. In Figure 11.2(a), the four phases of the PLC are applied to several products with which you are familiar:

1. *Introduction.* The introduction stage begins when the product reaches the marketplace. During this stage, marketers focus on making potential consumers aware of the product and its benefits. Because of extensive promotional and development costs, profits are nonexistent.
2. *Growth.* If the new product attracts and satisfies enough consumers, sales begin to climb rapidly. During this stage, the product begins to show a profit. Other firms in the industry move rapidly to introduce their own versions.
3. *Maturity.* Sales growth begins to slow. Although the product earns its highest profit level early in this stage, increased competition eventually leads to price cutting and lower profits. Toward the end of the stage, sales start to fall.
4. *Decline.* During this final stage, sales and profits continue to fall. New products in the introduction stage take away sales. Companies remove or reduce promotional support (ads and salespeople) but may let the product linger to provide some profits.

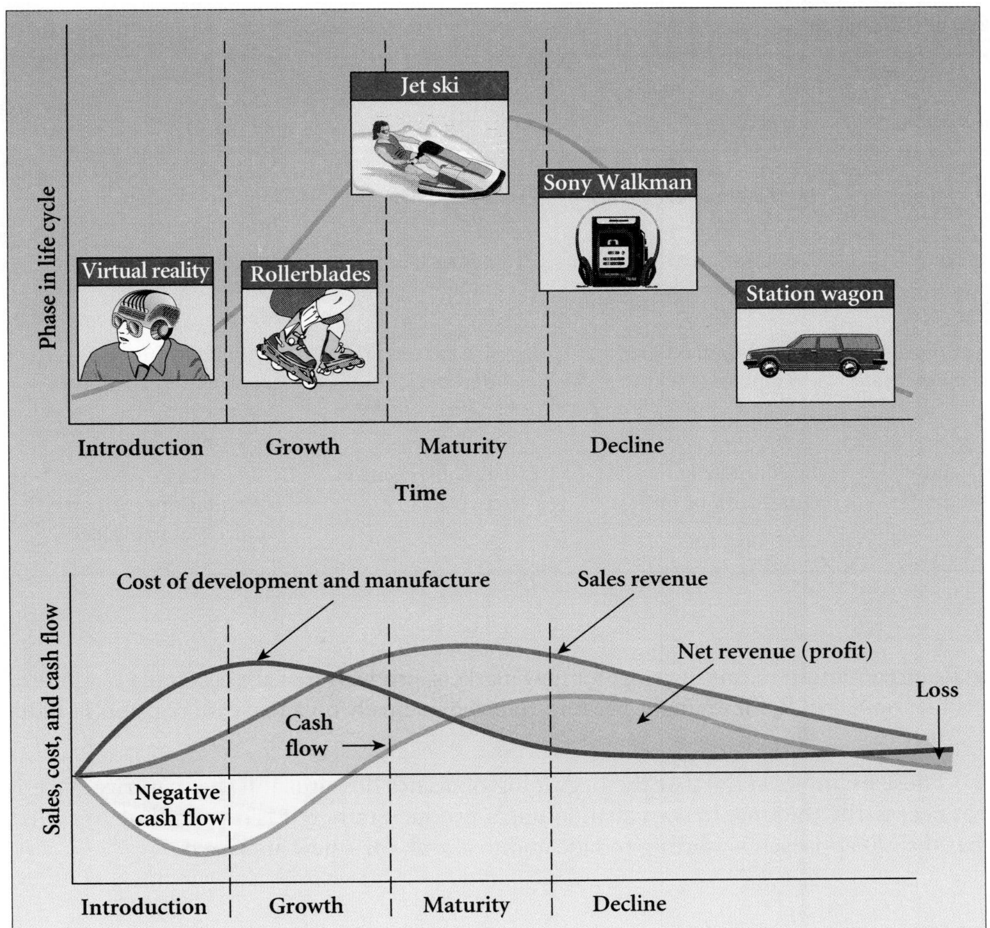

FIGURE 11.2(a) ◆ **Products in Life Cycle Stages**

FIGURE 11.2(b) ◆ **Life Cycle Stages: Sales, Cost, and Profit**

Figure 11.2(b) plots the relationship of the PLC to a product's typical sales, costs, and profits. As you can see, although the early stages of the PLC often result in negative cash flows, successful products will usually recover those losses and, in fact, will continue to generate profits until they enter the decline stage. Remember that, for most products, profitable life spans are short—thus the importance placed by so many firms on the constant replenishment of their product lines.

ADJUSTING MARKETING STRATEGY DURING THE LIFE CYCLE As a product passes from stage to stage, marketing strategy changes, too. Each aspect of the marketing mix—product, price, promotion, place (distribution)—is reexamined for each stage of the life cycle. Changes in strategy for all four life cycle stages are summarized in Table 11.1.

EXTENDING PRODUCT LIFE: AN ALTERNATIVE TO NEW PRODUCTS Not surprisingly, companies wish that they could maintain a product's position in the maturity stage for longer periods of time. Sales of television sets, for example, have been revitalized time and time again by introducing changes such as color, portability, miniaturization, and stereo capability. In fact, many companies have extended product life through a variety of creative means. Foreign markets, for example, offer three approaches to longer life cycles:

- In **product extension,** an existing product is marketed globally, instead of just domestically. Coca-Cola and Levi's 501 jeans are prime examples of successful international product extensions.
- With **product adaptation,** the basic product is modified to give it greater appeal in different countries. In Germany for example, the McDonald's meal includes beer, and Ford puts the steering wheel on the right side for exports to Japan. Because it involves product changes, this approach is usually more costly than product extension.

product extension Existing, unmodified product that is marketed globally

product adaptation Product modified to have greater appeal in foreign markets

TABLE 11.1 ◆ Marketing Strategy over the Life Cycle

	INTRODUCTION	GROWTH	MATURITY	DECLINE
Marketing strategy emphasis	Market development	Increase market share	Defend market share	Maintain efficiency in exploiting product
Pricing strategy	High price, unique product/cover introduction costs	Lower price with passage of time	Price at or below competitors'	Set price to stay profitable or decrease to liquidate
Promotion strategy	Mount sales promotion for product awareness	Appeal to mass market; emphasize features, brand	Emphasize brand differences, benefits, loyalty	Reinforce loyal customers; reduce promotion expenditures
Place strategy	Distribute through selective outlets	Build intensive network of outlets	Enlarge distribution network	Be selective in distribution; trim away unprofitable outlets

reintroduction Process of reviving for new markets products that are obsolete in older ones

- **Reintroduction** means reviving, for new markets, products that are becoming obsolete in older ones. NCR, for example, has reintroduced manually operated cash registers in Latin America.

These examples show that the beginning of a sales downturn in the maturity stage is not necessarily the time to start abandoning a product; rather, it is often a time to realize that the old approach is starting to fade and to search for a new approach.

TRENDS AND CHALLENGES

DEVELOPING A WILD LIFESTYLE

Whenever Disney develops a new attraction at its Disney World resort in Orlando, Florida, it does so with a great deal of thought and marketing pizzazz. The Animal Kingdom is no exception. With more than 1,000 live animals and 7 million annual visitors, the Kingdom is a high-stakes financial venture for Disney: Requiring nearly 10 years to develop and more than $1 billion to build, it is the most expensive theme park in the world.

As a product, the Animal Kingdom is a specialty service, and Disney took pains to get it right from the grand plan to the smallest detail. True to form, Disney CEO Michael Eisner was on hand at every stage of development. In fact, it was Eisner who liked the Animal Kingdom idea from the start and who ultimately took the advice of creative leader Joe Rohde to showcase a combination of live and imaginary animals in a spectacular, conservation-theme setting that would be both educational and fun. "It will be not merely live, real animals," Rohde told Eisner, "but all the animals we know and love. So the park is really about us. It's about our feeling about animals." The idea of building a $1 billion park on the basis of such vague sentiments created uncertainties as well as excitement. "It's always more frightening when it's different," admits Eisner. "But that's what makes it worthwhile in the end."

During one of his frequent visits to the park during its development, Eisner put his own mark on the Discovery River cruise. "It's a pretty sight," he observed, "but what's the intellectual content? What could we do to make it exciting?" The answer: Add another crew member to introduce guests to leeches, tarantulas, and other small animal wonders. "It's expensive," concedes Eisner. "You're adding an extra person on the boat, and there are a lot of boats. But it's worth it."

Eisner also helped develop the park's signature landmark—a 140-foot Tree of Life carved in the shape of animals. And he insisted on creating a park that looked "old." That meant new

IDENTIFYING PRODUCTS

As noted earlier, developing a product's features is only part of a marketer's job. Marketers must also encourage consumers to identify products. Two important tools for accomplishing this task are *branding* and *packaging*.

Branding Products

Coca-Cola is the best-known brand in the world. In fact, the *name* is so valuable that its executives like to say that if all of the company's other assets were obliterated, they could walk over to the bank and borrow $100 billion for rebuilding, just on the strength of the brand name.[7] Brand names such as Coca-Cola are symbols for characterizing products and distinguishing them from one another. They were originally introduced to simplify the process when consumers are faced with a wealth of purchase decisions. **Branding**, then, is a process of using symbols to communicate the qualities of a particular product made by a particular producer. Brands are designed to signal uniform quality: Customers who try and like a product can return to it by remembering its name.[8]

branding Process of using symbols to communicate the qualities of a product made by a particular producer

TYPES OF BRAND NAMES Virtually every product has a brand name. Generally, the different types of brand names—*national*, *licensed*, and *private brands*—increase buyers' awareness of the nature and quality of products that must compete with any number of other products. When the consumer is satisfied with the quality of a recognizable product, marketers work to achieve brand loyalty among the largest possible segment of repeat buyers.

- **National brands** are produced by, widely distributed by, and carry the name of the manufacturer. These brands (say, Scotch tape or Scope mouthwash) are often widely recognized by consumers because of national advertising campaigns. The costs of developing a positive image for a national brand are high. Some companies, therefore,

national brand Brand-name product produced by, widely distributed by, and carrying the name of a manufacturer

---

> "It's always more frightening when it's different. But that's what makes it worthwhile in the end."
>
> —Michael Eisner
> *CEO, Disney*

but cracked paint, purposefully dented boats with fresh coats of rust, and potholes in newly paved roads. "We created this motif of age, of erosion," explains Rohde. "It reminds us that no matter how great our efforts, nature is the most powerful force around us, and we should respect it. It's almost a moral tale."

But for all Disney *can* do, what power can it wield over wild animals? How could Disney magic make a giraffe or a lion or a gorilla perform on cue for busloads of tourists on Disney safari? Where there's a will—and there certainly is one at Disney—there's always a way. To attract giraffes to spots visible to passing tourists, engineers built revolving food trays high in the branches of artificial baobab trees and filled them with acacia leaves (regarded by the average giraffe as a four-star delicacy). "That way," says landscape architect Paul Comstock, "when people come by in the ride vehicles, there's Mr. and Mrs. Giraffe staring right in their faces, because the plants they like to eat, the candy, the Godiva chocolate of the plant world, are right there for the photo op. Bingo!"

Like other newly added Disney World attractions, including the Disney Institute for adults, a $100 million sports center, a late-night entertainment district, and nearly 12,000 new hotel rooms, the Animal Kingdom represents Disney's attempt to keep Disney World in the growth stage of the product life cycle. So far, these efforts are succeeding, and Disney World continues to be the most popular tourist attraction in the world.

At America Online (AOL), giving away free diskettes in newspapers (as well as in Rice Chex cereal boxes and United Airlines in-flight meals) is a means of strengthening the brand name. Technology companies such as AOL realize that strong brands can do for them the same sort of thing that they have long done for consumer-commodities firms: They can create loyal followings for new generations of products, and they reinforce a company's credibility when it launches new products or enters new markets.

use a national brand on several related products. Procter & Gamble, for instance, now markets Ivory shampoo, capitalizing on the widely recognized name of its bar soap and dishwashing liquid.

Most national brand names are valuable assets that signal product recognition. Not surprisingly, millions of dollars have been spent developing names such as Noxzema, Prudential, and Minute Maid. Millions more have been spent in getting consumers to attach meaning to these names. As a rule, therefore, they rarely change. At the same time, however, the product associated with the brand may very well change. The Smith Corona brand, for instance, has been associated with typewriters since 1886. Although the typewriter business, thanks to word processors, is all but dead, the Smith Corona brand is alive and well in the office-supplies business—on cordless phones and fax machines. The SC brand remains a valuable asset because 90 percent of Americans know it.[9]

- It has become increasingly common for nationally recognized companies (and even personalities) to sell the rights to place their names on products. These **licensed brands** are very big business today. Ferrari, for example, found that selling its name can be more profitable than selling its famous cars. According to Michele Scannavini, manager of sales and marketing, "Ferrari is as much style as substance . . . as much a legend as it is a car company." Marketers reconceived the company name as a brand to extend and exploit it. The famous stallion logo now appears on luxury goods, sportswear, toys, and school supplies. For 1997, says Scannavini, "we'll net $10 million on licensing"—as opposed to just $2 million from car sales—"and we should eventually be able to make $30 million to $35 million annually with very little commitment of capital."[10] Dilbert, the NFL, and *South Park* will all make millions on licensed products sales this year. Free advertising from licensed T-shirts and other clothing is an added bonus.

licensed brand Brand-name product for whose name the seller has purchased the right from an organization or individual

> **"We'll net $10 million on licensing, and we should eventually be able to make $30 million to $35 million annually with very little commitment of capital."**
>
> —Michele Scannavini
> *Manager of sales and marketing, Ferrari*

private brand (or private label) Brand-name product that a wholesaler or retailer has commissioned from a manufacturer

- When a wholesaler or retailer develops a brand name and has the manufacturer place that name on the product, the resulting product name is a **private brand** (or **private label**). One of the best-known sellers of private brands is Sears, which carries such lines as Craftsman tools, Canyon River Blues denim clothing, and Kenmore appliances.

Packaging Products

packaging Physical container in which a product is sold, advertised, or protected

With a few exceptions (fresh fruits and vegetables, structural steel), products need some form of **packaging** in which to be sold. More important, a package also serves as an in-store advertisement that makes the product attractive, displays the brand name, and identifies features and benefits. It also reduces the risk of damage, breakage, or spoilage and increases the difficulty of stealing small products. Recent advances in product usage and the materials available for packaging have created additional roles for packaging. For example, a paper-based material that can be used as a cooking container has made Budget Gourmet dinners a low-cost entry in the dinner-entree market. No-drip-spout bottles have enhanced sales and brand loyalty for Clorox bleach.

DETERMINING PRICES

In product development, managers decide what products the company will offer to customers. In **pricing**, the second major component of the marketing mix, managers decide what the company will receive in exchange for its products. In this section we first discuss the objectives that influence a firm's pricing decisions. Then we describe the major tools companies use to meet those objectives.

pricing Process of determining what a company will receive in exchange for its products

Pricing to Meet Business Objectives

Companies often price products to maximize profits, but sellers hope to attain other **pricing objectives,** or goals, in selling products. For example, some firms are more interested in dominating the market or securing high market share than in making the highest possible profits. Pricing decisions are also influenced by the need to survive in competitive marketplaces, by social and ethical concerns, and even by corporate image.[11]

pricing objectives Goals that producers hope to attain in pricing products for sale

PROFIT-MAXIMIZING OBJECTIVES Pricing to maximize profits is tricky. If prices are set too low, the company will probably sell many units of its product but may miss the opportunity to make additional profit on each unit (and may even lose money on each exchange). Conversely, if prices are set too high, the company will make a large profit on each item but will sell fewer units. Again, the firm loses money. In addition, it may be left with excess inventory and may have to reduce or even close production operations. To avoid these problems, companies try to set prices to sell the number of units that will generate the highest possible total profits.

In calculating profits, managers weigh receipts against costs for materials and labor. However, they also consider the capital resources (plant and equipment) that the company must tie up to generate that level of profit. The costs of marketing (such as maintaining a large sales staff) can also be substantial. Concern over the efficient use of these resources has led many firms to set prices so as to achieve a targeted level of return on sales or capital investment.

MARKET SHARE OBJECTIVES In the long run, of course, a business must make a profit to survive. Nevertheless, many companies initially set low prices for new products. They are willing to accept minimal profits, even losses, to get buyers to try products. In other words, they use pricing to establish **market share**—a company's percentage of the total market sales for a specific product type. Even with established products, market share may outweigh profits as a pricing objective. For a product such as Philadelphia Brand Cream Cheese, dominating a market means that consumers are more likely to buy it because they are familiar with a well-known, highly visible product. Market domination means the continuous sales of more units and thus higher profits even at a lower unit price.

market share As a percentage, total of market sales for a specific company or product

OTHER PRICING OBJECTIVES In some instances, neither profit maximizing nor market share is the best objective. During difficult economic times, for instance, loss containment and survival may become a company's main objectives. Thus in the mid-1980s, John Deere priced agricultural equipment low enough to ensure the company's survival in a severely depressed farm economy.

A still different objective might be to provide a benefit to customers. To introduce its services to industrial clients, for example, International Graffiti Control offered a *set-fee pricing system* (typically charging $60 a month per building) to owners who needed graffiti removed from building walls. This method shifted the risk from the customer to IGC. It appeals to customers who never know from day to day how much new graffiti will appear but who do know that removal is covered by a fixed fee.

Price-Setting Tools

Whatever a company's objectives, managers must measure the potential impact before deciding on final prices. Two basic tools are often used for this purpose: *cost-oriented pricing* and *breakeven analysis.* As a rule, these tools are combined to identify prices that will allow the company to reach its objectives.

Cost-Oriented Pricing Cost-oriented pricing considers the firm's desire to make a profit and takes into account the need to cover production costs. A music store manager, for instance, would begin to price CDs by calculating the cost of making them available to shoppers. Included in this figure would be store rent, employee wages, utilities, product displays, insurance, and, of course, the cost of buying CDs from the manufacturer.

markup Amount added to an item's cost to sell it at a profit

Let us assume that the cost from the manufacturer is $8 per CD. If the store sells CDs for this price, it will not make any profit. Nor will it make a profit if it sells CDs for $8.50 each or even $10 or $11. The manager must account for product and other costs and stipulate a figure for profit. Together, these figures constitute **markup.** In this case, a reasonable markup of $7 over costs would result in a $15 selling price. Markup is usually stated as a percentage of selling price. Markup percentage is thus calculated as follows:

$$\text{Markup percentage} = \frac{\text{Markup}}{\text{Sales price}}$$

In the case of our CD retailer, the markup percentage is 46.7:

$$\text{Markup percentage} = \frac{\$7}{\$15} = 46.7\%$$

In other words, out of every dollar taken in, 46.7 cents will be gross profit for the store. From this profit, of course, the store must still pay rent, utilities, insurance, and all other costs.

Markup can also be expressed as a percentage of cost: The $7 markup is 87.5 percent of the $8 cost of a CD ($7/$8).

variable cost Cost that changes with the quantity of a product produced or sold

fixed cost Cost unaffected by the quantity of a product produced or sold

breakeven analysis Assessment of the quantity of a product that must be sold before the seller makes a profit

Breakeven Analysis: Cost-Volume-Profit Relationships Using cost-oriented pricing, a firm will cover its **variable costs:** costs that change with the number of goods or services produced or sold. It will also make some money toward paying its **fixed costs:** costs that are unaffected by the number of goods or services produced or sold. But how many units must the company sell before all its fixed costs are covered and it begins to make a profit? To determine this figure, it needs a **breakeven analysis.**

To continue our music store example, suppose again that the variable cost for each CD (in this case, the cost of buying the CD from the producer) is $8. This means that the store's annual variable costs depend on how many CDs are sold—the number of CDs sold times $8 cost for each CD. Say that fixed costs for keeping the store open for 1 year are $100,000. These costs are unaffected by the number of CDs sold; costs for lighting, rent, insurance, and salaries are steady whether the store sells any CDs. Therefore, how many CDs must be sold to cover both fixed and variable costs and to generate some profit? The answer is the **breakeven point,** which is 14,286 CDs. We arrive at this number through the following equation:

breakeven point Quantity of a product that must be sold before the seller covers variable and fixed costs and makes a profit

$$\text{Breakeven point (in units)} = \frac{\text{Total fixed costs}}{\text{Price} - \text{Variable cost}}$$

$$= \frac{\$100{,}000}{\$15 - \$8} = 14{,}286 \text{ CDs}$$

Figure 11.3 shows the breakeven point graphically. If the store sells fewer than 14,286 CDs, it loses money for the year. If sales exceed 14,286 CDs, profits grow by $7 for each CD sold. If the store sells exactly 14,286 CDs, it will cover all its costs but will earn zero profit.

Zero profitability at the breakeven point can also be seen by using the profit equation:

$$\begin{aligned}\text{Profit} &= \text{Total revenue} - (\text{Total fixed cost} + \text{Total variable cost})\\ &= (14{,}286 \text{ CDs} \times \$15) - (\$100{,}000 \text{ Fixed cost} + [14{,}286 \text{ CDs} \times \$8 \text{ Variable cost}])\\ \$0 &= \$214{,}290 - (\$100{,}000 + \$114{,}288) \text{ (rounded to the nearest whole CD)}\end{aligned}$$

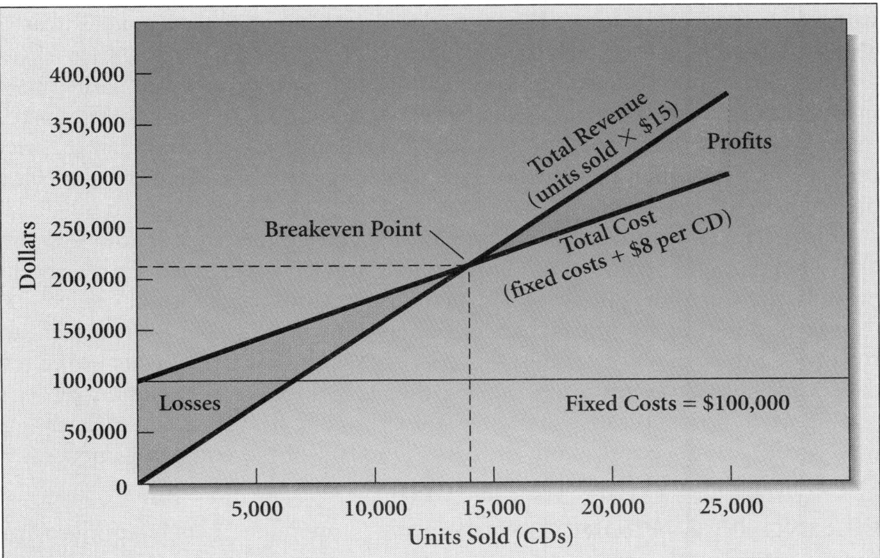

FIGURE 11.3 ◆ **Breakeven Analysis**

PRICING STRATEGIES AND TACTICS

The pricing tools discussed in the previous section are valuable in helping managers set prices on specific goods; however, they do not help in setting pricing philosophies. In this section, we discuss *pricing strategy*—that is, pricing as a planning activity. We then describe some basic *pricing tactics:* ways in which managers implement a firm's pricing strategies. We conclude this section by examining some of the common problems and solutions in pricing for international markets.

Pricing Strategies

We begin this section by addressing two questions. First, can a manager really identify a single best price for a product? Probably not. For example, a study of prices for popular nonaspirin pain relievers (such as Tylenol and Advil) found variations of 100 percent. In this market, some products sold for twice the price of other products with similar properties. Granted, such differences may reflect some differences in product costs; however, the issue is a little more complex. Such wide price differences reflect differing brand images that attract different types of customers. In turn, these images reflect vastly different pricing philosophies and strategies.

This brings us to our second question, which is how important is pricing as an element in the marketing mix? Because pricing has a direct and visible impact on revenues, it is extremely important to overall marketing plans. Moreover, it is a very flexible tool: It is certainly easier to change prices than to change products or distribution channels. In this section, we focus on the ways in which pricing strategies for both new and existing products can result in widely differing prices for very similar products.

PRICING EXISTING PRODUCTS A firm has three options for pricing existing products:

- Pricing above prevailing market prices for similar products
- Pricing below market prices
- Pricing at or near market prices

Pricing above the market plays on the common assumption that higher price means higher quality. For example, Curtis Mathes, which manufactures televisions, VCRs, and stereos, promotes itself as the most expensive television set in the United States—but worth it. Companies such as Bloomingdale's, Godiva chocolates, and Rolls-Royce have also succeeded with this pricing philosophy.

In contrast, both Budget and Dollar car rental companies promote themselves as low-priced alternatives to Hertz and Avis. Similarly, ads for Suave hair-care products argue that Suave does what theirs does for a lot less. Pricing below prevailing market price can succeed if a firm can offer a product of acceptable quality while keeping costs below those of higher-priced competitors.

price leader Dominant firm that establishes product prices that other companies follow

Finally, in some industries, a dominant firm called the **price leader** establishes product prices that other companies follow. This approach is called *market pricing*, and when it prevails, there are fewer price wars in an industry. Moreover, follower companies avoid the trouble of determining prices that consumers are willing to pay—the price leader has already done that. (Do not confuse this approach with *price fixing*, which occurs when producers illegally agree on prices among themselves.) Companies often resort to market pricing when products differ little in quality from one firm to another (for example, structural steel, gasoline, and many processed foods). These companies generally compete through promotion, personal selling, and service, not through price.

PRICING NEW PRODUCTS Companies introducing new products must often choose between two pricing policy options, selecting either very high prices or very low ones. The first option is called *price skimming*. The second is called *penetration pricing*.

price skimming Setting an initial high price to cover new product costs and generate a profit

Price Skimming. **Price skimming** may allow a firm to earn a large profit on each item sold. The cash income is often needed to cover development and introduction costs. Skimming works only if marketers can convince consumers that a product is truly different from those already on the market. Today's expensive high-definition television (HDTV) is an example. Moreover, the initial high profits will eventually attract competition. Like HDTVs, microwave ovens, calculators, video games, and video cameras were all introduced at high skim prices. Naturally, prices fell as soon as new companies entered the market. As you can see from Figure 11.4, the same is true of cellular phones. As the number of subscribers has skyrocketed in the last decade, the original price has plummeted accordingly: The average monthly cost for a cellular subscription, skim-priced at $275 in 1984, had fallen to under $50 just 13 years later.[12]

penetration pricing Setting an initial low price to establish a new product in the market

Penetration Pricing. In contrast, **penetration pricing** seeks to generate consumer interest and stimulate trial purchase of new products. For example, new food products (con-

FIGURE 11.4 ◆ **Price Skimming on Cellular Phones**

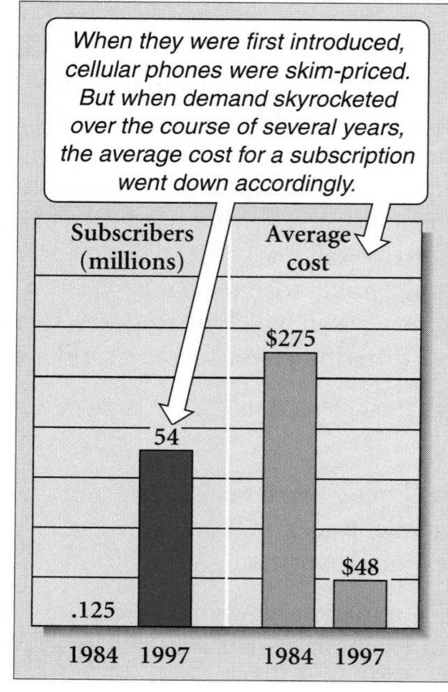

Since the end of the compact-disk boom in about 1994, the ranks of U.S. record store chains have been decimated by a long-running price war. It was started by Best Buy—which is an electronics store, not a record store. In the early 1990s, Best Buy tried to attract electronics customers by selling compact disks at discount prices—$2 to $3 less than what record store chains were charging. Circuit City—another electronics retailer—followed suit, and soon both chains were featuring discount-CD sections boasting 60,000 titles. Record stores could not match the selection or prices, and in 1995-1996, many—including the nation's largest chains—were forced to declare bankruptcy.

venience foods, cookies, and snacks) are often promoted at special low prices to stimulate early sales. Penetration pricing provides for minimal (if any) profit. Thus, it can succeed only if sellers can raise prices as consumer acceptance grows. Of course, increases must be managed carefully to avoid alienating customers.

Pricing Tactics

Regardless of its pricing strategy, a company may adopt one or more *pricing tactics*, such as *price lining* or *psychological pricing*. Managers must also decide whether to use *discounting tactics*.

PRICE LINING Companies selling multiple items in a product category often use **price lining,** offering all items in certain categories at a limited number of prices. A department store, for example, carries thousands of products. Obviously, setting separate prices for each brand and style of suit, glassware, or couch would take far too much time. With price lining, a store predetermines three or four *price points* at which a particular product will be sold. For men's suits, the price points might be $175, $250, and $400; thus, all men's suits in the store will be priced at one of these three points. The store's buyers, therefore, must select suits that can be purchased and sold profitably at one of these three prices.

price lining Setting a limited number of prices for certain categories of products

PSYCHOLOGICAL PRICING Customers are not completely rational when making buying decisions, and **psychological pricing** takes advantage of this fact. For example, one type of psychological pricing, **odd-even pricing,** proposes that customers prefer prices that are not stated in even dollar amounts. Thus, customers see prices of $1,000, $100, $50, and $10 as significantly higher than $999.95, $99.95, $49.95, and $9.95, respectively.

psychological pricing Pricing tactic that takes advantage of the fact that consumers do not always respond rationally to stated prices

odd-even pricing Psychological pricing tactic based on the premise that customers prefer prices not stated in even dollar amounts

DISCOUNTING Of course, the price that is eventually set for a product is not always the price at which it is sold. Often a seller must offer price reductions—**discounts**—to stimulate sales. At Filene's Basement, a Boston-based retail chain, this practice is the case more often than not. Filene's has built a profitable reputation by discounting designer clothing 20 to 60 percent below the prices charged by department stores. Analysts point out that this tactic accounts for Filene's success at times when larger upscale stores such as Macy's and Alexander's have suffered.

discount Price reduction offered as an incentive to purchase

International Pricing

When Procter & Gamble reviewed the possibilities for marketing products in new overseas markets, it encountered an unsettling fact: Because it typically priced products to cover hefty R&D costs, profitably priced items were out of reach for too many foreign consumers. The solution was, in effect, to reverse the process: Now P&G conducts research to find out what foreign buyers can afford and then develops products that they can buy. The strategy is to penetrate markets with lower-priced items and encourage customers to trade up as they become acquainted with and can afford higher-quality P&G products.

As P&G's experience shows, pricing products for sale in other countries is complicated because additional factors are involved. First, income and spending trends must be analyzed. In addition, the number of intermediaries varies from country to country, as does their effect on a product's cost. Exchange rates change daily, shipping costs may occur, import tariffs must be considered (Chapter 3), and different types of pricing agreements are permitted.

An alternative strategy calls for increasing foreign market share by pricing products below cost. As a result, a given product would be priced lower in a foreign market than in its domestic market. As we saw in Chapter 3, this practice is called *dumping*, which is illegal. In recent years, for example, the U.S. International Trade Commission has agreed that motorcycles made by Honda and Kawasaki were being dumped on the U.S. market, as were computer memory chips. As a result, special U.S. tariffs were imposed on these products.

Continued from page 271

The Joy of Take-It-or-Leave-It Shopping

Within months of introducing its buyer-driven service for airline tickets, priceline.com began offering hotel rooms and new cars and trucks on a "name your own price" basis. Like airline tickets, hotel rooms constitute a time-sensitive service and are subject to so-called "perishability losses": If they are not sold before a given date, the hotel cannot recover any portion of the room price or any profit for the date. To reduce such losses, hotels in 26 cities agreed to consider offers via the priceline.com network.

New cars and trucks are the first nonperishable products in the priceline.com system. Launched first in New York, New Jersey, and Connecticut, the service permits Internet consumers to buy new vehicles without ever talking to salespeople—and without haggling. Although there are other car-buying services on the Internet, including Auto-by-Tel and Microsoft CarPoint, they operate in a more traditional marketplace than priceline.com: They pay for the right to contact prospective customers and try to sell them vehicles. According to Gary Arlen, president of Arlen Communications, a research firm specializing in electronic media, "Priceline turns the car-buying process upside down. It takes advantage of the Web's capabilities by letting the buyer name the price and inviting dealers to take it or leave it."

How does priceline.com earn money? It charges customers $25 and dealers $75 once a sale is complete. To discourage browsing, consumers face a $200 penalty if they walk away after a dealer accepts an offer. Buyers who cannot break the haggling habit can use priceline.com to purchase vehicles and then argue with dealers about financing and trade-ins.

"Priceline turns the car-buying process upside down. It takes advantage of the Web's capabilities by letting the buyer name the price and inviting dealers to take it or leave it."

—Gary Arlen
President, Arlen Communications

Questions for Discussion

1. Priceline.com plans to expand its buyer-driven electronic commerce system into the rental car and home mortgage markets. How will the introduction of these new products be affected by the public's recognition of other priceline.com brands?
2. Why was an aggressive promotional campaign especially important during the introduction of priceline.com? What marketing advantages—and burdens—do innovative products face?
3. Why is priceline.com described as a "buyer-driven" electronic commerce system? Can you think of any other buyer-driven pricing systems?
4. Why is it important for sellers to keep priceline.com deals private?
5. Why would an airline reject any offer from a priceline.com customer on the day of a flight if the seat is likely to remain empty? Isn't selling inventory a primary pricing goal?
6. Why would a priceline.com customer be more likely to strike a deal for a car near the end of the model year rather than near the beginning of the year?

SUMMARY

1. **Identify a *product* and distinguish between *consumer* and *industrial products*.** Products are a firm's reason for being. Product features—the tangible and intangible qualities that a company builds into its products—offer benefits to buyers, whose purchases are the main source of most companies' profits. In developing products, firms must decide whether to produce *consumer goods* for direct sale to individual consumers or *industrial goods* for sale to other firms. Marketers must recognize that buyers will pay less for common, rapidly consumed convenience goods than for less frequently purchased *shopping* and *specialty goods.* In industrial markets, expense items are generally less expensive and more rapidly consumed than such capital items as buildings and equipment.

2. **Trace the stages of the *product life cycle*.** New products have a life cycle that corresponds to the following stages: *introduction* (the product reaches the marketplace and receives extensive promotion); *growth* (if it attracts and satisfies enough customers, it shows a profit); *maturity* (although it begins to earn its highest profits, the product's sales begin to slow); and *decline* (profits fall as sales are lost to new products in the introduction stage).

The fact that 9 of 10 new products will fail reflects the current *product mortality rate.* Among the strategies for increasing the likelihood of product success is *speed to market*—introducing new products to respond quickly to customer or market changes. In foreign markets, there are also three strategies for lengthening a product's life cycle: *product extension* (marketing an existing product globally instead of just domestically); *product adaptation* (modifying a product to give it greater appeal in other countries); and *reintroduction* (reviving for new markets a product that is becoming obsolete in old ones).

3. **Explain the importance of *branding* and *packaging*.** Each product is given an identity by its brand and the way it is packaged and labeled. The goal in developing *brands*—symbols to distinguish products and signal their uniform quality—is to increase the preference that consumers have for a product with a particular brand name. *National brands* are products that are produced and widely distributed by the same manufacturer. *Licensed brands* are items for whose names sellers have bought the rights from organizations or individuals. *Private brands* (or *private labels*) are developed by wholesalers or retailers and commissioned from manufacturers. *Packaging* provides an attractive container and advertises a product's features and benefits. It also reduces the risk of damage, spoilage, or theft.

4. **Identify the various *pricing objectives* that govern *pricing decisions* and describe the *price-setting tools* used in making these decisions.** A firm's *pricing decisions* reflect the *pricing objectives* set by its management. Although these objectives vary, they all reflect the goals that a seller hopes to reach in selling a product. They include *profit maximizing* (pricing to sell the number of units that will generate the highest possible total profits) and meeting *market share goals* (ensuring continuous sales by maintaining a strong percentage of the total sales for a specific product type). Other considerations include the need to survive in a competitive marketplace, social and ethical concerns, and even a firm's image.

   Price-setting tools are chosen to meet a seller's pricing objectives. *Cost-oriented pricing* recognizes the need to cover the variable costs of producing a product (costs that change with the number of units produced or sold). In determining the price level at which profits will be generated, *breakeven analysis* also considers *fixed costs* (costs, such as facilities and salaries, that are unaffected by the number of items produced or sold).

5. **Discuss *pricing strategies* and *tactics* for both existing and new products.** Either a *price-skimming strategy* (pricing very high) or a *penetration-pricing strategy* (pricing very low) may be effective for new products. Depending on the other elements in the marketing mix, existing products may be priced at, above, or below prevailing prices for similar products. Guided by a firm's pricing strategies, managers set prices using tactics such as *price lining* (offering items in certain categories at a set number of prices), *psychological pricing* (appealing to buyers' perceptions of relative prices), and *discounting* (reducing prices to stimulate sales).

QUESTIONS AND EXERCISES

Questions for Review

1. What are the various classifications of consumer and industrial products? Give an example of a good and a service for each category other than those discussed in the text.
2. List the four stages in the product life cycle and discuss some of the ways in which a company can extend product life cycles.
3. Explain how brand names and packaging can be used to foster brand loyalty.
4. How do cost-oriented pricing and breakeven analysis help managers measure the potential impact of prices?
5. What is the overall goal of price skimming? Of penetration pricing?

Questions for Analysis

6. How would you expect the branding and packaging of convenience, shopping, and specialty goods to differ? Why? Give examples to illustrate your answers.

7. Suppose that a small publisher selling to book distributors has fixed operating costs of $600,000 each year and variable costs of $3 per book. How many books must the firm sell to break even if the selling price is $6? If the company expects to sell 50,000 books next year and decides on a 40 percent markup, what will be the selling price?

8. Suppose your company produces industrial products for other firms. How would you go about determining the prices of your products? Describe the method you would use to arrive at a pricing decision.

APPLICATION EXERCISES

9. Interview the manager of a local manufacturing firm. Identify the company's different products according to their positions in the product life cycle.

10. Select a product with which you are familiar and analyze various possible pricing objectives for it. What information would you want to have if you were to adopt a profit-maximizing objective? A market share objective? An image objective?

BUILDING YOUR BUSINESS SKILLS

This exercise enhances the following SCANS workplace competencies: demonstrating basic skills, demonstrating thinking skills, exhibiting interpersonal skills, and working with information.

▼ GOAL

To encourage students to evaluate the ways in which branding affects their personal purchasing decisions.

▼ METHOD

STEP 1

Working individually, walk around your room and bathroom at school or at home with pencil and paper in hand. List the brands of the various items you have purchased. For example, do you own a gallon of Tide laundry detergent or a store-bought equivalent? Is your toothpaste Crest or a private drugstore brand? Does your favorite sweater have a private Kmart label or is it a designer brand? Divide the items on the list into two columns: national brands and private brands.

STEP 2

Join with three or four classmates to compare your lists. Analyze the extent to which private brands have made inroads into your own purchases and the purchases of group members. Discuss the reasons for your specific brand choices.

▼ FOLLOW-UP QUESTIONS

1. Looking at your list of national brands, what motivated you to make these purchases? Were you influenced by brand reputation, advertising, quality, or a combination of several factors?
2. Looking at your list of private brands, can you say what motivated you to make these purchases? Were you influenced mainly by price or were other factors involved?
3. Look at a specific item—soap, for example. When one group member purchased a national brand and other group members purchased private brands, what factors were responsible for the different choices?
4. Based on this exercise, are you likely to continue your current buying habits, to purchase more national brands, or to purchase more store brands? Explain your answer.

CRAFTING YOUR BUSINESS PLAN

SPICING UP THE PRODUCT DEVELOPMENT PROCESS

▼ The Purpose of the Assignment

1. To acquaint students with the process of navigating the Business PlanPro (BPP) software package.
2. To familiarize students with certain product development and product pricing issues that a sample firm faces in developing its business plan.
3. To demonstrate how four chapter topics—product line, product pricing, breakeven analysis, and packaging—affect the BPP planning environment.

▼ Assignment

After reading Chapter 11 in the textbook, open the BPP software and look around for information about product line, product pricing, packaging, and breakeven analysis as they apply to a sample firm: Salvadors Sauces Food Dis. Then respond to the following questions:*

1. Is Salvadors Sauces planning to offer consumer products or industrial products? Explain. [Sites to see in *BPP* (for this assignment): In the Task Manager screen, click on Initial Assessment. Then click on **6. Potential Customers.** After returning to Task Manager, click on Your Market and then on **2. Market Segmentation.** After returning to Task Manager, click on Your Sales Forecast and then on **1. Sales Strategy.** From the Task Manager screen, click on Finish and Polish and then on **5. Strategic Alliances.**]
2. How would you describe the pricing strategy that Salvadors Sauces plans to use? [Sites to see in *BPP:* In the Task Manager screen, click on Your Sales Forecast. Then click on **2. Pricing Strategy.**]
3. Suppose you want to help Salvadors Sauces set prices on the basis of cost-oriented pricing. Does the Salvadors plan contain enough data to allow this method of pricing? Explain why or why not. [Sites to see in *BPP:* In the Task Manager screen, click on The Bottom Line. Then click on **3. Profit and Loss Table.**]
4. What role does packaging play in the Salvadors plan? [Sites to see in *BPP:* In the Task Manager screen, click on The Business You're In. Then click on **2. Industry Participants.** After returning to the Task Manager screen, click on Your Marketing Plan and then on **4. Specific Marketing Programs.**]
5. Explain how product pricing relates to breakeven analysis in the Salvadors plan. [Sites to see in *BPP:* In the Task Manager screen, click on Initial Assessment. Then click on each of the following: **4. Breakeven Analysis** and **5. Explain Breakeven Analysis.**]

▼ For Your Own Business Plan

6. Many bankers and investors are interested in seeing evidence that a prospective business will be on solid (profitable) financial footing. Accordingly, your business plan will be stronger if you can project profits based on forecasts of sales, pricing, and breakeven analysis. Describe your pricing strategy and make sales forecasts. In which sections of the BPP document will you present this sort of information?

▼ *General Tips for Navigating in BPP

1. Open the BPP program, examine the Welcome screen, and click on **Open a Sample Plan.**
2. From the Open a Sample Plan dialogue box, click on a sample company name; then click on **Open.**
3. On the Task Manager screen, click on any of the lines (for example, **Your Company**).

4. You can always return to the Task Manager screen by going to the bottom of the screen and clicking on the **Task Manager** icon.
5. When you are finished with a sample company, close its Task Manager screen.
6. After finishing with a sample company, you can get to the next one by going to the top of the screen and clicking on **File** (on the menu bar). Then beneath that, select **Open Sample Plan.** This will exit you from the current company file and send you to the Open a Sample Plan dialogue box, where you can select your next example company.

EXPLORING THE NET

THE MARRIAGE OF PRODUCT AND PRICE

Every Web site is itself a product that competes in the marketplace. As with other products, consideration must be given to several factors, including the characteristics of the product offered by the site, the product line, the product life cycle, and pricing. To consider these variables in more detail, visit the following wedding-related site:

http://www.weddings-online.com/wol.html

Look first at the contents of the Home Page and then explore the site in detail by clicking on some of the service categories that interest you. Then consider the following questions:

1. Would you classify the overall "product" offered by this Web site as a "good" or a "service"? Explain.
2. Among the specific product offerings listed in the site, how many are "convenience" items? How many are "shopping" items? How many are "specialty" items? Explain.
3. How many "product lines" can you identify? What distinguishes any given product line from the others?

Now go to the bottom of the Home Page and click on **Please read our disclaimer.** Then click on **For information on how to be listed or linked, click here.** After reading those pages, consider the following questions:

4. What price did you pay for using this Web site? How can the site be maintained at this price? Do you believe this is a profitable Web site? Do you think that any of the price-setting tools described in this chapter of the text were used to determine this price? Explain why or why not.
5. What pricing objectives do you suppose are most important to the creator of this Web site?

PROMOTING AND DISTRIBUTING PRODUCTS

Log On and Get Rational

Please forgive us for using a phrase that most students love to hate, but it's the best way we know to describe the way in which traditional product-promotion strategies are changing in the era of the Internet: There has been a *paradigm shift*—the emergence of a new world view—in the way companies promote products in the virtual world. It is a shift that combines traditional promotional methods with new approaches geared to the interactivity of the Web.

Advertisers have discovered (often the hard way) that tried-and-true promotional tactics don't work on-line. For example, an emotion-filled vignette may be just right for television, but it has no impact in cyberspace, where on-line customers won't take the time to get involved. "You're not allowed to say or market anything on-line unless the customer wants to hear it," explains Chan Suh, CEO of Agency.com Ltd., an interactive consulting company. "In [cyberspace] marketing, the customer is in charge."

> **"You're not allowed to say or market anything online unless the customer wants to hear it. In cyberspace marketing, the customer is in charge."**
>
> —Chan Suh
> *CEO, Agency.com Ltd.*

According to research, the best way to reach on-line customers is through something called *rational marketing*—product promotions that provide concrete, interactive services. Consider a recent theme promoted on the MasterCard International Web site. "Shop Smart" is a program that guides on-line shoppers to retail sites with state-of-the-art credit card security systems. In contrast, the company's traditional marketing message for television uses the emotional tag line "Priceless" and shows Mark McGwire hitting his 62nd home run. Debra Coughlin, a member of MasterCard's Internet marketing team, explains the thinking behind the different approaches: "The TV user is looking for entertainment. The Internet user is online for more practical reasons. Our brand efforts reflect that end-user goal."

Marketers at General Motors' Saturn division use television and other traditional media to introduce consumers to the help they'll receive on-line. The Saturn Web site includes a lease-price calculator, a purchase-payment calculator, an interactive method for choosing options and seeing how they look on different cars, a dealer locator, and an on-line order form. The Web site is featured on a humorous television commercial that shows a college student ordering a Saturn from his dorm room as easily as he might order a pizza. The synergy created through the television and virtual promotions has tripled the number of annual visitors to the Saturn Web site.

Retailers have been especially successful in using rational marketing. On the Macy's Web site, on-line shoppers find a gift registry and a personal shopper, among other services. Shoppers, who learn of the site through TV and print ads, are younger than average store shoppers and more likely to be men. Clearly, says Kent Anderson, president of Macy's.com, "the Internet presence is extending our brand to shoppers we were not reaching with our stores. To us, that's classic brand building."

Not all products are equally promotable on the Web, as packaged-goods manufacturers have learned. Although marketers for Tide laundry detergent, Ragú sauces, and Clairol hair-care products have filled their sites with practical interactive help, they still use traditional channels for the bulk of their promotions. Fast-food companies are also taking a cautious promotional approach. Although

McDonald's does some marketing on the Web, marketing executives are waiting for the technology that allows full-motion video and audio programming before they make a greater commitment. As a promotional medium, explains David G. Green, McDonald's senior vice president for international marketing, the Internet "is more difficult for those of us who do not have a good or service that is transferable to a virtual experience."

Most marketers believe that, sooner rather than later, on-line marketing will be a critical element in their promotional and distribution strategies. In fact, as the on-line market grows, mastering the art of reaching on-line consumers through "rational marketing" and other methods may be necessary for corporate survival. The development and use of rational marketing demonstrates how flexible marketers must be in their approach to promotion and to the synergies that they must now develop among different promotional media. As you will see in this chapter, it is the challenge of marketers to meet their strategic goals by making the right promotional choices on all media and by linking these choices to both traditional and innovative methods of distribution. By focusing on the learning objectives of this chapter, you will become acquainted with the different approaches to promotional strategy and better understand when and why companies choose particular strategies and tools. You will also better understand the importance of distribution in the marketing process.

Our opening story is continued on page 314

After reading this chapter, you should be able to:

1. **Identify the important objectives of *promotion* and discuss the considerations entailed in selecting a *promotional mix*.**
2. **Describe the key *advertising media* available to marketing managers.**
3. **Outline the tasks involved in *personal selling*, describe the various types of *sales promotions*, and explain the uses of *publicity* and *public relations*.**
4. **Identify the different *channels of distribution*.**
5. **Identify the different types of *retail stores*.**
6. **Compare the five basic forms of *transportation*.**

THE IMPORTANCE OF PROMOTION

We begin by looking at the way in which a well-known company used an advertising campaign in response to threats in its marketing environment.

Starbucks, the upscale coffee vendor, needed to increase sales for continued growth. The company began an $8 million TV and radio campaign in May 1997, developed by Goodby, Silverstein & Partners, a San Francisco advertising agency. The campaign's objectives were to promote a cold drink—Frappuccino—and to define and build Starbucks' image as a friendly local purveyor of "coffee, tea, and sanity." Starbucks' previous ads were limited to outdoor efforts, newspaper ads, and occasional radio and TV ads to support its stores and beverages. But a change was needed for broader reach to keep up with Starbucks' growth; the current 1,200 stores in 25 states is expected to become 2,000 stores by 2000. Goodby has planned this new campaign as the first of a series of coordinated campaigns for the future. It includes three TV and three radio spots running for 8 weeks in 11 major North American markets. Each TV ad, using whimsical line drawings of animated characters, shows Starbucks' iced Frappuccino drink providing relief from the summer heat. The radio campaign features "Mr. Z," a man suffering in the heat, who finds relief with the iced drink. Frappuccino in particular was chosen for the campaign because Starbucks hopes the cold drink will increase sales during the normally slow summer period. The Goodby agency managed the entire campaign: the ad message and format, choice of media, number of spots, selection of markets, negotiation of the media purchases, and the timing for the ad appearances.[1]

promotion Aspect of the marketing mix concerned with the most effective techniques for selling a product

As noted in Chapter 10, **promotion** is any technique designed to sell a product. It is part of the communication mix: the total message any company sends to consumers about its product. Promotional techniques, especially advertising, must communicate the uses, features, and benefits of products. Sales promotions also include various programs that add value beyond the benefits inherent in the product. For example, it is nice to get a high-quality product at a reasonable price, but even better when the seller offers a rebate or a bonus pack with "20 percent more FREE." In promoting products, then, marketers have an array of tools at their disposal.[2]

Promotional Objectives

The ultimate objective of any promotion is to increase sales. In addition, marketers may use promotion to *communicate information*, *position products*, *add value*, and *control sales volume*.

COMMUNICATING INFORMATION Promotion is effective in communicating information from one person or organization to another. Of course, consumers cannot buy products unless they have been informed about them. Information may thus advise customers that a product exists or educate them about its features. Soon after the New Year's holiday, for example, the Physicians' Weight Loss Centers advertisement in *USA Today* not only announces the program's availability but also educates the public on its health advantages over diets. Information may be communicated in writing (in newspapers and magazines), verbally (in person or over the telephone), or visually (on television, matchbook covers, or billboards). Today, in fact, the communication of information about a company's goods or services is so important that marketers try to place it everywhere consumers can be found: Experts estimate that the average consumer comes into contact with approximately 1,500 bits of promotional information each day.

positioning Process of establishing an identifiable product image in the minds of consumers

POSITIONING PRODUCTS As we also saw in Chapter 10, **positioning** is the process of establishing an easily identifiable product image in the minds of consumers. Positioning a product is difficult because a company is trying to appeal to a specific segment of the market rather than to the market as a whole. First, therefore, it must identify which segments are likely to purchase its product and who are its competitors. Only then can it focus its strategy on differentiating its product from the competition's while still appealing to its target audience.

ADDING VALUE Today's value-conscious customers gain benefits when the promotional mix is shifted so that it communicates value-added benefits in its products. Burger King, for instance, shifted its promotional mix by cutting back on advertising dollars and using those funds for customer discounts: Receiving the same food at a lower price is "value-added" for BK's customers. Similarly, in upstate New York, Lawless Container Corp., whose customers are other companies that buy cardboard boxes and packaging materials, has shifted its emphasis to certain unique services such as special credit terms, storage, and delivery times that are valued by individual customers. Like BK's discounts, Lawless's new services add greater value for the dollar.

CONTROLLING SALES VOLUME Many companies, such as Hallmark Cards, experience seasonal sales patterns. By increasing promotional activities in slow periods, these firms can achieve more stable sales volume throughout the year. They can thus keep production and distribution systems running evenly. Promotions can even turn slow seasons into peak sales periods. For example, greeting card companies and florists together have done much to create Grandparents' Day. The result has been increased consumer demand for cards and flowers in the middle of what was once a slow season for both industries.

Promotional Strategies

Once its larger marketing objectives are clear, a firm must develop a promotional strategy to achieve them. Two fundamentally different strategies are often used:[3]

- A **pull strategy** is designed to appeal directly to consumers, who will demand the product from retailers. In turn, retailers will demand the product from wholesalers. When publishing a Stephen King novel, for example, Doubleday directs its promotions at horror story fans. If a bookstore does not stock the book, requests from readers will prompt it to order copies from Doubleday.
- Using a **push strategy,** a firm aggressively markets its product to wholesalers and retailers, who then persuade consumers to buy it. Brunswick Corp., for instance, uses a push strategy to promote Bayliner boats, directing its promotions at dealers and persuading them to order more inventory. Dealers are then responsible for stimulating demand among boaters in their respective districts.

pull strategy Promotional strategy designed to appeal directly to consumers who will demand a product from retailers

push strategy Promotional strategy designed to encourage wholesalers or retailers to market products to consumers

Many large firms use combination pull and push strategies. For example, General Foods uses advertising to create consumer demand (pull) for its cereals. At the same time, it pushes wholesalers and retailers to stock them.

The Promotional Mix

As noted in Chapter 10, there are four types of promotional tools: *advertising, personal selling, sales promotions,* and *publicity and public relations.* The best combination of these tools—that is, the best **promotional mix**—depends on many factors. The company's product, the characteristics of the target audience, and budget considerations are all important.

promotional mix Combination of tools used to promote a product

THE TARGET AUDIENCE: PROMOTION AND THE BUYER DECISION PROCESS An important consideration in establishing the promotional mix is matching the promotional tool with the relevant stage in the buyer decision process. As noted in Chapter 10, this process can be broken down into five steps:

1. Buyers must first recognize the need to make a purchase. At this stage, marketers must make sure the buyer is aware that their products exist. Thus, advertising and publicity, which can reach a large number of people very quickly, are quite important.
2. Buyers also want to learn more about available products. Advertising and personal selling are important in this stage because both can be used to educate the customer.

3. Buyers evaluate and compare competing products. Personal selling can be vital at this point: Sales representatives can demonstrate their product's quality and performance in direct relation to competitors' products.
4. Buyers decide on specific products and purchase them. Sales promotion is effective at this stage because it can give consumers an incentive to buy. Personal selling can also help by bringing products to convenient purchase locations.
5. Finally, buyers evaluate products after purchasing them. Advertising, or even personal selling, is sometimes used after the sale to remind consumers that they made a prudent purchase.

Figure 12.1 summarizes the effective promotional tools for each stage of the consumer buying process.

advertising Promotional tool consisting of paid, nonpersonal communication used by an identified sponsor to inform an audience about a product

ADVERTISING PROMOTIONS **Advertising** is paid, nonpersonal communication used by an identified sponsor to inform an audience about a product. In 1997, U.S. firms spent more than $187 billion on advertising, with $58 billion of this amount being spent by just 100 companies.[4] In this section we begin by describing some key elements in advertising strategy. Then we describe each of the different types of advertising media, noting both advantages and limitations of each.

Advertising Strategies. The advertising strategies used for a product most often depend on the stage of the product life cycle (see Chapter 10) occupied by the product. During the introduction stage, for example, informative advertising can help develop an awareness of the company and its product among buyers and help establish a demand for the product. Thus, when a new textbook is published, instructors receive direct-mail informative advertisements notifying them of the book's contents and availability.

advertising media Variety of communication devices for carrying a seller's message to potential customers

Advertising Media. Bombarded with thousands of advertisements, consumers tend to ignore the bulk of the ads they see or hear. Marketers therefore must find out who are their customers, which media get their attention, what message will appeal to them, and how to get their attention. Marketers thus use several different **advertising media**—specific communication devices for carrying a seller's message to potential customers. For example, IBM uses television ads to keep its name fresh in consumers' minds. It uses newspaper and magazine ads, however, to educate consumers on product features and uses trade publications to introduce new software. The following are the most common advertising media. Each medium has its own advantages and disadvantages.

- *Newspapers* are the most widely used medium, accounting for about 25 percent of all advertising expenditures. Because each local market has at least one daily newspaper, these provide excellent coverage. Each day, they reach more than 113 million U.S. adults. The main advantage of newspaper advertising is flexible, rapid coverage: Ads can easily be changed from day to day. However, newspapers are generally thrown out after one day, are usually not printed in color, and have poor reproduction quality. Moreover, because their readership is so broad, newspapers do not usually allow advertisers to target audiences very well.

FIGURE 12.1 ◆ **The Consumer Buying Process and the Promotional Mix**

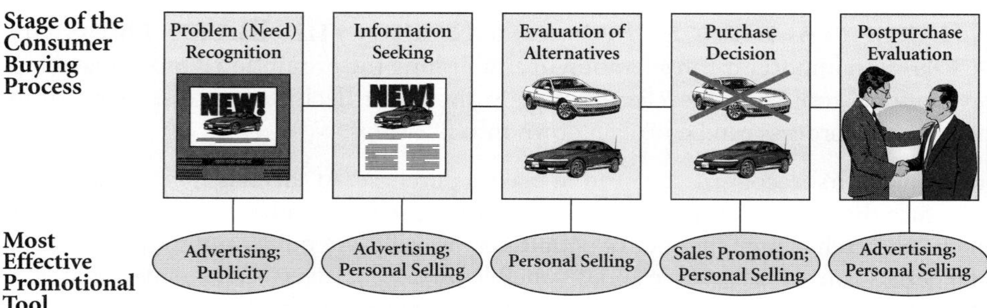

- *Television* accounts for about 22 percent of all advertising outlays. Figure 12.2 shows network TV advertising expenditures for some major U.S. firms.[5] In addition to the major networks, both spot TV (local) and cable television are important advertising media.

  Combining sight, sound, and motion, television appeals to a full complement of the viewer's senses. In addition, information on viewer demographics for a particular program allows advertisers to aim at target audiences. Television also reaches more people than any other medium. For example, recent Super Bowl games have consistently attracted over 40 million households and 115 million viewers. Unfortunately, the fact that there are so many commercials on television often causes viewers to confuse products. Finally, television is also the most expensive medium in which to advertise. Companies such as McDonald's, Frito-Lay, Nokia, Anheuser-Busch, and Quaker State now pay about $1.6 million for 30-second commercials during the Super Bowl. One company alone, Pepsi, spent $6.5 million to buy five 30-second spots for its flagship brand during the 1998 Super Bowl broadcast.[6] "If you're in the Super Bowl," reasoned one Nike executive, "you might as well give it your best shot."

> **"If you're in the Super Bowl, you might as well give it your best shot."**
>
> —*Nike executive*

- *Direct mail advertisements* account for 18 percent of all advertising outlays. **Direct mail** involves fliers or other types of printed advertisements mailed directly to consumers' homes or places of business. It allows the company to select its audience and personalize its message. In addition, although many people discard junk mail, advertisers can predict in advance how many recipients will take a mailing seriously. These people have a stronger-than-average interest in the product advertised and are more likely than most to buy the promoted product.

direct mail Advertising medium in which messages are mailed directly to consumers' homes or places of business

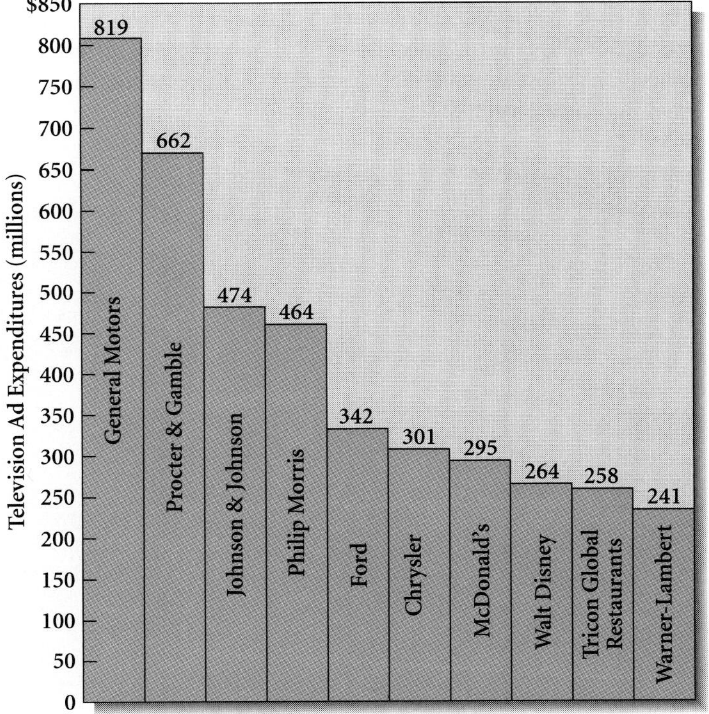

FIGURE 12.2 ◆ Top Ten Network TV Advertisers

- About 7 percent of all advertising outlays are for *radio advertising*. Over 180 million people in the United States listen to the radio each day, and radio ads are quite inexpensive. For example, a small business in a midwestern town of 100,000 people pays only about $20 for a 30-second local radio spot. (A television spot in the same area costs over $250.) In addition, stations are usually segmented into categories such as rock and roll, country and western, jazz, talk shows, news, and religious programming; thus, their audiences are largely segmented. Unfortunately, radio ads, like television ads, are over quickly. Furthermore, they provide only audio presentations, and people tend to use the radio as background while doing other things.
- *Magazine ads* account for roughly 5 percent of all advertising. The huge variety of magazines provides a high level of ready market segmentation. Magazines also allow advertisers plenty of space for detailed product information. In addition, they allow for excellent reproduction of photographs and artwork. Finally, because magazines have long lives and tend to be passed from person to person, ads get constantly increased exposure. Ads must be submitted well in advance, however, and there is often no guarantee of where an ad will appear within a magazine.
- *Outdoor advertising*—billboards, signs, and advertisements on buses, taxis, and subways—makes up about 1 percent of all advertising. These ads are inexpensive, face little competition for customers' attention, and are subject to high repeat exposure.
- The most recent advertising medium is, of course, the *Internet*, where such well-known names as 3M Corp., Burlington Coat Factory, Miller Genuine Draft, MCI Communications, and Reebok have all placed ads. Although Internet advertising is still in its infancy and offers high potential, most marketers recognize that it also has limitations: In particular, consumers do not want to wade through electronic pages looking at details about hundreds of products.[7] One expert offers the disappointing opinion that most of the commercial advertisements on the Internet may never be read by anyone. Even so, U.S. ad expenditures on the Net jumped from $301 million in 1996 to $545 million in 1997; Microsoft Corp. alone spent $31 million. Communication analysts are projecting that ad expenditures will rise to $23 billion by 2002.[8]
- *Other advertising channels*. A combination of many additional media, including catalogs, sidewalk handouts, Yellow Pages, skywriting, telephone calls, special events, and door-to-door communication, make up the remaining 22 percent of all U.S. advertising.

The Media Mix. The combination of media that a company chooses to advertise its products is called its **media mix.** As Table 12.1 suggests, different industries use very different mixes, and most depend on a variety of different media, rather than using just one, for reaching their target audiences.

media mix Combination of advertising media chosen to carry message about a product

In promoting Godzilla, *Sony Pictures Corp. opted for outdoor advertising because both the medium and the message were matters of size. When the market is clogged with heavily marketed big-budget films (and it has been nearly every summer since* Jaws *in 1975), studios feel the need to generate the impression of greater bigness—that the movie is so important that viewers must see it* right now. *Sony and its promotional partners spent $200 million to advertise* Godzilla*—about as much as it cost to make* Titanic*—and besides billboards, buses, and the sides of buildings, they put the title on about 3,000 products ranging from batteries to tacos.*

TABLE 12.1 ◆ **Media Mix by Industry**

INDUSTRY	MAGAZINE	NEWSPAPER	OUTDOOR	TELEVISION	RADIO
Retail stores	4.2%	61.1%	1.9%	27.8%	5.0%
Industrial materials	29.3	7.8	0.3	52.8	9.8
Insurance and real estate	11.1	53.5	2.2	29.3	3.9
Food	14.9	0.7	0.3	80.5	3.6
Apparel	50.5	1.8	0.5	45.8	1.4

Using the Services of an Advertising Agency. Advertising agencies assist in the development of advertising campaigns by providing specialized services. They are independent companies that provide some or all of their clients' advertising needs. The agency works together with the client company to determine the campaign's central message, create detailed message content, identify ad media, and negotiate media purchases.[9]

The advantage offered by agencies is expertise in developing ad themes, message content, and artwork, as well as in coordinating ad production and advising on relevant legal matters. Today, even more specialized agencies have emerged to cater to clients with very specific goals in specific industries or market segments. For example, Medicus Consumer/D.M.B.&B., Kallir Phillips Ross, and Sudler & Hennessey are agencies experienced in the marketing of pharmaceuticals. Burrell Communications Group is the largest African American advertising agency, and Conhill Advertising focuses on Hispanic consumers.

As payment for its services, the agency usually receives a percentage, traditionally 15 percent of the media purchase cost. For example, if an agency purchases a $1 million television commitment for a client's campaign, it would receive $150,000 for its services.

PERSONAL SELLING PROMOTIONS In **personal selling,** a salesperson communicates one-to-one with potential customers to identify their needs and to line them up with the seller's products. The oldest form of selling, it provides the personal link between seller and buyer and adds to a firm's credibility because it allows buyers to interact with and ask questions of the seller.[10] This professional intimacy is especially effective for relationship marketing: It places the seller closer to the buyer, it provides a clearer exposure of the customer's business, and the salesperson can then assist the buying company in creating value-adding services for the buyer's target customers.[11]

personal selling Promotional tool in which a salesperson communicates one-on-one with potential customers

Ha-Lo Industries sells things that have logos on them—desk clocks, sweatshirts, basketball goals. According to CEO Lou Weisbach, a one-time Ha-Lo salesman, the key to the company's success is a hard-driving, well-trained sales force. Ha-Lo's top salesperson will take home about $3 million per year, and Weisbach delayed entering the lucrative New York market until he had completed a $4 million upgrade on the order-processing system that his sales reps use.

However, because it involves personal interaction, personal selling requires a certain level of trust between buyer and seller—a relationship that must often be established over time. Moreover, because presentations are generally made to only one or two individuals at a time, personal selling is the most expensive form of promotion per contact. Expenses may include salespeople's compensation and their overhead, usually travel, food, and lodging. Indeed, the average cost of a single industrial sales call has been estimated at approximately $300.

Such high costs have prompted many companies to turn to *telemarketing:* using telephone solicitations to perform the personal selling process. Telemarketing can be used to handle any stage of the personal selling process or to set up appointments for outside salespeople. For example, it saves the cost of personal sales visits to industrial customers. Each industrial buyer requires an average of nearly four visits to complete a sale; some companies have thus realized savings in sales visits of $1,000 or more. Not surprisingly, such savings are stimulating the remarkable growth of telemarketing, which the Direct Marketing Association estimates will grow in sales to $600 billion, with as many as 5 million more people to be employed by the year 2000.[12]

Personal Selling Tasks. One important aspect of sales force management is overseeing salespeople as they perform the three basic tasks generally associated with personal selling: order processing, creative selling, and missionary selling. Depending on the product and company, sales jobs usually require individuals to perform all three tasks to some degree.

order processing Personal selling task in which salespeople receive orders and see to their handling and delivery

creative selling Personal selling task in which salespeople try to persuade buyers to purchase products by providing information about their benefits

missionary selling Personal selling tasks in which salespeople promote their firms and products rather than try to close sales

- *Order Processing.* In **order processing,** a salesperson receives an order and sees to its handling and delivery. Route salespeople, who call on regular customers to check their supplies, are often order processors: With the customers' consent, they may determine the sizes of reorders, fill them directly from their trucks, and even stack the customers' shelves.
- *Creative Selling.* When the benefits of a product are not entirely clear, **creative selling** can help to persuade buyers. Most industrial products involve creative selling, especially when a buyer is unfamiliar with a product or the features and uses of a specific brand. Personal selling is also crucial for high-priced consumer products, such as homes and cars, for which buyers comparison shop. Any new product can benefit from creative selling that works to differentiate it from competitors.
- *Missionary Selling.* A company may also use **missionary selling** when its purpose is to promote itself and its products rather than simply to close a sale. For example, drug company representatives promote drugs to doctors who, in turn, prescribe them to patients. The sale, then, is actually made at the drugstore. In this case, the goal of missionary selling may be to promote the company's long-term image as much as any given product. Another form of missionary selling is the after-sale technical assistance that companies offer for complex products. For example, IBM uses after-sale missionary selling both to ensure that customers know how to use IBM equipment and to promote goodwill.

sales promotion Short-term promotional activity designed to stimulate consumer buying or cooperation from distributors and sales agents

SALES PROMOTIONS Short-term promotional activities designed to stimulate consumer buying or cooperation from distributors, sales agents, or other members of the trade involve **sales promotions.** They are important because they increase the likelihood that buyers will try products. Sales promotions also enhance product recognition and can increase purchase size and amount. For example, soap is sometimes bound in packages of four with the promotion "Buy three and get one free."[13]

To be successful, sales promotions must be convenient and accessible when the decision to purchase occurs. For instance, if Harley-Davidson has a 1-week motorcycle promotion and you have no local dealer, the promotion is neither convenient nor accessible to you, and you will not buy. On the other hand, if Folgers offers a $1-off coupon that you can save for use later, the promotion is both convenient and accessible.

Types of Sales Promotions. The best-known forms of promotions are coupons, point-of-purchase displays, various purchasing incentives (especially free samples and premiums), trade shows, and contests and sweepstakes.

- A certificate that entitles the bearer to a stated savings off a regular price is a **coupon.** Coupons may be used to encourage customers to try new products, to attract customers away from competitors, or to induce current customers to buy more of a product. They appear in newspapers and magazines, are included with other products, and are often sent through direct mail.
- To grab customers' attention as they walk through stores, some companies use **point-of-purchase (POP) displays.** Located at the ends of aisles or near checkout counters, POP displays make it easier for customers to find products and easier for sellers to eliminate competitors from consideration.
- Free samples and premiums are *purchasing incentives.* Free samples allow customers to try products without risk. They may be given out at local retail outlets or sent by manufacturers to consumers by direct mail. **Premiums** are gifts, such as pens, pencils, calendars, and coffee mugs, that are given away to consumers in return for buying a specified product.
- Periodically, industries sponsor **trade shows** for members and customers. Trade shows allow companies to rent booths to display and demonstrate products to customers who have a special interest in them or who are ready to buy.
- Customers, distributors, and sales representatives may all be persuaded to increase sales by means of *contests.* For example, consumers may be asked to enter their cats in the Purina Cat Chow calendar contest by submitting entry blanks from the backs of cat food packages.

coupon Sales promotion technique in which a certificate is issued entitling the buyer to a reduced price

point-of-purchase (POP) display Sales promotion technique in which product displays are located in certain areas to stimulate purchase

premium Sales promotion technique in which offers of free or reduced-price items are used to stimulate purchases

trade show Sales promotion technique in which various members of an industry gather to display, demonstrate, and sell products

PUBLICITY AND PUBLIC RELATIONS Much to the delight of marketing managers with tight budgets, **publicity** is free. Moreover, because it is presented in a news format, consumers often see publicity as objective and highly believable. Thus, it is an important part of the promotional mix.

Public relations is company-influenced publicity that seeks to build good relations with the public and to deal with the effects of unfavorable events. It attempts to establish goodwill with customers (and potential customers) by performing and publicizing a company's public service activities. Anheuser-Busch's 1997 *Annual Report,* for example, proudly announces the company's role in alcohol-awareness efforts; independent studies show reduced drinking among high school seniors and drastic reductions in teenage drunk-driving fatalities nationwide during the past 15 years. During the 1990s alone, A-B invested more than $165 million in efforts to curb alcohol abuse, fight drunk driving, and discourage underage drinking. A-B recently joined forces with 7-Eleven—the country's largest beer retailer—to distribute ID-checking tools at all of 7-Eleven's 5,600 stores nationwide.

publicity Promotional tool in which information about a company or product is transmitted by general mass media

public relations Company-influenced publicity directed at building goodwill between an organization and potential customers

INTERNATIONAL PROMOTIONAL STRATEGIES As discussed in Chapter 3, recent decades have witnessed a profound shift from home-country marketing to multicountry and now to global marketing. Nowhere is this rapidly growing global orientation more evident than in marketing promotions, especially advertising.[14]

Emergence of the Global Perspective. Every company that markets its products in several countries faces a basic choice: use a decentralized approach with separate marketing management for each country or adopt a global perspective with a coordinated marketing program directed at one worldwide audience. The global perspective, therefore, is actually a company philosophy that directs marketing toward a worldwide rather than a local or regional market. The movement is in the global direction, but, due to national differences, "one world market" remains a concept more than a reality.

Universal Messages and Regional Variations. In recognizing national differences, many global marketers try to build on a universal advertising theme that nevertheless allows for variations. For example, KFC spends $80 million a year on non-U.S. advertising, including global branding campaigns. KFC has promoted a single message—its red and white three-letter logo—that is recognized around the world. At the same time, however, it still uses advertising variations for Europe, Asia, Latin America, and Australia that are developed by various ad agencies in different countries.

The Coca-Cola Co. earns no less than 80 percent of its profits from markets outside North America. The company's marketing strategy is essentially the same everywhere: Coke (which is really little more than flavored, carbonated, sweetened water) is positioned as unique. Something better than the next soft drink. "The real thing." The product itself, however, is not necessarily uniform. Its taste, for example, is often altered to suit local preferences. Channels of distribution differ, as of course, do prices, but Coke remains the best example of a global product and a global brand.

PROMOTIONAL PRACTICES IN SMALL BUSINESS From our discussion so far, you may think that only large companies can afford to promote their products. Although small businesses generally have fewer resources, cost-effective promotions can improve sales and allow small firms to compete with much larger firms.

Small-Business Advertising. The type of advertising chosen by a small business depends on the market that the firm is trying to reach: local, national, or international.

- *Local Markets.* Advertising in non-prime-time slots on local television or cable television offers great impact at a cost that many small firms can afford. More often, however, small businesses with local markets use newspaper, radio, and, increasingly, direct mail. Although billboards are beyond the means of many small businesses, outdoor store signs can draw strong responses from passersby.
- *National Markets.* Many businesses have grown from small to large by using direct mail, particularly catalogs. Sears & Roebuck was once a small mail-order house, as was L.L. Bean. By purchasing mailing lists of other companies' customers, a small firm can reduce costs by targeting its mailings. Advertising to a targeted audience in a specialized magazine is also effective for small businesses. For example, Turnquist Lumber Co. of Foster, Rhode Island, advertises its specialty, the exporting of quality red oak, in *Southern Lumberman*, a trade magazine for the lumber industry.
- *International Markets.* Television, radio, and newspapers are seldom viable promotional options for small businesses to use in reaching international markets. For one thing, they are too expensive for many small firms. Instead, most small firms find direct mail and carefully targeted magazine advertising the most effective tools.

The Role of Personal Selling in Small Business. Some small firms maintain sales forces to promote and sell their products in local markets, where clients can be quickly visited. Others prefer not to do their own selling, but contract with *sales agencies:* companies that handle the products of several clients to act on their behalf. For national and international markets, however, the costs of operating a sales force are high, so sales agencies and other methods such as telemarketing are used.

Small-Business Promotions. Small companies use the same sales promotion incentives as larger companies. However, larger firms tend to use more coupons, POP displays, and sales contests. Because these tools are expensive and difficult to manage, smaller firms rely on premiums and special sales. One successful company, however, uses a variety of promotions to encourage lasting relationships with its customers. Zane's Cycles, a bicycle retailer in Branford, Connecticut, offers free coffee and soft drinks to waiting customers, even some who drop in on Saturday mornings, drink coffee, read the paper, and leave after 20 minutes. With revenues expected to pass $2 million in 1997, Zane's also offers the ultimate promotional incentive: Free lifetime service on each bike it sells.[15]

■ DISTRIBUTING PRODUCTS

Businesses use many ways to get products to customers. As the fourth element in the marketing mix (place), distribution takes many forms.

The Distribution Mix

distribution mix The combination of distribution channels by which a firm gets its products to end users

intermediary Individual or firm that helps to distribute a product

We have already seen that a company needs an appropriate product mix. But the success of any product also depends on its **distribution mix:** the combination of distribution channels that a firm selects to get a product to end users. In this section, we consider some of the many factors that enter into the distribution mix. First, we look at the role of the target audience and explain the need for intermediaries.

INTERMEDIARIES AND DISTRIBUTION CHANNELS Once called *middlemen*, **intermediaries** are the individuals and firms who help to distribute a producer's goods.

They are generally classified as wholesalers or retailers. **Wholesalers** sell products to other businesses, who resell them to final consumers. **Retailers** sell products directly to consumers. Some firms rely on independent intermediaries, and others employ their own distribution networks and sales forces.

wholesaler Intermediary who sells products to other businesses for resale to final consumers

retailer Intermediary who sells products directly to consumers

distribution channel Network of interdependent companies through which a product passes from producer to end user

Distribution of Consumer Products. A **distribution channel** is the path that a product follows from producer to end user. Figure 12.3 shows how the six primary distribution channels can be identified according to the kinds of channel members who participate in getting products to their ultimate destinations. As we move through this discussion, note first that all channels begin with a manufacturer and end with a consumer or an industrial user. Channels 1 through 4 are most often used for the distribution of consumer goods and services.

CHANNEL 1: DIRECT DISTRIBUTION OF CONSUMER PRODUCTS. In a **direct channel,** the product travels from the producer to the consumer without intermediaries. Using their own sales forces, companies such as Avon, Fuller Brush, and Tupperware use this channel.

direct channel Distribution channel in which a product travels from producer to consumer without intermediaries

Dell Computer Corp., for example, sells personal computers over the phone and customers receive their purchases by direct mail. Today, Dell Computer boasts a yearly $3.4 billion business and the fourth-largest PC maker in the United States. By selling direct, Dell and rival Gateway 2000 have captured about 20 percent of the $45 billion PC market. Dell runs a bare-bones operation in Austin, Texas, where workers assemble off-the-shelf components into finished PCs as orders are received. As the first entrepreneur to sell computers by mail, Michael Dell feels confident that he knows his market better than anyone else. However, Dell's experience has also taught him that direct sales is more difficult than it looks: "It's not as easy as a couple of 1-800 lines and a bunch of picnic tables," he warns.

> **"It's not as easy as a couple of 1-800 lines and a bunch of picnic tables."**
>
> —Michael Dell
> *Computer entrepreneur*

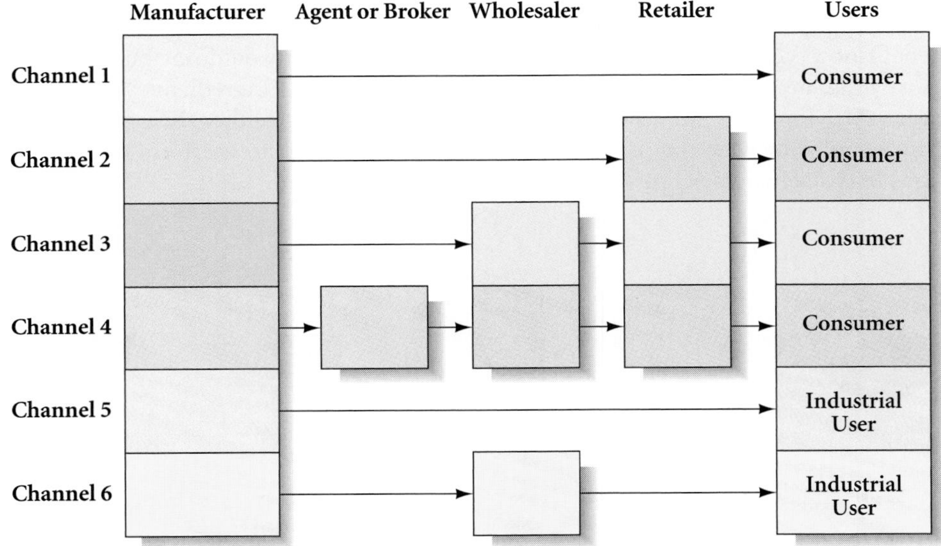

FIGURE 12.3 ◆ **Channels of Distribution**

Channel 2: Retail Distribution of Consumer Products. In channel 2, manufacturers distribute products through retailers. Goodyear, for example, maintains its own system of retail outlets. Levi's has its own outlets but also produces jeans for other retailers such as The Gap. Liz Claiborne, on the other hand, relies on more than 9,300 retailers to sell its apparel worldwide. Claiborne uses its sales force to sell products to the retailers, who then sell them over the counter to consumers.

Channel 3: Wholesale Distribution of Consumer Products. Until the mid-1960s, channel 2 was the most widely used method of nondirect distribution. It requires a large amount of floor space, however, both for storing merchandise and for displaying it in retail stores. Faced with the rising cost of retail space, many retailers found that they could not afford both retail and storage space. Thus, wholesalers entered the distribution network to take over more and more of the storage service. An example of channel 3 is combination convenience stores/gas stations. Approximately 90 percent of the space in these stores is used for merchandise displays; only about 10 percent is left for storage and office facilities. Merchandise in the store is stocked frequently by wholesalers.

sales agent/broker
Independent intermediary who usually represents many manufacturers and sells to wholesalers or retailers

Channel 4: Distribution through Sales Agents or Brokers. Channel 4 uses **sales agents,** or **brokers,** who represent manufacturers and sell to wholesalers, retailers, or both. They receive commissions based on the price of goods they sell. Agents generally deal in the related product lines of a few producers, serving as their sales representatives on a long-term basis. For example, travel agents represent airlines, car rental companies, and hotels. In contrast, brokers are hired to assist in buying and selling temporarily, matching sellers and buyers as needed. The real estate industry, for example, relies on brokers for matching buyers and sellers of property.

The Pros and Cons of Nondirect Distribution. Ultimately, each link in the distribution chain makes a profit by charging a markup or commission. Thus, nondirect distribution channels mean higher prices for end users: The more members in the channel—the more intermediaries—the higher the final price. Calculated as a percentage of cost, markups are applied each time a product is sold. Figure 12.4 highlights a series of markups as a product moves through the distribution channel. Markups may range from 10 to 40 percent for manufacturers, from 2 to 25 percent for wholesalers, and from 5 to 100 percent for retailers. Markup size depends on the particular industry and competitive conditions.

At the same time, however, intermediaries can save consumers both time and money. In doing so they provide added value for customers. Moreover, this value-adding activity continues and accumulates at each stage of the supply chain. In fact, intermediaries add value by making the right quantities of products available where and when you need them. For example, consider Figure 12.5, which illustrates the problem of making chili without benefit of a common intermediary—the supermarket. You would obviously spend a lot more time, money, and energy if you tried to gather all the ingredients yourself. Moreover, if we eliminated intermediaries, we would not eliminate either their functions or the costs entailed by what they do. Intermediaries exist because they perform necessary functions in cost-efficient ways.

FIGURE 12.4 ◆ Typical Sequence of Markups

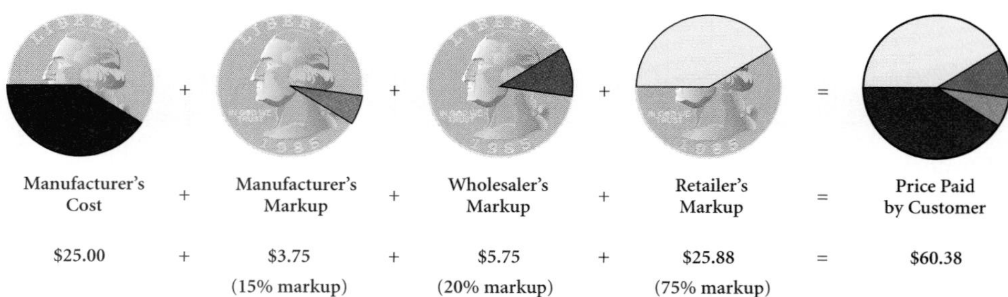

At Direct Casket, shoppers in Brooklyn can take advantage of retail coffin sales. The company is now one of about 50 firms nationwide that buy from manufacturers and sell directly to the public through showrooms, catalogs, and even the Internet. Markups are typically 100 percent—compared to about 350 percent at funeral homes. A cloth-covered wood casket that costs $150 wholesale will retail at Direct Casket for $395—considerably less than the $695 to $1,150 charged by funeral homes. Funeral homes, of course, offer convenience and services that storefront retailers do not, but as Direct Casket president Ray Silvas puts it, "Smart shoppers don't want to spend thousands of dollars that aren't necessary."

Distribution of Industrial Products. Industrial channels are important because every company is itself a customer that buys products from other companies. The Kellogg Co., for example, buys grain to make breakfast cereals, and Humana, a nationwide chain of for-profit hospitals, buys medicines and other supplies to provide medical services. **Industrial distribution,** therefore, is the network of channel members involved in the flow of manufactured goods to industrial customers. Unlike consumer products, industrial products are traditionally distributed through channels 5 or 6, shown in Figure 12.3.

industrial distribution Network of channel members involved in the flow of manufactured goods to industrial customers

CHANNEL 5: DIRECT DISTRIBUTION OF INDUSTRIAL PRODUCTS. Most industrial goods are sold directly by the manufacturer to the industrial buyer. Lawless Container Corp., for instance, produces packaging containers that are sold directly to such customers as Fisher-Price (toys), Dirt Devil (vacuum cleaners), Peak (anti-freeze), and Mr. Coffee (coffee makers). As contact points with their customers, manufacturers maintain **sales offices.** These offices provide all services for the company's customers and serve as headquarters for its salespeople.

sales office Office maintained by a manufacturer as a contact point with its customers

CHANNEL 6: WHOLESALE DISTRIBUTION OF INDUSTRIAL PRODUCTS. Wholesalers function as intermediaries between manufacturers and end users in a very small percentage of industrial channels. Brokers and agents are even rarer. Channel 6 is most often used for accessory equipment (computer terminals, office equipment) and supplies (floppy disks, copier paper). Whereas manufacturers produce these items in large quantities, companies buy them in small quantities. For example, few companies order truckloads of paper clips. As with consumer goods, then, intermediaries help end users by representing manufacturers or by breaking down large quantities into smaller sales units.

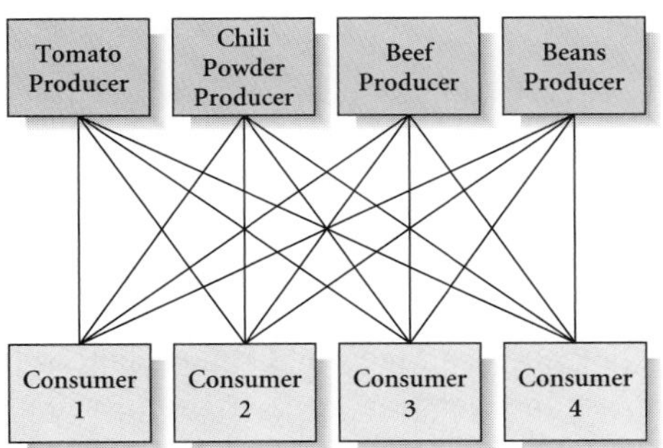

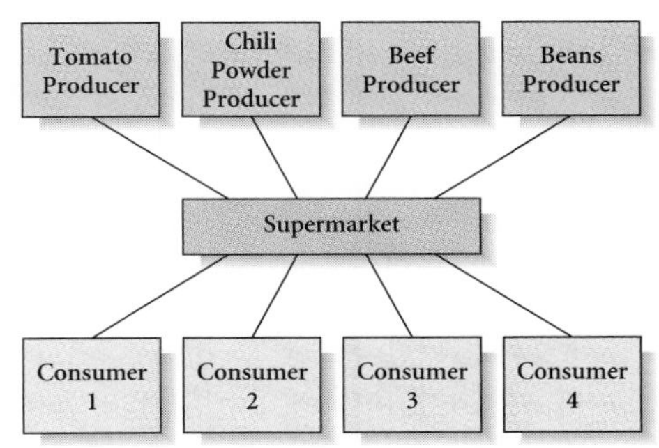

FIGURE 12.5 ◆ **Value-Adding Intermediary**

WHOLESALING Now that you know something about distribution channels, we can consider the role played by intermediaries in more detail. Wholesalers provide a variety of services to customers who are buying products for resale or business use. For example, in addition to storing and providing an assortment of products, wholesalers offer delivery, credit, and product information. Of course, not all wholesalers perform all these functions. Services offered depend on the type of intermediary involved—merchant wholesalers or agents and brokers.

merchant wholesalers
Intermediaries that buy products from manufacturers and sell them to other businesses

Merchant Wholesalers. Most wholesalers are independent operations that sell various consumer or business goods produced by a variety of manufacturers. **Merchant wholesalers,** the largest single group of wholesalers, play dual roles, buying products from manufacturers and selling them to other businesses. Merchant wholesalers purchase and own the goods that they resell. Usually, they also provide storage and delivery. In the United States, the merchant wholesaling industry employs 5 million people with a total yearly payroll of $140 billion.

Agents and Brokers. Agents and brokers serve as sales forces for various manufacturers. They are independent representatives of many companies' products. They work on commissions, usually about 4 to 5 percent of net sales. Unlike merchant wholesalers, they do not take title to (that is, they do not own) the merchandise they sell. Rather, they serve as sales and merchandising arms of manufacturers who do not have their own sales forces.

The value of agents and brokers lies primarily in their knowledge of markets and their merchandising expertise. They also provide a wide range of services, including shelf and display merchandising and advertising layout. Finally, they maintain product salability by removing open, torn, or dirty packages, arranging products neatly, and generally keeping them attractively displayed. Many supermarket products are handled through brokers.

TRENDS AND CHALLENGES

MAKING BOOK ON THE FUTURE

Arguably, the least "sexy" aspect of bookselling is distribution—the system of packing, shipping, and delivering books to bookstores and, directly, to on-line consumers. There are no multimillion dollar author deals, no book parties or book signings, and no awards. Instead, there is a decidedly unglamorous back-office function with the potential to turn one company into a winner and another into an also-ran. With industry sales growth projected at less than 5 percent a year in the nation's $8 billion consumer book market, the battleground for both industry superstars—Barnes & Noble and Amazon.com—and independent booksellers is increasingly in the distribution arena.

The competition nearly reached a boiling point when B&N announced that it would acquire the Ingram Book Co., the country's largest book distributor, for $600 million, a move that B&N claims will speed its ability to deliver books to both stores and on-line consumers overnight. Industry analysts also see other, more aggressively competitive motives for the purchase, including a desire to tie up Amazon.com's distribution system. Before the B&N/Ingram merger, Amazon.com received nearly 60 percent of its books from Ingram's 11 nationwide distribution centers. Following the merger announcement, Amazon.com declared its intention to diversify its supplier base. Warned Amazon.com CEO Jeff Bezos: "Everyone has to be worried that Barnes & Noble will use this to achieve an unfair advantage."

According to the American Booksellers Association, the industry trade association, the nation's independent bookstores have even more to worry about. With Ingram supplying independents with most of their books, small bookstore owners are naturally concerned that Ingram will give preference to B&N when a title is in short supply. With three B&N stores within 15 miles of R. J. Julia Booksellers in Madison, Connecticut, owner Roxanne Coady expects the worst: "I guess [Ingram] will give [books] to me when they feel like it."

Retailing

There are more than 2.5 million retail establishments in the United States. Most of them are small operations, often consisting of owners and part-time help. Indeed, over one-half of the nation's retailers account for less than 10 percent of all retail sales. Retailers also include huge operations such as Wal-Mart, the largest employer in the United States, and Sears. Although there are large retailers in many other countries—Kaufhof in Germany, Carrefour in France, and Daiei in Japan—more of the world's largest retailers are based in the United States than in any other country. In this section we describe in some depth the different types of outlets, both store and nonstore, that dot the U.S. retailing landscape.

TYPES OF RETAIL OUTLETS U.S. retail operations vary as widely by type as they do by size. They can be classified in various ways: by pricing strategies, location, range of services, or range of product lines. Choosing the right types of retail outlets is a crucial aspect of every seller's distribution strategy. In this section we describe U.S. retail stores by using two classifications: *product line retailers* and *bargain retailers.*[16]

Product Line Retailers. Retailers that feature broad product lines include *department stores, supermarkets,* and *hypermarkets; specialty stores* are typified by narrow product lines.

- *Department Stores.* As the name implies, **department stores** are organized into specialized departments: shoes, furniture, women's petite sizes, and so on. Department stores are usually large and handle a wide range of goods. In addition, they usually offer a variety of services, such as generous return policies, credit plans, and delivery. In the past, department stores differentiated themselves by what they sold and the prices they charged. Today, however, consumers report that ambiance and service levels differ more than merchandise and thus drive buyer preferences among stores.

department store Large product line retailer characterized by organization into specialized departments

- *Supermarkets.* The shift from the small corner grocery to supermarkets began in the second half of the 1930s. Like department stores, **supermarkets** are divided into departments of related products: food products, household products, and so forth. The emphasis is on low prices, self-service, and wide selection. The largest supermarkets are chain stores such as Safeway, Kroger, Lucky Stores, Winn-Dixie, A&P, and Albertson's.

supermarket Large product line retailer offering a variety of food and food-related items in specialized departments

> **"Everyone has to be worried that Barnes & Noble will use its merger with Ingram Book to achieve an unfair advantage."**
>
> —Jeff Bezos
> *CEO, Amazon.com*

Independents are also concerned about B&N's access to inside information about its competitors who do business with Ingram. Complains William Petrocelli, co-owner of Book Passage, a California-based independent: "They'll be able to find out what our sales are and what the profit margin is, and then find out just how vulnerable these stores are and then move in."

Responding to such concerns, John R. Ingram, who will continue to operate as Ingram's chairman, sent letters to more than 5,000 independent booksellers, urging them to trust in the company's history of ethics and fair play. "We've never shared information," says Ingram. "We have always operated with the highest degree of ethics and confidentiality, and that will absolutely continue. . . . I wouldn't have done the deal without those assurances."

Despite negative industrywide reaction to the deal, the purchase of Ingram may have been a financial necessity for B&N. With Amazon.com enjoying a commanding lead in the on-line book business (B&N does only about one-tenth as much on-line business as Amazon.com), many industry insiders believe that B&N purchased Ingram to remain competitive in the industry, not to monopolize it.

"If you go into a supermarket," says Gap Inc. CEO Mickey Drexler, "you would expect to find some fundamental items. I don't know why apparel stores should be any different." The Gap launched its Old Navy division in 1994 to compete with stores like Sears—except that Old Navy stores are louder, cheaper, and more playful. There are listening booths where customers can sample CDs, and refrigerator cases are stocked with shirts shrink-wrapped like pork chops. By 2003, the company expects sales at Old Navy outlets to outstrip those at Gap stores.

hypermarket Very large product line retailer carrying a wide variety of unrelated products

specialty store Small retail store carrying one product line or category of related products

- *Hypermarkets.* A phenomenon begun in the late 1970s, **hypermarkets** are much larger than supermarkets (up to 200,000 square feet) and sell a much wider variety of products. They also practice scrambled merchandising: carrying any product, whether similar or dissimilar to the store's original product offering, that promises to sell. In Dallas, for example, Hypermart U.S.A. sells a wide range of food and grocery items, including specialty foods and fresh bakery goods. It also offers television sets, auto accessories, and dry-cleaning services.
- *Specialty Stores.* **Specialty stores** are small stores that carry one line of related products. They serve clearly defined market segments by offering full product lines in narrow product fields and often feature knowledgeable sales personnel. Sunglass Hut International, for example, has 1,600 outlets carrying a deep selection of sunglasses at competitive prices. In the United States, Canada, Europe, and Australia, its stores are located in malls, airports, and anywhere else that is convenient for quick, one-stop shopping. "People's time," contends CEO Jack B. Chadsey, "is so limited, they don't want to walk through a maze of categories. If they're looking for electronics, they're going to go to an electronics specialty store. Sunglasses are no different."

> **"People's time is so limited, they don't want to walk through a maze of categories. If they're looking for electronics, they're going to go to an electronics specialty store. Sunglasses are no different."**
>
> —Jack B. Chadsey
> *CEO, Sunglass Hut*

bargain retailer Retailer carrying a wide range of products at bargain prices

discount house Bargain retailer that generates large sales volume by offering goods at substantial price reductions

Bargain Retailers. **Bargain retailers** carry wide ranges of products and come in many forms. Included in this category are *discount houses, off-price stores, catalog showrooms, factory outlets, warehouse clubs,* and *convenience stores.*

- *Discount Houses.* After World War II, some U.S. retailers began offering discounts to certain customers. These first **discount houses** sold large numbers of items such as televisions and other appliances by featuring substantial price reductions. As brand-name items became more plentiful in the early 1950s, discounters offered even better product assortments while still embracing a philosophy of cash-only sales conducted in low-rent facilities. As they became more firmly entrenched, they began moving to better locations, improving decor, and selling better-quality merchandise at higher prices. They also began offering a few department store services, such as credit plans and noncash sales.

- *Off-Price Stores.* The 1980s witnessed the growth of the discount house variation commonly called the **off-price store.** Off-price stores buy the excess inventories of well-recognized high-quality manufacturers and sell them at prices up to 60 percent off regular department store prices. They are often prohibited from using manufacturers' names in their advertising because producers fear that a product's marketplace value and prestige will be compromised. One of the more successful off-price chains is Marshall's, which reduces prices on brand-name apparel for men, women, and children.
- *Catalog Showrooms.* Another form of bargain store that has grown dramatically in recent years is the **catalog showroom.** These firms mail catalogs with color pictures, product descriptions, and prices to attract customers into their showrooms. Once there, customers view display samples, place orders, and wait briefly while clerks retrieve orders from attached warehouses. Service Merchandise, Best Products, and LaBelle's are major catalog showroom retailers.
- *Factory Outlets.* **Factory outlets** are manufacturer-owned stores that avoid wholesalers and retailers by selling merchandise directly from the factory to consumers. The first factory outlets featured apparel, linens, food, and furniture. Because they were usually located in warehouselike facilities next to the factories, distribution costs were quite low. Lower costs were passed on to customers as lower prices.
- *Warehouse Clubs.* The **warehouse club** (or **wholesale club**) offers large discounts on brand-name clothing, groceries, appliances, automotive supplies, and other merchandise. Unlike customers at discount houses and factory outlets, club customers pay annual membership fees. The first warehouse club, Price Club, opened in 1976. It merged with its rival Costco in 1993 to form the second-largest warehouse club in the nation (after Wal-Mart's Sam's Club).
- *Convenience Stores.* Neighborhood food retailers such as 7-Eleven and Circle K stores are successful convenience store chains. As the name suggests, **convenience stores** offer ease of purchase: They stress easily accessible locations with parking, extended store hours (in many cases 24 hours), and speedy service. They differ from most bargain retailers in that they do not feature low prices. Like bargain retailers, however, they control prices by keeping in-store service levels to a minimum.

off-price store Bargain retailer that buys excess inventories from high-quality manufacturers and sells them at discounted prices

catalog showroom Bargain retailer in which customers place orders for catalog items to be picked up at on-premises warehouses

factory outlet Bargain retailer owned by the manufacturer whose products it sells

warehouse club (or wholesale club) Bargain retailer offering large discounts on brand-name merchandise to customers who have paid annual membership fees

convenience store Retail store offering easy accessibility, extended hours, and fast service

NONSTORE RETAILING Of course, not all goods and services are sold in stores. In fact, some of the nation's largest retailers sell all or most of their products without stores. For example, certain types of consumer goods—soft drinks, candy, and cigarettes—lend themselves to distribution in vending machines. Even at $30 billion per year, however, vending machine sales still represent less than 5 percent of all U.S. retail sales.

Major Types of Nonstore Selling. In this section we survey a few of the more important forms of nonstore retailing. In particular, we examine **direct-response retailing,** in which firms make direct contact with customers both to inform them about products and to receive sales orders. This type of retailing includes *mail marketing, mail order, video marketing, telemarketing,* and *electronic shopping.* Another important form of nonstore retailing is *direct selling.*[17]

direct-response retailing Nonstore retailing by direct interaction with customers to inform them of products and to receive sales orders

- *Mail Marketing.* Direct mail and mail-order marketing result in billions of sales dollars annually in both retail and industrial sales. In retailing, the world's largest mail-order business is run by Otto Versand, a privately held company based in Hamburg, Germany. Company founder Werner Versand began in mail order back in 1950 by pasting pictures of shoes in hand-bound catalogs. Today, with annual sales topping $13 billion, Otto Versand has used mail order to build his company into one of the world's biggest multinational retailers. In addition to mail-order companies in Hungary, Japan, Italy, France, Britain, and Germany, Otto Versand owns 90 percent of Spiegel and its Eddie Bauer subsidiary in the United States.
- *Mail Order (or Catalog Marketing).* Firms that sell by **mail order** (or **catalog marketing**) typically send out splashy color catalogs describing a variety of merchandise. Currently, they garner sales of $45 billion to $60 billion in the United States each year. L. L.Bean alone ships more than 10 million packages to mail-order customers annually. As a whole,

mail order (or catalog marketing) Form of nonstore retailing in which customers place orders for catalog merchandise received through the mail

"We already changed our phone service to something or other last week, so we don't need whatever it is you have."

the world of interactive commerce is an incredibly busy place: Each year, for example, AT&T's 800-line unit generates 13 billion calls, and competitors carry another 9 billion.

Although mail-order firms have existed for a long time, computer technology and telephone charge transactions have made this a booming industry in recent years. Armed with 24-hour international toll-free phone lines, overnight delivery, inexpensive fax machines, and credit card offers, U.S.-based catalog marketing is now convenient and fast for consumers in Canada, Japan, Europe, and England. Japanese consumers can call a San Francisco outlet toll-free around the clock, talk with a Japanese-speaking telemarketer, avoid import tariffs, and receive express mail delivery.

video marketing Nonstore retailing to consumers via standard and cable television

telemarketing Nonstore retailing in which the telephone is used to sell directly to consumers

- *Video Marketing.* More and more companies have begun using television to sell many kinds of consumer commodities such as jewelry and kitchen accessories. Most cable systems offer **video marketing** through home-shopping channels that display and demonstrate products and allow viewers to phone in orders. One home-shopping network, QVC, has extended into international markets via agreements with British Sky Broadcasting to reach into England, Ireland, and parts of Europe and with Mexico's Grupo Telvisa to send live broadcasts to Mexico, Spain, Portugal, and South America.
- *Telemarketing.* **Telemarketing** is the use of the telephone to sell directly to consumers. WATS (wide area telephone service) lines can be used to receive toll-free calls from consumers responding to television and radio ads. Using live or automated dialing, message delivery, and order taking, telemarketers can also use WATS lines to call consumers to promote products and services. Telemarketing is used not only for consumer goods but also for industrial goods and insurance and accounting services. Currently, telemarketing is experiencing exceptional growth in the United States, Canada, and Great Britain. With sales having topped $360 billion in 1995, the industry expects sales of up to $600 billion by the year 2000.

- *Electronic Shopping.* **Electronic shopping** is made possible by computer information systems that allow sellers to connect to consumers' computers with information about products. With over 1 million subscribers, Prodigy, which was formed as a joint venture of IBM and Sears, is among the largest home networks. As an Internet service company, it provides members with computer access showing available products, which range from airplane reservations to financial services to consumer goods. The viewer can examine detailed descriptions, compare brands, send for free information, or purchase by credit card from home. As an industry leader in Internet shopping transactions, Prodigy operates beyond the United States with networks in Africa, Asia, and Latin America.

electronic shopping Nonstore retailing in which information about the seller's products and services is connected to consumers' computers, allowing consumers to receive the information and purchase the products in the home

- *Direct Selling.* Possibly the oldest form of retailing, **direct selling** is still used by more than 600 U.S. companies that sell door-to-door or through home-selling parties. For example, some of us have attended Tupperware parties at friends' houses.

  Office-to-office direct selling is also common in the wholesaling of such industrial goods as commercial copying equipment. Although direct selling is convenient and gives customers one-on-one attention, prices are usually driven up by labor costs (salespeople often receive commissions of 40 to 50 cents on every sales dollar). Even so, there are about 3.5 million direct salespeople in the United States, 80 percent of whom are women. Worldwide, 9 million direct salespeople now generate annual retail sales of $35 billion. In Japan alone, for instance, 1.2 million distributors have made Amway Corp. second only to Coca-Cola as the most profitable foreign retailer.

direct selling Form of nonstore retailing typified by door-to-door sales

Physical Distribution

Physical distribution refers to the activities needed to move products efficiently from manufacturer to consumer. The goals of physical distribution are to make goods available when and where consumers want them, to keep costs low, and to provide services that keep customers satisfied. Thus, physical distribution includes *warehousing* and *transporting operations.*

physical distribution Activities needed to move a product efficiently from manufacturer to consumer

WAREHOUSING OPERATIONS Storing, or **warehousing,** is a major part of distribution management. In selecting a strategy, managers must keep in mind both the different characteristics and costs of warehousing operations.

warehousing Physical distribution operation concerned with the storage of goods

Types of Warehouses. The two basic types of warehouses are *private* and *public.* Facilities can be further divided according to their use as *storage warehouses* or *distribution centers.*

- *Public and Private Warehouses.* **Private warehouses** are owned and used by a single manufacturer, wholesaler, or retailer. Most are operated by large firms that deal in mass quantities and need storage on a regular basis. J.C. Penney, for example, eases the movement of products to retail stores by maintaining its own warehouses.

  Public warehouses are independently owned and operated. Companies rent only the space they need. Public warehouses are popular with firms that need storage only during peak periods. They are also used by manufacturers needing multiple storage locations to get products to numerous markets.

private warehouse Warehouse owned by and providing storage for a single company

public warehouse Independently owned and operated warehouse that stores goods for many firms

- *Storage Warehouses and Distribution Centers.* **Storage warehouses** provide storage for an extended time. Producers of seasonal items, such as agricultural crops, use this type of warehouse. **Distribution centers** store products whose market demand is both constant and high. They are used by retail chains, wholesalers, and manufacturers that need to break down large quantities of merchandise into the smaller quantities that stores or customers demand.

  Distribution centers are common in the grocery and food industry. Kellogg, for example, stores virtually no products at its plants. Instead, it ships cereals from factories directly to regional distribution centers. As wholesalers place orders for combinations of products, warehouses fill and ship them. Because warehouses are regional, wholesalers receive orders quickly.

storage warehouse Warehouse providing storage for extended periods of time

distribution center Warehouse providing short-term storage of goods for which demand is both constant and high

TRANSPORTATION OPERATIONS The highest cost faced by many companies is the cost of physically moving a product. Thus, cost is a major factor in choosing a transportation method. Firms must also consider several other factors, such as the nature of the product, the distance it must travel, the speed with which it must be received, and customer wants and needs.[18]

Transportation Modes. Figure 12.6 compares the strengths of the major transportation modes: trucks, railroads, planes, water carriers, and pipelines. Not surprisingly, differences in cost are most directly related to delivery speed.

- *Trucks.* The advantages of trucks include flexibility, fast service, and dependability. Nearly all areas of the United States can be reached by truck. Because less breakage occurs than with railroad transport, trucked goods need less packing, which is a major cost savings. Trucks are a particularly good choice for short-distance distribution and for expensive products. They carry more freight than any other form of transport except rail carriers.
- *Railroads.* Railroads have been the backbone of the U.S. transportation system since the late 1800s. Until the 1960s, when trucking firms attracted many of their customers with lower rates, railroads were also fairly profitable. They are now used primarily to transport heavy, bulky items such as cars, steel, and coal. To regain market share, railroads have expanded services to include faster delivery times and piggyback service, in which truck trailers are placed on railcars. This service alone can save shippers up to one-half the cost of shipping by truck.
- *Planes.* Air is the fastest available mode of transportation. Other advantages include much lower costs in handling and packing and unpacking compared with other modes. Inventory carrying costs can also be reduced. Shipments of fresh fish, for example, can be picked up by restaurants each day, thus avoiding the risk of spoilage from packaging and storing. However, air freight is the most expensive form of transportation.

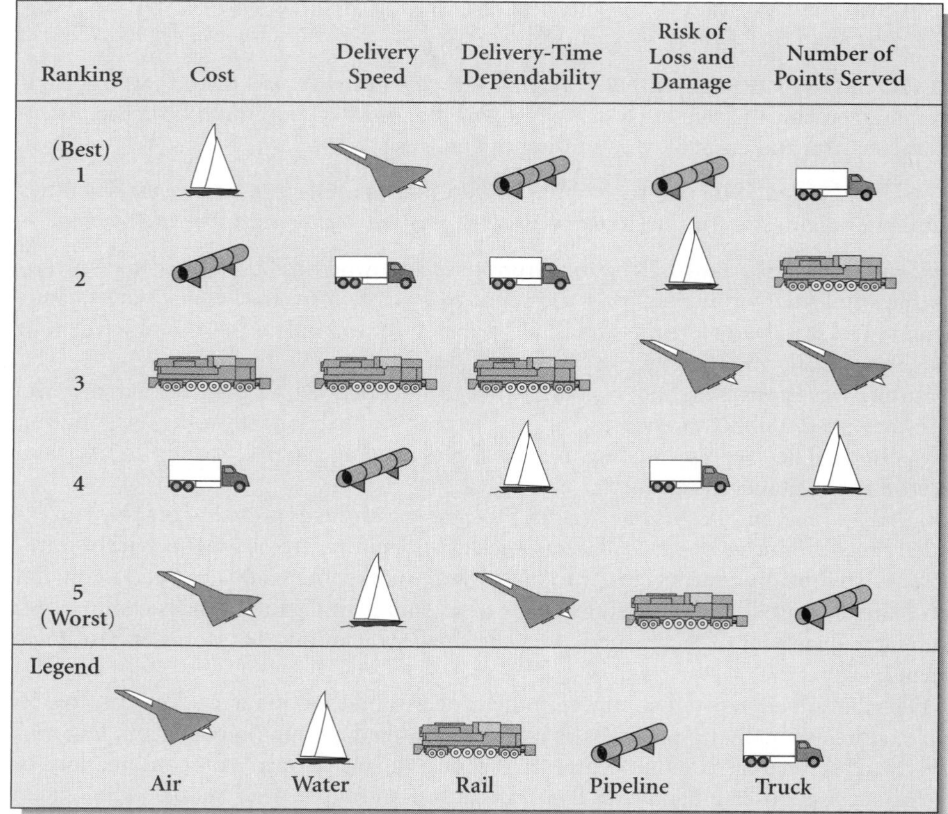

FIGURE 12.6 ◆ **Ranking Modes of Transportation**

- *Water Carriers.* Of all transport modes, water is the least expensive. Modern networks of internal waterways, locks, rivers, and lakes allow water carriers to reach many areas in the United States and throughout the world. Unfortunately, water transport is also the slowest mode. Thus, boats and barges are used mostly for heavy, bulky materials and products (such as sand, gravel, oil, and grain), for which delivery speed is unimportant. Today, companies use water carriers because many ships are now specially constructed to hold large standardized containers.
- *Pipelines.* Like water transportation, pipelines are slow. Used to transport liquids and gases, pipelines are also inflexible. But pipelines do provide a constant flow of products and are unaffected by weather conditions. The Alaska Pipeline, for example, transports oil through Alaska on its route to the lower 48 states. Lack of adaptability to other products makes pipelines an unimportant transportation method for most industries.

Changes in Transportation Operations. For many years, U.S. transport companies specialized in one mode or another. Since deregulation in 1980, however, this pattern has changed. New developments in cost efficiency and competitiveness include intermodal transportation, containerization, and information technology.

INTERMODAL TRANSPORTATION. **Intermodal transportation**—the combined use of different modes of transportation—has come into widespread use. For example, shipping by a combination of air and rail or truck is sometimes called *birdyback* transport. Large railroad companies, such as Burlington Northern and Union Pacific, are thus merging with trucking, air, and shipping lines. The goal is to offer simplified source-to-destination delivery by any necessary combination of methods.

intermodal transportation
Combined use of several different modes of transportation

CONTAINERIZATION. To make intermodal transport more efficient, **containerization** uses standardized heavy-duty containers in which many items are sealed at points of shipment and opened only at final destinations. On the trip, containers may be loaded onto ships for ocean transit, transferred onto trucks, loaded onto railcars (piggyback service), and delivered to final destinations by other trucks. Sealed containers are then unloaded and returned for future use.

containerization
Transportation method in which goods are sealed in containers at shipping sources and opened when they reach final destinations

INFORMATION TECHNOLOGY. Up-to-the-minute information about the location and progress of in-transit shipments can be just as important as the method of transportation. American President Cos., a large U.S.-based steamship and train operator, uses a high-tech computer system to monitor and guide transportation shipments for customers throughout the world. For example, containers of toys bound for Toys "R" Us are tracked from suppliers in Asia until they reach regional distribution centers in the United States. APC keeps Toys "R" Us headquarters informed electronically on where every container is and what's in it; they know as much as 2 weeks in advance what product types, sizes, and colors are in each container and what their exact destinations are, and they are advised of potential delays. This enables the toy company to reorder missing products or divert cargo from one destination to another to keep store shelves adequately stocked.

DISTRIBUTION AS A MARKETING STRATEGY Distribution is an increasingly important way of competing for sales. Instead of just offering advantages in product features and quality, price, and promotion, many firms have turned to distribution as a cornerstone of their business strategies. This approach means assessing and improving the entire stream of activities (wholesaling, warehousing, and transportation) involved in getting products to customers. Its importance is illustrated at Molex, a large manufacturer of electronic connectors and switches. The firm's 100,000 products are used by manufacturers of cars, computers, and consumer products who not only want fast, just-in-time delivery but who are becoming more and more globalized. To meet its customers' needs, Molex became the first connector manufacturer to sign distribution agreements on a global basis. Its relationships with Arrow Electronics and Avnet, the world's largest distributors of electronic components, allow Molex to better service customers who want a single worldwide source for their products.

Continued from page 293

The Rationale of Alienating Traditional Partners

Even though the Internet may be the most effective sales tool since the telephone, it also has the potential to throw a monkey wrench into traditional sales and distribution channels. Naturally, this prospect worries marketers who are aware that traditional methods, which rely on armies of sales representatives and retail partners, still account for at least 90 percent of most companies' orders.

Granted, on-line selling eliminates paperwork and sales commissions and can potentially reduce costs by as much as 15 percent. These savings, however, come out of the pockets of sales reps and distributors, many of whom wonder if they will survive the cybernetic future. As a result, companies wanting to maintain their current sales and distribution networks while simultaneously venturing onto the Web find themselves walking on egg shells. "In some cases," reports one business journalist, companies are "launching Web commerce sites with no publicity or limited merchandise offerings. In other cases, [they are] keeping online prices high, so traditional vendors can lead the way in offering discounts. Some manufacturers are even trying to placate dealers and salespeople with a cut of each Internet sale, regardless of whether they played a role in generating it."

Software maker Intuit Inc., wary of alienating its traditional distribution network by discounting Quicken, TurboTax, and other software programs on the Web, is leaving discounting to the retailers who are responsible for most of its sales. "We could decide to market aggressively on the Web," explains CEO William Harris, "but we don't do that in deference to our third-party resellers." Marketers at 3M Corp. also see the danger of Web-based selling and use the Web for promotion only, not for sales. Although the company's Web site lists hundreds of 3M products, it posts no order form—a policy that suits the traditional distribution network just fine. "We are very concerned about our distribution-channel structure," says a 3M Internet specialist. "We take care not to damage those relationships." In any case, most on-line orders would be relatively small by comparison with those brought in through current distributors (whereas a consumer might order a box of 10 floppy disks, a retailer like Staples will order in bulk). Obviously, 3M is also acting in its own economic best interest.

Meanwhile, however, other companies are moving rapidly into on-line discounting, despite the impact on traditional channels. When Compaq began selling computers at discounted prices on the Web, dealers saw a dramatic sales drop. "It's taking a chunk out of our business," admits Richard Wong, head of San Francisco–based Sefco Computers Inc. "We still have people ask us for bids on small business installations, but we don't win the orders anymore." The reason, says Wong, is pricing: Compaq's on-line site sells each machine for about $50 less than companies like Sefco can afford to sell them.

As the Internet becomes more sophisticated and its use more widespread, companies that are now resisting on-line sales and distribution may be forced to find ways of keeping traditional network members happy as they move onto the Web. "We'll learn as we go," says James Cyrier, head of medical sales and marketing for Hewlett-Packard. His hospital customers want the convenience of on-line shopping, but what does Cyrier do with the 500 HP sales reps and distributors who bring in more than $1 billion a year worldwide? There are no easy answers.

Questions for Discussion

1. What do you think of rational marketing as an approach to reaching Internet consumers?
2. Why is it necessary for marketers to introduce Internet sites on television and other media? Can marketers plan promotional strategies for one medium without considering others?
3. Why are sales representatives so concerned about Web-based marketing? Do you agree or disagree with their concerns? Explain.
4. Do you envision a changing role for direct mail in this era of on-line marketing? How do you think direct mail will be used in this new environment?
5. Argue for or against this statement: *Marketers will* always *look to traditional sales and distribution channels for the bulk of their orders.*
6. How do you think the Web will change the sale and distribution of consumer products? Of industrial products?

SUMMARY

1. **Identify the important objectives of *promotion* and discuss the considerations entailed in selecting a *promotional mix*.** Although the ultimate goal of a *promotion* is to increase sales, other goals include *communicating information, positioning a product, adding value,* and *controlling sales volume.* In deciding on the appropriate promotional mix, marketers must consider the good or service being offered, characteristics of the target audience and the buyer's decision process, and the promotional mix budget.

2. **Describe the key *advertising media* available to marketing managers.** Advertising managers may use various *advertising media,* or specific communication devices, for transmitting a seller's message to potential buyers. The most common media—*newspapers, television, direct mail, radio, magazines, outdoor advertising,* and, increasingly, the *Internet*—differ in their cost and their ability to segment target markets. The combination of media that a company chooses is called its *media mix.*

3. **Outline the tasks involved in *personal selling,* describe the various types of *sales promotions,* and explain the uses of *publicity* and *public relations.*** Personal selling tasks include *order processing, creative selling* (activities that help persuade buyers), and *missionary selling* (activities that promote firms and products rather than simply close sales).

   Coupons are a type of *sales promotion* that provide savings off the regular price of a product. *Point-of-purchase (POP) displays* are intended to grab attention and help customers find products in stores. *Purchasing incentives* include samples (which let customers try products without buying them) and *premiums* (rewards for buying products). At *trade shows,* sellers rent booths to display products to customers who already have an interest in buying. Contests are intended to increase sales by stimulating buyers' interest in products.

   Publicity—general mass-media information about a company or product—differs from other types of promotions in being free (though often uncontrollable). It is useful in ensuring the broad dissemination of a message. *Public relations* is company-influenced publicity whose purpose is to build good relations with the public and to deal with unfavorable events.

4. **Identify the different *channels of distribution.*** The first four *channels of distribution* are aimed at getting products to consumers, and the last two are aimed at getting products to industrial customers. Channel 1 involves direct sales to consumers. Channel 2 includes a *retailer.* Channel 3 involves both a retailer and a *wholesaler,* and channel 4 includes an *agent* or *broker* who enters the system before the wholesaler and retailer. Channel 5 involves a direct sale to an industrial user. Channel 6, which is used infrequently, entails selling to industrial users through wholesalers.

5. **Identify the different types of *retail stores.*** Retailers can be described according to two classifications: product line retailers and bargain retailers. *Product line retailers* include *department stores, supermarkets, hypermarkets,* and *specialty stores. Bargain retailers* include *discount houses, off-price stores, catalog showrooms, factory outlets, warehouse clubs,* and *convenience stores.* These retailers differ in terms of size, goods and services offered, and pricing. Some retailing also takes place without stores. Nonstore retailing may use direct mail catalogs, vending machines, video marketing, telemarketing, electronic shopping, and direct selling.

6. **Compare the five basic forms of *transportation.*** *Trucks, railroads, planes, water carriers* (boats and barges), and *pipelines* are the major transportation modes used in the distribution process. They differ in cost, availability, reliability, speed, and number of points served. Air is the fastest but most expensive mode; water carriers are the slowest but least expensive. Since transport companies were deregulated in 1980, they have become more cost efficient and competitive by developing such innovations as *intermodal transportation* and *containerization.*

QUESTIONS AND EXERCISES

QUESTIONS FOR REVIEW

1. What are the differences between push and pull strategies? Why would a firm choose one over the other?
2. What are the advantages of personal selling over other promotional tools?
3. Is publicity more or less available to small firms than to larger firms? Why?
4. From the manufacturer's point of view, what are the advantages and disadvantages of using intermediaries to distribute products? From the end user's point of view?
5. Identify the six channels of distribution. In what key ways do the four channels used for consumer products differ from the two channels used for industrial products?

QUESTIONS FOR ANALYSIS

6. Take a look at some of the advertising conducted by locally based businesses in your area. Choose two campaigns: one that you think is effective and one that you think is ineffective. What differences in the campaigns make one better than the other?
7. Select a good or a service that you have purchased recently. Try to retrace the relevant steps in the buyer decision process as you experienced it. Which steps were most important to you? Least important?
8. Give examples of five products that typify the sort of products sold by video shopping networks. Explain why this form of nonstore retailing is effective for each of these different products.

APPLICATION EXERCISES

9. Select a product that is sold nationally. Identify as many media used in its promotion as you can. Which medium is used most? On the whole, do you think the campaign is effective? Why or why not?
10. Interview the manager of a local manufacturing firm. Identify the firm's distribution strategy and the channels of distribution that it uses. Where applicable, describe the types of wholesalers or retail stores used to distribute the firm's products.

BUILDING YOUR BUSINESS SKILLS

ARE YOU SOLD ON THE NET?

This exercise enhances the following SCANS workplace competencies: demonstrating basic skills, demonstrating thinking skills, exhibiting interpersonal skills, and working with information.

▼ GOAL

To encourage students to consider the value of on-line retailing as an element in a company's distribution system.

▼ SITUATION

As the distribution manager of a privately owned clothing manufacturer that specializes in camping gear and outdoor clothing, you are convinced that your product line is perfect for on-line distribution. The owner of the company, however, is reluctant to expand distribution from a successful network of retail stores and a catalog operation. Your challenge is to convince the boss that retailing via the Internet can boost sales.

▼ METHOD

STEP 1

Join with four or five classmates to research the advantages and disadvantages of an on-line distribution system for your company. Among the factors to consider are the following:

- The likelihood that target consumers are Internet shoppers. Camping gear is generally purchased by young, affluent consumers who are comfortable with the Web.
- The industry trend to on-line distribution. Are similar companies doing it? Have they been successful?
- The opportunity to expand inventory without increasing the cost of retail space or catalog production and mailing charges.
- The opportunity to have a store that never closes.
- The lack of trust many people have about doing business on the Web. Many consumers are reluctant to provide credit card data on the Web.
- The difficulty electronic shoppers have in finding a Web site when they do not know the store's name.
- The frustration and waiting time involved in Web searches.
- The certainty that the site will not reach consumers who do not use computers or who are uncomfortable with the Web.

STEP 2

Based on your findings, write a persuasive memo to the company's owner stating your position about expanding to an on-line distribution system. Include information that will counter expected objections.

▼ FOLLOW-UP QUESTIONS

1. What place does on-line distribution have in the distribution network of this company?
2. In your view, is on-line distribution the wave of the future? Is it likely to increase in importance as a distribution system for apparel companies? Why or why not?

CRAFTING YOUR BUSINESS PLAN

HITTING THE SAUCE CUSTOMER

▼ THE PURPOSE OF THE ASSIGNMENT

1. To acquaint students with the process of navigating the Business PlanPro (BPP) software package.
2. To familiarize students with promotion- and distribution-related issues that a sample firm must address in developing its business plan.
3. To demonstrate how four chapter topics—promotional strategy, product positioning, channels of distribution, and personal selling—can be integrated as components of the BPP planning environment.

(continued)

▼ ASSIGNMENT

After reading Chapter 12 in the textbook, open the BPP software and look around for information about product promotion and distribution as it applies to a sample firm: Salvadors Sauces Food Dis. Then, respond to the following questions:*

1. As we saw in Chapter 12, product positioning is an important promotional objective. What are Salvadors Sauces' plans for positioning its products? [Sites to see in BPP (for this assignment): In the Task Manager screen, click on **Your Market.** Then click on **2. Market Segmentation.** After returning to the Task Manager screen, click on **The Business You're In.** Then click on each of the following in turn: **3. Distribution Patterns** and **4. Factors of Competition.** After returning to the Task Manager screen, click once again on **The Business You're In; *then click on*** **2. Industry Participants.** After again returning to the Task Manager screen, click on **Your Marketing Plan;** then click on **4. Specific Marketing Programs.**]
2. Describe Salvadors Sauces' promotional strategy. [Sites to see in BPP: In the Task Manager screen, click on **Your Sales Forecast.** Then click on **1. Promotion Strategy**. From the Task Manager screen, click on **The Business You're In** and then click on each of the following in turn: **3. Distribution Patterns** and **4. Factors of Competition.**]
3. Which channels of distribution does Salvadors Sauces plan to use? Can you suggest alternative channels that might improve the company's market position? [Sites to see in BPP: In the Task Manager screen, click on **Your Market.** Then click on each of the following in turn: **1. Summary and Introduction** and **2. Market Segmentation.** After returning to the Task Manager screen, click on **Initial Assessment;** then click on **6. Potential Customers.** After returning once again to the Task Manager screen, click on **Your Sales Forecast** and then on **6. Sales Programs.** Again from the Task Manager screen, click on **Your Marketing Plan;** then click on **3. Marketing Strategy Summary.** Returning again to the Task Manager screen, click on **Finish and Polish** and then click on **5. Strategic Alliances.** Finally, after returning one last time to the Task Manager screen, click on **Financial Plan** and then on **1. Financial Plan Summary.**]
4. What role does personal selling play in the promotional plans at Salvadors Sauces? Who will do the personal selling? Are these individuals qualified for the role? [Sites to see in BPP: In the Task Manager screen, click on **Your Sales Forecast.** Then click on each of the following in turn: **1. Sales Strategy** and **6. Sales Programs.** Return to the Task Manager screen and click on **Your Management Team.** Then click on each of the following in turn: **1. Management Summary** and **3. Management Team.**]

▼ FOR YOUR OWN BUSINESS PLAN

5. Consider the channels of distribution that could be used by the company for which your business plan is being developed. Explain how your choices of distribution channels might be appropriately presented in each of the following BPP sections: **Your Market** and **Your Marketing Plan.** In which section(s) of the document will you present your plans for channels of distribution?

▼ *GENERAL TIPS FOR NAVIGATING IN BPP

1. Open the BPP program, observe the Welcome screen, and click on **Open a Sample Plan.**
2. From the Open a Sample Plan dialogue box, click on a sample company name; then click on **Open.**
3. On the Task Manager screen, click onto any of the lines (for example, **Your Company**).

4. You can always return to the Task Manager screen by going to the bottom of the screen and clicking on the **Task Manager** icon.
5. When you are finished with a sample company, close its Task Manager screen.
6. After finishing with one sample company, you can get to the next one by going to the top of the screen and clicking on **File** (on the menu bar). Then beneath that, select **Open Sample Plan.** This will exit you from the current company file and send you to the Open a Sample Plan dialogue box, where you can select your next sample company.

EXPLORING THE NET

ARE YOU QUALIFIED?

To find out what some real-world companies would like you to know about their human resources policies and programs, log on to the following two Web sites:

- United Airlines, Flight Attendant Career Information:

  http://www.ualfltctr.com/docs/sw.html

- McDonald's, Careers:

  http://www.mcdonalds.com.

After you have read the material posted by these two companies, consider the following questions:

1. Do you qualify in terms of "Education/Work Experience" to apply to United's Flight Attendant training program? If you have had work experience that you consider relevant to United's "Work Experience" description, why do you think it would be an asset?
2. What part of United's training program do you think would be most challenging to you? Why?
3. What part of a flight attendant's job do you think you would enjoy the most? The least? Why?
4. Which of the skills listed by McDonald's would you list under your own strong points? Under your weak points? Which one or two skills do you think you need to focus on most conscientiously?
5. Why do you think McDonald's puts so much emphasis on career advancement within the company? Why does it put so much emphasis on the awards earned by the company's training program? In what respects are these important criteria for you?
6. What do you think the word *opportunities* should mean in a slogan like "McDonald's Means Opportunities"?

VIDEO EXERCISE 4.1

Showtime Channels Its Marketing Efforts

Learning Objectives

The purpose of this video is to help you

1. Understand the different marketing channels that businesses use.
2. Appreciate the role of public relations in marketing.

Background Information

Showtime spends considerable money and energy promoting its brand name and offerings. In a market of extreme competition, Showtime attempts to position itself as a network with premium programming available nowhere else. One way Showtime promotes itself is through its Web site, which allows viewers to provide feedback over the Internet. The site provides information about the company and its offerings while promoting the Showtime name and programs. Showtime also uses public relations as a means of promotion, which, it claims, has been 10 times more effective than its other promotional efforts.

The Video

Showtime is in many ways a marketing company, using different methods to talk about its products and services. This video provides an excellent example of how a focused public relations campaign can be an effective form of marketing. The choice of marketing channels can vary dramatically among businesses and across industries. In fact, businesses in the same industry often pursue different marketing strategies.

Discussion Questions

1. What are some of the keys to identifying a market?
2. Why is it so important to have an effective marketing strategy?
3. What are some of the keys to an effective marketing strategy?
4. What are some of the external factors that influence a company's marketing plan?

Follow-Up Assignment

Coke and Pepsi offer similar products but the companies have differing marketing strategies. Evaluate the marketing strategies of Coke and Pepsi. How would you describe each marketing strategy? What slogans do Coke and Pepsi currently use? Have their marketing strategies changed over time? Does each make sense? In your opinion, is one better than the other?

For Further Exploration

Go to Showtime's Web site

http://www.showtimeonline.com/

Examine Showtime's multifaceted approach to marketing. Take a specific look at its "Pick-A-Flick" contest. How does it work? Why do you think the company is running it?

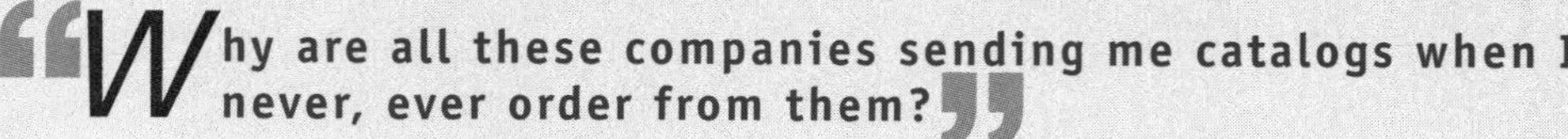

S.C.R.U.B.S.

"Why are all these companies sending me catalogs when I never, ever order from them?"

—*Lament of an average American consumer*

Learning Objectives

The purpose of this video exercise is to help you

1. Understand that *timing* is often the secret of success for a new business.
2. Realize that some very successful businesses started almost as a "hobby."
3. Become aware that a key decision when starting up a business is whether to add a partner.

Background Information

What is a *scrub?* It is the garment many workers in the health care industry wear. You've seen them in hospitals, and they are usually green, pale blue, or white. Well, Sue Callaway, a registered nurse, came to work one day wearing a scrub sewn from a flowery print, and her coworkers wanted one just like it. And so **S.C.R.U.B.S.**—which stands for Simply Comfortable Really Unique Basic Scrubs—was born.

Sue Callaway points out that she made these attractive new scrubs out of 100 percent cotton denim (rather than the polyester that hospitals use) for her colleagues for about 2 years before it dawned on her and her husband, Rocky, that this could be a *business.* "I was not in it for the money," Sue says. "I had nursing as my source of income." Nonetheless, as they moved into business, Sue and Rocky talked to Steve Epstein, a "business mind" who knew the garment industry. Other entrepreneurs featured in this videotape series will tell you that they were hesitant about—or absolutely opposed to—bringing in a partner. Why share the dream with other people? But Sue and Rocky were more than willing to bring in someone who knew the business.

The early years of the business were not smooth sailing. Rocky relates that he and Sue pushed their credit cards to the limit and borrowed from friends and family. There were times, he says, when the firm was "up to the edge," and the creators of **S.C.R.U.B.S.** wondered if the firm could last another month. But business always took a turn for the better.

The firm's computer programming analyst is interviewed, and we see two very important areas he must control on an almost minute-by-minute basis: customer orders and inventory. To handle his job, he says, "I am constantly developing new software." Of course, a firm wants to process a customer's order quickly, but processing an order for an item no longer in stock is wasteful and embarrassing. Controlling inventory closely is clearly a necessity. Hattie Bryant and Sue Callaway also discuss the costs of refilling an order when customers return merchandise.

The Video

Small Business 2000 Master Class, SB2000 Program #404.

Many business ventures—large and small—take years of planning. But that is not always the case. This video shows you that **S.C.R.U.B.S.** hero Sue Callaway started it all by making just *one* scrub in a flowery print for just *one* fellow employee. How that one garment evolved into a major company is what this tape covers.

Discussion Questions

1. Do you think that Sue and Rocky were wise to bring in Steve Epstein as a partner? Why or why not?
2. Consider Sue Callaway, who would love to sew scrubs for her friends. But now she's running an entire business, and no sewing takes place at the firm's Southern California headquarters. All the sewing is outsourced. What is your reaction to this situation?
3. Consider the closing thought on the videotape regarding a manager's need for a "tolerance for ambiguity." Explain what this concept means to you.
4. If a manager says to you, "I have a tolerance for ambiguity," does this mean that this manager is an unsure leader who does a poor job of directing workers and easily accepts sloppy work? Why or why not?
5. Prepare a brief statement on how the garment industry has changed, because disease may spread through dirty hands.
6. What seems to be the secret **S.C.R.U.B.S.** discovered for not wasting money by sending catalogs to everyone?
7. Explain why the computer programming analyst is so important to **S.C.R.U.B.S.**
8. Evaluate this statement made by a firm in a business similar to that of **S.C.R.U.B.S.** "We have a rather strict policy on returning of merchandise. Quite frankly, this return jazz is costing us too much!"
9. Explain the stance **S.C.R.U.B.S.** takes on the return of merchandise.

Follow-Up Assignment

The video explains that **S.C.R.U.B.S.** handles its sewing through *outsourcing*. Your assignment is to find out more about this term. Head for the library on your campus, talk to businesspeople, or ask any business professor. And while you're investigating *outsourcing*, you might look into *temporary employees* and *part-time employees*. These three phenomena are becoming more and more visible on the American business landscape, and they could well affect your employment opportunities—if they have not already. Look for positive and negative features of these three ways of handling business. They will continue to generate arguments between management and workers.

The Internet Connection and One Last Thing to Remember

You can contact **S.C.R.U.B.S.** on the Internet at

http://www.1scrubs.com

When most of us check our mailboxes, we ask: "Why are all these companies sending me catalogs when I never, ever order from them?" The catalog specialist at **S.C.R.U.B.S.** makes it clear that here is one firm that sends out catalogs in a logical and sensible manner. In short, sending a catalog to a customer who orders frequently is a high priority, while less important is sending a catalog to the occasional customer. And this firm does the research to determine just who is a frequent customer and who is not.

MANAGING OPERATIONS AND INFORMATION

The Millennium Bomb

Picture the ball dropping in New York City's Times Square on December 31, 1998, as millions celebrate the start of the last year of the twentieth century. Then picture thousands of weary technology and information managers who watch with a mixture of fear and dread. Are they Scrooges with little party spirit? It's possible. But it's more likely that they are preoccupied with the most serious and universal technology problem to hit business: getting the world's computers ready for the millennium, just 365 days away.

Facing these experts is a glitch that will wreak havoc on every aspect of business that operates via computer unless it is fixed in time. The problem goes by many names (the year 2000 bug, the millennium bomb, the Y2K problem) and will cost government, business, and individuals as much as $600 billion to repair (about $1 to $2 for every line of computer code). The federal government alone will spend at least $4 billion, Chase Manhattan Bank $250 million, Prudential Insurance $110 million, and FedEx $75 million.

WHY MM/DD/YY IS A PROBLEM

The seeds of the millennium bomb were planted in the 1970s when the computer industry was still in its infancy and when a megabyte of computer memory cost $600,000, as compared with 10 cents today. To control costs, programmers limited dates to only six spaces: two for the month, two for the day, and two for the year (MM/DD/YY). This system works well for months and days, but with only two digits rather than four to represent the year, the computer cannot handle the switch from the twentieth to the twenty-first century.

"The problem is that the computer doesn't interpret '00' as the year 2000 but rather 1900, and miscalculates all computations accordingly," explains Gary Fisher, a computer scientist with the Commerce Department's National Institute of Standards and Technology. This problem appears in mainframe computers and in the computer chips that control everything from ATMs to security systems.

How will this affect business? Examples of problems that have already surfaced tell a story of what lies ahead for companies that fail to find a workable solution:

- At a gourmet food store in Warren, Michigan, a customer tried to pay his bill with a credit card that expired in 2000. The simple act of swiping the card through the system caused the store's 10 computerized cash registers to lock shut for half a day.

- At Delta, American, and other airlines, problems associated with Y2K began in the mid-1990s, when maintenance cycles, pension programs, and even extended leaves of absence were being scheduled.
- When in 1997 a municipal sewage treatment plant tested Y2K changes, the fix failed and raw sewage spilled into a harbor, according to computer directions.

The year 2000 problem affects manufacturing and service companies that do long-term budget and production planning. At Reebok, the Massachusetts-based athletic shoe manufacturer, the year 2000 problem showed up when the company began its 18-month planning horizon on apparel and footwear. Banks, accounting firms, and other financial institutions may encounter automated computer backup routines that will overwrite new files with older, outdated information.

DEFINING THE PROBLEM

Most companies have gotten the message that if they ignore the problem, their computer systems may shut down or produce incorrect data that infect other systems. Sears, one of the country's retailing giants, has divided the problem into three parts.

The problem "is to bring the applications systems up to compliance level as well as the systems software that we have within our organization," explains chief information officer Joe Smialowski. "The second area is tougher to tackle: all those desktop applications we've all built . . . whether they be spreadsheets or data-base or word-processing applications. . . . In some cases, they are important to running the day-to-day business. We are focusing heavily on this area now.

"The third area concerns our suppliers, both merchandise suppliers and service providers. Hopefully, they're working toward compliance also. We have an active certification program that is under way that determines whether our suppliers are making the right level of progress on year 2000 compliance. Having a real year 2000 plan and being able to demonstrate it to our company is a condition to continue to do business with Sears. If you [can't do it], your business is at risk with Sears."

Computer analysts in other industries see the problem in the same way. Debbie Freedman, vice president of American Airlines' Sabre system, is particularly concerned about desktop PCs. "Imagine the impact when the simple little PC package purchased by the local office to produce monthly sales statistics suddenly fails or provides wrong information." Worse yet, the information technology department has no centralized control over these PCs.

> **"Imagine the impact when the simple little PC package purchased by the local office to produce monthly sales statistics suddenly fails or provides wrong information."**
>
> —Debbie Freedman
>
> *Vice President, American Airlines' Sabre system*

FIXING THE PROBLEM

In 1996, the International Air Transport Association established a Year 2000 Group (Y2KG) to coordinate efforts within the industry to solve the year 2000 problem on time. The group has defined seven steps to remedy the problem. These steps apply to other industries as well.

- *Recognize the problem.* This requires that everyone in an organization as well as clients, vendors, and even government officials acknowledge the problem and its deadline.
- *Inventory all software, hardware, and ancillary equipment run by computer chips.* In the case of the airline industry, that includes runway lights, which are operated with a computerized clock, security and access systems, and ticket machines.
- *Study options and risks.* This involves establishing a budget and prioritizing so that critical computer functions are handled first.
- *Plan the project.* Detailed plans and budgets are essential to meet the deadline, as is the development of controls to identify and correct problems that arise along the way.
- *Make the changes.* This phase is time consuming and requires a supply of trained computer programmers. According to Y2KG, the problems that are likely to arise at this stage include "missing or out-of-date documentation, lack of resources skilled in older technologies, and lack of knowledge of a system, especially the special 'fixes' that have been implemented over the years."
- *Test the fixes.* Experts agree that this will represent more than half of the entire effort because it involves internal systems as well as interactions with vendors, clients, and other business partners.
- *Set up a post-2000 watch.* Thorough testing will not produce a fail-safe system. Companies must expect minor to serious problems in the early months of the new millennium.

The Gartner Group, a market research firm based in Stamford, Connecticut, estimates that half of all businesses will not make the fix in time, creating potential chaos for every computer connected to their systems. Some companies may fail because of the shortage of trained programmers. Aware of this labor shortage, Reebok, Safeway, and other companies are using programmers in India and other developing countries.

To put it mildly, chief information officers are not happy with the millennium bug. They view it as a hurdle they must jump to do business in the twenty-first century. "It's an opportunity," said Office Depot CIO Bill Seltzer, "only if our competitors fail to execute."

WEB LINKS

The following Web sites highlight the Y2K problem. The information in these sites will help you answer the questions that follow.

- **American Institute of Certified Public Accountants**
  http://www.aicpa.org/
- **Apple Products: Mac OS**
  http://www.apple.com/macos/info/2000.html
- **IBM Year 2000 Home Page**
  http://www.ibm.com.IBM/year2000/
- **ITAA (Information Technology Association of America) Year 2000 Home Page**
  http://www.itaa.org/year2000.html
- **Survive 2000**
  http://www.sbhs.com/
- **Year 2000 Date Problem Support Centre**
  http://www.compinfo.co.uk/y2k.html
- **The Year 2000 Information Center/Millennium**
  http://www.year2000.com/
- **Ymark2000**
  http://www.nstl.com/

QUESTIONS FOR DISCUSSION

1. If a manufacturing company fails to fix its Y2K problem in time, how could the millennium bug affect operation processes? If a service company fails to fix its Y2K problem in time, how could the millennium bug affect operation processes?
2. How could the integrity and operation of a company's accounting system be affected by the Y2K problem? Why do you think the AICPA Web site pays so much attention to this issue?
3. Federal regulators are worried that some community banks and credit unions are not doing enough to handle their Y2K risk. As a chief financial officer, what steps would you take to safeguard the corporate accounting system if company assets were held by these institutions?
4. Some Y2K experts see the problem as an opportunity to upgrade a company's computer system. Considering what you learned in this case and on the Web links, do you consider this a feasible solution?
5. How are word-processing programs, spreadsheets, and database management programs at risk from this problem? In what ways are users' concerns reflected on the IBM and Apple Web sites?
6. Consider this statement: Managing the Y2K problem is a quality control issue. Do you agree or disagree? Explain your answer.

CHAPTER 13

*M*ANAGING *P*RODUCTION AND *I*MPROVING *Q*UALITY

A High-Concept Story about Bad Food

Remember when Demi Moore, Bruce Willis, Arnold Schwarzenegger, and Whoopi Goldberg were top box-office draws in Hollywood? If so, you undoubtedly remember when Planet Hollywood, the theme restaurant chain they helped start, was the hottest dinner ticket in town—the place to see and be seen if you wanted to partake of Hollywood-style glitz and glamour in any one of 87 locations around the world.

Hollywood fell in love with the idea that beautiful people could seduce diners. So did Wall Street. Build Planet Hollywoods, reasoned investors, and they will come. After all, everyone wants to get close to the stars, whether live or just on giant video screens. Given the chance, they'll wait hours for a table and be grateful for poor service once they get one. Moreover, they'll commemorate the experience with $18 T-shirts.

In the beginning, the buzz was right. Profits at Planet Hollywood took off and the chain built by the stars became the envy of the restaurant business. When the company went public in April 1996, stock analysts compared its brand-name potential to Disney, Nike, and Starbucks. "Strong buy" recommendations pushed the stock price up to $32.13 a share on its first trading day.

Certain that the concept had unlimited expansion potential, chairman and chief executive Robert Earl went on a construction binge. He built Planet Hollywoods in the glamour and tourist capitals of the world, including London, Paris, New York, Las Vegas, and Orlando. He also installed them in places with a bit less glamour—places like the Mall of America in Minneapolis and Gurnee Mills, a factory-outlet center in Illinois.

But then customers began to eat the food and experience the experience. They tried the $6.95 chicken strip appetizer with what *The Wall Street Journal* described as a "glazed-doughnut-over-a-McNugget taste." They looked for Demi and Bruce, Whoopi and Arnold, but of course they were nowhere in sight. They grew tired of squinting at each other through the harsh glare of halogen lights. Finally, they opted for other tourist restaurants in Orlando, Las Vegas, and Baltimore Harbor; after all, there were Planet Hollywoods everywhere, including back home.

"Not a whole lot to it," reported one diner after an evening at the Chicago Planet Hollywood. "I wouldn't make a point of coming back," added another. "The food was bad." The problem was pretty simple: Even a sexy restaurant won't make money without repeat business. By the second quarter of 1998, same-store sales had plummeted 17 percent from the previous year. With revenues in free fall, the company reported a 1997 loss of $1.4 million—versus a profit of $16.3 million a year earlier. Naturally, the stock price dropped, too—to under $4 a share. "This is a story of bad food," explained stock analyst Paul Marsh. "And the stars never came out after the grand openings."

> **"I wouldn't make a point of coming back. The food was bad."**
> —*Customer at Chicago Planet Hollywood*

Industry experts regard the Planet Hollywood story as a business no-brainer; if the chain hopes to survive, it will have to provide a level of quality that does not stand in such stark contrast to its image. It must improve its food

and service, and it must deliver on its implicit promise to furnish something of the Hollywood experience. It must also rethink its location strategies. Like any other business that has lost sight of production and quality controls, Planet Hollywood must return to basics and give customers value for their money. As you will see in this chapter, this is not a simple process. By focusing on the learning objectives of this chapter, you will better understand how complex it can be for producers of both goods and services.

Our opening story is continued on page 351

After reading this chapter, you should be able to:

1. **Identify the characteristics that distinguish *service operations* from *goods production* and explain the main differences in the *service focus*.**
2. **Describe the two ways of *classifying operations processes*.**
3. **Describe the factors involved in *operations planning* and *scheduling*.**
4. **Explain some of the activities involved in *operations control*, including *materials management* and the use of certain *operations control tools*.**
5. **Identify some of the key tools for *total quality management*, including strategies for getting closer to the customer.**

GOODS AND SERVICE OPERATIONS

service operations Business activities that provide tangible and intangible services

goods production Business operations that create tangible products

Everywhere you go today, you encounter business activities that provide goods and services to their customers. You wake up in the morning, for example, to the sound of your favorite radio station. You stop at the corner newsstand for a newspaper on your way to the bus stop, where you catch the bus to work or school. Your instructors, the bus driver, the clerk at the 7-Eleven store, and the morning radio announcer are all examples of people who work in **service operations.** They provide you with tangible and intangible service products, such as entertainment, transportation, education, and food preparation. Firms that make tangible products—radios, newspapers, buses, textbooks—are engaged in **goods production.**

Growth in the Service and Goods Sectors

Although the term *production* has historically referred to companies engaged in goods production, the concept as we now use it embraces services as well as goods. An abundance of necessities and conveniences on which we rely, from fire protection and health care to mail delivery and fast food, are all produced by service operations. Yet many experts admit that it is still hard to describe the economic value of the service sector in quantitative terms.

One problem, according to marketing consultant Fred Reichheld, is the traditional view of the economy. "Most people," charges Reichheld, "still view the world through manufacturing goggles." In other words, management and accounting practices still focus on the financial value of equipment, inventory, and other tangible assets. In the service sector, says Reichheld, the profit and loss statement should reflect such valuable assets as employee brainpower and sensitivity to customer needs.

> **"Most people still view the world through manufacturing goggles."**
>
> —Fred Reichheld
> *Marketing consultant*

In this view, service sector managers should focus less on such manufacturing-centered goals as equipment and technology. Rather, they should stress the human element in their activities, because success or failure depends on contact with the customer during service delivery. The provider's employees—their human resources—who deal directly with their customers affect the customer's feelings about the service. As we will see throughout this chapter, one of the main differences between production and service operations is the customer's involvement in the latter.

Manufacturing industries today still account for about 25 percent of all private sector jobs in the United States—just as they have for the past four decades. Nevertheless, the economic significance of manufacturing activity is rising. For example, real income from manufacturing has been rising steadily, increasing by over 30 percent in the past 10 years. So effective are new manufacturing methods, and so committed are U.S. manufacturers to using them, that in 1999 the United States remained ahead of Germany and Japan in manufactured exports, retaining the number-one spot for the sixth consecutive year.

Naturally, both goods and service industries are important to the economy. However, as you can see from Figures 13.1 and 13.2, services have grown far more rapidly since 1984. For one thing, employment has risen significantly in the service sector while remaining stagnant in goods production (Figure 13.1). In fact, by 1997 employment in private-sector service industries accounted for almost 80 percent of the total U.S. workforce: nearly 98 million jobs. Much of this growth has been in finance, food and retailing, insurance, real estate, and health care. Employment projections indicate that services will re-

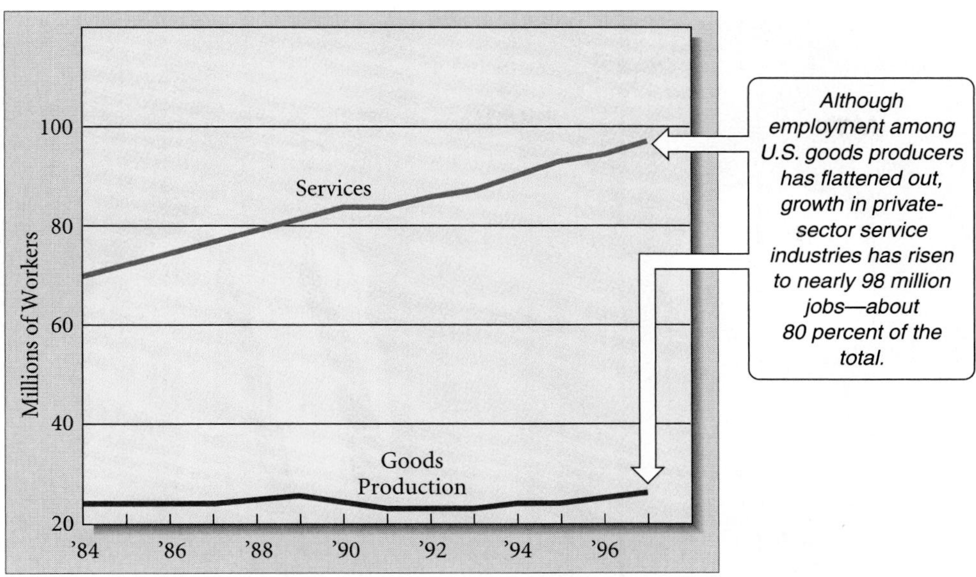

FIGURE 13.1 ◆ Employment in Goods and Service Sectors

main the faster-growing employment source in the immediate future.[1] With this growth, the gap in average wages between the two sectors has closed to just $19 per week more for goods-producing workers. More importantly, however, the distribution of high-paying and low-paying jobs in each sector is now equal.

By 1997, the service sector also provided nearly 55 percent of national income, as opposed to just over 50 percent in 1947. As Figure 13.2 shows, the service sector's share of the U.S. gross domestic product—the value of all the goods and services produced by the economy, excluding foreign income—has climbed since 1984 until it is now nearly 50 percent greater than that of the goods-producing sector. At the same time, the 20 percent of the U.S. workforce in manufacturing produces about 40 percent of the nation's GDP.[2] In China, by contrast, manufacturing employs 70 percent of the urban labor force but produces only 30 percent of the country's national income.[3]

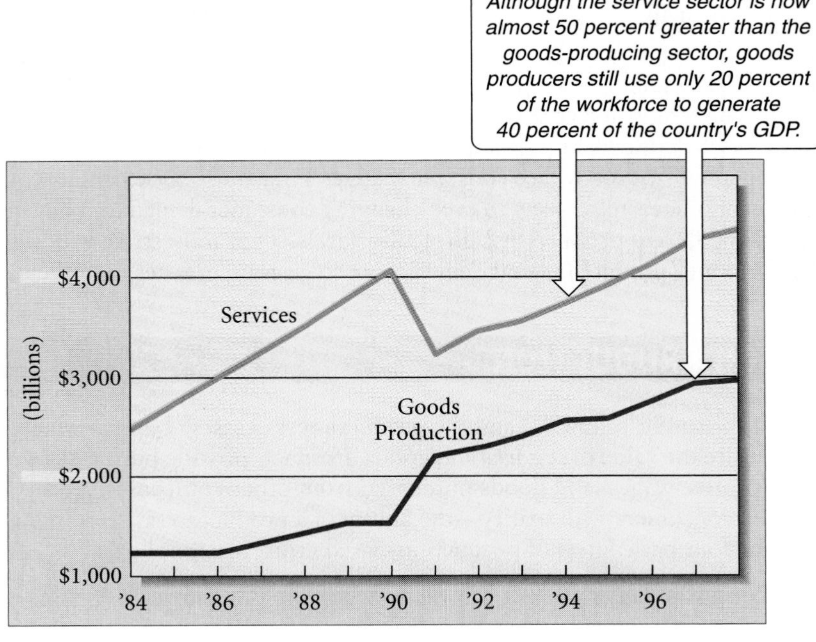

FIGURE 13.2 ◆ GDP from Goods and Services

Thomas O'Gara (left) runs an Ohio-based company that makes bulletproof, bombproof limousines. Jules B. Kroll is the founder of Kroll Associates, the world's leading business investigations firm. When they decided to combine forces as Kroll-O'Gara, they strengthened their respective hands in an industry—corporate and personal security—that includes both manufacturing (armored cars, satellite telephone kits, and other James Bond–like hardware) and services (security guards and antiterrorist driving lessons).

Remember that although companies are often classified as either goods producers or service providers, the distinction is often blurred. For one thing, all businesses are service operations to some extent. Consider Johnson Controls, a Milwaukee manufacturer of electronic controls for heating and cooling systems in schools, hospitals, and commercial buildings. Although Johnson has been making tangible products since 1883, it has prospered since 1989 in a brand-new but related area: It manages the lighting, security, and cleaning operations of office buildings. "It's a market worth tens of billions of dollars in the U.S. alone," says vice president Terry Weaver.

The Growth of Global Operations

Many countries have joined in the global competition that has reshaped production into a fast-paced, challenging business activity. Although the factory remains the centerpiece for manufacturing, it is virtually unrecognizable when compared with its counterpart of even just a decade ago. The smoke, grease, and danger have been replaced in many companies by glistening high-tech machines, computers, and "clean rooms" that are contaminant-free and carefully controlled for temperature. Instead of the need to maintain continuous mass production, firms today face constant change. They must, for example, constantly develop new technologies to respond to ever-changing consumer demands. They must produce varieties of different products at high-quality levels. They must strive to design new products, get them into production, and deliver them to customers faster than their competitors.

CREATING VALUE THROUGH PRODUCTION

Not surprisingly, to understand the production processes of a firm we need to know how to measure the value of services and goods. Products provide businesses with economic results: profits, wages, and goods purchased from other companies. At the same time, they provide consumers with **utility**—the ability of a product to satisfy a human want.

utility A product's ability to satisfy a human want

The four basic kinds of production-based utility are as follows:

- When a company turns out ornaments in time for Christmas, it creates *time utility;* that is, it makes products available when consumers want them.

- When a department store opens its annual Trim-a-Tree department, it creates *place utility:* It makes products available where they are convenient for consumers.
- By making a product available for consumers to own and use, production creates *ownership* or *possession utility*, which customers enjoy when they buy boxes of ornaments and decorate their trees.
- Above all, production makes products available in the first place: By turning raw materials into finished goods, production creates *form utility*, as when an ornament maker combines glass, plastic, and other materials to create tree decorations.

Because the term *production* was historically associated just with manufacturing, writers have recently replaced it with *operations*, a term that reflects both service and goods production. **Operations** (or **production**) **management** is the systematic direction and control of the processes that transform resources into finished services and goods. Thus, operations (or production) managers are ultimately responsible for creating utility for customers.

operations (or production) management Systematic direction and control of the processes that transform resources into finished products

As Figure 13.3 shows, **operations managers** must draw up plans to transform resources into products. First, of course, they must bring together basic resources: knowledge, physical materials, equipment, and labor. Naturally, they must put those resources to effective use in the production facility. As demand for a product increases, managers must schedule and control work to produce the required amounts of products. Finally, they must also control costs, quality levels, inventory, and facilities and equipment.

operations managers Managers responsible for production, inventory, and quality control

Although some production managers work in factories, others work in large and small offices and retail stores ranging from giant discount outlets to specialty shops. Farmers are also operations managers. They create utility by transforming soil, seeds, fuel, and other inputs into soybeans, milk, and other outputs. As production managers, they may employ crews of workers to plant and harvest. Or they may opt for automated machinery or some combination of workers and machinery. Naturally, these decisions affect costs, the role of buildings and equipment in their operations, and the quality and quantity of goods that they produce.

Operations Processes

An **operations process** is a set of methods and technologies used in the production of a good or a service. We classify various types of production according to differences in their operations processes. We can describe goods by the kind of transformation technology required to produce them. As we will see, we can describe services according to the extent of customer contact required.

operations process Set of methods and technologies used in the production of a good or service

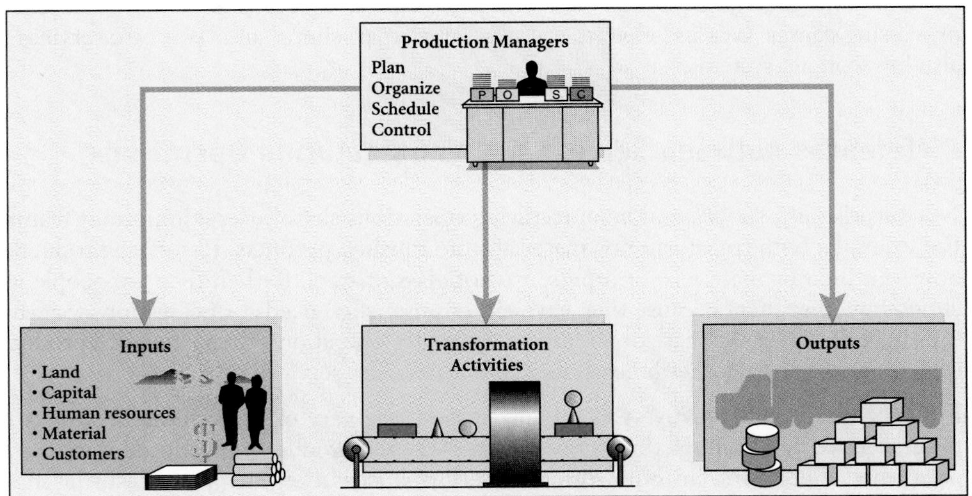

FIGURE 13.3 ◆ Transformation Process

TYPES OF GOODS MANUFACTURING Whether an independent businessperson or an employee of a multinational manufacturer, a production manager must control the process by which goods are produced. As defined, an operations process is the set of methods and technologies used in the production of a good or a service. All manufacturing processes can be classified by the type of *transformation technology* used during transformation.

Transformation Technology. Manufacturers use the following types of transformation processes to turn raw materials into finished goods:

In *chemical processes,* raw materials are chemically altered. Such techniques are common in the aluminum, steel, fertilizer, petroleum, and paint industries.

Fabrication processes mechanically alter the basic shape or form of a product. Fabrication occurs in the metal-forming, woodworking, and textile industries.

Assembly processes put together various components. These techniques are common in the electronics, appliance, and automotive industries.

In *transport processes,* goods acquire place utility by being moved from one location to another. For example, bicycles are routinely moved by trucks from manufacturing plants to consumers through warehouses and discount stores.

Clerical processes transform information. Combining data on employee absences and machine breakdowns into a productivity report is a clerical process, as is compiling inventory reports at a retail outlet.

TYPES OF SERVICE PROCESSES: EXTENT OF CUSTOMER CONTACT One way of classifying services is to ask whether a given service can be provided without the customer's being part of the production system. In answering this question, we classify services according to the extent of *customer contact.*

High-Contact Processes. Think for a moment about your local public transit system. The service provided is transportation, and when you purchase transportation, you must board a bus or train. For example, the Bay Area Rapid Transit System (BART) connects San Francisco with many of its outlying suburbs. Like all public transportation systems, BART is a **high-contact system:** To receive the service, the customer must be a part of the system. For this reason, BART managers must worry about the cleanliness of the trains and the appearance of the stations. This is usually not the case in low-contact systems, where large industrial concerns that ship coal in freight trains, for example, are generally not concerned with the appearance inside those trains.

high-contact system Level of service-customer contact in which the customer receives the service as part of the system

Low-Contact Processes. Now consider the check-processing operations at your bank. Workers sort the checks that have been cashed that day and dispatch them to the banks on which they were drawn. This operation is a **low-contact system:** Customers are not in contact with the bank while the service is performed. They receive the service—their funds are transferred to cover their checks—without ever setting foot in the check-processing center. Gas and electric utilities, auto repair shops, and lawn care services are also low-contact systems.

low-contact system Level of service-customer contact in which the customer need not be a part of the system to receive the service

Differences between Service and Manufacturing Operations

Not surprisingly, service and manufacturing operations share several important features. For example, both transform raw materials into finished products. In service production, however, the raw materials, or inputs, are not glass or steel. Rather, they are people who choose among sellers because they have either unsatisfied needs or possessions for which they need some form of care or alteration. In service operations, then, "finished products" or "outputs" are people with needs met and possessions serviced.

FOCUS ON PERFORMANCE Thus, at least one very obvious difference exists between service and manufacturing operations: Whereas goods are produced, services are performed. Therefore, customer-oriented performance is a key factor in measuring the effectiveness of a service company.

Wal-Mart, for example, sells to millions of people from California to Germany out of more than 3,000 stores. Its superstar status stems from an obsession with speedy product delivery that it measures not in days or even hours, but in minutes and seconds. Wal-Mart's keen customer focus emphasizes avoiding unnecessary inventories, getting fast responses from suppliers, streamlining transactions processes, and knowing accurately the sales and restocking requirements for keeping the right merchandise moving from warehouses to store shelves. To implement this strategy, Wal-Mart has made technology—namely, its vaunted computer and telecommunications system—a core competency.[4]

In many ways, the focus of service operations is more complex than that of goods production. First, service operations feature a unique link between production and consumption—between process and outcome. Second, services are *more intangible* and *more customized* and *less storable* than most products. Finally, quality considerations must be defined, and managed, differently in the service sector than in manufacturing operations.

Focus on Process and Outcome As we saw earlier, manufacturing operations focus on the outcome of the production process. The products offered by most service operations, however, are actually combinations of goods and services. Services, therefore, must focus on both the transformation *process* and its outcome—both on making a pizza and on delivering it to the buyer. Service operations thus require different skills from manufacturing operations. For example, local gas company employees may need the interpersonal skills necessary to calm and reassure frightened customers who have reported gas leaks. The job, therefore, can mean more than just repairing defective pipes. Factory workers who install gas pipes while assembling mobile homes are far less likely to need such skills.

Focus on Service Characteristics Service companies' transactions always reflect the fact that service products are characterized by three key qualities: *intangibility*, *customization*, and *unstorability*.

Intangibility. Often services cannot be touched, tasted, smelled, or seen. An important value, therefore, is the *intangible* value that the customer experiences in the form of pleasure, satisfaction, or a feeling of safety. For example, when you hire an attorney to resolve a problem, you purchase not only the intangible quality of legal expertise but also the equally intangible reassurance that help is at hand. Although all services have some degree of intangibility, some provide tangible elements as well. Your attorney, for example, can draw up the living will that you want to keep in your safe deposit box.

Customization. When you visit a physician, you expect to be examined for your symptoms. Likewise, when you purchase insurance, get your pet groomed, or have your hair cut, you expect these services to be designed for your needs. Typically, therefore, services are *customized.*

Unstorability. Services such as rubbish collection, transportation, child care, and house cleaning cannot be produced ahead of time and then stored. If a service is not used when available, it is usually wasted. Services, then, are typically characterized by a high degree of *unstorability.*

Focus on the Customer Service Link Because they transform customers or their possessions, service operations often acknowledge the customer as part of the operations process itself. For example, to purchase a haircut you must usually go to the barbershop or beauty salon.

As part of the operations process, consumers of services have a unique ability to affect that process. In other words, as the customer, you expect the salon to be conveniently located, to be open for business at convenient times, to offer needed services at reasonable prices, and to extend prompt service. Accordingly, the manager adopts hours of operation, available services, and an appropriate number of employees to meet the requirements of the customer.

FOCUS ON SERVICE QUALITY CONSIDERATIONS Consumers use different criteria to judge services and goods. Service managers must understand that quality of work and quality of service are not necessarily synonymous. For example, although your car may have been flawlessly repaired, you might feel dissatisfied with the service if you were forced to pick it up a day later than promised.

OPERATIONS PLANNING

Now that we've contrasted goods and services we can return to a more general consideration of production encompassing both goods and services. Like all good managers, we start with planning. Managers from many departments contribute to the firm's decisions about operations management. As Figure 13.4 shows, however, no matter how many decision makers are involved, the process can be described as a series of logical steps. The success of any firm depends on the final result of this logical sequence of decisions.

The overall business plan and forecasts developed by a company's top executives guide operations planning. The business plan outlines the firm's goals and objectives, including the specific goods and services that it will offer in the upcoming years. In this section we survey the development of the main parts of operations planning. We discuss the key planning activities that fall into one of five major categories: *capacity*, *location*, *layout*, *quality*, and *methods planning*.

capacity Amount of a product that a company can produce under normal working conditions

Capacity Planning

The amount of a product that a company can produce under normal working conditions is its **capacity.** The capacity of a goods or service firm depends on how many people it em-

FIGURE 13.4 ◆ Operations Planning and Control

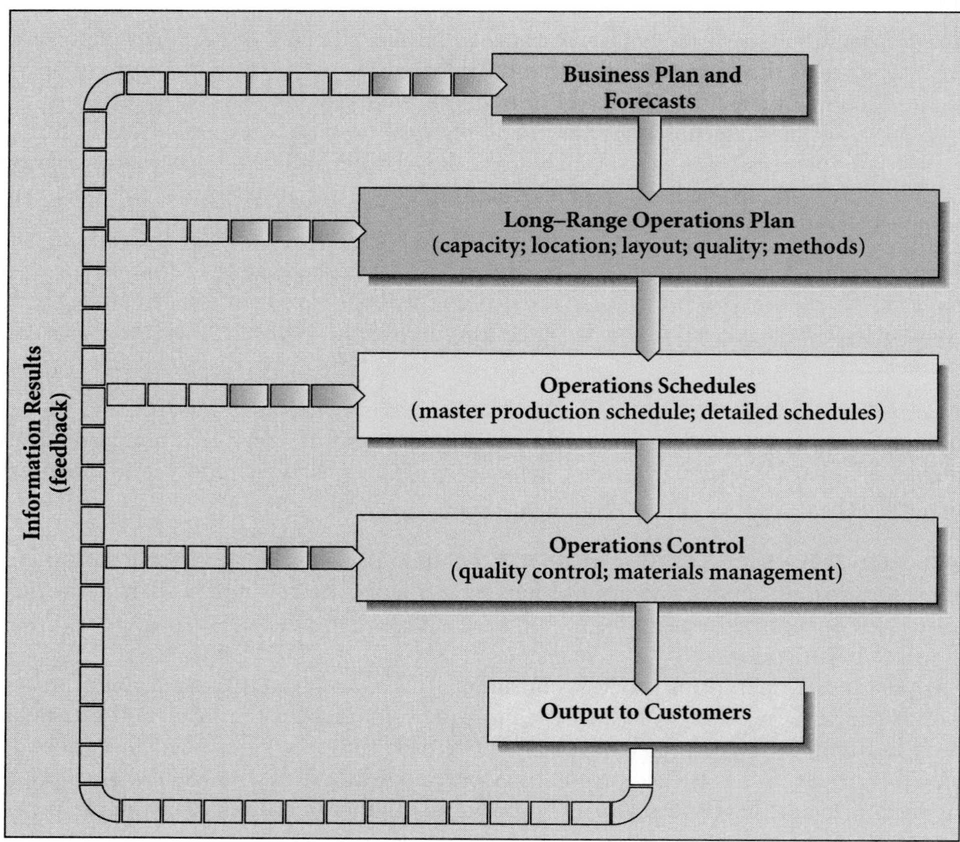

ploys and the number and size of its facilities. Long-range planning must take into account both current and future capacity.

Capacity Planning for Producing Goods Capacity planning for goods means ensuring that a manufacturing firm's capacity slightly exceeds the normal demand for its product. To see why this policy is best, consider the alternatives. If capacity is too small to meet demand, the company must turn away customers—a situation that not only cuts into profits but also alienates both customers and salespeople. If capacity greatly exceeds demand, then the firm is wasting money by maintaining a plant that is too large, by keeping excess machinery on-line, or by employing too many workers.

The stakes are high in the company's capacity decisions: While expanding fast enough to meet future demand and to protect market share from competitors, they must also weigh the increased costs of expanding. One reason that Intel Corp. enjoys more than 70 percent market share in the worldwide semiconductor business is the $11 billion it invested in capacity expansion between 1991 and 1995 (including $1.8 billion for its plant in Rio Rancho, New Mexico) and the additional $625 million to buy Digital Equipment's Hudson, Massachusetts, semiconductor plant in 1998. Will demand for semiconductors continue to grow even further? With so much invested thus far, Intel must decide whether the risks of additional capacity are worth the potential gains.[5]

Capacity Planning for Producing Services In low-contact processes, maintaining inventory lets managers set capacity at the level of *average demand.* For example, the J.C. Penney catalog sales warehouse may hire enough order fillers to handle 1,000 orders each day. When daily orders exceed this average demand, some orders are placed in inventory—set aside in a "to be done" file—to be processed on a day when fewer than 1,000 orders are received.

In high-contact processes, managers must plan capacity to meet *peak demand.* A supermarket, for instance, has far more cash registers than it needs on an average day; but on a Saturday morning or during the 3 days before Thanksgiving, all registers will be running full speed.

Location Planning

Because the location of a factory, office, or store affects its production costs and flexibility, sound location planning is crucial. Depending on the site of its facility, a company may be capable of producing a low-cost product or may find itself at an extreme cost disadvantage relative to its competitors.

Location Planning for Producing Goods Managers in goods-producing operations must consider many factors in location planning. Their location decisions are influenced by proximity to raw materials and markets, availability of labor, energy and transportation costs, local and state regulations and taxes, and community living conditions.

In 1998, for example, General Motors announced it would build new plants in North America to increase productivity and competitiveness. These agile, highly efficient assembly plants will rely on outside producers to supply large components such as fully assembled dashboards, stamped hoods, and other body parts. GM intends for production efficiencies to arise from a system in which each supplier specializes in making just one major component. To resupply GM assembly plants quickly and to reduce transportation costs, suppliers will locate factories nearby.[6]

Some location decisions are now being simplified by the rise of industrial parks. Created by cities interested in attracting new industry, these planned sites come with the necessary zoning, land, shipping facilities, utilities, and waste disposal outlets already in place. Such sites offer flexibility, often allowing firms to open new facilities before competitors can get started in the same area. The ready-made site also provides faster construction start-ups because it entails no lead time in preparing the chosen site.

LOCATION PLANNING FOR PRODUCING SERVICES In planning low-contact services, companies have some options: Services can be located near resource supplies, labor, or transportation outlets. For example, the typical Wal-Mart distribution center is located near the hundreds of Wal-Mart stores it supplies, not the companies that supply the distribution center. Distribution managers regard Wal-Mart stores as their customers. To better serve them, distribution centers are located so that truckloads of merchandise flow quickly to the stores.

On the other hand, high-contact services are more restricted. They must locate near the customers who are a part of the system. Accordingly, fast-food restaurants such as Taco Bell, McDonald's, and Burger King have begun moving into nontraditional locations with high traffic—dormitories, hospital cafeterias, and shopping malls. They can also be found in Wal-Mart outlets and Meijer Supermarkets that draw large crowds. Similarly, some McDonald's are located on interstate highway rest stops, and Domino's Pizza and KFC restaurants can be found on military bases.

The fundamental strategy establishes outlets where the customers are located. Observes Wayne Norbitz, president of Nathan's Famous Hotdogs: "You used to open a restaurant, advertise, and ask people to come to you. Today, the strategy is to find out where people already are and bring your product there."

"You used to open a restaurant, advertise, and ask people to come to you. Today, the strategy is to find out where people already are and bring your product there."

—Wayne Norbitz
President, Nathan's Famous Hotdogs

Layout Planning

Once a site has been selected, managers must decide on plant layout. Layout of machinery, equipment, and supplies determines whether a company can respond quickly and efficiently to customer requests for more and different products or finds itself unable to match competitors' production speed or convenience of service.

LAYOUT PLANNING FOR PRODUCING GOODS In facilities that produce goods, layout must be planned for three different types of space:

- *Productive facilities:* workstations and equipment for transforming raw materials, for example
- *Nonproductive facilities:* storage and maintenance areas
- *Support facilities:* offices, restrooms, parking lots, cafeterias, and so forth

In this section, we focus on productive facilities. Alternatives include *process, product,* and *cellular layouts.*

process layout Spatial arrangement of production activities that groups equipment and people according to function

product layout Spatial arrangement of production activities designed to move resources through a smooth, fixed sequence of steps

assembly line Product layout in which a product moves step-by-step through a plant on conveyor belts or other equipment until it is completed

Process Layouts. In a **process layout,** which is well suited to job shops that specialize in custom work, equipment and people are grouped according to function. In a custom cake bakery, for instance, machines blend batter in an area devoted to mixing, baking occurs in the oven area, and cakes are decorated on tables in a finishing area before boxing. The various tasks are each performed in specialized locations. Machine, woodworking, and dry cleaning shops also feature process layouts.

Product Layouts. In a **product layout,** equipment and people are set up to produce one type of good in a fixed sequence of steps and are arranged according to its production requirements. Product layouts often use **assembly lines:** A partially finished product moves

Boeing makes and sells more airplanes than anyone else and has only one worldwide competitor (a European consortium called Airbus Industrie). Though widely admired as a global company, Boeing has only recently taken steps to correct its notoriously inefficient assembly-line methods. In the past, for example, a customer could choose from among four configurations for duct holes in the cargo compartment. Once the choice was made, 990 pages of engineering plans had to be coded, and the placement of no fewer than 2,550 parts was affected. "We have $25,000 engine mounts that can't be finished," complains one parts supplier, "because we're waiting for $40 nuts and bolts." In one 20-month period, Boeing hired and trained 38,000 workers to meet commitments to customers and then had to lay off 12,000 as soon as assembly lines had been straightened out.

step by step through the plant on conveyor belts or other equipment, often in a straight line, until the product is completed. Automobile, food-processing, and computer assembly plants use product layouts.

Product layouts can be efficient and inexpensive because they simplify work tasks and use unskilled labor. However, they tend to be inflexible because they require a heavy investment in specialized equipment that is hard to rearrange for new applications. In addition, workers are subject to boredom, and when someone is absent or overworked, those farther down the line cannot help out.

Cellular Layouts. A newer workplace arrangement for some applications is called the **cellular layout.** Cellular layouts are used when families of products can follow similar flow paths. A clothing manufacturer, for example, may establish a cell, or designated area, dedicated to making a family of pockets—say, pockets for shirts, coats, blouses, trousers, and slacks. Although each type of pocket is unique in shape, size, and style, all go through the same production steps. Within the cell, therefore, various types of equipment (for cutting, trimming, and sewing) are arranged close together in the appropriate sequence. All pockets pass stage by stage through the cell from beginning to end, in a nearly continuous flow.

cellular layout Spatial arrangement of production facilities designed to move families of products through similar flow paths

Cellular layouts have several advantages. For example, because similar products require less machine adjustment, equipment setup time is reduced. Because flow distances are usually shorter, there is less material handling and transit time. Finally, inventories of goods in progress are lower and paperwork is simpler because material flows are more orderly.

LAYOUT PLANNING FOR PRODUCING SERVICES Service firms use some of the same layouts as goods-producing firms. In a low-contact system, for instance, the facility should be arranged to enhance the production of the service. A mail-processing facility at UPS or Federal Express, therefore, looks very much like a product layout in a factory: Machines and people are arranged in the order in which they are used in the mass processing of mail. In contrast, Kinko's Copy Centers use process layouts for different custom jobs: Specific functions such as photocopying, computing, binding, photography, and laminating are performed in specialized areas of the store.

High-contact systems should be arranged to meet customer needs and expectations. For example, Piccadilly Cafeterias focuses both layout and services on the groups that constitute its primary market: families and elderly people. As you can see in Figure 13.5, families enter to find an array of highchairs and rolling baby beds that make it convenient to wheel children through the line. Servers are willing to carry trays for elderly people and for those pushing strollers. Note, too, that customers must pass by the whole serving line

FIGURE 13.5 ◆ Layout of a Typical Piccadilly Cafeteria

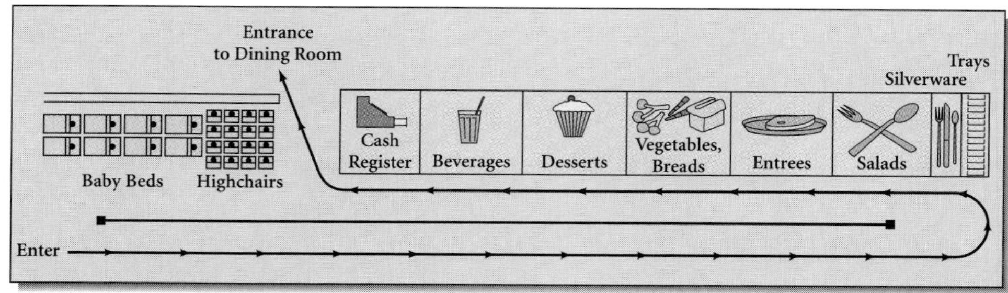

before making selections. Not only does this layout help them make up their minds; it also tempts them to select more.

Quality Planning

In planning production systems and facilities, managers must keep in mind the firm's quality goals. Thus, any complete operations plan must ensure that products are produced to meet the firm's standards of quality. The American Society for Quality Control defines **quality** as "the totality of features and characteristics of a product or service that bear on its ability to satisfy stated or implied needs."

quality A product's fitness for use; its success in offering features that consumers want

Such features may include a product's reasonable price and its consistent performance in delivering the benefit it promises. For example, Perrigo, the largest U.S. manufacturer of over-the-counter pharmaceuticals and personal-care products, treats quality planning as a central part of its competitive strategy. Quality is enhanced through the continuous improvement of manufacturing methods, the careful control of every step in production and packaging, and a quality improvement program that empowers employees to reduce waste and increase production capabilities.[7]

Methods Planning

In designing operations systems, managers must clearly identify every production step and the specific methods for performing them. They can then work to reduce waste, inefficiency, and poor performance by examining procedures on a step-by-step basis—an approach sometimes called *methods improvement.*

McDonald's claims that a new wrinkle in layout planning ranks with indoor seating and drive-through windows among the most important innovations in the company's first half century. The change is in the kitchen, where such nonmeat ingredients as bread, onions, and lettuce are now spared the wilting heat of holding bins and, more importantly, the microwave. Now only the meat is kept warm, and everything else is added after microwaving. McDonald's expects to increase sales by 1.2 percent and save $100 million per year in food costs, and customers will no longer have to wait several minutes if they don't want pickles or ketchup.

METHODS IMPROVEMENT IN GOODS Improvement of production for goods begins when a manager documents the current method. A detailed description, often using a diagram called the *process flow chart*, is usually helpful for organizing and recording all information. The process flow chart identifies the sequence of production activities, movements of materials, and work performed at each stage as the product flows through production. The flow can then be analyzed to identify wasteful activities, sources of delay in production flows, and other inefficiencies. The final step is implementing improvements.

Mercury Marine, for example, used methods improvement to streamline the production of stern-drive units for power boats. Examination of the process flow from raw materials to assembly (the final production step) revealed numerous wastes and inefficiencies. Each product passed through 122 steps, traveled nearly 21,000 feet (almost 4 miles) in the factory, and was handled by 106 people. Analysis revealed that only 27 steps actually added value to the product (for example, drilling, painting). Work methods were revised to eliminate nonproductive activities. Mercury ultimately identified potential savings in labor, inventory, paperwork, and space requirements. Because production lead time was also reduced, customer orders were filled faster.

METHODS IMPROVEMENT IN SERVICES In a low-contact process, managers can use methods improvements to speed services ranging from mowing lawns to filling prescriptions and drawing up legal documents. Dell Computer, for example, sells its computers on-line and over the phone, mostly to medium and large companies. Methods analysis eliminates unnecessary steps so that orders can be processed quickly for production and delivery. Dell's emphasis on efficient selling by means of electronic technology speeds its response time to provide customers with a specific value—extremely fast delivery service.[8]

Design for Customer Contact in Services. In a high-contact service, the demands on system designs are somewhat different. Here, managers must develop procedures that clearly spell out the ways in which workers interact with customers. These procedures must cover such activities as exchanging information or money, delivering and receiving materials, and even making physical contact. The next time you visit your dentist's office, for instance, notice the way dental hygienists scrub up and wear disposable gloves. They also scrub after patient contact, even if they intend to work on equipment or do paperwork, and they rescrub before working on the next patient. The high-contact system in a dental office consists of very strict procedures designed to avoid contact that can transmit disease.

OPERATIONS SCHEDULING

Once plans identify needed resources and how they will be used to reach a firm's goals, managers must develop timetables for acquiring resources for production. This aspect of operations is called *scheduling*.

Scheduling Goods Operations

Scheduling of goods production occurs on different levels within the firm. First, a top-level or *master production schedule* shows which products will be produced, when production will occur, and what resources will be used during specified time periods.

Consider the case of Logan Aluminum Inc. Logan produces coils of aluminum that its main customers, Atlantic Richfield and Alcan Aluminum, use to produce aluminum cans. Logan's master schedule extends out to 60 weeks and shows how many coils will be made each week. For various types of coils, the master schedule specifies how many of each will be produced. "We need this planning and scheduling system," says material manager Candy McKenzie, "to determine how much of what product we can produce each and every month."

This information, however, is not complete. For example, manufacturing personnel must also know the location of all coils on the plant floor and their various stages of production. Start-up and stop times must be assigned, and employees must be given scheduled work assignments. Short-term detailed schedules fill in these blanks on a daily basis. These schedules use incoming customer orders and information about current machine conditions to update the sizes and variety of coils to make each day.

Scheduling Service Operations

Service scheduling may involve both work and workers. In a low-contact service, work scheduling may be based either on desired completion dates or on the time of order arrivals. For example, several cars may be scheduled for repairs at a local garage. Thus, if your car is not scheduled for work until 3:30, it may sit idle for several hours even if it was the first to be dropped off. In such businesses, reservations and appointments systems can help smooth ups and downs in demand.

In contrast, if a hospital emergency room is overloaded, patients cannot be asked to make appointments and come back later. As we have seen, in high-contact services, the customer is part of the system and must be accommodated. Thus, precise scheduling of services may not be possible in high-contact systems.

In scheduling workers, managers must also consider efficiency and costs. McDonald's, for example, guarantees workers that they will be scheduled for at least 4 hours at a time. To accomplish this goal without having workers idle, McDonald's uses *overlapping shifts*—the ending hours for some employees overlap the beginning hours for others. The overlap provides maximum coverage during peak periods. McDonald's also trains employees to put off minor tasks, such as refilling napkin dispensers, until slow periods.

A 24-hour-a-day service operation, such as a hospital, can be an even greater scheduling challenge. Nurses, for example, must be on duty around the clock, 7 days a week. Few nurses, however, want to work on weekends or during the wee hours of the morning. Similarly, although enough nurses must be scheduled to meet emergencies, most hospitals are on tight budgets and cannot afford to have too many on-duty nurses. Thus, incentives are often used to entice nurses to work at times they might not otherwise choose. For example, would you choose to work 12 hours a day, 7 days a week? Probably not, but what if you were entitled to have every other week off in exchange for working such a schedule? A number of hospitals use just such a plan to attract nurses.

■ OPERATIONS CONTROL

operations control Process of monitoring and adjusting production performance by comparing results with plans

Once long-range plans have been put into action and schedules have been drawn up, **operations control** requires production managers to monitor production performance by comparing results with detailed plans and schedules. If schedules or quality standards are not met, these managers must take corrective action. *Follow-up*—checking to ensure that production decisions are being implemented—is an essential and ongoing facet of operations control.

Operations control features *materials management* and *production process control.* Both these activities ensure that schedules are met and that production goals are fulfilled, both in quantity and in quality. In this section, we consider the nature of materials management and look at some important methods of process control.

Materials Management

Both goods-producing and service companies use materials. For many manufacturing firms, material costs account for 50 to 75 percent of total product costs. For goods whose production uses little labor, such as petroleum refining, this percentage is even higher. Thus, companies have good reasons to emphasize materials management.

The process of **materials management** not only controls but also plans and organizes the flow of materials. Even before production starts, materials management focuses on product design by emphasizing materials **standardization**—the use of standard and uniform components rather than new or different components. Law firms, for example, maintain standardized forms and data files for estate wills, living wills, trust agreements, and various contracts that can be adjusted easily to meet your individual needs. In manufacturing, Ford's engine plant in Romeo, Michigan, uses common parts for several different kinds of engines rather than unique parts for each. Once components were standardized, the total number of different parts was reduced by 25 percent. Standardization also simplifies paperwork, reduces storage requirements, and eliminates unnecessary material flows.

materials management Planning, organizing, and controlling the flow of materials from design through distribution of finished goods

standardization Use, where possible, of standard and uniform components in the production process

Once the product has been designed, materials managers purchase the necessary materials and monitor the production process through the distribution of finished goods. The five major areas of materials management are *transportation*, *warehousing*, *purchasing*, *supplier selection*, and *inventory control:*

- *Transportation* includes the means of transporting resources to the company and finished goods to buyers.
- *Warehousing* is the storage of both incoming materials for production and finished goods for physical distribution to customers.
- **Purchasing** is the acquisition of all the raw materials and services that a company needs to produce its products; most large firms have purchasing departments to buy proper materials in the amounts needed.
- **Supplier selection** means finding and choosing suppliers of services and materials to buy from. It includes evaluating potential suppliers, negotiating terms of service, and maintaining positive buyer-seller relationships.
- **Inventory control** includes the receiving, storing, handling, and counting of all raw materials, partly finished goods, and finished goods. It ensures that enough materials inventories are available to meet production schedules.

purchasing The acquisition of raw materials and services that a company needs to produce its products

supplier selection Finding, choosing, and building relationships with suppliers of services and materials to buy from

inventory control Receiving, storing, handling, and counting of all raw materials, partly finished goods, and finished goods

Tools for Operations Process Control

Numerous tools assist managers in controlling operations. Chief among these are *worker training*, *just-in-time production systems*, *material requirements planning*, and *quality control.*

WORKER TRAINING Not surprisingly, customer satisfaction is closely linked to the employees who provide the service. Says Kip Tindell, chief operating officer at the Container Store, a Dallas-based retailer of storage products: "We are just wild-eyed fanatics when it comes to human resources and training." Naturally, effective customer relationships do not come about by accident: Service workers can be trained and motivated in customer-oriented attitudes and behavior. In service-product design, it is important to remember that most services are delivered by people: That is, service system employees are both the producers of the product and the salespeople. Thus, human relations skills are vital in anyone who has contact with the public. Tindell, who attributes the Container Store's high profits to effective employees, contends that human resources and training are "the most difficult and the most joyous part of the retail business." Like Tindell, more and more human resource experts now realize that without employees' trained relationship skills for pleasing their clients, businesses such as airlines, employment agencies, and hotels can lose customers to better-prepared competitors.

> "**Human resources and training are the most difficult and the most joyous part of the retail business.**"
>
> —Kip Tindell
>
> *Chief operating officer at Container Store*

Managers realize how easily service employees with a poor attitude can reduce sales. Conversely, the right attitude is a powerful sales tool. The Walt Disney Company has long recognized the vital link between its employees and its business success. Their methods for employee development are widely recognized by other firms who send managers to the Disney Institute to learn "The Disney Approach to People Management." The Disney organization does an excellent job of remembering that no matter what their jobs, service employees are all links to the public. Of the 35,000 employees at Disney World Resort in Buena Vista, Florida, some 20,000 have direct contact with guests. For example, Disney World has a team of sweepers constantly at work picking up bits of trash as soon as they fall to the ground. When visitors have questions about directions or time, they often ask one of the sweepers. Because their responses affect visitors' overall impressions of Disney World, sweepers are trained to respond in appropriate ways. Their work is evaluated and rewarded based on strict performance appraisal standards. A pleased customer is more likely to return.[9]

just-in-time (JIT) production system Production method that brings together all materials and parts needed at each production stage at the precise moment at which they are required

JUST-IN-TIME PRODUCTION SYSTEMS To minimize manufacturing inventory costs, some managers use **just-in-time (JIT) production systems.** JIT brings together all the needed materials and parts at the precise moment they are required for each production stage, not before. All resources are continuously flowing, from their arrival as raw materials to subassembly, final completion, and shipment of finished products. JIT reduces to practically nothing the number of goods in process (that is, goods not yet finished) and saves money by replacing stop-and-go production with smooth movement. Once smooth movements become the norm, disruptions become more visible and thus get resolved more quickly. Finding and eliminating disruptions by continuous improvement of production is a major objective of JIT.

By implementing JIT, Harley-Davidson reduced its inventories by over 40 percent, improved production work flows, and reduced its costs of warranty work, rework, and scrap by 60 percent. In addition, Harley motorcycles have retained their coveted quality reputation: The annual number of shipments more than doubled from 1988 to 1996. And, with the help of JIT, their Plan 2003 calls for another doubling of production for Harley's 100th anniversary in 2003.[10]

TRENDS AND CHALLENGES

THE FINE LINE BETWEEN BOLD MOVES AND DYSFUNCTIONAL MANEUVERS

Since 1995, business has been booming at Boeing, one of the world's two remaining suppliers of large commercial aircraft. In Boeing's case, however, the boom hasn't brought good times. Production problems and cost overruns have so far offset record orders that the company is on the verge of financial meltdown. In 1998, Boeing was forced to write off $4.45 billion in losses as net profits slumped to only $308 million—a dismal 1.2 percent of revenues. Needless to say, no one inside or outside the company could disagree with aerospace analyst Paul H. Nisbet, who prescribed "a thorough scrubbing of operations from top to bottom."

The scrubbing took the form of a management shakeup which, in the summer of 1998, brought new blood into Boeing's commercial, defense, and space divisions. It also brought a commitment to increase productivity, decrease costs, and improve profit margins. Of course, management must be more than merely committed. At Boeing, the new team must deliver in such areas as the following:

- Implementing a new computer system to streamline purchasing and create production efficiencies. With production costs topping historic levels, this project is a top priority.
- Resetting production goals. With 620 jets scheduled for production in 1999, management is trying to persuade customers to push back orders to 2001, when fewer deliveries are scheduled.
- Improving relationships with suppliers who have been stretched to the limit by Boeing's extraordinary, order-driven demand for parts and raw materials.

In recent years, Boeing has been accepting more orders than it can handle, primarily to protect market share from arch rival Airbus Industrie, a European consortium that enjoys government subsidies. Unfortunately, costs soared as the company geared up production and management scram-

MATERIAL REQUIREMENTS PLANNING Like JIT, **material requirements planning (MRP)** also seeks to deliver the right amounts of materials at the right place and the right time for goods production. MRP uses a *bill of materials* that is basically a recipe for the finished product. It specifies the necessary ingredients (raw materials and components), the order in which they should be combined, and the quantity of each ingredient needed to make one batch of the product (say, 2,000 finished telephones). The recipe is fed into a computer that controls inventory and schedules each stage of production. The result is fewer early arrivals, less frequent stock shortages, and lower storage costs. MRP is most popular among companies whose products require complicated assembly and fabrication activities, such as automobile manufacturers, appliance makers, and furniture companies.

material requirements planning (MRP) Production control method in which a bill of materials is used to ensure that the right amounts of materials are delivered to the right place at the right time

QUALITY CONTROL Another operation control tool is **quality control**—the management of the production process so as to manufacture goods or supply services that meet specific quality standards. McDonald's, for example, has been a pioneer in quality control in the restaurant industry since the early 1950s. The company oversees everything from the farming of potatoes for french fries to the packing of meat for Big Macs. Quality assurance staffers even check standards for ketchup sweetness and french fry length.

quality control Management of the production process designed to manufacture goods or supply services that meet specific quality standards

Teamwork. In their quest for quality control, many U.S. businesses have adopted **quality improvement teams** (patterned after the Japanese concept of **quality circles**)—groups of employees from various work areas who define, analyze, and solve common production problems. Teams meet regularly to discuss problems and keep management informed of the group's progress in addressing various issues.

quality improvement team (or quality circle) TQM tool in which groups of employees work together as a team to improve quality

Frito-Lay Inc., for instance, started such a program at its plant in Lubbock, Texas. Teams of 10, hourly workers oversee activities ranging from potato processing to machine maintenance. Their primary job, however, is to cut costs while improving quality. Thus, workers now assume such "managerial" responsibilities as rejecting products that fail to meet quality standards and sending home employees who are unneeded (for example, when machines break down). They also schedule work crews and even interview prospective employees. From a place in the bottom 20 of Frito-Lay's 48 U.S. plants, the Lubbock operation has jumped into the top 6 in terms of quality.

bled to deliver planes on time. The situation became financially dire when, to attract customers away from Airbus, Boeing agreed to discounts as high as 25 percent. It was a bold move, but Richard Aboulafia, director of aviation consulting for Teal Group Corp., is convinced that "it was one of the most dysfunctional maneuvers in the history of American business."

"The Boeing discount was one of the most dysfunctional maneuvers in the history of American business."

—Richard Aboulafia

Director of aviation consulting, Teal Group

To get back on track, Boeing must first deliver all the planes that customers want. It must then take a hard look at demand for aircraft in relationship to its production capacity. Putting too many demands on production traumatized the company once and reduced profit margins, and management obviously can't make the same mistake again. Boeing, says one industry executive, "is like a huge freight train that takes a couple of miles to slow down. They have to talk to their customers now about deferrals."

To solve the chronic production problems that forced the halt of 747 and 737 jet assembly for several weeks in 1998, Boeing has divided its commercial airplane unit into three separate divisions, each of which is responsible for its own profits and losses. It's another bold move. Indeed, *The New York Times* calls it "a revolutionary concept, since even top executives do not know how much it costs to make their planes."

"Productivity is up nine percent since I made everyone a vice-president."

Many companies report that improvement teams have not only raised quality levels but also increased productivity, reduced costs, and improved job satisfaction. At Xerox Business Services, employee satisfaction increased from a 63 percent favorable rating to 80 percent in a 3-year period. Both revenues and profits increased by more than 30 percent annually.[11] Remember, however, that improvement teams also involve risks. Not all employees, for example, want to participate. Moreover, management cannot always adopt group recommendations, no matter how much careful thought, hard work, and enthusiasm went into them. The challenge for production managers, then, is to make wise decisions about when and how to use quality improvement teams.

■ QUALITY IMPROVEMENT

It is not enough to measure production performance in terms of numbers of items produced. We must also take *quality* into account. For the past 50 years, the American Society for Quality Control (ASQC) has maintained standards for quality and provided services to assist U.S. industry's quality efforts.

Managing for Quality

total quality management (TQM) The sum of all activities involved in getting quality products into the marketplace

Total quality management (TQM) includes all the activities necessary for getting high-quality goods and services into the marketplace. It must consider all parts of the business, including customers, suppliers, and employees (Figure 13.6). Says John Kay, director of Oxford University's School of Management: "You can't run a successful company if you don't care about customers and employees, or if you are systematically unpleasant to suppliers."[12] To bring the interests of all these stakeholders together, TQM involves planning, organizing, directing, and controlling.

performance quality The performance features offered by a product

PLANNING FOR QUALITY Planning for quality begins *before* products are designed or redesigned. To ensure that their needs are not overlooked, customers may be invited to participate in the planning process. In the predesign stage, managers must set goals for both performance quality and quality reliability. **Performance quality** refers to the *performance features* of a product. For example, Maytag gets premium prices for its appliances because they are perceived as offering more advanced features and a longer life than competing brands. Through its advertising, the firm has made sure that consumers recognize the Maytag repairman as the world's loneliest service professional.

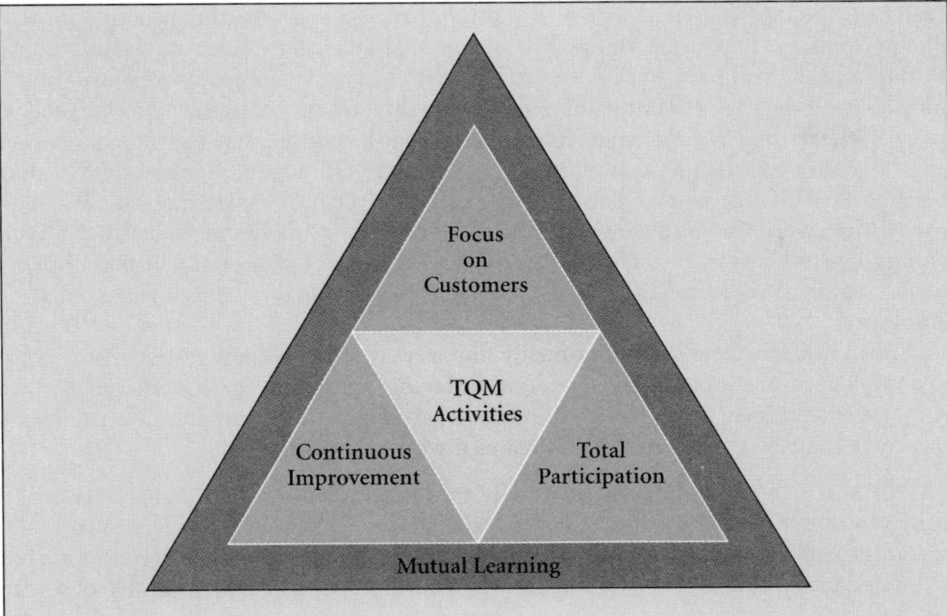

FIGURE 13.6 ◆ **ADAC Laboratories Quality System**

Performance quality may be related to a product's **quality reliability**—the *consistency* of product quality from unit to unit. Toyotas, for example, enjoy high quality reliability; the firm has a reputation for producing very few lemons. In services, consistency is important. Custom Research, Inc., a marketing research firm that received the 1996 Malcolm Baldrige National Quality Award, was applauded for 99 percent on-time delivery of final research reports to its clients. For both goods and services, consistency is achieved by controlling the quality of raw materials, encouraging conscientious work, and keeping equipment in good working order.

quality reliability Consistency of a product's quality from unit to unit

Some products offer both high quality reliability and high performance quality. Kellogg, for example, has a reputation for consistently producing cereals made of high-quality ingredients. To achieve any form of high quality, managers must plan for production processes (equipment, methods, worker skills, and materials) that will result in high-quality products.

ORGANIZING FOR QUALITY Perhaps most important to the quality concept is the belief that producing high-quality goods and services requires an effort from all parts of the organization. Having a separate "quality control" department is no longer enough. Everyone from the chairperson of the board to the part-time clerk—purchasers, engineers, janitors, marketers, machinists, and other personnel—must work to ensure quality. At Merrill Lynch Credit Corp., for example, all employees are responsible for taking initiative and responsibility in responding to customers' credit needs. They are also encouraged to be flexible in helping customers and in the development of their own employee skills. The overall goal is to reduce problems to a minimum by providing credit selectively and skillfully right from the beginning. As a result, the number of loans and market share are increasing while loan delinquencies are decreasing.

Although everyone in a company contributes to product quality, responsibility for specific aspects of total quality management is often assigned to specific departments and jobs. In fact, many companies have quality assurance or quality control departments staffed by quality experts. These people may be called in to help solve quality-related problems in any of the firm's other departments. They keep other departments informed of the latest developments in equipment and methods for maintaining quality. In addition, they monitor all quality control activities to identify areas for improvement.

DIRECTING FOR QUALITY Too often, firms fail to take the initiative in making quality happen. Directing for quality means that managers must motivate employees throughout the company to achieve quality goals. Managers companywide must help employees see how they affect quality and how quality affects both their jobs and the company. General Electric chairman John F. Welch, for example, has led the changeover to such a quality program by committing more than $1 billion and 3 years of effort to converting all of GE's divisions. The new program, says Welch, "has galvanized our company with an intensity the likes of which I have never seen in my 40 years at GE."[13] Welch's willingness to take drastic action to ensure the program's success was a visible display of a quality emphasis that had the added value of raising the quality consciousness of all GE's employees.

Like Welch, leaders must continually find ways to foster a quality orientation by training employees, encouraging involvement, and tying compensation to work quality. Ideally, if managers succeed, employees will ultimately accept **quality ownership:** the idea that quality belongs to each person who creates it while performing a job.

quality ownership Principle of total quality management that holds that quality belongs to each person who creates it while performing a job

CONTROLLING FOR QUALITY By monitoring its products and services, a company can detect mistakes and make corrections. First, however, managers must establish specific quality standards and measurements. For example, the control system for a bank's teller services might use the following procedure. Supervisors periodically observe the tellers' work and evaluate it according to a checklist. Specific aspects of each teller's work—appearance, courtesy, efficiency—are recorded. The results are reviewed with employees and either confirm proper performance or indicate changes needed to bring performance up to standards.

Tools for Quality Management

Many companies rely on proven tools to manage quality. Often, ideas for improving both the product and the production process come from **competitive product analysis.** For example, Toshiba might take apart a Xerox copier and test each component. Test results will then help managers decide which Toshiba product features are satisfactory, which features should be upgraded, and which operations processes need improvement. In this section, we survey three of the most commonly used tools for total quality management: statistical process control, quality/cost studies, and various means of getting closer to the customer.

competitive product analysis Process by which a company analyzes a competitor's products to identify desirable improvements in its own

STATISTICAL PROCESS CONTROL Although every company would like complete uniformity in its output, the goal is unattainable: Every business experiences unit-to-unit variations in products and services. Firms can better control product quality by understanding sources of variation. **Statistical process control (SPC)** refers to methods by which employees can gather data and analyze variations in production activities to determine when adjustments are needed.

statistical process control (SPC) Evaluation methods that allow managers to analyze variations in a company's production activities

The Glidden Co., for example, uses SPC to control paint-making processes more effectively. Litton Precision Gear uses SPC to ensure the quality of transmission gears installed in military helicopters. At Farbex, a plastics manufacturer, SPC analysts spot-check numerous standards such as the weight of samples of plastic pellets at several different points in the production process. Forty percent of all North American pulp and paper mills use SPC to reduce waste and increase productivity during production.

Control Charts. One of the most common SPC methods is the use of control charts. Knowing that a process is capable of meeting quality standards is not enough. Managers must still monitor the production process to prevent it from going astray. To detect the beginning of departures from normal conditions, employees can check production periodically and plot the results on a **control chart.** Three or four times a day, for example, a machine operator at Honey Nuggets might weigh several boxes of cereal together to determine the average weight. That average is then plotted on the control chart.

control chart Process control method that plots test sampling results on a diagram to determine when a process is beginning to depart from normal operating conditions

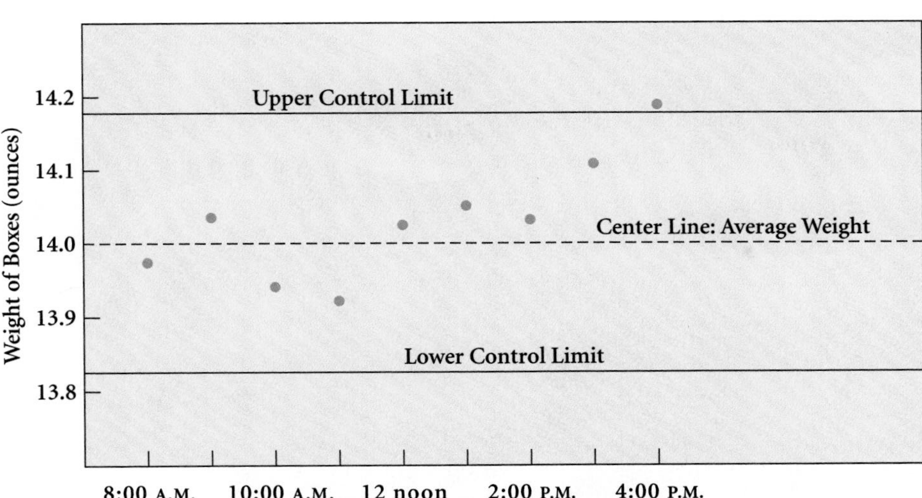

FIGURE 13.7 ◆ Process Control Chart

Figure 13.7 shows the control chart for Machine A at the Honey Nuggets plant. As you can see, the first five points are randomly scattered around the center line, indicating that the machine was operating well from 8 A.M. until noon. However, the points for samples 5 through 9 are all above the center line, indicating that something caused boxes to overfill. The last point falls outside the upper *control limit*, confirming that the process is out of control. At this point, the machine must be shut down so that an operator can investigate the cause of the problem—be it equipment, people, materials, or work methods. Control is completed when the problem is corrected and the process is restored to normal.

QUALITY/COST STUDIES Statistical process controls help keep operations up to existing capabilities. In today's competitive environment, however, firms must consistently raise quality capabilities. Any improvement in products or production processes also means additional costs, whether for new facilities, equipment, training, or other changes. Managers thus face the challenge of identifying the improvements that offer the greatest promise. **Quality/cost studies** are useful because they not only identify a firm's current costs but also reveal areas with the largest cost-savings potential.

quality/cost study Method of improving quality by identifying current costs and areas with the greatest cost-savings potential

Quality costs are associated with making, finding, repairing, or preventing defective goods and services. All of these costs should be analyzed in a quality/cost study. For example, Honey Nuggets must determine its costs for *internal failures.* These are expenses including the costs of overfilling boxes and the costs of sorting out bad boxes incurred during production and before bad products leave the plant. Studies indicate that many U.S. manufacturers incur costs for internal failures up to 50 percent of total costs.

Despite quality control procedures, however, some bad boxes may get out of the factory, reach the customer, and generate complaints from grocers and consumers. These *external failures* are discovered outside the factory. The costs of correcting them (refunds to customers, transportation costs to return bad boxes to the factory, possible lawsuits, and factory recalls) should also be tabulated in the quality/cost study.

The percentage of costs in the different categories varies widely from company to company. Thus, every firm must conduct systematic quality/cost studies to identify the most costly and often the most vital areas of its operations. Not surprisingly, these areas should be targets for improvement. Too often, however, firms substitute hunches and guesswork for data and analysis.

GETTING CLOSER TO THE CUSTOMER As one advocate of quality improvement puts it, "Customers are an economic asset. They're not on the balance sheet, but they should be." One of the themes of this chapter has been that struggling companies

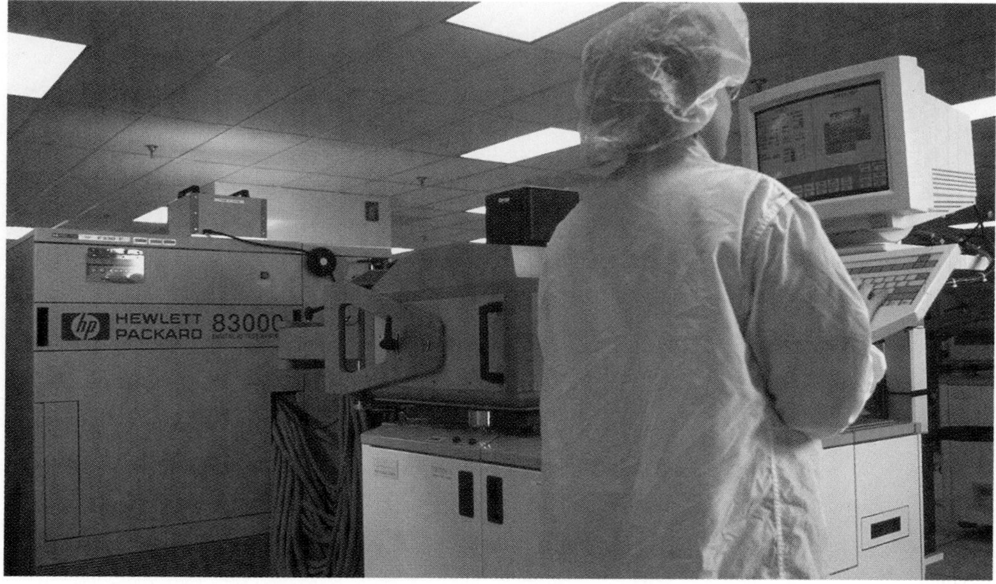

Depending on its complexity, a semiconductor wafer destined for a PC microprocessor can contain thousands of chips. At Hewlett-Packard, testing machines use miniscule probes to ensure that the electronic characteristics of every semiconductor are correct. Such systems are designed to check primarily for so-called "class defects"—problems that can affect a whole parade of products on the assembly line. One bad wafer at the end of the line can represent a waste of $10,000 in costs, and its commercial value is $0.00.

have often lost sight of customers as the driving force for all business activity. Perhaps they waste resources designing products that customers do not want. Sometimes they ignore customer reactions to existing products or fail to keep up with changing consumer tastes. By contrast, the most successful businesses keep close to their customers and know what they want in the products they consume.

> **"Customers are an economic asset. They're not on the balance sheet, but they should be."**
>
> *An advocate for quality improvement*

Continued from page 329

Planet Hollywood Tightens Its Stellar Orbit

To save Planet Hollywood from financial ruin, CEO Robert Earl shifted his focus from expansion to quality. First, he brought in William H. Baumhauer as chief operating officer and told him to start by improving the food. With a background in restaurant operations rather than celebrity marketing, Baumhauer brought strong operating experience to the troubled company. He also admitted from the outset that celebrity images alone could not keep the company going. "Planet Hollywood," he acknowledged, "does have a credibility problem. As a competitor, I wouldn't eat the damn food."

> **"Planet Hollywood does have a credibility problem. As a competitor, I wouldn't eat the damn food."**
>
> —William H. Baumhauer
> *Chief Operating Officer, Planet Hollywood*

To improve quality, the company plans to close unprofitable locations, listen to customer complaints, and attract better managers with a better pay scale. "We are 100-percent focused on fixing the problems at hand and maximizing the company's long-term potential," promises CEO Earl. Meanwhile expansion plans have been curtailed. Instead of nine projected openings in 1998, there were three. "Our focus," announced Earl, "is on creating renewed excitement in our Planet Hollywood brand."

Questions for Discussion

1. It can be argued that Planet Hollywood sells "experiences" instead of meals. If this is the case, why is it critical for management to focus on service production and quality issues?
2. How can heightened expectations lead to service disappointments? Why was the food only one of the quality problems at Planet Hollywood?
3. Why do you think management found it difficult to focus on quality and expansion at the same time?
4. How do crowds affect a service company's ability to deliver quality?
5. What were the flaws in the company's original location strategy?
6. How will listening to customers help Planet Hollywood make quality improvements?

SUMMARY

1. **Identify the characteristics that distinguish *service operations* from *goods production* and explain the main differences in the *service focus*.** Although the creation of both goods and services involves resources, transformations, and finished products, service operations differ from goods manufacturing in several important ways. In service production, the raw materials are people who choose among sellers because they have unsatisfied needs or possessions in need of care or alteration. Whereas goods are typically produced, services are performed.

   In addition, services are largely *intangible*, more likely than physical goods to be *customized* to meet the purchaser's needs, and more *unstorable* than most products. Service businesses, therefore, focus explicitly on these characteristics of their products. Because services are intangible, for instance, providers work to ensure that customers receive value in the form of pleasure, satisfaction, or a feeling of safety. Often, they also focus on both the transformation process and the final product—say, making a pizza as well as the pizza itself. Finally, service providers typically focus on the customer service link, often acknowledging the customer as part of the operations process.

2. **Describe the two ways of *classifying operations processes*.** Operations managers in manufacturing classify *operations processes* according to the type of *technology* used (*chemical, fabrication, assembly, transport*, or *clerical*) to transform raw materials into finished goods. Service operations are classified according to the extent of *customer contact*. In *high-contact systems*, the customer is part of the system. In *low-contact systems*, customers are not in contact with the service provider while the service is provided.

3. **Describe the factors involved in *operations planning* and *scheduling*.** *Operations planning* involves the analysis of five key factors. In *capacity planning*, the firm analyzes how much of a product it must be able to produce to stay ahead of normal demand. *Location planning* for goods involves analyzing proposed facility sites in terms of proximity to raw materials and markets, availability of labor, energy and transportation costs, regulations and taxes, and community living conditions. Location planning for high-contact services involves locating the service near customers.

   Layout planning involves designing department locations in a facility so as to enhance production efficiency. In *quality planning*, systems are developed to ensure that products meet a firm's quality standards. In *methods planning*, specific production steps and methods for performing them are identified. Once plans identify needed resources and specify means of using them, production timetables are developed in the form of schedules.

4. **Explain some of the activities involved in *operations control*, including *materials management* and the use of certain *operations control tools*.** *Materials management* refers to the planning, organizing, and controlling of the flow of materials. It focuses on the control of *transportation* (transporting resources to the manufacturer and products to customers), *warehousing* (storing both incoming raw materials and finished goods), *purchasing* (acquiring the raw materials and services that a manufacturer needs), and *inventory control*. To control inventory, operations managers use various methods. A *just-in-time (JIT)* production system brings together all materials and parts needed at each production stage at the precise moment that they are required. *Material requirements planning (MRP)* refers to a method for ensuring that the right amounts of materials are delivered to the right place at the right time. The use of *quality improvement teams* and worker training programs can assist in *quality control*—the management of the operations process so as to ensure products that meet specific quality standards.

5. **Identify some of the key tools for *total quality management*, including strategies for getting closer to the customer.** *Total quality management (TQM)* includes any activity for getting quality products to the marketplace. It involves all the key functions of management—planning, organizing, directing, and controlling. It often begins with *competitive product analysis*—the process whereby a company analyzes a competitor's products to identify desirable improvements in its own.

   TQM tools include *statistical process control (SPC)*—methods whereby employees gather data and analyze variations in production activities. The purpose of SPC is to identify needed adjustments. One SPC tool is the *control chart*, which plots test sampling results to identify when a process is beginning to depart from normal conditions. *Quality/cost studies* are useful because improvements in products or production processes always entail additional costs. This method helps manufacturers identify areas in which quality can be maintained with the greatest cost savings. Finally, an increasingly important area of quality improvement is the realization that heeding the needs and reactions of its customers is a good way of making the most cost-effective changes in a company's goods or services.

QUESTIONS AND EXERCISES

QUESTIONS FOR REVIEW

1. What are the four different kinds of production-based utility?
2. What are the major differences between goods-production operations and service operations?
3. What are the major differences between high-contact and low-contact service systems?
4. What are the five major categories of operations planning?
5. What activities are involved in total quality management?

QUESTIONS FOR ANALYSIS

6. What are the resources and finished products of the following services?
   - Real estate firm
   - Child care facility
   - Bank
   - City water department
   - Hotel
7. Analyze the layout of a local firm with which you do business—perhaps a restaurant or a supermarket. What problems do you see and what recommendations would you make to management?
8. Why is high quality in the service sector so difficult to achieve?

APPLICATION EXERCISES

9. Interview the owner of a local, small manufacturing firm. Classify the firm's operations processes and then identify its major operations problems. Propose some solutions to these problems.
10. Using a local company as an example, show how you would conduct a quality/cost study. Identify the cost categories and give some examples of the costs in each category. Which categories do you expect to have the highest and lowest costs? Why?

BUILDING YOUR BUSINESS SKILLS

MAKING YOUR BENCHMARK IN THE BUSINESS WORLD

This exercise enhances the following SCANS workplace competencies: demonstrating basic skills, demonstrating thinking skills, exhibiting interpersonal skills, and working with information.

▼ GOAL

To encourage students to understand ways in which benchmarking can improve quality and productivity.

▼ SITUATION

As the director of maintenance for a regional airline, you are disturbed to learn that the cost of maintaining your 100-plane fleet is skyrocketing. A major factor is repair time: When maintenance or repairs are required, work often proceeds slowly. As a result, additional aircraft are required to meet the schedule. To address the problem, you decide to use a powerful total quality management tool called *benchmarking:* You will approach your problem by studying ways in which other companies have successfully managed similar problems. Your goal is to apply the best practices to your own maintenance and repair operation.

(continued)

▼ METHOD

STEP 1

Working with three or four other students, choose your benchmarking target from among the following choices:

The maintenance and repair operations of a competing airline
The pit crew operations of an Indianapolis 500 race car team
The maintenance and repair operations of a nationwide trucking company

Write a memo explaining the reasons for your choice.

STEP 2

Write a list of benchmarking questions that will help you learn the best practices of your targeted company. Your goal is to ask questions that will help you improve your own operation. These questions will be asked during on-site visits.

STEP 3

As part of a benchmarking project, you will be dealing with your counterparts in other companies. You have a responsibility to prepare for these encounters, and you must remember that what you learn during the exchange process is privileged information. Given these requirements, describe the steps that you would take before your first on-site visit and outline your benchmarking code of ethics.

▼ FOLLOW-UP QUESTIONS

1. Why is benchmarking an important method for improving quality?
2. Why did you make your benchmarking choice? Explain why the company you selected holds more promise than other companies in helping you solve your internal maintenance problems.
3. What kind of information would help you improve the efficiency of your operations? Are you interested in management information, technical information, or both?
4. In an age of heightened competition, why do you think companies are willing to benchmark with each other?

CRAFTING YOUR BUSINESS PLAN

PRODUCING FOR QUALITY

▼ The Purpose of the Assignment

1. To acquaint students with the process of navigating the Business PlanPro (BPP) software package.
2. To familiarize students with the ways in which production and quality management considerations enter into the business planning framework in BPP.
3. To stimulate students' thinking about applying the textbook's information on operations management and quality improvement to the preparation of their business plan in BPP.

▼ Assignment

After reading Chapter 13 in the textbook, open the BPP software* and look around for information about the plans for managing production and implementing quality at a sample firm: Golf Pro Shop (Golf Master Pro Shops, Inc.). Then respond to the following questions:

1. What type of product—a physical good or a service—is Golf Master Pro Shops creating in its production process? Explain. [Sites to see in *BPP* (for this assignment): In the Task Manager screen, click on Finish and Polish. Then click on **6. Executive Summary.** After returning to the Task Manager screen, click on Initial Assessment. Next click on each of the following, in turn: **1. Objectives** and **2. Mission.** In the Task Manager screen, click on What You're Selling and then on **3. Competitive Positioning.** From the Task Manager screen, click on Your Marketing Plan. From there, click on **3. Marketing Strategy Summary.**]
2. Describe the characteristics of the transformation (operations) process that produces this company's products. [Sites to see in *BPP:* In the Task Manager screen, click on Your Company. Then click on each of the following, in turn: **1. The Company Summary** and **3. Start-Up Plan.** After returning to Task Manager, click on Your Management Team; then click on **2. Organizational Structure.** From the Task Manager screen, click on What You're Selling; then click on **3. Competitive Positioning.**]
3. Suppose that Golf Master wants to develop plans for measuring the quality of both its products and its production process. What kinds of measurements would you recommend? [Sites to see in *BPP:* In the Task Manager screen, click on Your Company. Then click on each of the following, in turn: **1. The Company Summary** and **6. Sales Literature.** After returning to Task Manager, click first on Your Management Team and then on **2. Organizational Structure.** From the Task Manager screen, click on What You're Selling. From there, click on each of the following in turn: **2. Detailed Description, 3. Competitive Positioning,** and **4. Sourcing and Fulfillment.**]
4. Identify and describe some issues and problems that Golf Master might face in developing a layout for its facilities. [Sites to see in *BPP:* In the Task Manager screen, click on Your Management Team. Then click on each of the following, in turn: **2. Organizational Structure** and **4. Gaps.** From the Task Manager screen, click on What You're Selling. From there, click on each of the following: **2. Detailed Description** and **6. Future Development.** After returning to Task Manager, click first on Finish and Polish and then on **6. Executive Summary.**]

(continued)

▼ For Your Own Business Plan

5. Consider the planning that would be appropriate for the following three aspects of production: (1) the steps involved in producing your company's product; (2) the types of equipment and facilities that will be used; and (3) the steps that will be taken to ensure product quality. Among these three aspects, which is most important to emphasize for your business plan? Which is least important? In how much detail will you cover each of these aspects in the writeup of your plan?

▼ *Tips for Navigating in BPP

1. Open the BPP program, observe the Welcome screen, and click on **Open a Sample Plan.**
2. From the Open a Sample Plan dialogue box, click on a sample company name; then click on **Open.**
3. On the Task Manager screen, click onto any lines (for example, **Your Company**).
4. You can always return to the Task Manager screen by going to the bottom of the screen and clicking on the **Task Manager** icon.
5. When you are finished with a sample company, close its Task Manager screen.
6. After finishing with a sample company, you can get to the next one by going to the top of the screen and clicking on **File** (on the menu bar). Then beneath that, select **Open Sample Plan.** This will exit you from the current company file and send you to the Open a Sample Plan dialogue box, where you can select your next sample company.

EXPLORING THE NET

BECOMING ACCULTURATED TO QUALITY

At a time when rigorous competition has driven many U.S. companies out of the electronics products business, Motorola has maintained its position as one of the industry's most successful firms. To learn more about the production of its products and the role played by quality assurance in a world-class company, log on to the Motorola website at

http://www.motorola.com

First browse the home page. Then explore the pages titled "Product Portfolio," "Motorola Store," and "Inside Motorola." Finally consider the following questions:

1. Would Motorola be best described as a "goods producer" or a "services provider"? Explain your answer using information that you located at this Web site.
2. From the "Motorola Store" page, click on **Customer Services.** Explain Motorola Store's customer service process. What steps (activities) are included in its operations? What types of utility does this service-production process provide for the customer?
3. From the "Inside Motorola" page, click on **Motorola University.** Next, select Site Navigator (at the top of the page). Now explore the window titled "About Motorola University." Is the product offered here a "good" or a "service"? Describe its transformation technology.
4. From the "Inside Motorola" page, click on **Motorola University.** Next, select "Site Navigator" (at the top of the page). Now explore the window titled "Motorola Quality Briefing." Describe Motorola's position on quality. Why do you suppose Motorola qualifies as an expert on quality?
5. This company is famous for its "six sigma" quality program. To find out more about six sigma, start at the page titled "Inside Motorola." At the top of this page, click on **Search;** then enter the words *six sigma* in the search engine. Explore the first few documents located by the search. How important is quality at Motorola?
6. Considering the nature of its six sigma program, would you say that Motorola is being realistic in its efforts to achieve for perfection? List the pros and cons of the company's approach to six sigma quality.
7. Still considering the role of the six sigma program in Motorola's quality culture, start again at the page titled "Inside Motorola"; at the top of the page, click on **Search.** Look in the left column and explore the title "TCS (Total Customer Satisfaction) Teams." Explain the role played by these teams in Motorola's quality culture.

Understanding Accounting and Information Systems

How Cooking the Books Left One Accountant with a Bad Taste

Let's say that you are the head of a corporation that is committing systematic fraud against the federal government worth hundreds of millions of dollars. Who's the last person you'd want on your team? Probably an ethical accountant, especially if that person is also determined and detail oriented. It would certainly be a mistake to ask this accountant to create two sets of accounting ledgers and thereby involve him directly in the fraud. That's the mistake that Columbia/HCA Healthcare Corp. and the Quorum Health Group made when they told hospital finance officer James F. Alderson to "cook the books." Alderson refused. He was fired but ultimately blew the whistle on his old employer to signal a federal lawsuit that has shaken the entire health care industry.

Alderson worked for years at North Valley Hospital in Whitefish, a ski town in northwest Montana. When the hospital's top administrator left in 1990, the board turned to Quorum Health Group to run the hospital. Quorum, a management company once affiliated with Columbia/HCA, got the account largely because of its promise to obtain maximum reimbursements for Medicare-related expenses.

Thus becoming a Quorum employee, Alderson was working on Medicare cost reports when he was told by his Quorum superiors to prepare two sets of books. The "official" set would aggressively claim expenses that never occurred. A second "unofficial" set, for internal use only, would be legitimate. This second set estimated the amount in claims made on the first set that Medicare might reject as bogus. A corresponding amount of money was placed in reserve. If there was no audit for 2 years, accountants would then credit these reserves as revenues.

Alderson advised his new employer that he "never did two tax returns for anyone" when he was a public accountant and "wasn't going to do two cost reports" now that he was a private accountant working for Quorum. Alderson suspected that the scheme in which he had been ordered to participate was standard practice not only at Quorum, but also at its former parent, Columbia/HCA. Both companies, he believed, were submitting false Medicare reports that were costing the taxpayers millions.

A few days later, Alderson was dismissed. Understandably outraged, he filed a wrongful termination suit against Quorum and began gathering evidence of the suspected fraud. At about this time, a friend told him about the federal whistle-blower law, which allows private citizens to file fraud-related lawsuits on behalf of the federal government and to receive a percentage of the money that the government ultimately recovers. By filing such a suit, Alderson instigated a government investigation during the course of which the Justice Department subpoenaed years' worth of Quorum cost and reserve reports. "I couldn't believe what I was seeing," said former Medicare auditor (and Alderson advisor) Nicholas L. Bordeau. "It was an organized system to take advantage of the Medicare system."

Years after he had initiated his original case, Alderson filed a new complaint in Florida, a state with millions of Medicare-aged residents and a history of fraud offenses involving Columbia/HCA. By 1997, the Federal Bureau of Investigation had indicted three Columbia executives in Florida, and a year later, on October 5, 1998, the federal government officially joined Alderson's case against Quorum and Columbia. At that point, his lawyer, Stephen Meagher, attempted to put 8 years of legal struggles into perspective: "A discovery made by one man at a small rural hospital ultimately unraveled a nationwide, systemwide scheme. One person can truly make a difference."

> "A discovery made by one man at a small rural hospital ultimately unraveled a nationwide, systemwide scheme. One person can truly make a difference."
>
> —Stephen Meagher
> *Attorney*

This chapter will introduce you to the work performed by accountants and to the basic financial reports of economic activity that are the primary reason for accounting. As you will see in this chapter, accounting goes hand in hand with information management. In today's complex business environment, the need to manage information efficiently and quickly is crucial. Information, of course, can take many forms—information about expenses and assets, information about customers' locations and order patterns, information about supplies and finished goods on hand, information about workers' pay and productivity, information about products in development, and information about competitors and customers.

Our opening story is continued on page 383

After reading this chapter, you should be able to:

1. **Explain the role of *accountants* and the kinds of work they do.**
2. **Explain how the following three concepts are used in *record keeping: accounting equation*, *double-entry accounting*, and *T-accounts for debits and credits*.**
3. **Describe two important *financial statements* and show how they reflect the activity and financial condition of a business.**
4. **Explain how computing key *financial ratios* can help in analyzing the financial strengths of a business.**
5. **Identify the role played in computer systems by *databases* and describe four important types of *business application programs*.**
6. **List some trends in the application of technology to *business information management* and discuss the effect of the *Internet* and *World Wide Web* on information management.**

WHAT IS ACCOUNTING AND WHO USES ACCOUNTING INFORMATION?

accounting Comprehensive system for collecting, analyzing, and communicating financial information

bookkeeping The recording of accounting transactions

accounting system Organized means by which financial information is identified, measured, recorded, and retained for use in accounting statements and management reports

Accounting is a comprehensive system for collecting, analyzing, and communicating financial information. It is a system for measuring business performance and translating those measures into information for management decisions. Accounting also uses performance measures to prepare performance reports for owners, the public, and regulatory agencies. To meet these objectives, accountants keep records of such transactions as taxes paid, income received, and expenses incurred. They also analyze the effects of these transactions on particular business activities. By sorting, analyzing, and recording thousands of transactions, accountants can determine how well a business is being managed and how financially strong it is.[1]

Bookkeeping, which is sometimes confused with accounting, is just one phase of accounting—the recording of accounting transactions. Clearly, accounting is much more comprehensive than bookkeeping because accounting involves more than just the recording of information.

Because businesses engage in many thousands of transactions, ensuring consistent, dependable financial information is mandatory. This is the job of the **accounting system:** an organized procedure for identifying, measuring, recording, and retaining financial information so that it can be used in accounting statements and management reports. The system includes all the people, reports, computers, procedures, and resources for compiling financial transactions.

Users of Accounting Information

On November 18, 1997, Noranda Inc., Canada's biggest natural resource company, announced plans to refocus on the mining and metals side of its activities by selling its forest products and oil and natural gas interests. In preparation for the announcement, corporate officers relied on accounting to provide information for everyone who might be interested in the firm's activities. Its 49-percent ownership of Norcen Energy Resources Ltd. will be sold. Its oil and gas subsidiary, Canadian Hunter Exploration Ltd., will be distributed as a dividend to Noranda shareholders, as will its interest in Noranda Forest Inc., a forest products company. A statement was issued to shareholders and the public to show clearly how much each of the three segments contributed to Noranda's overall sales, expenses, and earnings. Current and potential stockholders also had to be told how the new stock shares would be distributed.[2]

Noranda accountants must tabulate financial projections for the separation because stakeholders have important questions about each of the three companies destined for separation: Do the business prospects indicate that as separate companies they are good credit risks? As investments, will they pay sufficient financial returns to owners? Have adequate arrangements been made for employee retirement funds and benefits? Do their business prospects look healthy enough to support current employment levels? Upon receiving accounting answers to questions such as these, different information users (owners, employees, regulatory agencies, lenders, and the public) are better prepared to make decisions for themselves and for their organizations.

As the Noranda example illustrates, there are numerous users of accounting information:

- *Business managers* use accounting information to set goals, develop plans, set budgets, and evaluate future prospects.
- *Employees and unions* use accounting information to get paid and to plan for and receive such benefits as health care, insurance, vacation time, and retirement pay.
- *Investors and creditors* use accounting information to estimate returns to stockholders, determine a company's growth prospects, and determine whether it is a good credit risk before investing or lending.

The Broadway musical Ragtime *was a hit—but not* that *big a hit. It seems that Toronto-based Livent Inc., the show's producer, used some creative accounting tactics to bolster the success of various projects. According to analysts, one "irregular" technique permitted Livent to buy advertising, scenery, and costumes without deducting them from the bottom line. Merely resorting to looser Canadian accounting standards enabled Livent head Garth Drabinsky to reduce one year's loss from $38 million to $29 million. It did not, however, prevent Wall Street from reckoning the firm's debt at $130 million and total value at $120 million.*

- *Tax authorities* use accounting information to plan for tax inflows, determine the tax liabilities of individuals and businesses, and ensure that correct amounts are paid on time.
- *Government regulatory agencies* rely on accounting information to fulfill their duties. The Toronto Stock Exchange in Canada and the Securities and Exchange Commission in the United States, for example, require firms to file financial disclosures so that potential investors have valid information about a company's financial status.

WHO ARE ACCOUNTANTS AND WHAT DO THEY DO?

At the head of the accounting system is the *controller*, who manages all the firm's accounting activities. As chief accounting officer, the controller ensures that the accounting system provides the reports and statements needed for planning, controlling, and decision-making activities. This broad range of activities requires different types of accounting specialists. In this section we begin by distinguishing between the two main fields of accounting: *financial* and *managerial.* Then we discuss two of the most important services offered by accountants—*auditing* and *tax services.*

Financial versus Managerial Accounting

In any company, two fields of accounting (financial and managerial) can be distinguished by the different users they serve. As we have just seen, it is both convenient and accurate to classify users of accounting information as users outside the company and users inside the company. This same distinction allows us to categorize accounting systems as either *financial* or *managerial.*

financial accounting system Field of accounting concerned with external users of a company's financial information

managerial (or **management**) **accounting** Field of accounting that serves internal users of a company's financial information

FINANCIAL ACCOUNTING A firm's **financial accounting system** is concerned with external users of information: consumer groups, unions, stockholders, and government agencies. It prepares and publishes income statements and balance sheets at regular intervals, as well as other financial reports that are published for shareholders and the general public.[3] All of these documents focus on the activities of the company as a whole, rather than on individual departments or divisions.

MANAGERIAL ACCOUNTING In contrast, **managerial** (or **management**) **accounting** serves internal users. Managers at all levels need information to make decisions for their departments, to monitor current projects, and to plan for future activities. Other employees also need accounting information. Engineers, for instance, want to know the costs for materials and production so that they can make product or operations improvements. To set performance goals, salespeople need data on past sales by geographic region. Purchasing agents use information on materials costs to negotiate terms with suppliers.[4]

Accounting Services

certified public accountant (CPA) Accountant licensed by the state and offering services to the public

Certified public accountants (CPAs) offer accounting services to the public. CPAs are licensed at the state level after passing a 3-day written exam prepared by the American Institute of Certified Public Accountants (AICPA), which is the national professional organization of CPAs. The AICPA also provides technical support to members and discipline in matters of professional ethics. Virtually all CPA firms, whether consisting of 10,000 employees in 100 nationwide offices or just one person in a small private facility, provide auditing, tax, and management services. Larger firms earn 60 to 70 percent of their revenue from auditing services. Smaller firms typically earn most of their income from tax and management services.

audit Systematic examination of a company's accounting system to determine whether its financial reports fairly present its operations

AUDITING An **audit** examines a company's accounting system to determine whether its financial reports fairly present its operations. Companies must normally provide audit reports when applying for loans or selling stock. In 1998, for example, the chief accounting officer and an internal auditing team at newly formed Cendant Corp. uncovered an accounting scandal involving more than $250 million. Cendant had been formed by the merger of CUC International, a catalog buying-club business, and HFS Inc., owner of hotel chains (Days Inn and Howard Johnson) and real estate brokerages (Century 21 and Caldwell Bankers). After the merger, the Cendant team reported a problem with CUC's net income reported for 1997: Sixty percent of it did not exist! An immediate result of the disclosure was a 50 percent plunge in the share price of Cendant stock. Company officials hastened to report that the irregularities were a result of inadequate checks and balances in CUC's accounting procedures (before the merger), not of any fraudulent management conduct.[5]

generally accepted accounting principles (GAAP) Accepted rules and procedures governing the content and form of financial reports

The auditor must also ensure that the client's accounting system follows **generally accepted accounting principles (GAAP):** rules and procedures governing the content and form of financial reports. These principles are formulated by the Financial Accounting Standards Board (FASB) of the AICPA.[6] By using GAAP, the audit should determine whether a firm has controls to prevent errors and fraud. Ultimately, the auditor will certify whether the client's financial reports comply with GAAP, although the principles are not foolproof. Recently, for example, the Securities and Exchange Commission has expressed concern that some companies and their accountants are using "accounting hocus-pocus" to inflate their earnings reports, so that bottom lines do not reflect actual operations. According to SEC Chairman Arthur Levitt, "We're seeing greater evidence of these illusions or tricks, and we intend to step in and turn around some of these practices." Some companies, for instance, use a practice called "revenue recognition" to increase their reported earnings prematurely: They figure these prospective revenues into earnings reports before a sale is completed, before a product is delivered, or before the customer has made a binding commitment to buy.[7]

"We're seeing greater evidence of these illusions or tricks, and we intend to step in and turn around some of these practices."

—Arthur Levitt
Chairman, Securities and Exchange Commission

Tax Services Tax laws are immensely complex. Tax services thus include assistance not only with tax return preparation but also with tax planning. A CPA's advice, for example, can help a business structure (or restructure) operations and investments and perhaps save millions of dollars in taxes. To best serve their clients, accountants must stay abreast of changes in tax laws, which is no simple matter. Legislators made more than 70 pages of technical corrections to the 1986 Tax Reform Act before it even became law. But no matter how detailed the tax code itself, different interpretations still result in controversy over how much tax write-offs the law allows. In 1998, for example, the Securities and Exchange Commission blocked America Online (AOL), the world's biggest Internet company, from publishing its fourth-quarter earnings report for 2 months. According to the SEC, AOL tried to write off excessive amounts of "research and development" assets for two companies that it had bought during the year. After reaching agreement with SEC, AOL published an earnings report with a substantially lower tax write-off than originally planned.[8]

TOOLS OF THE ACCOUNTING TRADE

All accountants rely on record keeping, either manual or electronic, to enter and track business transactions. Underlying all record-keeping procedures are the three key concepts of accounting: *the accounting equation*, *double-entry accounting*, and *T-accounts* for debits and credits.

Record Keeping with Journals and Ledgers

As Figure 14.1 shows, record keeping begins with initial records of a firm's financial transactions. These transactions include sales orders, invoices for incoming materials, employee time cards, and customer installment payments. Large companies receive and process tens of thousands of these documents every day. For example, before switching to credit cards with magnetic strips, Amoco Oil Co. received 650,000 sales receipts daily. Each receipt represented a transaction. Of course, few companies today are deluged with such waves of paper, but even in the age of digitized information flows, managers can track and control a company's progress only if its transactions are analyzed and classified in an orderly fashion.

Journals and Ledgers As *initial records* are received, they are sorted and entered into a **journal:** a chronological record of financial transactions, including a brief description of each. They are now *intermediate records.* Most companies keep specialized journals for different transactions, such as cash receipts, sales, and purchases.

journal Chronological record of a firm's financial transactions, including a brief description of each

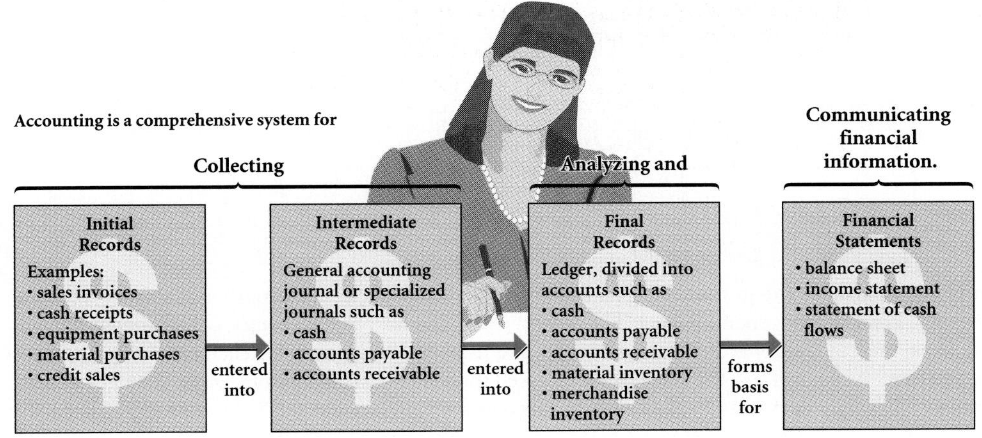

FIGURE 14.1 ◆ **Accounting and Record Keeping**

ledger Record, divided into accounts and usually compiled on a monthly basis, containing summaries of all journal transactions

Journal transactions are summarized, usually on a monthly basis, in a *final record* called the **ledger.** In the term *auditing the books*, the *book* is the ledger. Like specialized journals, the ledger is divided into *accounts*, such as *cash*, *inventories*, and *receivables*. The cash account, for example, is a detailed record of all the firm's changes in cash. Other accounts record changes in each type of asset and liability. Ledgers also feature an important column labeled "balance," which shows the current total dollar amount in each account. If a balance in a given account is unexpectedly high or low, tracking backward to the corresponding journal entry should reveal the cause of the unexpected figure.

fiscal year Twelve-month period designated for annual financial reporting purposes

FINANCIAL REPORTS AND THE FISCAL YEAR At the end of the year, all the accounts in the ledger are totaled, and the firm's financial status is assessed. This summation is the basis for annual financial reports. With the preparation of reports, the old accounting cycle ends and a new cycle begins. The timing of the annual accounting cycle is called the **fiscal year:** the 12-month period used for financial reporting purposes. Although most companies adopt the calendar year, many companies use 12-month periods that reflect the seasonal nature of their industries. For example, to close its fiscal year at the completion of harvesting, a fruit orchard may select the period from September 1, 1999, to August 31, 2000.

As an example of the record-keeping process, consider Figures 14.2 and 14.3, which illustrate a portion of the process for Perfect Posters Inc., a hypothetical wholesaler. In Figure 14.2, a check from Eye-Poppers (an initial record) is entered in Perfect Posters' general accounting journal (an intermediate record).

FIGURE 14.2 ◆ Entering a Check in the General Journal

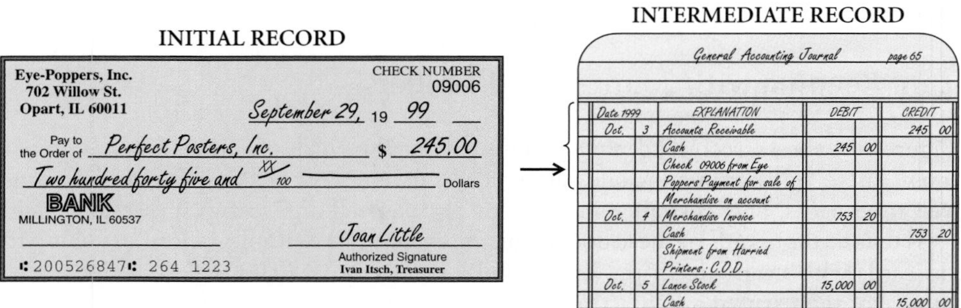

INITIAL RECORD

Eye-Poppers, Inc.
702 Willow St.
Opart, IL 60011

CHECK NUMBER 09006

September 29, 19 99

Pay to the Order of Perfect Posters, Inc. $ 245.00

Two hundred forty five and xx/100 Dollars

BANK
MILLINGTON, IL 60537

Joan Little
Authorized Signature
Ivan Itsch, Treasurer

⑆200526847⑆ 264 1223

INTERMEDIATE RECORD

General Accounting Journal page 65

Date 1999		EXPLANATION	DEBIT		CREDIT	
Oct.	3	Accounts Receivable			245	00
		Cash	245	00		
		Check 09006 from Eye				
		Poppers Payment for sale of				
		Merchandise on account				
Oct.	4	Merchandise Invoice	753	20		
		Cash			753	20
		Shipment from Harried				
		Printers: C.O.D.				
Oct.	5	Lance Stock	15,000	00		
		Cash			15,000	00

Entering a check in the general journal. The transaction begins when Perfect Posters receives a check from Eye-Poppers. Along with a brief explanation, the amount of the check is entered on the *debit* side of the Perfect Posters general accounting journal. Note that the amount, $245, has also been entered on Oct. 3 as an *accounts receivable.* The accountant has noted both a *decrease* in the company's assets (money owed Perfect Posters by Eye-Poppers) and an *increase* (money paid to Perfect Posters by Eye-Poppers). As we will see, these entries will be balanced in the firm's general ledger (Figure 14.3).

FIGURE 14.3 ◆ Entering a Check in the General Ledger

General Ledger Page 19
Accounts Receivable Account

Date 1999			Debit		Credit		Balance	
Sept.	30						4546	61
Sept.	30	No Blond Looks			324	46	4222	15
Oct.	3	Eye Poppers			245	00	3977	15
Oct.	6	Walls R Us	5131	32			9108	47
Oct.	10	Cover All			123	45	8985	02

General Ledger
Cash Account

Date 1999			Debit		Credit		Balance	
Oct.	3						98,563	43
Oct.	3	Eye Poppers	245	00			98,808	43
Oct.	4	Harried Printers			753	20	98,055	23
Oct.	5	Lance			15,000	00	83,055	23
Oct.	5	Walls R Us			5,131	20	77,924	03

Entering a check in the general ledger. Perfect Poster's accountant now transfers the entry from the general journal to the general ledger. The ledger is divided into two accounts: *accounts receivable* and cash. Note that a new column, *balance*, also appears; total dollar amounts for each type of account are entered here. As we will see, the accountant has used the *double-entry accounting system:* The $245 check from Eye-Poppers decreases Perfect Posters' accounts receivable account (it is no longer owed the money) *and* increases its cash account. On the company's balance sheet (Figure 14.5), both balances will appear as *current assets.*

In Figure 14.3, this entry eventually turns up in Perfect Posters' general ledger, where it becomes a final record showing a cash account balance of $98,808.43. In the next section we see how this entry is ultimately reflected in the financial reports that Perfect Posters submits to its stockholders and its bank.

The Accounting Equation

At various points in the year, accountants use the following equation to balance the data in journals and ledgers:

Assets = Liabilities + Owners' equity

To understand the importance of this equation, we must first understand the terms *assets*, *liabilities*, and *owners' equity*.[9]

ASSETS AND LIABILITIES Charm and intelligence are often said to be assets, and a nonswimmer is no doubt a liability on a canoeing trip. Accountants apply these same terms to items with quantifiable value. Thus, an **asset** is any economic resource that is expected to benefit a firm or an individual who owns it. Assets include land, buildings, equipment, inventory, and payments due the company (accounts receivable). A **liability** is a debt that the firm owes to an outside organization or individual.

asset Any economic resource expected to benefit a firm or individual who owns it

liability Debt owed by a firm to an outside organization or individual

OWNERS' EQUITY You may also have heard someone speak of the equity that he or she has in a home—that is, the amount of money that could be made by selling the house and paying off the mortgage. Similarly, **owners' equity** is the amount of money that owners would receive if they sold all of a company's assets and paid all of its liabilities. We can rewrite the accounting equation to show this definition:

owners' equity Amount of money owners would receive if they sold all of a firm's assets and paid all of its liabilities

Assets − Liabilities = Owners' equity

If a company's assets exceed its liabilities, owners' equity is *positive:* If the company goes out of business, the owners will receive some cash (a gain) after selling assets and paying off liabilities. If liabilities outweigh assets, however, owners' equity is *negative:* Assets are insufficient to pay off all debts. If the company goes out of business, the owners will get no cash and some creditors will not be paid. Owners' equity is a meaningful number to both investors and lenders. For example, before lending money to owners, lenders want to know the amount of owners' equity existing in a business.

Owners' equity consists of two sources of capital:

- The amount that the owners originally invested
- Profits earned by and reinvested in the company

When a company operates profitably, its assets increase faster than its liabilities. Owners' equity, therefore, will increase if profits are retained in the business instead of paid out as dividends to stockholders. Owners' equity can also increase if owners invest more of their own money to increase assets. However, owners' equity can shrink if the company operates at a loss or if the owners withdraw assets.

Double-Entry Accounting

If your business purchases inventory with cash, you decrease your cash and increase your inventory. Similarly, if you purchase supplies on credit, you increase your supplies and increase your accounts payable. If you invest more money in your business, you increase the company's cash and increase your owners' equity. In other words, *every transaction affects two accounts.* Accountants thus use a **double-entry accounting system** to record the dual effects of financial transactions.

double-entry accounting system Bookkeeping system that balances the accounting equation by recording the dual effects of every financial transaction

Recording dual effects ensures that the accounting equation always balances. As the term implies, the double-entry system requires at least two bookkeeping entries for each transaction. This practice keeps the accounting equation in balance.

FIGURE 14.4 ◆ **The T-Account and Accounting Equation**

ACCOUNTING EQUATION	Assets		=	Liabilities		+	Owners' Equity	
RULES OF THE T-ACCOUNT	Debit for Increase	Credit for Decrease		Debit for Decrease	Credit for Increase		Debit for Decrease	Credit for Increase

Debits and Credits: The T-Account

T-account Bookkeeping format for recording transactions that takes the shape of a *T* whose vertical line divides the account into debits (left side) and credits (right side)

Another accounting tool uses debits and credits as a universal method for keeping accounting records. To understand debits and credits, we first need to understand the **T-account.** The format for recording transactions takes the shape of a *T* whose vertical line divides the account into two sides. As pictured below, for example, Perfect Posters' general accounting journal has the following T format:

Cash	
Left side	**Right side**
Debit	Credit

debit Bookkeeping entry in a T-account that records increases in assets

credit Bookkeeping entry in a T-account that records decreases in assets

In bookkeeping, **debit** and **credit** refer to the side on which account information is to be entered. The left column of any T-account is called the *debit* side, and the right column is the *credit* side:

debit = left side
credit = right side

When an asset increases, it is entered as a debit. When it decreases, it is entered as a credit. Thus, when Perfect Posters received payment from Eye-Poppers, it received more cash—an asset. It thus debited the general accounting journal (Figure 14.2) by placing $245 on the left side of that T-account.

Figure 14.4 shows how the rules of the T-account are consistent with the terms of the accounting equation. Debits and credits provide a system of checks and balances. Every debit entry in a journal must have an offsetting credit entry elsewhere. If not, the books will not balance because some error (or deliberate deception) has been introduced in the record keeping. To ensure accurate financial records, accountants must find and correct such errors.

T-accounts and the double-entry system, therefore, provide an important method of accounting control. At the end of the accounting cycle, debits and credits must balance; total debits must equal total credits in the account balances recorded in the general ledger. An imbalance indicates improper accounting that must be corrected. Balancing the books, then, is a control procedure to ensure that proper accounting has been used.

■ FINANCIAL STATEMENTS

financial statement Any of several types of reports summarizing a company's financial status to aid in managerial decision making

As noted earlier, the primary purposes of accounting are to summarize the results of a firm's transactions and to issue reports to help managers make informed decisions. Among the most important reports are **financial statements,** which fall into two broad categories—*balance sheets* and *income statements.*[10]

Balance Sheets

balance sheet Financial statement detailing a firm's assets, liabilities, and owners' equity

Balance sheets supply detailed information about the accounting equation factors: assets, liabilities, and owners' equity. Because they also show a firm's financial condition at one point in time, balance sheets are sometimes called *statements of financial position.* Figure 14.5 shows the balance sheet for Perfect Posters.

FIGURE 14.5 ◆ Perfect Posters' Balance Sheet

Perfect Posters, INC.
555 RIVERVIEW, CHICAGO, IL 60606

Perfect Posters, Inc.
Balance Sheet
As of December 31, 1999

Assets			
Current Assets:			
Cash		$7,050	
Marketable securities		2,300	
Accounts receivable	$26,210		
Less: Allowance for doubtful accounts	(650)	25,560	
Merchandise inventory		21,250	
Prepaid expenses		1,050	
Total current assets			$ 57,210
Fixed assets:			
Land		18,000	
Building	65,000		
Less: Accumulated depreciation	(22,500)	42,500	
Equipment	72,195		
Less: Accumulated depreciation	(24,815)	47,380	
Total fixed assets			107,880
Intangible assets:			
Patents	7,100		
Trademarks	900		
Total intangible assets			8,000
Total assets			$173,090

Liabilities and Owners' Equity		
Current liabilities:		
Accounts payable	$16,315	
Wages payable	3,700	
Taxes payable	1,920	
Total current liabilities		$ 21,935
Long-term liabilities:		
Notes payable, 8% due 2001	10,000	
Bonds payable, 9% due 2003	30,000	
Total long-term liabilities		40,000
Total liabilities		**$ 61,935**
Owners' Equity:		
Common stock, $5 par	40,000	
Additional paid-in capital	15,000	
Retained earnings	56,155	
Total owners' equity		111,155
Total liabilities and owners' equity		**$173,090**

Perfect Posters' balance sheet as of December 31, 1999. Perfect Posters' balance sheet shows clearly that the firm's total assets equal its total liabilities and owners' equality.

ASSETS As we have seen, an asset is any economic resource that a company owns and from which it can expect to derive some future benefit. From an accounting standpoint, most companies have three types of assets: *current*, *fixed*, and *intangible*.

Current Assets. The **current assets** include cash and assets that can be converted into cash within the following year. They are normally listed in order of **liquidity:** the ease with which they can be converted into cash. Business debts, for example, can usually be satisfied only through payments of cash. A company that needs but cannot generate cash—in other words, a company that is not liquid—may thus be forced to sell assets at sacrifice prices or even go out of business.

current asset Asset that can be converted into cash within the following year

liquidity Ease with which an asset can be converted into cash

By definition, cash is completely liquid. *Marketable securities* purchased as short-term investments are slightly less liquid but can be sold quickly if necessary. Marketable securities include stocks or bonds of other companies, government securities, and money market certificates. There are three other important nonliquid assets held by many companies: *accounts receivable*, *merchandise inventory*, and *prepaid expenses*.

ACCOUNTS RECEIVABLE. The **accounts receivable** are amounts due from customers who have purchased goods on credit. Most businesses expect to receive payment within 30 days of a sale. In our hypothetical example, the entry labeled *Less: Allowance for doubtful accounts* in Figure 14.5 indicates $650 in receivables that Perfect Posters does not expect to collect. Total accounts receivable assets are decreased accordingly.

accounts receivable Amount due from a customer who has purchased goods on credit

MERCHANDISE INVENTORY. Following accounts receivable on the Perfect Posters balance sheet is **merchandise inventory**—the cost of merchandise that has been acquired for sale to customers and is still on hand. Accounting for the value of inventories on the balance sheet is difficult because inventories are flowing in and out throughout the year. Therefore, assumptions must be made about which ones were sold and which ones remain in storage.

merchandise inventory Cost of merchandise that has been acquired for sale to customers and that is still on hand

prepaid expense Expense, such as prepaid rent, that is paid before the upcoming period in which it is due

PREPAID EXPENSES. The **prepaid expenses** include supplies on hand and rent paid for the period to come. They are assets because they have been paid for and are available to the company. In all, Perfect Posters' current assets as of December 31, 1999, totaled $57,210.

fixed asset Asset with long-term use or value, such as land, buildings, and equipment

depreciation Process of distributing the cost of an asset over its life

Fixed Assets. The next major classification on the balance sheet is usually **fixed assets.** Items in this category have long-term use or value (for example, land, buildings, and equipment). As buildings and equipment wear out or become obsolete, their value decreases. To reflect decreasing value, accountants use **depreciation** to spread the cost of an asset over the years of its useful life. Depreciation means calculating an asset's useful life in years, dividing its worth by that many years, and subtracting the resulting amount each year. Each year, therefore, the asset's remaining value decreases on the books. In Figure 14.5, Perfect Posters shows fixed assets of $107,880 after depreciation.

intangible asset Nonphysical asset, such as a patent or trademark, that has economic value in the form of expected benefit

goodwill Amount paid for an existing business above the value of its other assets

Intangible Assets. Although their worth is hard to set, intangible assets have monetary value. **Intangible assets** usually include the cost of obtaining rights or privileges such as patents, trademarks, copyrights, and franchise fees. **Goodwill** is the amount paid for an existing business beyond the value of its other assets.

A purchased firm, for example, may have a particularly good reputation or location. In fact, a company's goodwill may be worth more than its tangible assets. For example, when Ford purchased Jaguar for $2.5 billion, $2 billion was recorded as goodwill. Similarly, when General Motors paid $5 billion for Hughes Aircraft, only $1 billion could be associated with assets on Hughes's balance sheet; the remaining $4 billion was paid for goodwill.

Perfect Posters has no goodwill assets; however, it does own trademarks and patents for specialized storage equipment. These are intangible assets worth $8,000. Larger companies, of course, have intangible assets that are worth much more.

current liability Debt that must be paid within the year

accounts payable Current liabilities consisting of bills owed to suppliers, plus wages and taxes due within the upcoming year

long-term liability Debt that is not due for at least a year

paid-in capital Additional money, above proceeds from stock sale, paid directly to a firm by its owners

retained earnings Earnings retained by a firm for its use rather than paid as dividends

LIABILITIES Like assets, liabilities are often separated into different categories. **Current liabilities** are debts that must be paid within 1 year. These include **accounts payable:** unpaid bills to suppliers for materials as well as wages and taxes that must be paid in the coming year. Perfect Posters has current liabilities of $21,935.

Long-term liabilities are debts that are not due for at least a year. These normally represent borrowed funds on which the company must pay interest. Perfect Posters's long-term liabilities are $40,000.

OWNERS' EQUITY The final section of the balance sheet in Figure 14.5 shows owners' equity broken down into *common stock, paid-in capital,* and *retained earnings.* When Perfect Posters was formed, the declared legal value of its common stock was $5 per share. By law, this $40,000 ($5 × 8,000 shares) cannot be distributed as dividends. **Paid-in capital** is additional money invested in the firm by its owners. Perfect Posters has $15,000 in paid-in capital.

Retained earnings are net profits minus dividend payments to stockholders. Retained earnings accumulate when profits, which could have been distributed to stockholders, are kept instead for use by the company. At the close of 1999, Perfect Posters had retained earnings of $56,155.

Income Statements

income statement (or **profit-and-loss statement**) Financial statement listing a firm's annual revenues, expenses, and profit or loss

The **income statement** is sometimes called a **profit-and-loss statement,** because its description of revenues and expenses results in a figure showing the firm's annual profit or loss. In other words,

Revenues – Expenses = Profit (or loss)

Popularly known as "the bottom line," profit or loss is probably the most important figure in any business enterprise. Figure 14.6 shows the 1999 income statement for Perfect Posters, whose bottom line that year was $12,585. Like the balance sheet, the income statement is divided into three major categories: *revenues, cost of goods sold,* and *operating expenses.*

Perfect Posters, INC.
555 RIVERVIEW, CHICAGO, IL 60606

Perfect Posters, Inc.
Income Statement
Year Ended December 31, 1999

Revenues (gross sales)			$256,425
Cost of goods sold:			
Merchandise inventory, January 1, 1999.	$22,380		
Merchandise purchases during year	103,635		
Goods available for sale		$126,015	
Less: Merchandise inventory December 31, 1999		21, 250	
Cost of goods sold			104,765
Gross profit			151,660
Operating expenses:			
Selling and repackaging expenses:			
Salaries and wages	49,750		
Advertising	6,380		
Depreciation—warehouse and repackaging equipment	3,350		
Total selling and repackaging expenses		59, 480	
Administrative expenses:			
Salaries and wages	55,100		
Supplies	4,150		
Utilities	3,800		
Depreciation—office equipment	3,420		
Interest expense	2,900		
Miscellaneous expenses	1,835		
Total administrative expenses		71,205	
Total operating expenses			130,685
Operating income (income before taxes)			20,975
Income taxes			8,390
Net income			$12,585

Perfect Posters' income statement for year ended December 31, 1999. The final entry on the income statement, the bottom line, reports the firm's profit or loss.

FIGURE 14.6 ◆ Perfect Posters' Income Statement

REVENUES When a law firm receives $250 for preparing a will or when a supermarket collects $65 from a customer buying groceries, both are receiving **revenues:** the funds that flow into a business from the sale of goods or services. In 1999, Perfect Posters reported revenues of $256,425 from the sale of art prints and other posters.

revenues Funds that flow into a business from the sale of goods or services

COST OF GOODS SOLD In Perfect Posters' income statement, the **cost of goods sold** category shows the costs of obtaining materials to make the products sold during the year. Perfect Posters began 1999 with posters valued at $22,380. Over the year, it spent another $103,635 to purchase posters. During 1999, then, the company had $126,015 worth of merchandise available to sell. By the end of the year, it had sold all but $21,250 of those posters, which remained as merchandise inventory. The cost of obtaining the goods sold by the firm was thus $104,765.

cost of goods sold Total cost of obtaining materials for making the products sold by a firm during the year

Gross Profit (or Gross Margin). To calculate **gross profit** (or **gross margin**), subtract cost of goods sold from revenues. Perfect Posters' gross profit in 1999 was $151,660 ($256,425 – $104,765). Expressed as a percentage of sales, gross profit is 59.1 percent ($151,660/$256,425).

gross profit (or **gross margin**) Revenues from goods sold minus cost of goods sold

Gross profit percentages vary widely across industries. In retailing, for instance, Safeway's gross profit percentage is 27 percent; in food processing, General Mills' is 48 percent; and in the software industry, Microsoft's gross margin is 80 percent. For companies with low gross margins, product costs are a big expense. If a company has a high gross margin, it probably has low cost of goods sold but high selling and administrative expenses.

OPERATING EXPENSES In addition to costs directly related to acquiring goods, every company has general expenses ranging from erasers to the president's salary. Like cost of goods sold, **operating expenses** are resources that must flow out of a company for it to earn revenues. As you can see from Figure 14.6, Perfect Posters had 1999 operating expenses of $130,685. This figure consists of $59,480 in selling and repackaging expenses and $71,205 in administrative expenses.

operating expenses Costs, other than the cost of goods sold, incurred in producing a good or service

Selling expenses result from activities related to selling the firm's goods or services. These may include salaries for the sales force, delivery costs, and advertising expenses. *General and administrative expenses*, such as management salaries, insurance expenses, and maintenance costs, are expenses related to the general management of the company.

Operating and Net Income. Sometimes managers must determine **operating income,** which compares the gross profit from business operations against operating expenses. This calculation for Perfect Posters (\$151,660 – \$130,685) reveals an operating income, or *income before taxes*, of \$20,975. Subtracting income taxes from operating income (\$20,975 – \$8,390) reveals **net income** (also called **net profit** or **net earnings**). In 1999, Perfect Posters' net income was \$12,585.

■ ANALYZING FINANCIAL STATEMENTS

Financial statements present a great deal of information, but what does it all mean? How, for example, can statements help investors decide what stock to buy or help managers decide whether to extend credit? Statements provide data, which can in turn be applied to various ratios (comparative numbers). These ratios can then be used to analyze the financial health of one or more companies. They can also be used to check a firm's progress by comparing current with past statements.

Ratios are normally grouped into three major classifications:

- **Solvency ratios,** both short- and long-term, estimate risk.
- **Profitability ratios** measure potential earnings.
- **Activity ratios** reflect management's use of assets.

Depending on the decisions to be made, a user may apply none, some, or all the ratios in a particular classification.

solvency ratio Financial ratio, both short and long term, for estimating the risk in investing in a firm

profitability ratio Financial ratio for measuring a firm's potential earnings

activity ratio Financial ratio for evaluating management's use of a firm's assets

liquidity ratio Solvency ratio measuring a firm's ability to pay its immediate debts

Short-Term Solvency Ratios

In the short run, a company's survival depends on its ability to pay its immediate debts. Such payments require cash. Short-term solvency ratios measure a company's relative liquidity and thus its ability to pay immediate debts. The higher a firm's **liquidity ratios,** then, the lower the risk involved for investors.

current ratio Solvency ratio that determines a firm's creditworthiness by measuring its ability to pay its current obligations

CURRENT RATIO The most commonly used liquidity ratio is the current ratio, which has been called the "banker's ratio" because it concerns a firm's creditworthiness. The **current ratio** measures a company's ability to meet current obligations out of current assets. It thus reflects a firm's ability to generate cash to meet obligations through the normal, orderly process of selling inventories and collecting accounts receivable. It is calculated by dividing current assets by current liabilities.

As a rule, a current ratio is satisfactory if it is 2:1 or higher—that is, if current assets more than double current liabilities. A smaller ratio may indicate that a company will have difficulty paying its bills. Note, however, that a larger ratio may imply that assets are not being used productively and should be invested elsewhere.

How does Perfect Posters measure up? Look again at the balance sheet in Figure 14.5. Judging from its current assets and current liabilities at the end of 1999, we see that

$$\frac{\text{Current assets}}{\text{Current liabilities}} = \frac{\$57{,}210}{\$21{,}935} = 2.61$$

How does Perfect Posters' ratio compare with those of other companies? Not bad: It is higher than those of Johnson & Johnson (1.83), Boeing (1.41), and Northeast Utilities (0.95). Although Perfect Posters may be holding too much uninvested cash, it looks like a good credit risk.

Long-Term Solvency Ratios

To survive in the long run, a company must be able to meet both its short-term (current) debts and its long-term liabilities. These latter debts usually involve interest payments. A firm that cannot meet them is in danger of collapse or takeover—a risk that makes creditors and investors quite cautious. The 1998 Asian financial crisis was fueled by a loss of confidence by investors in large firms in Japan and Korea that could not meet their long-term cash obligations.[11]

DEBT-TO-OWNERS' EQUITY RATIO To measure the risk that a company may encounter this problem, we use the *long-term solvency ratios* called **debt ratios.** The most commonly used debt ratio is the **debt-to-owners' equity ratio** (or **debt-to-equity ratio**), which describes the extent to which a firm is financed through borrowed money. It is calculated by dividing **debt**—total liabilities—by owners' equity.

This ratio is commonly used to compare a given company's status with industry averages. For example, companies with debt-to-equity ratios above 1 are probably relying too much on debt. Such firms may find themselves owing so much debt that they lack the income needed to meet interest payments or to repay borrowed money.

In the case of Perfect Posters, we can see from the balance sheet in Figure 14.5 that the debt-to-equity ratio works out as follows:

$$\frac{\text{Debt}}{\text{Owners' equity}} = \frac{\$61,935}{\$111,155} = 0.56$$

debt ratio Solvency ratio measuring a firm's ability to meet its long-term debts

debt-to-owners' equity ratio (or **debt-to-equity ratio**) Solvency ratio describing the extent to which a firm is financed through borrowing

debt A firm's total liabilities

Profitability Ratios

Although it is important to know that a company is solvent in both the long and the short term, safety or risk alone is not an adequate basis for investment decisions. Investors also want some measure of the returns they can expect. *Return on equity* and *earnings per share* are two commonly used profitability ratios.

RETURN ON EQUITY Owners are interested in the net income earned by a business for each dollar invested. **Return on equity** measures this performance by dividing net income (recorded in the income statement, Figure 14.6) by total owners' equity (recorded in the balance sheet, Figure 14.5).[12] For Perfect Posters, the return-on-equity ratio in 1999 can be calculated as follows:

$$\frac{\text{Net income}}{\text{Total owners' equity}} = \frac{\$12,585}{\$111,155} = 11.3\%$$

return on equity Profitability ratio measuring income earned for each dollar invested

Is this figure good or bad? There is no set answer. If Perfect Posters' ratio for 1999 is higher than in previous years, owners and investors should be encouraged. But if 11.3 percent is lower than the ratios of other companies in the same industry, they should be concerned.

EARNINGS PER SHARE Defined as net income divided by the number of shares of common stock outstanding, **earnings per share** determines the size of the dividend that a company can pay its shareholders. Investors use this ratio to decide whether to buy or sell a company's stock. As the ratio gets higher, the stock value increases, because investors know that the firm can better afford to pay dividends. Naturally, stock will lose market value if the latest financial statements report a decline in earnings per share. For Perfect Posters, we can use the net income total from the income statement in Figure 14.6 to calculate earnings per share as follows:

$$\frac{\text{Net income}}{\text{Number of common shares outstanding}} = \frac{\$12,585}{8,000} = \$1.57 \text{ per share}$$

earnings per share Profitability ratio measuring the size of the dividend that a firm can pay shareholders

As a baseline for comparison, note that Gucci's recent earnings were $2.86 per share. The Walt Disney Co. earned $0.89.

Activity Ratios

The efficiency with which a firm uses resources is linked to profitability. As a potential investor, then, you want to know which company gets more mileage from its resources. Activity ratios measure this efficiency. For example, say that two firms use the same amount of resources or assets. If Firm A generates greater profits or sales, it is more efficient and thus has a better activity ratio.

inventory turnover ratio Activity ratio measuring the average number of times that inventory is sold and restocked during the year

INVENTORY TURNOVER RATIO Certain specific measures can be used to explain how one firm earns greater profits than another. One of the most important is the **inventory turnover ratio,** which measures the average number of times that inventory is sold and restocked during the year—that is, how quickly it is produced and sold.[13] First, you need to know your *average inventory:* the typical amount of inventory on hand during the year. You can calculate average inventory by adding end-of-year inventory to beginning-of-year inventory and dividing by 2. You can now find your inventory turnover ratio, which is expressed as the cost of goods sold divided by average inventory:

$$\frac{\text{Cost of goods sold}}{\text{Average inventory}} = \frac{\text{Cost of goods sold}}{(\text{Beginning inventory} + \text{Ending inventory})/2}$$

A high inventory turnover ratio means efficient operations: Because a smaller amount of investment is tied up in inventory, the company's funds can be put to work elsewhere to earn greater returns. However, inventory turnover must be compared with both prior years and industry averages. An inventory turnover rate of 5, for example, might be excellent for an auto supply store, but it would be disastrous for a supermarket, where a rate of about 15 is common. Rates can also vary within a company that markets a variety of products. To calculate Perfect Posters' inventory turnover ratio for 1999, we take the merchandise inventory figures for the income statement in Figure 14.6. The ratio can be expressed as follows:

$$\frac{\$104{,}765}{(\$22{,}380 + \$21{,}250)/2} = 4.8 \text{ times}$$

In other words, new merchandise replaces old merchandise every 76 days (365 days/4.8). The 4.8 ratio is below the average of 7.0 for comparable wholesaling operations, indicating that the business is slightly inefficient.

INFORMATION MANAGEMENT: AN OVERVIEW

Accounting information is a vital element in modern business. Business information, however, can take many forms in addition to the financial aspects—information about customers' locations and order patterns, information about supplies and finished goods on hand, information about workers' pay and productivity, information about products in development, and information about competitors and customers, for example. Not surprisingly, the computer is at the forefront of contemporary information management. In this section, we explore the ways in which companies manage information with computers and related information technologies.

Businesspeople are bombarded with facts and figures. Modern communications permit businesses to receive up-to-the-minute information from remote plants, branches, and sales offices. To find the information that they need to make critical decisions, managers must often sift through a virtual avalanche of reports, memos, magazines, and phone calls. How can businesses get useful information to the right people at the right time?

information managers Managers responsible for designing and implementing systems to gather, organize, and distribute information

Most businesses regard their information as a private resource—an asset that they plan, develop, and protect. It is not surprising, then, that companies have **information managers,** just as they have production, marketing, and finance managers. Information management is an internal operation that determines business performance and outcomes. Consider, for example, Chaparral Steel—a technologically advanced steel mill that produces structural products from recycled steel. Chaparral's performance—customer service, delivery times, sales, profits, and customer loyalty—has been boosted by an information system that gives customers fast access to lists of the steel products that are currently available in Chaparral's inventories. The technology that allows customers to shop electronically through its storage yards gives Chaparral greater agility, and because it can respond more rapidly than its competitors, it gets more sales.

Data versus Information

Although businesspeople often complain that they get too much information, what they usually mean is that they get too many data. **Data** are raw facts and figures. **Information** is the useful interpretation of data.

data Raw facts and figures

information The useful interpretation of data

For example, consider the following data:

- Last year, casino gambling was available in 32 states in the United States.
- Eighty-five percent of Americans live within a 3-hour drive of a casino.
- In the past 3 years, visitor growth, especially of wealthy Asian gamblers, has been flat.
- In the last 2 years, Las Vegas has added $6 billion to its gaming capacity.
- Since Congress passed the 1988 Indian Gaming Regulation Act, some 23 states offer some form of Native American casino gambling.

If all these data were put together in a meaningful way, they might produce information about what sells gaming and, in particular, whether entertainment companies should construct new hotels and casinos to meet increasing demand. The challenge for businesses, then, is to turn a flood of data into manageable information.

Management Information Systems

One response to this challenge has been the growth of the **management information system (MIS):** a system for transmitting and transforming data into information that can be used in decision making. Those charged with running a company's MIS must first determine what information will be needed. Then they must gather the data and provide ways to convert data into desired information. They must also control the flow of information so that it goes only to people who need it.[14]

management information system (MIS) System for transforming data into information that can be used in decision making

Information supplied to employees and managers varies according to such factors as the functional areas in which they work (say, accounting or marketing) and the levels of management they occupy. The quality of the information transmitted to all levels depends increasingly on an organization's technological resources and on the people who manage it. In this section we discuss the evolution of the technology that processes information and then describe the information requirements in today's organization.

■ DATABASES AND APPLICATIONS PROGRAMS

As noted, all computer processing is the processing of data. This processing is carried out by programs—instructions that tell the computer to perform specified functions. In this section we begin by briefly describing the nature of computer data and databases. We then discuss a few of the specialized applications programs designed for business use.

Data and Databases

Computers convert data into information by organizing them in some meaningful manner. Within a computer system, chunks of data—numbers, words, and sentences—are stored in a series of related collections called *fields*, *records*, and *files*. Taken together, all these data files constitute a **database:** a centralized, organized collection of related data.

database Centralized, organized collection of related data

Processing Once data are entered into the database, they can be manipulated, sorted, combined, or compared. In **batch processing,** data are collected over some time period and then processed as groups or batches. Payrolls, for example, are usually run in

batch processing Method of collecting data over a period of time and then computer processing them as a group or batch batches: Because most employees get paid on either a weekly or a biweekly basis, the data (the hours worked) are accumulated over the pay periods and processed at one time.

real-time processing Method of entering data and computer processing them immediately

Batch processing was once the only type of computer processing. Although it is still widely used, companies today have such choices as **real-time processing,** in which data are entered and processed immediately. This system is always used when the results of each entry affect subsequent entries. For example, if you book seat F6 on Continental Flight 253 on December 23, the computer must thereafter keep other passengers from booking the same seat.

Application Programs

Increasingly inexpensive equipment and software have made computers an irresistible option for businesses of all types and sizes. Moreover, programs are available for a huge variety of business-related tasks. Some of these programs address such common, long-standing needs as accounting, payroll, and inventory control. Others have been developed for application to an endless variety of specialized needs. Most business application programs fall into one of four categories—*word processing, spreadsheets, database management,* and *graphics.*[15] Of all PC software applications, 70 percent are designed for the first three types of programs.

word-processing program Application program that allows computers to store, edit, and print letters and numbers for documents created by users

WORD PROCESSING Popular **word-processing programs** such as Microsoft Word for Windows, Corel WordPerfect, and Lotus Word Pro allow computer users to store, edit, display, and print documents. Sentences or paragraphs can be added or deleted without retyping or restructuring an entire document, and mistakes are easily corrected. At *USA Today,* for example, hundreds of reporters and editors use word processing to write, edit, and store articles on computer terminals that are linked to a central system. Within minutes after stories are completed, the system sends typeset text via satellite to printing sites throughout the United States, where the paper is printed and distributed to newsstands each day.

TRENDS AND CHALLENGES

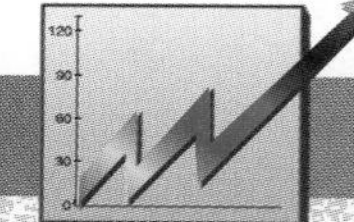

Y2K? WHAT, ME WORRY?

Osman Arpad, controller at EDPA USA Inc., a New York City–based textile and apparel trading company, may not have heard about the so-called Y2K problem back in the early 1990s, but he certainly knows about it today. Since the beginning of 1998, nearly 70 of his customers, vendors, and bankers have sent him questionnaires asking about EDPA's Y2K compliance. They want to know what steps the company is taking to ensure that its computers will be ready for business as usual at the start of the millennium.

The Y2K problem (aka the "Year 2000 Bug" and the "Millennium Bomb") involves the computer industry's cost-related decision in the 1970s to limit computer space for calculating dates to only six spaces: two for the month, two for the day, and two for the year (*MM/DD/YY*). The system works well for months and days, but with only two digits to represent the year rather than four, the computer cannot handle the switch from the twentieth to the twenty-first century. "The problem," explains Commerce Department computer scientist Gary Fisher, "is that the computer doesn't interpret '00' as the year 2000 but rather 1900, and miscalculates all computations accordingly." In other words, your computer has room only for the digits denoting given years (say, the *99* in *1999*); it has no place to deal with the digits denoting the century (the *19* in *1999*).

Y2K concerns are already affecting both manufacturing and service companies that do long-term budget and production planning. Well before the start of the millennium, firms that relied on older computers were unable to input information for 2000 and beyond. It seems that automated computer backup routines insisted on overwriting new files with outdated data. As you can see from the following true stories, the problem threatens to be especially serious for small businesses:

- After a long airplane flight, a Japanese businessman arrived at a small hotel in New York at about 1:30 A.M. Exhausted and hoping for a rapid check-in, he handed the clerk a credit card that happened to expire in 2000. The computer rejected the card, and the weary traveler was forced to move to another hotel—one that had Y2K-compliance software.
- At a gourmet food store in Warren, Michigan, a customer tried to pay with a credit card that expired in 2000. The sim-

SPREADSHEETS **Electronic spreadsheets** spread data across and down the page in rows and columns. Users enter data, including formulas, at row and column intersections, and the computer automatically performs the necessary calculations. Payroll records, sales projections, and a host of other financial reports can be prepared in this manner.

Spreadsheets are useful planning tools because they allow managers to see how making a change in one item will affect related items. For example, a manager can insert various operating cost percentages, tax rates, or sales revenues into the spreadsheet. The computer will automatically recalculate all the other figures and determine net profit. Three popular spreadsheet packages are Lotus 1-2-3, Quattro Pro, and Microsoft Excel for Windows.

electronic spreadsheet Application program with a row-and-column format that allows users to compare the effect of changes from one category to another

DATABASE MANAGEMENT Such **database management programs** as Microsoft Access for Windows, Paradox for Windows (from Borland), and dBase (also from Borland) can keep track of all of a firm's relevant data. They can then sort and search through data and integrate a single piece of data into several different files. Figure 14.7 shows how a database management program might be used at a company called Artists' Frame Service. In this case, the program is integrating the file for customer orders with the company's inventory file. When sales to Jones and Smith are entered into the customer orders file, the database system automatically adjusts the frame inventory file; the quantities of materials B5 and A3 are reduced because those materials were used in making the frames for Jones and Smith.

database management program Application program for creating, storing, searching, and manipulating an organized collection of data

GRAPHICS **Computer graphics programs** convert numeric and character data into pictorial information such as charts, graphs, and cartoon characters. These programs make computerized information easier to use and understand in two ways. First, graphs and charts summarize data and allow managers to detect problems, opportunities, and relationships more easily. Second, graphics are valuable in creating clearer and more persuasive reports and presentations.

computer graphics program Application program that converts numeric and character data into pictorial information, such as graphs and charts

ple act of swiping the card through the system locked the store's 10 computerized cash registers for half a day.

Despite such problems, however, most small-business owners are taking a wait-and-see attitude. One survey conducted for Wells Fargo Bank revealed just how pervasive "noncompliance" is. "We are dismayed to learn," announced a Wells Fargo spokesman, "that half of all small-business owners, though aware of the Year 2000 problem, have no plans to reduce their risk. They need to realize this is a business problem and not a technology problem." Adds consultant Claire McAuliff: "There is a sense of security among small businesses because they don't consider their offices to be a technology powerhouse."

"We are dismayed to learn that half of all small-business owners, though aware of the Year 2000 problem, have no plans to reduce their risk. They need to realize this is a business problem and not a technology problem."

—Wells Fargo spokesperson

But even if small-business owners are in denial about Y2K, their bankers are not. Bankers—like the ones who loaned that money to EDPA—are asking credit customers to outline the specific steps they will take to head off problems and to draw up timetables for taking them. Bankers themselves are being pushed by bank regulators to toughen lending terms on all new loans and to avoid high-risk loans for companies with too much Y2K exposure.

Fearing that serious computer problems may snowball, large companies are also insisting on compliance from the small businesses with whom they deal. And in turn, of course, these companies are passing on the same demands to their suppliers. How serious are the repercussions? Unfortunately, predicts computer consultant Bob Dusmore, "some companies will go out of business because they might not have the finances available to fix the problem."

FIGURE 14.7 ◆ **Artists' Frame Service Database Management Program**

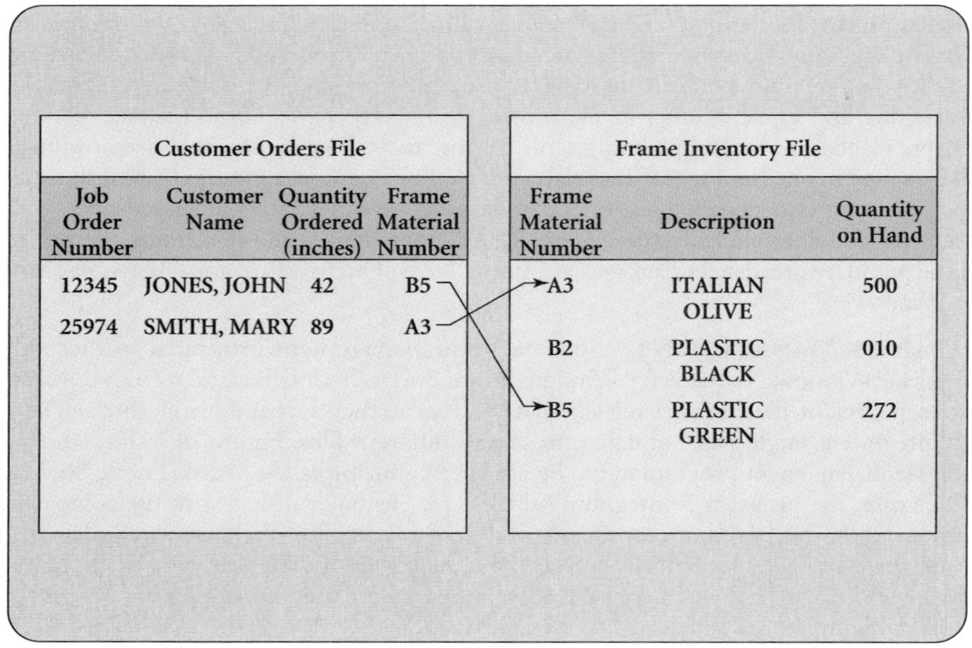

Customer Orders File

Job Order Number	Customer Name	Quantity Ordered (inches)	Frame Material Number
12345	JONES, JOHN	42	B5
25974	SMITH, MARY	89	A3

Frame Inventory File

Frame Material Number	Description	Quantity on Hand
A3	ITALIAN OLIVE	500
B2	PLASTIC BLACK	010
B5	PLASTIC GREEN	272

presentation graphics software Applications that allow users to create visual presentations integrating animation and sound

Presentation graphics software such as Microsoft PowerPoint for Windows, Corel Presentations, Corel-Draw, and Visio uses slides, video, and sound splices for professional presentations. The ability to vary color and size, and to use pictures and charts with three-dimensional effects, shadows, and shading with animation and sound is more visually interesting than static presentations.

Computer graphics capabilities extend beyond mere data presentation. They also include stand-alone programs for artists, designers, and special effects designers. Everything from simple drawings to fine art, television commercials, and motion picture special effects are now created by computer graphics software. The realism of the sinking in *Titanic* and the physical appearance of the space creatures in the new Star Wars movie *Episode One: The Phantom Menace* are special effects created with computer graphics.

This fashion designer is using a graphic tablet to design a dress on her computer. The initial design can easily be changed electronically to try new features and styles. The final design is stored for future use. Graphics programs and applications can now create everything from a simple slide presentation to award-winning special effects for film and television.

Some of the latest software for **desktop publishing** combines word-processing and graphics capability to produce typeset-quality text with stimulating visual effects from personal computers. Quark XPress, for example, is able to manipulate text, graphics, and full-color photographs. Desktop publishing eliminates costly printing services for reports and proposals, and Quark is also used by ad agencies such as J. Walter Thompson, whose computer-generated designs offer greater control over color and format. Other specialized desktop publishing packages include Microsoft Publisher and Adobe Systems PageMaker for Windows.

desktop publishing Process of combining word-processing and graphics capability to produce typeset-quality text from personal computers

■ THE MARRIAGE OF INFORMATION AND COMMUNICATION TECHNOLOGY

Although computing is constantly evolving, some of its foundational elements are well established: *artificial intelligence, expert systems, office information technologies, executive information systems, operations information systems, data communication networks*, and *multimedia communication systems*. The most powerful vehicle for using these elements to their full potential is the marriage of computers to communication technologies. Thanks to lower-cost, higher-capacity networks, the joining of computers, communication, and the mass media is already in its first stages.

This marriage promises to change the future of business—indeed, of society itself. "Personal computing," observes Microsoft's Bill Gates, "was qualitatively a very, very different thing than the computing that came before. The advances in communication likewise will create new ways of using communication for learning, education, and commerce that go far beyond anything done to date." Both independently and through joint ventures, companies such as Microsoft, AT&T, Hewlett-Packard, Oracle Corp., and Telecommunications Inc. are pursuing such products as personal digital assistants, digital TVs, digital photography, and devices for tapping into high-bandwidth networks, multimedia information, and on-line services. In this section we briefly discuss the progress of some of these projects.

> **"Personal computing was qualitatively a very, very different thing than the computing that came before. The advances in communication likewise will create new ways of using communication for learning, education, and commerce that go far beyond anything done to date."**
>
> Bill Gates
> *CEO of Microsoft*

Artificial Intelligence

Artificial intelligence (AI) can be defined as the construction and programming of computers to imitate human thought processes. In developing components and programs for AI, computer scientists are trying to design computers capable of reasoning so that computers, instead of people, can perform useful activities.

artificial intelligence (AI) Construction and programming of computers to imitate human thought processes

Robotics is one category of AI. With their "reasoning" capabilities, robots can "learn" repetitive tasks such as painting, assembling components, and inserting screws. Furthermore, they avoid repeating mistakes by "remembering" the causes of past mistakes and, when those causes reappear, adjusting or stopping until adjustments are made.

Computer scientists are also designing AI systems that possess sensory capabilities (vision with lasers, as well as hearing and feeling). In addition, as machines become more sophisticated in processing natural languages, humans will be able to give instructions and ask questions just by speaking to the computer.

Using the latest techniques in knowledge engineering and computer technology, this GE Capital Services team was able to put together in one program all the loan and collateral requirements, cash flow analyses, market reports, risk factors, and other criteria that go into a complex real estate investment decision. Thanks to this expert system, which can be accessed with a laptop, GE field staff will now be able to quote, underwrite, and review a real estate deal more quickly and effectively, helping to reduce overall cycle time by two-thirds.

Expert Systems

expert system Form of artificial intelligence that attempts to imitate the behavior of human experts in a particular field

A special form of artificial intelligence programs, the **expert system,** tries to imitate the behavior of human experts in a particular field.[16] Expert systems incorporate the rules that an expert applies to specific types of problems. In effect, they supply everyday users with "instant expertise." General Electric's Socrates Quick Quote, for example, places a package of technical knowledge about real estate transactions at the fingertips of real estate dealers on GE's private computer network. A system called Magic incorporates 6,000 government regulations for human services and related agencies. MOCA (Maintenance Operations Center Advisor) schedules routine maintenance for American Airlines' entire fleet.

Office Information Technologies

Office information technologies (OIT) are the computer-based devices and applications whose function is to enhance the performance and productivity of general office activities. In this section we survey three of the most solidly entrenched innovations in today's automated office: *fax machines, voice mail,* and *e-mail.*

fax machine Machine that can transmit copies of documents over telephone lines

FAX MACHINES The **fax machine** (short for *facsimile-transceiver machine*) can transmit text documents, drawings, and photograph images over telephone lines in a matter of seconds, thus permitting written communication over long distances. Fax machines are popular with both large and small firms because of speed and low cost.

voice mail Computer-based system for receiving and delivering incoming telephone calls

VOICE MAIL A computer-based system for receiving and delivering incoming telephone calls is **voice mail.** Incoming calls are never missed because a voice responds to the caller, invites a message, and stores it. A company with voice mail has each employee's phone networked for receiving, storing, and forwarding calls.

Voice mail software links the communication device (telephone) with a computer. The input from the telephone is sent to the computer, which uses software to digitize the voice data and stores it on a disk. The employee can then call the voice mail center to retrieve from storage a recording of waiting calls and voice messages. By combining technologies, voice mail can receive and store an incoming fax message until the recipient requests that the fax be printed.

electronic mail (e-mail) Computer system that electronically transmits information between computers

E-MAIL An **electronic mail** (or **e-mail**) system electronically transmits letters, reports, and other information between computers, whether in the same building or in another country. It is also used for voice transmission and for sending graphics and videos

The new Railway Control and Management System, developed by GE–Harris Railway Electronics and demonstrated here by one of the firm's scientists, can coordinate the movement of all trains and work crews across an entire railroad network, allowing railroads to make the best use of existing lines and to avoid expensive investments in new rail infrastructure. The improved flow of train traffic will allow for better on-time performance as well. This is a prime example of how computers can assist in operations information systems.

from one computer to another. E-mail thus substitutes for the flood of paper and telephone calls that threatens to engulf many offices.

Operations Information Systems

Computer technology is having a major impact on production and manufacturing through the use of **operations information systems,** which includes *computer-aided design* (*CAD*), *computer-aided manufacturing* (*CAM*), and computer operation control. CAD assists in designing products by simulating the real product and displaying it in three-dimensional graphics. Immersion's MicroScribe-3D software (<http://www.immerse.com>), for example, uses a penlike tool to scan the surface of any three-dimensional object, such as a football helmet, and electronically transforms it into a 3D graphic. The helmet designer can then try different shapes and surfaces for the helmet in the computer and observe the new designs on the video monitor.[17] Products ranging from cell phones to auto parts are created using CAD because it creates faster designs at lower cost than manual modeling methods. The older method—making handcrafted prototypes (trial models) of wood, plastic, or clay—is replaced with "rapid prototyping" (RP): The CAD computer electronically transfers instructions to the computer-controlled machine that automatically builds the prototype.[18]

operations information system Computer system used to manage production and manufacturing operations

CAM is a similar tool, but it is used for designing the manufacturing equipment, facilities, and plant layouts for better product flows and productivity. *Computer operations control* refers to any system for managing the day-to-day production activities for either goods or service production. Hospitals use computer-based scheduling for preparing patients' meals, just as manufacturers do for making autos, clocks, and paper products.

Data Communication Networks

Gaining popularity on both home and business computers are public and private **data communication networks:** global networks that carry streams of digital data (electronic messages, documents, and other forms of video and sound) back and forth quickly and economically on telecommunication systems. The most prominent networks, the Internet and the World Wide Web, have emerged as powerful communication technologies.

data communications network Global network (such as the Internet) that permits users to send electronic messages and information quickly and economically

Internet Global data communications network serving thousands of computers with information on a wide array of topics and providing communications flows among certain private networks

THE INTERNET The **Internet** (or "the Net," for short) is the largest public network, serving millions of computers with information on business, science, and government and providing communication flows among certain private networks, including CompuServe

"Dennis, I would like to talk to you for a minute—off line."

and MCI Mail. Originally commissioned by the Pentagon as a communication tool for use during war, the Internet allows personal computers in virtually any location to be linked together by means of large computers known as network servers. The Net has gained in popularity because it makes available an immense wealth of academic, technical, and business information. Another major attraction is its capacity to transmit e-mail. For thousands of businesses, therefore, the Net is joining—and even replacing—the telephone, the fax machine, and express mail as a standard means of communication.

In 1995, more than 25 million people and 22,000 businesses had access to the Net. In 1998, more than 40 million Net users were active with links to over 150 countries. Usage continues to grow because the Net offers new opportunities for computing enhancements. Consider Java by Sun Microsystems, Inc. Java is a software language that can be used by software developers on any type of PC. By instantaneously connecting software writers with software users on the Internet, it provides an entirely new, convenient way of creating, selling, delivering, and using software. Software writers like Java because they can create a new tool and then send it to users via the Net. When the program arrives, it automatically self-loads and runs on the requestor's PC. Thus, the user avoids having to install a big program. Suppose, for instance, that you want to create a Web site but are not a programmer. Just use Java to call up "Webra" and you'll get assistance. If you want to add animation to your site, use Java to call up "Dimension X" for programs to create animation with just a few mouse clicks. Each time the program is needed, you call up Java, which comes across the Net and then leaves when you are finished. Like Java, numerous so-called applets (short applications or mini-programs) can be retrieved from many suppliers' Web sites. Like Java, too, they perform a specific function and then disappear when the user is finished.

The Net's power to change the way business is conducted has already been amply demonstrated. Digital Equipment Corp., for instance, is a heavy Internet user: With more than 31,000 computers connected to the network, DEC's monthly e-mail volume has jumped to an average of 700,000 messages. DEC also linked its Alpha AXP high-speed business computer to the Internet so that potential buyers and software developers can spend time using and evaluating it. Gail Grant, Internet administrator at DEC, reports that in just a few months, 2,500 computer users in 27 countries took advantage of the opportunity to explore the Alpha AXP.

The Net has also benefited small companies, especially as a means of expanding market research, improving customer service, and as a source of information. In San Leandro, California, TriNet Employer Group subscribes to Ernst & Young's on-line consulting program, called Ernie. For $3,500 a year, TriNet controller Lyle DeWitt sends questions from his computer and gets an answer from an Ernst & Young expert within 48 hours. Aiming for small clients who cannot afford big-name consulting advice, Ernie answers questions on health insurance, benefit plans, immigration issues, and payroll taxes. For clients such as

TriNet, the convenience of on-line consulting is a blessing. Says DeWitt: "Ernie is kind of like having 50 consultants in my pocket—and for a phenomenally inexpensive rate."[19]

> "Ernie is kind of like having 50 consultants in my pocket—and for a phenomenally inexpensive rate."
>
> Lyle DeWitt
>
> *Controller at TriNet on her on-line consulting program*

World Wide Web Subsystem of computers providing access to the Internet and offering multimedia and linking capabilities

WORLD WIDE WEB Thanks to a subsystem of 7,000 computers known as the **World Wide Web** (WWW, or simply "the Web"), the Internet is easier to use than ever before. It has made the Internet usable to a general audience, rather than to only technical users. The Federal Express Web site, for example, gives customers access to the FedEx package-tracking database. Among the more than 2 million customers who depend on timely deliveries each day, thousands look through the FedEx Web pages and find out the status of their packages without any help from FedEx employees. Its customer self-help program saves FedEx over $2 million each year.

The computers linked by the Web are known as Web servers. They are owned by corporations, colleges, government agencies, and other large organizations. Today there are well over 650,000 such sites serving up hundreds of millions of pages of publicly accessible information. The user can connect with the Web by means of browser software (such as Netscape, Yahoo!, Lycos, WebExplorer, and Mosaic). **Browsers** support the graphics and linking capabilities needed to navigate the Web. The user must simply point and click, and experts predict that as more people become familiar with browsers, the number of Net users will grow by up to 10 to 15 percent a month. Netscape Navigator has enjoyed as much as an 80 percent market share, although it is being challenged by others, including its own Netscape Communicator and Microsoft Corp.'s Explorer.

browser Software supporting the graphics and linking capabilities necessary to navigate the World Wide Web

Among the most successful enterprises to take advantage of the Web are those that operate *search engines*. Companies such as Excite, InfoSeek, Lycos, and Yahoo! maintain free-to-use public directories of the Web's ever-increasing content. These indexes constantly scan the Web to stay current. A search engine may respond to more than 10 million inquiries per day. It is thus no surprise that search engines are packed with paid ads placed by companies such as Honda and AT&T. At the beginning of 1999, Yahoo! was the leader in *portal sites* (sites used by Net surfers as a primary home page), although Lycos was closing fast on Yahoo! for tops in number of users.[20]

intranet Private network of internal Web sites and other sources of information available to a company's employees

INTRANETS The success of the Internet has led some companies to extend the Net's technology internally, for browsing internal Web sites containing information throughout the firm. These private networks, or **intranets,** are accessible only to employees via entry through electronic firewalls.[21] At Compaq Computer Corp., the intranet allows employees to shuffle their retirement savings among various investment funds. Ford Motor Co.'s intranet connects 120,000 workstations in Asia, Europe, and the United States to thousands of Ford Web sites containing private information on Ford activities—in production, engineering, distribution, and marketing. Sharing the information has helped reduce the lead time for getting models into production from 36 months to 24 months. Ford's next step, scheduled for the end of 1999, is fast response to customers, or so-called manufacturing on demand: The Mustang of your choice that required 50 days' delivery time in 1996 will become available in less than 2 weeks after you order it. The savings to Ford will be billions of dollars in inventory and fixed costs.[22]

Multimedia Communication Systems

Today's information systems include not only computers but also multimedia communication systems. These systems are connected networks of communication appliances such as faxes, televisions, sound equipment, cell phones, printing machines, and photocopiers that may also be linked with such mass media as TV and radio broadcast programming, news and other print publications, and library collections. Not surprisingly, the integration of these elements is already changing the ways we live our lives and manage our businesses. A good example is T. Rowe Price's TeleAccess, a customer service in which investors make their own financial transactions by interacting with a computer on the phone, or use their home computers to track their investments and electronically change their portfolios.

MULTIMEDIA TECHNOLOGY Multimedia communication technology is profoundly expanding the applications of PCs. Today's programs incorporate sound, animation, and photography as well as ordinary graphics and text. Communication power has multiplied through on-line information services such as Prodigy and CompuServe that provide instant access to financial and news data. Electronic discussion groups and business meetings display interactive dialogue on screens for the benefit of conference callers in widespread locations. America Online, for example, has some 14,000 chat rooms that allow PC users to exchange electronic messages in real time. Today's PCs have built-in TV circuits so that you can tune in your favorite TV show on the computer monitor, watch movies from CD-ROMs, and listen to your favorite music.

Communication Channels. Communication channels are the media that make all these transmissions possible. These include coaxial and fiber-optic cable and infrared, microwave, and satellite transmission. In particular, the use of satellite channels is increasing to meet the growing demand for wireless transmission. GE's Technical Response Center, for example, demonstrates the value of satellites for improving aircraft engine maintenance and safety. With wireless systems instead of fiber cables underground, laser beams or radio waves will transmit signals from satellite to satellite. Using satellite networks under development by McCaw, Hughes, Motorola, AT&T, and Loral, the Net becomes accessible in remote areas where underground cable is not feasible; all the world is within instant reach on the Internet. Most of us use communication channels when we use some type of telephone system. Even today, however, the bulk of telephone transmissions are data, not conversations. Fax data account for 90 percent of all telephone signals between the United States and Japan.

The need for more capacity in communication channels is the biggest factor in the push toward more sophisticated wireless technology. In conjunction with electronics and communication giants such as IBM, Motorola, BellSouth, and McCaw Cellular Communications, specialty firms such as Ardis, Ram Mobile Data, Metricom, and Orbcomm are developing wireless devices that use credit card–size modems to transmit data over radio signals traveling from tiny PCs to a series of strategically placed receivers. Experts anticipate that such devices will find a ready market among businesspeople who cannot afford to be out of touch.

Continued from page 359

Is Whistle-Blowing a Growth Industry?

The federal lawsuit against Columbia/HCA Healthcare and Quorum Health Group alleges that more than 200 hospitals systematically submitted false Medicare expense reports over a 14-year period. With Alderson's case being just one of about a dozen against the companies, the cost to Columbia and Quorum—in back payments, interest, and fines—could reach $1 billion. The various whistle-blowers who brought suit stand to receive 15 percent of the recovered sum—about $150 million.

The size of this reward bothers James Blumstein, director of the Health Policy Center at Vanderbilt University, who questions whether it is in the public's best interest. "The profit motive," says Blumstein, "gives whistle-blowers the incentive not to overlook even the most benign technical violation of the Medicare rules." In theory, hospitals could be prosecuted for violation of anti-kickback rules for providing doctors with free breakfast doughnuts.

Not surprisingly, as the financial incentives for reporting fraud have increased, so have the number of whistle-blower suits and the money the government has recovered. In 1988, a mere 60 suits netted $355,000 in penalties. In 1997, 534 suits recovered $625 million. Six of 10 of the current suits involve the health care industry and unscrupulous practices in Medicare and Medicaid billing.

Questions for Discussion

1. What's wrong with keeping two sets of accounting books?
2. Why are government programs, such as Medicare and Medicaid, so often the target of corporate accounting fraud?
3. How do audits protect against fraud?
4. What would you have done if you were in Alderson's place? Do you think Alderson is unusual?
5. Evaluate the merits and problems with the federal whistle-blower law.

SUMMARY

1. **Explain the role of *accountants* and describe the kinds of work they do.** By collecting, analyzing, and communicating financial information, accountants provide business managers and investors with an accurate picture of the firm's financial health. *Financial accounting* is concerned with external users of information; *managerial accounting* serves internal users. *Certified public accountants* (*CPAs*) are licensed professionals who provide auditing, tax, and management advisory services for other firms and individuals.

2. **Explain how the following three concepts are used in *record keeping: accounting equation, double-entry accounting,* and *T-accounts for debits and credits.*** The *accounting equation* (assets = liabilities + owners' equity) is used to balance the data in both *journals* and *ledgers. Double-entry accounting* acknowledges the dual effects of financial transactions and ensures that the accounting equation always balances. Using the *T-account,* accountants record financial transactions in the shape of a *T,* with the vertical line dividing the account into *debit* and *credit* columns. These tools enable accountants to enter and track transactions.

3. **Describe two important *financial statements* and show how they reflect the activity and financial condition of a business.** The *balance sheet,* also called the *statement of financial condition,* summarizes a company's assets, liabilities, and owners' equity at a given point in time. The *income statement,* also known as the *profit-and-loss statement,* details revenues and expenses for a given period of time and identifies any profit or loss.

4. **Explain how computing key *financial ratios* can help in analyzing the financial strengths of a business.** Drawing upon data from financial statements, ratios can help creditors, investors, and managers assess a firm's finances. The *current ratio* measures short-term solvency—a firm's ability to pay its debt in the short run. The *debt-to-owners' equity ratio* measures long-term solvency. *Return on equity* and *earnings per share* both measure profitability. *Inventory turnover ratios* show how efficiently a firm is using its inventory funds.

5. **Identify the role played in computer systems by *databases* and describe four important types of *business application programs*.** Through computer sequences of instructions called *programs*, computers are able to process data and perform specific functions. Once *data* (raw facts and figures) are centralized and organized into meaningful *databases*, they can be manipulated, sorted, combined, and/or compared according to program instructions.

   Four major types of application programs for businesses are *word processing* (which allows computers to act like sophisticated typewriters), *electronic spreadsheets* (which enter data in rows and columns and perform calculations), *database management* (which organizes and retrieves a company's relevant data), and *graphics* (which convert numeric and character data into pictorial information).

6. **List some trends in the application of computer technology to *business information management* and discuss the effect of the *Internet* and *World Wide Web* on information management.** The latest generation of computers includes *artificial intelligence* (programming computers to imitate human thought processes); *expert systems* (which try to imitate the behavior of experts in a given field); *office automation* (which includes machine technology—fax machines, e-mail, and the like—that streamlines communications); *data communications networks* (which permit users to send electronic messages and video and audio information quickly and economically); and *operations information systems* (which increase operations productivity). All of these technologies help businesspeople make decisions and solve problems.

   The Internet and World Wide Web carry information from documents, video, and sound back and forth quickly and economically on telecommunication systems. They give millions of people and companies access to remote technical and commercial information for improving business operations. Instant communication through e-mail provides up-to-the-minute status reports. Business transactions, from beginning dialogue through product exposure to closing the sale, can be conducted nearly instantaneously through remote video and sound interaction. Users can access Web sites to discover various companies' product offerings, make purchases, and network with remote groups in electronic chat rooms. For software developers and users, the Internet provides a new channel for the quick distribution, retrieval, and temporary use of numerous new applications programs (applets), thus avoiding the cost of buying and permanently installing them on the user's computer.

QUESTIONS AND EXERCISES

Questions for Review

1. How does the double-entry system reduce the chances of mistakes or fraud in accounting?
2. What are the two basic financial statements and what major information items does each contain?
3. Identify the three major classifications of financial statement ratios and give an example of one ratio in each category.
4. Why does a business need to manage information as a resource?
5. How can an e-mail system increase office productivity and efficiency?

Questions for Analysis

6. Suppose that Inflatables Inc., makers of air mattresses for swimming pools, has the following transactions during the week:
   - Sale of three deluxe mattresses to Al Wett (paid $75 in cash) on 7/16
   - Received check on 7/13 from Ima Flote in payment for mattresses bought on credit ($90) on 7/13
   - Received new shipment of 200 mattresses from Airheads Mfg. (total cost, $2,000) on 7/17

Construct a journal for Inflatables, Inc.

7. Dasar Co. reports the following data in its September 30, 1999, financial statements:

Gross sales	$225,000
Current assets	40,000
Long-term assets	100,000
Current liabilities	16,000
Long-term liabilities	44,000
Owners' equity	80,000
Net income	7,200

Compute the following financial measures: current ratio, debt-to-equity ratio, and return on owners' equity.

APPLICATION EXERCISES

8. Describe the types of work or activities for which a local department store might choose to use batch processing. Do the same for real-time processing.
9. Interview the manager of a local retail or wholesale business about taking inventory. What is the firm's primary purpose in taking inventory? How often is it done?
10. Visit a small business in your community to investigate the ways it is presently using computers. How does it play to use them in the future? Prepare a report for presentation in class.

BUILDING YOUR BUSINESS SKILLS

THE ART AND SCIENCE OF POINT-AND-CLICK RESEARCH

This exercise enhances the following SCANS workplace competencies: demonstrating basic skills, demonstrating thinking skills, exhibiting interpersonal skills, working with information, applying systems knowledge, and using technology.

▼ GOAL

To introduce students to World Wide Web search sites.

▼ BACKGROUND

In a recent survey of nearly 2,000 Web users, two-thirds stated that they used the Web to obtain work-related information. With an estimated 320 million pages of information on the Web, the challenge for business users is fairly obvious: how to find what they're looking for.

▼ METHOD

You'll need a computer and access to the World Wide Web to complete this exercise.

STEP 1

Get together with three other classmates and decide on a business-related research topic. Choose a topic that interests you, for example, "Business Implications of the Year 2000 Census," "Labor Disputes in Professional Sports," or "Marketing Music Lessons and Instruments to Parents of Young Children."

(continued)

STEP 2

Search the following sites for information on your topic. Divide the sites among group members to speed the process:

- Yahoo! http://www.yahoo.com
- Hotbot http://www.hotbot.com
- Alta Vista http://www.altavista.net
- Excite http://www.excite.com
- Infoseek http://www.infoseek.com
- Lycos http://www.lycos.com
- Metacrawler http://www.metacrawler.com
- Dogpile http://www.dogpile.com
- Ask Jeeves http://www.askjeeves.com
- Northern Light http://www.nlsearch.com
- Internet Sleuth http://www.isleuth.com

Take notes as you search so that you can explain your findings to other group members.

STEP 3

Working as a group, answer the following questions about your collective search:

1. Which sites were the easiest to use?
2. Which sites offered the most helpful results? What specific factors made these sites better than the others?
3. Which sites offered the least helpful results? What were the problems?
4. Why is it important to learn the special code words or symbols, called *operators*, that target a search? (Operators are words like AND, OR, and NOT that narrow search queries. For example, using AND in a search tells the system that all words must appear in the results—American AND Management AND Association.)

▼ Follow-Up

1. Research the differences between search *engines* and search *directories.* Then place the sites listed above in each category. Did you find search engines or directories more helpful in this exercise?
2. Why is it important to learn to use the search-site "Help" function?
3. Based on your personal career goals, how do you think that mastering Web research techniques might help you in the future?

CRAFTING YOUR BUSINESS PLAN

THE PROFITABILITY OF PLANNING

▼ The Purpose of the Assignment

1. To acquaint students with the process of navigating the Business PlanPro (BPP) software package.
2. To familiarize students with issues involving accounting and information systems that a sample firm faces in developing its business plan.
3. To demonstrate how four chapter topics—application software programs, computer graphics programs, financial ratios, and the profit-and-loss statement—can be integrated as components in the BPP planning environment.

▼ Assignment

After reading Chapter 14 in the textbook, open the BPP software and search for information about accounting and information systems as it applies to a sample firm: AMT Computer Store (American Management Technologies). Then respond to the following questions:*

1. As we saw in Chapter 14, various kinds of software exist for different applications. Would you classify the Business PlanPro (BPP) software as an "application program"? Explain why or why not.

2. Evaluate the computer graphics capabilities of the Business PlanPro (BPP) software package. Will its graphics help you develop a better business plan than you otherwise might develop? Explain why or why not. [Sites to see in BPP (for this assignment): In the Task Manager screen, click on **The Bottom Line.** Then click on **5. Benchmarks Chart.** After returning to the Task Manager screen, click on **Cash is King.** Next, click on **2. Cash Plan Chart.** While you are in this section, go to the top of the window and click on **Chart** in the toolbox. You will now see your options for setting up charts.]

3. AMT Computer Store is planning on large changes in annual net profits in the coming 3 years. Based on the company's planned profit-and-loss statement, identify the key factors—changes in the revenues and expenses categories—that account for changes in planned net profits from year to year. [Sites to see in BPP: In the Task Manager screen, click on **The Bottom Line.** Then click on **3. Profit and Loss Table.**]

4. What do the financial ratios in its business plan tell you about the financial activities and conditions that AMT Computer Store expects over the next 3 years? Specifically, explain the information that is revealed by three of these ratios: inventory turnover, current, and return on equity. Next, choose any three other ratios and explain how they are calculated. [Sites to see in BPP: In the Task Manager screen, click on **Financial Plan.** Then click on each of the items in **3. Business Ratios.** On the screen above the ratios, click on the **Table Help** folder tab. Finally, return to the list of ratios and click on any one of them. Now you can read its definition and see how to calculate it.]

▼ For Your Own Business Plan

5. Make an initial assessment of revenues versus expenses by preparing a trial income (profit-and-loss) statement for your business plan. You can prepare this pro forma (projected) document for at least the first year (month-by-month) using BPP's **Profit and Loss** spreadsheet in the section entitled **"The Bottom Line."**

▼ *General Tips for Navigating in BPP

1. Open the BPP program, examine the Welcome screen, and click on **Open a Sample Plan.**

2. From the Open a Sample Plan dialogue box, click on a sample company name; then click on **Open.**

3. On the Task Manager screen, click onto any of the lines (for example, **Your Company**).

4. You can always return to the Task Manager screen by going to the bottom of the screen and clicking on the **Task Manager** icon.

5. When you are finished with a sample company, close its Task Manager screen.

6. After finishing with one sample company, you can get to the next one by going to the top of the screen and clicking on **File** (on the menu bar). Then beneath it select **Open Sample Plan.** This will exit you from the current company file and send you to the Open a Sample Plan dialogue box, where you can select your next example company.

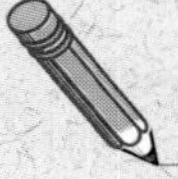

EXPLORING THE NET

FIELD TRIP TO THE AICPA

Most business practitioners belong to professional associations that provide services for members. The American Institute of Certified Public Accountants (AICPA) is one of accounting's best-known associations. To learn about the purpose of the AICPA and the activities that it offers, visit its Web site at

http://www.aicpa.org/

Spend some time navigating through the home page. To get an idea of the variety of topics covered and services offered for AICPA members, enter each of the subject gates (point the mouse to the title and click) ranged up and down the page. Next, scroll down the page into the Site Directory and select, for example, **AICPA Conferences.** After reviewing the area that you selected, consider the following questions:

1. Examine the list of AICPA conferences sorted by date. Notice the variety of conference topics and locations throughout the year. Are any of the topics or locations of interest to you? Do you think that anyone other than accountants might get some value from attending a conference? Explain.
2. Look at the AICPA Software offerings (in the Site Directory). Why does the AICPA offer this software to its members? As you scan down the AICPA Software screen, click on **Product Highlights** and examine the various product offerings. Identify at least three different kinds of software and explain what they do for the user.
3. After returning to the Site Directory, scan down the page and click on **Students.** Explore the Career section. From a career standpoint, which of the items (the aspects of accounting life) are appealing to you and which are not? Return to the Students page and scan down to **About Becoming a CPA.** Now go to **FAQs (Frequently Asked Questions) on Accounting Careers.** What is your opinion about the "150-hour education program"? What are its pros and cons?

VIDEO EXERCISE 5.1

Networking Information

Learning Objectives

1. Understand the role of information in the management process.
2. Appreciate the need to evaluate information to determine what is needed and how to use it most effectively.
3. Understand the power and limitations of the Internet as a business tool.

Background Information

Today's managers sometimes find it difficult to identify and manage needed information. Showtime's difficulty in managing information is a case to contrast with other low-tech or high-tech firms. Managers often mismanage and fail to understand the use of information systems and the Internet. The Internet in particular has become an effective business tool. It is important to understand the many things that companies must consider—and manage—in using the Internet to conduct business.

The Video

Showtime is a good example of the complexities of operating a large, multidimensional company. Logistics, production costs, quality, salaries, communication, and technological trends all affect Showtime managers on a daily basis. Managing this type of operation effectively requires managers to understand what information they need and what is "noise" in the system. Showtime uses an intranet—an internal information system—to link employees and systems. Showtime links to affiliates and customers via an extranet, which provides these affiliates and customers with information but not its private company data.

Discussion Questions

1. What are some of the major issues in managing operating expenses?
2. What steps can a business owner take to maximize use of resources?
3. What is the value of organizing workers into teams?

Follow-Up Assignment

The success of the Internet as a business tool has driven many companies to quickly create Web sites. However, in their haste, many businesses have created sites without focus or strategy. Use any resources at your disposal (articles, experts, information on the Internet) to develop a list of "do's and don'ts" for creating business Web sites.

For Further Exploration

Evaluate Showtime's Web site along with those of its competitors, HBO and Cinemax.

http://www.showtimeonline.com/
http://www.hbo.com/
http://www.cinemax.com/

Assess each company's goals and strategies for using the Internet. Compare Showtime's Web site with those of HBO and Cinemax.

Brewing Up Business at Silocaf of New Orleans

> "Work smarter, not harder!"
> —Commentator Jim Shell

Learning Objectives

The purpose of this video exercise is to help you

1. Recognize that almost all successful business ventures have started when some creative entrepreneurs spotted a *need* and then proceeded to fill that need.
2. Understand how important it can be for founders of a new business to *complement* one another.
3. Fully understand that keeping up with technology is vital to business's success or even its *survival.*

Background Information

Hostess Hattie Bryant introduces us to **Silocaf of New Orleans, Inc.** The firm, with annual sales of around $10 million, handles coffee in bulk, which is known in the business as "forwarding." When ships come to New Orleans with their holds full of coffee beans, Silocaf provides a place to hold the beans, cleans them, and eventually ships them out to their clients, who are the major coffee manufacturers. Nowhere in the videotape does Silocaf reveal where the coffee is headed, which is likely a good business move. At no time can it be said that Silocaf *owns* the coffee beans.

Hattie Bryant first talks to Federico Pacorini, a member of the company's founding family. Federico provides details of the firm's start in Trieste, Italy. Noting how much raw coffee was shipped into New Orleans, Federico's father investigated acquiring an old silo close to the waterfront. In fact, the company had a first customer lined up before purchasing the silo. Federico discusses some of the matters that spring up in a family business. For example, Federico's brother had sharp disagreements with the father over what direction the firm should be taking. However, when that brother and Federico took over from the father, the brothers worked out a well-balanced approach.

Hattie Bryant follows the systems and resources manager around the facility. That manager explains that the company normally holds 30 to 40 million pounds of coffee, valued at around $50 million. The coffee never sits at Silocaf for more than 2 weeks. As we view how the beans are processed, it becomes clear that Silocaf is a capital-intensive operation, with computerized technology at its heart. The systems and resources manager explains the PC LAN (personal computer local area network) to Hattie. Commentator Paul Nelson tells us that the company's technology actually enables the firm to seem more personal because it allows Silocaf to be far more intelligent when responding to calls from clients/customers. Silocaf developed its technology very slowly, and commentator Jim Shell tells us that what has really changed over the last 25 years is not the technology itself, but the *employees*—with their new attitudes, independence, and different ideas on company loyalty.

Federico comes back to assure us that Silocaf believes in its service and its product. He admits that a major coffee manufacturer could expand its own operations to include the services performed by Silocaf, but he believes that the manufacturers are satisfied with Silocaf handling the task.

The Video

SMALL BUSINESS 2000 MASTER CLASS, SB2000 SHOW #109. ALTHOUGH FEW COFFEE DRINKERS HAVE EVER HEARD OF **SILOCAF,** millions of people have consumed the coffee that the firm has processed. This video points out that significant firms with large operations can often operate beyond the view of the consumer.

Discussion Questions

1. Explain the working relationship between Federico and his brother. Is that relationship a good definition of the term *teamwork?*
2. Looking back at the early days of Silocaf in New Orleans, point out places where the whole concept could have gone down the drain. Would Silocaf have been wise to line up numerous clients before acquiring the silo at New Orleans?
3. Does Silocaf own the coffee beans that come through its facilities? What is the likelihood that a major coffee manufacturer will develop its own facilities to handle what Silocaf now does?
4. What were some of the advantages of Silocaf building up its technology gradually? Could a firm acquire technology slowly today? Why or why not?
5. What is your reaction to the coffee taster (in the context of quality control) who revealed that he is not a big coffee drinker?
6. What are some of the reasons that commentator Jim Shell gave to back up his statement that the main difference from 25 years ago is not technology? What, then, is so different today?
7. Comment on how much Federico and his colleagues believe in their services and the product they process.
8. Commentator Jim Shell said that in past years "elbow grease" was all you needed to succeed in a small business. What does it take now?

Follow-Up Assignment

To better understand various aspects of **Silocaf of New Orleans, Inc.,** familiarize yourself with the following concepts in the textbook:

- Today's global context (Chapter 3)
- Small-business operations (Chapter 7)
- Managing human resources (Chapter 9)
- Quality control (Chapter 13)
- Production technology (Chapter 13)
- Information technology (Chapter 14)
- Marketing channels (Chapter 12)

The Internet Connection and One Last Thing to Remember

You can contact Silocaf on the Internet at

http://www.pacorini.it

The videotape points out that "hard work is not enough." This view seems different from traditional thinking, which tells us that if you're willing to put in the necessary hard work, you will succeed. The videotape states, rather, that you should work smarter, not harder.

Jim Shell points out that employees have changed over the past 25 years. And today's managers must learn to understand these employees if the business is to succeed. Despite the many changes in employees and technology, Silocaf has held on to a timeless value: The company believes in the services it provides and in the product it handles.

UNDERSTANDING FINANCIAL ISSUES

Lettuce and Loans

It's 10 A.M. on Saturday morning—a good time to have some coffee, if only you had the sugar and cream that make it taste so good. Your refrigerator is empty, you're yearning for caffeine, and the supermarket beckons. And so does the market's in-store banking center, where you plan to spend a few extra minutes depositing your paycheck and applying for a home equity loan.

Welcome to the new world of banking, where full-service supermarket branches are located right down the aisle from Kellogg's cereals and where branch managers are learning to sell as hard as Coke and Pepsi. There are now more than 5,000 in-store banks across the country, and the number is climbing every year. "It's a concept whose time has come," says John W. Garnett, president of International Banking Technologies, an Atlanta-based consulting firm. "There's tremendous potential for new business and the bank does not have to spend one nickel to advertise to bring the people in."

Barely a blip on bankers' radar screens just a few years ago, supermarket banking is now the location of choice for many of the country's largest banks, including Wells Fargo, Bank of America, Barnett Banks, NationsBank, and First Union. San Francisco–based Wells Fargo already has more than 700 supermarket sites and is so confident of its location strategy that it is selling its branch real estate.

Supermarket branches have helped level the playing field for community banks, which lack the resources to go head-to-head with larger competitors in the normal branch system. For a mere $100,000, instead of $1 million or more for a stand-alone branch, a small bank can set up shop in a supermarket and compete with the big guys.

BRANCH OUT INTO SUPERMARKETS AND THEY WILL COME

Supermarket branches make sense because they give customers what they want: the ability to bank while shopping. As they become more popular, they are forcing bankers to redefine the branch concept. In a 300-square-foot space in the corner of a supermarket, the focus is no longer on operations, but on customer service. "The real issue is, 'Is the customer changing?' " contends Don Horner, vice chairperson of First Hawaiian Bank. "And, if so, how can we better serve him and what facility can we use to do it?"

Research has shown that customers want convenience in the form of one-stop banking and that they are willing to use technology to expedite service. At Barnett Bank in Jacksonville, Florida, self-service delivery channels, including ATMs and voice mail systems, account for half of all transactions. Some banks use video technology to augment in-store staff. At the Bank of Oklahoma in Tulsa, a two-way video unit is connected to the bank's call center, via a high-speed (ISDN) telephone hookup. Customers who want to open an account or apply for a loan dial into the system. The machine can even print temporary checks and ATM cards.

Thanks to this technology, banks are providing full service with fewer employees. Wells Fargo runs its in-store branches with only six employees, half the number in a typical stand-alone branch. But customers don't seem to mind because they can make transactions, set up new accounts, arrange for home and auto loans, and buy insurance and investments without leaving the market.

WHAT HAPPENED TO ALL THOSE STUFFY BANKERS?

If Christopher H. Stephenson is typical, bankers aren't what they used to be. At age 25, Stephenson is a supermarket branch manager for National Commerce Bancorp in suburban Memphis. In a typical month, he and his staff must sell 26 new checking accounts, 26 new money market accounts, as well as other banking products. If the business doesn't come to the window, Stephenson walks the aisles to find it in the market.

This go-out-and-find-the-customer attitude is echoed at the in-store operation of National City Bank in Dublin, Ohio. Since the branch opened in the Big Bear supermarket in 1996, monthly sales, including those produced by telemarketing, have averaged 250 products. A top seller is the home equity loan, which, in just 8 months, has brought in more than $1.2 million.

The greatest challenge this new breed of bankers face is to entice new customers to give them a try. Although supermarket shoppers average 2.5 visits a week, 80 percent have never used an in-store bank. Experience has shown that traditional bank sales strategies don't work in the supermarket setting.

What does work? The same dynamic sales techniques used by food marketers. Francie Henry, vice president and regional manager of Cincinnati-based Fifth Third Bancorp, has learned that banks, like food stores, must capture consumer interest before they can make sales. "We have a product-of-the-month promotion and we always decorate to match the theme," said Henry. "The goal is to keep the message fresh and to keep moving around." She means that literally. Bank employees discuss loans in the bakery aisle, open money market accounts in the meat department, and arrange for certificates of deposit next to containers of Clorox Bleach.

WILL THE SUPERMARKET BE TOMORROW'S ONE-STOP BANKING CENTER?

As the popularity of in-store branches grows, their product lines are also growing from federally insured vehicles, such as bank money market accounts, to uninsured vehicles, including mutual funds. Large banks, which see themselves as financial supermarkets, are expanding their product lines in both branch and in-store settings.

This worries the National Association of Securities Dealers (NASD), which cites the potential for consumer confusion in the small space of a supermarket bank. NASD spokesman Michael Robinson explains: "If you walk into a [regular] bank, it's pretty easy to understand that in one section they sell treasury bonds that are federally insured, while in other areas they sell mutual funds. In a supermarket branch, it's much more difficult to make that distinction."

Sandra Deem, a spokesperson for Connecticut-based First Union Corp., considers this distinction unnecessary because most First Union customers use in-store branches for check cashing and other simple transactions. "People don't often come in to talk about a mutual fund," said Deem. "The people who are coming in to shop for groceries often don't generate the type of business we are looking for."

Despite First Union's skepticism, industry analysts expect approximately 7,500 in-store branches by the year 2000. Will banking and banking relationships ever be the same?

WEB LINKS

The following Web sites will help you examine the issues that surround in-store banking and answer the questions that follow.

- **American Banker Online**
  http://www.americanbanker.com/
- **Barnett Bank**
  http://www.barnett.com
- **NationsBank**
  http://www.nationsbank.com/
- **New York Stock Exchange**
  http://www.nyse.com/
- **Wells Fargo**
  http://www.wellsfargo.com/home/
- **U.S. Securities and Exchange Commission**
  http://www.sec.gov/

QUESTIONS FOR DISCUSSION

1. In an environment where millions of Americans are taking money out of banks to invest in the stock market (via mutual funds and individual stocks), can you make an argument that supermarket banking is critical to the survival of the banking industry? Explain your answer. (Consult the New York Stock Exchange Web site for investor information.)
2. Do you think that the same consumers who use on-line banking services are likely to use supermarket banking services? Why or why not? (See bank Web sites for information about on-line banking.)
3. Do you agree or disagree with the concerns of the National Association of Securities Dealers about consumer confusion between insured and uninsured investments in the small space of a supermarket bank? What role do you think the U.S. Securities and Exchange Commission should play in addressing these concerns? (See the SEC Web site for information on the agency's regulatory activities.)
4. What effect do you think the Interstate Banking Efficiency Act of 1994 has had on the spread of in-store banks?
5. Do you agree that in-store banking puts small banks on an equal footing with larger institutions?
6. As banks achieve greater efficiencies and lower costs by closing stand-alone branches in favor of in-store branches, how do you think bank stock prices will change? How important do you think these efficiencies are in maintaining a high stock price?
7. Should banks target specific in-store branches for small-business owners? What kinds of financial products should they sell?
8. What risks does Wells Fargo face in closing traditional branches in favor of supermarket branches?

CHAPTER 15

UNDERSTANDING MONEY AND BANKING

A Popular Bank in a Big Niche

The American Dream is to rise from poverty to wealth—or at least comfort—through hard work, determination, business savvy, and other virtues given meaning by opportunity. It is the dream not only of people who can trace their roots back to the *Mayflower* but also of new Hispanic immigrants to America who speak English as a second language. For many, the dream has long been possible because the American banking system loaned money to buy homes and build and expand businesses. For others, however, particularly minorities, loans were often hard to get, and insufficient financial help doomed plans for both families and businesses.

Reflecting on the state of the American Dream, at least one bank recognized opportunity in this situation. Instead of classifying low- to moderate-income Hispanics as credit risks to be avoided at all costs, Puerto Rico–based Banco Popular saw them as an untapped market for personal and business banking services. When he looks at the multiethnic New York City neighborhoods that many mainstream banks are reluctant to enter, Jose Antonio Torres, Banco Popular's New York/New Jersey general manager, sees "strong retail areas with good, growing neighborhoods and housing stock. They are the kind of communities where we have done well before."

> **"Multiethnic New York City districts are strong retail areas with good, growing neighborhoods and housing stock. They are the kind of communities where we have done well before."**
>
> —Jose Antonio Torres
> *Banco Popular, New York/New Jersey General Manager*

Indeed, Banco Popular's historical mission has been to serve the banking needs of Hispanic Americans. The bank entered the New York market in 1961 and through growth and acquisitions now boasts 39 metropolitan-area branches. In addition to New York, Banco Popular has always focused on the five states with the largest Hispanic populations: California, Florida, Illinois, New Jersey, and Texas. Every acquisition that the bank makes keeps this market in mind. For example, Banco Popular acquired Houston-based Citizens National Bank in 1997 because its customer base was predominantly Hispanic. Citizens National Bank, explains Mike Cart, president at the time of the acquisition, had already "become lenders to ethnic minorities in low- to moderate-income areas all over Houston in the single family mortgage finance business. We already served the market that satisfied Banco Popular's strategic plans."

In the New York area, which is home to 3.4 million Hispanics and 70,000 Hispanic-owned businesses, the bank found a niche in lending to small and midsize companies and is the metropolitan region's top provider of Small Business Administration–backed loans in terms of dollar volume ($32 million in 1998). One of the bank's new financing programs is aimed at second-generation, family-owned Hispanic groceries. It centers around loans to adult children who want to expand existing businesses run by their parents.

Having witnessed Banco Popular's success in New York's Hispanic communities, mainstream banks such as Chase Manhattan and Citibank are also moving aggressively into the Hispanic market. Chase, for example, recently opened a small-business development center in the Bronx, equipped with a multilingual business library and a staff offering management help. Chase also took part in a 2-year SBA pilot program to speed and simplify the lending process to minority businesses.

With a larger presence and more marketing money to spend than Banco Popular, will banks such as Chase and Citi ultimately dominate New York's minority banking market? Although the answer to that question remains unclear, it is clear that many Hispanics prefer a bank with ethnic roots. Roberto Reyes, owner of Jeselvi Travel in the Bronx, may be typical. When he opened his agency, he had a choice of banking with Chase or Banco Popular. He chose Banco Popular because he wanted to do business with Hispanics.

Whether it caters to the minority communities of Los Angeles, Houston, Jersey City, or Miami or to nonminority communities across the United States, a complex system of financial institutions, especially banks, is needed to meet the money requirements of individuals and businesses. By focusing on the learning objectives of this chapter, you will better understand the environment for banking in the United States and the different kinds of institutions that conduct business in it.

Our opening story continues on page 417

After reading this chapter, you should be able to:

1. **Define *money* and identify the different forms that it takes in the nation's money supply.**
2. **Describe the different kinds of *financial institutions* that comprise the U.S. financial system and explain the services they offer.**
3. **Explain how banks create money and describe the means by which they are regulated.**
4. **Discuss the functions of the *Federal Reserve System* and describe the tools that it uses to control the money supply.**
5. **Identify three important ways in which the financial industry is changing.**

■ WHAT IS MONEY?

When someone asks you how much money you have, do you count the dollar bills and coins in your pockets? Do you include your checking and savings accounts? What about stocks and bonds? Do you count your car? Taken together, the value of all these things is your "personal wealth." Not all of it, however, is "money." In this section, we consider more precisely what *money* is and does.

The Characteristics of Money

money Any object that is portable, divisible, durable, and stable and serves as a medium of exchange, a store of value, and a unit of account

Modern money often takes the form of stamped metal or printed paper—U.S. dollars, British pounds, French francs, Japanese yen—issued by governments. Theoretically, however, just about any object can serve as **money** if it is *portable, divisible, durable,* and *stable.* To appreciate these qualities, imagine using something that lacks them—say, a 70-pound salmon:

- *Portability.* Try lugging 70 pounds of fish from shop to shop. In contrast, modern currency is light and easy to handle.
- *Divisibility.* Suppose that you want to buy a hat, a book, and some milk from three different stores. How would you divide your fish-money? Is a pound of its head worth as much as, say, two gills? Modern currency is easily divisible into smaller parts, each with a fixed value. A dollar, for example, can be exchanged for four quarters. More important, units of money can be easily matched with the value of all goods.
- *Durability.* Regardless of whether you "spend" it, your salmon will lose value every day (in fact, it will eventually be too smelly to be worth anything). Modern currency, however, neither dies nor spoils, and if it wears out, it can be replaced. It is also hard to counterfeit—certainly harder than catching more salmon.
- *Stability.* If salmon were in short supply, you might be able to make quite a deal for yourself. In the middle of a salmon run, however, the market would be flooded with fish. Sellers of goods would soon have enough fish and would refuse to produce anything for which they could get only salmon. Goods would become scarcer, but the salmon would continue (or cease) running, regardless of the plenitude or scarcity of buyable goods. The value of our paper money also fluctuates, but it is considerably more stable than salmon. Its value is related to what we can buy with it.

The Functions of Money

Imagine a successful fisherman who needs a new sail for his boat. In a barter economy—one in which goods are exchanged directly for one another—he would have to find someone who not only needs fish but who is also willing to exchange a sail for it. If no sailmaker wants fish, the fisherman must find someone else—say, a shoemaker—who wants fish. Then the fisherman must hope that the sailmaker will trade for his new shoes. Clearly, barter is inefficient in comparison with money. In a money economy, the fisherman would sell his catch, receive money, and exchange the money for such goods as a new sail.

Money serves three functions:[1]

- *Medium of exchange.* Like the fisherman "trading" money for a new sail, we use money as a way of buying and selling things. Without money, we would be bogged down in a system of barter.
- *Store of value.* Pity the fisherman who catches a fish on Monday and wants to buy a few bars of candy on, say, the following Saturday, by which time the fish would have spoiled and lost its value. In the form of currency, however, money can be used for future purchases and so "stores" value.
- *Unit of account.* Money lets us measure the relative values of goods and services. It acts as a unit of account because all products can be valued and accounted for in terms of money.

Of all the Asian nations struck by the financial crisis of 1997–1998, perhaps Indonesia was hardest hit. In an 8-month period, the value of the Indonesian currency, the rupiah, fell from 3,000 to the dollar to 15,000. As usual, the hardest hit among the hard-hit are the poor, who find the local money worth more when it's pounded into jewelry than when it's held as a medium of exchange.

For example, the concepts of "$1,000 worth of clothes" or "$500 in labor costs" have universal meaning because everyone deals with money every day.

The Spendable Money Supply: M-1

For money to serve its basic functions, both buyers and sellers must agree on its value. That value depends in part on its *supply*—on how much money is in circulation. When the money supply is high, the value of money drops. When it is low, that value increases.

Unfortunately, it is not easy to measure the supply of money. One of the most commonly used measures, known widely as **M-1,** counts only the most liquid, or spendable, forms of money: currency, demand deposits, and other checkable deposits. These are all noninterest-bearing or low-interest-bearing forms of money. As of July 1998, M-1 in the United States totaled just over $1 trillion.[2]

M-1 Measure of the money supply that includes only the most liquid (spendable) forms of money

CURRENCY Paper money and metal coins are **currency** issued by the government. Currency is widely used for small exchanges. As the U.S. dollar bill states, currency is "legal tender for all debts, public and private"—that is, the law requires creditors to accept it in payment of debts. The average adult in the United States carries about $45 in currency. As of July 1998, currency in circulation in the United States amounted to $441 billion, or about 41 percent of M-1. Traveler's checks, bank cashier's checks, and money orders, which are all accepted as currency, accounted for another $8 billion.

currency Government-issued paper money and metal coins

DEMAND DEPOSITS A **check** is essentially an order instructing a bank to pay a given sum to a "payee." Checks permit buyers to make large purchases without having to carry large amounts of cash. Although not all sellers accept them as payment, many do. Checks are usually acceptable in place of cash because they are valuable only to specified payees and can be exchanged for cash. Checking accounts, which are known as **demand deposits,** are counted in M-1 because funds may be withdrawn at any time—"on demand." Eighty-four percent of all U.S. households have checking accounts. As of July 1998, demand deposits accounted for $379 billion, or about 35 percent of M-1.

check Demand deposit order instructing a bank to pay a given sum to a specified payee

demand deposit Bank account funds that may be withdrawn at any time

OTHER CHECKABLE DEPOSITS Other checkable deposits—those on which checks can be written—include automated teller machine (ATM) account balances and *negotiable order of withdrawal (NOW)* accounts, which are interest-bearing accounts that can be held only in savings banks and savings and loan associations by individuals and nonprofit organizations. As of July 1998, checkable deposits in the United States exceeded $245 billion, or 23 percent of M-1.

M-1 Plus the Convertible Money Supply: M-2

M-2 Measure of the money supply that includes all the components of M-1 plus the forms of money that can be easily converted into spendable form

M-2 includes everything in M-1 plus items that cannot be spent directly but are easily converted to spendable forms. The major components of M-2 are M-1, *time deposits, money market mutual funds,* and *savings deposits.* Totaling over $4.2 trillion in July 1998, M-2 accounts for nearly all the nation's money supply. It thus measures the store of monetary value available for financial transactions. As this overall level of money increases, more is available for consumer purchases and business investment. When the supply is tightened, less money is available, and financial transactions, spending, and business activity thus slow down.

time deposit Bank funds that cannot be withdrawn without notice or transferred by check

TIME DEPOSITS Unlike demand deposits, **time deposits** require prior notice of withdrawal and cannot be transferred by check. However, time deposits pay higher interest rates. The supply of money in time deposits, such as certificates of deposit (CDs) and savings certificates, grew rapidly in the 1970s and 1980s after government ceilings on interest rates were removed. Depositors can now invest for both short and long periods of time. Time deposits in M-2 include only accounts of less than $100,000 that can be redeemed on demand with small penalties. Large time deposits, usually those made by businesses, cannot be redeemed early and are not included in M-2. As of July 1998, U.S. time deposits amounted to nearly $959 billion—almost 23 percent of M-2.

money market mutual fund Fund of short-term, low-risk financial securities purchased with the assets of investor-owners pooled by a nonbank institution

MONEY MARKET MUTUAL FUNDS Operated by investment companies that bring together pools of assets from many investors, **money market mutual funds** buy a collection of short-term, low-risk financial securities. Ownership of and profits (or losses) from the sale of these securities are shared among the fund's investors.

Money market funds attracted many investors in the 1980s because they paid high rates and often allowed investors to write checks against their shares. Why do mutual funds pay higher returns than most individuals can get on their own? There are two reasons:

1. Funds can buy into higher-paying securities that require larger investments than most individuals can afford.
2. They are managed by professionals who monitor changing investment opportunities.

Shortly after being introduced in 1974, money market mutual funds had attracted $1.7 billion. As of July 1998, they totaled $675 billion—16 percent of M-2.

SAVINGS DEPOSITS In the wake of new, more attractive investments, traditional savings deposits, such as passbook savings accounts, have declined in popularity. Savings deposits represented 40 percent of M-2 in 1971 but less than 36 percent by 1998. Figure 15.1 shows how the two measures of money, M-1 and M-2, have grown since 1959. For many years, M-1 was the traditional measure of liquid money. Because it was closely related to gross domestic product, it served as a reliable predictor of the nation's economic health. This situation changed in the early 1980s, however, with the introduction of new types of investments and easier transfer of money among investment funds to gain higher interest returns. As a result, M-2 today is a more reliable measure than M-1 and is often used by economists for economic planning.

Credit Cards

Citicorp is the world's largest credit card issuer, with more than 49 million accounts worldwide. More than 124 million U.S. cardholders carry more than 1.4 billion cards. Spending with general-purpose credit cards in the United States reached $991 billion in 1996 and is projected to reach $1.6 trillion—almost half of all transactions—by the year 2000.[3] Indeed, the use of cards such as Visa, MasterCard, American Express, Discover, and Diners Club has become so widespread that many people refer to them as "plastic money."

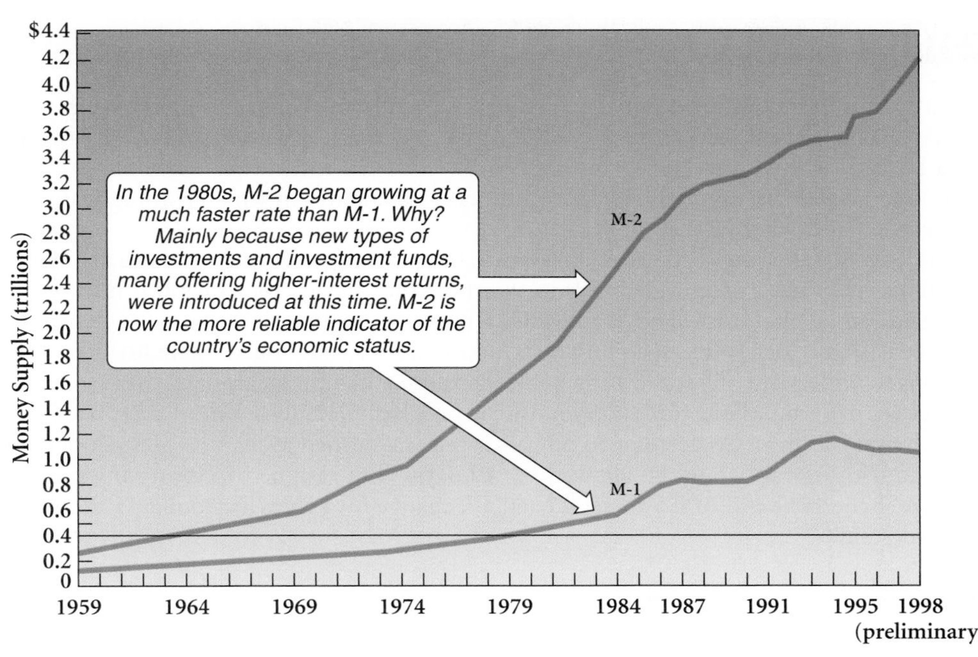

FIGURE 15.1 ◆ Money-Supply Growth, 1959–1998

Credit cards are big business for two basic reasons. First, they are convenient. Second, they are extremely profitable for issuing companies. Profits derive from two sources:

1. Some cards charge annual fees to holders. All charge interest on unpaid balances. Depending on the issuer, and on certain state regulations, cardholders pay interest rates ranging from 11 to 20 percent.
2. Merchants who accept credit cards pay fees to card issuers. Depending on the merchant's agreement with the issuer, 2 to 5 percent of total credit sales dollars goes to card issuers.

Credit card loans have been increasing at the rate of 20 percent per year since 1994. As of 1997, it is estimated that households were carrying $450 billion of credit card debt on which they were paying interest; it is projected to increase to $780 billion in the year 2000. Why are banks and other card issuers so willing to grant this kind of credit? Returns are up to three times higher than those from other forms of banking.[4]

In 1998, U.S. banks and credit card issuers launched a full-scale attack on British borrowers, whose own financial industry lags behind in the area of consumer-credit marketing. According to one executive at American Express, the European industry went from cash to checking to debit cards without pausing for revolving credit like that offered by AmEx, Visa, and MasterCard. "European banks," he believes, "have missed a big profit opportunity," and companies like AmEx are willing to risk a tougher regulatory climate to distribute credit cards throughout Great Britain and continental Europe.

THE U.S. FINANCIAL SYSTEM

Many forms of money, especially demand deposits and time deposits, depend on the existence of financial institutions to provide a broad spectrum of services to both individuals and businesses. Just how important are reliable financial institutions to both businesses and individuals? Try asking financial consumers in a country in which commercial banking can be an adventure.

In Russia, for example, there is almost no banking regulation and no way to distinguish qualified from unscrupulous bankers in the thousands of different financial institutions, large and small, that exist. The Moscow City Bank has no deposit insurance, no customer service desk, no loan officers, and no cash machine. Businesses need stable financial institutions to underwrite modernization and expansion, and individuals need them to handle currency. Imagine, then, the disappointment of Vladimir Shcherbakov, who needed to withdraw $500 from his account to buy a car but was turned away by a sign announcing that no withdrawals would be allowed for 10 days. "I'm resigned to losing my money," sighed Shcherbakov. "But if I do get it back, I'll change my rubles into dollars and hold on to it myself."[5]

> **"I'm resigned to losing my money. But if I do get it back, I'll change my rubles into dollars and hold on to it myself."**
>
> —Vladimir Shcherbakov
> *Russian bank customer*

In the sections that follow, we describe the major types of financial institutions, explain how they work when they work as they are supposed to, and survey some of the special services that they offer. We also explain their role as creators of money and discuss the regulation of the U.S. banking system.

Financial Institutions

The main function of financial institutions is to ease the flow of money from sectors with surpluses to those with deficits.[6] They do this by issuing claims against themselves and using the proceeds to buy the assets of—and thus invest in—other organizations. A bank, for instance, can issue financial claims against itself by making available funds for checking and savings accounts. In turn, its assets will be mostly loans invested in individuals and businesses and perhaps government securities. In this section, we discuss each of the major types of financial institutions: *commercial banks, savings and loan associations, mutual savings banks, credit unions,* and various organizations known as *nondeposit institutions.*

commercial bank Federal- or state-chartered financial institution accepting deposits that it uses to make loans and earn profits

COMMERCIAL BANKS The United States today boasts nearly 10,000 **commercial banks**—companies that accept deposits that they use to make loans and earn profits. Commercial banks range from the very largest institutions in New York, such as Citigroup and Chase Manhattan, to tiny banks dotting the rural landscape. Bank liabilities include checking accounts and savings accounts. Assets consist of a wide variety of loans to individuals, businesses, and governments.

state bank Commercial bank chartered by an individual state

national bank Commercial bank chartered by the federal government

All commercial banks must be *chartered.* Until 1863, all banks were chartered by individual states. Today nearly 70 percent of all commercial banks remain **state banks.** Most of the largest U.S. banks, however, are **national banks,** chartered by the federal government. The 10 largest U.S. commercial banks are all nationally chartered. As of 1997, these 10 institutions had combined profits of $22 billion. Combined, all state and national banks hold $4.6 trillion in domestic assets and $2.8 trillion in loans.[7]

Diversification and Mergers. Many observers today believe that traditional banking has become a "mature" industry, one whose basic operations have expanded as broadly as they can. For instance, 1993 marked the first year in which the money invested in mutual funds—almost $2 trillion—equaled the amount deposited in U.S. banks. Thus, financial industry competitors in areas such as mutual funds are growing, sometimes rapidly.

As consumers continue to look for alternatives to traditional banking services, commercial banks and savings and loan associations find themselves with a dwindling share of market. In fact, nonbank competitors have increased their share of the market to about 70 percent. The investment bank Merrill Lynch, for example, has originated billions of dollars in commercial loans, formerly the province of commercial banks. Savers, too, have been putting their savings into the money market funds, stocks, and bonds offered by companies such as Charles Schwab instead of into the traditional savings accounts offered by banks. Many observers contend that to compete, banks, too, must diversify their offerings. The only way that they can compete, says banking analyst Thomas Brown, "is to transform themselves into successful retailers of financial services, which involves dramatic, not incremental change."

> **"The only way banks can compete is to transform themselves into successful retailers of financial services, which involves dramatic, not incremental change."**
>
> —Thomas Brown
> *Banking analyst*

A related option seems to be to get bigger. In efforts to regain competitiveness, banks have been merging at a record-setting pace in the 1990s. When commercial banks merge with investment banks, the resulting companies hold larger shares of the financial market, and the lines become blurred between traditional banking and nonbank financial institutions. Chase Manhattan Corp., which became the largest U.S. bank when it merged with Chemical Banking Corp. in 1996, has already been dwarfed by sprawling Citigroup Inc., the result of a 1998 merger between Citicorp (a commercial bank) and Travelers Group (which includes investment bank Salomon Smith Barney). With $700 billion in assets, Citigroup plans to offer one-stop shopping on a global scale for both consumers and businesses, including private banking, credit card services, mortgages, mutual funds, stock brokerage services, insurance, and loans.

Bank of America Corp., created from the merger of NationsBank and BankAmerica, is the first coast-to-coast bank in the United States, with a presence in 22 states and assets of $570 billion. Internationally, Germany's Deutsche Bank AG is primarily a commercial banking firm that wants to become a major U.S. investment bank. Deutsche has thus offered to purchase Bankers Trust Corp., an investment bank that ranks eighth among all American banks. Mergers are the trend, and fewer but larger banks are offering a wide range of financial products. The strategy streamlines operations to reduce costs and focuses on providing products that will win back customers from nonbank competitors.[8]

Commercial Interest Rates. Every bank receives a major portion of its income from interest paid on loans by borrowers. As long as terms and conditions are clearly revealed to borrowers, banks are allowed to set their own interest rates. Traditionally, the lowest rates were made available to the bank's most creditworthy commercial customers. That rate is called the **prime rate.** Most commercial loans are set at markups over prime. However, the prime rate is no longer a strong force in setting loan rates. Borrowers can now get funds less expensively from other sources, including foreign banks that set lower interest rates. To remain competitive, therefore, U.S. banks now offer some commercial loans at rates below prime.

prime rate Interest rate available to a bank's most creditworthy customers

savings and loan association (S&L) Financial institution accepting deposits and making loans primarily for home mortgages

SAVINGS AND LOAN ASSOCIATIONS Like commercial banks, **savings and loan associations (S&Ls)** accept deposits and make loans. They lend money primarily for home mortgages. Most S&Ls were created to provide financing for homes. Many of them, however, have ventured into other investments, with varying degrees of success. S&Ls in the United States now hold $1 trillion in assets and deposits of $728 billion.[9]

mutual savings bank Financial institution whose depositors are owners sharing in its profits

MUTUAL SAVINGS BANKS In **mutual savings banks,** all depositors are considered owners of the bank. All profits, therefore, are divided proportionately among depositors, who receive dividends. Like S&Ls, mutual savings banks attract most of their funds in the form of savings deposits, and funds are loaned out in the form of mortgages. Although 90 percent of all mutual savings bank deposits are held in five northeastern states, these institutions have nearly the same volume of total assets as S&Ls.

credit union Financial institution that accepts deposits from, and makes loans to, only its members, usually employees of a particular organization

CREDIT UNIONS In **credit unions,** deposits are accepted only from members who meet specific qualifications, usually working for a particular employer. Most universities, for example, run credit unions, as do the U.S. Navy and the Pentagon. Credit unions make loans for automobiles and home mortgages, as well as other types of personal loans. More than 12,000 credit unions now operate in the United States, nearly double the number operating in 1945. They hold $327 billion in savings and checking accounts for more than 72 million members.[10]

NONDEPOSIT INSTITUTIONS A variety of other organizations take in money, provide interest or other services, and make loans. Four of the most important are *pension funds, insurance companies, finance companies,* and *securities dealers.*[11]

pension fund Nondeposit pool of funds managed to provide retirement income for its members

Pension Funds. A **pension fund** is essentially a pool of funds managed to provide retirement income for its members. *Public pension funds* include Social Security and $1 trillion in retirement programs for state and local government employees. *Private pension funds,* operated by employers, unions, and other private groups, cover about 80 million people and have total assets of $5.4 trillion. The Teachers Insurance and Annuity Association (TIAA) operates the largest private fund in the United States, with assets of $214 billion in 1998.

insurance company Nondeposit institution that invests funds collected as premiums charged for insurance coverage

Insurance Companies. **Insurance companies** collect large pools of funds from the premiums charged for coverage. Funds are invested in stocks, real estate, and other assets. Earnings pay for insured losses, such as death benefits, automobile damage, and health care expenses. Insurance companies now hold total assets of more than $3 trillion.[12]

finance company Nondeposit institution that specializes in making loans to businesses and consumers

Finance Companies. **Finance companies** specialize in making loans to businesses and individuals. *Commercial finance companies* lend to businesses needing capital or long-term funds. They may, for instance, lend to a manufacturer that needs new assembly-line equipment. *Consumer finance companies* devote most of their resources to small noncommercial loans to individuals. Consumer finance companies take greater risks and generally charge higher interest rates than banks. Most loans pay for such items as cars, appliances, medical bills, and vacations. As of June 1998, U.S. finance companies had issued credit totaling $832 billion.[13]

securities investment dealer (broker) Nondeposit institution that buys and sells stocks and bonds both for investors and for its own accounts

Securities Dealers. **Securities investment dealers (brokers),** such as Merrill Lynch and A.G. Edwards & Sons, buy and sell stocks and bonds on the New York and other stock exchanges for client investors. They also invest in securities—they buy stocks and bonds for their own accounts in hopes of reselling them later at a profit. These companies hold large sums of money for transfer between buyers and sellers. *Investment bankers* match buyers and sellers of newly issued securities and receive commissions for the service. They, too, are thus financial intermediaries. U.S. investment dealers and investment bankers now hold $629 billion in assets.[14] (We discuss the activities of brokers and investment bankers more fully in Chapter 16.)

Special Financial Services

The finance business today is a highly competitive industry. No longer is it enough for commercial banks to accept deposits and make loans. Most, for example, now offer bank-issued credit cards and safe-deposit boxes. In addition, many offer pension, trust, international, and brokerage services and financial advice. Most offer ATMs and electronic money transfer.

PENSION SERVICES Most banks help customers establish savings plans for retirement. **Individual retirement accounts (IRAs)** are pension funds that wage earners and their spouses can set up to supplement other retirement funds. All wage earners can invest up to $2,000 of earned income annually in an IRA. They offer a significant tax benefit: Under many circumstances, taxes on principal and earnings are deferred until funds are withdrawn upon retirement. Under the 1997 tax changes, some IRAs are entirely tax-free. Banks serve as financial intermediaries by receiving funds and investing them as directed by customers. They also provide customers with information on investment vehicles available for IRAs (deposit accounts, mutual funds, stocks, and so forth).

Banks also assist customers in establishing **Keogh plans.** Though similar to IRAs, Keogh plans can be opened only by self-employed people, such as doctors, small-business owners, and consultants. Taxes on Keogh plans are always deferred until earners withdraw the funds. If a depositor needs to withdraw funds from a Keogh or an IRA before age 59 1/2, the Internal Revenue Service will impose a penalty of 10 percent on the withdrawn amount.

TRUST SERVICES Many commercial banks offer **trust services**—the management of funds left "in the bank's trust." In return for a fee, the trust department will perform such tasks as making your monthly bill payments and managing your investment portfolio. Trust departments also manage the estates of deceased persons.

INTERNATIONAL SERVICES The three main international services offered by banks are *currency exchange, letters of credit,* and *banker's acceptances.* Suppose, for example, that a U.S. company wants to buy a product from a French supplier. For a fee, it can use one or more of three services offered by its bank:

1. It can exchange U.S. dollars for French francs at a U.S. bank and then pay the French supplier in francs.
2. It can pay its bank to issue a **letter of credit**—a promise by the bank to pay the French firm a certain amount if specified conditions are met.
3. It can pay its bank to draw up a **banker's acceptance,** which promises that the bank will pay some specified amount at a future date.

A banker's acceptance requires payment by a particular date. Letters of credit are payable only after certain conditions are met. The French supplier, for example, may not be paid until shipping documents prove that the merchandise has been shipped from France.

FINANCIAL ADVICE AND BROKERAGE SERVICES Many banks, both large and small, help their customers manage their money. Depending on the customer's situation, the bank may recommend different investment opportunities. The recommended mix might include CDs, mutual funds, stocks, and bonds. Many banks also serve as securities intermediaries, using their own stockbrokers to buy and sell securities and their own facilities to hold them. Bank advertisements often stress the role of banks as financial advisers.

AUTOMATED TELLER MACHINES **Electronic automated teller machines (ATMs)** allow customers to withdraw money and make deposits 24 hours a day, 7 days a week. They also allow transfers of funds between accounts and provide information on account status. Some banks offer cards that can be used in affiliated nationwide systems. About 175,000 machines are now located at bank buildings, grocery stores, airports, shopping malls, and other locations, and forecasters anticipate up to 220,000 machines by the year 2000. U.S. bank customers conduct more than 12 billion ATM transactions a year, withdrawing an average of $50 per transaction.[15]

This Manhattan outlet looks like a branch bank, but there are no ATMs at Chase Checks-To-Cash Clubs. At this location, tellers simply exchange cash for payroll checks (for a fee, of course). Institutions such as Chase have entered the check-cashing business, which now processes $60 billion worth of payroll and government checks every year. In industry lingo, customers are ALICs: people who are "asset limited, income constrained."

individual retirement account (IRA) Tax-deferred pension fund with which wage earners supplement other retirement funds

Keogh plan Tax-deferred pension plan for the self-employed

trust services Bank management of an individual's investments, payments, or estate

letter of credit Bank promise, issued for a buyer, to pay a designated firm a certain amount of money if specified conditions are met

banker's acceptance Bank promise, issued for a buyer, to pay a designated firm a specified amount at a future date

automated teller machine (ATM) Electronic machine that allows customers to conduct account-related activities 24 hours a day, 7 days a week

Citibank has realized a big payoff from its 20-year commitment to consumer banking technology—that is, to the world's most advanced ATM technology. In one recent year, for example, the consumer banking division earned more than all the bank's other divisions combined. That's why Citibank now has consumer banking outlets in 41 countries, where it strives to make its once specialized products universal. At this ATM machine in Budapest, Hungary, for example, Americans can access their U.S. accounts in English. Then, says Victor Meneszes, head of Citibank's U.S./Europe consumer banking operations, "they can withdraw cash and go across the street to McDonald's. They feel completely at home."

Increasingly, ATMs are also becoming global fixtures. In fact, among the world's 545,000 ATMs, 80 percent are located outside the United States. The world total is expected to reach nearly 950,000 machines by the year 2000. Many U.S. banks now offer international ATM services. Citicorp installed Shanghai's first 24-hour ATM and is the first foreign bank to receive approval from the People's Bank of China to issue local currency through ATMs. Elsewhere, Citibank machines feature touch screens that take instructions in any of 10 languages.

electronic funds transfer (EFT) Communication of fund-transfer information over wire, cable, or microwave

ELECTRONIC FUNDS TRANSFER ATMs are the most popular form of **electronic funds transfer (EFT).** These systems transfer many kinds of financial information via electrical impulses over wire, cable, or microwave. In addition to ATMs, EFT systems include automatic payroll deposit, bill payment, and automatic funds transfer. Such systems can help a businessperson close an important business deal by transferring money from San Francisco to Miami within a few hours.

Banks as Creators of Money

In the course of their activities, financial institutions provide a special service to the economy—they create money. This is not to say that they mint bills and coins. Rather, by taking in deposits and making loans, they *expand the money supply.*[16]

As Figure 15.2 shows, the money supply expands because banks are allowed to loan out most (although not all) of the money they take in from deposits. Suppose that you deposit $100 in your bank. If banks are allowed to loan out 90 percent of all their deposits, then your bank will hold $10 in reserve and loan $90 of your money to borrowers. (You, of course, still have $100 on deposit.) Meanwhile, borrowers—or the people they pay—will deposit the $90 loan in their own banks. Together, the borrowers' banks will then have $81 (90 percent of $90) available for new loans. Banks, therefore, have turned your original $100 into $271 ($100 + $90 + $81). The chain continues, with borrowings from one bank becoming deposits in the next.

Regulation of Commercial Banking

Because commercial banks are critical to the creation of money, the government regulates them to ensure a sound and competitive financial system. Later in this chap-

DEPOSIT	MONEY HELD IN RESERVE BY BANK	MONEY TO LEND	TOTAL SUPPLY
$100.00	$10.00	$90.00	$190.00
90.00	9.00	81.00	271.00
81.00	8.10	72.90	343.90
72.90	7.29	65.61	409.51
65.61	6.56	59.05	468.56

FIGURE 15.2 ◆ How Banks Create Money

ter, we will see how the Federal Reserve System regulates many aspects of U.S. banking. Other federal and state agencies also regulate banks to ensure that the failure of some banks as a result of competition will not cause the public to lose faith in the banking system itself.

Federal Deposit Insurance Corporation (FDIC) Federal agency that guarantees the safety of all deposits up to $100,000 in the financial institutions that it insures

FEDERAL DEPOSIT INSURANCE CORPORATION The **Federal Deposit Insurance Corporation (FDIC)** insures deposits in member banks. More than 99 percent of the nation's commercial banks pay fees for membership in the FDIC. In return, the FDIC guarantees, through its Bank Insurance Fund (BIF), the safety of all deposits up to the current maximum of $100,000. If a bank collapses, the FDIC promises to pay its depositors—through the BIF—for losses up to $100,000 per person. (A handful of the nation's 10,000 commercial banks are insured by states rather than by the BIF.)

To insure against multiple bank failures, the FDIC maintains the right to examine the activities and accounts of all member banks. Such regulation was effective from 1941 through 1980, when fewer than 10 banks failed per year. At the beginning of the 1980s, however, banks were deregulated, and between 1981 and 1990, losses from nearly 1,100 bank failures depleted the FDIC's reserve fund. In recent years, the FDIC has thus raised the premiums charged to member banks to keep up with losses incurred by failed banks.

■ THE FEDERAL RESERVE SYSTEM

Perched atop the U.S. financial system and regulating many aspects of its operation is the Federal Reserve System. Established by Congress in 1913, the **Federal Reserve System** (or **the Fed**) is the nation's central bank. In this section, we describe the structure of the Fed, its functions, and the tools that it uses to control the nation's money supply.

Federal Reserve System (the Fed) Central bank of the United States, which acts as the government's bank, serves member commercial banks, and controls the nation's money supply

The Structure of the Fed

The Federal Reserve System consists of a board of governors, a group of reserve banks, and member banks. As originally established by the Federal Reserve Act of 1913, the system consisted of 12 relatively autonomous banks and a seven-member committee whose powers were limited to coordinating their activities. By the 1930s, however, both the structure and function of the Fed had changed dramatically.

THE BOARD OF GOVERNORS The Fed's board of governors consists of seven members appointed by the president for overlapping terms of 14 years. The chair of the board serves on major economic advisory committees and works actively with the administration to formulate economic policy. The board plays a large role in controlling the money supply. It alone determines the reserve requirements, within statutory limits, for depository institutions. It also works with other members of the Federal Reserve System to set discount rates and handle the Fed's sale and purchase of government securities.

RESERVE BANKS The Federal Reserve System consists of 12 administrative areas and 12 banks. Each Federal Reserve bank holds reserve deposits from and sets the discount rate for commercial banks in its region. Reserve banks also play a major role in the nation's check-clearing process.

MEMBER BANKS All nationally chartered commercial banks are members of the Federal Reserve System, as are some state-chartered banks. The accounts of all member bank depositors are automatically covered by the FDIC/BIF. Although many state-chartered banks do not belong to the Federal Reserve System, most pay deposit insurance premiums and are covered by the FDIC.

The Functions of the Fed

In addition to chartering national banks, the Fed serves as the federal government's bank and the "bankers' bank," regulating a number of banking activities. Most importantly, however, it controls the money supply. In this section, we describe these functions in some detail.

THE GOVERNMENT'S BANK Two of the Fed's activities are producing the nation's paper currency and lending money to the government. The Fed, for example, decides how many bills to produce and how many to destroy. To lend funds to the government, the Fed buys bonds issued by the Treasury Department. The borrowed money is then used to help finance the national deficit.

THE BANKERS' BANK Individual banks that need money can borrow from the Federal Reserve and pay interest on the loans. In addition, the Fed provides storage for commercial banks, which are required to keep funds on reserve at a Federal Reserve bank.

Check Clearing. The Fed also *clears checks*, some 65 billion of them each year, for commercial banks. To understand the check-clearing process, imagine that you are a photographer living in New Orleans. To participate in a workshop in Detroit, you must send a check for $50 to the Detroit studio. Figure 15.3 traces your check through the clearing process:

1. You send your check to the Detroit studio, which deposits it in its Detroit bank.
2. The Detroit bank deposits the check in its own account at the Federal Reserve Bank of Chicago.
3. The check is sent from Chicago to the Atlanta Federal Reserve Bank for collection because you, the check writer, live in the Atlanta district.
4. Your New Orleans bank receives the check from Atlanta and deducts the $50 from your personal account.
5. Your bank then has $50 deducted from its deposit account at the Atlanta Federal Reserve Bank.
6. The $50 is shifted from Atlanta to the Chicago Federal Reserve Bank. The studio's Detroit bank gets credited, whereupon the studio's account is then credited $50. Your bank mails the canceled check back to you.

Depending on the number of banks and the distances between them, a check will clear in 2 to 6 days. Until the process is completed, the studio's Detroit bank cannot spend the $50 deposited there. Meanwhile, your bank's records will continue to show $50 in your account. Each day, approximately $1 billion in checks is processed by the system. The term **float** refers to all the checks in the process at any one time.

float Total amount of checks written but not yet cleared through the Federal Reserve

OVERSEEING THE BANKING COMMUNITY The Federal Reserve System is empowered to examine all banks in its system. In reality, however, it examines only the state banks because national banks are examined by the Comptroller of the Currency and the

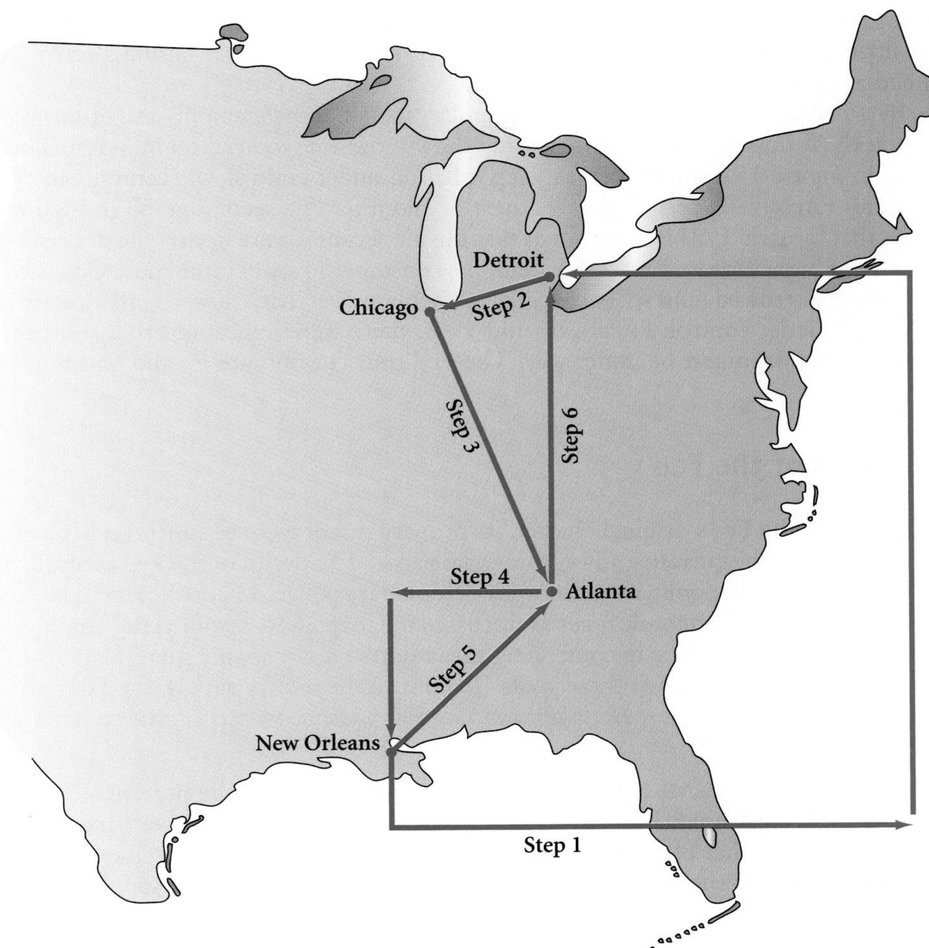

FIGURE 15.3 ◆ Clearing a Check

FDIC. Together these auditing efforts ensure the safety and stability of the state and national banks that are members of the Federal Reserve System.

CONTROLLING THE MONEY SUPPLY The Federal Reserve System is responsible for the conduct of U.S. **monetary policy**—the management of the nation's economic growth by managing money supply and interest rates. By controlling these two factors, the Fed influences the ability and willingness of banks throughout the country to loan money.

monetary policy Policies by which the Federal Reserve manages the nation's money supply and interest rates

Inflation Management. As defined in Chapter 1, *inflation* is a period of widespread price increases throughout an economic system. It occurs if the money supply grows too large. Demand for goods and services increases, and the prices of everything rise. (In contrast, too little money means that an economy will lack the funds to maintain high levels of employment.) Because commercial banks are the main creators of money, much of the Fed's management of the money supply takes the form of regulating the supply of money through commercial banks.

Consider the following illustration.

In July 1995, the Fed announced a decrease in the federal funds rate, the interest rate charged on overnight loans made among banks, from 6 percent to 5.75 percent. Inflationary trends had been easing since early 1994, and the step was intended to keep the economy from slowing down too much. Thus, the Fed's action completed a classic cycle of rate changes that it had begun in 1990, when the Fed had decreased interest rates to stimulate the then-recessionary economy. The Fed steadily cut rates until September 1992, when it became apparent that its actions were having the desired effect—consumer and business borrowing were increasing and business activity showed signs of increasing during 1993. At that point, therefore, the Fed stopped decreasing the rate. The decision was effective. Although the rate was unchanged throughout 1993, business activity continued to grow.

By 1994, however, the Fed perceived indications that the economy might be growing *too* quickly. It thus began gently increasing the interest rate to head off inflation. The first graph in Figure 15.4 shows that, to keep inflation under control, the central bank raised the funds rate seven times during the next 17 months. The second graph in Figure 15.4 shows that by early 1995 it was evident that the higher rates were having the desired effect. Because of higher interest rates, for example, consumer loans became more expensive. As consumers borrowed (and spent) less, overall economic activity slowed. Inflationary pressures were under control. Finally, by mid-1995, there were indications that another economic slowdown might be under way. The Fed thus cut the rate for the first time since 1992.[17]

The Tools of the Fed

According to the Fed's original charter, its primary duties were to supervise banking and to manage both the currency and commercial paper. The duties of the Fed evolved, however, along with a predominant philosophy of monetary policy. That policy includes an emphasis on the broad economic goals as discussed in Chapter 1—stability, full employment, and growth. The Fed's role in controlling the nation's money supply stems from its role in setting policies to help reach these goals. To control the money supply, the Fed uses four primary tools: *reserve requirements, discount rate controls, open-market operations,* and *selective credit controls.*

reserve requirement Percentage of its deposits that a bank must hold in cash or on deposit with the Federal Reserve

RESERVE REQUIREMENTS The **reserve requirement** is the percentage of its deposits a bank must hold, in cash or on deposit, with a Federal Reserve bank. High requirements mean that banks have less money to lend. Thus, a high reserve requirement reduces the money supply. Conversely, low requirements permit the supply to expand. Because the Fed sets requirements for all depository institutions, it can adjust them to make changes in the overall supply of money to the economy.

discount rate Interest rate at which member banks can borrow money from the Federal Reserve

DISCOUNT RATE CONTROLS As the "bankers' bank," the Fed loans money to banks. The interest rate on these loans is known as the **discount rate.** If the Fed wants to reduce the money supply, it increases the discount rate, making it more expensive for banks to borrow money and less attractive for them to loan it. Conversely, low rates encourage borrowing and lending and expand the money supply.

open-market operations The Federal Reserve's sales and purchases of securities in the open market

OPEN-MARKET OPERATIONS The third instrument for monetary control is probably the Fed's most important tool. **Open-market operations** refer to the Fed's sale and purchase of securities (usually U.S. Treasury notes and bonds) in the open market. Open-market operations are particularly effective because they act quickly and predictably on the money supply. How so? The Fed buys securities from dealers. Because the dealer's bank account is credited for the transaction, its bank has more money to lend, and so expands the money supply. The opposite happens when the Fed sells securities.

selective credit controls Federal Reserve authority to set both margin requirements for consumer stock purchases and credit rules for other consumer purchases

SELECTIVE CREDIT CONTROLS The Federal Reserve can exert considerable influence on business activity by exercising **selective credit controls.** The Fed may set special requirements for consumer stock purchases and credit rules for other consumer purchases.

As we will see in Chapter 16, investors can set up credit accounts with stockbrokers to buy stocks and bonds. A *margin requirement* set by the Fed stipulates the amount of credit that the broker can extend to the customer. For example, a 60 percent margin rate means that approved customers can purchase stocks having $100,000 market value with $60,000 in cash (60 percent of $100,000) and $40,000 in loans from the dealer. If the Fed wants to

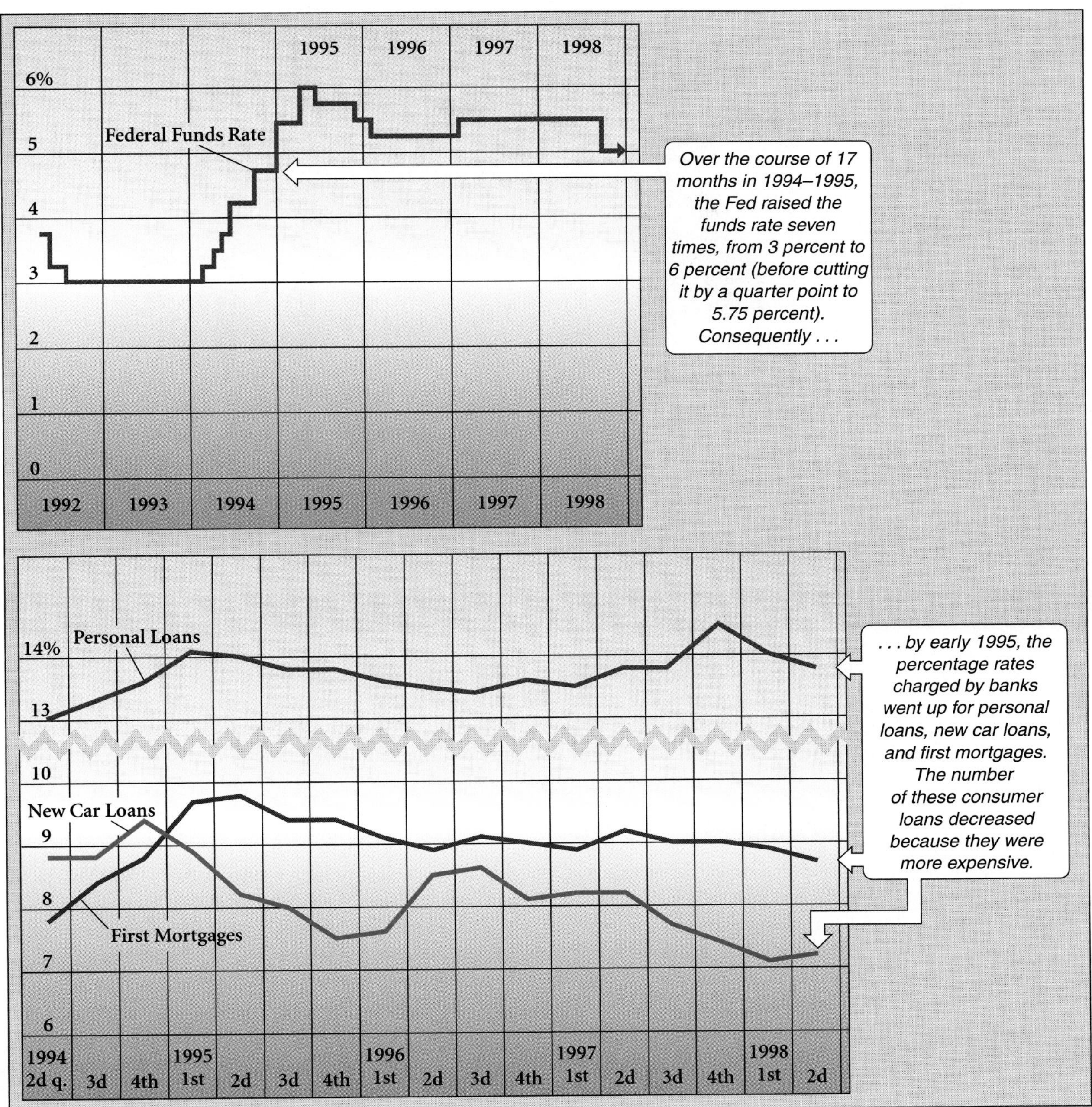

FIGURE 15.4 ◆ **The Fed and the Federal Funds Rate**

increase securities transactions, it can lower the margin requirement. Customers can then borrow greater percentages of their purchase costs from dealers, thus increasing their purchasing power and the amount of securities that they can buy.

Within stipulated limits, the Fed is also permitted to specify the conditions of certain credit purchases. This authority extends to such conditions as allowable down payment percentages for appliance purchases and repayment periods on automobile loans. The Fed has chosen to not use these powers in recent years.

"Money doesn't trickle down unless there's a damn leak."

■ THE CHANGING MONEY AND BANKING SYSTEM

The U.S. money and banking systems have changed in recent years and continue to change today. Deregulation and interstate banking, for example, have increased competition not only among banks but also between banks and other financial institutions. Electronic technologies affect how you obtain money and how much interest you pay for it.

Deregulation

The Depository Institutions Deregulation and Monetary Control Act (DIDMCA) of 1980 brought many changes to the banking industry. Before its passage, there were clear distinctions between the types of services offered by different institutions. For example, although all institutions could offer savings accounts, only commercial banks could offer checking accounts, and S&Ls and mutual savings banks generally could not make consumer loans. The DIDMCA and subsequent laws sought to promote competition by eliminating many such restrictions.

Under deregulation, many banks were unable to survive in the new competitive environment. In the 1980s, more than 1,000 banks—1 more than 7 percent of the total—failed, as did 835 savings and loans. Many economists, however, regard some bank closings as a beneficial weeding out of inefficient competitors.

Interstate Banking

The Interstate Banking Efficiency Act was passed into law in September 1994, thus allowing banks to enter (gradually) into interstate banking—the operation of banks or branches across state lines. It also mandates regulation by government agencies to ensure proper operation and competition. The key provisions in this act include the following:

- Limited nationwide banking is permitted, beginning in 1995. Bank holding companies can acquire subsidiaries in any state.
- The ultimate *size* of any company is limited. No one company can control more than 10 percent of nationwide insured deposits. No bank can control more than 30 percent of a state's deposits (each state is empowered to set its own limit).

- Beginning in 1995, banks can provide limited transactions for affiliated banks in other states. They can thus accept deposits, close loans, and accept loan payments on behalf of other affiliated banks. (They cannot, however, *originate* loans or *open* deposit accounts for affiliates.)
- Beginning in June 1997, banks can convert affiliates into full-fledged interstate branches.

Interstate banking offers certain efficiencies. For example, it allows banks to consolidate services and eliminate duplicated activities. Opponents, however, remain concerned that some banks will gain undue influence, dominate other banks, and hinder competition.

The Impact of Electronic Technologies

Like so many other businesses, banks are increasingly investing in technology as a way to improve efficiency and customer service levels. Many banks offer ATMs and EFT systems. Some offer TV banking, in which customers use television sets and terminals—or home computers—to make transactions. The age of electronic money has arrived. Digital money is replacing cash in stores, taxi cabs, subway systems, and vending machines. Each business day, more than $2 trillion exists in and among banks and other financial institutions in purely electronic form. Each year, the Fed transfers electronically more than $250 trillion in transactions.

DEBIT CARDS One of the most recent electronic offerings from the financial industry is the debit card. Unlike credit cards, **debit cards** allow only the transfer of money between accounts. They do not increase the funds at an individual's disposal. They can, however, be used to make retail purchases.

For example, in stores with **point-of-sale (POS)** terminals, customers insert cards that transmit to terminals information relevant to their purchases. The terminal relays the information directly to the bank's computer system. The bank automatically transfers funds from the customer's account to the store's account.

debit card Plastic card that allows an individual to transfer money between accounts

point-of-sale (POS) terminal Electronic device that allows customers to pay for retail purchases with debit cards

smart card Credit-card-size computer programmed with electronic money

SMART CARDS The so-called **smart card** is a credit-card-size computer that can be programmed with "electronic money." Also known as "electronic purses" or "stored-value cards," smart cards have existed for more than a decade. Phone callers and shoppers in Europe and Asia are the most avid users, holding the majority of the nearly 1 billion cards in circulation in 1998. Analysts expect 3 billion cards to be in use by the year 2000.[18]

Why are smart cards increasing in popularity today? For one thing, the cost of producing them has fallen dramatically, from as much as $10 to as little as $1. Convenience is equally important, notes Donald J. Gleason, president of Electronic Payment Services' Smart Card Enterprise division. "What consumers want," Gleason contends, "is convenience, and if you look at cash, it's really quite inconvenient."[19]

"What customers want is convenience, and if you look at cash, it's really quite inconvenient."

—Donald J. Gleason

President, Electronic Payment Services' Smart Card Enterprise Division

Smart cards can be loaded with money at ATM machines or, with special telephone hookups, even at home. After using your card to purchase an item, you can then check an electronic display to see how much money your card has left. Analysts predict that in the near future, smart cards will function as much more than electronic purses. For example, travel industry experts predict that people will soon book travel plans at home on personal computers and then transfer their reservations onto their smart cards. The cards will then serve as airline tickets and boarding passes. As an added benefit, they will allow travelers to avoid waiting in lines at car rental agencies and hotel front desks.

E-cash Electronic money that moves among consumers and businesses via digital electronic transmissions

E-CASH A new, revolutionary world of electronic money has begun to emerge with the rapid growth of the Internet. Electronic money, known as **E-cash,** is money that moves along multiple channels of consumers and businesses via digital electronic transmissions. E-cash moves outside the established network of banks, checks, and paper currency overseen by the Federal Reserve. Companies as varied as new start-up Mondex and giant Citicorp are developing their own forms of electronic money that allow consumers and businesses to spend money more conveniently, quickly, and cheaply than they can through the banking system. In fact, some observers predict that by the year 2005, as much as 20 percent of all household expenditures will take place on the Internet. "Banking," comments one investment banker, "is essential to the modern economy, but banks are not."

> **"Banking is essential to the modern economy, but banks are not."**
>
> —Investment banker

How does E-cash work? Traditional currency is used to buy electronic funds, which are downloaded over phone lines into a PC or a portable "electronic wallet" that can store and transmit E-cash. E-cash is purchased from any company that issues (sells) it, including companies such as Mondex, Citicorp, and banks. When shopping on-line—say, to purchase jewelry—a shopper sends digital money to the merchant instead of using traditional cash, checks, or credit cards. Businesses can purchase supplies and services electronically from any merchant that accepts E-cash. It flows from the buyer's into the seller's E-cash funds, which are instantaneously updated and stored on a microchip. One system, operated by CyberCash, tallies all E-cash transactions in the customer's account and, at the end of the day, converts the E-cash balance back into dollars in the customer's conventional banking account.

Although E-cash transactions are cheaper than handling checks and the paper records involved with conventional money, there are some potential problems. Hackers, for example, may break into E-cash systems and drain them instantaneously. Moreover, if the issuer's

TRENDS AND CHALLENGES

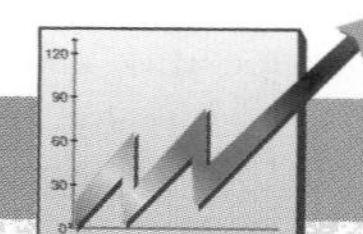

THE CONTINENT BRACES FOR THE ERA OF THE EURO

While earthquakes tend to be explosive and revolutions bloody, so-called "upheavals" can also be civil, planned, and quiet yet still powerful enough to change the landscape of a continent. Such a peaceful upheaval took place in 11 European countries on January 4, 1999, with the introduction of the euro, Europe's new common currency.

Participating in the switch from national currencies to the euro are Austria, Belgium, Finland, France, Germany, Ireland, Italy, Luxembourg, the Netherlands, Portugal, and Spain. Between 1999 and 2002, only banks and other financial institutions and large companies will be required to use euros for all transactions. After 2002, ordinary citizens will trade in their German marks, Spanish pesetas, French francs, and Italian liras for euro bills and coins.

How will a common currency affect European companies? As with any upheaval, there are advantages. For example:

- Gone are worries about currency exchange rates that affect profitability (see Chapter 3). "Competition," promises Santo Versace, chairman of the Italian company Gianni Versace, "will come from the product—like quality and customer service—and not from the currency." Adds Armin Muller, finance director of Italian apparel manufacturer Jil Sander: "We produce 100 percent of our men's collection and about 85 percent of our women's collection in Italy. We invoice in lira, and there have been big fluctuations in the exchange rate. The euro will certainly bring some sort of stability in terms of currency."

> **"Competition will come from the product—like quality and customer service—and not from the currency."**
>
> —Santo Versace
>
> *Chairman, Gianni Versace*

computer system crashes, it is conceivable that money "banked" in memory may be lost forever. Finally, regulation and control of E-cash systems remain largely nonexistent; there is virtually none of the protection that covers government-controlled money systems.

■ INTERNATIONAL BANKING AND FINANCE

Along with international banking networks, electronic technologies now permit nearly instantaneous financial transactions around the globe. The economic importance of international finance is evident from both the presence of foreign banks in the U.S. market and the sizes of certain banks around the world. In addition, each nation tries to influence its currency exchange rates for economic advantage in international trade. The subsequent country-to-country transactions result in an *international payments* process that moves money among buyers and sellers on different continents.

The International Payments Process

When transactions are made among buyers and sellers in different countries, exactly how are payments made? Payments are simplified through the services provided by their banks. For example, payments from buyers flow through a local bank that converts them from the local currency into the foreign currency of the seller. The local bank receives and converts incoming money from the banks of foreign buyers. The payments process is shown in Figure 15.5.

- *Step 1.* A U.S. olive importer withdraws $1,000 from its checking account to buy olives from a Greek exporter. The local U.S. bank converts those dollars into Greek drachmas at the current exchange rate (230 drachmas per dollar).
- *Step 2.* The U.S. bank sends a check for 230,000 drachmas (230 × 1,000) to the exporter in Greece.

- The euro will make it a lot easier for European industries to compete with one another on the European continent. Manufacturers will be able to export finished goods freely among European Union (EU) members. The elimination of red tape at border crossings will permit goods to move quickly from one country to the next, thereby lowering costs. With quotas gone and cheaper financing available (when banks deal in one currency instead of 11, costs drop), imported European goods will also be cheaper for U.S. importers and U.S. consumers.
- A single currency makes possible the merger of banks and businesses across national boundaries. The expansion of capital markets across the continent will encourage the growth of entrepreneurial ventures and new alliances.

And, of course, disadvantages:

- With corporate consolidation will come restructuring, cost cutting, and layoffs. Corporate failures will also be inevitable among companies that resist change or fail to meet the challenges of their new environment.
- Branded goods from the United States may be diverted from lower-cost EU countries, such as Italy, to higher-cost countries, such as Sweden, thereby underselling local distributors. This practice will become possible with the removal of duties among EU nations.
- With retailers required to list prices in both national and euro currencies, price labeling will increase in complexity. As many as eight different currencies, for example, may be listed on a dress or suit.

Each company's preparation for the era of the euro will affect its success as a business competitor. Anticipating the computer problems associated with the switch, some companies are spending millions for new systems. "Suddenly," admits Sander's Muller, "we'll have to be able to invoice in two currencies—the original currency plus the euro—and that's something the systems can't currently cope with." With European computers also facing the Y2K problem, firms have added worries. "The good thing with the year 2000, compared with the introduction of the euro," opines Muller, "is that at least we know when it will happen."

FIGURE 15.5 ◆ **The International Payments Process**

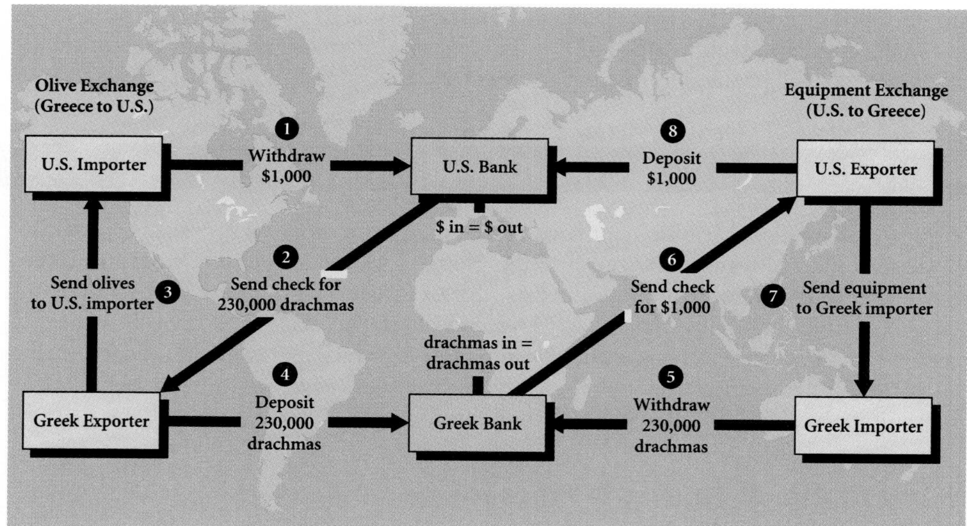

- *Steps 3 and 4.* The exporter sends olives to its U.S. customer and deposits the check in its local Greek bank. The exporter now has drachmas that can be spent in Greece, and the importer has olives to sell in the United States.

At the same time, a separate transaction is being made between a U.S. machine exporter and a Greek olive oil producer. This time, importer/exporter roles are reversed between the two countries: The Greek firm needs to import a $1,000 olive oil press from the United States.

- *Steps 5 and 6.* Drachmas (230,000) withdrawn from a local Greek bank account are converted into $1,000 U.S. dollars and sent via check to the U.S. exporter.
- *Steps 7 and 8.* The olive oil press is sent to the Greek importer, and the importer's check is deposited in the U.S. exporter's local bank account.

In this example, trade between the two countries is in balance. Money inflows and outflows are equal for both countries. When such a balance occurs, *money does not actually have to flow between the two countries.* Within each bank, the dollars spent by local importers offset the dollars received by local exporters. In effect, therefore, the dollars have simply flowed from U.S. importers to U.S. exporters. Similarly, the drachmas have moved from Greek exporters to Greek importers.

Continued from page 397

Extending Credit Where Credit Is Due

Banco Popular, the largest issuer of credit cards in Puerto Rico, is expanding its card operation to the 50 states. It's a natural step for the bank, which is continuing to expand personal and business banking services to Hispanic clients at the same time that it enters the credit card market. "We have an understanding of the language and culture," explains Donald R. Simanoff, president of Banco Popular's U.S. card division, "and targeting the Hispanic consumer is what we do for a living."

> **"We have an understanding of the language and culture, and targeting the Hispanic consumer is what we do for a living."**
>
> —Donald R. Simanoff
> *President, Banco Popular's U.S. Card Division*

Since 1997, when Banco Popular officially entered the market, it has opened nearly 150,000 credit card accounts, 25 percent of which are secured accounts with credit lines backed by customer bank deposits. Thus three-fourths of the bank's credit card portfolio is unsecured because the customers are considered good credit risks.

Ironically, one of the main challenges facing Banco Popular is convincing the nearly half of all Hispanic consumers who have no access to credit through cards or other banking services that credit can be a good thing. To attract customers, Banco Popular offers card-related discounts on products popular in the Hispanic community, including Western Union money orders and purchases at Kmart pharmacies. It is also negotiating a discounted long-distance calling plan.

With a keen understanding of the cultural needs of the Hispanic market, and with a clear strategic plan, Banco Popular is optimistic about future success in its primary New York, New Jersey, Texas, California, Florida, and Illinois markets. At the same time, however, managers realize that they are learning new things about the market every day. Recently, for example, the bank discovered that 4 of 10 people who call the bank choose to speak English instead of Spanish. Many Hispanic customers read English better than they do Spanish. This information convinced Banco Popular to issue credit card solicitations and statements in both English and Spanish and to make sure that every customer service representative is proficient in both languages.

Questions for Discussion

1. What are the demographic reasons underlying the growing importance of the Hispanic market to all U.S. banks?
2. Why have many mainstream U.S. banks thus far minimized their exposure in minority markets? What do you think of this business decision, and why do you think that many banks are now seeking a greater presence in these communities?
3. Why do you think a "cultural fit" is so important to many individual and small-business customers?
4. What do you think of Banco Popular's strategy to focus on the six states with the largest Hispanic populations instead of moving into all states?
5. Why is it smart—at least in the short and long run—for Banco Popular to issue secured credit cards to people who would otherwise be ineligible for credit?

SUMMARY

1. **Define *money* and identify the different forms that it takes in the nation's money supply.** Any item that is portable, divisible, durable, and stable satisfies the four basic characteristics of *money.* Money also serves three functions: it is a medium of exchange, a store of value, and a unit of account. The nation's money supply is often determined by two measures. M-1 includes liquid (or spendable) forms of money: currency (bills and coins), demand deposits, and other checkable deposits (such as ATM account balances and NOW accounts). M-2 includes M-1 plus items that cannot be directly spent but that can be easily converted to spendable forms, namely, time deposits, money market funds, savings deposits, and overnight transactions. Credit cards must also be considered as a factor in the money supply.

2. **Describe the different kinds of *financial institutions* that comprise the U.S. financial system and explain the services they offer.** The U.S. financial system includes federal- and state-chartered *commercial banks*, *savings and loan associations*, *mutual savings banks*, *credit unions*, and *nondeposit institutions*, such as pension funds and insurance companies. These institutions offer a variety of services, including pension, trust, and international services, financial advice and brokerage services; and convenient electronic funds transfer (EFT), including automated teller machines.

3. **Explain how banks create money and describe the means by which they are regulated.** By taking in deposits and making loans, banks *expand the money supply*. The overall supply of money, however, is governed by several federal agencies. The *Federal Reserve System* is the primary agency responsible for ensuring a sound, competitive financial system.

4. **Discuss the functions of the *Federal Reserve System* and describe the tools it uses to control the money supply.** The *Federal Reserve System* (or *the Fed*) is the nation's central bank. As the government's bank, the Fed produces currency and lends money to the government. As the "bankers' bank," it lends money (at interest) to member banks, stores required *reserve funds* for banks, and clears checks for them. The Fed is empowered to audit member banks and sets U.S. *monetary policy* by controlling the country's money supply. To control the money supply, the Fed specifies *reserve requirements* (the percentage of deposits a bank must hold with the Fed). It sets the discount rate at which it loans money to banks and conducts *open-market operations* to buy and sell securities. It also exerts influence through *selective credit controls* (such as margin requirements governing the credit granted to buyers by securities brokers).

5. **Identify three important ways in which the financial industry is changing.** Many changes have affected the financial system in recent years. *Deregulation*, especially of interest rates, and the rise of *interstate banking* have increased competition. *Electronic technologies* offer a variety of new financial conveniences to customers. *Debit cards* are plastic cards that permit users to transfer money between bank accounts. *Smart cards* are credit-card-size computers that can be loaded with "electronic money" at ATMs or over special telephone hookups. *E-cash* is money that can be moved among consumers and businesses via digital electronic transmissions.

QUESTIONS AND EXERCISES

QUESTIONS FOR REVIEW

1. What are the components of M-1 and M-2?
2. Explain the roles of commercial banks, savings and loan associations, and nondeposit institutions in the U.S. financial system.
3. Explain the types of pension services that commercial banks provide for their customers.
4. Describe the structure of the Federal Reserve System.
5. Show how the Fed uses the federal funds rate to manage inflation in the U.S. economy.

QUESTIONS FOR ANALYSIS

6. Do you think that credit cards should be counted in the money supply? Why or why not? Support your argument by using the definition of money.
7. Should commercial banks be regulated, or should market forces be allowed to determine the money supply? Why?
8. Identify a purchase made by you or a family member in which payment was made by check. Draw a diagram to trace the steps in the clearing process followed by that check.

APPLICATION EXERCISES

9. Start with a $1,000 deposit and assume a reserve requirement of 15 percent. Trace the amount of money created by the banking system after five lending cycles.
10. Interview the manager of a local commercial bank. Identify several ways in which the Fed either helps the bank or restricts its operations.

BUILDING YOUR BUSINESS SKILLS

FOUR ECONOMISTS IN A ROOM

This exercise enhances the following SCANS workplace competencies: demonstrating basic skills, demonstrating thinking skills, exhibiting interpersonal skills, working with information, and applying system knowledge.

▼ GOAL

To encourage students to understand the economic factors considered by the Federal Reserve Board in determining current interest rates.

▼ BACKGROUND

One of the Federal Reserve's most important tools in setting monetary policy is the adjustment of the interest rates it charges member banks to borrow money. To determine interest rate policy, the Fed analyzes current economic conditions from its 12 districts. Its findings are published eight times a year in a report commonly known as the *Beige Book.*

▼ METHOD

STEP 1

Working with three other students, access the Federal Reserve Web site at <http://www.bog.frb.fed.us/>. Look for the heading "Federal Open Market Committee," and then click on the subheading **Beige Book.** When you reach that page, click on **Summary** of the **Current Report.**

STEP 2

Working with group members, study each of the major summary sections:

- Consumer spending
- Manufacturing
- Construction and real estate
- Banking and finance
- Nonfinancial services
- Labor market, wages, and pricing
- Agriculture and natural resources

Working with team members, discuss ways in which you think that key information contained in the summary might affect the Fed's decision to raise, lower, or maintain interest rates.

STEP 3

At your library find back issues of *Barron's*, the highly respected weekly financial publication. Look for the issue published immediately following the appearance of the most recent *Beige*

(continued)

Book. Search for articles analyzing the report. Discuss with group members what the articles say about current economic conditions and interest rates.

STEP 4

Based on your research and analysis, what factors do you think the Fed will take into account to control inflation? Working with group members, explain your answer in writing.

STEP 5

Working with group members, research what the Federal Reserve chairperson says next about interest rates. Do the chairperson's reasons for raising, lowering, or maintaining rates agree with your group's analysis?

FOLLOW-UP QUESTIONS

1. What are the most important factors in the Fed's interest rate decision?
2. Consider the old joke about economists that goes like this: *When there are four economists in a room analyzing current economic conditions, there are at least eight different opinions.* Based on your research and analysis, why do you think economists have such varying opinions?

CRAFTING YOUR BUSINESS PLAN

HOW TO BANK ON YOUR MONEY

▼ THE PURPOSE OF THE ASSIGNMENT

1. To acquaint students with the process of navigating the Business PlanPro (BPP) software package.
2. To familiarize students with banking issues that a sample firm faces in developing its business plan.
3. To demonstrate how two chapter topics—bank services and interest rates—can be integrated as components in the BPP planning environment.

▼ ASSIGNMENT

After reading Chapter 15 in the textbook, open the BPP *software* and search for information about the marketing plan of a sample firm:* Flower Importer *(Fantastic Florals, Inc.). Then respond to the following questions:*

1. Consider the interest rates that are assumed in the business plan. Are the short-term and long-term rates reasonable in today's economy? Explain. [Sites to see in *BPP* (for this assignment): In the Task Manager screen, click on The Bottom Line, then click on **1. General Assumptions Table.** Also, read the Instructions section near the top of the screen.]
2. Identify some international banking services that would benefit FFI in its daily operations. [Sites to see in *BPP:* In the Task Manager screen, click on Finish and Polish, then click on 6. Executive Summary. Return to the Task Manager and click on What You're Selling, then click on each of **4. Sourcing and Fulfillment** and **6. Future Development.**]
3. From FFI's financial plan, can you see any need for bank credit? When, during the planning horizon, might the firm need a line of credit and how much? To meet what financial needs? [Sites to see in *BPP:* In the Task Manager screen, click on Financial Plan, then click on each of **1. Financial Plan Summary** and **6. Start-up Chart.**]

4. Does FFI plan to have excess cash that can be deposited in the bank to earn interest? When, during the planning horizon, might the firm accumulate excess cash and how much? [Sites to see in *BPP:* In the Task Manager screen, click on Your Sales Forecast, then click on **4. Sales Forecast.** Return to the Task Manager screen, click on Cash is King, then click on **1. Cash Plan Table.** Observe the cash balance at the bottom of the table.]

▼ For Your Own Business Plan

5. Planning for cash is an important part of your financial plan. To get started, go to the BPP section entitled "**Cash is King**"; then explore each of the cash-flow tools and tables. After filling in projected cash inflows and outflows for your company, select the cash-flow document that you think will best demonstrate your planned cash position.

▼ * General Tips for Navigating in *BPP*

1. Open the BPP program, examine the Welcome screen, and click on **Open a Sample Plan.**
2. From the Open a Sample Plan dialogue box, click on a sample company name; then click on **Open.**
3. On the Task Manager screen, click on any of the lines (for example, **Your Company**).
4. You can always return to the Task Manager screen by going to the bottom of the screen and clicking on the **Task Manager** icon.
5. When you are finished with one sample company, close its Task Manager screen.
6. After finishing with one sample company, you can get to the next one by going to the top of the screen and clicking on **File** (on the menu bar). Then beneath that, select **Open Sample Plan.** This will exit you from the current company file and send you to the Open a Sample Plan dialogue box, where you can select your next example company.

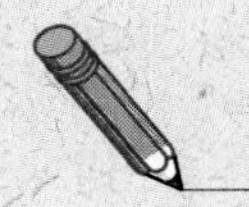

EXPLORING THE NET

BANKING ON THE FED

The Federal Reserve Board, as the central controlling figure in the U.S. banking system, actively rules on a variety of banking issues. To find out about some of the Fed's recent activities, log on to its Web site at

http://www.bog.frb.fed.us.

Working from the left column of the home page, you are asked to explore two areas—"Domestic and Foreign Banking Cases" and "Enforcement Actions"—as described here.

- Scroll down to Press Releases; then click on **Domestic and foreign banking cases.** Scan the summaries of the 20 most-recent cases and then consider the following questions:
  1. Describe the various *types of actions* taken by the Fed.
  2. How many of the cases involve *bank mergers?*
  3. How many involve *international activities?*
  4. Select a case that interests you, click on the date, and read the detailed press release. Then prepare a brief report for class that identifies the main banking issue, the business firms involved, the action taken by the Fed, and the economic significance of the case.
- Scroll down to Press Releases; then click on **Enforcement Actions.** Scan the summaries of any 10 recent cases. Describe the types of actions taken by the Fed in those cases.
- Next, select a case that interests you, click on the date, and read the detailed press release. Then prepare a report on the following:
  1. Describe the *banking issue* involved in the case.
  2. Who are the *contestants* in the case?
  3. Explain the *enforcement actions* taken by the Federal Reserve Board in this case.

UNDERSTANDING SECURITIES AND INVESTMENTS

"Give Me 1,000 Shares of Dramamine"

Like the space-age roller coaster rides at Disney World and Coney Island, today's stock market promises a little nerve-shattering volatility for everyone with the guts to hop a ride. The best advice for the timid—or those prone to motion sickness—is stay away, especially if the swings that characterized the market in the summer and fall of 1998 are here to stay.

Why are today's market swings so violent? Why, for example, did the Dow Jones Industrial Average plunge more than 19 percent between July 17 and August 31, 1998, only to recoup its losses and then some just 3 months later? Why did the Dow shoot up nearly 300 points in a single half hour in October 1998 after the Federal Reserve Board announced that it would cut interest rates by a quarter of a percentage point? Why did the Dow surge nearly 400 points on a single day a month earlier, only to give it all back on the following 2 days? Market volatility can be traced to several factors, including technology, large pools of available cash, and global financial interrelationships.

Technology, of course, has transformed Wall Street. Every stock exchange, financial services company, and public corporation has invested heavily in faster computers and faster transmission lines, all of which increase both the number of shares traded and their potential volatility. The companies and organizations that comprise Wall Street now spend more than $10 billion a year on information technology, with Merrill Lynch alone accounting for 15 percent of that figure.

On Black Monday—the day in 1987 when the stock market dropped 508 points—*only* 684 million shares were traded on the New York Stock Exchange. Eleven years later, that volume is nothing special. In fact, between August and October 1998, there were 11 days with trading volumes higher than 900 million shares. The New York Stock Exchange is now prepared to handle 2 billion trades a day and by the millennium will have the computer power to process 5 billion daily trades. "The speed of transactions," says Mike Holland, chairman of Holland & Co., a private investment company, "is increasing geometrically as information and technology allow it. That volatility is here to stay," he adds, especially with the proliferation of on-line brokers.

> **"The speed of transactions is increasing geometrically as information and technology allow it. That volatility is here to stay."**
>
> —Mike Holland
> *Chairman, Holland & Co.*

James B. Lee, vice chairman of Chase Manhattan Bank, agrees: "Today," he notes, "everything happens at a faster rate than it did 10 years ago. What took a year to happen in 1990 . . . occurred [in Fall 1998] in 90 days. It may be the speed and breadth of information was that much slower, that much narrower, then, so it took a year to filter through the system. Now it takes less time."

Large pools of available cash also add to market volatility. Few Americans store their money in savings accounts at local banks or savings and loans the way their parents did. Today, we invest and shift available cash in and out of mutual funds and individual stocks. "Years ago," observes Jeremy Siegel, professor of finance at the Wharton School, "if you wanted to make a stock purchase, you'd have to go to the bank, draw the money or get a bank check, then go and give it to your brokerage. Now you just call up and say, 'Give me 1,000 shares of IBM.' "

Split-second decision making by individuals and institutional investors is encouraged by a web of global finan-

cial relationships that are instantly reported on 24-hour business television, telephone, and Internet services. Never before in history have the personal finances of Americans been so inextricably linked to the financial health of countries halfway around the world. When the Indonesian, Korean, and Japanese economies collapsed in 1997 and 1998, investors in U.S. companies doing business there added to market volatility by abandoning risky stocks. When concern over economic problems in Southeast Asia eased in the fall of 1998, the stock market rebounded. Investors, for example, dumped Intel in July, August, and September but bought their stock in November and December when Intel reported that Asian orders had stabilized. "Japan," an Intel spokesman reassured them, "remains pretty crummy, but it isn't getting any worse."

Stock market volatility, then, may be just another expression of the fast pace of modern life. It's a pace that American investors seem willing to tolerate, perhaps because of their fundamental faith in the U.S. economy or perhaps because they have few investment alternatives. As you will see in this chapter, investing in U.S. and international companies through the purchase of stocks and bonds is now an integral part of many Americans' plans for acquiring and building wealth. By focusing on the learning objectives of this chapter, you will better understand the importance of the marketplaces in which securities are traded and the nature of such investment vehicles as stocks and bonds, mutual funds, and commodities.

Our opening story is continued on page 443

After reading this chapter, you should be able to:

1. **Explain the difference between *primary* and *secondary securities markets*.**
2. **Discuss the value to shareholders of *common* and *preferred stock*, and describe the secondary market for each type of security.**
3. **Distinguish among various types of *bonds* in terms of their issuers, safety, and retirement.**
4. **Describe the investment opportunities offered by *mutual funds* and *commodities*.**
5. **Explain the process by which securities are bought and sold.**
6. **Explain how securities markets are regulated.**

SECURITIES MARKETS

securities Stocks and bonds representing secured, or asset-based, claims by investors against issuers

Stocks and bonds are known as **securities** because they represent *secured*, or *asset-based*, claims on the part of investors. In other words, holders of stocks and bonds have a stake in the business that issued them. As we saw in Chapter 2, stockholders have claims on some of a corporation's assets (and a say in how the company is run) because each share of stock represents part ownership.

In contrast, *bonds* represent strictly financial claims for money owed to holders by a company. Companies sell bonds to raise long-term funds. The markets in which stocks and bonds are sold are called *securities markets*.

Primary and Secondary Securities Markets

primary securities market Market in which new stocks and bonds are bought and sold

In **primary securities markets,** new stocks and bonds are bought and sold by firms and governments.[1] Sometimes new securities are sold to single buyers or small groups of buyers. These so-called *private placements* are desirable because they allow issuers to keep their plans confidential.

Each year, more than $100 billion in new private placements are purchased in the United States by large pension funds and other institutions that privately negotiate prices with sellers.[2] Because private placements cannot be resold in the open market, buyers generally demand higher returns from the issuers.

Securities and Exchange Commission (SEC) Federal agency that administers U.S. securities laws to protect the investing public and maintain smoothly functioning markets

investment bank Financial institution engaged in issuing and reselling new securities

INVESTMENT BANKING Most new stocks and some bonds are sold on the wider public market. To bring a new security to market, the issuing firm must get approval from the **Securities and Exchange Commission**—the government agency that regulates securities markets. It also needs the services of an **investment bank**—a financial institution that specializes in issuing and reselling new securities. Such investment banking firms as Merrill Lynch and Morgan Stanley provide three important services:

1. They advise companies on the timing and financial terms of new issues.
2. By *underwriting*—that is, buying—new securities, they bear some of the risks of issuing them.
3. They create the distribution networks for moving new securities through groups of other banks and brokers into the hands of individual investors.

secondary securities market Market in which stocks and bonds are traded

In 1997, U.S. investment bankers brought to the market $118 billion in new corporate stocks and $641 billion in new corporate bonds.[3] New securities, however, represent only a minute portion of traded securities. Existing stocks and bonds are sold in the **secondary securities market,** which is handled by such familiar bodies as the New York Stock Exchange. We consider the activities of these markets later in this chapter.

In 1995, after a 10-year struggle in Silicon Valley, Samir Arora founded a Web software maker called Net-Objects Inc. The company was on the verge of bankruptcy by early 1997, when it caught the eye of IBM, which decided to invest by buying some stock. For a 50 percent stake, IBM paid $100 million, and 31-year-old Arora was a multimillionaire. "It's weird," admits Arora. "You have to ask, 'Why is this happening to me?' "

■ STOCKS

Each year, financial managers, with millions of individual investors, buy and sell the stocks of thousands of companies. This widespread ownership has become possible because of the availability of different types of stocks and because markets have been established for conveniently buying and selling them. In this section, we focus on the value of *common* and *preferred stock* as securities. We also describe the *stock exchanges* on which they are bought and sold.[4]

Common Stocks

Individuals and other companies purchase a firm's common stock in the hope that it will increase in value, provide dividend income, or both. But how is the *value* of a common stock determined? Stock values are expressed in three different ways—as *par, market,* and *book value.*

PAR VALUE The face value of a share of stock at the time it is originally issued is the **par value.** It is set by the issuing company's board of directors. To receive their corporate charters, all companies must declare par values for their stocks. Each company must preserve the par value money in its retained earnings, and it cannot be distributed as dividends. However, because this procedural protection is largely a formality, par value usually bears no relationship to a stock's true value.

par value Face value of a share of stock, set by the issuing company's board of directors

In 1997, for example, Rayovac, a company that manufactures batteries, issued stock with a par value of only $0.01 per share. The firm proceeded to sell the stock to the public for $14 a share.[5] The choice of $14 reflects the price that Rayovac management believed investors would be willing to pay based on Rayovac's assets and earnings potential.

MARKET VALUE A stock's real value, then, is its **market value**—the current price of a share in the stock market. Rayovac shares, for example, sold for up to $23 a share in 1998, indicating that investors value the stock at much more than the original $14. Market value, therefore, reflects buyers' willingness to invest in a company. It depends on a firm's history of dividend payments, its earnings potential, and on investors' expectations of **capital gains**—profits to be made from selling the stock for more than it cost. Investors, then, are concerned primarily with market value.

market value Current price of a share of stock in the stock market

capital gain Profit earned by selling a share of stock for more than it cost

BOOK VALUE Recall from Chapter 14 our definition of *stockholders' equity*—the sum of a company's common stock par value, retained earnings, and additional paid-in capital. The **book value** of common stock represents stockholders' equity divided by the number

book value Value of a common stock expressed as total shareholders' equity divided by the number of shares of stock

In 1993, Heather Beach began work as a receptionist at Siebel Systems Inc., a start-up maker of sales-information software located in East Palo Alto, California. She was paid only $28,000 a year, but in addition to stock options—the right to purchase a specific number of company shares at a specific price during a given period of time—Beach also chose to receive part of her paycheck in Siebel stock. Siebel went public at $17 per share, quadrupled in value inside of 6 months, and for every dollar that Beach took in stock, she realized a minimum of $40.

of shares. In 1997, for example, Rayovac had stockholders' equity of $61.6 million. There were 27.4 million shares outstanding.[6] Thus, the book value of the stock was $2.25 per share ($61.6 / 27.4).

Book value is used as a comparison indicator because, for successful companies, the market value is usually greater than its book value. Thus, when market price falls to near book value, some investors buy the stock on the principle that it is underpriced and will increase in the future.

INVESTMENT TRAITS OF COMMON STOCK Common stocks are among the riskiest of all securities. Uncertainties about the stock market itself, for instance, can quickly change a given stock's value. Furthermore, when companies have unprofitable years, they often cannot pay dividends. Shareholder income, therefore—and perhaps share price—drops. At the same time, however, common stocks offer high growth potential. Naturally the prospects for growth in various industries change from time to time, but the **blue-chip stocks** of well-established, financially sound firms such as Ralston Purina and Exxon have historically provided investors steady income through consistent dividend payouts.

blue-chip stock Common stock issued by a well-established company with a sound financial history and a stable pattern of dividend payouts

Preferred Stock

Preferred stock is usually issued with a stated par value, and dividends are typically expressed as a percentage of par value. For example, if a preferred stock with a $100 par value pays a 6 percent dividend, holders will receive an annual dividend of $6 per share.

Some preferred stock is *callable.* The issuing firm can call in shares by requiring preferred stockholders to surrender them in exchange for cash payments. The amount of this payment—the *call price*—is specified in the purchase agreement between the firm and its preferred stockholders.

INVESTMENT TRAITS OF PREFERRED STOCK Because preferred stock has first rights to dividends, income is less risky than income from the same firm's common stock. Moreover, most preferred stock is **cumulative preferred stock,** which means that any missed dividend payments must be paid as soon as the firm is able to do so. In addition, the firm cannot pay any dividends to common stockholders until it has made up all late payments to preferred stockholders. Let us take the example of a firm with preferred stock having a $100 par value and paying a 6 percent dividend. If the firm fails to pay that dividend for 2 years, it must make up arrears of $12 per share to preferred stockholders before it can pay dividends to common stockholders.

cumulative preferred stock Preferred stock on which dividends not paid in the past must be paid to stockholders before dividends can be paid to common stockholders

Stock Exchanges

Most of the secondary market for stocks is handled by organized stock exchanges. In addition, a dealer or the over-the-counter market handles the exchange of some stocks. A **stock exchange** is an organization of individuals formed to provide an institutional setting in which stock can be bought and sold. The exchange enforces certain rules to govern its members' trading activities. Most exchanges are nonprofit corporations established to serve their members.

stock exchange Organization of individuals formed to provide an institutional setting in which stock can be traded

To become a member, an individual must purchase one of a limited number of memberships, called *seats,* on the exchange. Only members (or their representatives) are allowed to trade on the exchange. In this sense, because all orders to buy or sell must flow through members, members of the exchange have a legal monopoly. Memberships can be bought and sold like other assets.

THE TRADING FLOOR Each exchange regulates the places and times at which trading may occur. Trading is allowed only at an actual physical location called the trading floor. The floor is equipped with a vast array of electronic communications equipment for conveying buy-and-sell orders or confirming completed trades. A variety of news services furnish up-to-the-minute information about world events and business developments. Any change in these factors, then, may be swiftly reflected in share prices.

BROKERS Some of the people on the trading floor are employed by the exchange. Others are trading stocks for themselves. Many, however, are **brokers,** who receive and execute buy-and-sell orders from nonexchange members. Although they match buyers with sellers, brokers do not own the securities. They earn commissions from the individuals and organizations for whom they place orders.

broker Individual or organization who receives and executes buy-and-sell orders on behalf of other people in return for commissions

As with many products, brokerage assistance can be purchased at either discount prices or at full-service prices.

Discount broker Charles Schwab & Co., for example, offers well-informed individual investors a fast, low-cost way to participate in the market. Schwab's customers know what they want to buy or sell, and they usually make trades simply by using personal computers or Schwab's automated telephone order system without talking with a broker. Why are discount brokerage services low cost? For one thing, their sales personnel receive fees, not commissions. Unlike many full-service brokers, they offer no investment advice and hold no person-to-person sales conversations. They do, however, offer automated on-line services such as stock research, industry analysis, and screening for types of stocks you might request using your personal computer.

The discount approach has filled a previously neglected niche among investors. At Schwab alone, active accounts rose from about 1 million in 1988 to more than 5 million in 1998. Why are investors coming to Schwab? The reason, at least according to Tom D. Seip, Schwab's vice president for branch services, is fairly simple. "Many people come to us—it sounds sad, but it's true—after they have been shafted somewhere else." Today Schwab's competition includes other discount brokers, such as Fidelity Brokerage Services and National Discount Brokerage, which have already undercut some of Schwab's fees. On-line trading, offered by Schwab and such specialty firms as E*TRADE®, allows investors to manage their own portfolios while paying low commissions for trading stocks on the Web.[7]

There remains an important market for full-service brokerages to advise new, uninformed investors and for experienced investors who don't have time to keep up on the latest stock market developments. When you deal with busy people who want to invest successfully, says Joseph Grano of Paine Webber, "you can't do it through a telephone response system. In a world that's growing more and more complicated, the advice and counsel of a broker will be more important, not less important."[8]

> **"Many people come to us—it sounds sad, but it's true—after they have been shafted somewhere else."**
>
> —Tom D. Seip
>
> *Schwab's Vice President for Branch Services*

THE MAJOR EXCHANGES AND THE OTC MARKET The two major stock exchanges in the United States are the New York and American Stock Exchanges. The New York Stock Exchange, the largest exchange in the United States, has recently begun to face stiff competition from both smaller regional U.S. exchanges and larger foreign exchanges, especially in London.

The New York Stock Exchange. For many people, "the stock market" means the New York Stock Exchange (NYSE). Founded in 1792 and located at the corner of Wall and Broad Streets in New York City, the largest of all U.S. exchanges is, in fact, the model for exchanges worldwide. An average of 527 million shares change hands each day; about 40 percent of all shares traded on U.S. exchanges are traded here.

"Hello, we're Mathers, Thorpe and Beneke. Can your husband come out and play the market?"

Only firms meeting certain minimum requirements—earning power, total value of outstanding stock, and number of shareholders—are eligible for listing on the NYSE. The stocks of more than 3,100 companies are traded on the NYSE, with total market values of $12 trillion. At mid-1997, General Electric's common shares had the highest market value: $169 billion. NYSE trading volume in 1998 was over 160 billion shares.[9]

TRENDS AND CHALLENGES

WHERE VIRTUAL INVESTING IS A REALITY

In just a few short years, the Internet has transformed the world of personal investing. The best Web sites give home-based investors access to more and better information than anyone could imagine back when the Internet made its first appearance. Today, thanks to the latest generation of high-speed modems, access is fast and truly painless. "It's a cliché," observes financial writer Kathy Yakal, "that the Internet provides individuals with what once was available only on Wall Street trading desks. Actually, it offers more."

> **"It's a cliché that the Internet provides individuals with what once was available only on Wall Street trading desks. Actually, it offers more."**
>
> —Kathy Yakal
> *Financial Writer*

Each year, *Barron's*, one of the country's most respected financial publications, rates the top 10 investment Web sites. Editors look for standard data (stock and bond tables, earnings reports, and portfolio trackers), interactivity, and more. Here are their top choices. While some are free, others charge monthly subscription fees:

1. **Microsoft MoneyCentral (http://www.moneycentral.com)** Among the features of this four-star service are free real-time quotes, a personal portfolio graph, news and analysis (updated five times daily by *The Wall Street Journal*), and access to Securities and Exchange Commission filings. MoneyCentral's Research Wizard teaches new investors how to research securities. Another advantage is the site won't overload you with too many features and information, and the design facilitates use.
2. **CBS MarketWatch (http://www.cbsmarketwatch.com)** The strength of this site, says *Barron's*, is in reporting and analyzing breaking news and in a feature selection that offers value for beginners to pros. It also has a good portfolio tracker and direct links to data from Hoover's and other securities-research companies.
3. **Yahoo! Finance (http://www.quote.yahoo.com)** "Nobody," says *Barron's*, "has yet bettered the design, at least in

The American Stock Exchange. The second-largest U.S. exchange, the American Stock Exchange (AMEX), is also located in New York. It accounts for about 3 percent of all shares traded on U.S. exchanges. Like the NYSE, the AMEX has minimum requirements for listings. They are, however, less stringent. The minimum number of publicly held shares, for example, is 500,000 versus 1.1 million for the NYSE. The AMEX currently lists about 900 stocks of companies around the world. Indeed, in 1997, foreign stocks made up nearly 7 percent of the total market value for the 24 million shares traded daily on the AMEX. As firms grow, they often transfer their listings from the AMEX to the NYSE. Well-known companies with stocks listed on the AMEX include Turner Broadcasting, TWA, and The New York Times Co.

Regional Stock Exchanges. Established long before the advent of modern communications, the seven regional stock exchanges were organized to serve investors in places other than New York. The largest regional exchanges are the Midwest Stock Exchange in Chicago and the Pacific Stock Exchange in Los Angeles and San Francisco. Other exchanges are located in Philadelphia, Boston, Cincinnati, and Spokane. Many corporations list their stocks both regionally and on either the NYSE or the AMEX.

Foreign Stock Exchanges. As recently as 1980, the U.S. market accounted for more than half the value of the world market in traded stocks. Indeed, as late as 1975, the equity of IBM alone was greater than the national market equities of all but four countries. Market activities, however, have shifted as the value of shares listed on foreign exchanges continues to grow. The annual dollar value of trades on exchanges in London, Tokyo, and other cities is in the trillions. In fact, the London exchange exceeds even the NYSE in number of stocks listed; in market value, transactions on U.S. exchanges are now second to those on Japanese exchanges. Relatively new exchanges are also beginning to flourish in cities from Shanghai to Warsaw.

In Muscat, the capital of Oman, a tiny sultanate on the Arabian peninsula, the tax laws have been changed to encourage more foreign investment. One immediate result has been a 62 percent increase in activity on the Muscat Securities Exchange, where "high-tech" accoutrements still consist of telephones and (for interested local parties stationed in the gallery) binoculars.

terms of financial information." Among the tools you'll find here are a stock screener, message boards, a stock chat room, and a pager service triggered by your own buy and sell prices. Personal portfolio pages include related stock quotes and charts, news, and user messages.

4. **CNNfn (http://www.cnnfn.com)** This site has a tremendous volume of news, data, and analysis. Its partnership with Quicken.com links investors to such additional investment tools as a portfolio tracker and the Lipper Mutual Fund Report.
5. **Quicken.com (http://www.quicken.com)** In addition to posting the same data and analysis as most other sites, this full-service personal finance site also looks at banking, mortgages, and insurance.
6. **Morningstar.Net (http://www.morningstar.net)** This site is divided into six sections: Learn (a step-by-step tutorial for beginners); Plan (information on developing your own financial plan); Research (data and analysis on specific securities); Invest (get advice, make trades); Monitor (portfolio tracking and market updates); and Socialize (message boards for investment topics and company information).
7. **The Street (http://www.thestreet.com)** The strength of this site is its expert investment analysis and numerous features on companies in the news. Virtual investors will find the standard package of investment tools, including a portfolio tracker and stock and mutual fund charting.
8. **ZD Interactive Investor (http://www.zdii.com)** The strong data and editorial content of this site links investors to breaking financial stories, analyses of global and U.S. markets, company profiles and competitors, SEC filings, and more.
9. **Stockpoint (http://www.stockpoint.com)** This easy-to-use site includes market data screens, securities quotes (accompanied by analysts' ratings), and interactive data screens.
10. **The Motley Fool (http://www.fool.com)** An ideal site for beginners, Motley Fool uses a commonsense approach to teach 13 steps to investing. Known for its sense of community, the site's message boards are filled with lively opinions.

With the novelty of the Web long gone, *Barron's* judged these sites on content, design, and usefulness rather than on their *potential* to deliver information and interact with investors. Although only one site is rated best, *Barron's* makes it clear that independent-minded investors can be the clear winners on any of them.

over-the-counter (OTC) market Organization of securities dealers formed to trade stock outside the formal institutional setting of the organized stock exchanges

Over-the-Counter Market: NASDAQ and NASD. The **over-the-counter (OTC) market** is so called because its original traders were somewhat like retailers. They kept supplies of shares on hand and sold them over the office counter to interested buyers as opportunities arose. Even today, the OTC market has no trading floor. Instead, it consists of many people in different locations who hold an inventory of securities that are not listed on NASDAQ or any of the national U.S. securities exchanges. Unlike brokers, the OTC consists of independent dealers who own the securities they buy and sell, at their own risk.

Separate from the OTC market is the National Association of Securities Dealers (NASD), which has nearly 5,500 member firms. NASD includes dealers (not brokers) who have joined to coordinate investment activities. They must pass qualification exams and meet certain standards for financial soundness. The privilege of trading in the market is granted by federal regulators and by NASD. Their electronic communication system includes the **National Association of Securities Dealers Automated Quotation (NASDAQ) system,** which operates the NASDAQ Stock Market. Currently, the NASD is working with officials in an increasing number of countries, especially in Asia and Latin America, who want to replace the trading floors of traditional exchanges with electronic networks like NASDAQ.

National Association of Securities Dealers Automated Quotation (NASDAQ) system Organization of over-the-counter dealers who own, buy, and sell their own securities over a network of electronic communications

Although NASD and AMEX have merged to become the NASD-AMEX Market Group, they are continuing to operate as separate markets (NASDAQ and AMEX). Some 5,400 companies' stocks are traded by NASDAQ. Newer firms are often listed here when their stocks first become available in the secondary market. Many of these later become well known, including companies such as MCI Communications, Apple Computer, and Yellow Freight, along with many high-technology stocks in such industries as biotechnology, medical advancements, and electronics.

In October 1997, NASDAQ became the first U.S. stock market to trade more than 1 billion shares in a day and reached a record high of 2,040 in December 1998. Although the number of shares traded surpasses the New York Stock Exchange volume, the market value of NASDAQ stocks is only about one-fifth of those on the NYSE.

Figure 16.1 shows the number of shares traded on the various exchanges and the NASDAQ system.

FIGURE 16.1 ◆ **Trading Levels, Billions of Shares Per Year**

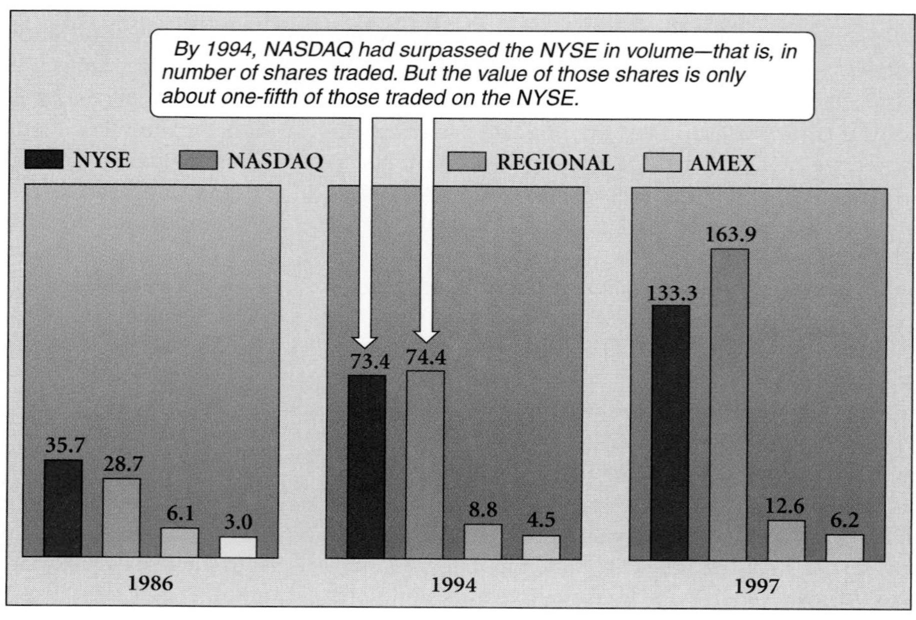

In the battle for premier companies, both the New York Stock Exchange and NASDAQ have taken to marketing themselves much more aggressively. Each, for example, has expanded operations at its broadcast center and permitted more and more TV stations to air real-time stock prices. A virtual high-tech market site, the NASDAQ center features 100 video monitors and provides a showplace to impress new or prospective companies.

■ BONDS

A **bond** is an IOU—a promise by the issuer to pay the buyer a certain amount of money by a specified future date, usually with interest paid at regular intervals. The U.S. bond market is supplied by three major sources—the U.S. government, municipalities, and corporations. Bonds differ in terms of maturity dates, tax status, and level of risk versus potential yield.[10]

bond Security through which an issuer promises to pay the buyer a certain amount of money by a specified future date

To aid bond investors in making purchase decisions, several services rate the quality of bonds. Table 16.1, for example, shows the systems of two well-known services, Moody's and Standard & Poor's. Ratings measure default risk—the chance that one or more promised payments will be deferred or missed altogether. The highest grades are AAA and Aaa, the lowest C and D. Low-grade bonds are usually called *junk bonds*.

U.S. Government Bonds

The U.S. government is the world's largest debtor. New federal borrowing from the public exceeded $38 billion in 1997, when the total U.S. debt reached $5.5 trillion.[11] To finance its debt, the federal government issues a variety of government bonds. The U.S. Treasury issues Treasury bills (T-bills), Treasury notes, and Treasury bonds (including U.S. savings bonds). Many government agencies (for example, the Federal Housing Administration) also issue bonds.

Government bonds are among the safest investments available. Securities with longer maturities are somewhat riskier than short-term issues because their longer lives expose them to more political, social, and economic changes. All federal bonds, however, are backed by the U.S. government. Government securities are sold in large blocks to

government bond Bond issued by the federal government

TABLE 16.1 ◆ **Bond Rating Systems**

	HIGH GRADES	MEDIUM GRADES (INVESTMENT GRADES)	SPECULATIVE	POOR GRADES
Moody's	Aaa, Aa	A, Baa	Ba, B	Caa to C
Standard & Poor's	AAA, AA	A, BBB	BB, B	CCC to D

institutional investors who buy them to ensure desired levels of safety in their portfolios. As investors' needs change, they may buy or sell government securities to other investors.

Municipal Bonds

municipal bond Bond issued by a state or local government

State and local governments issue **municipal bonds** to finance school and transportation systems and a variety of other projects. In 1997, new municipal bonds were issued at a value of more than $214 billion.

Some bonds, called *obligation bonds*, are backed by the issuer's taxing power. A local school district, for example, may issue $50 million in obligation bonds to fund new elementary and high schools. The issuer intends to retire the bonds from future tax revenues. In contrast, *revenue bonds* are backed only by the revenue generated by a specific project. In 1998, for example, the Alaska Industrial Development and Export Authority issued $100 million in revenue bonds to finance the purchase of the Snettisham Hydroelectric Project from the U.S. Department of Energy. The facility generates and sells electricity, and the resulting operating revenues will eventually pay off the indebtedness. Payment of the principal and interest is due at various dates from 2000 through 2034.[12]

The most attractive feature of municipal bonds is the fact that investors do not pay taxes on interest received. Commercial banks invest in bonds nearing maturity because they are relatively safe, liquid investments. Pension funds, insurance companies, and even private citizens also make longer-term investments in municipals.

Corporate Bonds

corporate bond Bond issued by a company as a source of long-term funding

Although the U.S. government and municipalities are heavy borrowers, corporate long-term borrowing is even greater. **Corporate bonds** issued by U.S. companies are a large source of financing, involving more money than government and municipal bonds combined. U.S. companies raised nearly $641 billion from new bond issues in 1997. Bonds have traditionally been issued with maturities ranging from 20 to 30 years. In the 1980s, 10-year maturities came into wider use.

Like municipal bonds, longer-term corporate bonds are somewhat riskier than shorter-term bonds. To help investors evaluate risk, Standard & Poor's and Moody's rate both new and proposed issues on a weekly basis. Remember, however, that negative ratings do not necessarily keep issues from being successful. Rather, they raise the interest rates that issuers must offer. Corporate bonds may be categorized (1) in terms of the method of interest payment or (2) in terms of whether they are *secured* or *unsecured.*

registered bond Bond bearing the name of the holder and registered with the issuing company

bearer (or coupon) bond Bond requiring the holder to clip and submit a coupon to receive an interest payment

secured bond Bond backed by pledges of assets to the bondholders

debenture Unsecured bond for which no specific property is pledged as security

INTEREST PAYMENT: REGISTERED AND BEARER BONDS **Registered bonds** register the names of holders with the company, which simply mails out checks. Certificates are of value only to registered holders. **Bearer** (or **coupon**) **bonds** require bondholders to clip coupons from certificates and send them to the issuer to receive payment. Coupons can be redeemed by anyone, regardless of ownership.

SECURED BONDS With **secured bonds,** issuers can reduce the risk to holders by pledging assets in case of default. Bonds can be backed by first mortgages, other mortgages, or other specific assets. In 1994, for example, Union Pacific Railroad Co. issued $76 million in bonds to finance the purchase and renovation of equipment. Rated Aaa (prime) by Moody's and maturing in 2012, the bonds are secured by the newly purchased and rehabilitated equipment itself—80 diesel locomotives, 1,300 hopper cars, and 450 auto-rack cars.

DEBENTURES Unsecured bonds are called **debentures.** No specific property is pledged as security. Rather, holders generally have claims against property not otherwise pledged in the company's other bonds. Thus, debentures are said to have "inferior claims" on a corporation's assets. Financially strong firms often use debentures. An example is Boeing's $175 million debenture issued in 1993, with maturity on April 15, 2043. Similar issues by weaker companies often receive low ratings and may have trouble attracting investors.

Secondary Markets for Bonds

Nearly all secondary trading in bonds occurs in the OTC market rather than on organized exchanges. Thus, precise statistics about annual trading volumes are not recorded. As with stocks, however, market values and prices change daily. The direction of bond prices moves *opposite* to interest rate changes. As interest rates move up, bond prices tend to go down. The prices of riskier bonds fluctuate more widely than those of higher-grade bonds.

OTHER INVESTMENTS

Stocks and bonds are not the only marketable securities available to businesses. Financial managers are also concerned with financial opportunities in *mutual funds* and *commodities.*

Mutual Funds

Companies called **mutual funds** pool investments from individuals and organizations to purchase a portfolio of stocks, bonds, and other securities. Investors are thus part owners of the portfolio. For example, if you invest $1,000 in a mutual fund with a portfolio worth $100,000, you own 1 percent of that portfolio. Investors in **no-load funds** are not charged sales commissions when they buy into or sell out of funds. Investors in **load funds** generally pay commissions of 2 to 8 percent.

mutual fund Company that pools investments from individuals and organizations to purchase a portfolio of stocks, bonds, and short-term securities

no-load fund Mutual fund in which investors pay no sales commissions when they buy in or sell out

load fund Mutual fund in which investors are charged sales commissions when they buy in or sell out

REASONS FOR INVESTING The total assets invested in U.S. mutual funds has grown significantly every year since 1991, to a total of $5 trillion in more than 9,500 different funds.[13] Why do investors find them so attractive? Remember first of all that mutual funds vary in their investment goals. Naturally, different funds are designed to appeal to the different motives and goals of investors. Funds stressing safety often include money market mutual funds and other safe issues offering immediate income. Investors seeking higher current income must generally sacrifice some safety. Typically, these people look to long-term municipal bond, corporate bond, and income mutual funds that invest in common stocks with good dividend-paying records.

Mutual funds that stress growth include balanced mutual funds—portfolios of bonds and preferred and common stocks, especially the common stocks of established firms. Aggressive growth funds seek maximum capital appreciation. They sacrifice current income and safety and invest in stocks of new (and even troubled) companies and other high-risk securities. Figure 16.2 shows how total assets in mutual funds are divided among different types of mutual fund investments.[14] As you can see, the distribution of assets has shifted since the early 1980s to meet changing investor goals and attitudes toward financial risk.

Commodities

Individuals and businesses can buy and sell commodities as investments. **Futures contracts**—agreements to purchase specified amounts of commodities at given prices on set dates—can be bought and sold in the **commodities market.** These contracts are available not only for stocks but also for commodities ranging from coffee beans and hogs to propane and platinum. Because selling prices reflect traders' estimates of future events and values, futures prices are quite volatile and trading is risky.

futures contract Agreement to purchase specified amounts of a commodity at a given price on a set future date

commodities market Market in which futures contracts are traded

To clarify the workings of the commodities market, let us look at an example. On March 2, 1998, the price of gold on the open market was $299 per ounce. Futures contracts for December 1998 gold were selling for $307 per ounce. This price reflected investors' judgment that gold prices would be higher the following December. Now suppose that you purchased a 100-ounce gold futures contract in March for $30,700 ($307 × 100). If in May 1998 the December gold futures sold for $332, you could sell your contract for $33,200. Your profit after the 2 months would be $2,500.

FIGURE 16.2 ◆ **Types of Mutual Funds**

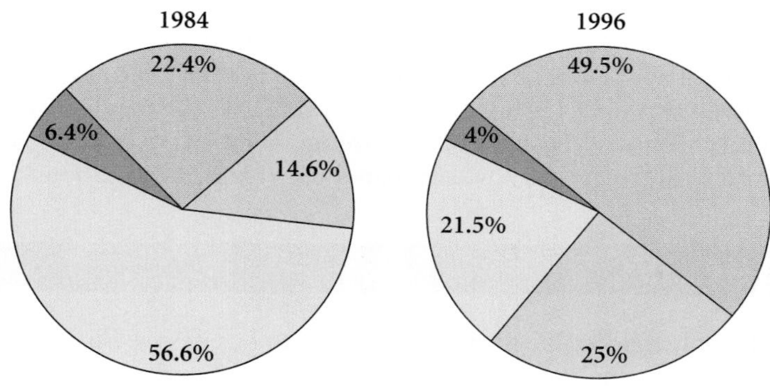

- = Equity Funds
- = Bond and Income Funds
- = Taxable Money Market Funds
- = Tax-Exempt Money Market Funds

margin Percentage of the total sales price that a buyer must put up to place an order for stock or futures contracts

MARGINS Usually, buyers of futures contracts need not put up the full purchase amount. Rather, the buyer posts a smaller amount—the **margin**—that may be as little as $3,000 for contracts up to $100,000. Let us look again at our gold futures example. As we saw, if you had posted a $3,000 margin for your December gold contract, you would have earned a $2,500 profit on that investment of $3,000 in only 2 months.

However, you also took a big risk involving two big ifs: If you had held onto your contract until December, and if gold had dropped, say to $291 (as it really did by December 1998), you would have lost $1,600 ($30,700–29,100). If you had posted a $3,000 margin to buy the contract, you would have lost $1,600 of it and would receive back only $1,400 of your original $3,000 investment. In fact, between 75 and 90 percent of all small-time investors lose money in the futures market. For one thing, the action is fast and furious, with small investors trying to keep up with professionals ensconced in seats on the major exchanges. Although the profit potential is exciting, experts recommend that most novices retreat to safer stock markets. Of course, as one veteran financial planner puts it, commodities are tempting. "After trading commodities," he reports, "trading stocks is like watching the grass grow."

> **"After trading commodities, trading stocks is like watching the grass grow."**
>
> —*A veteran financial planner*

Most commodities investors have no intention of ever taking possession of the commodities in question. Some companies, however, buy futures to protect the prices of commodities important to their businesses. Hormel Meats, for example, trades in hog futures to protect the prices of pork and pork products.

■ SECURITIES AND LONG-TERM FUNDING

Firms need long-term funding to finance expenditures on fixed assets: the buildings and equipment necessary for conducting their business. They may seek long-term funds through *debt financing* (borrowing from outside the firm) or through *equity financing* (drawing on internal sources). We will compare both options in this section, as well as a middle ground called *hybrid financing*.

Debt Financing

Long-term borrowing from sources outside the company—**debt financing**—is a major component of most firms' long-term financial planning. Long-term debts are obligations that are payable more than a year after they were originally issued. The two primary sources of such funding are long-term loans (see Appendix I) and the sale of corporate bonds.

debt financing Long-term borrowing from sources outside a company

CORPORATE BONDS As we have seen, a corporate bond, like commercial paper, is a contract—a promise by the issuer to pay the holder a certain amount of money on a specified date. Unlike issuers of commercial paper, however, bond issuers do not pay off quickly. In many cases, bonds may not be redeemable for 30 years. Also, unlike commercial paper, most bonds pay bondholders a stipulated sum of annual or semiannual interest. If the company fails to make a bond payment, it is said to be in default.

Bonds are the major source of long-term debt financing for most corporations. They are attractive when firms need large amounts for long periods of time. The issuing company also gains access to large numbers of lenders through nationwide bond markets and stock exchanges. On the other hand, bonds entail high administrative and selling costs. They may also require stiff interest payments, especially if the issuing company has a poor credit rating.

Equity Financing

Although debt financing often has strong appeal, looking inside the company for long-term funding is sometimes preferable. In small companies, for example, founders may increase personal investments in their own firms. In most cases, **equity financing** means issuing common stock or retaining the firm's earnings. Both options involve putting the owners' capital to work.

equity financing Use of common stock and/or retained earnings to raise long-term funding

COMMON STOCK People who purchase common stock seek profits in two forms—dividends and appreciation. Overall, shareholders hope for an increase in the market value of their stock (appreciation) because the firm has profited and grown. By issuing shares of stock, the company gets the funds it needs for buying land, buildings, and equipment.

Hybrid Financing: Preferred Stock

A middle ground between debt financing and equity financing is the use of preferred stock. Preferred stock is a hybrid because it has some of the features of both corporate bonds and common stocks. As with bonds, for instance, payments on preferred stock are fixed amounts such as $6 per share per year. Unlike bonds, however, preferred stock never matures; like common stock, it can be held indefinitely. In addition, preferred stocks have first rights (over common stock) to dividends.

A major advantage to the issuer is the flexibility of preferred stock. Because preferred stockholders have no voting rights, the stock secures funds for the firm without jeopardizing corporate control of its management. Furthermore, corporations are not obligated to repay the principal and can withhold payment of dividends in lean times.

BUYING AND SELLING SECURITIES

The process of buying and selling securities is complex. First, you need to find out about possible investments and match them to your investment objectives. Then you must select a broker and open an account. Only then can you place orders and make different types of transactions.

Financial Information Services

Have you ever looked at the financial section of your daily newspaper and wondered what all those tables and numbers mean? It is a good idea to know how to read stock, bond, and mutual fund quotations if you want to invest in issues. Fortunately, this skill is easily mastered.

STOCK QUOTATIONS Daily transactions for NYSE securities are reported in most city newspapers. Figure 16.3, for instance, shows part of a listing from *The Wall Street Journal*, with columns numbered 1 through 12. Let us analyze the listing for the company at the top, The Gap Inc.:

- The first two columns ("High" and "Low") show the highest and lowest prices paid for one share of The Gap stock *during the past year.* Note that stock prices throughout are expressed *in dollars per share*, with the smallest fraction of a dollar being 1/16, or 6 1/4 cents. In the past year, then, The Gap's stock ranged in value from $36.50 to $20.50 per share. This range reveals a fairly volatile stock price.
- The third column ("Stock") is the abbreviated company name. (Sometimes the notation "pf" appears after the company's name to show that the stock is *preferred*, not common. The listing reveals that GeminiII offers both a preferred stock and a common stock.)
- The NYSE *symbol* for the stock is listed in column 4 ("Sym").
- The fifth column ("Div") indicates that The Gap pays an annual *cash dividend* of $0.30 per share. This amount can be compared with payouts by other companies.
- Column 6 ("Yld %") is the *dividend yield* expressed as a percentage of the stock's current price (shown in column 11). The Gap's dividend yield is 1.0 percent (0.30/30.125, rounded). Potential buyers can compare this yield with returns they might get from alternative investments.
- Column 7 ("PE") shows the **price-earnings ratio**—the current price of the stock divided by the firm's current annual earnings per share. On this day, The Gap's PE is 21, meaning that investors are willing to pay $21 for each dollar of reported profits to own The Gap stock. This figure can be compared with PE ratios of other stocks to decide which is the best investment.
- The last five columns detail the day's trading. Column 8 ("Vol 100s") shows the *number of shares* (in hundreds) that were traded—in this case 11,822. Some investors interpret increases in trading volume as an indicator of forthcoming price changes in a stock.
- Column 9 ("High") shows the highest price paid *that day*—$30.625. Column 10 ("Low") shows the lowest price paid *that day*, $30.00.

price-earnings ratio Current price of a stock divided by the firm's current annual earnings per share

FIGURE 16.3 ◆ **Reading a Stock Quotation**

	①	②	③	④	⑤	⑥	⑦	⑧	⑨	⑩	⑪	⑫
	52 Weeks					Yld		Vol				Net
	High	Low	Stock	Sym	Div	%	PE	100s	High	Low	Close	Chg
s	36½	20½	Gap Inc	GPS	.30	1.0	21	11822	30⅝	30	30⅛	+ ¼
▲	28¼	18¾	GaylrdEntn	GET	.36b	1.8	15	1352	19⅞	19⅝	19¾	– ⅛
	27¼	23⅜	Geminill	GMI	.11e	.4	...	139	27¾	27⅜	27¾	+ ¼
	10¾	9½	Geminill pf		1.40	14.5	...	88	9¾	9⅝	9⅝	+ ⅛
	17	10¼	GenCorp	GY	.60	3.7	22	3287	16⅜	15¾	16⅜	+ ½
	55⅜	50⅜	Genentech	GNE		...	49	460	53⅞	53⅝	53⅞	+ ¼
	23½	19⅛	GenAmInv	GAM	.32e	1.4	...	201	23½	23¼	23½	+ ⅜
n	21	16⅝	GenlChemGp	GCG	.08e	.4	...	555	19	18⅜	18½	– ¼
	21⅞	9⅛	GenData	GDC		...	dd	662	10¾	10¼	10½	+ ⅛
	72	56⅜	GenDynam	GD	1.64	2.4	15	2315	67¾	66¾	67¼	+ ¼
▲	99⅜	63⅜	GenElec	GE	1.84	1.8	24	27767	101⅝	98⅝	101⅝	+2⅞

- Column 11 ("Close") shows that The Gap's *last sale of the day* was for $30.125.
- The final column ("Net Chg") shows the *difference between the previous day's close and the close on the day being reported.* The closing price of The Gap stock is 1/4 higher than it was on the previous business day. Day-to-day changes are indicators of recent price stability or volatility.

Finally, look back at the far-left column, which has no heading. This column reports unusual conditions of importance to investors. Note, for example, the *s* to the left of the "52-Week High" column for The Gap. This symbol indicates either a *stock split* (a division of stock that gives stockholders a greater number of shares but that does not change each individual's proportionate share of ownership) or an *extra stock dividend* paid during the past 52 weeks. The *n* accompanying the General Chemical Group indicates that this stock was *newly issued* during the past 52 weeks. The dagger symbol (†) indicates new 52-week highs in the prices of Gaylord and General Electric stocks.

BOND QUOTATIONS Daily quotations on corporate bonds from the NYSE are also widely published. Bond quotations contain essentially the same type of information as stock quotations. One difference, however, is that the year in which it is going to mature is listed beside each bond.

OTC QUOTATIONS Most OTC (NASDAQ) stock quotations are reported in the same format as listed stock quotations. Some OTC trades, however, are reported in terms of "bid" and "asked" quotations. For example, a quotation might show 7 1/4 as the bid price and 7 3/4 as the asked price. The **bid price** is the amount that the OTC dealer pays to obtain each share. The **asked price** is the amount the dealer charges clients to buy a share. The difference between bid and asked prices—in this case, 1/2—is the dealer's gain for making the transaction.

bid price Price that an OTC broker pays for a share of stock

asked price Price that an OTC broker charges for a share of stock

MUTUAL FUNDS QUOTATIONS Selling prices for mutual funds are reported daily in most city newspapers. Additional investor information is also available in the financial press. Figure 16.4 shows how to read a typical weekly mutual funds quotation.

- Column 1 is the net asset value (NAV), or the value of a single share as calculated by the fund.
- Column 2 shows the net asset value change, the gain or loss based on the previous day's NAV.
- Column 3 lists the fund family at the top and the individual fund names beneath the family name.
- Column 4 reports each fund's objective. The "IB" code stands for an intermediate-term bond fund; "GR" indicates a growth stock fund. This allows readers to compare the performance of funds with similar objectives.
- The next five columns report each fund's recent and long-term performance, and rank the funds within each investment objective. These numbers reflect the percentage change in NAV plus accumulated income for each period, assuming that all distributions are reinvested in the fund. These five columns show the return of the fund for the year to date, the last 4 weeks, 12 months, 3 years, and 5 years. The numbers for periods exceeding a year show an average annual return for the period, and are followed by letters indicating the fund's performance relative to other funds with the same objective. "A" means the fund was among the top 20 percent of funds in that category, "B" indicates the second 20 percent, and so on.
- The next column reports the maximum initial sales commission, expressed in percent, which the investor would have to pay to purchase shares in the fund.
- The last column shows the fund's average annual expenses, as a percentage of the fund's assets, paid annually by investors in the fund.

MARKET INDEXES Although they do not indicate the status of particular securities, **market indexes** provide useful summaries of trends, both in specific industries and in the stock market as a whole. Market indexes, for example, reveal bull and bear market trends.

market index Summary of price trends in a specific industry and/or the stock market as a whole

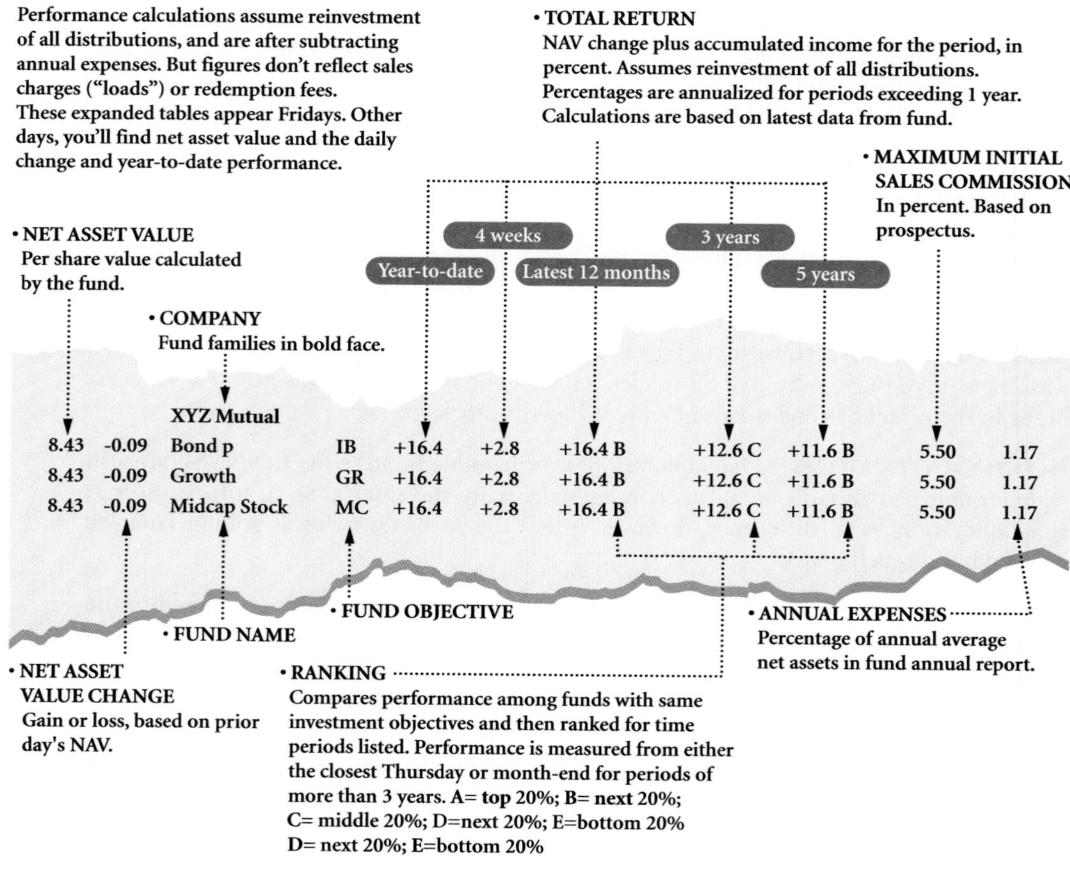

FIGURE 16.4 ◆ **Reading Mutual Funds Quotations**

bull market Period of rising stock prices

bear market Period of falling stock prices

Bull markets are periods of rising stock prices. Periods of falling stock prices are called **bear markets.**

As Figure 16.5 shows, for example, the years 1981 to 1998 boasted a strong bull market, the longest in history. Inflation was under control as business flourished in a healthy economy. In contrast, the period 1972 to 1974 was characterized by a bear market. The Mideast oil embargo caused a business slowdown, and inflation was beginning to dampen economic growth. As you can see, the data that characterize such periods are drawn from two leading market indexes—the Dow Jones and Standard & Poor's.

Dow Jones Industrial Average Market index based on the prices of 30 of the largest industrial firms listed on the NYSE

The Dow and S&P. The **Dow Jones Industrial Average** is the most widely cited U.S. index. The "Dow" is the sum of market prices for 30 of the largest industrial firms listed on the NYSE. By tradition, it is an indicator of blue-chip stock price movements.

In February 1995, the Dow topped 4,000 for the first time ever. In November 1996, it broke the 6,400 barrier for the first time, and then surpassed 9,300 in November 1998. For the first time ever, the Dow gained more than 20 percent a year for 3 consecutive years, from 1995 to 1997. Why such optimism on the part of investors? What does the Dow's performance say about attitudes toward the economy? Though unable to pinpoint one single reason for the Dow's performance, experts cited at least three factors in the surge:

1. Continued (and surprising) growth in corporate profits
2. Continued acquisition and merger activity among corporations
3. Indications from the Federal Reserve that inflation is under control and that interest rates will remain at present levels

As you can see in Figure 16.6, the Dow's movement has generally been *opposite the trend for interest rates on long-term bonds,* because as bond rates decrease, investors tend to

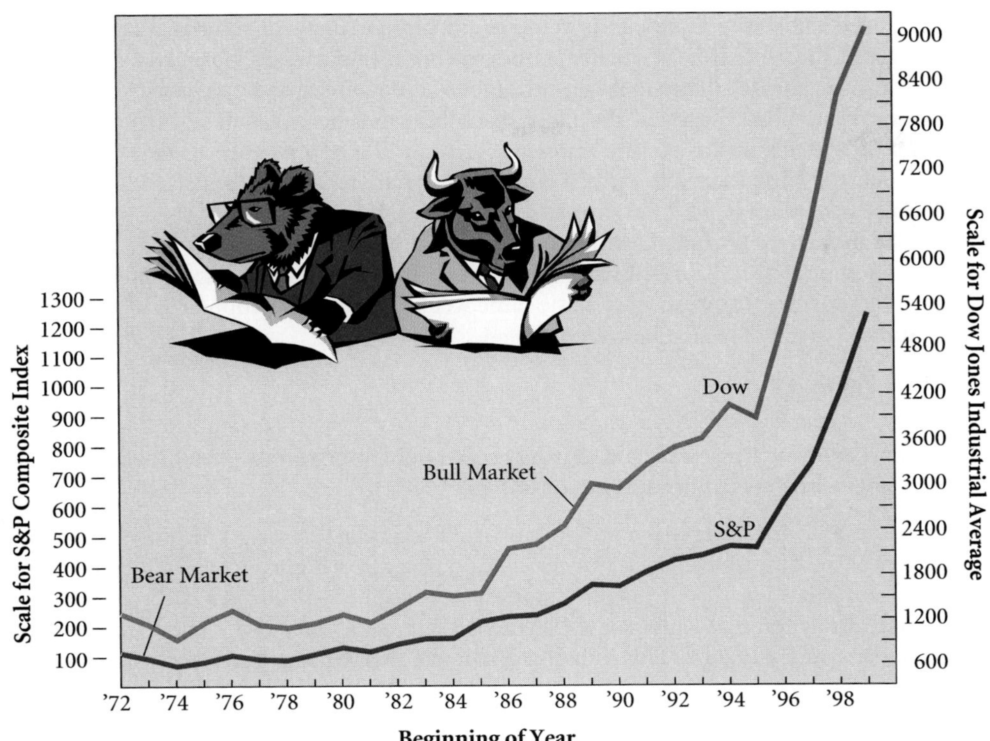

FIGURE 16.5 ◆ **Bull and Bear Markets**

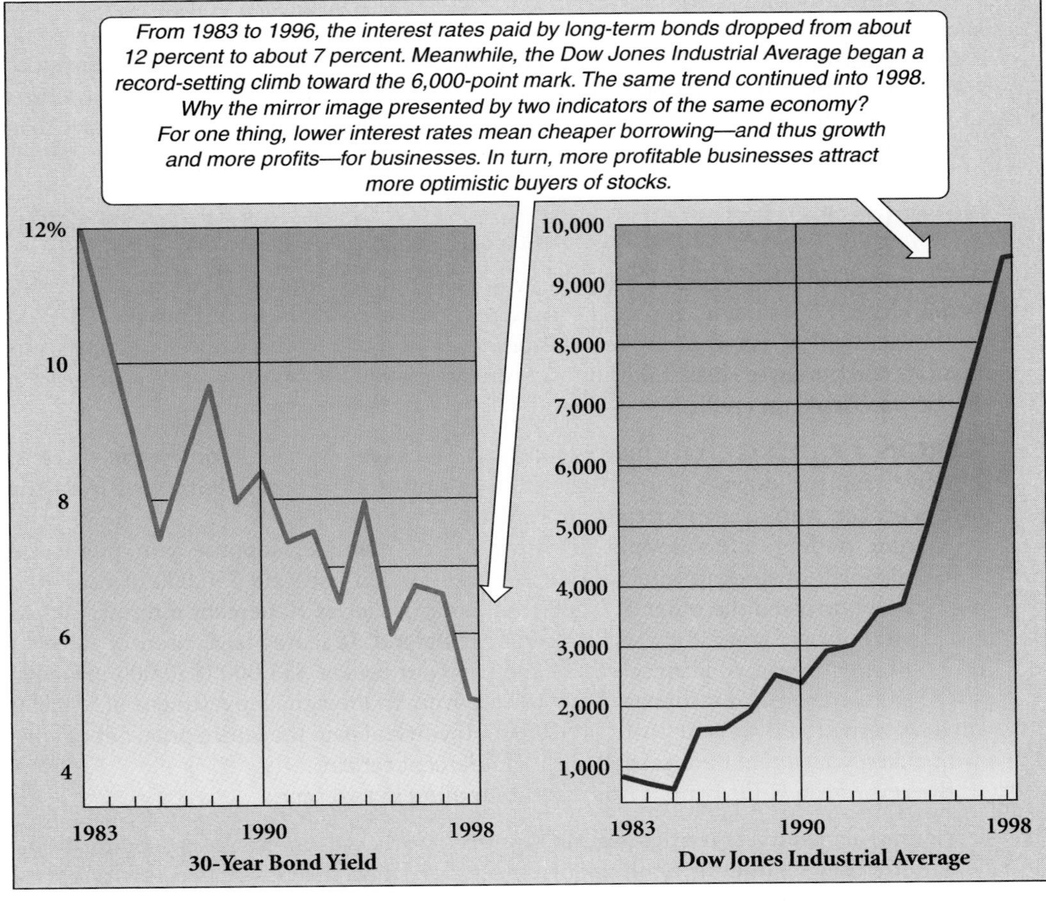

FIGURE 16.6 ◆ **Dow and Interest Rates**

become more interested in stocks as vehicles for higher financial returns. Furthermore, because lower interest rates mean cheaper borrowing for businesses, business expenses are reduced and businesses become more profitable. Thus, investor hopes for even greater profits continue. How high will the Dow reach before it begins to fall? No one knows. Says Jack Bogle, chairman of the Vanguard Group, "Hope can turn to fear and greed pretty quickly. I think there's too much confidence in the market at these [1996] levels."[15]

Standard & Poor's Composite Index Market index based on the performance of 400 industrial firms, 40 utilities, 40 financial institutions, and 20 transportation companies

Because it considers very few firms, the Dow is a limited gauge of the overall stock market. **Standard & Poor's Composite Index** is a broader report. It consists of 500 stocks, including 400 industrial firms, 40 utilities, 40 financial institutions, and 20 transportation companies. Interestingly, in the same week that the Dow topped 9,300, the S&P Index jumped to 1,193, also a new record.

Placing Orders

After doing your own research and getting recommendations from your broker, you can choose to place several different types of orders:

market order Order to buy or sell a security at the market price prevailing at the time the order is placed

limit order Order authorizing the purchase of a stock only if its price is equal to or less than a specified amount

stop order Order authorizing the sale of a stock if its price falls to or below a specified level

round lot Purchase or sale of stock in units of 100 shares

odd lot Purchase or sale of stock in fractions of round lots

- A **market order** requests that a broker buy or sell a certain security at the prevailing market price at the time of the order. For example, look again at Figure 16.3. On that day, your broker would have sold your Gap Inc. stock for between $30.00 and $30.625 per share.

  Note, however, that when you gave your order to sell, you did not know exactly what the market price would be. This situation can be avoided with limit and stop orders, which allow for buying and selling only if certain price conditions are met.
- A **limit order** authorizes the purchase of a stock only if its price is less than or equal to a specified limit. For example, an order to buy at $30 a share means that the broker is to buy if and only if the stock becomes available for a price of $30 or less. A **stop order** instructs the broker to sell if a stock price falls to a certain level. For example, an order of $25 on a particular stock means that the broker is to sell that stock if and only if its price falls to $25 or below.
- Orders also differ by size. An order for a **round lot** requests 100 shares of a particular stock or some multiple thereof. Fractions of round lots are called **odd lots.** Because an intermediary—*an odd-lot broker*—is often involved, odd-lot trading is usually more expensive than round-lot trading.

Financing Purchases

When you place a buy order of any kind, you must tell your broker how you will pay for the purchase. For example, you might maintain a cash account with your broker. Then, as you buy and sell stocks, your broker adds proceeds to your account while deducting commissions and purchase costs. Like almost every product in today's economy, securities can also be purchased on credit.

MARGIN TRADING Like futures contracts, stocks can be bought on *margin*—that is, the buyer can put down a portion of the stock's price. The rest is borrowed from the buyer's broker, who secures special-rate bank loans with stock.

Margin trading offers several advantages. For example, suppose you purchased $100,000 worth of stock in Intel Corp. Let's also say that you paid $50,000 of your own money and borrowed the other $50,000 from your broker at 10 percent interest. Valued at its market price, your stock serves as your collateral. If shares have risen in value to $115,000 after 1 year, you can sell them and pay your broker $55,000 ($50,000 principal plus $5,000 interest). You will have $60,000 left over. Your original investment of $50,000 will have earned a 20 percent profit of $10,000. If you had paid the entire price out of your own pocket, you would have earned only a 15 percent return.

Brokers, meanwhile, benefit from margin trading in two ways:

1. Because it encourages more people to buy more stock, brokers earn more commissions.
2. Because they charge buyers higher interest rates than they pay banks, brokers earn profits on their loans.

Although investors often recognize possible profits to be made in margin trading, they sometimes fail to consider that losses, too, can be amplified. Suppose, for example, that you decided on June 26, 1996, to buy 1,000 shares of Acme Electric, a producer of power conversion equipment, for $36 per share. You put up $18,000 of your own money and borrow $18,000 from your broker. As the stock rises, you reason, the loan will enable you to profit from twice as many shares. Now let us say that, shortly after you purchase your stock, Acme's market price begins to fall. You decide to hold on until it recovers. By June 26, 1997, when the price has fallen to $8.50 a share, you give up hope and sell.

Now let us see how margin trading has amplified your losses. If you had invested your own $18,000 instead of borrowing it, you would recover $8,500 of your $36,000 investment (excluding commissions). Your loss, therefore, would be 76 percent ($27,500 loss / $36,000 invested). By trading on margin, however, even though you still recover $8,500 of your $18,000 investment, you must repay the $18,000 that you borrowed, plus $1,800 in loan interest (at a 10-percent annual rate). In this case, your losses total $29,300 ($37,800 in outlays less $8,500 recovered). The percentage loss is 163 percent of your investment ($29,300 loss / $18,000 investment)—much greater than the 76-percent loss you would have suffered without margin trading.[16]

short sale Stock sale in which an investor borrows securities from a broker to be sold and then replaced at a specified future date

SHORT SALES In addition to lending money, brokerages also lend securities. A **short sale** begins when you borrow a security from your broker and sell it (one of the few times that it is legal to sell something that you do not own). At a given point in the future, you must restore an equal number of shares of that issue to the brokerage, along with a fee.

We now return to our Gap Inc. example. Suppose that in January you believe the price of Gap stock will soon fall. You therefore order your broker to "sell short" 100 shares at the market price of $30.125 per share. Your broker will make the sale and credit $3,012.50 to your account. If The Gap's price falls to $25 per share in July, you can buy 100 shares for $2,500 and use them to repay your broker. You will have made a $512.50 profit (before commissions). Your risk, of course, is that The Gap's price will not fall. If it holds steady or rises, you will take a loss.

SECURITIES MARKET REGULATION

program trading Large purchase or sale of a group of stocks, often triggered by computerized trading programs that can be launched without human supervision or control

One oft-cited cause of sudden market fluctuations is **program trading**—the purchase or sale of a group of stocks valued at $1 million or more, often triggered by computerized trading programs that can be launched without human supervision or control. It works in the following way. As market values change and economic events transpire during the course of a day, computer programs are busy recalculating the future values of stocks. Once a calculated value reaches a critical point, the program automatically signals a buy or sell order. Because electronic trading could cause the market to spiral out of control, the NYSE has set up "circuit breakers" that suspend trading for a preset length of time (usually an hour). The interruption provides a "cooling-off" period that slows trading activity and allows computer programs to be revised or shut down.

The Securities and Exchange Commission

Securities and Exchange Commission (SEC) Federal agency that administers U.S. securities laws to protect the investing public and maintain smoothly functioning markets

prospectus Registration statement filed with the SEC before the issuance of a new security

To protect the investing public and to maintain smoothly functioning markets, the **Securities and Exchange Commission (SEC)** oversees many phases in the process through which securities are issued. The SEC regulates the public offering of new securities by requiring that all companies file prospectuses before proposed offerings commence. To protect investors from fraudulent issues, a **prospectus** contains pertinent information about both the offered security and the issuing company. False statements are subject to criminal penalties.

Unfortunately, to ensure full disclosure, the typical prospectus is highly technical and not easily understood by most investors. To overcome this difficulty and to make the document more user friendly, the SEC is encouraging experimentation with a "profile prospectus." Currently this new abbreviated document is being tested by mutual fund companies. It contains summarized information about the fund's goals, risks, investment strategy, and past performance so investors can compare it with other funds. It also fits on one piece of paper instead of requiring an entire booklet. At the very least, says A. Michael Lipper of Lipper Analytical Securities Corp., "This prospectus could save trees and lower costs to investors, and that's positive."

> **"This prospectus could save trees and lower costs to investors, and that's positive."**
>
> —A. Michael Lipper
> *Lipper Analytical Securities Corp.*

insider trading Illegal practice of using special knowledge about a firm for profit or gain

The SEC also enforces laws against **insider trading**—the use of special knowledge about a firm for profit or gain. In 1998, for example, the SEC filed suit in U.S. District Court against four New York–area residents on charges of using insider information and gaining $1.55 million in illegal profits by buying and selling shares of 13 companies. One defendant allegedly had access to advance, nonpublic information about the 13 firms through her former job in a Wall Street investment firm. She allegedly sold the information to the other defendants, who, in turn, tipped others, all of whom used the information to make their buy-and-sell decisions and thereby realize handsome profits.[17]

Along with the SEC's enforcement efforts, the stock exchanges cooperate in detecting and stopping insider action. In any given year, for example, NASD may refer more than 100 cases to the SEC for possible insider trading. In addition, NASD's self-regulation results in actions ranging from fining member firms and officers to barring or suspending them. In 1998, for example, Hampton Capital Management Corp. was suspended from membership and fined, and its principal officer was fined and barred from any association with any NASD member in any capacity: The firm had refused to allow the NASD staff to enter and examine the firm's books and records. The New York Stock Exchange and the other exchanges, too, have spent millions on self-regulation. They use sophisticated surveillance methods that electronically monitor transactions to detect unusual trading patterns. In May 1996, for example, the Pacific Stock Exchange asked the SEC to investigate the trading patterns of several investors believed to have had ties to toymaker Hasbro Inc. The investigation began when the exchange observed a sudden rise in their trading of Hasbro stock just before Mattel Inc. announced its failed bid to purchase Hasbro. To stem the increase in illegal insider trading, the SEC is also using tougher enforcement, including criminal prosecution against offenders.[18]

blue-sky laws Laws requiring securities dealers to be licensed and registered with the states in which they do business

State governments also regulate the sale of securities. For example, commenting that some promoters would sell stock "to the blue sky itself," one legislator's speech led to the phrase **blue-sky laws** and the passage of statutes requiring securities to be registered with state officials. In addition, securities dealers must be registered and licensed by the states in which they do business. Finally, states may prosecute the sale of fraudulent securities.

Continued from page 423

The Forces that Might *Have Been at Work*

Never before in history have investors had such immediate access to financial market information and analysis. From such sources as Reuters financial news services, we can access our home PCs for real-time securities quotes and financial news from any market in the world. We can plug into hundreds of Internet-based on-line brokers for both analysis and full-color graphic explanations. We can watch CNBC's 24-hour cable operation or listen to the Bloomberg financial radio network for news and trends. We can get a copy of Fed chairman Alan Greenspan's latest speech by clicking on the Fed's Web site. The media give us not only instant information, but an instant "feedback loop" through which our reactions to facts, expectations, and rumors have the power to influence market swings.

Media analysts who feel compelled to give their spin on market changes also affect volatility. Without analysis, the business report would be little more than a recitation of numbers that would sell very few newspapers or hold the attention of very few viewers. "It's impossible to know why the stock market rose or fell," admits Associated Press business editor Rick Gladstone, "when there's no . . . obvious news. It may have nothing to do with the news or with anything. But reporters are obliged to say what might've been at work." This penchant for public speculation is the stuff that rumors, inflated expectations, and volatility are made of.

Immediate media access has turned many avid investors into 24-hour-a-day tradaholics. Securities are traded among investors in New York, Tokyo, London, and Buenos Aires any time day or night. When investors wake up in the morning, they can learn the latest dollar-yen relationship or assess what the price of Standard & Poor's Index futures means to the trading day. The pace is exhausting and so is the volatility.

Questions for Discussion

1. How do you think stock market volatility will affect today's investors in both the short term and in the long term?
2. What is the relationship between the growth of privately managed retirement accounts, in the form of Individual Retirement Accounts, Roth IRAs, and 401(K) pension plans, and stock market volatility?
3. In a volatile stock market, why is it important for investors to assess their reaction to financial risk and to put together short-term and long-term financial plans?
4. Is increasingly more sophisticated computer technology necessarily a good thing for the market? Explain your answer.
5. Computer programs now use mathematical formulas to make buy-and-sell decisions for large institutions without benefit of human intervention. Is this progress? Explain your answer.
6. What do you think about the media's role in stock market volatility?

SUMMARY

1. **Explain the difference between *primary* and *secondary securities markets*.** *Primary securities markets* involve the buying and selling of new securities, either in public offerings or *through private placements* (sales to single buyers or small groups of buyers). *Investment bankers* specialize in issuing securities in primary markets. *Secondary markets* involve the trading of stocks and bonds through such familiar bodies as the New York and American Stock Exchanges.

2. **Discuss the value to shareholders of *common* and *preferred stock*, and describe the secondary market for each type of security.** *Common stock* affords investors the prospect of *capital gains* and/or dividend income. Common stock values are expressed in three ways: as *par value* (the face value of a share when it is issued), *market value* (the current market price of a share), and *book value* (the value of shareholders' equity divided by the number of shares). Market value is most important to investors. *Preferred stock* is less risky. Cumulative preferred stock entitles holders to missed dividends as soon as the company is financially

capable of paying. It also offers the prospect of steadier income. Shareholders of preferred stock must be paid dividends before shareholders of common stock.

Both common and preferred stock are traded on *stock exchanges* (institutions formed to conduct the trading of existing securities) and in *over-the-counter (OTC) markets* (dealer organizations formed to trade securities outside stock exchange settings). "Members" who hold seats on exchanges act as *brokers*—agents who execute buy-and-sell orders—for nonmembers. Exchanges include the New York, American, and regional and foreign exchanges. In the OTC market, licensed dealers serve functions similar to those of exchange members.

3. **Distinguish among various types of *bonds* in terms of their issuers, safety, and retirement.** The issuer of a *bond* promises to pay the buyer a certain amount of money by a specified future date, usually with interest paid at regular intervals. U.S. *government bonds* are backed by government institutions and agencies such as the Treasury Department or the Federal Housing Administration. *Municipal bonds*, which are offered by state and local governments to finance a variety of projects, are also usually safe, and the interest is ordinarily tax exempt. *Corporate bonds* are issued by companies to gain long-term funding. They may be secured (backed by pledges of the issuer's assets) or unsecured, and offer varying degrees of safety. The safety of bonds issued by various borrowers is rated by Moody's and Standard & Poor's.

4. **Describe the investment opportunities offered by *mutual funds* and *commodities*.** Like stocks and bonds, *mutual funds*—companies that pool investments to purchase portfolios of financial instruments—offer investors different levels of risk and growth potential. *Load funds* require investors to pay commissions of 2 to 8 percent. *No-load funds* do not charge commissions when investors buy in or out. *Futures contracts*—agreements to buy specified amounts of commodities at given prices on preset dates—are traded in the *commodities market*. Commodities traders often buy on *margins*—percentages of total sales prices that must be put up to order futures contracts.

5. **Explain the process by which securities are bought and sold.** Investors generally use such *financial information* services as newspaper stock, bond, and OTC quotations to learn about possible investments. *Market indexes* such as the Dow Jones Industrial Average and Standard & Poor's Composite Index provide useful summaries of trends, both in specific industries and in the market as a whole. Investors can then place different types of orders. *Market orders* are orders to buy or sell at current prevailing prices. Because investors do not know exactly what prices will be when market orders are executed, they may issue *limit* or *stop orders* that are to be executed only if prices rise to or fall below specified levels. *Round lots* are purchased in multiples of 100 shares. Odd lots are purchased in fractions of round lots. Securities can be bought on margin or as part of *short sales*—sales in which investors sell securities that are borrowed from brokers and returned at a later date.

6. **Explain how securities markets are regulated.** To protect investors, *the Securities and Exchange Commission (SEC)* regulates the public offering of new securities and enforces laws against such practices as *insider trading* (using special knowledge about a firm for profit or gain). To guard against fraudulent stock issues, the SEC lays down guidelines for *prospectuses*—statements of information about stocks and their issuers. Many state governments also prosecute the sale of fraudulent securities as well as enforce *blue-sky laws*, which require dealers to be licensed and registered where they conduct business.

QUESTIONS AND EXERCISES

Questions for Review

1. What are the purposes of the primary and secondary markets for securities?
2. Which of the three measures of common stock value is most important? Why?
3. How do government, municipal, and corporate bonds differ from one another?

4. How might an investor lose money in a commodities trade?
5. How does the Securities and Exchange Commission regulate securities markets?

Questions for Analysis

6. What are your personal financial goals for the future? What types of stocks, bonds, or mutual funds would be best for meeting those goals? Why?
7. Which type of mutual fund would be most appropriate for your investment purposes at this time? Why?
8. Using a newspaper, select an example of a recent day's transactions for each of the following: a stock on the NYSE, a stock on the AMEX, an OTC stock, a bond on the NYSE, and a mutual fund. Explain the meaning of each element in the listing.

Application Exercises

9. Interview the financial manager of a local business or your school. What are the investment goals of this person's organization? What securities does it use? What advantages and disadvantages do you see in its portfolio?
10. Either in person or through a toll-free number, contact a broker and request information about setting up a personal account for trading securities. Prepare a report on the broker's policies regarding the following: buy/sell orders, credit terms, cash account requirements, services available to investors, and commissions/fees schedules.

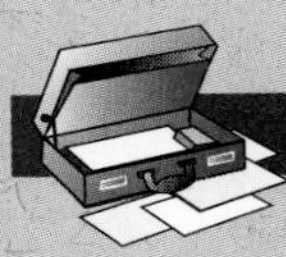

BUILDING YOUR BUSINESS SKILLS

MARKET UPS AND DOWNS

This exercise enhances the following SCANS workplace competencies: demonstrating basic skills, demonstrating thinking skills, exhibiting interpersonal skills, and working with information.

▼ Goal

To encourage students to understand the forces that affect fluctuations in stock price.

▼ Background

Investing in stocks requires an understanding of the various factors that affect stock price. These factors may be intrinsic to the company itself or part of the external environment.

- Internal factors relate to the company itself, such as an announcement of poor or favorable earnings, earnings that are more or less than expected, major layoffs, labor problems, management issues, and mergers.
- External factors relate to world or national events, such as a threatened war in the Persian Gulf, the Asian currency crisis, weather conditions that affect sales, the Federal Reserve Board's adjustment of interest rates, and employment figures that were higher or lower than expected.

By analyzing these factors, you will often learn a lot about why a stock did well or why it did poorly. Being aware of these influences will help you anticipate future stock movements.

▼ Method

STEP 1

Working alone, choose a common stock that has experienced considerable price fluctuations in the past few years. Here are several examples, but there are many others: IBM, Chase Manhattan Bank, AT&T, Southern New England Telephone, Oxford Health Care, and Apple

(*continued*)

Computer. Find the symbol for the stock (for example, Chase Manhattan Bank is CMB) and the exchange on which it is traded (CMB is traded on the New York Stock Exchange).

STEP 2

At your library, find the *Daily Stock Price Record*, a publication that provides a historical picture of daily stock closings. There are separate copies for the New York Stock Exchange, the American Stock Exchange, and the OTC markets. Find your stock and study its trading pattern.

STEP 3

Find 4 or 5 days over a period of several months or even a year when there have been major price fluctuations in the stock. (A two- or three-point price change from one day to the next is considered major.) Then research what happened on that day that might have contributed to the fluctuation. The best place to begin is with *The Wall Street Journal* or on the business pages of a national newspaper, such as *The New York Times* or *The Washington Post.*

STEP 4

Write a short analysis that links changes in stock price to internal and external factors. As you analyze the data, be aware that sometimes it is difficult to know why a stock price fluctuates.

STEP 5

Get together with three other students who studied different stocks. As a group, discuss your findings, looking for fluctuation patterns.

▼ Follow-Up Questions

1. Do you see any similarities in the movement of the various stocks during the same period? For example, did the stocks move up or down at about the same time? If so, do you think the stocks were affected by the same factors? Explain your thinking.
2. Based on your analysis, did internal or external factors have the greatest impact on stock price? Which factors had the most long-lasting effect? Which factors had the shortest effect?
3. Why do you think it is so hard to predict changes in stock price on a day-to-day basis?

CRAFTING YOUR BUSINESS PLAN

UNDERSTANDING SECURITIES AND INVESTMENTS

▼ Purpose of the Assignment

1. To acquaint students with the process of navigating the Business PlanPro (BPP) software package.
2. To familiarize students with securities and investments issues that a sample firm may face in developing its business plan.
3. To demonstrate how three chapter topics—equity financing, debt financing, and securities markets—can be integrated as components in the BPP planning environment.

▼ Assignment

After reading Chapter 16 in the textbook, open the BPP software and look around for information about financial plans, equity financing, and debt financing as they apply to a sample firm: Sample Software Company. Then respond to the following questions:*

1. Evaluate Sample Software's use of debt and equity to finance its operations. Does the company have any outstanding stock? Does it plan to issue stock in the future? Explain the basis for your answers. [Sites to see in *BPP* (for this assignment): In the Task Manager screen, click on Financial Plan. Then click on **1. Financial Plan Summary.**]
2. Evaluate the soundness of Sample Software's plans for using debt versus equity capital. How much financing will be needed according to this plan, and at what points in time? What equity sources are available for meeting the firm's financial needs? What debt sources are available? [Sites to see in *BPP:* In the Task Manager screen, click on The Bottom Line. Then click on **2. Explain Your Assumptions.** Next click on Finish and Polish and then on **6. Executive Summary.**]
3. Based on the company's "net profit" projections, at what points in time will Sample Software be able to pay dividends or repay its debt obligations? [Sites to see in *BPP:* In the Task Manager screen, click on The Bottom Line. Then click on **3. Profit and Loss Table** and **4. Profit and Loss Text.**]
4. According to the company's plans, will Sample Software qualify for listing on a stock exchange? If so, which exchange is best suited for it? If it will not qualify, explain why. [Sites to see in *BPP:* In the Task Manager screen, click on Financial Plan. Then click on **1. Financial Plan Summary.**]

▼ For your Own Business Plan

5. What type of financing—debt or equity—are you going to propose in the business plan that you are developing? How will you explain in your plan the reasons for your choice? In what section(s) of the BPP planning document will you present your plans for financing your business?

▼ *General Tips for Navigating in BPP

1. Open the BPP program, examine the Welcome screen, and click on **Open a Sample Plan.**
2. From the Open a Sample Plan dialogue box, click on a sample company name. Then click on **Open.**
3. On the Task Manager screen, click onto any of the lines (for example, **Your Company**).
4. You can always return to the Task Manager screen by going to the bottom of the screen and clicking on the **Task Manager** icon.
5. When you are finished with a sample company, close its Task Manager screen. After finishing with one sample company, you can get to the next one by going to the top of the screen and clicking on **File** (on the menu bar). Then beneath that, select **Open Sample Plan.** This will exit you from the current company file and send you to the Open a Sample Plan dialogue box, where you can select your next sample company.

EXPLORING THE NET

WHAT TO DO DURING TRADING HOURS

Because stock market action can be fast and furious, up-to-date information is a must for most investors. Current regulations allow information about sales to become publicly available only minutes after transactions have been made on the stock markets. To get an idea of the types of information available on the Internet, access the Web site maintained by NASDAQ at

http://www.nasdaq.com.

To observe the process and results of trading activity, both current and past, explore the diverse information that this Web site provides to potential investors. Accessing it during actual daytime trading hours enables you to see minute-to-minute changes. On the initial NASDAQ-AMEX screen, for example, examine "Site Map and Tour" for an overview of the NASDAQ system. Explore the **Symbol Look-up** option as well as **Quotes for NASDAQ, AMEX & NYSE.** The **Reference** option accesses foreign stock exchanges throughout the world. Now consider the following questions:

1. What is the NASDAQ Composite Index? How many and what types of companies are included in it? Compare it with the Dow Jones Industrial Average Index. Which of the indexes is more representative of overall market activity? Why?
2. Select any two stocks (from the newspaper or other source). Using the **Symbol Look-up** option on the initial screen, examine the volatility of the stocks' values during the past 6 months. Which stock was most volatile? What was the percentage change (from high to low) during the 6 months? [To get there, first look up the stock's symbol, enter it, and click on **Get InfoQuotes.** Then click on **Charting,** set the selector on **6 month,** then click on **Get Chart.**]
3. Select any two mutual funds (from the newspaper or other source). Using the **Symbol Look-up** option on the initial screen, examine the volatility of the funds' values during the past 6 months. Which of the funds was most volatile? What was the percentage change (from high to low) during the 6 months?
4. Compare and contrast the operations of any major U.S. stock exchange (NYSE, AMEX, NASDAQ) with other exchanges by accessing the **Reference** option on the initial screen. In addition to the U.S. Regional group, how many groups of foreign exchanges are available for examination? Select any two exchanges from different groups and examine their operations as described in their Web sites. In what ways are they similar to and in what ways do they differ from the U.S. stock exchanges?
5. Select the **News** option and explore some current news releases. How recently were these news items published? Why do you think NASDAQ displays these news releases at its Web site?
6. Using the **News** option, can you find a news release that might influence investors to buy or sell the stock of a particular company? An item that might influence investors to trade the stocks of companies in a particular industry?

Show Me the Money

Learning Objectives

The purpose of this video is to help you

1. Understand the challenges all businesses face in raising capital.
2. Appreciate how the financial management process varies among different businesses.

Background Information

Like all businesses, Showtime is confronted by two primary financial issues. The first is how Showtime manages its financial affairs. The second is how Showtime acquires the tremendous amounts of capital required for its many projects. Showtime relies on its track record to persuade investors that the next generation of programming will hit its mark with viewers.

The Video

Raising capital for growth is a significant challenge for many businesses. Showtime certainly has options that other smaller, less-established businesses do not. The issues discussed in Part Six of this video can be a way to show how the financial management at Showtime differs from the financial management of other types of businesses.

Discussion Questions

1. What are some of the issues that a company must face in raising capital for expansion?
2. Why is it important to identify and manage the risks inherent in a business?

Follow-Up Assignment

Review the information you gathered about Intel from doing the follow-up assignment in Part Two of the Showtime video. Discuss how financial management at Showtime differs from Intel. What issues are of primary concern at Showtime? What issues would require the most attention at Intel? If you were responsible for hiring a chief financial officer at Intel, how would you feel about hiring Showtime's current CFO?

For Further Exploration

Go to the Business Finance Web site:

http://www.businessfinance.com/propres.shtml

Read the information provided in the Funding Workbook. What are some of the most important issues in raising capital for a small business? What are some of the common pitfalls? What are some key issues in preparing income projections?

VIDEO EXERCISE 6.2

SMALL BUSINESS 2000

On Target Supplies and Logistics

Learning Objectives

The purpose of this video exercise is to help you

1. See that getting a new business started can sometimes require a very long day.
2. Understand that just as important as serving customers is providing a satisfying work environment for employees.
3. Gain an understanding about the importance of networking.

Background Information

We are introduced to Albert Black, MBA, the founder of **On Target Supplies and Logistics** of Dallas, Texas. The business furnishes its customers with copy paper and computer paper, and it also provides virtual warehousing services. To stress the point that small businesses often need big businesses for clients, we learn that **On Target Supplies and Logistics** services such giants as EDS (Electronic Data Systems), Texas Instruments, Southwestern Bell, Texas Utilities, Lone Star Gas, and NationsBank. In delivering its products, Black explains, **On Target** doesn't just deliver to the client's company—it delivers to the desktops of individuals in the client's firm.

Meeting Albert Black is an inspiring experience. Raised in the ghetto, he took on his first business venture at age 8, renting a push mower and cutting grass for 50 cents a yard. After finishing college, he wanted to establish a business in the inner city that would create jobs so that people living there could improve their lives. He saw this as "God's work." But getting started was not easy. He could not live on what **On Target** could pay, so to supplement that income he worked in the computer facilities of Texas Utilities from 5:00 P.M. until 1:00 A.M. He would then work at **On Target** from 7:00 A.M. until 5:00 P.M. We learn that he kept up this two-job arrangement for 10 years. Clearly, Albert Black is no ordinary man.

Albert's heavy voluntary involvement in community-oriented activities aimed at improving the inner city has given his firm visibility. It also enabled him to attract EDS executive John Castle as chairman of the board of directors for **On Target.** John Castle tells us he is impressed by Albert's willingness to learn, and Albert says of John: "He's an angel who has flown into my Christian life."

Albert freely admits that he gets involved in the lives of his employees. **On Target** has a 401K plan, and he encourages his workers to save 20 percent of their pay for future needs. He really pushes education, and **On Target** pays people to go on to college. Black says he is just "doing those things that God would have us do."

The Video

SMALL BUSINESS 2000 MASTER CLASS, SB2000 SERIES 2, SHOW #12. Meeting Albert Black is a very worthwhile experience. You'll learn plenty about running a highly successful business operation. But there is so much more here. Albert Black provides his employees with not only a place to earn a living but also the opportunity to see life itself in a totally different way.

Discussion Questions

1. Recall that Albert Black was working two full-time jobs at the same time. Do you think such an investment is necessary for a new entrepreneur to succeed? Why or why not?

2. Consider and discuss the impact that Albert's father, mother, and grandmother had on his growing up and on his present way of life.
3. Hattie Bryant's strategist indicates in his short commentary that "warehousing will become obsolete." What did he see replacing it? Where will manufactured products be stored?
4. We meet John Castle of EDS, chairman of the board of directors of **On Target.** Explain how important the relationship between Albert and John has been to **On Target.** With that fine relationship in mind, comment on this statement: "You know, really, no one can ever serve as a *mentor* unless that *mentor* has someone who is *willing to learn.*"
5. Think back to the moment on the videotape when Albert Black talks about suggesting to an employee that that person continue with education. Just how strong do employees consider such a suggestion to be?
6. Albert Black speaks of "educational income" from working with his firm. What does he mean by this term?
7. Comment upon Hattie Bryant's mention that small businesses need big businesses as customers. When this does occur, is it a good idea to have executives of the big businesses sitting on the boards of the small businesses? Why or why not?
8. Explain how you think Albert Black's networking around Dallas has been essential to his success with **On Target.**

Follow-Up Assignment

Find out more about firms in your area that follow the **On Target** example by paying for their employees to take college courses. When you complete your bachelor's degree and take a full-time job, you could very well be interested in obtaining a master's degree. The effort would be far easier if your boss encouraged you. Ask your business professor about it, and then contact some prospective employers. For sure, **On Target** is not the only firm in America offering this golden opportunity.

The Internet Connection and One Last Thing to Remember

As we went to press, **On Target Supplies and Logistics** was in the process of developing its Web site. To find out when they're ready, you could call 214-941-1505.

Albert Black is a religious man, and he is not afraid for you to know it, as he accomplishes "those things that God would have us do." He makes clear to us his priorities: God first, family second, and everything else somewhere after that. Can a man so openly religious make it in today's business world? At least in the case of Albert Black, the answer is obvious.

APPENDIX I

Understanding Financial and Risk Management

THE ROLE OF THE FINANCIAL MANAGER

finance (or **corporate finance**) Activities concerned with determining a firm's long-term investments, obtaining the funds to pay for them, conducting the firm's everyday financial activities, and managing the firm's risks

The business activity known as **finance** (or **corporate finance**) typically entails four responsibilities:

- Determining a firm's long-term investments
- Obtaining funds to pay for those investments
- Conducting the firm's everyday financial activities
- Helping to manage the risks that the firm takes

financial manager Manager responsible for planning and controlling the acquisition and dispersal of a firm's financial resources

As we saw in Chapter 13, production managers plan and control the output of goods and services. In Chapter 10, we saw that marketing managers plan and control the development and marketing of products. Similarly, **financial managers** plan and control the acquisition and dispersal of a firm's financial resources. In this section, we will see in some detail how those activities are channeled into specific plans for protecting—and enhancing—a firm's financial well-being.

Responsibilities of the Financial Manager

Financial managers collect funds, pay debts, establish trade credit, obtain loans, control cash balances, and plan for future financial needs. But a financial manager's overall objective is to increase a firm's value—and thus stockholders' wealth. Whereas accountants create data to reflect a firm's financial status, financial managers make decisions for improving that status. Financial managers, then, must ensure that a company's earnings exceed its costs—in other words, that it earns a profit. In sole proprietorships and partnerships, profits translate directly into increases in owners' wealth. In corporations, profits translate into an increase in the value of common stock.

The various responsibilities of the financial manager in increasing a firm's wealth fall into two general categories: *cash-flow management* and *financial planning*.

cash-flow management Management of cash inflows and outflows to ensure adequate funds for purchases and the productive use of excess funds

CASH-FLOW MANAGEMENT To increase a firm's value, financial managers must ensure that it always has enough funds on hand to purchase the materials and human resources that it needs to produce goods and services. At the same time, of course, there may be funds that are not needed immediately. These must be invested to earn more money for the firm. This activity—**cash-flow management**—requires careful planning. If excess cash balances are allowed to sit idle instead of being invested, a firm loses the cash returns that it could have earned.

How important to a business is the management of its idle cash? One study has revealed that companies averaging $2 million in annual sales typically hold $40,000 in noninterest-bearing accounts. Larger companies hold even larger sums. More and more companies, however, are learning that these idle funds can become working funds. By locating idle cash and putting it to work, for instance, they can avoid borrowing from outside sources. The savings on interest payments can be substantial.

financial plan A firm's strategies for reaching some future financial position

FINANCIAL PLANNING The cornerstone of effective financial management is the development of a financial plan. A **financial plan** describes a firm's strategies for reaching some future financial position. In constructing the plan, a financial manager must ask several questions:

- What amount of funds does the company need to meet immediate needs?
- When will it need more funds?
- Where can it get the funds to meet both its short- and long-term needs?

To answer these questions, a financial manager must develop a clear picture of why a firm needs funds. Managers must also assess the relative costs and benefits of potential funding sources. In the sections that follow, we will examine the main reasons for which companies generate funds and describe the main sources of business funding, both for the short term and the long term.

WHY DO BUSINESSES NEED FUNDS?

Every company must spend money to survive: According to the simplest formula, funds that are spent on materials, wages, and buildings eventually lead to the creation of products, revenues, and profits. In planning for funding requirements, financial managers must distinguish between two different kinds of expenditures: *short-term (operating)* and *long-term (capital) expenditures.*

Short-Term (Operating) Expenditures

Short-term expenditures are incurred regularly in a firm's everyday business activities. To manage these outlays, managers must pay special attention to *accounts payable*, *accounts receivable*, and *inventories.* We will also describe the measures used by some firms in managing the funds known as *working capital.*

ACCOUNTS PAYABLE In Chapter 14, we defined *accounts payable* as unpaid bills owed to suppliers plus wages and taxes due within the upcoming year. For most companies, this is the largest single category of short-term debt. To plan for funding flows, financial managers want to know *in advance* the amounts of new accounts payable as well as when they must be repaid. For information about such obligations and needs—say, the quantity of supplies required by a certain department in an upcoming period—financial managers must rely on other managers.

ACCOUNTS RECEIVABLE As we also saw in Chapter 14, *accounts receivable* consist of funds due from customers who have bought on credit. A sound financial plan requires financial managers to project accurately both how much and when buyers will make payments on these accounts. For example, managers at Kraft Foods must know how many dollars' worth of cheddar cheese Kroger's supermarkets will order each month; they must also know Kroger's payment schedule. Because they represent an investment in products for which a firm has not yet received payment, accounts receivable temporarily tie up its funds. Clearly, the seller wants to receive payment as quickly as possible.

INVENTORIES Between the time a firm buys raw materials and the time it sells finished products, it ties up funds in **inventory**—materials and goods that it will sell within the year.

inventory Materials and goods which are held by a company but which will be sold within the year

Failure to manage inventory can have grave financial consequences. Too little inventory of any kind can cost a firm sales. Too much inventory means tied-up funds that cannot be used elsewhere. In extreme cases, a company may have to sell excess inventory at low profits simply to raise cash.

WORKING CAPITAL Basically, **working capital** consists of a firm's current assets on hand. It is a liquid asset out of which current debts can be paid. A company calculates its working capital by adding up the following:

working capital Liquid current assets out of which a firm can pay current debts

- Inventories—that is, raw materials, work-in-process, and finished goods on hand
- Accounts receivable (minus accounts payable)

How much money is tied up in working capital? Fortune 500 companies typically devote 20 cents of every sales dollar—about $800 billion total—to working capital. What are the benefits of reducing these sums? There are two very important pluses:

1. Every dollar that is not tied up in working capital becomes a dollar of more useful cash flow.
2. Reduction of working capital raises earnings permanently.

The second advantage results from the fact that money costs money (in interest payments and the like). Reducing working capital, therefore, means saving money.

Long-Term (Capital) Expenditures

In addition to needing funds for operating expenditures, companies need funds to cover long-term expenditures on fixed assets. As we saw in Chapter 14, *fixed assets* are items with long-term use or value, such as land, buildings, and machinery.

Long-term expenditures are usually more carefully planned than short-term outlays because they pose special problems. They differ from short-term outlays in the following ways, all of which influence the ways that long-term outlays are funded:

- Unlike inventories and other short-term assets, they are not normally sold or converted into cash.
- Their acquisition requires a very large investment.
- They represent a binding commitment of company funds that continues long into the future.

■ SOURCES OF SHORT-TERM FUNDS

Firms can call on many sources for the funds they need to finance day-to-day operations and to implement short-term plans. These sources include *trade credit* and *secured* and *unsecured loans.*

Trade Credit

trade credit Granting of credit by one firm to another

open-book credit Form of trade credit in which sellers ship merchandise on faith that payment will be forthcoming

Accounts payable are not merely expenditures. They also constitute a source of funds for the buying company. Until it pays its bill, the buyer has the use of *both* the purchased product *and* the price of the product. This situation results when the seller grants **trade credit,** which is effectively a short-term loan from one firm to another. The most common form of trade credit, **open-book credit,** is essentially a "gentlemen's agreement." Buyers receive merchandise along with invoices stating credit terms. Sellers ship products on faith that payment will be forthcoming.

Secured Short-Term Loans

secured loan Loan for which the borrower must provide collateral

collateral Borrower-pledged legal asset that may be seized by lenders in case of nonpayment

For most firms, bank loans are a very important source of short-term funding. Such loans almost always involve promissory notes in which the borrower promises to repay the loan plus interest. In **secured loans,** banks also require **collateral:** a legal interest in certain assets that can be seized if payments are not made as promised.

Secured loans allow borrowers to get funds when they might not qualify for unsecured credit. Moreover, they generally carry lower interest rates than unsecured loans. Collateral may be in the form of inventories or accounts receivable, and most businesses have other types of assets that can be pledged. Some, for instance, own marketable securities, such as stocks or bonds of other companies (see Chapter 16). Many more own fixed assets, such as land, buildings, or equipment. Fixed assets, however, are generally used to secure long-term rather than short-term loans. Most short-term business borrowing is secured by inventories and accounts receivable.

When a loan is made with inventory as a collateral asset, the lender loans the borrower some portion of the stated value of the inventory. When accounts receivable are used as collateral, the process is called **pledging accounts receivable.** In the event of nonpayment, the lender may seize the receivables—that is, funds owed the borrower by its customers.

pledging accounts receivable Using accounts receivable as loan collateral

Unsecured Short-Term Loans

With an **unsecured loan,** the borrower does not have to put up collateral. In many cases, however, the bank requires the borrower to maintain a *compensating balance:* the borrower must keep a portion of the loan amount on deposit with the bank in a noninterest-bearing account.

unsecured loan Loan for which collateral is not required

The terms of the loan—amount, duration, interest rate, and payment schedule—are negotiated between the bank and the borrower. To receive an unsecured loan, then, a firm must ordinarily have a good banking relationship with the lender. Once an agreement is made, a promissory note will be executed and the funds transferred to the borrower. Although some unsecured loans are one-time-only arrangements, many take the form of *lines of credit, revolving credit agreements,* or *commercial paper.*

A **line of credit** is a standing agreement between a bank and a business in which the bank promises to lend the firm a specified amount of funds on request. **Revolving credit agreements** are similar to consumer bank cards. A lender agrees to make some amount of funds available on demand and on a continuing basis. The lending institution guarantees that these funds will be available when sought by the borrower. In return for this guarantee, the bank charges the borrower a *commitment fee* for holding the line of credit open. This fee is payable even if the customer does not borrow any funds. It is often expressed as a percentage of the loan amount (usually 0.5 to 1 percent of the committed amount).

line of credit Standing arrangement in which a lender agrees to make available a specified amount of funds upon the borrower's request

revolving credit agreement Arrangement in which a lender agrees to make funds available on demand and on a continuing basis

Finally, some firms can raise short-term funds by issuing **commercial paper**—short-term securities, or notes, containing the borrower's promise to pay. Because it is backed solely by the issuing firm's promise to pay, commercial paper is an option for only the largest and most creditworthy firms.

commercial paper Short-term securities, or notes, containing a borrower's promise to pay

How does commercial paper work? Corporations issue commercial paper with a certain face value. Buying companies pay *less* than that value. At the end of a specified period (usually 30 to 90 days, but legally up to 270 days), the issuing company buys back the paper—*at face value.* The difference between the price paid and the face value is the buyer's profit. For the issuing company, the cost is usually lower than prevailing interest rates on short-term loans.

■ SOURCES OF LONG-TERM FUNDS

Firms need long-term funding to finance expenditures on fixed assets: the buildings and equipment necessary for conducting their business. They may seek long-term funds through *debt financing* (that is, from outside the firm) or through *equity financing* (by drawing on internal sources). We will discuss both options in this section, as well as a middle ground called *hybrid financing.* We will also analyze some of the options that enter into decisions about long-term financing, as well as the role of the *risk-return relationship* in attracting investors to a firm.

Debt Financing

debt financing Long-term borrowing from sources outside a company

Long-term borrowing from sources outside the company—**debt financing**—is a major component of most firms' long-term financial planning. Long-term debts are obligations that are payable more than 1 year after they were originally issued. The two primary sources of such funding are *long-term loans* and the sale of *corporate bonds*.

LONG-TERM LOANS Most corporations get long-term loans from commercial banks, usually those with which they have developed longstanding relationships. Credit companies (such as Household Finance Corp.), insurance companies, and pension funds also grant long-term business loans.

Long-term loans are attractive to borrowers for several reasons:

- Because the number of parties involved is limited, loans can often be arranged very quickly.
- The firm need not make public disclosure of its business plans or the purpose for which it is acquiring the loan. (In contrast, the issuance of corporate bonds requires such disclosure.)
- The duration of the loan can easily be matched to the borrower's needs.
- If the firm's needs change, loans usually contain clauses making it possible to change terms.

Long-term loans also have some disadvantages. Borrowers, for instance, may have trouble finding lenders to supply large sums. Long-term borrowers may also face restrictions as conditions of the loan. For example, they may have to pledge long-term assets as collateral or agree to take on no more debt until the loan is paid.

CORPORATE BONDS As we saw in Chapter 16, a *corporate bond*, like commercial paper, is a contract—a promise by the issuer to pay the holder a certain amount of money on a specified date. Unlike issuers of commercial paper, however, bond issuers do not pay off quickly. In many cases, bonds may not be redeemable for 30 years. Also, unlike commercial paper, most bonds pay bondholders a stipulated sum of annual or semiannual interest. If the company fails to make a bond payment, it is said to be *in default*.

Bonds are the major source of long-term debt financing for most corporations. They are attractive when firms need large amounts for long periods of time. The issuing company also gains access to large numbers of lenders through nationwide bond markets and stock exchanges. On the other hand, bonds entail high administrative and selling costs. They may also require stiff interest payments, especially if the issuing company has a poor credit rating.

Equity Financing

equity financing Use of common stock and/or retained earnings to raise long-term funding

Although debt financing often has strong appeal, looking inside the company for long-term funding is sometimes preferable. In small companies, for example, founders may increase personal investments in their own firms. In most cases, **equity financing** means issuing common stock or retaining the firm's earnings. Both options involve putting the owners' capital to work.

COMMON STOCK People who purchase common stock seek profits in two forms—dividends and appreciation. Overall, shareholders hope for an increase in the market value of their stock (appreciation) because the firm has profited and grown. By issuing shares of stock, the company gets the funds it needs for buying land, buildings, and equipment.

Suppose, for example, that Sunshine Tanning's founders invested $10,000 by buying the original 500 shares of common stock (at $20 per share) in 1990. The company used these funds to buy equipment, and it succeeded financially. By 1996, then, it needed funds for expansion. A pattern of profitable operations and regularly paid dividends now allows Sunshine to raise $50,000 by selling 500 new shares of stock at $100 per share. This $50,000 would constitute *paid-in capital*—additional money, above the par value of its original stock sale, paid directly to a firm by its owners (see Chapter 14). As Table AI.1 shows, this additional paid-in capital would increase total stockholders' equity to $60,000.

RETAINED EARNINGS Again, recall our discussion in Chapter 14, where we defined *retained earnings* as profits retained for the firm's use rather than paid out in dividends. If

TABLE AI.1 ◆ **Stockholders' Equity for Sunshine Tanning**

COMMON STOCKHOLDERS' EQUITY, 1990	
Initial common stock (500 shares issued @ $20 per share, 1990)	$10,000
Total stockholders' equity	$10,000
COMMON STOCKHOLDERS' EQUITY, 1996	
Initial common stock (500 shares issued @ $20 per share, 1990)	$10,000
Additional paid-in capital (500 shares issued @ $100 per share, 1996)	50,000
Total stockholders' equity	$60,000

a company uses retained earnings as capital, it will not have to borrow money and pay interest. If a firm has a history of reaping profits by reinvesting retained earnings, it may be very attractive to some investors. Retained earnings, however, mean smaller dividends for shareholders. In this sense, then, the practice may decrease the demand for—and thus the price of—the company's stock.

For example, if Sunshine Tanning had net earnings of $50,000 in 1996, it could pay a $50-per-share dividend on its 1,000 shares of common stock. Let's say, however, that Sunshine plans to remodel at a cost of $30,000, intending to retain $30,000 in earnings to finance the project. Only $20,000—$20 per share—will be available for shareholders.

Hybrid Financing: Preferred Stock

A middle ground between debt financing and equity financing is the use of preferred stock (see Chapter 16). Preferred stock is a "hybrid" because it has some of the features of both corporate bonds and common stocks. As with bonds, for instance, payments on preferred stock are fixed amounts such as $6 per share per year. Unlike bonds, however, preferred stock never matures; like common stock, it can be held indefinitely. In addition, preferred stocks have first rights (over common stock) to dividends.

A major advantage to the issuer is the flexibility of preferred stock. Because preferred stockholders have no voting rights, the stock secures funds for the firm without jeopardizing corporate control of its management. Furthermore, corporations are not obligated to repay the principal and can withhold payment of dividends in lean times.

Choosing between Debt and Equity Financing

Needless to say, an aspect of financial planning is striking a balance between debt and equity financing. Because a firm relies on a mix of debt and equity to raise the cash needed for capital outlays, that mix is called its **capital structure.** Financial plans thus contain targets for capital structure; an example would be 40 percent debt and 60 percent equity. But choosing a target is not easy. A wide range of mixes is possible, and strategies range from conservative to risky.

capital structure Relative mix of a firm's debt and equity financing

The most conservative strategy is all-equity financing and no debt: a company has no formal obligations to make financial payouts. As we have seen, however, equity is an expensive source of capital. The riskiest strategy is all-debt financing. Although less expensive than equity funding, indebtedness increases the risk that a firm will be unable to meet its obligations (and even go bankrupt). Somewhere between the two extremes, financial planners try to find mixes that will increase stockholders' wealth with a reasonable exposure to risk.

The Risk-Return Relationship

While developing plans for raising capital, financial managers must be aware of the different motivations of individual investors. Why, for example, do some individuals and firms invest in stocks while others invest only in bonds? Investor motivations, of course, determine who is willing to buy a given company's stocks or bonds. Investors give money to firms and, in return, anticipate receiving future cash flows. Thus everyone who invests money is expressing a personal preference for safety versus risk.

In other words, some cash flows are more certain than others. Investors generally expect to receive higher payments for higher uncertainty. They do not generally expect large returns for secure investments like government-insured bonds. Each type of investment, then, has a **risk-return relationship** reflecting the principle that whereas safer investments tend to offer lower returns, riskier investments tend to offer higher returns.

risk-return relationship Principle that, whereas safer investments tend to offer lower returns, riskier investments tend to offer higher returns

Risk-return differences are recognized by financial planners, who try to gain access to the greatest funding at the lowest possible cost. By gauging investors' perceptions of their riskiness, a firm's managers can estimate how much they must pay to attract funds to their offerings. Over time, a company can reposition itself on the risk continuum by improving its record on dividends, interest payments, and debt repayment.

■ FINANCIAL MANAGEMENT FOR SMALL BUSINESS

As we saw in Chapter 7, new business success and failure are often closely related to adequate or inadequate funding. For example, one study of nearly 3,000 new companies revealed a survival rate of 84 percent for new businesses with initial investments of at least $50,000. Unfortunately, those with less funding have a much lower survival rate. Why are so many start-ups underfunded? For one thing, entrepreneurs often underestimate the value of establishing *bank credit* as a source of funds and use trade credit ineffectively. In addition, they often fail to consider *venture capital* as a source of funding, and they are notorious for not planning *cash-flow needs* properly.

ESTABLISHING BANK AND TRADE CREDIT Some banks have liberal credit policies and offer financial analysis, cash-flow planning, and suggestions based on experiences with other local firms. Some provide loans to small businesses in bad times and work to keep them going. Some, of course, do not. Obtaining credit, therefore, begins with finding a bank that can—and will—support a small firm's financial needs. Once a line of credit is obtained, the small business can seek more liberal credit policies from other businesses. Sometimes, for instance, suppliers give customers longer credit periods—say, 45 or 60 days rather than 30 days. Liberal trade credit terms with their suppliers let firms increase short-term funds and avoid additional borrowing from banks.

LONG-TERM FUNDING Naturally, obtaining long-term loans is more difficult for new businesses than for established companies. With unproven repayment ability, start-up firms can expect to pay higher interest rates than older firms. If a new enterprise displays evidence of sound financial planning, however, the Small Business Administration (see Chapter 7) may support a guaranteed loan.

VENTURE CAPITAL Many newer businesses—especially those undergoing rapid growth—cannot get the funds they need through borrowing alone. They may, therefore, turn to **venture capital:** outside equity funding provided in return for part ownership of the borrowing firm. *Venture capital firms* actively seek chances to invest in new firms with rapid growth potential. Because failure rates are high, they typically demand high returns, which are now often 20 to 30 percent.

venture capital Outside equity financing provided in return for part ownership of the borrowing firm

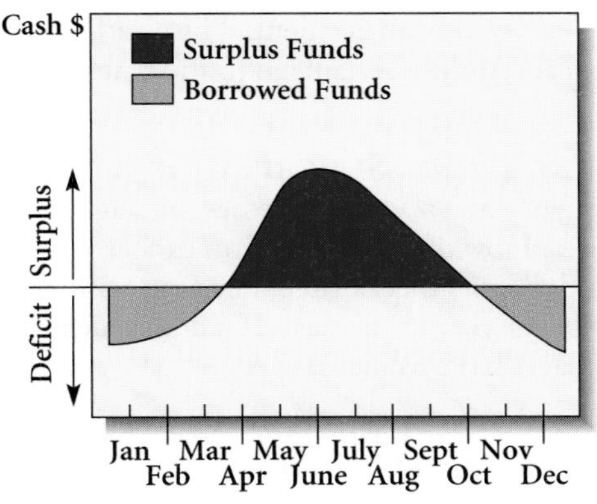

FIGURE AI.1 ◆ **Projected Cash Flow for Slippery Fish Bait Supply Co.**

Planning for Cash-Flow Requirements

Although all businesses should plan for their cash flows, this planning is especially important for small businesses. Success or failure may hinge on anticipating those times when either cash will be short or excess cash can be expected.

Figure AI.1 shows possible cash inflows, cash outflows, and net cash position (inflows minus outflows) month by month for Slippery Fish Bait Supply—a highly seasonal business. As you can see, bait stores buy heavily from Slippery during the spring and summer months. Revenues outpace expenses, leaving surplus funds that can be invested. During the fall and winter, however, expenses exceed revenues. Slippery must borrow funds to keep going until revenues pick up again in the spring. Comparing predicted cash inflows from sales with outflows for expenses shows the firm's expected monthly cash-flow position.

Such knowledge can be invaluable for the small business manager. By anticipating shortfalls, for example, a financial manager can seek funds in advance and minimize their cost. By anticipating excess cash, a manager can plan to put the funds to work in short-term, interest-earning investments.

■ RISK MANAGEMENT

Financial risks are not the only risks faced every day by companies (and individuals). In this section, we will describe various other types of risks that businesses face and analyze some of the ways in which they typically manage them.

Coping with Risk

Businesses constantly face two basic types of **risk**—that is, uncertainty about future events. **Speculative risks,** such as financial investments, involve the possibility of gain or loss. **Pure risks** involve only the possibility of loss or no loss. Designing and distributing a new product, for example, is a speculative risk. The product may fail, or it may succeed and earn high profits. In contrast, the chance of a warehouse fire is a pure risk.

For a company to survive and prosper, it must manage both types of risk in a cost-effective manner. We can thus define the process of **risk management** as "conserving the firm's earning power and assets by reducing the threat of losses due to uncontrollable events." In every company, each manager must be alert for risks to the firm and their impact on profits. The risk-management process usually entails five steps.

risk Uncertainty about future events

speculative risk Risk involving the possibility of gain or loss

pure risk Risk involving only the possibility of loss or no loss

risk management Process of conserving the firm's earning power and assets by reducing the threat of losses due to uncontrollable events

STEP 1: IDENTIFY RISKS AND POTENTIAL LOSSES Managers analyze a firm's risks to identify potential losses. For example, a firm with a fleet of delivery trucks can expect that one of them will eventually be involved in an accident. The accident may cause bodily injury to the driver or others, may cause physical damage to the truck or other vehicles, or both.

STEP 2: MEASURE THE FREQUENCY AND SEVERITY OF LOSSES AND THEIR IMPACT To measure the frequency and severity of losses, managers must consider both past history and current activities. How often can the firm expect the loss to occur? What is the likely size of the loss in dollars? For example, our firm with the fleet of delivery trucks may have had two accidents per year in the past. If it adds trucks, however, it may reasonably expect the frequency of accidents to increase.

STEP 3: EVALUATE ALTERNATIVES AND CHOOSE THE TECHNIQUES THAT WILL BEST HANDLE THE LOSSES Having identified and measured potential losses, managers are in a better position to decide how to handle them. With this third step, they generally have four choices: *risk avoidance*, *control*, *retention*, or *transfer*.

risk avoidance Practice of avoiding risk by declining or ceasing to participate in an activity

Risk Avoidance. A firm opts for **risk avoidance** by declining to enter or by ceasing to participate in a risky activity. For example, the firm with the delivery trucks could avoid any risk of physical damage or bodily injury by closing down its delivery service. Similarly, a pharmaceutical maker may withdraw a new drug for fear of liability suits.

risk control Practice of minimizing the frequency or severity of losses from risky activities

Risk Control. When avoidance is not practical or desirable, firms can practice **risk control**—say, the use of loss-prevention techniques to minimize the frequency of losses. A delivery service, for instance, can prevent losses by training its drivers in defensive-driving techniques, mapping out safe routes, and conscientiously maintaining its trucks.

risk retention Practice of covering a firm's losses with its own funds

Risk Retention. When losses cannot be avoided or controlled, firms must cope with the consequences. When such losses are manageable and predictable, they may decide to cover them out of company funds. The firm is thus said to "assume" or "retain" the financial consequences of the loss: hence the practice known as **risk retention.** For example, our firm with the fleet of trucks may find that vehicles suffer vandalism totaling $100 to $500 per year. Depending on its coverage, the company may find it cheaper to pay for repairs out of pocket rather than to submit claims to its insurance company.

risk transfer Practice of transferring a firm's risk to another firm

Risk Transfer. When the potential for large risks cannot be avoided or controlled, managers often opt for **risk transfer.** They transfer the risk to another firm—namely, an insurance company. In transferring risk to an insurance company, a firm pays a sum called a premium. In return, the insurance company issues an insurance policy—a formal agreement to pay the policyholder a specified amount in the event of certain losses. In some cases, the insured party must also pay a deductible—an agreed-upon amount of the loss that the insured must absorb prior to reimbursement. Thus, our hypothetical company may buy insurance to protect itself against theft, physical damage to trucks, and bodily injury to drivers and others involved in an accident.

STEP 4: IMPLEMENT THE RISK-MANAGEMENT PROGRAM The means of implementing risk-management decisions depends on both the technique chosen and the activity being managed. For example, risk avoidance for certain activities can be implemented by purchasing those activities from outside providers—say, hiring delivery services instead of operating delivery vehicles. Risk control might be implemented by training employees and designing new work methods and equipment for on-the-job safety. For situations in which risk retention is preferred, reserve funds can be set aside out of revenues. When risk transfer is needed, implementation means selecting an insurance company and buying the right policies.

STEP 5: MONITOR RESULTS Because risk management is an ongoing activity, follow-up is always essential. New types of risks, for example, emerge with changes in customers, facilities, employees, and products. Insurance regulations change, and new types of insurance become available. Consequently, managers must continually monitor a company's risks, reevaluate the methods used for handling them, and revise them as necessary.

Insurance as Risk Management

To deal with some risks, both businesses and individuals may choose to purchase one or more of the products offered by insurance companies. Buyers find insurance appealing for a very basic reason: in return for a relatively small sum of money, they are protected against certain losses, some of them potentially devastating. In this sense, buying insurance is a function of risk management. To define it as a management activity dealing with insurance, we can thus amplify our definition of *risk management* to say that it is the logical development and implementation of a plan to deal with chance losses.

With insurance, then, individuals and businesses share risks by contributing to a fund out of which those who suffer losses are paid. But why are insurance companies willing to accept these risks for other companies? Insurance companies make profits by taking in more **premiums** than they pay out to cover policyholders' losses. Quite simply, although many policyholders are paying for protection against the same type of loss, by no means all of them will suffer such a loss.

premium Fee paid by a policyholder for insurance coverage

INSURABLE VERSUS UNINSURABLE RISKS Like every business, insurance companies must avoid certain risks. Insurers thus divide potential sources of loss into *insurable* and *uninsurable risks*. Obviously, they issue policies only for insurable risks. Although there are some exceptions, an insurable risk must meet the four criteria described in the following sections.

Predictability. The insurer must be able to use statistical tools to forecast the likelihood of a loss. For example, an auto insurer needs information about the number of car accidents in the past year to estimate the expected number of accidents for the following year. With this knowledge, the insurer can translate expected numbers and types of accidents into expected dollar losses. The same forecast, of course, also helps insurers determine premiums charged to policyholders.

Casualty. A loss must result from an accident, not from an intentional act by the policyholder. Obviously, insurers do not have to cover damages if a policyholder deliberately sets fire to corporate headquarters. To avoid paying in cases of fraud, insurers may refuse to cover losses when they cannot determine whether policyholders' actions contributed to them.

Unconnectedness. Potential losses must be random and must occur independently of other losses. No insurer can afford to write insurance when a large percentage of those who are exposed to a particular kind of loss are likely to suffer such a loss. One insurance company, for instance, would not want all the hurricane coverage in Miami or all the earthquake coverage in Los Angeles. By carefully choosing the risks that it will insure, an insurance company can reduce its chances of a large loss or even insolvency.

Verifiability. Finally, insured losses must be verifiable as to cause, time, place, and amount. Did an employee develop emphysema because of a chemical to which she was exposed or because she smoked 40 cigarettes a day for 30 years? Did the policyholder pay the renewal premium before the fire destroyed his factory? Were the goods stolen from company offices or from the president's home? What was the insurable value of the destroyed inventory? When all these points have been verified, payment by the insurer goes more smoothly.

THE INSURANCE PRODUCT Insurance companies are often distinguished by the types of insurance coverage they offer. Whereas some insurers offer only one area of coverage—life insurance, for example—others offer a broad range. In this section, we describe the four major categories of business insurance: *liability*, *property*, *life*, and *health*.

Liability Insurance. As we will see in Appendix II, *liability* means responsibility for damages in case of accidental or deliberate harm to individuals or property. **Liability insurance** covers losses resulting from damage to people or property when the insured party is judged liable.

liability insurance Insurance covering losses resulting from damage to people or property when the insured is judged responsible

workers' compensation coverage Coverage provided by a firm to employees for medical expenses, loss of wages, and rehabilitation costs resulting from job-related injuries or disease

property insurance Insurance covering losses resulting from physical damage to or loss of the insured's real estate or personal property

WORKERS' COMPENSATION. A business is liable for any injury to an employee when the injury arises from activities related to occupation. When workers are permanently or temporarily disabled by job-related accidents or disease, employers are required by law to provide **workers' compensation coverage** for medical expenses, loss of wages, and rehabilitation services. U.S. employers now pay out approximately $60 billion in workers' compensation premiums each year, much of it to public insurers.

Property Insurance. Firms purchase **property insurance** to cover injuries to themselves resulting from physical damage to or loss of real estate or personal property. Property losses may result from fire, lightning, wind, hail, explosion, theft, vandalism, or other destructive forces. Losses from fire alone in the United States come to over $10 billion per year.

BUSINESS INTERRUPTION INSURANCE. In some cases, loss to property is minimal in comparison to loss of income. A manufacturer, for example, may have to close down for an extended time while repairs to fire damage are being completed. During that time, of course, the company is not generating income. Even so, however, certain expenses—such as taxes, insurance premiums, and salaries for key personnel—may continue. To cover such losses, a firm may buy **business interruption insurance.**

business interruption insurance Insurance covering income lost during times when a company is unable to conduct business

life insurance Insurance paying benefits to the policyholder's survivors

group life insurance Insurance underwritten for a group as a whole rather than for each individual in it

Life Insurance. Insurance can also protect a company's human assets. As part of their benefits packages, many businesses purchase **life insurance** for employees. Life insurance companies accept premiums in return for the promise to pay beneficiaries after the death of insured parties. A portion of the premium is used to cover the insurer's own expenses. The remainder is invested in various types of financial instruments such as corporate bonds and stocks.

GROUP LIFE INSURANCE. Most companies buy **group life insurance,** which is underwritten for groups as a whole rather than for each individual member. The insurer's assessment of potential losses and its pricing of premiums are based on the characteristics of the whole group. Johnson & Johnson's benefit plan, for example, includes group life coverage with a standard program of protection and benefits—a master policy purchased by J & J—that applies equally to all employees.

health insurance Insurance covering losses resulting from medical and hospital expenses as well as income lost from injury or disease

Health Insurance. **Health insurance** covers losses resulting from medical and hospital expenses as well as income lost from injury or disease. It is, of course, no secret that the cost of health insurance has skyrocketed in recent years. In one recent year, for example, companies paid an average of $3,781 per employee on health insurance premiums to both commercial insurers like Prudential, Metropolitan, and Nationwide and special health insurance providers like Blue Cross/Blue Shield and other organizations called *health maintenance organizations* and *preferred provider organizations.*

disability income insurance Insurance providing continuous income when disability keeps the insured from gainful employment

DISABILITY INCOME INSURANCE. **Disability income insurance** provides continuous income when disability keeps the insured from gainful employment. Many health insurance policies cover "short-term" disabilities, sometimes up to 2 years. Coverage for permanent disability furnishes some stated amount of weekly income—usually 50 to 70 percent of the insured's weekly wages—with payments beginning after a 6-month waiting period. Group policies account for over 70 percent of all disability coverage in the United States.

SPECIAL HEALTH CARE PROVIDERS. Instead of reimbursement for a health professional's services, Blue Cross/Blue Shield, which is made up of nonprofit health care membership groups, provides specific service benefits to its subscribers. Many other commercial insurers do the same. What is the advantage to the subscriber or policyholder? No matter what the service actually costs, the special health care provider will cover the cost. In contrast, when policies provide reimbursement for services received, the policyholder may pay for a portion of the expense if the policy limit is exceeded. Other important options include *HMOs* and *PPOs:*

- A **health maintenance organization (HMO)** is an organized health care system providing comprehensive medical care to its members for a fixed, prepaid fee. In an HMO, all members agree that, except in emergencies, they will receive their health care through the organization.
- A **preferred provider organization (PPO)** is an arrangement whereby selected hospitals and/or doctors agree to provide services at reduced rates and to accept thorough review of their recommendations for medical services. The objective of the PPO is to help control health care costs by encouraging the use of efficient providers' health care services.

health maintenance organization (HMO) Organized health care system providing comprehensive care in return for fixed membership fees

preferred provider organization (PPO) Arrangement whereby selected professional providers offer services at reduced rates and permit thorough review of their service recommendations

SPECIAL FORMS OF BUSINESS INSURANCE Many forms of insurance are attractive to both businesses and individuals. For example, homeowners are as concerned about insuring property from fire and theft as are businesses. Businesses, however, have some special insurable concerns. In this section, we will discuss two forms of insurance that apply to the departure or death of key employees or owners.

Key Person Insurance. Many businesses choose to protect themselves against loss of the talents and skills of key employees. For example, if a salesperson who annually rings up $2.5 million dies or takes a new job, the firm will suffer loss. It will also incur recruitment costs to find a replacement and training expenses once a replacement is hired. **Key person insurance** is designed to offset both lost income and additional expenses.

Business Continuation Agreements. Who takes control of a business when a partner or associate dies? Surviving partners are often faced with the possibility of having to accept an inexperienced heir as a management partner. This contingency can be handled in **business continuation agreements,** whereby owners make plans to buy the ownership interest of a deceased associate from his or her heirs. The value of the ownership interest is determined when the agreement is made. Special policies can also provide survivors with the funds needed to make the purchase.

business continuation agreement Special form of business insurance whereby owners arrange to buy the interests of deceased associates from their heirs

APPENDIX II

Understanding the Legal Context of Business

In this appendix, we describe the basic tenets of U.S. law and show how these principles work through the court system. We will also survey a few major areas of business-related law. By focusing on the learning objectives of this appendix, you will see that laws may create opportunities for business activity just as readily as they set limits on them.

THE U.S. LEGAL AND JUDICIAL SYSTEMS

If people could ignore contracts or drive down city streets at any speed, it would be unsafe to do business on Main Street—or even to set foot in public. Without law, people would be free to act "at will," and life and property would constantly be at risk. **Laws** are the codified rules of behavior enforced by a society. In the United States, laws fall into three broad categories according to their origins: *common*, *statutory*, and *regulatory*. After discussing each of these types of laws, we will briefly describe the three-tier system of courts through which the judicial system administers the law in the United States.

Types of Law

Law in the United States originates primarily with English common law. Its sources include the U.S. Constitution, state constitutions, federal and state statutes, municipal ordinances, administrative agency rules and regulations, executive orders, and court decisions.

common law Body of decisions handed down by courts ruling on individual cases

COMMON LAW Court decisions follow *precedents*, or the decisions of earlier cases. Following precedent lends stability to the law by basing judicial decisions on cases anchored in similar facts. This principle is the keystone of **common law:** the body of decisions handed down by courts ruling on individual cases. Although some facets of common law predate the American Revolution (and even hearken back to medieval Europe), common law continues to evolve in the courts today.

statutory law Law created by constitutions or by federal, state, or local legislative acts

STATUTORY LAW Laws created by constitutions or by federal, state, or local legislative acts constitute **statutory law.** For example, Article I of the U.S. Constitution is a statutory law that empowers Congress to pass laws on corporate taxation, the zoning authority of municipalities, and the rights and privileges of business operating in the United States.

State legislatures and city councils also pass statutory laws. Some state laws, for example, prohibit the production or sale of detergents containing phosphates, which are believed to be pollutants. Nearly every town has ordinances specifying sites for certain types of industries or designating areas where cars cannot be parked during certain hours.

regulatory (or administrative) **law** Law made by the authority of administrative agencies

REGULATORY LAW Statutory and common law have long histories. Relatively new is **regulatory** (or **administrative**) **law:** law made by the authority of administrative agencies. By and large, the expansion of U.S. regulatory law has paralleled the nation's economic and technological development. Lacking the technical expertise to develop specialized legislation for specialized business activities, Congress established the first administrative agencies to create and administer the needed laws in the late 1800s. Before the early 1960s, most agencies concerned themselves with the *economic* regulation of specific areas of business—say, transportation or securities. Since then many agencies have been established to pursue narrower *social* objectives. They focus on issues that cut across different sectors of the economy—clean air, for example, or product testing.

Today a host of agencies, including the Equal Employment Opportunity Commission (EEOC), the Environmental Protection Agency (EPA), the Food and Drug Administration (FDA), the Federal Trade Commission (FTC), and the Occupational Safety and Health Administration (OSHA), regulate U.S. business practices.

In this section, we look briefly at the nature of regulatory agencies and describe some of the key legislation that makes up administrative law in this country. We also discuss an area of increasing importance in the relationship between government and business: *regulation*—or, more accurately, *deregulation.*

Agencies and Legislation. Although Congress retains control over the scope of agency action, once passed, regulations have the force of statutory law. Government regulatory agencies act as a secondary judicial system, determining whether regulations have been violated and imposing penalties. A firm that violates OSHA rules, for example, may receive a citation, a hearing, and perhaps a heavy fine. Much agency activity consists of setting standards for safety or quality and monitoring the compliance of businesses. The FDA, for example, is responsible for ensuring that food, medicines, and even cosmetics are safe and effective.

Regulatory laws have been on the books for nearly a century. As early as 1906, for example, the Pure Food and Drug Act mandated minimum levels of cleanliness and sanitation for food and drug companies. More recently, the Children's Television Act of 1990 requires that broadcasters meet the educational and informational needs of younger viewers and limit the amount of advertising broadcast during children's programs. In 1996, a sweeping new law to increase competition in the communications industry required television makers to install a "V-chip," which allows parents to block undesirable programming. And Congress continues to debate the possibility of regulating the Internet.

Congress has created many new agencies in response to pressure to address social issues. In some cases, agencies were established in response to public concern about corporate behavior. The activities of these agencies have sometimes forced U.S. firms to consider the public interest almost as routinely as they consider their own financial performance.

The Move toward Deregulation. Although government regulation has benefited U.S. business in many ways, it is not without its drawbacks. Businesspeople complain—with some justification—that government regulations require too much paperwork. To comply with just one OSHA regulation for a year, Goodyear once generated 345,000 pages of computer reports weighing 3,200 pounds. It now costs Goodyear $35.5 million each year to comply with the regulations of six government agencies, and it takes 36 employee-years annually (the equivalent of one employee working full time for 36 years) to fill out the required reports.

Not surprisingly, many people in both business and government support broader **deregulation:** the elimination of rules that restrict business activity. Advocates of both regulation and deregulation claim that each acts to control business expansion and prices, increase government efficiency, and right wrongs that the marketplace cannot or does not handle itself. Regulations such as those enforced by the EEOC, for example, are supposed to control undesirable business practices in the interest of social equity. In contrast, the court-ordered breakup of AT&T was prompted by a perceived need for greater market efficiency. For these and other reasons, the federal government began deregulating certain industries in the 1970s.

It is important to note that the United States is the only industrialized nation that has deregulated key industries—financial services, transportation, telecommunications, and a host of others. A 1996 law, for instance, allowed the seven "Baby Bells"—regional phone companies created when AT&T was broken up—to compete for long-distance business. It also allowed cable television and telephone companies to enter each other's markets by offering any combination of video, telephone, and high-speed data communications services. Many analysts contend that such deregulation is now and will become an even greater advantage in an era of global competition. Deregulation, they argue, is a primary incentive to innovation.

According to this view, deregulated industries are forced to innovate in order to survive in fiercely competitive industries. Those firms that are already conditioned to compete by being more creative will outperform firms that have been protected by regulatory climates in their home countries. "What's important," says one economist, "is that competition energizes new ways of doing things." The U.S. telecommunications industry, proponents of this view say, is twice as productive as its European counterparts because it is the only such industry forced to come out from under a protective regulatory umbrella.

The U.S. Judicial System

Laws are of little use unless they are enforced. Much of the responsibility for law enforcement falls to the courts. Although few people would claim that the courts are capable of resolving every dispute, there often seem to be more than enough lawyers to handle them all: Indeed, there are 140 lawyers for every 100,000 people in the United States. Litigation is a significant part of contemporary life, and we have given our courts a voice in a wide range of issues, some touching profoundly personal concerns, some ruling on matters of public policy that affect all our lives. In this section, we look at the operations of the U.S. judicial system.

THE COURT SYSTEM As Figure AII.1 shows, there are three levels in the U.S. judicial system—*federal*, *state*, and *local*. These levels reflect the *federalist* structure of a system in which a central government shares power with state or local governments. Federal courts were created by the U.S. Constitution. They hear cases on questions of constitutional law, disputes relating to maritime laws, and violations of federal statutes. They also rule on regulatory actions and on such issues as bankruptcy, postal law, and copyright or patent violation. Both the federal and most state systems embody a three-tiered system of *trial*, *appellate*, and *supreme courts*.

trial court General court that hears cases not specifically assigned to another court

Trial Courts. At the lowest level of the federal court system are the **trial courts,** general courts that hear cases not specifically assigned to another court. A case involving contract violation would go before a trial court. Every state has at least one federal trial court, called a *district court*.

FIGURE AII.1 ◆ **The U.S. Judicial System**

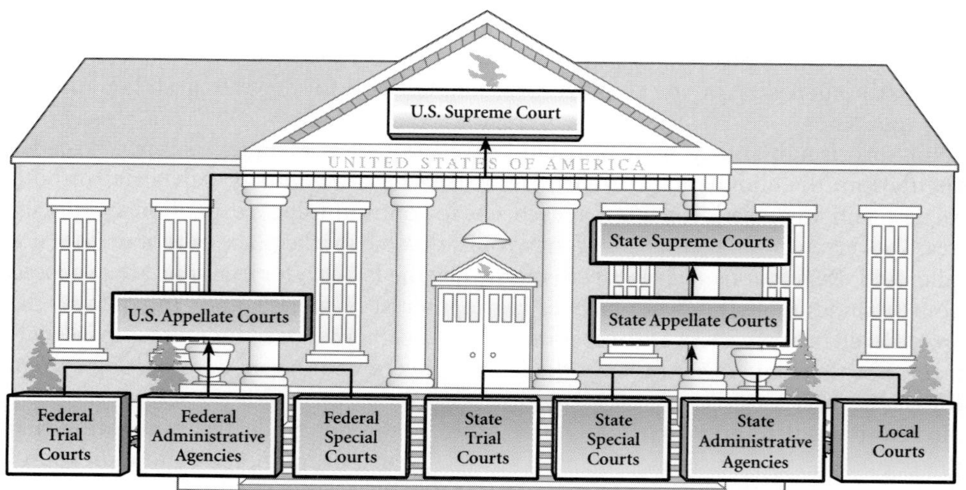

Trial courts also include special courts and administrative agencies. *Special courts* hear specific types of cases, such as cases involving tax evasion, fraud, international disputes, or claims against the U.S. government. Within their areas of jurisdiction, administrative agencies also make judgments much like those of courts.

Courts in each state system deal with the same issues as their federal counterparts. However, they may rule only in areas governed by state law. For example, a case involving state income tax laws would be heard by a state special court. Local courts in each state system also hear cases on municipal ordinances, local traffic violations, and similar issues.

Appellate Courts. A losing party may disagree with a trial court ruling. If that party can show grounds for review, the case may go before a federal or state **appellate court.** These courts consider questions of law, such as possible errors of legal interpretation made by lower courts. They do not examine questions of fact. There are now 13 federal courts of appeal, each with 3 to 15 judges. Cases are normally heard by three-judge panels.

appellate court Court that reviews case records of trials whose findings have been appealed

Supreme Courts. Cases still not resolved at the appellate level can be appealed to the appropriate state supreme courts or to the U.S. Supreme Court. If it believes that an appeal is warranted or that the outcome will set an important precedent, the U.S. Supreme Court also hears cases appealed from state supreme courts. Each year, the U.S. Supreme Court receives about 5,000 appeals but typically agrees to hear fewer than 200.

■ BUSINESS LAW

Most legal issues confronted by businesses fall into one of six basic areas: *contract, tort, property, agency, commercial,* or *bankruptcy law.* These areas cover a wide range of business activity.

Contract Law

A **contract** is any agreement between two or more parties that is enforceable in court. As such, it must meet six conditions. If all these conditions are met, one party can seek legal recourse from another if the other party breaches (that is, violates) the terms of the agreement.

1. *Agreement.* Agreement is the serious, definite, and communicated offer and acceptance of the same terms. Let us say that an auto parts supplier offers in writing to sell rebuilt engines to a repair shop for $500 each. If the repair shop accepts the offer, the two parties have reached an agreement.
2. *Consent.* A contract is not enforceable if any of the parties has been affected by an honest mistake, fraud, or pressure. For example, a restaurant manager orders a painted sign, but the sign company delivers a neon sign instead.
3. *Capacity.* To give real consent, both parties must demonstrate legal **capacity** (competence). A person under legal age (usually 18 or 21) cannot enter into a binding contract.
4. *Consideration.* An agreement is binding only if it exchanges **considerations,** that is, items of value. If your brother offers to paint your room for free, you cannot sue him if he changes his mind. Note that "items of value" do not necessarily entail money. For example, a tax accountant might agree to prepare a homebuilder's tax return in exchange for a new patio. Both services are items of value. Contracts need not be "rational," nor must they provide the "best" possible bargain for both sides. They need only include "legally sufficient" consideration. The terms are met if both parties receive what the contract details.
5. *Legality.* A contract must be for a lawful purpose and must comply with federal, state, and local laws and regulations. For example, an agreement between two competitors to engage in price fixing—that is, to set a mutually acceptable price—is not legal.
6. *Proper form.* A contract may be written, oral, or implied from conduct. It must be written, however, if it involves the sale of land or goods worth more than $500. It must be

capacity Competence required of individuals entering into a binding contract

considerations Any item of value exchanged between parties to create a valid contract written if the agreement requires more than a year to fulfill—say, a contract for employment as an engineer on a 14-month construction project. All changes to written contracts must also be in writing.

BREACH OF CONTRACT What can one party do if the other fails to live up to the terms of a valid contract? Contract law offers a variety of remedies designed to protect the reasonable expectations of the parties and, in some cases, to compensate them for actions taken to enforce the agreement.

As the injured party to a breached contract, any of the following actions might occur:

- You might cancel the contract and refuse to live up to your part of the bargain. For example, you might simply cancel a contract for carpet shampooing if the company fails to show up.
- You might sue for damages up to the amount that you lost as a result of the breach. Thus, you might sue the original caterer if you must hire a more expensive caterer for your wedding reception because the original company canceled at the last minute.
- If money cannot repay the damage you suffered, you might demand specific performance—that is, require the other party to fulfill the original contract. For example, you might demand that a dealer in classic cars sell you the antique Stutz Bearcat he agreed to sell you and not a classic Jaguar instead.

Tort Law

tort Civil injury to people, property, or reputation for which compensation must be paid

Tort law applies to most business relationships *not governed by contracts.* A **tort** is a *civil*—that is, noncriminal—injury to people, property, or reputation for which compensation must be paid. For example, if a person violates zoning laws by opening a convenience store in a residential area, he or she cannot be sent to jail as if the act were a criminal violation. But a variety of other legal measures can be pursued, such as fines or seizure of property. Trespass, fraud, defamation, invasion of privacy, and even assault can be torts, as can interference with contractual relations and wrongful use of trade secrets. In this section, we explain three classifications of torts: *intentional, negligence,* and *product liability.*

intentional tort Tort resulting from the deliberate actions of a party

INTENTIONAL TORTS **Intentional torts** result from the deliberate actions of another person or organization—for instance, a manufacturer knowingly fails to install a relatively inexpensive safety device on a product. Similarly, refusing to rectify a product design flaw, as in the case of the space shuttle *Challenger* disaster, can render a firm liable for an intentional tort. The actions of employees on the job may also constitute intentional torts—say, an overzealous security guard who wrongly accuses a customer of shoplifting. To remedy torts, courts will usually impose **compensatory damages:** payments intended to redress an injury actually suffered. They may also impose **punitive damages:** fines that exceed actual losses suffered by plaintiffs and that are intended to punish defendants.

compensatory damages Monetary payments intended to redress injury actually suffered because of a tort

punitive damages Fines imposed over and above any actual losses suffered by a plaintiff

In 1992, for example, a jury awarded $300,000 in compensatory damages plus $4 million in punitive damages to a couple who alleged that a two-way mirror in their penthouse suite had allowed strangers to spy on them at a local hotel. The compensatory damages were awarded because the jury agreed that the couple's privacy had been invaded. The large punitive award cited the plaintiff's emotional distress in the aftermath of the incident. (The case was later settled for $1 million in total damages.)

negligence Conduct falling below legal standards for protecting others against unreasonable risk

NEGLIGENCE TORTS Ninety percent of tort suits involve charges of **negligence,** conduct falling below legal standards for protecting others against unreasonable risk. If a company installs a pollution-control system that fails to protect a community's water supply, it may later be sued by an individual who gets sick from drinking the water.

Negligence torts may also result from employee actions. For example, if the captain of a supertanker runs aground and spills 11 million gallons of crude oil into coastal fishing waters, the oil company may be liable for potentially astronomical damages. Thus in September 1994, a jury in Alaska ordered Exxon Corp. to pay $5 billion in punitive damages to 34,000 fishermen and other plaintiffs as a consequence of the *Exxon Valdez* disaster of 1989. (Plaintiffs had asked for $15 billion.) A month earlier, the jury had awarded plaintiffs $287 million in compensatory damages. In 1993, the firm responsible for pipeline operations at the Valdez, Alaska, terminal (which is partially owned by Exxon) agreed to pay plaintiffs in the same case $98 million in damages. In a separate case, Exxon paid $20 million in damages to villages whose food supply had been destroyed. A separate state jury will consider another $120 million in claims by Alaskan corporations and municipalities. Even before any of these awards was handed down, Exxon had spent $2.1 billion on the cleanup effort and paid $1.3 billion in civil and criminal penalties.

PRODUCT LIABILITY TORTS In cases of **product liability**, a company may be held responsible for injuries caused by its products. Product liability is an issue in each of the following situations:

product liability tort Tort in which a company is responsible for injuries caused by its products

- In a raft of recent lawsuits, plaintiffs have charged that certain three-wheel all-terrain vehicles are unsafe; they contend that they are unstable and too easily overturned. They argue that manufacturers are liable for injuries suffered by drivers operating those vehicles.
- In 1997, several suits were filed against Mattel. During the preceding Christmas season, the toymaker had sold thousands of Cabbage Patch dolls with a brand-new feature: the dolls could "chew" play food. Unfortunately, they were also prone to gnaw on the hair of young children.

According to a special government panel on product liability, about 33 million people are injured and 28,000 killed by consumer products each year. Even so, U.S. courts seem to be taking a harder look at many product liability claims, especially when they are based on "soft" science:

- An appeals court overturned a $1 million award to a psychic who claimed that a CAT scan destroyed her special abilities.
- A federal judge barred as "unreliable" medical testimony linking carpal tunnel syndrome to a computer keyboard made by Unisys.
- Another federal judge dismissed a case claiming that cellular phone use caused a woman's brain tumor.

Strict Product Liability. Since the early 1960s, businesses have faced a number of legal actions based on the relatively new principle of **strict product liability:** the principle that liability can result not from a producer's negligence but from a defect in the product itself. An injured party need show only that

strict product liability Principle that liability can result not from a producer's negligence but from a defect in the product itself

1. The product was defective.
2. The defect was the cause of injury.
3. The defect caused the product to be unreasonably dangerous.

Many recent cases in strict product liability have focused on injuries or illnesses attributable to toxic wastes or other hazardous substances that were legally disposed of. Because plaintiffs need not demonstrate negligence or fault, these suits frequently succeed. Not surprisingly, the number of such suits promises to increase.

Property Law

As the name implies, *property law* concerns property rights. But what exactly is "property"? Is it the land under a house? The house itself? A car in the driveway? A dress in the closet? The answer in each case is yes: In the legal sense, **property** is anything of value to which a person or business has sole right of ownership. Indeed, property is technically those *rights.*

property Anything of value to which a person or business has sole right of ownership

Within this broad general definition, we can divide property into four categories. In this section, we define these categories and then examine more fully the legal protection of a certain kind of property—intellectual property.

tangible real property Land and anything attached to it

tangible personal property Any movable item that can be owned, bought, sold, or leased

- **Tangible real property** is land and anything attached to it. A house and a factory are both tangible real property, as are built-in appliances or the machines inside the buildings.
- **Tangible personal property** is any movable item that can be owned, bought, sold, or leased. Examples are automobiles, clothing, stereos, and cameras.

intangible personal property Property that cannot be seen but that exists by virtue of written documentation

intellectual property Property created through a person's creative activities

- **Intangible personal property** cannot be seen but exists by virtue of written documentation. Examples are insurance policies, bank accounts, stocks and bonds, and trade secrets.
- **Intellectual property** is created through a person's creative activities. Books, articles, songs, paintings, screenplays, and computer software are all intellectual property.

PROTECTION OF INTELLECTUAL RIGHTS The U.S. Constitution grants protection to intellectual property by means of copyrights, trademarks, and patents. Copyrights and patents apply to the tangible expressions of an idea—not to the ideas themselves. Thus, you could not copyright the idea of cloning dinosaurs from fossil DNA. Michael Crichton could copyright his novel, *Jurassic Park*, which is a tangible result of that idea, and sell the film rights to producer-director Steven Spielberg. Both creators are entitled to the profits, if any, that may be generated by their tangible creative expressions.

copyright Exclusive ownership right belonging to the creator of a book, article, design, illustration, photo, film, or musical work

Copyrights. **Copyrights** give exclusive ownership rights to the creators of books, articles, designs, illustrations, photos, films, and music. Computer programs and even semiconductor chips are also protected. Copyrights extend to creators for their entire lives and to their estates for 50 years thereafter. All terms are automatically copyrighted from the moment of creation.

trademark Exclusive legal right to use a brand name or symbol

Trademarks. Because the development of products is expensive, companies must prevent other firms from using their brand names. Often they must act to keep competitors from seducing consumers with similar or substitute products. A producer can apply to the U.S. government for a **trademark—**the exclusive legal right to use a brand name.

Trademarks are granted for 20 years and may be renewed indefinitely if a firm continues to protect its brand name. If a firm allows the brand name to lapse into *common usage*, it may lose protection. Common usage takes effect when a company fails to use the ® symbol to indicate that its brand name is a registered trademark. It also takes effect if a company seeks no action against those who fail to acknowledge its trademark. Recently, for example, the popular brand-name sailboard Windsurfer lost its trademark. Like *trampoline*, *yo-yo*, and *thermos*, *windsurfer* has become the common term for the product and can now be used by any sailboard company. In contrast, Formica Corp. successfully spent the better part of a decade in court to protect the name *Formica* as a trademark. The Federal Trade Commission had contended that the word had entered the language as a generic name for any similar laminate material.

patent Exclusive legal right to use and license a manufactured item or substance, manufacturing process, or object design

Patents. **Patents** provide legal monopolies for the use and licensing of manufactured items, manufacturing processes, substances, and designs for objects. A patentable invention must be *novel*, *useful*, and *nonobvious*. Since June 1995, U.S. patent law has been in harmony with that of most developed nations. For example, patents are now valid for 20 years rather than 17 years. In addition, the term now runs from the date on which the application was *filed*, not the date on which the patent itself was *issued*.

Although the U.S. Patent Office issues about 1,200 patents a week, requirements are stringent, and U.S. patents actually tend to be issued at a slow pace. While Japan and most European countries have installed systems to speed up patent filing and research, the U.S. system can extend the process to years. Other observers argue that American firms trail their foreign counterparts in patents because of the sluggishness with which U.S. companies move products through their own research and development programs.

About 50 percent of all U.S. patents granted each year are awarded to foreign companies. However, the percentage of patents awarded to U.S. companies is increasing as U.S. companies become more aggressive. In 1992, for example, Digital Equipment Corp. won 223 U.S. patents, up from a mere 20 in 1985. Intel Corp. increased the number of its filings from 100 in 1990 to 400 in 1993.

RESTRICTIONS ON PROPERTY RIGHTS Property rights are not always absolute. For example, rights may be compromised under any of the following circumstances:

- Owners of shorefront property may be required to permit anglers, clam diggers, and other interested parties to walk near the water.

- Utility companies typically have rights called easements, such as the right to run wire over private property or to lay cable or pipe under it.
- Under the principle of **eminent domain,** the government may, upon paying owners fair prices, claim private land to expand roads or erect public buildings.

Agency Law

The transfer of property—whether the deeding of real estate or the transfer of automobile title—often involves agents. An **agent** is a person who acts for, and in the name of, another party, called the **principal.** The most visible agents are those in real estate, sports, and entertainment. Many businesses, however, use agents to secure insurance coverage and handle investments. Every partner in a partnership and every officer and director in a corporation is an agent of that business. Courts have also ruled that both a firm's employees and its outside contractors may be regarded as its agents.

agent Individual or organization acting for, and in the name of, another party

principal Individual or organization authorizing an agent to act on its behalf

AUTHORITY OF AGENTS Agents have the authority to bind principals to agreements. They receive that authority, however, from the principals themselves; they cannot create their own authority. An agent's authority to bind a principal can be express, implied, or apparent. The following illustration involves all three forms of agent authority:

> Ellen is a salesperson in Honest Sam's Used Car Lot. Her written employment contract gives her **express authority** to sell cars, to provide information to prospective buyers, and to approve trade-ins up to $2,000. Derived from the custom of used-car dealers, she also has **implied authority** to give reasonable discounts on prices and to make reasonable adjustments to written warranties. Furthermore, Ellen may—in the presence of Honest Sam—promise a customer that she will match the price offered by another local dealer. If Honest Sam assents—perhaps merely nods and smiles—Ellen may be construed to have the **apparent authority** to make this deal.

express authority Agent's authority, derived from written agreement, to bind a principal to a certain course of action

implied authority Agent's authority, derived from business custom, to bind a principal to a certain course of action

apparent authority Agent's authority, based on the principal's compliance, to bind a principal to a certain course of action

RESPONSIBILITIES OF PRINCIPALS Principals have several responsibilities to their agents. They owe agents reasonable compensation, must reimburse them for related business expenses, and should inform them of risks associated with their business activities. Principals are liable for actions performed by agents *within the scope of their employment.* Thus, if agents make untrue claims about products or services, the principal is liable for making amends. Employers are similarly responsible for the actions of employees. In fact, firms are often liable in tort suits because the courts treat employees as agents.

Businesses are increasingly being held accountable for *criminal* acts by employees. Court findings, for example, have argued that firms are expected to be aware of workers' propensities for violence, to check on their employees' pasts, and to train and supervise employees properly. Suppose, for instance, that a delivery service hires a driver with a history of driving while intoxicated. If the driver has an accident with a company vehicle while under the influence of alcohol, the company may be liable for criminal actions.

Commercial Law

Managers must be well acquainted with the most general laws affecting commerce. Specifically, they need to be familiar with the provisions of the *Uniform Commercial Code,* which sets down rules regarding *warranties.*

THE UNIFORM COMMERCIAL CODE For many years, companies doing business in more than one state faced a special problem: Laws governing commerce varied, sometimes widely, from state to state. In 1952, however, the National Conference of Commissioners on Uniform State Laws and the American Law Institute drew up the **Uniform Commercial Code (UCC).** Subsequently accepted by every state except Louisiana, the UCC describes the rights of buyers and sellers in transactions.

Uniform Commercial Code Body of standardized laws governing the rights of buyers and sellers in transactions

For example, buyers who believe that they have been wronged in agreements with sellers have several options. They can cancel contracts, refuse deliveries, and demand the return of any deposits. In some cases, they can buy the same products elsewhere and sue the original contractors to recover any losses incurred. Sellers, too, have several options. They can cancel contracts, withhold deliveries, and sell goods to other buyers. If goods have already been delivered, sellers can repossess them or sue the buyers for purchase prices.

warranty Seller's promise to stand by its products or services if a problem occurs after the sale

express warranty Warranty whose terms are specifically stated by the seller

implied warranty Warranty, dictated by law, based on the principle that products should fulfill advertised promises and serve the purposes for which they are manufactured and sold

Warranties. A **warranty** is a seller's promise to stand by its products or services if a problem occurs after the sale. Warranties may be *express* or *implied.* The terms of an **express warranty** are specifically stated by the seller. For example, many stereo systems are expressly warranted for 90 days. If they malfunction within that period, they can be returned for full refunds.

An **implied warranty** is dictated by law. Implied warranties embody the principle that a product should (1) fulfill the promises made by advertisements and (2) serve the purpose for which it was manufactured and sold. If you buy an advertised frost-free refrigerator, the seller implies that the refrigerator will keep your food cold and that you will not have to defrost it. It is important to note, however, that warranties, unlike most contracts, are easily limited, waived, or disclaimed. Consequently, they are the source of more and more tort action, as dissatisfied customers seek redress from producers.

Bankruptcy Law

bankruptcy Permission granted by the courts to individuals and organizations not to pay some or all of their debts

At one time, individuals who could not pay their debts were jailed. Today, however, both organizations and individuals can seek relief by filing for **bankruptcy—**the court-granted permission not to pay some or all debts.

Hundreds of thousands of individuals and tens of thousands of businesses file for bankruptcy each year, and their numbers continue to increase. Filings have doubled since 1985, peaking in 1996 at 1.1 million (a 25 percent increase over 1995). Why do individuals and businesses file for bankruptcy? Cash-flow problems and drops in farm prices caused many farmers, banks, and small businesses to go bankrupt. In recent years, large enterprises such as Continental Airlines and R. H. Macy have sought the protection of bankruptcy laws as part of strategies to streamline operations, cut costs, and regain profitability.

Three main factors account for the increase in bankruptcy filings:

1. The increased availability of credit
2. The "fresh-start" provisions in current bankruptcy laws
3. The growing acceptance of bankruptcy as a financial tactic

involuntary bankruptcy Bankruptcy proceedings initiated by the creditors of an indebted individual or organization

voluntary bankruptcy Bankruptcy proceedings initiated by an indebted individual or organization

In some cases, creditors force an individual or firm into **involuntary bankruptcy** and press the courts to award them payment of at least part of what they are owed. Far more often, however, a person or business chooses to file for court protection against creditors. In general, individuals and firms whose debts exceed total assets by at least $1,000 may file for **voluntary bankruptcy.**

BUSINESS BANKRUPTCY A business bankruptcy may be resolved by one of three plans:

- Under a *liquidation plan,* the business ceases to exist. Its assets are sold and the proceeds used to pay creditors.
- Under a *repayment plan,* the bankrupt company simply works out a new payment schedule to meet its obligations. The time frame is usually extended, and payments are collected and distributed by a court-appointed trustee.
- *Reorganization* is the most complex form of business bankruptcy. The company must explain the sources of its financial difficulties and propose a new plan for remaining in business. Reorganization may include a new slate of managers and a new financial strategy. A judge may also reduce the firm's debts to ensure its survival. Although creditors naturally dislike debt reduction, they may agree to the proposal, since 50 percent of one's due is better than nothing at all.

New legislation passed in 1994 has made some major revisions in bankruptcy laws. For example, it is now easier for individuals with up to $1 million in debt to make payments under installment plans instead of liquidating assets immediately. In contrast, the new law restricts how long a company can protect itself in bankruptcy while continuing to do business. Critics have charged, for instance, that many firms have succeeded in operating for many months under bankruptcy protection. During that time, they were able to cut costs and prices, not only competing with an unfair advantage but dragging down overall industry profits. The new laws place time limits on various steps in the filing process. The intended effect is to speed the process and prevent assets from being lost to legal fees.

■ THE INTERNATIONAL FRAMEWORK OF BUSINESS LAW

Laws can vary dramatically from country to country, and many businesses today have international markets, suppliers, and competitors. It follows that managers need a basic understanding of the international framework of business law that affects the ways in which they can do business.

National laws are created and enforced by countries. The creation and enforcement of international law is more complicated. For example, if a company shipping merchandise between the United States and Mexico breaks an environmental protection law, to whom is that company accountable? The answer depends on several factors. Which country enacted the law in question? Where did the violation occur? In which country is the alleged violator incorporated?

Issues such as pollution across borders are matters of **international law:** the very general set of cooperative agreements and guidelines established by countries to govern the actions of individuals, businesses, and nations themselves. In this section, we examine the various sources of international law. We then discuss some of the important ways in which international trade is regulated and place some key U.S. trade laws in the international context in which they are designed to work.

international law Set of cooperative agreements and guidelines established by countries to govern actions of individuals, businesses, and nations

Sources of International Law

International law has several sources. One source is custom and tradition. Among countries that have been trading with each other for centuries, many customs and traditions governing exchanges have gradually evolved into practice. Although some trading practices still follow ancient unwritten agreements, there has been a clear trend in more recent times to approach international trade within a more formal legal framework. Key features of that framework include a variety of formal trade agreements.

TRADE AGREEMENTS In addition to subscribing to international rules, virtually every nation has formal trade treaties with other nations. A *bilateral agreement* is one involving two countries; a *multilateral agreement* involves several nations.

General Agreement on Tariffs and Trade. The **General Agreement on Tariffs and Trade (GATT)** was first signed shortly after the end of World War II. Its purpose is to reduce or eliminate trade barriers, such as tariffs and quotas. It does so by encouraging nations to protect domestic industries within internationally agreed-upon limits and to engage in multilateral negotiations.

General Agreement on Tariffs and Trade (GATT) International trade agreement to encourage the multilateral reduction or elimination of trade barriers

In December 1994, the U.S. Congress ratified a revision of GATT that had been worked out by 124 nations over a 12-year period. Still, many issues remain unresolved—for example, the opening of foreign markets to most financial services. Governments may still provide subsidies to manufacturers of civil aircraft, and no agreement was reached on limiting the distribution of American cultural exports—movies, music, and the like—in Europe. With those agreements that have been reached, however, one international economic group predicts that world commerce will have increased by $270 billion by 2002.

North American Free Trade Agreement (NAFTA) Agreement to gradually eliminate tariffs and other trade barriers between the United States, Canada, and Mexico

North American Free Trade Agreement. The **North American Free Trade Agreement (NAFTA)** was negotiated to remove tariffs and other trade barriers among the United States, Canada, and Mexico. NAFTA also included agreements to monitor environmental and labor abuses. It took effect on January 1, 1994, and immediately eliminated some tariffs; others will disappear after 5-, 10-, or 15-year intervals.

In the first year after its passage, observers agreed that, by and large, NAFTA achieved what it was supposed to: a much more active North American market. The following were among the results after 1 year:

- Direct foreign investment increased. U.S. and Canadian firms, for example, accounted for 55 percent of all foreign investment in Mexico, investing $2.4 billion. Companies from other nations—for instance, Toyota Motor Corp.—also made new investments, such as expanding production facilities, to take advantage of the freer movement of goods in the new market.
- U.S. exports to Mexico increased by about 20 percent. Procter & Gamble, for example, enjoyed an increase of nearly 75 percent, and the giant agribusiness firm of Archer Daniels Midland reported a tripling of its exports to Mexico. Mexico passed Japan as the second largest buyer of U.S. goods, and trade with Canada rose 10 percent (twice the gain in Europe and Asia).
- U.S. imports from Mexico and Canada rose even faster than rates in the opposite direction, setting records of $48 billion and $120 billion, respectively. In particular, electronics, computers, and communications products came into the United States twice as fast as they went out. "We pointed out," says one NAFTA opponent, "that there was a fairly sophisticated manufacturing base in Mexico that pays peanuts, and the numbers bear that out."
- NAFTA created fewer jobs than proponents had hoped. Although the U.S. economy added 1.7 million new jobs in 1994, the Labor Department estimates that only 100,000 jobs were NAFTA related. At the same time, however, the flood of U.S. jobs to Mexico predicted by Ross Perot and other NAFTA critics, especially by labor union officials, did not occur. In fact, the president of Ford Motor Co.'s Mexico operations has boasted that his activities "have created jobs here and in the U.S." His reasoning: Ford's exports of Mexican-made vehicles to the United States are up 30 percent, and 80 percent of all components in those cars are made in the United States. Ford also reports that its exports of American-made cars to Mexico rose from 1,200 to 30,000 in NAFTA's first year.

European Union (EU) Agreement among major Western European nations to elimzinate or make uniform most trade barriers affecting group members

European Union. Originally called the Common Market, the **European Union (EU)** includes the principal Western European nations. These countries have eliminated most quotas and have set uniform tariff levels on products imported and exported within their group. In 1992, virtually all internal trade barriers were eliminated, making the European Union the largest free marketplace in the world.

NOTES, SOURCES, AND CREDITS

Reference Notes

Chapter 1

[1]Karl E. Case and Ray C. Fair, *Principles of Economics*, 5th ed. (Upper Saddle River, NJ: Prentice Hall, 1999), pp. 69–70.

[2]Jane Perlez, "Decidedly Un-Communist Goals for the Young of Central Europe," *The New York Times*, January 1, 1998, pp. A1, A6; Perlez, "Post-Marxist Hungarian Bus Maker Takes to Capitalist Road," *The New York Times*, August 10, 1995, p. D3.

[3]Carol Kaesuk Yoon, "Chocoholics Take Note: Beloved Bean in Peril," *The New York Times*, May 4, 1998, pp. A1, A15.

[4]See Nancy A. Kubasek, Bartley A. Brennan, and M. Neil Browne, *The Legal Environment of Business: A Critical Thinking Approach*, 2nd ed. (Upper Saddle River, NJ: Prentice Hall, 1999), Chap. 13.

[5]Norman N. Scarborough and Thomas W. Zimmerer, *Essentials of Entrepreneurship and Small Business Management*, 2nd ed. (Upper Saddle River, NJ: Prentice Hall, 1998), pp. 9–10.

[6]Steve Hamm with Amy Cortese and Peter Burrows, "No Letup—And No Apologies," *Business Week*, October 26, 1998, pp. 58–60+.

[7]Kim Clark, "These *Are* the Good Old Days," *Fortune*, June 9, 1997, pp. 74–82.

[8]See Nina Munk, "The New Organization Man," *Fortune*, March 16, 1998, pp. 62–66+.

[9]Michael J. Mandel, "Why the Pace Has to Pick Up," *Business Week*, August 31, 1998, pp. 136–139.

[10]Case and Fair, *Principles of Economics*, pp. 55–56.

[11]Richard W. Stevenson, "Red Ink No More," *The New York Times*, October 1, 1998, pp. C1, C23.

[12]Seth Faison, "China to Prime Economic Pump With Mammoth Building Outlay," *The New York Times*, March 6, 1998, pp. A1, A6.

Chapter 2

[1]See Philip Kotler and Gary Armstrong, *Principles of Marketing*, 8th ed. (Upper Saddle River, NJ: Prentice Hall, 1999), pp. 14–16.

[2]U.S. Bureau of the Census, *Statistical Abstract of the United States: 1997* (Washington, DC, 1998), p. 537.

[3]Nancy A. Kubasek, Bartley A. Brennan, and M. Neil Browne, *The Legal Environment of Business: A Critical Thinking Approach*, 2nd ed. (Upper Saddle River, NJ: Prentice Hall, 1999), pp. 335–338.

[4]*Statistical Abstract of the United States: 1997*, p. 537.

[5]"Fortune 5 Hundred Largest U.S. Corporations," *Fortune*, April 27, 1998, pp. F1–F20; see also "Infoseek Company Profile: ASARCO Incorporated." On-Line. Internet. Accessed 6 November 1998. Available World Wide Web: *http://www.infoseek.com/Content?arn=10133&qt=Asarco&col=HV&svx=1hscaps*

[6]Reed Abelson, "Proxy Peace," *The New York Times*, May 28, 1998, pp. D1, D2.

[7]Reed Abelson, "Outspoken and Out the Door," *The New York Times*, August 26, 1998, pp. D1, D5.

Chapter 3

[1]See Karen P. Gonçalves, *Services Marketing: A Strategic Approach* (Upper Saddle River, NJ: Prentice Hall, 1998), pp. 12–13.

[2]*International Monetary Fund Annual Report: 1998*, p. 10.

[3]"The Other Side of Prosperity: India," *The Economist*, June 21, 1997, p. 45.

[4]Geri Smith and Elisabeth Malkin, "Why Mexico Scares the UAW," *Business Week*, August 3, 1998, pp. 37–38.

[5]Donald A. Ball and Wendell H. McCulloch Jr., *International Business: The Challenge of Global Competition*, 7th ed. (Boston: Irwin McGraw-Hill, 1999), pp. 146–147.

[6]Warren J. Keegan, *Global Marketing Management*, 6th ed. (Upper Saddle River, NJ: Prentice Hall, 1999), pp. 145–146.

[7]See Karl E. Case and Ray C. Fair, *Principles of Economics*, 5th ed. (Upper Saddle River, NJ: Prentice Hall, 1999), pp. 813–817; and Dominick Salvatore, *International Economics*, 6th ed. (Upper Saddle River, NJ: Prentice Hall, 1998), Chap. 2.

[8]*Hoover's Handbook of World Business: 1998* (Austin, TX: Hoover's Business Press, 1998), p. 56.

[9]See James C. Baker, *International Finance: Management, Markets, and Institutions* (Upper Saddle River, NJ: Prentice Hall, 1998), pp. 51–59.

[10]See Arthur J. Keown et al., *Foundations of Finance: The Logic and Practice of Financial Management*, 2nd ed. (Upper Saddle River, NJ: Prentice Hall, 1998), pp. 507–512.

[11]See "Caterpillar, UAW Face Renewed Hurdles," *The Wall Street Journal*, February 24, 1998, p. A2.

[12]Brian Zajac, "Yankee Travelers," *Forbes*, July 27, 1998, pp. 162–163.

[13]Paul J. Deveney, "International World Watch," *The Wall Street Journal*, May 5, 1998, p. A16.

[14]Jeff Gerth and Eric Schmitt, "Chinese Said to Reap Gains in U.S. Export Policy Shift," *The New York Times*, October 19, 1998, pp. A1, A14.

[15]See Ball and McCulloch, *International Business*, pp. 96–97.

Chapter 4

[1]See Gerald F. Cavanaugh, *American Business Values: With International Perspectives*, 4th ed. (Upper Saddle River, NJ: Prentice Hall, 1998), pp. 69–83.

[2]Julia Flynn, "Astra: It's Not Over Yet," *Business Week*, February 23, 1998, pp. 50–51; Jane Sasseen, "Abuse of Power," *Business Week*, May 13, 1996, pp. 86–89+; and Mark Maremont, "Sex, Lies, and Home Improvements?" *Business Week*, March 31, 1997, p. 40.

[3]David Sheff, "Levi's Changes Everything," *Fast Company*, June/July 1996, 65–69+.

[4]Randall Smith and Steven Lipin, "Are Companies Using Restructuring Costs to Fudge the Figures?" *The Wall Street Journal*, January 30, 1996, pp. A1, A11.

[5]Andrew C. Revkin, "Who Cares about a Few Degrees?" *The New York Times*, December 12, 1997 (A Preview to the Kyoto Conference: Global Warming), pp. F1, F4.

[6]See Rogene A. Buchholz and Sandra B. Rosenthal, *Business Ethics: The Pragmatic Path beyond Principles to Process* (Upper Saddle River, NJ: Prentice Hall, 1998), Chap. 10.

[7]Daniel Machalaba, "As Old Pallets Pile Up, Critics Hammer Them as a New Eco-Menace," *The Wall Street Journal*, April 1, 1998, p. A1.

[8]See Buchholz and Rosenthal, *Business Ethics*, Chap. 13.

[9]Joseph Weber with John Carey, "Did Denture Creams Put Users at Risk?" *Business Week*, April 22, 1996, pp. 92, 94+.

[10]Bryan Gruley and Joseph Pereira, "FTC Antitrust Case Accuses Toys "R" Us," *The Wall Street Journal*, May 23, 1996, pp. A3, A4.

[11]See Buchholz and Rosenthal, *Business Ethics*, Chaps. 14 and 15.

[12]Lee Gomes, "A Whistle-Blower Finds Jackpot at the End of His Quest," *The Wall Street Journal*, April 27, 1998, pp. B1, B12.

[13]Tom Lowry, "Merger Mania Revives Insider Trading," *USA Today*, August 11, 1998, p. A1.

Chapter 5

[1]Marc Ballon, "Extreme," *Inc.*, July 1998, pp. 60–71.

[2]Patricia Sellers, "The 50 Most Powerful Women in American Business," *Fortune*, October 12, 1998, pp. 76–95.

[3]Randall F. Stross, "How Yahoo! Won the Search Wars," *Fortune*, March 2, 1998, pp. 148–150+; "Yahoo! The Company, the Strategy, the Stock," *Business Week*, September 7, 1998, pp. 66–76.

[4]Shaifali Puri, "A Cut Above," *Fortune*, August 4, 1997, pp. 55–59.

[5]See Fred R. David, *Strategic Management: Concepts and Cases*, 7th ed. (Upper Saddle River, NJ: Prentice Hall, 1999), pp. 178–184.

[6]"Nike Plans to Swoosh into Sports Equipment, But It's a Tough Game," *The Wall Street Journal*, January 16, 1998, pp. A1, A10.

[7]Nancy Austin, "The Cultural Evolution," Inc. 500 1997, May 1997, pp. 72–80.

Chapter 6

[1]Robert L. Simison, "Ford Rolls Out New Model of Corporate Culture," *The Wall Street Journal*, January 13, 1999, pp. B1, B4.

[2]See Gary Dessler, *Management: Leading People and Organizations in the 21st Century* (Upper Saddle River, NJ: Prentice Hall, 1998), pp. 212–213.

[3]See Richard Daft, *Organizational Theory and Design*, 6th ed. (St. Paul, MN: West, 1998).

[4]See Stephen P. Robbins, *Organizational Behavior: Concepts, Controversies, Applications*, 8th ed. (Upper Saddle River, NJ: Prentice Hall, 1998), pp. 478–480.

[5]Andy Reinhardt and Seanna Browder, "Can a New Crew Buoy Boeing?" *Business Week*, September 14, 1998, p. 53; Frederic Biddle and John Helyar, "Behind Boeing's Woes: Clunky Assembly Line

and Price War with Airbus," *The Wall Street Journal*, April 4, 1998, pp. A1, A16.
[6]*Hoover's Handbook of American Business 1999* (Austin, TX: Hoover's Business Press, 1998), pp. 778–779.
[7]Alex Taylor III, "How Toyota Defies Gravity," *Fortune*, December 8, 1997, pp. 100–108.
[8]See Robbins, *Organizational Behavior*, pp. 483–484.
[9]See Stephen P. Robbins and Mary Coulter, *Management*, 6th ed. (Upper Saddle River, NJ: Prentice Hall, 1999), pp. 318–319.
[10]Thomas J. Peters and Robert H. Waterman, *In Search of Excellence* (New York: Harper & Row, 1982).

Chapter 7
[1]U.S. Department of Commerce, *Statistical Abstract of the United States* (Washington, DC: Bureau of the Census, 1997), p. 540.
[2]*The Wall Street Journal Almanac 1999* (New York: Ballantine Books, 1998), p. 185.
[3]"Small Business 'Vital Statistics.'" Internet. Online. Accessed 8 February 1999. Available World Wide Web: *http://www.sba.gov/aboutsba/.*
[4]"Small Business 'Vital Statistics.'" Internet. Online. Accessed 8 February 1999. Available World Wide Web: *http://www.sba.gov/aboutsba/.*
[5]See Chuck Salter, "Insanity, Inc.," *Fast Company*, January 1999, pp. 100–108.
[6]John Milward, "A Five-Year Journey to a Better Mousetrap," *The New York Times*, May 24, 1998, p. 8.
[7]Liza Potter, "The Need for Speed," *Entrepreneur*, February 1999, pp. 164–165.
[8]Wendy Zellner, "Peace, Love, and the Bottom Line," *Business Week*, December 7, 1998, pp. 79–82.
[9]Debra Nussbaum, "Giving Birth to a Web Business," *The New York Times*, October 15, 1998, p. G5.
[10]Nussbaum, "Giving Birth to a Web Business," p. G5.
[11]Lawrence M. Fisher, "Sailing for the Masses: Wind, Water, Plastic," *The New York Times*, October 7, 1998, pp. C1, C4.
[12]See Marc J. Dollinger, *Entrepreneurship: Strategies and Resources*, 2nd ed. (Upper Saddle River, NJ: Prentice Hall, 1999), pp. 4–19.
[13]Emily Esterson, "A Shock to the System," *Inc. Tech 1998*, no. 1, pp. 50–58.
[14]Dana Canedy, "The Courtship of Black Consumers," *The New York Times*, August 1998, pp. D1, D5.
[15]See *The Wall Street Journal Almanac 1999*, pp. 179, 182.
[16]Noelle Knox, "Women Entrepreneurs Attract New Financing," *The New York Times*, July 26, 1998, p. 10.
[17]Michael Hopkins, "The Antihero's Guide to the New Economy," *Inc.*, January 1998, pp. 36–48.
[18]See also Thomas W. Zimmerer and Norman M. Scarborough, *Essentials of Entrepreneurship and Small Business Management*, 2nd ed. (Upper Saddle River, NJ: Prentice Hall, 1998), pp. 23–27.
[19]See *The Wall Street Journal Almanac 1999*, p. 186.
[20]Donna Fenn, "A League of Your Own," *Inc. State of Small Business 1998*, pp. 103–108.

Chapter 8
[1]See Stephen P. Robbins, *Organizational Behavior: Controversies, Applications*, 8th ed. (Upper Saddle River, NJ: Prentice Hall, 1998), pp. 151–158.
[2]Timothy Schellhardt, "An Idyllic Workplace under a Tycoon's Thumb," *The Wall Street Journal*, November 23, 1998, pp. B1, B4.
[3]Linda Grant, "Happy Workers, High Returns," *Fortune*, January 12, 1998, p. 81.
[4]"Perks That Work," *Time*, November 9, 1998.
[5]See Ruth R. Gordon, *Organizational Behavior: A Diagnostic Approach*, 6th ed. (Upper Saddle River, NJ: Prentice Hall, 1999), pp. 88–107.
[6]See Gary Dessler, *Human Resource Management*, 7th ed. (Upper Saddle River, NJ: Prentice Hall, 1997), pp. 325–332.
[7]See Eileen K. Aranda and Luis Aranda, *Teams: Structure, Process, Culture, and Politics* (Upper Saddle River, NJ: Prentice Hall, 1998), pp. 12–14.
[8]Ralph King, Jr., "Levi's Factory Workers Are Assigned to Teams, and Morale Takes a Hit," *The Wall Street Journal*, May 20, 1998, pp. A1, A6.
[9]Jon R. Katzenbach, *Teams at the Top* (Boston: Harvard Business School Press, 1998).
[10]See Gordon, *Organizational Behavior*, pp. 436–443.
[11]See Dessler, *Human Resource Management*, pp. 312–315; Gordon, *Organizational Behavior*, pp. 443–445.
[12]Laura Koss-Feder, "Perks That Work," *Time*, November 9, 1998, pp. 46–49.
[13]"How Trilogy Software Trains Its Raw Recruits to Be Risk Takers," *The Wall Street Journal*, September 21, 1998, pp. A1, A10; "Insanity, Inc.," *Fast Company*, January 1999, pp. 100–108.
[14]See Gary Yukl, *Leadership in Organizations*, 4th ed. (Upper Saddle River, NJ: Prentice Hall, 1998), pp. 265–292.
[15]See Anne Marie Francesco and Barry Allen Gold, *International Organizational Behavior: Texts, Readings, Cases, and Skills* (Upper Saddle River, NJ: Prentice Hall, 1998), pp. 151–154.

Chapter 9
[1]See Stephen P. Robbins, *Organizational Behavior, Concepts, Controversies, Applications*, 8th ed. (Upper Saddle River, NJ: Prentice Hall, 1998), pp. 552–553.
[2]See Luis R. Gómez-Mejía, David B. Balkin, and Robert L. Cardy, *Managing Human Resources*, 2nd ed. (Upper Saddle River, NJ: Prentice Hall, 1998), pp. 151–171.
[3]"Recruiters Work Hard to Showcase Fun Side of Job," *USA Today*, December 29, 1997, p. 5B.
[4]Justin Martin, "So, You Want to Work for the Best," *Fortune*, January 12, 1998, pp. 77–78.
[5]See P. Nick Blanchard and James W. Thacker, *Effective Training: Systems, Strategies, and Practices* (Upper Saddle River, NJ: Prentice Hall, 1999), esp. pp. 277–311; Robbins, *Organizational Behavior*, pp. 559–580.
[6]John Helyar and Joann Lublin, "Corporate Coffers Gush with Currency of an Opulent Age," *The Wall Street Journal*, August 10, 1998, pp. B1, B4.
[7]See Nancy A. Kubasek, Bartley A. Brennan, and M. Neil Browne, *The Legal Environment of Business: A Critical Thinking Approach*, 2nd ed. (Upper Saddle River, NJ: Prentice Hall, 1999), pp. 449–452.
[8]Dorothy Rabinowitz, "The 'Seinfeld' Firing," *The Wall Street Journal*, May 11, 1998, p. A20.
[9]See Kubasek, Brennan, and Browne, *The Legal Environment of Business*, pp. 444–449.
[10]*The Wall Street Journal Almanac 1999* (New York: Ballantine Books, 1999), pp. 238, 241.
[11]Marc Adams, "Building a Rainbow, One Stripe at a Time," *HR Magazine*, August 1998, pp. 72–78.
[12]*The Wall Street Journal Almanac 1999*, p. 243.
[13]See E. Edward Herman, *Collective Bargaining and Labor Relations*, 4th ed. (Upper Saddle River, NJ: Prentice Hall, 1998), pp. 35–54.
[14]See Herman, *Collective Bargaining and Labor Relations*, Chaps. 8 and 9.

Chapter 10
[1]"Harley Owners Group." On-line. Internet. Accessed 16 November 1998. Available World Wide Web: *http://www.magicnet.mni/hog.html.*
[2]Stephen Baker, "SAP's Expanding Universe," *Business Week*, September 14, 1998, pp. 168, 170.
[3]Glenn Collins, "Updating an Icon, Carefully," *The New York Times*, November 17, 1995, D1, D4; "Campbell Earnings Rise on Strong Soup Sales," November 18, 1998 (Camden, NJ: Reuters News Service).
[4]Betsy Morris, "Doug Is It," *Fortune*, May 25, 1998, pp. 70–74+.
[5]Allen St. John, "Baseball's Billion-Dollar Question: Who's on Deck," *American Demographics*, October 1998, pp. 60–62, 65–69.
[6]Lauren Goldstein, "Dressing Up an Old Brand," *Fortune*, November 9, 1998, pp. 154–156.
[7]Jane Perlez, "Joy of Debts: Eastern Europe on Credit Fling," *The New York Times*, May 30, 1998, p. A3.
[8]See Michael R. Solomon, *Consumer Behavior: Buying, Having, and Being*, 4th ed. (Upper Saddle River, NJ: Prentice Hall, 1999), pp. 4–7.
[9]*Statistical Abstract of the United States* (Washington, DC: U.S. Department of Commerce, 1997), pp. 537, 769, 774, 777, 778.
[10]*Statistical Abstract of the United States*, pp. 297, 300; Leslie Wayne, "The Shrinking Military Complex," *The New York Times*, February 27, 1998, pp. D1, D6.
[11]See Edward G. Brierty, Robert W. Eckles, and Robert B. Reeder, *Business Marketing*, 3rd ed. (Upper Saddle River, NJ: Prentice Hall, 1998), Chaps. 4 and 5.
[12]See Warren J. Keegan, *Global Marketing Management*, 6th ed. (Upper Saddle River, NJ: Prentice Hall, 1999), Chaps. 12–16.
[13]See Thomas W. Zimmerer and Norman M. Scarborough, *Essentials of Entrepreneurship and Small Business Management*, 2nd ed. (Upper Saddle River, NJ: Prentice Hall, 1998), Chaps. 5–6.

Chapter 11
[1]See John Burnett and Sandra Moriarty, *Introduction to Marketing Communication: An Integrated Approach* (Upper Saddle River, NJ: Prentice Hall, 1998), pp. 34–40.
[2]"To Market, to Market," *Beverage Industry*, December 1996, pp. 43–46.
[3]Tom Vierhile, "New Products Fared Well in '97," *Beverage Industry*, March 1998, pp. 44–46; David Castle, "New Improved American Dream," *Grocer*, January 18, 1997, p. 15.
[4]Josephine Lee, "A New Medium for the Masses," *Forbes*, July 27, 1998, p. 89.
[5]See James C. Anderson and James A. Narus, *Business Market Management: Understanding, Creating, and Delivering Value* (Upper Saddle River, NJ: Prentice Hall, 1999), pp. 203–206.
[6]Philip Kotler and Gary Armstrong, *Principles of Marketing*, 8th ed. (Upper Saddle River, NJ: Prentice Hall, 1999), p. 288. See also Edward G. Brierty, Robert W. Eckles, and Robert R. Reeder, *Business Marketing*, 3rd ed. (Upper Saddle River, NJ: Prentice Hall, 1998), pp. 259–269.
[7]Betsy Morris, "The Brand's the Thing," *Fortune*, March 4, 1996, p. 72.

[8]See Kevin Lane Keller, *Strategic Brand Management: Building, Measuring, and Managing Brand Equity* (Upper Saddle River, NJ: Prentice Hall, 1998), pp. 2–7.

[9]Claudia Deutsch, "Using a Key That Still Works," *The New York Times*, March 23, 1998, D1, D7.

[10]Peter Passell, "Ferrari's Road to Success Is Its Name," *The New York Times*, July 5, 1997, pp. 35, 36.

[11]See also Karen P. Gonçalves, *Services Marketing: A Strategic Approach* (Upper Saddle River, NJ: Prentice Hall, 1998), pp. 64–77.

[12]Elizabeth Jensen, "Sprint PCS' Subscriber Count Nears One Million, at High End of Estimates," *The Wall Street Journal*, February 3, 1998, p. B5(E); Cellular One Web site. Online. Internet. Accessed 5 January 1999. Available World Wide Web: *http://www.cellularone.com/site/press/pr_index.html;* Alan Pearce, "Wireless Would Grow if Pricing Changed, Fell," *America's Network*, June 1, 1996, p. 54.

Chapter 12

[1]Alice Z. Cuneo, "Starbucks Breaks Largest Ad Blitz," *Advertising Age*, May 19, 1997, pp. 3, 84.

[2]See William Wells, John Burnett, and Sandra Moriarty, *Advertising: Principles and Practice*, 4th ed. (Upper Saddle River, NJ: Prentice Hall, 1998), pp. 94–97.

[3]See Philip Kotler and Gary Armstrong, *Principles of Marketing*, 8th ed. (Upper Saddle River, NJ: Prentice Hall, 1999), pp. 435–437.

[4]R. Craig Endicott, "Leaders Swell Spending by 8.6%, to $58 Billion," *Advertising Age*, September 28, 1998, p. s3.

[5]Endicott, "Leaders Swell Spending," p. s38.

[6]Louise Kramer, "Pepsi Brand Takes a Pass on Super Bowl," *Advertising Age*, January 11, 1999, pp. 1, 40.

[7]See E. Wainright Martin et al., *Managing Information Technology: What Managers Need to Know*, 3rd ed. (Upper Saddle River, NJ: Prentice Hall, 1999), pp. 254–263.

[8]Endicott, "Leaders Swell Spending," pp. s49–s50; "Internet Stock Reports with Steve Harmon." 25 December 1998. Online. Internet. Accessed 23 February 1999. Available World Wide Web: http://www.internet news.com/stocks/.

[9]See Wells, Burnett, and Moriarty, *Advertising*, pp. 104–139.

[10]See John Burnett and Sandra Moriarty, *Introduction to Marketing Communication: An Integrated Approach* (Upper Saddle River, NJ: Prentice Hall, 1998), pp. 410–415.

[11]See Michael D. Hutt and Thomas W. Speh, *Business Marketing Management*, 6th ed. (New York: Dryden Press, 1998), pp. 504–505.

[12]John F. Yarborough, "Dialing for Dollar$," *Marketing Management*, January 1997, p. 60.

[13]See Burnett and Moriarty, *Marketing Communications*, pp. 312–318.

[14]See Warren J. Keegan, *Global Marketing Management*, 6th ed. (Upper Saddle River, NJ: Prentice Hall, 1999), pp. 457–474.

[15]Michael Barrier, "Ties That Bind," *Nation's Business*, August 1997, p. 12.

[16]See also Barry Berman and Joel R. Evans, *Retail Management: A Strategic Approach*, 7th ed. (Upper Saddle River, NJ: Prentice Hall, 1998), pp. 147–158.

[17]See Berman and Evans, *Retail Management*, pp. 178–188.

[18]See Edward G. Brierty, Robert W. Eckles, and Robert R. Reeder, *Business Marketing*, 3rd ed. (Upper Saddle River, NJ: Prentice Hall, 1998), pp. 373–376.

Chapter 13

[1]*Monthly Labor Review* (Washington, DC: U.S. Department of Labor, October 1998), p. 52.

[2]*Survey of Current Business* (Washington, DC: U.S. Department of Commerce, January 1999), p. D-3.

[3]Richard Tomlinson, "China's Reform: Now Comes the Hard Part," *Fortune*, March 1, 1999, p. 159.

[4]Eryn Brown, "America's Most Admired Companies," *Fortune*, March 1, 1999, pp. 68, 70–73.

[5]"Digital and Intel Complete Sale of Digital Semiconductor Manufacturing Operations," *Intel Press Release* (Santa Clara, CA, and Maynard, MA, May 18, 1998).

[6]Keith Bradsher, "General Motors Plans to Build New, Efficient Assembly Plants," *The New York Times*, August 6, 1998, pp. A1, D3.

[7]*Perrigo: 1998 Annual Report* (Allegan, MI: Perrigo, 1998).

[8]Brown, "America's Most Admired Companies," pp. 69–70.

[9]See "The Disney Institute." Internet. Online. Accessed 15 February 1999. Available World Wide Web: http://www.disney.go.com/business_info/index.html.

[10]Gina Imperato, "Harley Shifts Gears," *Fast Company*, June-July 1997, pp. 104–105+.

[11]Internet. Online. Accessed 15 February 1999. Available World Wide Web: http://www.asq.org/abtquality/awards/baldrige/97briefs.html.

[12]Joel Kurtzman, "Is Your Company Off Course? Now You Can Find Out Why," *Fortune*, February 17, 1997, p. 133.

[13]Claudia Deutsch, "Six Sigma Enlightenment," *The New York Times*, December 7, 1998, pp. C1, C7.

Chapter 14

[1]Charles T. Horngren, Walter T. Harrison, Jr., and Linda Smith Bamber, *Accounting*, 4th ed. (Upper Saddle River, NJ: Prentice Hall, 1999), pp. 6–7.

[2]Mark Heinzl, "Noranda to Shed Interests in Forestry and Energy, Refocusing on Mining," *The Wall Street Journal*, November 19, 1997, pp. A3, A6.

[3]See Walter T. Harrison, Jr., and Charles T. Horngren, *Financial Accounting*, 3rd ed. (Upper Saddle River, NJ: Prentice Hall, 1998), pp. 7–10; George H. Bodnar and William S. Hopwood, *Accounting Information Systems*, 7th ed. (Upper Saddle River, NJ: Prentice Hall, 1998), pp. 410–411.

[4]See Charles T. Horngren, Gary L. Sundem, and William O. Stratton, *Cost Accounting: A Managerial Emphasis*, 9th ed. (Upper Saddle River, NJ: Prentice Hall, 1996), pp. 4–5.

[5]Amy Barrett, "Cendant: Who's to Blame?" *Business Week*, August 17, 1998, pp. 70–71; David J. Morrow, "Cendant Finds $115 Million Accounts Error," *The New York Times*, April 16, 1998, pp. D1, D4; Tom Lowry, "Cendant Hopes Canceling Merger Allows Growth," *USA Today*, October 19, 1998, p. 9B.

[6]See Horngren, Harrison, and Bamber, *Accounting*, pp. 10–12.

[7]Melody Petersen, "'Trick' Accounting Draws Levitt Criticism," *The New York Times*, September 29, 1998, p. C8.

[8]Saul Hansell, "S.E.C. Crackdown on Technology Write-Offs," *The New York Times*, September 29, 1998, pp. C1, C8.

[9]See Horngren, Harrison, and Bamber, *Accounting*, pp. 12–14.

[10]See Harrison and Horngren, *Financial Accounting*, pp. 15–23.

[11]See Paul Krugman, "Saving Asia: It's Time to Get Radical," *Fortune*, September 7, 1998, pp. 74–80.

[12]See Horngren, Harrison, and Bamber, *Accounting*, pp. 562–563; Arthur J. Keown et al., *The Foundations of Finance: The Logic and Practice of Financial Management*, 2nd ed. (Upper Saddle River, NJ: Prentice Hall, 1998), pp. 89–95.

[13]See Horngren, Harrison, and Bamber, *Accounting*, pp. 201–202.

[14]See Kenneth C. Laudon and Jane Price Laudon, *Essentials of Management Information Systems* (Upper Saddle River, NJ: Prentice Hall, 1999), pp. 46–51.

[15]See E. Wainright Martin et al., *Managing Information Technology: What Managers Need to Know*, 3rd ed. (Upper Saddle River, NJ: Prentice Hall, 1999), pp. 61–68.

[16]See Martin et al., *Managing Information Technology*, pp. 225–227.

[17]Joshua Macht, "The Ultimate Head Trip," *Inc. Technology*, no. 3 (1997), p. 77.

[18]Gene Bylinsky, "Industry's Amazing Instant Prototypes," *Fortune*, January 12, 1998, pp. 120 (B-D).

[19]Steve Kaufman, "Querying Experts by Keystroke," *Nation's Business*, November 1998, pp. 37–39.

[20]David Kirkpatrick, "Why Have Investors Ignored Lycos for So Long?" *Fortune*, February 1, 1999, p. 150; Matt Lake," "Desperately Seeking Susan OR Suzie NOT Sushi," *The New York Times*, September 8, 1998, pp. G1, G7.

[21]See Martin et al., *Managing Information Technology*, pp. 204–206.

[22]Mary J. Cronin, "Ford's Intranet Success," *Fortune*, March 30, 1998, p. 158.

Chapter 15

[1]See Karl E. Case and Ray C. Fair, *Principles of Economics*, 5th ed. (Upper Saddle River, NJ: Prentice Hall, 1999), pp. 610–611.

[2]The data in this section come from *Federal Reserve Bulletin* (Washington, DC: Board of Governors of the Federal Reserve System, October 1998), pp. A12, A13.

[3]Citicorp. Online. Internet. Accessed 28 November 1998. Available World Wide Web: *http://www.citicorp.com;Statistical Abstract of the United States* (Washington, DC: Bureau of the Census, 1997), p. 520.

[4]Anita Womack, "The High Cost of Credit Card Debt," *Bank Marketing*, March 1998, p. 10; *Statistical Abstract of the United States*, p. 520.

[5]Richard W. Stevenson, "In New Economy, Russians Cannot Rely on Their Banks," *The New York Times*, September 12, 1995, pp. A1, A10; Charles Clover, "Arrears and Barter Return as Bank Credit Dries Up," *The Financial Times*, August 26, 1998, p. 2.

[6]See Frank J. Fabozzi, Franco Modigliani, and Michael G. Ferri, *Foundations of Financial Markets and Institutions*, 2nd ed. (Upper Saddle River, NJ: Prentice Hall, 1998), Chap. 4.

[7]*Fortune*, April 27, 1998, p. F-46; *Statistical Abstract of the United States*, p. 515.

[8]"Sizing Up the Megabanks," *Nation's Business*, November 1, 1998, p. 14; Paul Beckett, "Deal Is Likely to Take Deutsche Bank on a Bumpy Ride," *The Wall Street Journal*, November 27, 1998, p. B4. See also Bank of America Corp. Online. Internet. Accessed 8 December 1998. Available World Wide Web: *http://www.bankamerica.com/news/merger_news.html.*

[9]*Statistical Abstract of the United States*, p. 517.

[10]*Statistical Abstract of the United States*, p. 517. See also Credit Union National Association. Online. Internet. Accessed 8 December 1998. Available World Wide Web: *http://www.cuna.org*.

[11]See Fabozzi, Modigliani, and Ferri, *Foundations of Financial Markets and Institutions*, Chaps. 7–9.

[12]*Statistical Abstract of the United States*, p. 510.

[13]*Federal Reserve Bulletin*, p. A33.

[14]*Statistical Abstract of the United States*, p. 510.

[15]Joe Asher, "The Second ATM Revolution," *ABA Banking Journal*, May 1998, pp. 51–56.

[16]See Fabozzi, Modigliani, and Ferri, *Foundations of Financial Markets and Institutions*, Chap. 5.

[17]This material has been updated from Keith Bradsher, "Federal Reserve Trims a Key Rate; First Cut since '92," *The New York Times*, July 7, 1995, pp. A1, D1, D4.

[18]Bill Orr, "Will It Be Smart or Debit?" *ABA Banking Journal*, September 1998, pp. 54–58. See also Smart Card Forum. Online. Internet. Accessed 8 December 1998. Available World Wide Web: *http://www.smartcrd.com/index.htm*.

[19]Kelly Holland and Greg Burns, "Plastic Talks," *Business Week*, February 14, 1994, pp. 105–107; Saul Hansell, "An End to the 'Nightmare' of Cash," *The New York Times*, September 6, 1994, pp. D1, D5; Thomas McCarroll, "No Checks. No Cash. No Fuss?" *Time*, May 9, 1994, pp. 60–62; Marla Matzer, "Plastic Mania," *Forbes*, October 24, 1994, pp. 281–282.

Chapter 16

[1]See Arthur J. Keown et al., *Foundations of Finance: The Logic and Practice of Financial Management* (Upper Saddle River, NJ: Prentice Hall, 1998), pp. 40–42.

[2]*Federal Reserve Bulletin* (Washington, DC: Board of Governors of the Federal Reserve System, November 1998), p. A31.

[3]*Federal Reserve Bulletin*, November 1998, p. A31.

[4]See David F. Scott, Jr., et al., *Basic Financial Management*, 8th ed. (Upper Saddle River, NJ: Prentice Hall, 1999), pp. 291–292, 296–300.

[5]*Prospectus: Rayovac® Common Stock* (Madison, WI: Rayovac), November 20, 1997.

[6]*Prospectus: Rayovac® Common Stock*.

[7]You can visit the Web sites to examine these online investing services at *http://www.etrade.com* and *http://www.schwab.com*.

[8]Erick Schonfield, "Schwab Puts It All Online," *Fortune*, December 7, 1998, pp. 94–96+; "Schwab Reports Market Activity Highlights," *PRNewswire*, November 12, 1998 (San Francisco).

[9]"New York Stock Exchange." Online. Internet. Accessed 10 December 1998. Available World Wide Web: *http://www.nyse.com*.

[10]See Scott, Jr., et al., *Basic Financial Management*, pp. 266–270.

[11]*Federal Reserve Bulletin*, November 1998, pp. A27, A28, A31, A37.

[12]*$100,000,000 Alaska Industrial Development and Export Authority Power Revenue Bonds, First Series* (John Nuveen & Co. Inc., Goldman, Sachs & Co., Prudential Securities Inc., August 6, 1998).

[13]*Wiesenberger Mutual Funds Update* (Rockville, MD: CDA Investment Technologies, June 30, 1997), p. iii; Greg Carlson, "Trading Works," *Mutual Funds*, September 1998, p. 18.

[14]*Statistical Abstract of the United States: 1997* (Washington, DC: U.S. Department of Commerce, 1997), Table No. 822.

[15]David Barboza, "Stocks Race Past New Milestone as Dow Breaks 7,000 Barrier," *The New York Times*, February 14, 1997, pp. A1, D6.

[16]This illustration is based on Bill Alpert, "The Times Are Risky, the Game Is Dangerous," *The New York Times*, August 27, 1995, sec. 3, p. 3.

[17]SEC Website. Online. Internet. Accessed 9 December 1998. Available World Wide Web: *http://www.sec.gov*.

[18]Michael Schroeder and Amy Barrett, "A Bigger Stick Against Inside Traders," *Business Week*, May 27, 1996, pp. 34–35; NASD Web site. Internet. Online. Accessed 9 December 1998. Available World Wide Web: *http://www.nasdr.com/2700b.htm*.

Source Notes

Part 1

Web Case Study: *The Beanie Baby Business* Joseph Berger, "Goodbye, Tickle Me Elmo; Hello, Beanie Babies," *The New York Times*, March 14, 1997, p. B1; William L. Hamilton, "The Short, Sweet Life of Peanut the Elephant," *The New York Times*, October 30, 1997, p. F1; David Leonhardt, "Hey Kid, Buy This," *Business Week*, June 30, 1997, p. 62; Gary Samuels, "Mystique Marketing," *Forbes*, October 21, 1996, p. 276; Joanna Sullivan, "Bank Offers Hot Investment: Teeny Beanie Babies," *American Banker*, May 19, 1997, p. 17; Rod Taylor et al., "The Beanie Factor," *Brandweek*, June 16, 1997, p. 22; Randy Weston, "Beanie Babies Blitz IS," *Computerworld*, April 28, 1997, p. 1.

Chapter 1

Who Do You Think I Am, Your Concierge?/The Customized Concierge Marc Ballon, "Concierge Makes Hay in Corporate Fields," *Inc.*, September 1998, pp. 23–25; Donna Fenn, "Perks: Buying Time for Employees," *Inc.*, January 1996, p. 85; Susan Greco, "The Road to One-to-One Marketing," *Inc.*, October 1995, p. 56+; Capitol Concierge. Online. Internet. Accessed 26 October 1998. Available World Wide Web: *www.capitolconcierge.com*. **Cartoon** © The New Yorker Collection 1992, Leo Cullum. From cartoonbank.com. All rights reserved. **Figure 1.1** John J. Wild, Kenneth L. Wild, and Jerry C. Y. Han, *International Business: An Integrated Approach* (Upper Saddle River, NJ: Prentice Hall, 2000). **Figure 1.2 (a,b,c)** Carol Kaesuk Yoon, "Chocoholics Take Note: Beloved Bean in Peril," *The New York Times*, May 4, 1998, pp. A1, A15. **Trends and Challenges: *The Deflation Dilemma*** Ram Charan, "With Capacity Growing, Currencies Tumbling, and Prices Slipping, the Rules Have Changed," *Fortune*, March 16, 1998, pp. 159–162; James K. Glassman, "If Prices Fall Too Far, Duck," *U.S. News & World Report*, October 27, 1997, p. 65; James R. Healey, "Some '99 Model Cars Offer Dramatic Price Cuts," *USA Today*, September 16, 1998, p. 1B; Joseph Nocera, "Requiem for the Bull," *Fortune*, September 28, 1998, p. 78+; Rohwer, Jim, "Why the Global Storm Will Zap the U.S. Economy," *Fortune*, September 28, 1998, p. 34+; N. Gregory Mankiw, "Should Alan Greenspan Be Worrying about Deflation?" *Fortune*, December 7, 1998, pp. 54–55. **Building Your Business Skills: *Teaching an Old Dog to Bypass Long-Distance Carriers*** Seth Schiesel, "The Formerly Staid Ma Bell Hatches a Secret Offspring," *The New York Times*, October 7, 1998, pp. A1, C5; Stephanie N. Mehta, "Dog Teaches New Trick to AT&T," *The Wall Street Journal*, October 7, 1998, pp. B1, B4.

Chapter 2

Fiddling Around with Alliances/Alliance by Location Doreen D. Fitzpatrick, "Making Connections," *Crain's New York Business*, September 14, 1998, pp. 25+; Jon Kalish, "Woodworkers Profit by Becoming Joiners," *Crain's New York Business*, September 14, 1998, p. 28; Twin Computer Training, Inc. Online. Internet. Accessed 7 October 1998. Available World Wide Web: www.twincomputers.com. **Cartoon** © 1999 Joseph Farris from cartoonbank.com. All rights reserved. **Figure 2.2** Data from U.S. Bureau of the Census, *Statistical Abstract of the United States: 1997* (Washington, DC, 1998), p. 537. **Figure 2.2** Based on Henry R. Cheeseman, *The Legal and Regulatory Environment: Contemporary Perspectives in Business* (Upper Saddle River, NJ: Prentice Hall, 1997), p. 335. Reprinted by permission of Prentice Hall Inc., Upper Saddle River, NJ. **Figure 2.3** Based on Nancy A. Kubasek, Bartley A. Brennan, and M. Neil Browne, *The Legal Environment of Business* 3rd ed. (Upper Saddle River, NJ: Prentice Hall, 1999), p. 346. Reprinted by permission of Prentice Hall Inc., Upper Saddle River, NJ. **Trends and Challenges: *Banking, Too, Makes Strange Bedfellows*** Maricris G. Briones, "Citigroup: Cross-Selling Products Could Put Firm at Cross Purposes," *Marketing News*, May 11, 1998, p. 2; Aaron Elstein and Jacqueline S. Gold, "Citi-Travelers CEOs Find Opposites Attract," *American Banker*, April 7, 1998, p. 4+; Jacqueline S. Gold, "Bank's Retail Clients Have Misgivings about One-Stop Financial Shopping," *American Banker*, April 8, 1998, p. 1+; Leah Nathans Spiro and Gary Silverman, "Where Does the Buck Stop at Citi?" *Business Week*, November 16, 1998, pp. 180–182+; Carol J. Loomis, "Citigroup: A Progress Report," *Fortune*, November 23, 1998, pp. 33–34; Michael Schrage, "IT and the Citigroup Gamble," *Computerworld*, April 27, 1998, p. 37; Robert Teitelman, "Man and Machine," *Institutional Investor*," May 1998, p. 7.

Chapter 3

Chrysler Gets Under the Hood with Daimler-Benz/How Polo Shirts Came to Tuscaloosa William J. Holstein, "Chrysler's New Identity Crisis," *U.S. News & World Report*, October 26, 1998, pp. 50–52; Karen Lowry Miller with Joann Muller, "The Auto Baron," *Business Week*, November 16, 1998, pp. 82–84+; Douglas A. Blackmon, "A Factory in Alabama Is the Merger in Microcosm," *The Wall Street Journal*, May 8, 1998, p. B1; Lawrence Ingrassia and Brandon Mitchener, "I Was Thinking That, Too, Said Mr. Eaton—And the Talks Were On," *The Wall Street Journal*, May 8, 1998, p. A1; Steven Lipin and Brandon Mitchener, "Daimler-Chrysler Merger to

Produce $3 Billion in Savings, Revenue Gains within 3 to 5 Years," *The Wall Street Journal*, May 8, 1998, p. A10. **Cartoon:** © The New Yorker Collection 1980, Peter Steiner. From cartoonbank.com. All rights reserved. **Figures 3.4 and 3.5** Bureau of Economic Analysis, "International Accounts Data: Trade in Goods and Services." Online. Internet. Accessed 11 December 1998. Available World Wide Web: *http://www.bea.doc.gov/bea/di/tradgs-d.htm* **Trends and Challenges: *It Can't Hurt to Say "Skinny Latte" in Chinese*** Seanna Browder, "Reheating Starbucks," *Business Week*, June 12, 1998, pp. 66–67; "Making Customers Come Back for More," *Fortune*, March 16, 1998, p. 156; Howard Schultz and Dori Jones Yang, "Starbucks: Making Values Pay," *Fortune*, September 29, 1997, pp. 261–272; Joanne Lee-Young, "Starbucks' Expansion in China Is Slated," *The Wall Street Journal*, October 5, 1998, p. A27. **Building Your Business Skills: *"I Intend to Be a Global Company"*** Maria Atanasov, "Taking Her Business on the Road," *Fortune*, April 13, 1998, pp. 158–160.

Chapter 4
The Side Effects of Power Stats/Are There Big Bucks in Big Mac's Future? Thomas Hayden and Karen Springen, "McGwire's Power Supply," *Newsweek*, September 7, 1998, p. 61; Joannie M. Schrof, "McGwire Hits the Pills," *U.S. News & World Report*, September 7, 1998, pp. 53–54; Mark Fitzgerald, "Furor Follows AP Disclosure on McGwire," *Editor & Publisher*, August 29, 1998, p. 10+; Mark Hyman, "Holy Cow, Was That a $25 Million Homer?" *Business Week*, September 21, 1998, p. 104; Gary Mihoces, "Debate over 'Andro' Builds," *USA Today*, August 25, 1998, p. 3C; "ESPN Withdrew Muscle-Supplement Ads," *Communications Daily*, September 25, 1998; Bruce Horovitz, "Sales of Nutrition Supplement Out of Ballpark," *USA Today*, August 27, 1998, p. 1B; "Toss Out the Pills," *St. Louis Post Dispatch*, August 25, 1998, p. B6; Sam Walker, "Home-Run Heroes Bring in Few Endorsements," *The Wall Street Journal*, October 21, 1998, p. B1. © 1999 Robert Mankoff from cartoonbank.com. All rights reserved. **Figure 4.1** Based on Gerald F. Cavanaugh, *American Business Values; With International Perspectives*, 4th ed. (Upper Saddle River, NJ: Prentice Hall, 1998), p. 71. **Trends and Challenges: *Nike Sweats Some Unpleasant Details*** (Gina Binole, "Protesters Prepare for International Nike Day of Protest," *Business Journal-Portland*, October 17, 1997, p. 16; Joanna Ramey, "Anti-Sweatshop Effort at Nike to Be Expanded," *Women's Wear Daily*, May 12, 1998, p. 2; Ramey, "Nike Unfurls Anti-Sweatshop Measures," *Footwear News*, May 18, 1998, p. 4; Ramey, "Religious Investors Ask Nike, Reebok to Hire Offshore Factory Worker Wages," *Women's Wear Daily*, May 21, 1948, p. 4; Bill Richards, "Tripped Up by Too Many Shoes, Nike Regroups," *The Wall Street Journal*, March 3, 1998, p. B1. **Figure 4.2** Based on Andrew C. Revkin, "Who Cares about a Few Degrees?" *The New York Times*, December 12, 1997 (A Preview to the Kyoto Conference: Global Warming), p. F1. **Table 4.1** Data from The Foundation Center, "50 Largest Corporate Foundations by Total Giving." Online. Internet. Accessed 3 December 1998. Available World Wide Web: *http://fdncenter.org/grantmaker/trends/top50giving.htm.*

Part 2
Web Case Study: *Cape Cod Revival* Linda Grant, "A Passion for Potato Chips," *Fortune*, August 18, 1997, p. 228; Dan McGraw, "Salting Away the Competition: Frito-Lay Launches a Powerful Snack Attach and Crunches the Competition," *U.S. News & World Report*, September 16, 1996, p. 71; Bernard Pacyniak, "Cape Cod Redux," *Snack & Bakery Foods*, March 1997, p. 33; Dale D. Buss, "Hello, Mr. Chips," *Income Opportunities*, August 1997; Cape Cod Potato Chip Press Releases, "As Potato Chip Companies Try to Gain an Edge in the Snack Food Industry, Cape Cod Looks to the Russet," "Cape Cod Potato Chips' Success Wasn't Just by Accident," and "Just as Eaters Seem to Have Given Up Hope in the Taste of Low-Fat Foods, Cape Cod Potato Chips Finds the Answer."

Chapter 5
The Management Equivalent of Juggling/Management by Posting Pictures Timothy Aeppel, "A 3Com Factory Hires a Lot of Immigrants, Gets Mix of Languages," *The Wall Street Journal*, March 30, 1998, p. A1; Eric Benhamou, "Let the Good Times Roll," *PC Week*, October 5, 1998, p. 95; Christopher Elliott, "3Com Gets Back to Basics," *Journal of Business Strategy*, September-October 1998, p. 33. **Figure 5.1** Based on Stephen P. Robbins and Mary Coulter, *Management*, 6th ed. (Upper Saddle River, NJ: Prentice Hall, 1999), p. 239. **Cartoon:** DILBERT reprinted by permission of United Features Syndicate, Inc. **Trends and Challenges: *What's Your Emotional Intelligence Quotient?*** Sharon Begley, "The Boss Feels Your Pain," *Newsweek*, October 12, 1998, p. 74; Daniel Goleman, *Working with Emotional Intelligence* (New York: Bantam Books, 1998). **Building Your Business Skills: *Skillful Talking*** Information from Justin Martin, "How You Speak Shows Where You Rank," *Fortune*, February 2, 1998, p. 156.

Chapter 6
The Agony and Ecstasy of Delegating/My Name Is Anita, and I'm a Micromanager Scott Bistayi, "Delegate—Or Not?" *Forbes*, April 21, 1997, p. 20+; Norm Brodsky, "Necessary Losses," *Inc.*, December 1997, p. 116+; Linda Formichelli, "Letting Go of the Details," *Nation's Business*, November 1997, p. 50+. **Cartoon:** © 1999 Charles Barsotti, from cartoonbank.com. All rights reserved. **Trends and Challenges: *Star Tracking: The Next Generation*** John Beeson, "Succession Planning: Building the Management Corps," *Business Horizons*, September-October 1998, p. 61+; Eve Golden, "Nothing Succeeds Like Succession," *Across the Board*, June 1998, p. 36+. **Building Your Business Skills: *Holding On to Qualified Computer Programmers*** Amy Harmon, "Software Jobs Go Begging, Threatening Technology Boom," *The New York Times*, January 13, 1998, p. A1.

Chapter 7
Please Turn to Chapter 11/The Next Installment Patti Bond, "Chapter 11 on Musical Page with Onyx Deal," *Atlanta Journal Constitution*, March 27, 1998, p. H1; Bond "Retail Shapes Metro Atlanta's Horizon," *Atlanta Journal Constitution*, July 27, 1998, p. E7; Jeffrey A. Tannenbaum, "Small Bookseller Beats the Giants at Their Own Game," *The Wall Street Journal*, November 4, 1997, p. B1. **Figure 7.1** U.S. Department of Commerce, *Statistical Abstract of the United States* (Washington, DC: Bureau of the Census, 1997), p. 540. **Figure 7.2** *Hoover's Handbook of American Business 1999* (Austin, TX: Hoover's Business Press, 1999). **Figure 7.3** *The Wall Street Journal Almanac 1999* (New York: Ballantine Books, 1999). **Figure 7.4** *1996 Facts on Women-Owned Businesses* © 1996/National Foundation for Women Business Owners. **Figure 7.5** Adapted from NFIB Foundation/VISA Business Card Primer (Washington, DC). **Cartoon:** © The New Yorker Collection 1998, Michael Maslin from cartoonbank.com. All rights reserved. **Trends and Challenges: *Cashing In on Cuban Nostalgia*** Mirta Ojito, "A Nightclub Bottles Cuba, Before the Revolution," *The New York Times*, October 13, 1998, p. A12; Hillary Stout, "Fidel Meets Naomi, or Cashing In on the Cuban Craze," *The Wall Street Journal*, March 2, 1998, p. B1.

Part 3
Web Case Study: *The Wacky World of Southwest Airlines* Ann Bruce, "Southwest: Back to the FUNdamentals," *HR Focus*, March 1997, p. 11; Anne Fisher, "The 100 Best Companies to Work for in America," *Fortune*, January 12, 1998, p. 69; Kristin Dunlap Godsey, "Slow Climb to New Heights; Combine Strict Discipline with Goofy Antics and Make Billions," *Success*, October 1996, p. 20; Polly LaBarre, "Lighten Up! Blurring the Link between Fun and Work Not Only Humanizes Organizations but Strengthens the Bottom Line," *Industry Week*, February 5, 1996, p. 53; Robert Levering and Milton Moskowitz, "The 100 Best Companies to Work for in America," *Fortune*, January 12, 1998, p. 84; Ronald B. Lieber, "Why Employees Love These Companies," *Fortune*, January 12, 1998, p. 72; Justin Martin, "So, You Want to Work for the Best," *Fortune*, January 12, 1998, p. 77; Allen R. Myerson, "Air Herb," *The New York Times Magazine*," November 9, 1997, p. 36; Donald J. McNerney, "Employee Motivation: Creating a Motivated Workforce," *HR Focus*, August 1996, p. 1; Dan Reed, "Flying Like a Madman," *Sales & Marketing Management*, October 1997, p. 92.

Chapter 8
Do Stock Options Make It Happen?/The Price of Repricing Edward O. Welles, "Motherhood, Apple Pie and Stock options," *Inc.*, February 1998, p. 84+; Jonathan D. Epstein, "Chase to Lavish Stock Options on 67,000 Employees," *American Banker*, December 18, 1996, p. 1+; Arthur H. Kroll, "Exploring Options," *HRMagazine*, October 1997, p. 96+; Shaifali Puri, "Pay for Underperformance: The Problem with Stock Options," *Fortune*, December 8, 1997, p. 52+. **Figure 8.1** Linda Grant, "Happy Workers, High Returns," *Fortune*, January 12, 1998, p. 81. Reprinted from the January 12, 1998 issue of FORTUNE by special permission; copyright 1998, Time, Inc. **Figure 8.2** "Corporations That Prize Skills and Hands-On Experience Are Adapting at the Fringes," Time, November 9, 1998), p. 21. **Cartoon:** © The New Yorker Collection 1991, Leo Cullum, from the cartoonbank.com. All rights reserved. **Trends and Challenges: *How to Energize a Global Manager*** Pico Iyer, "The New Business Class," *The New York Times Magazine*, March 8, 1998, pp. 37–40; Hal Lancaster, "Global Managers Need Boundless Sensitivity, Rugged Constitutions," *The Wall Street Journal*, October 13, 1998, p. B1. **Building Your Business Skills: *Too Much of a Good Thing*** Information about George Uhe Co. from Dan Morse, "For Family Firm Uhe, Paternalism Signaled Stagnation," *The Wall Street Journal*, March 3, 1998, p. B2.

Chapter 9
Labor Rolls the Dice in Las Vegas/Membership Is Job #1 Vivienne Walt, "Labor's Big Bet," *U.S. News & World Report*, February 9, 1998, pp. 52–53; Franklin Foer, "Winners & Losers," *U.S. News & World Report*, November 16, 1998, p. 37; Aaron

Bernstein, "Meet the Al Dunlap of the Union Hall," *Business Week*, February 17, 1997, p. 62; Bernstein, "Sweeney's Blitz," *Business Week*, February 17, 1997, pp. 56–62. **Trends and Challenges: *Conducting Romances in Parallel Universes (And Other Places)*** William C. Symonds, "Sex on the Job," *Business Week*, February 16, 1998, pp. 30–31; Linda Himelstein, "Breaking Through," *Business Week*, February 17, 1997, pp. 64–70; Eric Konigsberg, "The Cheating Kind," *The New York Times Magazine*, March 8, 1998, p. 65. **Table 9.1** *The Wall Street Journal Almanac 1999* (New York: Balantine Books, 1998), p. 234. Data from U.S. Bureau of Labor Statistics. **Figure 9.3** Michele Galen with Anne Therese Palmer, "White, Male, and Worried," *Business Week*, January 31, 1994), p. 53. **Figure 9.4** *The Wall Street Journal Almanac 1999* (New York: Balantine Books, 1998), p. 241. Data from U.S. Bureau of Labor Statistics. **Figure 9.5** *USA Today*, April 11, 1997. **Figure 9.6** *The Wall Street Journal Almanac 1999* (New York: Balantine Books, 1998), p. 243. Data from U.S. Bureau of Labor Statistics.

Part 4

Web Case Study: *Off to the Races* Al Heller, "Motorsports Mania," *Inside Media*, June 26, 1996, p. 30; Tony Molla, "Motorsports Marketing: Race on Sunday, Sell on Monday." *Motor Age*, March 1997, p. 52; "NASCAR Is Becoming a Leader in Motorsports Entertainment," *Aftermarket Business*, November 1, 1996, p. 70; Bill Vlasic, "Speedways without Smoke," *Business Week*, July 21, 1997; Lee Walczak, "Speed Sells," *Business Week*, August 11, 1997; Interview with M. J. Castelo, Sponsorship Manager, Texaco/Havoline Motorsports Program, October 9, 1996.

Chapter 10

Baggy Brands and Deep Pockets/Between the Barbie Doll and the Driver's License Lisa Bannon, "As Children Become More Sophisticated, Marketers Think Older," *The Wall Street Journal*, October 13, 1998, p. A1; Nina Munk, "How Teens Buy," *Fortune*, April 13, 1998, pp. 28–30; Jennifer Steinhauer, "Lulu and Her Friends Are, Therefore They Shop," *The New York Times*, April 29, 1998, p. 6. **Figure 10.3** Erick Schonfield, "Changes in the U.S. Population: Betting on the Boomers," *Fortune*, December 25, 1995, pp. 78–80. Reprinted from the December 25, 1995 issue of FORTUNE by special permission; copyright 1995, Time Inc. **Figure 10.4** Paul C. Judge, "Technographics Variables: Are Tech Buyers Different?" *Business Week*, January 26, 1998, p. 65. Reprinted from the January 26, 1998 issue of Business Week by special permission © 1998 by the McGraw-Hill Companies, Inc. **Cartoon:** © 1999 William Hamilton from cartoonbank.com. All rights reserved. **Trends and Challenges: *How to Tell a Fast Forward from a Hand-Shaker*** Paul C. Judge, "Are Tech Buyers Different?" *Business Week*, January 26, 1998, pp. 64–68; "Forrester Forum to Explore On-Line Marketing Strategies and the Virtual Audience," *Business Wire*, July 14, 1998, p. 7141371; Andy Hines, "Do You Know Your Technology Type?" *The Futurist*, September/October 1997, pp. 10+; "The NPD Group to Incorporate Forrester's Technographics into the NPD Online Panel and SiteSelect," *Business Wire*, May 14, 1998, p. 5141052.

Chapter 11

Everybody Has a Price/The Joy of Take-It-or-Leave-It Shopping Katherine T. Beddingfield, "Airfare Roulette," *U.S. News & World Report*, April 27, 1998, p. 75; "For the First Time, Consumers Can Use the Power of the Internet to Name Their Own Price for Major Purchases," *Business Wire*, February 11, 1998, p. 2111120; "Priceline.com Expands 'Name Your Own Price' Service with an Entirely New Way to Buy a Car or Truck," *Business Wire*, July 6, 1998, p. 7061006; "Priceline.com Issued U.S. Patent No. 5,794,207 for the World's First Buyer-Driven E-Commerce System," *Business Wire*, August 11, 1998, p. 8110066; "Priceline.com Keeps Affordable Leisure Airline Tickets within Reach of Nation's Budget-Conscious Travelers," *Business Wire*, August 19, 1998, p. 8191346; Bob Wallace, "Pick a Car, Name Your Price," *Computerworld*, July 27, 1998, p. 45. **Cartoon:** © The New Yorker Collection 1996. William Hamilton from cartoonbank.com. All rights reserved. **Figure 11.2** Jay Heizer and Barry Render, *Operations Management*, 5th ed. (Upper Saddle River, NJ: Prentice Hall, 1999), p. 197. **Trends and Challenges: *Developing a Wild Life Style*** Marc Gunther, "Disney's Call of the Wild," *Fortune*, April 13, 1998, pp. 120–124.

Chapter 12

Log On and Get Rational/The Rationale of Alienating Traditional Partners George Anders, "Some Big Companies Long to Embrace Web but Settle for Flirtation," *The Wall Street Journal*, November 4, 1998, p. A1; Ellen Neuborne and Robert D. Hof, "Branding on the Net," *Business Week*, November 9, 1998, pp. 76–86. **Figure 12.2** R. Craig Endicott, "Leaders Swell Spending by 8.6% to $58 Billion," *Advertising Age*, September 28, 1998, p. s38. **Table 12.1** Craig Endicott, "Top Marketers Invest $47.3 Billion in '95 Ads," *Advertising Age*, November 30, 1996, p. s54. **Cartoon:** © The New Yorker Collection 1998. George Booth from cartoonbank.com. All rights reserved. **Trends and Challenges: *Making Book on the Future*** Doreen Carvajal, "Once upon a Frenzy," *The New York Times*, November 18, 1998, p. C1; Yahlin Chang, "Books Caught in the Web," *Newsweek*, November 23, 1998, p. 85; William J. Holstein, "A New Chapter in Publishing," *U.S. News & World Report*, November 23, 1998, p. 53.

Part 5

Web Case Study: *The Millenium Bomb* Danna K. Henderson, "To Meet the Millennium, Airlines Are Taking Steps to Deal with Computer Complications Accompanying the Approaching Year 2000," *Air Transport World*, September 1997, p. 96; Kris Hunter, "Getting Ready for the Big One: Business Prepares for 'Millennium Bug.'" *Memphis Business Journal*, August 26, 1996, p. 1; "Millennium Blues," *Chain Store Age Executive with Shopping Center Age*, October 1997, p. 8B; "Millennium Dilemma Could Cause Big Problems as Early as 1999, Fitch CPAs Say," *Software Industry Report*, March 3, 1997, p. 1; Paul Minkin and Adrienne Guistwite, "Are You Ready for the Next Millennium?" *Telephony*, June 24, 1996, p. 72; Ruth Morris, "Labor Shortage Looms over Year 2000 Problem," Reuters, January 26, 1998; Tariq K. Muhammad, "The 2000 Year Glitch: Will Your Computer Be Able to Usher in the New Millennium?" *Black Enterprise*, May 1997, p. 38; Andrea Rock and Tripp Reynolds, "The Year 2000 Bug," *Money*, February 1998, p. 49.

Chapter 13

A High-Concept Story about Bad Food/Planet Hollywood Tightens Its Stellar Orbit Richard Gibson, "Fame Proves Fleeting at Planet Hollywood as Fans Avoid Reruns," *The Wall Street Journal*, October 7, 1998, p. A1; Richard L. Papiernik, "Investors Say 'Haasta la Vista' after Planets Cites Falling Numbers," *Nation's Restaurant News*, February 2, 1998, p. 11. **Figure 13.1** Data from *Monthly Labor Review* (Washington, DC: U.S. Dept. of Labor, October 1998), p. 52. **Figure 13.2** Data from *Survey of Current Business* (Washington, DC: U.S. Dept. of Commerce, January 1999), p. D-3. **Cartoon:** © The New Yorker Collection, 1995, Ed Fisher from cartoonbank.com. All rights reserved. **Trends and Challenges: *The Fine Line between Bold Moves and Dysfunctional Maneuvers*** Andy Reinhardt, "Fly, Damn It, Fly," *Business Week*, November 9, 1998, p. 150–156; Laurence Zuckerman, "Boeing's Man in the Line of Fire," *The New York Times*, November 8, 1998, sec. 3, p. 2. **Figure 13.6** ADAC Laboratories, "Total Quality Management (TQM)." Online. Internet. Accessed 2 March 1999. Available World Wide Web: *http://www.adaclabs.com/about/ quality.html.*

Chapter 14

How Cooking the Books Left One Accountant with a Bad Taste/Is Whistleblowing a Growth Industry? Kurt Eichenwald, "He Blew the Whistle, and Health Giant Quaked," *The New York Times*, October 18, 1998, sec. 3, p. 1; Pamela Sherrid, "How to Really Make a Killing in Health Care," *U.S. News & World Report*, November 2, 1998, p. 48. **Cartoon:** © The New Yorker Collection 1994 Mort Gerberg from cartoonbank.com. All rights reserved. **Trends and Challenges: *Y2K? What, Me Worry?*** Ellen Depasquale, "For Smaller Firms, It's Comply or Else," *Crain's New York Business*, September 14, 1998, p. 39; "It's 1998. Do You Know What Your Y2K Status Is?" *Inc.*, March 15, 1998, p. 16; Sougata Mukherjee, "Small Business Putting Off Dealing with Y2K Problem," *San Francisco Business Times*, June 5, 1998, p. 8; Rose-Robin Pedone, "Y2K May Hurt Small Firms," *LI Business News*, April 20, 1998, p. 1; Jeffrey A. Tannenbaum, "Small Firms Face Tighter Credit Due to Y2K Threat," *The Wall Street Journal*, November 10, 1998, p. B2. **Building Your Business Skills: *The Art and Science of Point-and-Click Research*** Information on search sites from Matt Lake, "Desperately Seeking Susan OR Suzie NOT Sushi," *The New York Times*, September 3, 1998, p. G1; Thomas E. Weber, "Who, What, Where: Putting the Internet in Perspective," *The Wall Street Journal*, April 16, 1998, p. B12.

Part 6

Web Case Study: *Lettuce and Loans* Brett Chase, "Banks Race to Expand Chicago Supermarket Networks," *American Banker*, January 22, 1997, p. 5; Garey Gillam, "Supermarket Branches Ring Up Another Big Year," *American Banker*, January 8, 1997, p. 7; Julie Monahan, "The Branch Is Dead. Long Live the Branch!" *ABA Banking Journal*, April 1997, p. S2; Stephen Timewell, "Shopping for Money," *The Banker*, August 1996, p. 18; Jeffrey Zack, "National Commerce Points Way to Success in the Supermarkets," *American Banker*, May 6, 1996, p. 4A; Danna Christine Blank, "Are Consumers Confused?" *Progressive Grocer*, July 1996, p. 14.

Chapter 15

A Popular Bank in a Big Niche/Extending Credit Where Credit Is Due Tami Luhby, "Bank Vies for Popularity with Minority Businesses," *Crain's New York Business*, November 16, 1998, pp. 43–44; Lisa Fickenscher, "Banco Popular Targets U.S. Mainland Card Market," *American Banker*, October 19, 1998, p. 7; Monica Perin, "Puerto Rican Bank Gains Share of Hispanic Market," *Houston Business Journal*, September 26, 1997, pp. 1+. **Figures 15.1, 15.2, 15.3** Data compiled and updated from *Federal Reserve Bulletin* **Cartoon:** © The New Yorker Collection 1997 William Hamilton from cartoonbank.com. All rights reserved. **Trends and Challenges: *The Continent Braces for the Era of the Euro*** John Tagliabue, "No

Banker's Holiday for Europe," *The New York Times*, December 5, 1998, pp. C1, C2; Samantha Conti, "The Simple Life: Europe's Fashion Firms Await the Era of the Euro," *WWD*, July 22, 1997, pp. 84+; Alana Cowell, "Plotting the Center of the New Europe," *The New York Times*, October 20, 1998, p. C1; Thomas Kamm, "As the Euro's Arrival Nears, Europe Braces for Lots of Headaches," *The Wall Street Journal*, November 30, 1998, p. A1; Jane Bryant Quinn, "Here Comes the Euro," *Newsweek*, October 26, 1998, p. 63; Irving Vigdor, "The New Money: How the Euro Will Aid Apparel Makers," *Apparel Industry Magazine*, May 1998, pp. 14+.

Chapter 16

"Give Me 1000 Shares of Dramamine"/The Forces That* Might *Have Been at Work E. S. Browning, Greg Ip, and Leslie Scism, "With Dazzling Speed, Market Roars Back to Another New High," *The Wall Street Journal*, November 24, 1998, p. A1; Trevor Nelson, "How Now Dow Jones: Dubious Reporting on Why the Market Moves," *Columbia Journalism Review*, March-April 1994, p. 9+; James M. Pethokoukis and Mind Charski, "Lessons Learned: The Volatile Market Is Trying to Tell Us Something," *U.S. News & World Report*, September 21, 1998, pp. 65+; James M. Pethokoukis and Kim Clarke, "Panic Buying on Wall Street?" *U.S. News & World Report*, p. 76; Fred Vogelstein and William J. Holstein, "Fasten Your Seat Belts," *U.S. News and World Report*, October 26, 1998, pp. 43–46. **Cartoon:** © 1999 Robert Mankoff from cartoonbank.com. All rights reserved. **Trends and Challenges: *Where Virtual Testing Is a Reality*** Kathy Yakal, "Web Masters," *Barron's*, October 26, 1998, p. 31–38. **Figure 16.1** New York Stock Exchange. Online. Internet. Accessed 7 December 1998. Available World Wide Web: <nyse.com>. NASDAQ. Online. Internet. Accessed 7 December 1998. Available World Wide Web: <nasdaq.com>.

Photo Credits

Chapter 1
Page 3: AP/Wide World Photos
Page 7: Per Breiehagen
Page 11: C. Bruce Forster/Viewfinders
Page 19: John Stanmewer/SABA Press Photos, Inc.
Page 21: Wolf/Visum/SABA Press Photos, Inc.
Page 22: AP/Wide World Photos
Page 26: 10-10-345 Lucky Dog

Chapter 2
Page 31: Twin Computer Training, Inc.
Page 32: Carnegie Library of Pittsburgh
Page 33: Lewis W. Hine/Library of Congress
Page 35: Rex Rystedt/Rex Rystedt Photography
Page 37: William Mercer McLeod/William Mercer McLeod

Chapter 3
Page 53: John Stilwell/AP/Wide World Photos
Page 58: Andy Freeberg Photography
Page 60: Munshi Ahmed Photography
Page 66: Klaus D. Francke/Bilderberg Archiv der Fotografen
Page 69: Eric Bouvet/Agence Ernoult Features
Page 74: Cristina Nunez/Grazia Neri/Sygma

Chapter 4
Page 79: James A. Finley/AP/Wide World Photos
Page 81: Edward Keating/New York Times Pictures
Page 82: Les Stone/Sygma
Page 86: Ch. Simonpietri/Sygma

Chapter 5
Page 103: Ed Quinn/SABA Press Photos, Inc.
Page 107: AP/Wide World Photos
Page 116: Courtesy Boeing Commercial Airplane Group
Page 119: Douglas Levere/Douglas Levere Photography
Page 120: Diana Lixenberg/(Z) Photographic

Chapter 6
Page 129: Martin Benjamin/Black Star
Page 132: Sygma
Page 138: Cook/Jenshel

Chapter 7
Page 149: Adam Taylor/Barbara Babbit Kaufman
Page 154: Cathlyn Melloan/Tony Stone Images
Page 162: Yunghi Kim/Yunghi Kim
Page 166: Terry Wild Studio

Chapter 8
Page 177: Southwest Airlines Co.
Page 181: Craig Hammell/The Stock Market
Page 182: Todd Buchanan
Page 192: Layne Kennedy/Corbis
Page 195: Brian Moriarty/Brian Moriarty
Page 198: David Woo/The Dallas Morning News

Chapter 9
Page 207: William Mercer McLeod/William Mercer McLeod
Page 209: Len Rubenstein/Len Rubenstein Photography
Page 215: Evan Kafka
Page 218: Wolfgang Knapp/Agentur THEMA
Page 223: Mark Richards/Mark Richards
Page 227: Joel Rennich/AP/Wide World Photos

Chapter 10
Page 241: AP/Wide World Photos
Page 246: Omron Management Center of America, Inc./Courtesy of Omron Corp.
Page 247: Jake Wallis/Courtesy of United Parcel Service
Page 247: Chris Steinocher/Tampa Bay Partnership
Page 249: Monty Davis/AP/Wide World Photos
Page 250: Michael L. Abramson Photography
Page 256: R. Maiman/Sygma
Page 261: Greg Girard/Contact Press Images Inc.
Page 263: Nancy Price/Black Star
Page 264: David M. Barron/Oxygen Group Photography

Chapter 11
Page 272: Jody Dole/Price Waterhouse LLP
Page 276: Patrick Harbron
Page 280: John Abbott Photography
Page 285: James Schnepf Photography, Inc.

Chapter 12
Page 298: Tobias Everke/Liaison Agency, Inc.
Page 299: Michael L. Abramson Photography
Page 302: Jeffrey Aaronson/Network Aspen
Page 305: Keith Meyers/New York Times Pictures
Page 308: Andrew Garn

Chapter 13
Page 325: Bob Sacha Photography
Page 329: Albert Ferreira/AP/Wide World Photos
Page 332: Mark Lyons/New York Times Pictures
Page 339: Louis Psihoyos/Matrix International, Inc.
Page 340: Nancy Siesel/New York Times Pictures
Page 350: Ray Ng

Chapter 14
Page 359: Rich Frishman Photography and Videograph Inc.
Page 361: Sara Krulwich/New York Times Pictures
Page 376: Michael Newman/PhotoEdit
Page 378: Tracy Kroll/Tracy Kroll
Page 379: Brownie Harris/Brownie Harris, Photographer

Chapter 15
Part 393: Mark Richards/PhotoEdit
Page 397: Steinway/Banco Popular
Page 399: Ed Wrang/AP/Wide World Photos
Page 401: SABA Press Photos, Inc.
Page 405: Greg Miller/Greg Miller Photography
Page 406: Peter Korniss/Peter Korniss

Chapter 16
Page 423: Jonathan Saunders/Jonathan Saunders
Page 424: Mark Richards/Mark Richards
Page 425: Mark Richards
Page 429: Dod Miller/SABA Press Photos, Inc.
Page 431: Richard B. Levine/Frances M. Roberts

Cover: Sittler/REA/SABA Press Photos, Inc.

GLOSSARY

absolute advantage The ability to produce something more efficiently than any other country can [58]

accountability Liability of subordinates for accomplishing tasks assigned by managers [135]

accounting Comprehensive system for collecting, analyzing, and communicating financial information [360]

accounting system Organized means by which financial information is identified, measured, recorded, and retained for use in accounting statements and management reports [360]

accounts payable Current liabilities consisting of bills owed to suppliers, plus wages and taxes due within the upcoming year [368]

accounts receivable Amount due from a customer who has purchased goods on credit [367]

acquisition The purchase of one company by another [43]

Active Corps of Executives (ACE) SBA program in which currently employed executives work with small businesses on a volunteer basis [164]

activity ratio Financial ratio for evaluating management's use of a firm's assets [370]

advertising media Variety of communication devices for carrying a seller's message to potential customers [296]

affirmative action program Legally mandated program for recruiting qualified employees belonging to racial, gender, or ethnic groups that are underrepresented in an organization [216]

agent Individual or organization acting for, and in the name of, another party [471]

apparent authority Agent's authority, based on the principal's compliance, to bind a principal to a certain course of action [471]

appellate court Court that reviews case records of trials whose findings have been appealed [467]

articles of incorporation Document detailing the corporate governance of a company, including its name and address, its purpose, and the amount of stock it intends to issue [41]

artificial intelligence (AI) Construction and programming of computers to imitate human thought processes [377]

asked price Price that an OTC broker charges for a share of stock [437]

assembly line Product layout in which a product moves step-by-step through a plant on conveyor belts or other equipment until it is completed [338]

asset Any economic resource expected to benefit a firm or individual who owns it [365]

audit Systematic examination of a company's accounting system to determine whether its financial reports fairly present its operations [362]

authority Power to make the decisions necessary to complete a task [135]

autocratic style Managerial style in which managers generally issue orders and expect them to be obeyed without question [197]

automated teller machine (ATM) Electronic machine that allows customers to conduct account-related activities 24 hours a day, 7 days a week [405]

balance of payments Flow of all money into or out of a country [59]

balance of trade Economic value of all products a country imports minus the economic value of all products it exports [58]

balance sheet Financial statement detailing a firm's assets, liabilities, and owners' equity [366]

banker's acceptance Bank promise, issued for a buyer, to pay a designated firm a specified amount at a future date [405]

bankruptcy Permission granted by the courts to individuals and organizations not to pay some or all of their debts [472]

bargain retailer Retailer carrying a wide range of products at bargain prices [308]

batch processing Method of collecting data over a period of time and then computer processing them as a group or batch [373]

bear market Period of falling stock prices [438]

bearer (or coupon) bond Bond requiring the holder to clip and submit a coupon to receive an interest payment [432]

benefits Compensation other than wages and salaries [214]

bid price Price that an OTC broker pays for a share of stock [437]

blue-chip stock Common stock issued by a well-established company with a sound financial history and a stable pattern of dividend payouts [426]

blue-sky laws Laws requiring securities dealers to be licensed and registered with the states in which they do business [442]

board of directors Governing body of a corporation that reports to its shareholders and delegates power to run its day-to-day operations, but remains responsible for sustaining its assets [42]

bond Security through which an issuer promises to pay the buyer a certain amount of money by a specified future date [431]

bonus Individual performance incentive in the form of a special payment made over and above the employee's salary [213]

book value Value of a common stock expressed as total shareholders' equity divided by the number of shares of stock [425]

bookkeeping The recording of accounting transactions [360]

boycott Labor action in which workers refuse to buy the products of a targeted employer [228]

branch office Foreign office set up by an international or multinational firm [67]

brand competition Competitive marketing that appeals to consumer perceptions of similar products [249]

brand loyalty Pattern of regular consumer purchasing based on satisfaction with a product [257]

branding Process of using symbols to communicate the qualities of a product made by a particular producer 279]

breakeven analysis Assessment of the quantity of a product that must be sold before the seller makes a profit [282]

breakeven point Quantity of a product that must be sold before the seller covers variable and fixed costs and makes a profit [282]

broker Individual or organization who receives and executes buy-and-sell orders on behalf of other people in return for commissions [427]

browser Software supporting the graphics and linking capabilities necessary to navigate the World Wide Web [381]

budget deficit Situation in which a government body spends more money than it takes in [23]

bull market Period of rising stock prices [438]

business An organization that provides goods or services to earn profits [7]

business continuation agreement Special form of business insurance whereby owners arrange to buy the interests of deceased associates from their heirs [463]

business ethics Ethical or unethical behaviors by a manager or employer of an organization [80]

business interruption insurance Insurance covering income lost during times when a company is unable to conduct business [462]

business practice laws Laws or regulations governing business practices in given countries [70]

bylaws Document detailing corporate rules and regulations, including election and responsibilities of directors and procedures for issuing new stock [41]

cafeteria benefits plan Benefits plan that establishes dollar amount of benefits per employee and allows employees to choose from a variety of alternative benefits [214]

capacity Amount of a product that a company can produce under normal working conditions [336]

capacity Competence required of individuals entering into a binding contract [467]

capital The funds needed to create and operate a business enterprise [8]

capital gain Profit earned by selling a share of stock for more than it cost [425]

capital item Expensive, long-lasting, infrequently purchased industrial product such as a building [273]

capital structure Relative mix of a firm's debt and equity financing [457]

capitalism Market economy that provides for private ownership of production and encourages entrepreneurship by offering profits as an incentive [9]

cartel Association of producers whose purpose is to control supply and prices [70]

cash-flow management Management of cash inflows and outflows to ensure adequate funds for purchases and the productive use of excess funds [452]

catalog showroom Bargain retailer in which customers place orders for catalog items to be picked up at on-premises warehouses [309]

cellular layout Spatial arrangement of production facilities designed to move families of products through similar flow paths [339]

centralized organization Organization in which most decision-making authority is held by upper-level management [136]

certified public accountant (CPA) Accountant licensed by the state and offering services to the public [362]

chain of command Reporting relationships within a company [131]

check Demand deposit order instructing a bank to pay a given sum to a specified payee [399]

check kiting Illegal practice of writing checks against money that has not yet been credited at the bank on which the checks are drawn [90]

chief executive officer (CEO) Top manager hired by the board of directors to run a corporation [42]

classical theory of motivation Theory holding that workers are motivated solely by money [184]

closed promotion system System by which managers decide, often informally, which workers are considered for promotions [211]

closed shop Workplace in which an employer may hire only workers already belonging to a union [226]

collateral Borrower-pledged legal asset that may be seized by lenders in case of nonpayment [454]

collective bargaining Process by which labor and management negotiate conditions of employment for workers represented by the union [223]

collusion Illegal agreement between two or more companies to commit a wrongful act [88]

commercial bank Federal- or state-chartered financial institution accepting deposits that it uses to make loans and earn profits [402]

commercial paper Short-term securities, or notes, containing a borrower's promise to pay [455]

committee and team authority Authority granted to committees or work teams involved in a firm's daily operations [138]

commodities market Market in which futures contracts are traded [435]

common law Body of decisions handed down by courts ruling on individual cases [464]

common stock Stock that pays dividends and guarantees corporate voting rights, but offers last claims over assets [41]

comparable worth Principle that women should receive the same pay for traditionally "female" jobs of the same worth to a company as traditionally "male" jobs [218]

comparative advantage The ability to produce some products more efficiently than others [58]

compensation system Total package offered by a company to employees in return for their labor [212]

compensatory damages Monetary payments intended to redress injury actually suffered because of a tort [468]

competition Vying among businesses for the same resources or customers [15]

competitive product analysis Process by which a company analyzes a competitor's products to identify desirable improvements in its own [348]

compulsory arbitration Method of resolving a labor dispute in which both parties are legally required to accept the judgment of a neutral party [229]

computer graphics program Application program that converts numeric and character data into pictorial information, such as graphs and charts [375]

conceptual skills Abilities to think in the abstract, diagnose and analyze different situations, and see beyond the present situation [117]

considerations Any item of value exchanged between parties to create a valid contract [467]

consumer behavior Various facets of the decision process by which customers come to purchase and consume products [257]

consumer goods Products purchased by consumers for personal use [246]

consumerism Form of social activism dedicated to protecting the rights of consumers in their dealings with businesses [88]

containerization Transportation method in which goods are sealed in containers at shipping sources and opened when they reach final destinations [313]

contingency approach Approach to managerial style holding that the appropriate behavior in any situation is dependent (contingent) on the unique elements of that situation [198]

contingent worker Temporary employee hired to supplement an organization's permanent workforce [222]

control chart Process control method that plots test sampling results on a diagram to determine when a process is beginning to depart from normal operating conditions [348]

controlling Management process of monitoring an organization's performance to ensure that it is meeting its goals [113]

convenience good/service Inexpensive product purchased and consumed rapidly and regularly [273]

convenience store Retail store offering easy accessibility, extended hours, and fast service [309]

copyright Exclusive ownership right belonging to the creator of a book, article, design, illustration, photo, film, or musical work [470]

corporate bond Bond issued by a company as a source of long-term funding [432]

corporate culture The shared experiences, stories, beliefs, and norms that characterize an organization [121]

corporate governance Roles of shareholders, directors, and other managers in corporate decision making [41]

corporation Business that is legally considered an entity separate from its owners and is liable for its own debts; owners' liability extends to the limits of their investments [38]

cost of goods sold Total cost of obtaining materials for making the products sold by a firm during the year [369]

coupon Sales promotion technique in which a certificate is issued entitling the buyer to a reduced price [301]

creative selling Personal selling task in which salespeople try to persuade buyers to purchase products by providing information about their benefits [300]

credit Bookkeeping entry in a T-account that records decreases in assets [366]

credit union Financial institution that accepts deposits from, and makes loans to, only its members, usually employees of a particular organization [404]

cumulative preferred stock Preferred stock on which dividends not paid in the past must be paid to stockholders before dividends can be paid to common stockholders [426]

currency Government-issued paper money and metal coins [399]

current asset Asset that can be converted into cash within the following year [367]

current liability Debt that must be paid within the year [368]

current ratio Solvency ratio that determines a firm's creditworthiness by measuring its ability to pay its current obligations [370]

customer departmentalization Departmentalization according to types of customers likely to buy a given product [133]

data communications network Global network (such as the Internet) that permits users to send electronic messages and information quickly and economically [379]

database Centralized, organized collection of related data [373]

database management program Application program for creating, storing, searching, and manipulating an organized collection of data [375]

debenture Unsecured bond for which no specific property is pledged as security [432]

debit Bookkeeping entry in a T-account that records increases in assets [366]

debit card Plastic card that allows an individual to transfer money between accounts [413]

debt A firm's total liabilities [371]

debt financing Long-term borrowing from sources outside a company [435]

debt financing Long-term borrowing from sources outside a company [455]

debt ratio Solvency ratio measuring a firm's ability to meet its long-term debts [371]

debt-to-owners' equity ratio (or **debt-to-equity ratio**) Solvency ratio describing the extent to which a firm is financed through borrowing [371]

decentralized organization Organization in which a great deal of decision-making authority is delegated to levels of management at points below the top [136]

decision-making skills Skills in defining problems and selecting the best courses of action [118]

delegation Assignment of a task, responsibility, or authority by a manager to a subordinate [135]

demand The willingness and ability of buyers to purchase a good or service [13]

demand and supply schedule Assessment of the relationships between different levels of demand and supply at different price levels [13]

demand curve Graph showing how many units of a product will be demanded (bought) at different prices [13]

demand deposit Bank account funds that may be withdrawn at any time [399]

democratic style Managerial style in which managers generally ask for input from subordinates but retain final decision-making power [197]

demographic variables Characteristics of populations that may be considered in developing a segmentation strategy [253]

departmentalization Process of grouping jobs into logical units [132]

department store Large product line retailer characterized by organization into specialized departments [307]

depreciation Process of distributing the cost of an asset over its life [368]

depression Particularly severe and long-lasting recession [19]

derived demand Demand for industrial products that results from demand for consumer products [260]

desktop publishing Process of combining word-processing and graphics capability to produce type-set-quality text from personal computers [377]

direct channel Distribution channel in which a product travels from producer to consumer without intermediaries [303]

direct investment Arrangement in which a firm buys or establishes tangible assets in another country [67]

direct mail Advertising medium in which messages are mailed directly to consumers' homes or places of business [297]

direct selling Form of nonstore retailing typified by door-to-door sales [311]

direct-response retailing Nonstore retailing by direct interaction with customers to inform them of products and to receive sales orders [309]

directing Management process of guiding and motivating employees to meet an organization's objectives [113]

disability income insurance Insurance providing continuous income when disability keeps the insured from gainful employment [462]

discount Price reduction offered as an incentive to purchase [285]

discount house Bargain retailer that generates large sales volume by offering goods at substantial price reductions [308]

discount rate Interest rate at which member banks can borrow money from the Federal Reserve [410]

distribution center Warehouse providing short-term storage of goods for which demand is both constant and high [311]

distribution channel Network of interdependent companies through which a product passes from producer to end user [303]

distribution Part of the marketing mix concerned with getting products from producers to consumers [252]

distribution mix The combination of distribution channels by which a firm gets its products to end users [302]

diversity training Programs designed to improve employee awareness of differences in attitudes and behaviors of coworkers from different racial, ethnic, or gender groups [222]

divestiture Selling of one or more corporate business units [45]

division Department that resembles a separate business in producing and marketing its own products [139]

divisional organization Organizational structure in which corporate divisions operate as autonomous businesses under the larger corporate umbrella [139]

double-entry accounting system Bookkeeping system that balances the accounting equation by recording the dual effects of every financial transaction [365]

double taxation Situation in which taxes may be payable both by a corporation on its profits and by shareholders on dividend incomes [39]

Dow Jones Industrial Average Market index based on the prices of 30 of the largest industrial firms listed on the NYSE [438]

dumping Practice of selling a product abroad for less than the cost of production [70]

E-cash Electronic money that moves among consumers and businesses via digital electronic transmissions [414]

earnings per share Profitability ratio measuring the size of the dividend that a firm can pay shareholders [371]

economic strike Strike usually triggered by stalemate over one or more mandatory bargaining items [228]

economic system A nation's system for allocating its resources among its citizens [7]

electronic funds transfer (EFT) Communication of fund-transfer information over wire, cable, or microwave [406]

electronic mail (e-mail) Computer system that electronically transmits information between computers [378]

electronic shopping Nonstore retailing in which information about the seller's products and services is connected to consumers' computers, allowing consumers to receive the information and purchase the products in the home [311]

electronic spreadsheet Application program with a row-and-column format that allows users to compare the effect of changes from one category to another [375]

embargo Government order banning exportation and/or importation of a particular product or all products from a particular country [69]

emotional motives Reasons for purchasing a product that are based on nonobjective factors [259]

employee stock ownership plan (ESOP) Arrangement in which a corporation holds its own stock in trust for its employees, who gradually receive ownership of the stock and control its voting rights [45]

entrepreneur Businessperson who accepts both the risks and the opportunities involved in creating and operating a new business venture [155]

environmental analysis Process of scanning the business environment for threats and opportunities [111]

equal employment opportunity Legally mandated nondiscrimination in employment on the basis of race, creed, sex, or national origin [215]

equity financing Use of common stock and/or retained earnings to raise long-term funding [435]

equity financing Use of common stock and/or retained earnings to raise long-term funding [456]

equity theory Theory of motivation holding that people evaluate their treatment by employers relative to the treatment of others [188]

ethical behavior Behavior conforming to generally accepted social norms concerning beneficial and harmful actions [80]

ethics Beliefs about what is right and wrong or good and bad in actions that affect others [80]

European Union (EU) Agreement among major Western European nations to eliminate or make uniform most trade barriers affecting group members [474]

exchange rate Rate at which the currency of one nation can be exchanged for the currency of another country [59]

expectancy theory Theory of motivation holding that people are motivated to work toward rewards that they want and that they believe they have a reasonable chance of obtaining [187]

expense item Industrial product purchased and consumed rapidly and regularly for daily operations [273]

expert system Form of artificial intelligence that attempts to imitate the behavior of human experts in a particular field [378]

export Product made or grown domestically but shipped and sold abroad [54]

exporter Firm that distributes and sells products to one or more foreign countries [65]

express authority Agent's authority, derived from written agreement, to bind a principal to a certain course of action [471]

express warranty Warranty whose terms are specifically stated by the seller [472]

external environment Outside factors that influence marketing programs by posing opportunities or threats [247]

factors of production Resources used in the production of goods and services—natural resources, labor, capital, and entrepreneurs [8]

factory outlet Bargain retailer owned by the manufacturer whose products it sells [309]

Fair Labor Standards Act (1938) Federal law setting minimum wage and maximum number of hours in the workweek [226]

fax machine Machine that can transmit copies of documents over telephone lines [378]

feature Tangible quality that a company builds into a product [272]

Federal Deposit Insurance Corporation (FDIC) Federal agency that guarantees the safety of all deposits up to $100,000 in the financial institutions that it insures [407]

Federal Reserve System (the Fed) Central bank of the United States, which acts as the government's bank, serves member commercial banks, and controls the nation's money supply [407]

finance (or **corporate finance**) Activities concerned with determining a firm's long-term investments, obtaining the funds to pay for them, conducting the firm's everyday financial activities, and managing the firm's risks [452]

finance company Nondeposit institution that specializes in making loans to businesses and consumers [404]

financial accounting system Field of accounting concerned with external users of a company's financial information [361]

financial manager Manager responsible for planning and controlling the acquisition and dispersal of a firm's financial resources [452]

financial plan A firm's strategies for reaching some future financial position [452]

financial statement Any of several types of reports summarizing a company's financial status to aid in managerial decision making [366]

first-line managers Managers responsible for supervising the work of employees [115]

fiscal policies Government economic policies that determine how the government collects and spends its revenues [24]

fiscal year Twelve-month period designated for annual financial reporting purposes [364]

fixed asset Asset with long-term use or value, such as land, buildings, and equipment [368]

fixed cost Cost unaffected by the quantity of a product produced or sold [282]

flextime programs Method of increasing job satisfaction by allowing workers to adjust work schedules on a daily or weekly basis [193]

float Total amount of checks written but not yet cleared through the Federal Reserve [408]

franchise Arrangement in which a buyer (franchisee) purchases the right to sell the good or service of the seller (franchiser) [165]

free-rein style Managerial style in which managers typically serve as advisers to subordinates who are allowed to make decisions [197]

functional departmentalization Departmentalization according to groups' functions or activities [133]

functional organization Form of business organization in which authority is determined by the relationships between group functions and activities [139]

futures contract Agreement to purchase specified amounts of a commodity at a given price on a set future date [433]

gain-sharing plan Incentive program for distributing bonuses to employees whose performances improve productivity [214]

General Agreement on Tariffs and Trade (GATT) International trade agreement to encourage the multilateral reduction or elimination of trade barriers [473]

general partnership Business with two or more owners who share in both the operation of the firm and in financial responsibility for its debts [36]

generally accepted accounting principles (GAAP) Accepted rules and procedures governing the content and form of financial reports [362]

geographic departmentalization Departmentalization according to areas served by a business [133]

geographic variables Geographical units that may be considered in developing a segmentation strategy [253]

globalization Process by which the world economy is becoming a single interdependent system [54]

goal Objective that a business hopes and plans to achieve [108]

goods production Business operations that create tangible products [330]

goodwill Amount paid for an existing business above the value of its other assets [368]

government bond Bond issued by the federal government [431]

gross domestic product (GDP) The value of all goods and services produced in a year by a nation's economy through domestic factors of production [22]

gross national product (GNP) The value of all goods and services produced by an economic system in a year regardless of where the factors of production are located [20]

gross profit (or **gross margin**) Revenues from goods sold minus cost of goods sold [369]

group life insurance Insurance underwritten for a group as a whole rather than for each individual in it [462]

growth Increase in the amount of goods and services produced by a nation's resources [20]

guaranteed loans program Program in which the SBA guarantees to repay 75 to 85 percent of small-business commercial loans up to $750,000 [163]

Hawthorne effect Tendency for productivity to increase when workers believe they are receiving special attention from management [185]

health insurance Insurance covering losses resulting from medical and hospital expenses as well as income lost from injury or disease [462]

health maintenance organization (HMO) Organized health care system providing comprehensive care in return for fixed membership fees [463]

hierarchy of human needs model Theory of motivation describing five levels of human needs and arguing that basic needs must be fulfilled before people work to satisfy higher-level needs [185]

high-contact system Level of service-customer contact in which the customer receives the service as part of the system [334]

human relations Interactions between employers and employees and their attitudes toward one another [182]

human relations skills Skills in understanding and getting along with people [117]

human resource management Development and administration of programs to enhance the quality and performance of a company's workforce [208]

human resource managers Managers responsible for hiring, training, evaluating, and compensating employees [208]

hypermarket Very large product line retailer carrying a wide variety of unrelated products [308]

immediate participation loans program Program in which small businesses are loaned funds put up jointly by banks and the SBA [163]

implied authority Agent's authority, derived from business custom, to bind a principal to a certain course of action [471]

implied warranty Warranty, dictated by law, based on the principle that products should fulfill advertised promises and serve the purposes for which they are manufactured and sold [472]

import Product made or grown abroad but sold domestically [54]

importer Firm that buys products in foreign markets and then imports them for resale in its home country [65]

incentive program Special compensation program designed to motivate high performance [213]

income statement (or **profit-and-loss statement**) Financial statement listing a firm's annual revenues, expenses, and profit or loss [368]

independent agent Foreign individual or organization that agrees to represent an exporter's interests [66]

individual retirement account (IRA) Tax-deferred pension fund with which wage earners supplement other retirement funds [405]

industrial distribution Network of channel members involved in the flow of manufactured goods to industrial customers [305]

industrial goods Products purchased by companies to produce other products [246]

industrial market Organizational market consisting of firms that buy goods that are either converted into products or used during production [259]

Industrial Revolution Major mid-eighteenth century change in production characterized by a shift to the factory system, mass production, and the specialization of labor [32]

inelastic demand Demand for industrial products that is not largely affected by price changes [260]

inflation Phenomenon of widespread price increases throughout an economic system [18]

informal organization Network, unrelated to the firm's formal authority structure, of everyday social interactions among company employees [141]

information managers Managers responsible for designing and implementing systems to gather, organize, and distribute information [372]**data** Raw facts and figures [373]

information The useful interpretation of data [373]

insider trading Illegal practice of using special knowledge about a firm for profit or gain [442]

institutional investors Large investors, such as mutual funds and pension funds, that purchase large blocks of corporate stock [46]

institutional market Organizational market consisting of such nongovernmental buyers of goods and services as hospitals, churches, museums, and charitable organizations [260]

insurance company Nondeposit institution that invests funds collected as premiums charged for insurance coverage [404]

intangible asset Nonphysical asset, such as a patent or trademark, that has economic value in the form of expected benefit [368]

intangible personal property Property that cannot be seen but that exists by virtue of written documentation

intellectual property Property created through a person's creative activities [470]

intentional tort Tort resulting from the deliberate actions of a party [468]

intermediary Individual or firm that helps to distribute a product [302]

intermediate goals Goals set for a period of 1 to 5 years into the future [109]

intermodal transportation Combined use of several different modes of transportation [313]

international competition Competitive marketing of domestic products against foreign products [250]

international firm Firm that conducts a significant portion of its business in foreign countries [65]

international law Set of cooperative agreements and guidelines established by countries to govern actions of individuals, businesses, and nations [473]

international organizational structures Approaches to organizational structure developed in response to the need to manufacture, purchase, and sell in global markets [140]

Internet Global data communications network serving thousands of computers with information on a wide array of topics and providing communications flows among certain private networks [379]

intranet Private network of internal Web sites and other sources of information available to a company's employees [381]

intranet Private network of internal Web sites and other sources of information available to a company's employees [398]

intrapreneuring Process of creating and maintaining the innovation and flexibility of a small-business environment within the confines of a large organization [142]

inventory Materials and goods which are held by a company but which will be sold within the year [453]

inventory control Receiving, storing, handling, and counting of all raw materials, partly finished goods, and finished goods [343]

inventory turnover ratio Activity ratio measuring the average number of times that inventory is sold and restocked during the year [372]

investment bank Financial institution engaged in issuing and reselling new securities [426]

involuntary bankruptcy Bankruptcy proceedings initiated by the creditors of an indebted individual or organization [472]

job analysis Evaluation of the duties and qualities required by a job [208]

job description Outline of the objectives, tasks, and responsibilities of a job [208]

job enrichment Method of increasing job satisfaction by adding one or more motivating factors to job activities [192]

job redesign Method of increasing job satisfaction by designing a more satisfactory fit between workers and their jobs [192]

job relatedness Principle that all employment decisions should be based on the requirements of the jobs in question [208]

job satisfaction Degree of enjoyment that people derive from performing their jobs [182]

job specialization The process of identifying the specific jobs that need to be done and designating the people who will perform them [131]

job specifications Description of the skills, education, and experience required by a job [208]

joint venture Collaboration between two or more organizations on an enterprise [45]

journal Chronological record of a firm's financial transactions, including a brief description of each [363]

just-in-time (JIT) production system Production method that brings together all materials and parts needed at each production stage at the precise moment at which they are required [344]

Keogh plan Tax-deferred pension plan for the self-employed [405]

labor (or **human resources**) The physical and mental capabilities of people as they contribute to economic production [8]

labor union Group of individuals working together formally to achieve shared job-related goals [223]

Labor-Management Relations Act (Taft-Hartley Act) (1947) Federal law defining certain union practices as unfair and illegal [226]

Labor-Management Reporting and Disclosure Act (Landrum-Griffin Act) (1959) Federal law imposing regulations on internal union procedures, including elections of national leaders and filing of financial disclosure statements [227]

law of demand Principle that buyers will purchase (demand) more of a product as its price drops and less as its price increases [13]

law of supply Principle that producers will offer (supply) more of a product for sale as its price rises and less as its price drops [13]

leadership Process of motivating others to work to meet specific objectives [196]

ledger Record, divided into accounts and usually compiled on a monthly basis, containing summaries of all journal transactions [364]

letter of credit Bank promise, issued for a buyer, to pay a designated firm a certain amount of money if specified conditions are met [405]

liability Debt owed by a firm to an outside organization or individual [365]

liability insurance Insurance covering losses resulting from damage to people or property when the insured is judged responsible [461]

licensed brand Brand-name product for whose name the seller has purchased the right from an organization or individual [280]

licensing arrangement Arrangement in which firms choose foreign individuals or organizations to manufacture or market their products in another country [66]

life insurance Insurance paying benefits to the policyholder's survivors [462]

limit order Order authorizing the purchase of a stock only if its price is equal to or less than a specified amount [440]

limited liability Legal principle holding investors liable for a firm's debts only to the limits of their personal investments in it [39]

line authority Organizational structure in which authority flows in a direct chain of command from the top of the company to the bottom [137]

line department Department directly linked to the production and sales of a specific product [137]

line of credit Standing arrangement in which a lender agrees to make available a specified amount of funds upon the borrower's request [455]

liquidity Ease with which an asset can be converted into cash [367]

liquidity ratio Solvency ratio measuring a firm's ability to pay its immediate debts [370]

load fund Mutual fund in which investors are charged sales commissions when they buy in or sell out [433]

local content law Law requiring that products sold in a particular country be at least partly made there [70]

local development companies (LDCs) program Program in which the SBA works with local for-profit or nonprofit organizations seeking to boost a community's economy [163]

lockout Management tactic whereby workers are denied access to their workplace [228]

long-term goals Goals set for an extended time, typically 5 years or more into the future [109]

long-term liability Debt that is not due for at least a year [368]

low-contact system Level of service-customer contact in which the customer need not be a part of the system to receive the service [334]

M-1 Measure of the money supply that includes only the most liquid (spendable) forms of money [399]

M-2 Measure of the money supply that includes all the components of M-1 plus the forms of money that can be easily converted into spendable form [400]

mail order (or catalog marketing) Form of nonstore retailing in which customers place orders for catalog merchandise received through the mail [309]

management Process of planning, organizing, directing, and controlling an organization's resources to achieve its goals [112]

management by objectives (MBO) Set of procedures involving both managers and subordinates in setting goals and evaluating progress [190]

management consultant Independent outside specialist hired to help managers solve business problems [164]

management information system (MIS) System for transforming data into information that can be used in decision making [373]

managerial (or **management) accounting** Field of accounting that serves internal users of a company's financial information [361]

managerial style Pattern of behavior that a manager exhibits in dealing with subordinates [197]

margin Percentage of the total sales price that a buyer must put up to place an order for stock or futures contracts [434]

market Mechanism for exchange between buyers and sellers of a particular good or service [9]

market economy Economy in which individuals control production and allocation decisions through supply and demand [8]

market index Summary of price trends in a specific industry and/or the stock market as a whole [437]

market order Order to buy or sell a security at the market price prevailing at the time the order is placed [440]

market price (or **equilibrium price**) Profit-maximizing price at which the quantity of goods demanded and the quantity of goods supplied are equal [13]

market segmentation Process of dividing a market into categories of customer types [252]

market share As a percentage, total of market sales for a specific company or product [281]

market value Current price of a share of stock in the stock market [425]

marketing The process of planning and executing the conception, pricing, promotion, and distribution of ideas, goods, and services to create exchanges that satisfy individual and organizational objectives [246]

marketing concept Idea that a business must focus on identifying and satisfying consumer wants in order to be profitable [34]

marketing mix The combination of product, pricing, promotion, and distribution strategies used to market products [250]

markup Amount added to an item's cost to sell it at a profit [282]

material requirements planning (MRP) Production control method in which a bill of materials is used to ensure that the right amounts of materials are delivered to the right place at the right time [245]

materials management Planning, organizing, and controlling the flow of materials from design through distribution of finished goods [343]

matrix structure Organizational structure in which teams are formed and team members report to two or more managers [140]

media mix Combination of advertising media chosen to carry message about a product [298]

mediation Method of resolving a labor dispute in which a third party advises on, but does not impose, a settlement [229]

merchandise inventory Cost of merchandise that has been acquired for sale to customers and that is still on hand [367]

merchant wholesalers Intermediaries that buy products from manufacturers and sell them to other businesses [306]

merger The union of two corporations to form a new corporation [43]

merit salary system Incentive program linking compensation to performance in nonsales jobs [213]

middle managers Managers responsible for implementing the strategies, policies, and decisions made by top managers [115]

minority enterprise small-business investment company (MESBIC) Federally sponsored company that specializes in financing businesses that are owned and operated by minorities [163]

mission statement Organization's statement of how it will achieve its purpose in the environment in which it conducts its business [109]

missionary selling Personal selling tasks in which salespeople promote their firms and products rather than try to close sales [300]

mixed market economy Economic system featuring characteristics of both planned and market economies [10]

monetary policies Government economic policies that determine the size of a nation's money supply [24]

monetary policy Policies by which the Federal Reserve manages the nation's money supply and interest rates [409]

money market mutual fund Fund of short-term, low-risk financial securities purchased with the assets of investor-owners pooled by a nonbank institution [400]

monopolistic competition Market or industry characterized by numerous buyers and relatively numerous sellers trying to differentiate their products from those of competitors [16]

monopoly Market or industry in which there is only one producer, which can therefore set the prices of its products [17]

morale Overall attitude that employees have toward their workplace [182]

motivation The set of forces that cause people to behave in certain ways [184]

multinational firm Firm that designs, produces, and markets products in many nations [65]

municipal bond Bond issued by a state or local government [432]

mutual fund Company that pools investments from individuals and organizations to purchase a portfolio of stocks, bonds, and short-term securities [433]

mutual savings bank Financial institution whose depositors are owners sharing in its profits [404]

National Association of Securities Dealers Automated Quotation (NASDAQ) system Organization of over-the-counter dealers who own, buy, and sell their own securities over a network of electronic communications [430]

national bank Commercial bank chartered by the federal government [402]

national brand Brand-name product produced by, widely distributed by, and carrying the name of a manufacturer [279]

national debt Total amount that a nation owes its creditors [23]

National Labor Relations Act (Wagner Act) (1935) Federal law protecting the rights of workers to form unions, bargain collectively, and engage in strikes to achieve their goals [226]

National Labor Relations Board (NLRB) Federal agency established by the National Labor Relations Act to enforce its provisions [226]

natural monopoly Industry in which one company can most efficiently supply all needed goods or services [17]

natural resources Materials supplied by nature—for example, land, water, mineral deposits, and trees [8]

negligence Conduct falling below legal standards for protecting others against unreasonable risk [468]

networking Interactions among businesspeople for the purpose of discussing mutual problems and opportunities and perhaps pooling resources [164]

no-load fund Mutual fund in which investors pay no sales commissions when they buy in or sell out [433]

Norris-LaGuardia Act (1932) Federal law limiting the ability of courts to issue injunctions prohibiting certain union activities [225]

North Amercian Free Trade Agreement (NAFTA) Agreement to gradually eliminate tariffs and other trade barriers between the United States, Canada, and Mexico [474]

Occupational Safety and Health Administration (OSHA) Federal agency that sets and enforces guidelines for protecting workers from unsafe conditions and potential health hazards in the workplace [219]

odd lot Purchase or sale of stock in fractions of round lots [440]

odd-even pricing Psychological pricing tactic based on the premise that customers prefer prices not stated in even dollar amounts [285]

off-price store Bargain retailer that buys excess inventories from high-quality manufacturers and sells them at discounted prices [309]

off-the-job training Training conducted in a controlled environment away from the work site [211]

oligopoly Market or industry characterized by a handful of (generally large) sellers with the power to influence the prices of their products [16]

on-the-job training Training, sometimes informal, conducted while an employee is at work [211]

open-book credit Form of trade credit in which sellers ship merchandise on faith that payment will be forthcoming [454]

open-market operations The Federal Reserve's sales and purchases of securities in the open market [410]

open promotion system System by which employees apply, test, and interview for available jobs, requirements of which are posted [211]

operating expenses Costs, other than the cost of goods sold, incurred in producing a good or service [369]

operational plans Plans setting short-term targets for daily, weekly, or monthly performance [112]

operations control Process of monitoring and adjusting production performance by comparing results with plans [342]

operations information system Computer system used to manage production and manufacturing operations [379]

operations (or production) management Systematic direction and control of the processes that transform resources into finished products [333]

operations managers Managers responsible for production, inventory, and quality control [333]

operations process Set of methods and technologies used in the production of a good or service [333]

order processing Personal selling task in which salespeople receive orders and see to their handling and delivery [300]

organization chart Diagram depicting a company's structure and showing employees where they fit into its operations [131]

organizational analysis Process of analyzing a firm's strengths and weaknesses [111]

organizational structure Specification of the jobs to be done within an organization and the ways in which they relate to one another [130]

organizing Management process of determining how best to arrange an organization's resources and activities into a coherent structure [113]

over-the-counter (OTC) market Organization of securities dealers formed to trade stock outside the formal institutional setting of the organized stock exchanges [430]

owners' equity Amount of money owners would receive if they sold all of a firm's assets and paid all of its liabilities [365]

packaging Physical container in which a product is sold, advertised, or protected [280]

paid-in capital Additional money, above proceeds from stock sale, paid directly to a firm by its owners [368]

par value Face value of a share of stock, set by the issuing company's board of directors [425]

participative management and empowerment Method of increasing job satisfaction by giving employees a voice in the management of their jobs and the company [191]

patent Exclusive legal right to use and license a manufactured item or substance, manufacturing process, or object design [470]

pay-for-knowledge plan Incentive program to encourage employees to learn new skills or become proficient at different jobs [214]

pay-for-performance (or variable pay) Individual incentive that rewards a manager for especially productive output [214]

penetration pricing Setting an initial low price to establish a new product in the market [284]

pension fund Nondeposit pool of funds managed to provide retirement income for its members [404]

performance appraisal Evaluation, often in writing, of an employee's job performance [211]

performance quality The performance features offered by a product [246]

person-job matching Process of matching the right person to the right job [208]

personal selling Promotional tool in which a salesperson communicates one-on-one with potential customers [299]

physical distribution Activities needed to move a product efficiently from manufacturer to consumer [311]

picketing Labor action in which workers publicize their grievances at the entrance to an employer's facility [228]

planned economy Economy that relies on a centralized government to control all or most factors of production and to make all or most production and allocation decisions [8]

planning Management process of determining what an organization needs to do and how best to get it done [112]

pledging accounts receivable Using accounts receivable as loan collateral [455]

point-of-purchase (POP) display Sales promotion technique in which product displays are located in certain areas to stimulate purchase [301]

point-of-sale (POS) terminal Electronic device that allows customers to pay for retail purchases with debit cards [413]

positioning Process of establishing an identifiable product image in the minds of consumers [294]

preferred provider organization (PPO) Arrangement whereby selected professional providers offer services at reduced rates and permit thorough review of their service recommendations [463]

preferred stock Stock that guarantees its holders fixed dividends and priority claims over assets but no corporate voting rights[41]

premium Sales promotion technique in which offers of free or reduced-price items are used to stimulate purchases [301]

premium Fee paid by a policyholder for insurance coverage [461]

prepaid expense Expense, such as prepaid rent, that is paid before the upcoming period in which it is due [367]

presentation graphics software Applications that allow users to create visual presentations integrating animation and sound [376]

price leader Dominant firm that establishes product prices that other companies follow [284]

price lining Setting a limited number of prices for certain categories of products [285]

price-earnings ratio Current price of a stock divided by the firm's current annual earnings per share [438]

price skimming Setting an initial high price to cover new product costs and generate a profit [284]

pricing Process of determining what a company will receive in exchange for its products [281]

pricing objectives Goals that producers hope to attain in pricing products for sale [281]

primary securities market Market in which new stocks and bonds are bought and sold [424]

prime rate Interest rate available to a bank's most creditworthy customers [403]

principal Individual or organization authorizing an agent to act on its behalf [471]

private brand (or private label) Brand-name product that a wholesaler or retailer has commissioned from a manufacturer [280]

private corporation Corporation whose stock is held by only a few people and is not available for sale to the general public [39]

private enterprise Economic system that allows individuals to pursue their own interests without undue governmental restriction [14]

private property rights The right to buy, own, use, and sell almost any form of property [15]

private warehouse Warehouse owned by and providing storage for a single company [311]

privatization Process of converting government enterprises into privately owned companies [10]

process departmentalization Departmentalization according to production processes used to create a good or service [133]

process layout Spatial arrangement of production activities that groups equipment and people according to function [338]

product Good, service, or idea that is marketed to fill consumer needs and wants [250]

product adaptation Product modified to have greater appeal in foreign markets [277]

product departmentalization Departmentalization according to specific products being created [133]

product differentiation Creation of a product or product image that differs enough from existing products to attract consumers [250]

product extension Existing, unmodified product that is marketed globally [277]

product layout Spatial arrangement of production activities designed to move resources through a smooth, fixed sequence of steps [338]

product liability tort Tort in which a company is responsible for injuries caused by its products [469]

product life cycle (PLC) Series of stages in a product's profit-producing life [276]

product line Group of similar products intended for a similar group of buyers who will use them in similar ways [273]

product mix Group of products that a firm makes available for sale [273]

product use variables Consumer characteristics based on the ways in which a product is used, the brand loyalty it enjoys, and the reasons for which it is purchased [257]

production era Period during the early twentieth century in which U.S. business focused primarily on improving productivity and manufacturing efficiency [34]

productivity Measure of economic growth that compares how much a system produces with the resources needed to produce it [22]

profit center Separate company unit responsible for its own costs and profits [132]

profit-sharing plan Incentive program for distributing bonuses to employees for company profits above a certain level [214]

profitability ratio Financial ratio for measuring a firm's potential earnings [370]

profits The difference between a business's revenues and its expenses [7]

program trading Large purchase or sale of a group of stocks, often triggered by computerized trading programs that can be launched without human supervision or control [441]

promotion Aspect of the marketing mix concerned with the most effective techniques for selling a product [294]

promotional mix Combination of tools used to promote a product [295]

property Anything of value to which a person or business has sole right of ownership

property insurance Insurance covering losses resulting from physical damage to or loss of the insured's real estate or personal property [462]

prospectus Registration statement filed with the SEC before the issuance of a new security [441]

protectionism Practice of protecting domestic business against foreign competition [70]

proxy Authorization granted by a shareholder for someone else to vote his or her shares [41]

psychographic variables Consumer characteristics, such as lifestyles, opinions, interests, and attitudes, that may be considered in developing a segmentation strategy [256]

psychological pricing Pricing tactic that takes advantage of the fact that consumers do not always respond rationally to stated prices [285]

public corporation Corporation whose stock is widely held and available for sale to the general public [38]

public relations Company-influenced publicity directed at building goodwill between an organization and potential customers [301]

public warehouse Independently owned and operated warehouse that stores goods for many firms [311]

publicity Promotional tool in which information about a company or product is transmitted by general mass media [301]

pull strategy Promotional strategy designed to appeal directly to consumers who will demand a product from retailers [295]

punitive damages Fines imposed over and above any actual losses suffered by a plaintiff [468]

purchasing The acquisition of raw materials and services that a company needs to produce its products [343]

pure competition Market or industry characterized by numerous small firms producing an identical product [15]

pure risk Risk involving only the possibility of loss or no loss [459]

push strategy Promotional strategy designed to encourage wholesalers or retailers to market products to consumers [295]

quality A product's fitness for use; its success in offering features that consumers want [340]

quality control Management of the production process designed to manufacture goods or supply services that meet specific quality standards [245]

quality/cost study Method of improving quality by identifying current costs and areas with the greatest cost-savings potential [349]

quality improvement team (or quality circle) TQM tool in which groups of employees work together as a team to improve quality [345]

quality ownership Principle of total quality management that holds that quality belongs to each person who creates it while performing a job [348]

quality reliability Consistency of a product's quality from unit to unit [347]

quota Restriction on the number of products of a certain type that can be imported into a country [69]

rational motives Reasons for purchasing a product that are based on a logical evaluation of product attributes [259]

real gross national product (real GNP) Gross national product adjusted for inflation and changes in the value of a country's currency [21]

real-time processing Method of entering data and computer processing them immediately [374]

recession Period characterized by decreases in employment, income, and production [19]

registered bond Bond bearing the name of the holder and registered with the issuing company [432]

regulatory (or administrative) **law** Law made by the authority of administrative agencies[464]

reinforcement Theory that behavior can be encouraged or discouraged by means of rewards or punishments [190]

relationship marketing Marketing strategy that emphasizes lasting relationships with customers and suppliers [247]

reseller market Organizational market consisting of intermediaries who buy and resell finished goods [260]

reserve requirement Percentage of its deposits that a bank must hold in cash or on deposit with the Federal Reserve [410]

responsibility Duty to perform an assigned task [135]

retailer Intermediary who sells products directly to consumers [303]

retained earnings Earnings retained by a firm for its use rather than paid as dividends [368]

return on equity Profitability ratio measuring income earned for each dollar invested [371]

revenues Funds that flow into a business from the sale of goods or services [369]

reverse discrimination Practice of discriminating against well-represented groups by overhiring members of underrepresented groups [217]

revolving credit agreement Arrangement in which a lender agrees to make funds available on demand and on a continuing basis [455]

risk Uncertainty about future events [459]

risk avoidance Practice of avoiding risk by declining or ceasing to participate in an activity [460]

risk control Practice of minimizing the frequency or severity of losses from risky activities [460]

risk management Process of conserving the firm's earning power and assets by reducing the threat of losses due to uncontrollable events [459]

risk retention Practice of covering a firm's losses with its own funds [460]

risk transfer Practice of transferring a firm's risk to another firm [460]

risk-return relationship Principle that, whereas safer investments tend to offer lower returns, riskier investments tend to offer higher returns [458]

round lot Purchase or sale of stock in units of 100 shares [440]

royalty Payment made to a license holder in return for the right to market the licenser's product [66]

salary Compensation in the form of money paid for discharging the responsibilities of a job [212]

sales agent/broker Independent intermediary who usually represents many manufacturers and sells to wholesalers or retailers [304]

sales office Office maintained by a manufacturer as a contact point with its customers [305]

sales promotion Short-term promotional activity designed to stimulate consumer buying or cooperation from distributors and sales agents [300]

savings and loan association (S&L) Financial institution accepting deposits and making loans primarily for home mortgages [404]

secondary securities market Market in which stocks and bonds are traded [424]

secured bond Bond backed by pledges of assets to the bondholders [432]

secured loan Loan for which the borrower must provide collateral [454]

securities Stocks and bonds representing secured, or asset-based, claims by investors against issuers [424]

Securities and Exchange Commission (SEC) Federal agency that administers U.S. securities laws to protect the investing public and maintain smoothly functioning markets [424]

Securities and Exchange Commission (SEC) Federal agency that administers U.S. securities laws to protect the investing public and maintain smoothly functioning markets [441]

securities investment dealer (broker) Nondeposit institution that buys and sells stocks and bonds both for investors and for its own accounts [404]

selective credit controls Federal Reserve authority to set both margin requirements for consumer stock purchases and credit rules for other consumer purchases [410]

Service Corps of Retired Executives (SCORE) SBA program in which retired executives work with small businesses on a volunteer basis [164]

service operations Business activities that provide tangible and intangible services [330]

services Intangible products, such as time, expertise, or an activity, that can be purchased [246]

shopping good/service Moderately expensive, infrequently purchased product [273]

short sale Stock sale in which an investor borrows securities from a broker to be sold and then replaced at a specified future date [441]

short-term goals Goals set for the very near future, typically less than 1 year [110]

shortage Situation in which quantity demanded exceeds quantity supplied [13]

Small Business Administration (SBA) Federal agency charged with assisting small businesses [150]

Small Business Development Center (SBDC) SBA program designed to consolidate information from various disciplines and make it available to small businesses [164]

small business Independently owned and managed business that does not dominate its market [150]

Small Business Institute (SBI) SBA program in which college and university students and instructors work with small-business owners to help solve specific problems [164]

small-business investment company (SBIC) A government-regulated investment company that borrows money from the SBA to invest in or lend to a small business [163]

smart card Credit-card-size computer programmed with electronic money [413]

social audit Systematic analysis of a firm's success in using funds earmarked for meeting its social responsibility goals [92]

social obligation approach Approach to social responsibility by which a company meets only minimum legal requirements in its commitments to groups and individuals in its social environment [91]

social reaction approach Approach to social responsibility by which a company, if specifically asked to do so, exceeds legal minimums in its commitments to groups and individuals in its social environment [91]

social response approach Approach to social responsibility by which a company actively seeks opportunities to contribute to the well-being of groups and individuals in its social environment [91]

social responsibility The attempt of a business to balance its commitments to groups and individuals in its environment, including customers, other businesses, employees, and investors [83]

socialism Planned economic system in which the government owns and operates only selected major sources of production [10]

sole proprietorship Business owned and usually operated by one person who is responsible for all of its debts [35]

solvency ratio Financial ratio, both short and long term, for estimating the risk in investing in a firm [370]

span of control Number of people supervised by one manager [136]

specialty good/service Expensive, rarely purchased product [273]

specialty store Small retail store carrying one product line or category of related products [308]

speculative risk Risk involving the possibility of gain or loss [459]

speed to market Strategy of introducing new products to respond quickly to customer or market changes [276]

spin-off Setting up one or more corporate units as new, independent corporations [45]

stability Condition in which the balance between the money available in an economy and the goods produced in it are growing at about the same rate [18]

staff authority Authority based on expertise that usually involves advising line managers [138]

staff members Advisors and counselors who aid line departments in making decisions but do not have the authority to make final decisions [138]

Standard & Poor's Composite Index Market index based on the performance of 400 industrial firms, 40 utilities, 40 financial institutions, and 20 transportation companies [440]

standardization Use, where possible, of standard and uniform components in the production process [343]

state bank Commercial bank chartered by an individual state [402]

statistical process control (SPC) Evaluation methods that allow managers to analyze variations in a company's production activities [348]

statutory law Law created by constitutions or by federal, state, or local legislative acts [464]

stock Share of ownership in a corporation [41]

stock exchange Organization of individuals formed to provide an institutional setting in which stock can be traded [426]

stockholder (or **shareholder**) Owner of shares of stock in a corporation [41]

stop order Order authorizing the sale of a stock if its price falls to or below a specified level [440]

storage warehouse Warehouse providing storage for extended periods of time [311]

strategic alliance (or joint venture) Arrangement in which a company finds a foreign partner to contribute approximately half of the resources needed to establish and operate a new business in the partner's country [67]

strategic goals Long-term goals derived directly from a firm's mission statement [111]

strategic plans Plans reflecting decisions about resource allocations, company priorities, and steps needed to meet strategic goals [112]

strategy formulation Creation of a broad program for defining and meeting an organization's goals [110]

strict product liability Principle that liability can result not from a producer's negligence but from a defect in the product itself [469]

strike Labor action in which employees temporarily walk off the job and refuse to work [228]

strikebreaker Worker hired as permanent or temporary replacement for a striking employee [229]

subsidy Government payment to help a domestic business compete with foreign firms [69]

substitute product Product that is dissimilar to those of competitors but that can fulfill the same need [249]

supermarket Large product line retailer offering a variety of food and food-related items in specialized departments [307]

supplier selection Finding, choosing, and building relationships with suppliers of services and materials to buy from [343]

supply The willingness and ability of producers to offer a good or service for sale [13]

supply curve Graph showing how many units of a product will be supplied (offered for sale) at different prices [13]

surplus Situation in which quantity supplied exceeds quantity demanded [13]

T-account Bookkeeping format for recording transactions that takes the shape of a *T* whose vertical line divides the account into debits (left side) and credits (right side) [366]

tactical plans Generally short-range plans concerned with implementing specific aspects of a company's strategic plans [112]

tangible personal property Any movable item that can be owned, bought, sold, or leased [469]

tangible real property Land and anything attached to it [469]

target market Group of people that has similar wants and needs and that can be expected to show interest in the same products [252]

tariff Tax levied on imported products [69]

technical skills Skills needed to perform specialized tasks [117]

telecommuting Form of flextime that allows people to perform some or all of a job away from standard office settings [194]

telemarketing Nonstore retailing in which the telephone is used to sell directly to consumers [310]

tender offer Offer to buy shares made by a prospective buyer directly to a target corporation's shareholders, who then make individual decisions about whether to sell [39]

Theory X Theory of motivation holding that people are naturally irresponsible and uncooperative [185]

Theory Y Theory of motivation holding that people are naturally responsible, growth oriented, self-motivated, and interested in being productive [185]

time deposit Bank funds that cannot be withdrawn without notice or transferred by check [400]

time management skills Skills associated with the productive use of time [119]

top managers Managers responsible to the board of directors and stockholders for a firm's overall performance and effectiveness [115]

tort Civil injury to people, property, or reputation for which compensation must be paid [468]

total quality management (TQM) The sum of all activities involved in getting quality products into the marketplace [346]

trade credit Granting of credit by one firm to another [454]

trade deficit Situation in which a country's imports exceed its exports, creating a negative balance of trade [59]

trademark Exclusive legal right to use a brand name or symbol [470]

trade show Sales promotion technique in which various members of an industry gather to display, demonstrate, and sell products [301]

trade surplus Situation in which a country's exports exceed its imports, creating a positive balance of trade [59]

trial court General court that hears cases not specifically assigned to another court [466]

trust services Bank management of an individual's investments, payments, or estate [405]

two-factor theory Theory of motivation holding that job satisfaction depends on two types of factors, hygiene and motivation [186]

unemployment Level of joblessness among people actively seeking work [19]

unethical behavior Behavior which does not conform to generally accepted social norms concerning beneficial and harmful actions [80]

Uniform Commercial Code Body of standardized laws governing the rights of buyers and sellers in transactions [471]

unlimited liability Legal principle holding owners responsible for paying off all debts of a business [36]

utility A product's ability to satisfy a human want [332]

variable cost Cost that changes with the quantity of a product produced or sold [282]

venture capital Outside equity financing provided in return for part ownership of the borrowing firm [458]

venture capital company Group of small investors that invest money in companies with rapid growth potential [163]

vestibule training Off-the-job training conducted in a simulated environment [211]

video marketing Nonstore retailing to consumers via standard and cable television [310]

voice mail Computer-based system for receiving and delivering incoming telephone calls [378]

voluntary arbitration Method of resolving a labor dispute in which both parties agree to submit to the judgment of a neutral party [229]

voluntary bankruptcy Bankruptcy proceedings initiated by an indebted individual or organization [472]

wages Compensation in the form of money paid for time worked [212]

warehouse club (or wholesale club) Bargain retailer offering large discounts on brand-name merchandise to customers who have paid annual membership fees [309]

warehousing Physical distribution operation concerned with the storage of goods [311]

warranty Seller's promise to stand by its products or services if a problem occurs after the sale [472]

whistleblower Employee who detects and tries to put an end to a company's unethical, illegal, or socially irresponsible actions by publicizing them [89]

wholesaler Intermediary who sells products to other businesses for resale to final consumers [303]

word-processing program Application program that allows computers to store, edit, and print letters and numbers for documents created by users [374]

work sharing (or job sharing) Method of increasing job satisfaction by allowing two or more people to share a single full-time job [193]

workers' compensation coverage Coverage provided by a firm to employees for medical expenses, loss of wages, and rehabilitation costs resulting from job-related injuries or disease [462]

workers' compensation insurance Legally required insurance for compensating workers injured on the job [214]

workforce diversity Range of workers' attitudes, values, and behaviors that differ by gender, race, and ethnicity [220]

working capital Liquid current assets out of which a firm can pay current debts [453]

World Wide Web Subsystem of computers providing access to the Internet and offering multimedia and linking capabilities [381]

yellow-dog contracts Requirements that workers state that they did not belong to and would not join a union [226]

NAME, COMPANY, AND PRODUCT INDEX

SUBJECT INDEX